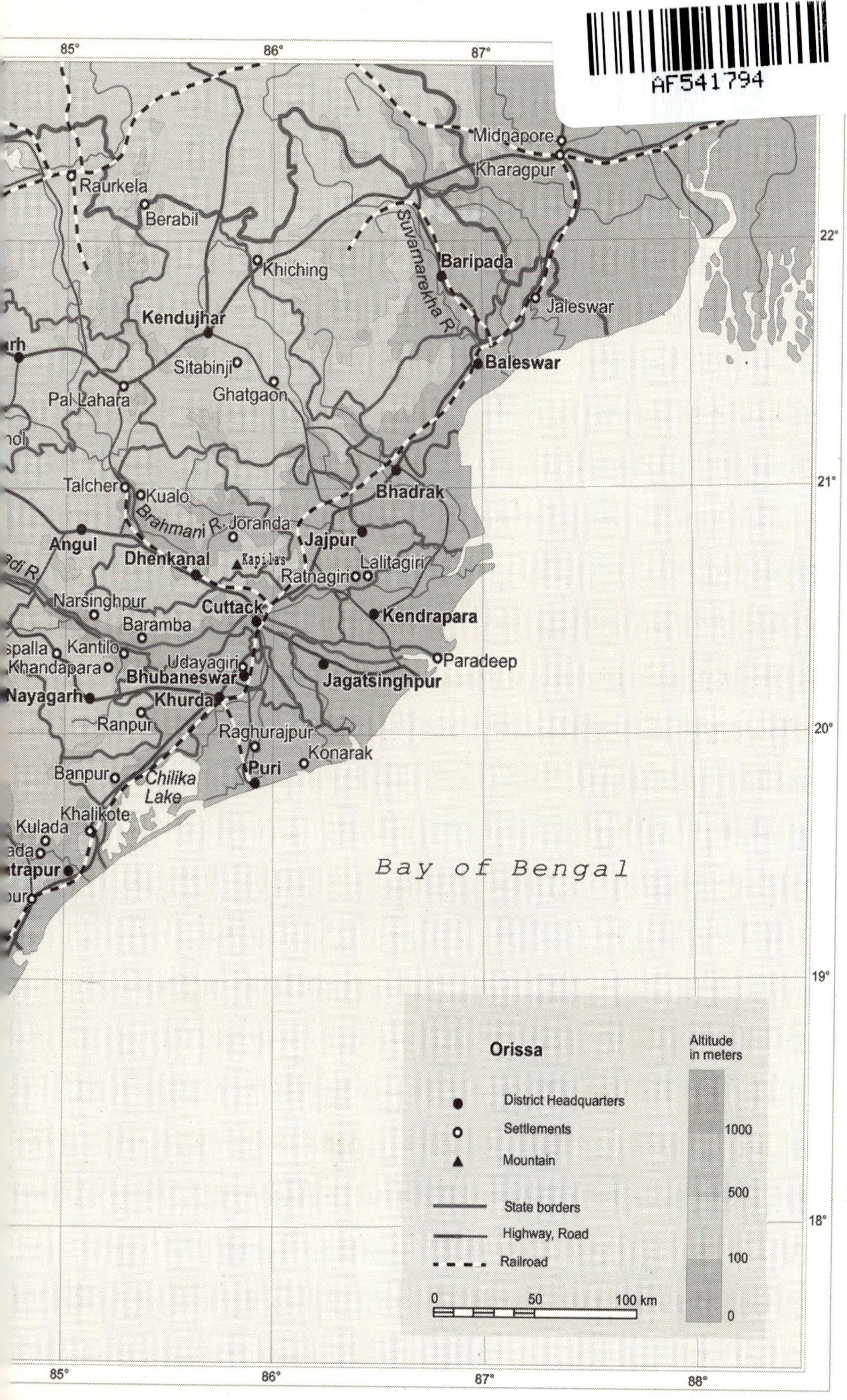

y, University of Tübingen, Germany.

CENTRES OUT THERE?

STUDIES IN ORISSAN SOCIETY, CULTURE AND HISTORY

Editors: HERMANN KULKE and BURKHARD SCHNEPEL

Vol. 1: Jagannatha Revisited: Studying Society, Religion and the State in Orissa, edited by Hermann Kulke and Burkhard Schnepel

Vol. 2: The Jungle Kings: Ethnohistorical Aspects of Politics and Ritual in Orissa, by Burkhard Schnepel

Vol. 3: Text and Context in History, Literature and Religion of Orissa, edited by Angelika Malinar, Johannes Beltz and Heiko Frese

Vol. 4: Altar of Power: The Temple and the State in the Land of Jagannatha, by Yaaminey Mubayi

Vol. 5: The Aghria: A Peasant Caste on a Tribal Frontier, by Uwe Skoda

Vol. 6: Time in India: Concepts and Practices, edited by Angelika Malinar

Vol. 7: Periphery and Centre: Studies in Orissan History, Religion and Anthropology, edited by Georg Pfeffer

Vol. 8: Popular Religion and Ascetic Practices: New Studies on Mahima Dharma, edited by Ishita Banerjee-Dube and Johannes Beltz

Vol. 9: Bhima Bhoi: Verses from the Void—Mystic Poetry of an Oriya Saint, edited by Bettina Bäumer and Johannes Beltz

Vol. 10: Descriptive Topographical Catalogue of Orissan Inscriptions, by Snigdha Tripathy

Vol. 11: Centres Out There? Facets of Subregional Identities in Orissa, edited by Hermann Kulke and Georg Berkemer

Vol. 11: Jagannatha and the Gajapati Kings of Orissa: A Compendium of Late Medieval Texts (*Rajabhog*, *Sevakarmani*, *Deshakhanja* and Other Minor Texts), edited by Gaganendra Nath Dash

CENTRES OUT THERE?

Facets of Subregional Identities in Orissa

Edited by

HERMANN KULKE

GEORG BERKEMER

MANOHAR
2011

First published 2011

ISBN 978-81-7304-906-4

Published by
Ajay Kumar Jain *for*
Manohar Publishers & Distributors
4753/23 Ansari Road, Daryaganj
New Delhi 110 002

Typeset by
Digigrafics
New Delhi 110 049

Printed at
Salasar Imaging Systems
Delhi 110 035

Contents

Acknowledgements

On the occasion of the publication of the last volume of the proceedings of international conferences of the second Orissa Research Project,[1] it is our pleasure to express again on behalf of its members our thanks to the government, research institutions and scholars in India, especially in Orissa, who generously welcomed and supported our academic endeavours. As already mentioned in the acknowledgements of a previous volume, we hope to pay back with these volumes at least a little of what this country has given to us. To conduct two comprehensive research projects in Orissa from 1970-75[2] and 1999-2005 was possible not only by the continuous support and help of scholars, many of whom have become our friends over the years. We are also gratefully remembering the numerous villagers, officers and chaprasis in research institutions who enabled our fieldwork and archive studies. A priceless gain for all German members of the ORPs is, thanks to the people of Orissa, our intimate acquaintance with their great culture and the experience of the warm hospitality bestowed upon us.

We are grateful to Robert Parkin, Oxford, for copy-editing our articles and to Niels Aulike, Nicole Pohland and Tim Schwabedissen for their work on the manuscripts and for their painstaking administrative work during the final years of the project at its head office at Kiel University. We are particularly grateful to Ramesh Jain and Siddharth Chowdhury, Manohar Publishers & Distributors, for their support and patience to bring out this volume, too, as the above-mentioned contributions of the ORPs since 1978.[3] And last but not least, we wish to thank the German Research Council (DFG) for its generous support of the project and its annual conferences with our Indian colleagues at the stately manor house at Salzau/Kiel.

HERMANN KULKE — GEORG BERKEMER
Kiel — *Berlin*

[1] H. Kulke and B. Schnepel (eds.), *Jagannath Revisited: Studies in Society, Religion and the State in Orissa* (2001); A. Malinar, J. Beltz and H. Frese (eds.), *Text and Context in the History, Literature and Religion of Orissa* (2004); G. Pfeffer (ed.), *Periphery and Centre: Studies in Orissan History, Religion and Anthropology* (2007); A. Malinar (ed.), *Time in India: Concepts and Practises* (2007); I. Banerjee-Dube and J. Beltz (ed.), *Popular Religion and Ascetic Practices: New Studies on Mahima Dharma* (2008); G. Pfeffer and D.K. Behera (eds.), *Structure and Exchange in Tribal India and Beyond* (2009); http://orp.uni-kiel.de

[2] A. Eschmann, H. Kulke and G.C. Tripathi (eds.), *The Cult of Jagannath and the Regional Tradition of Orissa* (1978).

[3] Except G. Pfeffer and D.K. Behera (eds.), 2009, published by Concept Publishing Company, New Delhi.

Introduction

HERMANN KULKE AND GEORG BERKEMER

From 1969 to 1974 the first Orissa Research Project (ORP), financed by the German Research Council and conducted by the South Asia Institute of Heidelberg University, revealed vital elements of Oriya identity and culture through its extensive research on the cult of Jagannath and the temple city of Puri. In a time when the discourses on Indian civilization were dominated by bipartite concepts like Redfield's 'great and little tradition', Singer's 'parochialization' and 'universalization' or Srinivasa's 'Sanskritization', the major theoretical quest of the project was to establish through its paradigmatical studies on Orissa the importance of India's great regional traditions not only as the central portion of the uninterrupted cultural continuum between the many local and the pan-Indian traditions but also as their genuine 'melting pot' or 'transmission belt'. Its results were published in a large number of research articles, monographs,[1] and a final report on the cult of Jagannath and the regional tradition.[2]

In June 1997, about 25 years after the former ORP undertook its field research, a group of German and Indian scholars of Orissan studies, among them five members of the former project, met at a conference at Heidelberg, entitled *Jagannath Revisited: Studying Society, Religion and the State in Orissa.*[3] It was planned as a kind of a state of the arts survey of research on Orissa and a stock-taking of its progress during the last two decades. It was during this conference that the decision was taken to conceive of a new research scheme on Orissa. In 1999 the second ORP, 'Various Identities: Socio-Cultural Profiles of Orissa in Historical and Regional Perspectives', coordinated at the Department of History at Kiel University, was sanctioned by the German Research Council until 2005. Although it was based on, and continued in many ways, the research of the former project, there was a clear shift of emphasis from the coastal region to the hinterland with the tribal and folk traditions of its various local and subregional identities. Whereas the former project focused on the dominant discourses of coastal Orissa, the second project was periphery oriented in a double sense. Geographically it extended its studies to the hinterland and periphery of coastal Orissa, and sociologically it gave a stronger emphasis on its peripheral or subaltern folk and tribal groups. With these

[1] See http://orp.uni-kiel.de.

[2] A. Eschmann, H. Kulke and G.C. Tripathi 1978.

[3] H. Kulke and B. Schnepel 2001.

complementary studies the second ORP attempts to give a more comprehensive view of the polymorphic and polycentric pattern of the great regional tradition of Orissa.[4] It also hopes to reveal the inherent vitality and dynamics of India's regional traditions by its paradigmatic studies on the genesis, historical development, competition and integration of various local and subregional traditions of Orissa.

From 2000 to 2003 the ORP conducted four annual conferences at the palatial manor house, the Landes-Kulturzentrum of the Federal State Schleswig-Holstein, at Salzau near Kiel. They were followed in 2004 by a final round of the members of the project in Civita Castellana in Italy. The four Salzau conferences were greatly enriched by the contributions of altogether about two dozen scholars from abroad, primarily from Orissa. Each of these conferences took up a special subject which was of central importance for the general theme of the project and related discourses. In its quest for reinterpretation of existing and the discovery of new sources for the study of Orissa's various identities, one of its grand theme, the notion of 'text', was taken up by the 2000 conference under the title *Text and Context in Orissa and Beyond*.[5] The following conference in 2001 focused with a strong anthropological emphasis on another theme of crucial importance for the project, the multi-faceted relations of *Periphery and Centre*.[6] The 2002 conference *Time in India: Concepts and Practices*[7] scrutinized Indian perceptions of 'time' as major markers of identity construction in Orissa.

The present volume *Centres Out There? Facets of Subregional Identities in Orissa* contains the proceedings of the fourth Salzau conference in 2003.[8] Its title is a deliberate borrowing from Victor Turner, not only to emphasize the two seemingly contradictory aspects of centrality and remoteness in the phenomena under study here. It was also meant as an invitation to see—similar to Turner's own approach[9]—the creation and functioning of the multiple centres not only as attempts to achieve social stability, but as processes, in which change and conflict are at least as much integral elements.

The title requires a qualification insofar as the dominant perception of Oriya identity usually associates its centres with coastal Orissa, particularly its 'Golden Triangle' of Bhubaneswar, Puri and Konarak. The 2003 conference

[4]See in this context also K.K. Basa 2004.

[5]A. Malinar, J. Beltz and H. Frese 2004.

[6]G. Pfeffer (ed.) 2007. Other contributors from among the participants in the project were P. Berger, R. Hardenberg, T. Otten, U. Skoda and C. Strümpell (see below and the references).

[7]A. Malinar 2007.

[8]P. Yule's preliminary report of the third archaeological field season of the Kiel group of the ORP in the year 2002 was again lectured by him at the 17th Conference of the European Association of South Asian Archaeologists at Bonn in July 2003 and published in its proceedings; see Yule et al. (2005), Yule (2006) and Brandtner et al. (2007).

[9]V. Turner 1973, 192.

and this volume, however, focus on their hinterland and periphery. Despite its size of about two-thirds of present-day Orissa with 62 distinct tribal communities and the history and culture of the former 24 Feudatory or Princely States[10] as well as the famous monuments of art and architecture of their predecessors, the early medieval *mandala* states, the so-called 'hinterland' of coastal Orissa remained until recently the stepchild of historical and socio-cultural research, the only notable exception being anthropological studies.[11] The present volume attempts primarily to emphasize this noticeable need and, if possible, to partly satisfy it.

A look at the history of Orissa clearly shows that the emergence of local and subregional identities had its roots in early medieval processes of state formation when tribal polities emerged in the periphery of the coastal kingdoms as autonomous *mandala* states. They were not just disruptive factors in the politics of these kingdoms but through processes of adaptation and inclusion became integral parts of them, strengthening their coherence and helping to extend the borders of their realm. The development of Orissa's little kingdoms as Garhjat or 'fort born' polities became a statewide phenomenon in the mountainous hinterland of coastal Mugalbandi since the seventeenth century and culminated in the rise of their successors, the Feudatory states in colonial Orissa. It is therefore no coincidence that more than half of the present papers pertain to the Feudatory states of Orissa and their early medieval predecessors, a subject which had already been taken up by G. Berkemer and B. Schnepel in the context of their studies of little kingdoms in Orissa.[12]

The volume opens with three introductory papers, viz., B.D. Chattopadhyaya's critical reasoning of the location and space of subregional centres and traditions in Indian history, B.P. Sahu's detailed and paradigmatic study of the emergence and early history of Dakshina Koshala as a subregional centre and H. Kulke's depiction of Orissa's Feudatory states as 'centres out there'. In his search for a model which can both locate cultural dynamics of integration and take note of diversities of separate communities, Chattopadhyaya takes us back to post-Vedic *janapadas* and the *tinai* eco-zones of Tamil Nadu in the *Sangam* age. The connecting links between the four levels, the subcontinent, its regions, subregions and localities, as 'basic sites of elements of diversity', he introduces the concept of 'imitable models' which emerged in the course of history and had varying lives in the process of circulation. He concludes his exploration with the hope that 'the perspective of looking at the Indian civilizational entity from above will be turned upside down, and the effort should rather be made to look for the historical processes involved in the making of a larger entity rather than for widely distributed sites of diversity as all derived from one tradition'. B.P. Sahu analyses the early history and

[10]L.E.B. Cobden Ramsay 1910.

[11]E.g. Bailey 1960; Sinha 1962, Mahapatra 1987.

[12]G. Berkemer 1993, 1997 and (together with M. Frenz) 2003; B. Schnepel 2002 (see his bibliography for his further studies on this subject); see also H. Kulke 1977.

cultural development of Dakshina Koshala, an area situated in present-day western Orissa and eastern Chhattisgarh, in order to examine how this 'socially unified space came to acquire discernible qualities which more or less defined it as a historico-cultural unit'. He admits that he used the terms 'regional' and 'subregional' interchangeably throughout his paper as 'the subregion, like the region, is a category which is easy to understand but rather difficult to define'. But he concludes his presentation with the helpful definition of subregions as 'a part of a region but with no single unit constituting it. In other words, they are in it and yet out of it, and in this are embedded the historical roots of contestation and negotiations within regions'. In his plea for stronger appreciation of the contributions of the Feudatory states to the cultural development of Orissa, H. Kulke points out that, in contrast to their early medieval *mandala* forerunners on the one hand and their often rather inglorious role under British rule on the other, their history, between the downfall of the imperial Gajapati kingdom in 1568 and British conquest of Orissa in 1803 remains outside the mainstream of Orissan historiography. But it was exactly during this decisive post-Gajapati period that the Garhjat states emerged as 'centres out there', when Orissa had come under Mughal and Maratha rule and Khurda struggled desperately for recognition as successors to the erstwhile imperial Gajapatis.

The wide spectrum of various socio-cultural facets of the Garhjat and Feudatory states of Orissa from centres of tribal integration to centres learning and emerging subregional identities is highlighted by several contributions of this volume. The two papers of C. Mallebrein on integration of tribal deities as tutelary deities of royal courts and on the famous coronation ritual with the raja sitting on tribal chief's lap[13] depict paradigmatically the enduring vividness of the tribal heritage of Orissan Feudatory states. In regard to their nature and emergence as 'centres out there' it is essential that these traditions focus on the 'capital' with its royal court as microcosm of the realm. Mallebrein's unique combination of visual media, interest in material culture and historiographical method provide insight into the subregion of central Orissa. Her contributions in the present volume concentrate on historical and religious aspects of some former feudatory states there, while elsewhere she has published and exhibited representative examples of Orissa's rich regional cultures.[14]

Whereas Mallebrein derives her examples primarily from the mountainous regions of western and northern Orissa, N. Gutschow's paper refers to Manikesvari, the powerful tribal tutelary goddess of Ranpur at the border of coastal Orissa. Her dominant role in the royal rituals is essential for the ritual centrality of Ranpur in its little kingdom. However, as pointed out by C.P. Nanda in his paper on Gangpur, a 'true' centre out there in far-off western Orissa, local traditions also preserve symbolic examples of tribal resistance

[13]See also C.P. Nanda forthcoming.

[14]For details to the newest publications see the references section of this chapter and otherwise the references of her contributions.

against their rulers in the shape of the presiding tribal deity. The traditions of these powerful tribal goddesses about their usually miraculous discovery and their deeds in favour of the rulers and the ruled are essential ingredients of local and subregional identities. As in the case of Gangpur and Ranpur, the legends of their 'Divine Play on the Earth'[15] found their way into local chronicles. As these were usually produced in the courts as dynastic or 'royal chronicles' (*rāja-vaṃśāvalī*), they further influenced the courtly nature of subregional identities.[16] Another aspect of religious life in the areas away from Orissa's coastal belt is the movement of Mahima Dharma. It has been studied by Anncharlott Eschmann in the first Orissa Project[17] and has been subject of extensive research in the second project.[18]

Several papers illustrate the rise of local Garhjat polities to truly 'centres out there' during seventeenth and eighteenth centuries. N. Gutschow's paper is instructive in this matter, too.[19] As an architect and historian of South Asian architecture, he traces the Ranpur's 'formation of a centre out there' through a study of its town-planning. Although its powerful tutelary goddess Maninagesvari is mentioned in inscriptions since a millennium, Ranpur's emergence as a subregional Garhjat state is linked with the rise of neighbouring Khurda as contested successor to the imperial Gajapatis in late sixteenth century. With the 'Great Street' (*baḍa daṇḍa*) for the annual car festival in front of the centrally located Jagannatha temple (sixteenth century) and the palace, it copied during the following two centuries systematically the Puri model. Ranpur's subregional centrality is moreover well documented by the annual Pancadolayatra festival when mobile images (*calanti pratimā*) of 108 deities from all over the State congregate in small portable shrines on Ranpur's ceremonial ground around its tutelary deity Maninagesvari.

G.C. Tripathi's case study of Keonjhar's rise to a powerful Feudatory state and a prominent seat of Brahmanical learning and Vedic studies is particularly revealing.[20] Bhanja kings are known to have ruled in the vicinity of Keonjhar since mid-first millennium CE and local tradition dates its foundation with the support of Bhuiyan tribe and tutelary goddesses of purely tribal origin in the early twelfth century. But its rise began with Govindabhanja around 1500, who became a staunch devotee of Jagannatha and whom Tripathi rightly calls 'harbinger of a new era'. In the late seventeenth century Lakshminarayana Bhanjadeva constructed in the capital Keonjhargarh the monumental Balabhadra temple, Orissa's second highest Vishnu temple after Puri's Jagannatha temple,

[15]This is the title of companion guide to the recent exhibition on tribal art and culture in Orissa at the Völkerkunde-Museum (Museum of Anthropology) at Heidelberg, see C. Mallebrein and H. von Stietencron 2008.

[16]H. Kulke 2004.

[17]A. Eschmann 1978.

[18]This research was done mainly by J. Beltz and L.J. Guzy; see Banerjee-Dube and Beltz 2008, Beltz 2007 and Guzy 2004, 2007.

[19]See also N. Gutschow, H. Kulke and R. Vasavada, in preparation.

[20]See also B. Schnepel, P.K. Nayak and H. Kulke, forthcoming.

and established five *sasana* villages for Brahmans whom he invited from all over Orissa. His successors collected and copied systematically manuscripts and laid the foundation stone of Keonjhar's fame as a centre of learning with its still existing unique library of palm-leaf manuscripts.

The rise of the Feudatory states as 'centres of learning' during this period, which Kulke, too, tries to document in his paper by a survey of the places of origin of the palm-leaf manuscripts of the Orissa State Museum, is further validated by the paper of G.N. Dash on Ghumsar in South Orissa. Its high estimate as the cultural centre of South Orissa is linked with Upendra Bhanja in early eighteenth century, the greatest late-medieval Oriya poet, and with his grandfather Dhananjaya. The major emphasis of Dash' erudition is a critical evaluation of the statement of John Beames, that the language of Ghumsar represents standard Oriya or 'the purest form' of the speech. S.K. Panda's paper on the *Kosalananda Kavyam* shows that already in mid-seventeenth century Sambalpur in western Orissa had even become a 'centre of attraction' for learned Brahmans. Gangadhar Mishra from a *sasana* village near Puri accepted the invitation of Raja Baliardeva to settle at Sambalpur and to compose Orissa's first historical Sanskrit poem on his dynasty.

Panda's article is relevant in regard to another matter of central importance of this volume, the creation of subregional identities by the emerging royal 'centres out there'. As already shown by S. Sinha in 1962 in a seminal article, the mostly tribal little kingdoms in the mountainous regions of eastern India experienced in the sixteenth to seventeenth centuries a wave of 'Rajputization' by adopting the Rajput model of state formation and the creation of genealogies and chronicles tracing their Rajput origin.[21] The most famous case in Orissa are the Chauhan Rajput kingdoms of Patnagarh-Bolangir, Sonpur, Sambalpur and Khariar in western Orissa. The earliest and in fact the major source of their deeply rooted Rajput identity till today is the *Kosalananda Kavyam*, whose historicity is fully accepted by historians of Orissa. Panda, however, for the first time comes forward with very convincing arguments that it was an 'invented tradition' by Gangadhar Mishra. The papers of C.P. Nanda and U. Skoda also refer to the 'Rajput myth' in the context of Gangpur and Bonai.

S. Arp takes up another important, most likely similarly controversial case of an invention of tradition, the legend of Yayati Kesari's invitation of ten thousand Brahmans from Kanauj for the performance of ten horse sacrifices at Jajpur. The great legendary deeds of Yayati Kesari, Orissa's most popular hero of pre-Gajapati history, at Jajpur and Puri[22] are unanimously associated

[21] S. Sinha 1962.

[22] H. Kulke (in print), argues that Yayati Kesari's Puri legend of the renewal of the Jaganntha cult and his construction of the first Jagannath temple at Puri is a legendary projection of the late sixteenth century. The legend moves Ramachandra of Khurda's renewal of the cult back into the 'hoary past'.

by Orissan historians with the historical Somavamsa king Yayati I and/or Yayati II (ninth and tenth centuries respectively). However, Arp advances emphatically strong arguments that Jajpur's Yayati Kesari legend, the foundation myth of the Kanauj origin of Orissa's Brahmans, is most likely not older than late eighteenth century. If the rather recent origin of Jajpur's and Puri's Yayati Kesari legends can be further verified, they validate the importance of the post-Gajapati period for the creation of important identity markers in coastal Orissa and its 'hinterland' alike.

B. Pati interrogates in his paper on colonial Orissa 'constructions of post-Orientalist Orientalism that tend to romanticize princely rulers' and depicts a very different picture of Orissa's 'Princely States' during late nineteenth and early twentieth centuries.[23] He explores the socio-economic order of seven states as 'centres of exploitation' which were closely integrated into the colonial system and processes of colonial underdevelopment. But he admits that 'it is not so clear how social practices associated with caste and patriarchy were preserved and reinforced in order to maintain social hierarchies, acquire legitimacy and thus obtain access to resources'.

Pati's work is a significant contribution to socio-historic questions at the tribal-state interface. While the tribals[24] and other non-Hindu minorities are increasingly marginalized in the course of modernization by the colonial state, the state administrations of the princely states, and later Indian governments, they still retain their particular world-view. The telling description of the conflicting moral orders of gatherer-hunters, tribals and the political society of the state in U. Demmer's contribution illustrates the fact that without a basic comprehension of tribal social norms even the most well meaning state administrator or development worker will fail to understand the consequences of the even the most well-intended interventions.

As has been shown by studies of ORP members which are not included in this volume, the most glaring contrasts exist in areas where mining and heavy industry exist as islands of 'progress' in a rural and tribal world. This aspect of social co-existence and conflict has been studied by C. Strümpell.[25] Details about the way of life under such different moral orders can be gleaned from P. Berger's studies on the Gadaba,[26] R. Hardenberg on the Kondh,[27] T. Otten on the Rona,[28] G. Pfeffer on the structure of tribal society.[29]

[23]See also B. Pati 2007.

[24]We are well aware of the fact that the term 'tribal' is considered old fashioned and even derogatory outside the Indian context. Within, it has significant legal connotations due to its occurrence in Article 342 of the Constitution of India and in the Fifth Schedule [The Constitution (Scheduled Tribes) Order, 1950].

[25]C. Strümpell 2006, 2007.

[26]P. Berger 2004, 2007.

[27]R. Hardenberg 2003, 2007.

[28]The Rona are an OBC group, not a scheduled tribe; see T. Otten 2006, 2007.

[29]G. Pfeffer 1998, 1998a, 2004; special mention should be made of the series of volumes

The 2003 conference was too early to raise the issue of the fate of tribals as traditional or converted non-Hindus *versus* an increasingly aggressive militant fringe of nationalist 'religiosity', as recently introduced into Orissa by the Sangh Parivar, who utilize social tensions between Tribals and Dalits for their aims.

Tribal-state co-existence in precolonial and early colonial times was neither always peaceful nor a field of permanent conflict.[30] Warfare and revolts did occur, as discussed by C.P. Nanda, and were part of claims and counter-claims for land and status, and sometimes, as B. Pati emphasizes, fights for sheer survival. U. Skoda, on the other hand, shows in his present contribution and in his earlier work,[31] a still existing tribal-caste interface left relatively undisturbed by the most recent economic and religious upheavals. Here, a peasant caste, the Aghria, immigrated into a tribal area, and social change came about without the destruction of the former moral order. In so far, this example is one of the paradigmatic types of Orissan little kingdoms. The already mentioned Feudatory state of Ranpur has been taken up by recent research as another such type.[32] Others are Gangpur/Bonai (Nanda, Skoda), Mayurbhanj/Keonjhar (Kulke, Tripathi) and Khurda (Tanabe). Others such as Kalahandi (Mallebrein) and Parlakhemundi (Berkemer) can be found in previous volumes of the Salzau conferences series.

Then there is L.J. Guzy's description of music as part of village rituals in western Orissa and its more recent social function in the formation of a Koshal identity. Here, a living tradition at the Hindu-tribal frontier is being reformulated in the context of regional identity formation. The agency taken over by a modern political discourse, village culture becomes both city folklore and an expression of a new subregional identity which seeks to construct its history by turning living but marginal traditions into its own fictitious past. This contribution and S.K. Panda's article on the Sanskrit poem *Koshalananda Kavyam* both give us an insight in the history of a text: its repeated re-creation as a depository of knowledge, its reflection of the dominant discourse during stages of its development, and finally its fate in the modern political and social contexts of the area it represents.

A second paradigmatic text for the creation of identity in Orissa is

---

published by Pfeffer and Behera called *Contemporary Society: Tribal Studies, Prof. Satya Narayana Ratha Felicitation Volumes.* This is an archive of work on tribal life and its changes in contemporary Orissa.

[30]See C. Mallebrein's articles on traditional tribal/state rituals of co-existence, but also G. Berkemer's contribution on Tekkali (Berkemer 1997), whose royal *vamsavali* hints at generations-long wars over land between Hindu settlers and tribal groups.

[31]U. Skoda 2003, 2005.

[32]This former little kingdom has been studied by several authors, among whom N. Gutschow's angle is unique (2003, 2004 and under preparation); see also Kulke 2004, Mallik/Kulke (in preparation).

Saraladasa's Oriya rendering of the *Mahabharata*. This text which is written by a low caste author is being discussed by B.K. Mallik. His focus is on caste tensions and the question of the life of widows in pre-modern Orissa. Mallik's contribution combines literary and social history with a gender issue.[33]

The gender aspect in religious ritual is being introduced by B. Hauser through her study on women's possession in south Orissa, thus bringing to our mind to what extent the female perspective, but also gender issues in general have so far been neglected in Orissan studies.[34]

There are other topics shared by several contributors: the question of historiography is prominent among them. It occurs in various contexts and combinations with textual studies, art, history, subaltern studies, anthropology, archaeology and various political critiques throughout this volume. The construction of the past, as it is done by chroniclers and astrologers, ritual specialists and family elders, bards and musicians, scribes and Brahmans, politicians, little kings and other wielders of power, and last but not least by historians and other academics, permeates all these contributions. Some criticize politically motivated attempts at history-building, or show that schoolbook history can be a very one-sided narrative of the past.[35]

After having described a host of real and academic challenges, the editors intend to end this introduction on a positive note: From A. Tanabe's[36] studies on the changing world of a little kingdom at the border between the former worlds of the traditional state and the tribal hinterland, a picture of slowly changing social formations emerges. Even though focusing on coastal Orissa, it can be very well put together with C.P. Nanda's, U. Skoda's and G.C. Tripathi's studies on the royal/tribal interface in western Orissa. Social change is not just a question of modernization, but runs more deeply in such social institutions which provide the integrative force for the coherence of otherwise very disparate worlds: what change other authors find in texts, narratives and rituals, is present here as well. The integration of both worlds as described by Tanabe is one of the most fascinating ongoing studies in Orissan research. The focus on proto-nationalism or 'patriotism in a primordial sense' shows us social integration which is deeply rooted in a living past and leads into a possible non-Western modernity.

[33]See also e.g. B.K. Mallik 1996, 2004.

[34]B. Hauser 2005, 2006, 2007; the gender aspect has also been studied by E. Hust 2002 and T. Otten 2007. The question of gender has not played much of a role in Orissan studies inside and outside the Orissa project (cf. however Behera/Nanda 1997, Tanabe 1999 and Tokita-Tanabe 1997 in the references). In Orissan studies, 'gender' is rarely distinguished from 'sex' and almost inevitably refers to 'woman'.

[35]See G. Berkemer in the present volume and H. Frese (2004).

[36]For references see A. Tanabe 2005, 2006, 2006a, 2007 in this chapter and his own references in the present volume.

REFERENCES

Bailey, Frederick G. 1960. *Tribe, Caste and Nation: A Study of Political Activity and Political Change in Highland Orissa*, Manchester: Manchester University Press.

Banerjee-Dube, Ishita and Johannes Beltz (eds.) 2008. *Popular Religion and Ascetic Practices: New Studies on Mahimā Dharma*, Delhi: Manohar.

Basa, Kishor K. 2004. 'Imagining Orissa: Archaeology, Art History and Cultural Identity', in A. Malinar, J. Beltz and H. Frese (eds.) 2004, 307-30.

Behera, Deepak Kumar and Namita Nanda 1997. 'Gender Inequalities in a Tribal Context: Some Reflections on Orissa', in G. Pfeffer and D.K. Behera (eds.) 1997, 149-62.

Beltz, Johannes 2007. 'Contested Authorities, Disputed Centres, and Rejected Norms: Situating Mahimā Dharma in its Regional Diversity', in G.F. Pfeffer (ed.) 2007, 79-104.

Berger, Peter 2004. *Füttern, Speisen und Verschlingen: Ritual und Gesellschaft im Hochland von Orissa, Indien*, Berlin: Lit-Verlag.

———2007. 'Sacrificial Food, the Person and the Ritual System of the Gadaba', in G. Pfeffer (ed.) 2007, 199-221.

Berkemer, Georg 1993. *Little Kingdoms in Kalinga. Ideologie, Legitimation und Politik Regionaler Eliten*, Stuttgart: Franz Steiner Verlag.

———1997. 'The Chronicle of a Little Kingdom: Some Reflections on the Tekkali-taluka Jamimdarla Vamsavali', in B. Kölver (ed.), *Recht, Staat und Verwaltung im klassischen Indien. The State, the Law and Administration in Classical India*, Munich: R. Oldenbourg Verlag, 65-95.

———2003. 'Borders, Lines and Cases: From Sīma to Sīmānta in South Orissa and Beyond. K.C. Panigrahi Memorial Lecture 2002, Ravenshaw College, Cuttack', *Ravenshaw Historical Journal* 3.

———2004. 'Jaypur - Parlakimedi - Vizianagaram: The Southern Gajapatis', in A. Malinar, J. Beltz and H. Frese (eds.) 2004, 93-117.

———2007. 'The King's Two Kingdoms or How the Maharaja of Parlakimedi Finally Became the Ruler of Orissa', in G. Pfeffer (ed.) 2007, 341-59.

Berkemer, G. and M. Frenz (eds.) 2003. *Sharing Sovereignty: The Little Kingdom in South Asia*, Berlin: Klaus Schwarz.

Brandtner, Martin, B. Misra, P. Mohanty and Paul Yule 2007. 'Survey in Western Orissa: Preliminary Report', in G. Pfeffer (ed.) 2007, 15-25.

Cobden Ramsay, L.E.B. 1910. *Feudatory States of Orissa*, Calcutta: The Bengal Secretariat Book Depot (rpt. 1950, 1982).

Eschmann, A., H. Kulke and G.C. Tripathi (eds.) 1978. *The Cult of Jagannath and the Regional Tradition of Orissa*, Delhi: Manohar.

Eschmann, Anncharlott 1978. 'Mahimā Dharma: An Autochthonous Hindu Reform Movement', in A. Eschmann, H. Kulke and G.C. Tripathi (eds.) 1978, 375-410.

Frese, Heiko 2004. 'Anecdotes of History: Reflections on Contexts and (Hi)stories', in A. Malinar, J. Beltz and H. Frese (eds.) 2004, 119-42.

Gutschow, Niels 2003. 'Ranpur – The Centre of a Little Kingdom', in G. Berkemer and M. Frenz (eds.) 2003, 137-64.

———2004. 'Ranpur Resolved: Spatial Analysis of a Town in Orissa Based on a Chronicle', in A. Malinar, J. Beltz and H. Frese (eds.) 2004, 67-92.

Gutschow, N., H. Kulke and R. Vasavada (in preparation). *Ranpur: History and Settlement Patterns of a 'Little Kingdom' of Orissa*, Heidelberg: Savifa, the Virtual South Asia Library (http://www.savifa.uni-hd.de/home_en.html).

Guzy, Lidia Julianna 2004. '*Babas* and *Alekhs*: A Religion in the Making', in C. Mallebrein and L.J. Guzy (eds.) 2004, 105-11.

———2007. 'Babas and Alekhs: Notes on Concepts of Time and Social Change in a Contemporary Ascetic Doctrine', in A. Malinar (ed.) 2007, 81-98.

———2008. '*Theaphony*: On Music, Religion and the Goddess in Western Orissa', in L.J. Guzy (ed.), *Religion and Music: Proceedings of the Interdisciplinary Workshop at the Institute for Scientific Studies of Religions, Freie Universität Berlin, May 2006*. Berlin: Weißensee-Verlag, 89-106.

Hardenberg, Roland 2003. 'Friendship and Violence among the Dongria Kond', *Baessler-Archiv* 51, 45-57.

———2007. 'Context and Values: A Discussion of Concepts', in G. Pfeffer (ed.) 2007, 153-72.

Hauser, Beatrix 2005. 'Travelling Through the Night: Living Mothers and Divine Daughters at an Orissan Goddess Festival', *Paideuma* 51, 221-33.

———2006. 'Divine Play or Subversive Comedy: Reflections on Costuming and Gender at a Hindu Festival', in U. Rao and J. Hutnyk (eds.), *Celebrating Transgression: Method and Politics in Anthropological Studies of Culture*, New York, Oxford: Berghahn, 129-44.

———2007. 'Tribal or Tantric: Reflections on the Classification of Goddesses in Southern Orissa', in G. Pfeffer (ed.) 2007, 131-52.

Hust, Evelin 2002. *Political Representation and Empowerment: Women in the Institutions of Local Government in Orissa after the 73rd Amendment to the Indian Constitution.* South Asia Inst., Dep. of Political Science, Univ. of Heidelberg. (Heidelberg Papers in South Asian and Comparative Politics. Working Paper No. 6; URL: http://www.ub.uni-heidelberg.de/archiv/4098).

Kulke, H. 1977. 'Early State Formation and Royal Legitimation in Late Ancient India', in M.N. Das (ed.), *Sidelights on History and Culture of Orissa*, Cuttack.

———1993. *Kings and Cults: State Formation and Legitimation in India and Southeast Asia*, Delhi: Manohar.

———2004. 'The Making of a Local Chronicle: The *Ranapura Rajavamsa Itihasa*', in A. Malinar, J. Beltz and H. Schnepel (eds.) 2004, 43-66.

———forthcoming. 'Yayati Kesari Revisited: Ramachandra of Khurda and Puri's Yayati Kesari Legend', in P. Berger, R. Hardenberg and E. Kattner (eds.), *The Anthropology of Values: Festschrift in Honour of Georg Pfeffer*, Delhi: Manohar.

Kulke, H. and B. Schnepel (eds.) 2001. *Jagannath Revisited: Studying Society, Religion and the State in Orissa*, Delhi: Manohar.

Mahapatra, L.K. 1987. 'Ex-Princely States of Orissa: Mayurbhanj, Keonjhar and Bonai', in S. Sinha (ed.), *Tribal Polities and State Systems in Pre-Colonial Eastern and North Eastern India*, Calcutta: K.P. Bagchi.

Malinar, Angelika (ed.) 2007. *Time in India: Concepts and Practices*, Delhi: Manohar.

Malinar, Angelika, Johannes Beltz and Heiko Frese (eds.) 2004. *Text and Context in the History, Literature and Religion of Orissa*, Delhi: Manohar.

Mallebrein, Cornelia and Lidia Julianna Guzy (eds.) 2004. *Facets of Orissan Studies*, Delhi: Kamla-Raj Enterprises (*Journal of Social Sciences* 8, 2 (Special Issue), March 2004).

Mallebrein, Cornelia and H. von Stietencron 2008. *The Divine Play on Earth: Religious Aestetics and Ritual in Orissa, India*, Heidelberg: Synchron.

Mallik, Basanta Kumar 1996. *Medieval Orissa: Literature, Society, Economy* (*Circa 1500-1600 A.D.*), Bhubaneswar: Mayur.

———2004. *Paradigms of Dissent and Protest: Social Movements in Eastern India* (*c. A.D. 1400-1700*), Delhi: Manohar.

Mallik, Basanta Kumar and H. Kulke (eds., in preparation). *Ranapura Rajavamshavali: A Dynastic History of the 'Little Kingdom' Ranpur in Orissa by Damodar Singh Deo,*

Heidelberg: Savifa, the Virtual South Asia Library (http://www.savifa.uni-hd.de/home_en.html).

Nanda, C.P. 2008. *Vocalizing Silence: Political Protests in Orissa, 1930-42*, Delhi, Thousand Oaks: Sage.

———forthcoming. 'Politicising 'Theatre': Sitting on the Lap of a Bhuiyan. Coronation Ceremonies in Keonjhar/Orissa', in H. Kulke and U. Skoda (eds.), *Rituals and the State in India*, Wiesbaden: Harrassowitz.

Nanda, C.P. and H. Kulke forthcoming. *Locating Local History: Identity Politics of Kudmis of Orissa*, Delhi: Manohar.

Otten, Tina 2006. *Heilung durch Rituale: Vom Umgang mit Krankheit bei den Ronā im Hochland Orissa*, Berlin: Lit.

———2007. 'Cosmic Time and Its Influence on Rona Girls and Women', in A. Malinar (ed.), 137-56.

Pati, Biswamoy 2007. 'The Order of Legitimacy: Princely Orissa, 1850-1947', in B. Pati and W. Ernst (eds), *India's Princely States: People, Princes and Colonialism*, London: Routledge, 85-98.

Pati, B. and M. Harrison (eds.) 2001. *Health, Medicine and Empire: Perspectives on Colonial India*, Delhi: Orient Longman.

Pfeffer, Georg F. 1998. 'The Indian State and the Tribes of India', *Journal of the Indian Anthropological Society* 33, 1, 77-86.

———1998a. 'The Own and the Other: Construction of Identity in Orissa', *The Fourth World* No. 8, 15-25.

———2004. 'Tribal Society of Highland Orissa, Highland Burma, and Elsewhere', in A. Malinar, J. Beltz and H. Frese (eds.) 2004, 427-56.

Pfeffer, Georg F. (ed.) 2007. *Periphery and Centre: Studies in Orissan History, Religion and Anthropology*, Delhi: Manohar.

Pfeffer, Georg F. and Deepak Kumar Behera (eds.) 1996. *Contemporary Society: Childhood and Complex Order. Prof. Satya Narayana Ratha Festschrift*, Delhi: Manak.

Pfeffer, Georg F. and Deepak Kumar Behera (eds.) 1997. *Contemporary Society: Tribal Studies. Prof. Satya Narayana Ratha Felicitation Volumes*, vol. I: *Structure and Process*, Delhi: Concept.

Sahu, Bhairabi Prasad 2003. *Legitimation, Ideology and State in Early India.* Presidential Address, Ancient India Section, Indian History Congress, Sixty-fourth Session, Mysore University, Mysore: Indian History Congress.

———2003a. 'The Early State in Orissa: From the Perspective of Changing Forms of Patronage and Legitimation', in B. Pati, B.P. Sahu and T.K. Venkatasubrahmanian (eds.), *Negotiating India's Past: Essays in Memory of Partha Sarathi Gupta*, Delhi: Tulika Books, 29-51.

———2006. 'Ways of Seeing: History and Historiography of the State in Early India', in M. Brandtner and S.K. Panda (eds.), *Interrogating History: Essays for Hermann Kulke*, Delhi: Manohar, 63-82.

Schnepel, B. 2002. *The Jungle Kings: Ethnohistorical Aspects of Politics and Ritual in Orissa*, Delhi: Manohar (transl. of *Die Dschungelkönige: Ethnohistorische Aspekte von Politik und Ritual in Südorissa/Indien*, Stuttgart: Steiner).

Schnepel, B. and P.K. Nayak, with contributions by H. Kulke, C.P. Nanda and R. Vasavada (in preparation). *Keonjhar: Ethnohistory of a Little Kingdom in Northern Orissa*, Heidelberg: Savifa, the Virtual South Asia Library (http://www.savifa.uni-hd.de/home_en.html).

Sinha, Surajit 1962. 'State Formation and Rajput Myth in Tribal Central India', *Man in India* 42, 35-80.

Skoda, Uwe 2003. 'On a Tribal Frontier: Aghriā-Gauntiā as Village Kings', in G. Berkemer and M. Frenz (eds.) 2003, 181-203.

———2005. *The Aghriā: A Peasant Caste on a Tribal Frontier*, Delhi: Manohar.

Strümpell, Christian 2006. '*Wir arbeiten zusammen, wir essen zusammen*': *Konvivium und soziale Peripherie in einer indischen Werkssiedlung*, Berlin, Münster: Lit.

———2007. 'Chatamput: An Industrial "Camp" in the Tribal Zone', in G. Pfeffer (ed.) 2007, 319-39.

Tanabe, Akio 2005. 'The System of Entitlements in Eighteenth-century Khurda, Orissa: Reconsidering "Caste" and "Community" in Late Pre-colonial India', *South Asia* 28, 3, 345-85.

———2006. 'Early Modernity and Colonial Transformation: Rethinking the Role of the King in Eighteenth and Nineteenth Century Orissa, India', in M. Kimura and A. Tanabe (eds.), *The State in India: Past and Present*, Delhi: Oxford University Press, 202-28.

———2006a. 'Recast(e)ing Identity: Transformation of Inter-caste Relationships in Post-colonial Rural Orissa', *Modern Asian Studies* 40, 3, 761-96.

———2007. 'Toward Vernacular Democracy: Moral Society and Post-Postcolonial Transformation in Rural Orissa, India', *American Ethnologist* 34, 3, 558-74.

Tokita-Tanabe, Yumiko 1996. 'Village Politics and Women: Towards a Gendered Analysis of "Faction" in Rural Orissa', *Journal of the Japanese Association for South Asian Studies* 8, 90-122.

Turner, Victor W. 1973. 'The Centre Out There: Pilgrims Goal', *History of Religions* 12, 3, 191-230.

Yule, Paul, P.K. Behera, M. Brandtner, D. Modarressi and B.K. Rath 2005. 'Preliminary Report on the Third Field Season, 2002: Contexting Early Historic Western Orissa', in U. Franke-Vogt and H.-J. Weisshaar (eds.), *South Asian Archaeology 2003*, Bonn, 7-11 July 2003, Aachen: Linden Soft, 307-18.

———2006. *Early Historic Sites in Orissa*, Delhi: Paragon.

CHAPTER 1

Space, History and Cultural Process: Some Ideas on the Ingredients of Subregional 'Identity'

BRAJADULAL CHATTOPADHYAYA

> The major concern of the sceptical discourse on culture is that the concept suggests boundedness, homogeneity, coherence, stability, and structure whereas social reality is characterized by variability, inconsistencies, conflict, change, and individual agency. . . .
>
> CHRISTOPH BRUMANN (1999, 52)

The concern that underlies the sceptical discourse on culture also applies to generalizations concerning space, since culture is in essence envisioned in the context of its spatial dimensions or its communities, whatever the nature of that space may be. Any discourse on India, stated even in historiographical terms, starts by invoking a by now hallowed convention of invoking a unique image of the country as a 'unity in diversity'. The present chapter attempts to understand to what extent available historical studies reflect this image and also evaluates the directions of suggested departures. This attempt will not be anchored in the context of any specific region except by way of providing examples. Instead, it will limit itself to consideration of some aspects of historiography relating to how India and its territorial components are viewed, and making references to textual and other ways of thinking about culture in relation to space.

THE HISTORIOGRAPHY OF INDIA AND ITS SPATIAL COMPONENTS

Since the idea of India as a unit of historical study is colonial in origin,[1] the unit was in essence viewed from a political perspective. This view took the form of an Indian State and of the Indian subcontinent as the space for that state. The history of the state, however, was dissected; the fragments, in chronological order, were Hindu, Muslim and British (not Christian). Some form of dichotomy between pre-Islamic and Islamic historiographical traditions

[1] Of the many studies available on the origins of modern Indian historiography, particularly on the shift to the history of India, see Chatterjee 1999, 1-49; also, Chattopadhyaya 2003, Chapter 1.

may have existed earlier, but dividing up the history of the subcontinent in religious terms was certainly a colonial invention. On two counts the relationship between space and history made a break from early Indian traditions: (i) by making the subcontinent the space of study. This space was different from Bharatavarsa, the land of the Bharatas, with its varying geographical connotations,[2] (ii) the traditional way of writing history with reference to 'sovereign rulers' and of the uninterrupted succession of sovereign families. This break must be stressed in particular because the relationship of the Cakravarti or sovereign ruler was to *sarva-bhumi* (all land), which comprised all the spaces (*janapada*s) of different communities. To put it briefly, in the new historiography, when regions become the units of study, they devolve from the larger space, which should be a stable space. The historical pattern of regions and formats of regional history are therefore replicas of general histories of India. The colonial break was not remade by anti-colonial nationalist enterprise. The 'fundamental unity' of India[3] being the base with which to start historical studies, the components of India, which were integrated through an elaborate system of networks of ideas and other cultural ingredients, came to be recognized essentially by the extent of which they were the representatives of the 'pan-Indian' pattern or deviations from this ideal. The perspective reminds one of W.B. Yeats's famous lines in 'The Second Coming' (1920):

> Things fall apart; the centre cannot hold;
> Mere anarchy is loosed upon the world.

What, then, about the much talked-about diversities? One notices here, if one observes carefully in retrospect, that there was a real mismatch between history and the various surveys—ethnographic, linguistic and in other areas—at ground level.[4] To repeat, region was a fractured space, a part of a larger one. To be fair, regional studies were built upon meticulous investigations into, and acquisition of, source material,[5] in attempting to identify major segments of what were considered regions and, more significantly, by some of the following:

[2]This is drawn from my ongoing work on 'Bharatavarsa, its Connotations and Historiographical Implications'.

[3]This expression was used as the title of a short but profoundly influential work by R.K. Mookerji (2003).

[4]One has in mind here the impressive series of ethnographic monographs, by both European and Indian scholars, presenting the results of fieldwork among tribes and other communities, with details of belief systems, kinship and marriage structures, ritual, subsistence and resources—the production pattern—and so on. For linguistic survey, see the comprehensive eleven-volume survey by G.A. Grierson published between 1903 and 1928 in Calcutta, Central Publication Branch.

[5]Source material, at the early stage of historical writing, was fairly well defined but varied. It included archaeological material, particularly monuments and art historical artefacts, inscriptions, coins, texts in manuscripts, archival records—all of which, expertly reported, edited and most times translated, constituted a vast corpus drawn upon by historians, even today, with occasional additions.

(i) icons of a region in the form of its mainly political heroes; (ii) attempted early chronologies of civilizations and kingdoms of which the region was the locus; (iii) rivals as homeland of such major figures as Kalidasa or Jayadeva; and (iv) the uniqueness of its sacred centre or centres and the form of worship. Even defined in terms of certain traits, regions were simply units of bounded space and were constructs similar to the construct of India as a given unit. For the historian, the problem with such constructs is that there are no pointers to the ways in which India would have evolved over time as a recognizable space, though not a homogeneous cultural space as a 'fundamental' entity. Similarly, in most studies, a region is a permanently homogeneous entity, not accommodating variations and mutations.

The problem, then, is one of developing a model for historical trajectories which can both locate cultural dynamics by pointing to modes and scales of integration and take note of diversities in the large number of communities that separate themselves in relation to others, in the areas of language and dialect differences and differences in religious practices and beliefs, and also of, in general, incorporating all these into a historical narrative. This does not mean switching from a grand mega-narrative to the microscopic views of fragments. The dynamics implied in any historical and cultural process have to be grasped, to start with, by taking into consideration the following dimensions of a possible interrelationship:

Spaces	Historical/cultural processes	Formation of cultural spaces and networks

With an interrelationship at this basic level being in the reckoning, the Indian subcontinent as a culture-space cannot be presupposed as a way of then looking for its diversities. The method should be the other way round: to look at the process and chronology of the formation of cultural zones and of networks of interaction, and further, to examine whether historically larger spatial formations could and did emerge over time. Thus, the three basic elements in this interrelationship were not isolated historically, but were in fact in a constant state of varying forms of interaction:

Spaces	Historical/cultural processes	Formation of cultural zones and networks

REGIONS AND THEIR COMPONENTS IN GEOGRAPHY AND ANTHROPOLOGY

Before we proceed further along this line of thinking, it may be worth taking account of how the components—geographical and cultural—constituting India have been defined and viewed in their interrelationships by geographers and anthropologists. Unlike historians, who start with an assumption of unity and then proceed to the presumed constituent components, geographers talk of diversities at both the macro and micro levels—mainly in terms of physical traits, but also of the historical possibilities of a complex of traits.[6] Thus regional traits are often seen to correspond to an order of hierarchy, in which perennial nuclear regions can be contrasted with march regions, areas of relative isolation, areas of isolation, and so on. Applied to the study of archaeology and history,[7] the concept of nuclear regions in relation to other not-so-nuclear areas has been found useful in explaining the location and spread of archaeological cultures, the emergence of kingdoms and empires, of cities and urban growth, as well as in suggesting directions of population movements and civilizational progress. There are, however, two limitations of this kind of ordering: (i) the static character of the nuclearity of space embedded in it does not explain why nuclear regions may cease to be nuclear over time, and other categories of space down the hierarchy emerge as centres of rapid change;[8] and (ii) the issue of nuclearity and non-nuclearity in history, in which different patterns of culture may co-exist, may be one of several perspectives, and one must therefore be specific about which particular pattern is taken to represent nuclearity. If one is analysing the pattern of interaction in simple societies, nuclearity will have a different implication than it would have in a complex society. These limitations, however, do not, as I shall try to show later, make the notion of hierarchy redundant; one still has to contend with the issue of the historical emergence of centres and networks, even though not as static points on cultural landscapes. In the context of the study of Indian society in its diversity and interrelationships, the notion of networks first came to be articulated effectively by anthropologists, and it is necessary to note, for the present context, of how they viewed the problem of spatial relationships in cultural terms. In a seminal article first published in 1958 and entitled 'Networks and Centers in the Integration of Indian Civilization', B. Cohn and M. Marriott[9] started by stating

[6]See, for example, Spate and Learmouth 1972.

[7]For an elaborate early attempt to analyse archaeological data in terms of a hierarchized order of regions, following geographical studies, see Subbarao 1958, Chapters 2, 6-8 in particular. For new ways of analysing archaeological cultures in spatial terms in general, see the collection edited by Wagstaff 1987. There have been several attempts to discuss ways in which regions can be conceptualized in the Indian context. See Crane 1967, Fox 1977, for studies of 'power' in relation to their regional dimensions. For other bibliographical references, see also Chattopadhyaya 1984.

[8]For example, although Radha in Bengal, with its extension to the Bhagirathi, was the nuclear region of proto- and early-historical cultures; in the Gupta period Pundravardhana in north Bengal, with its poorly documented settlement history in an earlier phase, was definitely the nuclear region. In the early centuries of the Christian Era, the shift from the nuclear Mahanadi basin to the comparatively inhospitable coast in the south of Orissa and Andhra is epigraphically documented. For a detailed study of how, in the Kakatiya period, there was a shifting of focus from the Krishna-Godavari delta to west and central Andhra, with Warangal emerging as the core of a new empire, see Talbot 2001.

[9]Included in Cohn 1998, 78-87; see also idem 1998b.

that 'both socially and culturally' India represented a combination and partial integration of very diverse elements. Since 'integration' is an assumed premise in this statement, the patterns of integration focused on 'networks' of relationships and relationships with centres. For this purpose, India needed to be viewed at four levels at least: (i) All India: The subcontinent, (ii) The Region: generally defined by a literary language and distinctive caste-patterning, (iii) The Subregion, (iv) The local level.

The regions and subregions do not correspond to political divisions, and, in any case, so far as level (i) is concerned, 'the nation of India is, of course, a recent unity'. The distinct contribution of the notion of the levels is that 'integration' is not seen as a reassemblage of the parts of a broken whole, but as the recognition of the presence of complex sets of 'social commonalities' such as caste structure and certain shared elements of culture such as language. 'In each division there is also likely to be a shared and characteristic variant of Hinduism, a body of distinctive historic tradition, and a common style in many matters of daily life'.

The notion of 'integration' implies the existence of 'centres', and indeed Cohn and Marriott believe that 'India's civilizational centres may be seen as formed and functioning in relationship to such networks, against the background of extreme social and cultural diversity. Reference to 'centres' rather than to a 'centre' takes the focus away from a single steady 'centre' as the pole star of Indian history and '[c]entres then contribute to India's diversity even in the process of organizing that diversity'.

Two points emerging from the voluminous contributions of geographers and anthropologists towards the understanding of diversities are (i) centres as nodes for networks, and (ii) the implied relationship between a 'centre' and spatial hierarchies which are conditioned geographically. From the perspective of historical time spans, the points, although of heuristic value, have to be checked against historical evidence, since both geographical and anthropological works tend to view hierarchies, networks and centres as congealed in time and as not shaping and re-shaping themselves. The historical exercise may begin with a brief statement of the spatial and cultural components constituting Indian space in early textual perception.

JANAPADAS AND *NADUS*

In Sanskritic perceptions about spaces, one can see a shift from landmarks like rivers or mountains as signifiers of space to *janapada*s, or settlements of people (literally, 'foot of the people'). An early Buddhist text gives us a list of sixteen major *janapada*s, distributed between the north-west and the Godavari valley in the Deccan.[10] *Janapada*s arranged according to directions (*dis*), later became an elaborate cosmographic scheme in which Bharatavarsa was the

[10] See Raychaudhuri 1958, particularly the chapter, 'Puranic Cosmography'.

macro-unit. Despite its varying uses and substitution by other, more official terms in some parts of contemporary India, *janapada* has come to be used again but mainly to denote district-level administrative units. What did *janapada*s denote in spatial and cultural terms? What, for example, would be the difference between Gandhara, Kuru, Koshala, Magadha or Anga in the period of the Buddha? At this stage it seems to have been more political and ethnic than cultural, although later texts do bring out the particular cultural traits of different regions. The difference as perceived was the difference—real or imagined—between sets of people who inhabited their respective *janapadas*; hence the interchangeability of the *janapada* name with 'ethnic' name.[11]

However, a *janapada* was not a homogeneous space, neither its ethnic composition. It is therefore necessary to understand the meanings of the term as they are suggested by the texts. *Janapada* space was not uniform, and a major difference was between *aranya* (forest) and what could be considered as proper inhabited space. Inhabited space too was differentiated in terms of varieties of villages (*grama*), market places (*nigama*), cities (*nagara*) and big cities (*mahanagara*), with cities and big cities expectedly functioning as 'centres' where networks converged.[12]

The multiplicity of *janapada*s and multiplicity of 'centres' thus constituted the landscape of Bharatavarsa with their differentiated and hierarchical structures. The total number of *janapada*s would vary from text to text, as would the number of divisions within which they were grouped, their number varying from five to nine.

To continue with the issue of the difference between *janapadas*, it is doubtful whether material culture, as revealed by archaeology, made any major difference. If one considers the material cultures of the major *janapada*s in the period of the Buddha, it would perhaps be impossible to distinguish between the Vatsa, Koshala, Kasi and Magadha *janapadas*.[13] There is, of course, a highlighting of particular resources for particular *janapada*s. Kalinga, for example, was, along with a few other *janapadas*, marked as an area of covetable textile production. Elephants too constituted one of its resources.[14] In Kalidasa's *Raghuvamsam*, the particular resources of the Malaya areas, namely the land in the southern hills, were items like black pepper (*marica*), cardamom

[11] Although H.C. Raychaudhuri considered them to be 'states of considerable extent and power' in the period of the Buddha, his detailed discussion on the *janapada*s of the period leaves no doubt that the texts use these names interchangeably with the people who inhabited them. Raychaudhuri 1997, pts. I-III.

[12] For the settlement structure of a *janapada*, see Ghosh 1973, Chapter 3.

[13] This will be evident from the nature of archaeological material culture of the middle Ganga basin of the period of the Buddha. For a synthesis of the material, see Sharma 1983, Chapters 4 and 6.

[14] *Arthasastra*, 2. 20: the elephants of Kalinga, along with those of Anga, Purvadesa, Cedi and Karusa, were considered to be the best. A reference to Kalingaka or cotton textiles is to be found in 2. 11.

(*elaphala*) and sandalwood (*candana*).[15] In Brahmanical notions, however, it was not material culture or resources which marked off one *janapada* from the other, but the extent to which they were close, both spatially and culturally, to where the ideal moral or social order prevailed. This was *madhyadesa* or *aryavarta*. The centrality of the 'firmly established' *madhyadesa*, dating to the text *Aitareya Brahmana*,[16] is expressed in *Manu-Samhita* thus:[17]

> Where the black antelope ranges by nature, that should be known as the country fit for sacrifices; and beyond it is the country of the barbarians (*mlecchas*).

The impurity associated with marginal areas is also evident in *Baudhayana Dharmasutra*'s injunction:[18]

> If someone travels to the land of the Kalingas, he commits a sin through his feet. The seers have prescribed the Vaisvanari sacrifice as an expiation for him.

The geographical limits of Madhyadesa could change, but its centrality did not. In the tenth century the writer Rajasekhara would consider Aryavarta to be the source of all *sadacara* (honest behaviour), with its foundation resting on four *varnas* and *asramas*; the literary codes too that could be emulated were those of the Aryavarta.[19]

Although the cultural ingredients of individual *janapadas* are not really spelt out, they do sometimes make their appearance in the form of references to peculiarities of speech, particular social habits, and even the display of personality traits of individuals representing peculiar human personal traits of a *janapada*,[20] extending to the imagined desirable or undesirable qualities of women to be seduced as sexual partners.[21]

Janapada, which would roughly correspond to a *nadu* in the context of south India, did not mean a region. Like *janapada*, the term *nadu* too could have various connotations.[22] It could mean the domain of a ruling power as in

[15] Devadhar 1984: IV. 26-86.

[16] Cf. the expression *dhruvayam madhyamayam paitisthayam disi*, *Aitareya Brahmana*, 8. 14.

[17] *Manu-Samhita*, 2. 17-24.

[18] *Baudhayana Dharmasutra*, 1. 2. 9-14.

[19] This is what Rajasekhara, in the *desavibhaga* section (17) of his *Kavyamimansa* says with regard to the Aryavarta: *tasmin caturvaryam caturasramyam ca tanmulasca sadacara tatratyo vyavahara prayena kavinam*, i.e. 'there prevail four *varnas* and four *ashramas*; it is the source of good behaviour, the poets follow the practices of this (region)'.

[20] See, for example, the allegorical play *Prabodha Candrodaya* by Krsna Misra, written in the eleventh century. This refers to a character from *Daksina Radha-Pradesa* who is a personification of *ahamkara* (egoism) and who, appropriately, calls everyone around him a fool: *murkha-bahulam jagat*, i.e. 'the world is full of fools', II. 2-18.

[21] See, for example, the monologue-play (*bhana*) *Padataditaka* by Saumilaka, which refers to Barbari women desired by men from Surashtra, who are themselves like monkeys; women from Lata; Yavani, woman enamoured of a male from Malava; M. Ghosh 1975, 155-7; for some sexual proclivities, see *Kamasutram*, V. 5, V. 6.

[22] See Subbarayalu 1973, Chapter 5; Stein 1980, Chapter 3. However, their characterization

Hoysala-nadu, but it was, like *janapada*, a basic unit of human settlement, distinguishable from other *nadus* and with a heterogeneous structure. Both *janapada* and *nadu* would correspond to what I have elsewhere called locality or 'settlement locality',[23] and, thus, Cohn's 'locality' in his schema of four-tiered spatial arrangement.

The rationale for the above exercise was the search for possible sources of diversities in the composition of the Indian entity, and *janapada* and *nadu* and the various meanings they carry may provide some useful insights into the making of Indian regions and subregions. Being basic and enduring units, they were in a sense autonomous (although internally differentiated), and while their incorporation into larger units or patterns of interaction with varying networks would surely change their character, traits which were local could remain at the core of what changed. One word of caution is called for here. While space is stable, a *janapada* name was not. For example, in Orissa, Kalinga was the settlement space of the Kalinga people in the littoral tract in early recorded history. In Major Rock Edict 13 of Asoka, Kalinga is used in both singular and plural,[24] possibly to refer to the Kalinga people and their settlement spaces interchangeably, as in cases of the Colas, Pandyas, Ceras and Satiyaputas. The two nodes of Kalinga, Tosali and Samapa, were located respectively in the delta of the Mahanadi Valley and on the banks of the Rishikulya. But the connotation of Kalinga underwent major modifications indicating an actual geographical shift of the name to the south.[25] This should serve as a mild reminder against the notion of the fixity of any variables in history.

REGIONS, SUBREGIONS AND 'IMITABLE MODELS'

It has already been noted that *janapadas* were not regions in the way human groups assert their spatial identity and cultural affiliation today. Modern regions like Bengal, Maharashtra, or Rajasthan would not have existed throughout Indian history. Historical evidence and perspective therefore demand that we look for the processes that went into the making of regions and the particular characteristics associated with them. The processes and characteristics, or, in other words, the history of the formation of regions, would obviously vary from one region to another, and the chronology and ingredients too may have differed. For example, whereas the formation of most regions is recognizable at a much later stage, Tamil Nadu may serve as an example of a 'historical'

---

of *nadu* as peasant macro-regions, that is, as basic units of the agrarian landscape, does not take into consideration other meanings of the term, including possible comparisons with such terms as *badi*.

[23] Chattopadhyaya 2003a.

[24] Major Rock Edict XIII; for text see Sircar 1965b, 34-7.

[25] Ganguly 1975, Chapter 1; Brandtner 2001, 179-210.

region.[26] Tamilaham, the early name, was marked by the presence of three major chiefdoms, Cola, Pandya and Cera. Despite their being mentioned as communities, along with other communities in Asokan edicts (Coda, Pada, Satiyaputo, Ketalaputo), their poetic image as the major representatives of the space give Tamilaham a certain measure of cohesion. More importantly, there was the language in which bards—men and women—composed their songs and sang them. The term *Sangam*, which is of later origin, carried the memory of a tradition of the poetic assemblies at Madurai, the seat of the Pandya chief.

That language and script came to be the most important ingredients of the formation of regions is suggested by historical evidence. The slow transition to modern Indian scripts through several historical stages is revealed by epigraphic documents, supplemented at a later stage by manuscripts from different regions.[27] Proto-regional scripts, later to mature into regional scripts, appear in the early medieval period. Whereas in epigraphy the appearance of local words in Sanskrit-language inscriptions slowly gives way to regional languages, their articulation in literary compositions is more spectacular. Regional languages did not completely displace Sanskrit, but they and their literary products having become more accessible, regional literary products now came to contest the dominance of Sanskrit. It has been surmised that in Andhra, the 'emergence of vernacular to a high literary status' did not 'take place in the centres of high culture' but in 'isolated regions'.[28] However, by the thirteenth century the Telugu language had come to be recognized as equivalent to the land of the Andhras. Languages now denoted places.[29] The identification of a language with a region, which was visible in the early medieval period, now remained everywhere the major binding force in Indian history. In the nineteenth century, the Oriya writer Fakirmohan Senapati creatively articulating in his autobiography his agony over the neglect of Oriya, recorded the efforts he and his associates had made to contest the dominance of the Bengali language over Oriya-speaking people.[30] In the twentieth century, the creation of linguistic states in India, and the more recent emergence of Bangladesh as a sovereign country are a testimony to the abiding sensitivity of language as identity, and as a source of conflict and tension. This, however, should not make us unconcerned about other potentials of identity formation and modes of mutation of identities. To this I shall return later.

The ambiguity in the meaning of *janapada* makes it difficult to suggest that it may stand for what we would call a subregion today. But present regions

[26]The term 'historical region' is used by B.S. Cohn 1998a.

[27]Sircar 1965a, 46-60; also Salomon 1998, 39-41.

[28]See Nagaraju 1995, 8-23; see also Cynthia Talbot 2001, 34-7 for some details of the inscriptional spread of Telugu.

[29]Talbot 2001, 36-7.

[30]Senapati 1977.

are comprised of a number of distinct subregions, which are visible in the historical records at different points in time, and some of them are indeed listed as *janapadas* in varieties of texts. The distinction between 'locality' and 'subregions', both modern terms, is hard to make in historical times; one may suppose that interaction between and the coming together of some localities was a prerequisite for the formation of the distinctive personalities of subregions.

Before I proceed to some later examples of what might correspond to modern subregions, I would like to provide a unique example, again, from early Tamil texts. This is to underline how even a coherent space like Tamilaham could comprise different segments, each segment corresponding to an 'eco-zone', and each being, as it were, 'worlds in themselves'.[31] Early Tamil poems, codified and indexed in the technical work *Tolkappiyar*, are grouped—taking into account both *akam* (poems of the interior) and *puram* (poems of the exterior)—in terms of their being related to several eco-zones. These are *Kurinci* (the hilly region), *Mullai* (region of 'pasturelands and open terraces'), *Marutam* ('riverine-agrarian' region), *Neytal* (coastal region), and *Palai* (uncultivated dry region). The differences between these segments were not simply geographical but went deeper into their respective subsistence patterns, and in their respective 'behaviour patterns' (*tinai*) in love and war too. If *Kurinci* overall represented the subsistence pattern of hill-cultivation and hunting and gathering, the *Neytal* communities had fish and salt as their major resources; *Marutam* was the region of settled agriculture, with the centres of their three major chiefs. The respective deities of the eco-zones were different: *Kurinci* had Murugan as its major cult; *Mullai* was represented by Mayon; for *Palai*, oscillating between the geographical characteristics of different regions, it was the fierce goddess Kottravai. The segments, which in today's terminology may be called subregions of Tamilaham, perhaps convey a notion of hierarchy in terms of the resources available in each, but more importantly, they were not segments in isolation. Note the following poem in a *Sangam* anthology, *Porunarattrupadai*:[32]

> Those selling honey and roots eatable
> Exchange them for fish's fat and wine
> They barter sugarcane and roasted rice
> Fr toddy and deer flesh. The fisher folk
> sing hillmen's song, while hillmen
> wear garlands of fragrant blooms that grow along the coast.
> The dwellers of the desert sing the songs
> of those in fertile lands, and these in turn
> Praise forest lands where grows the *mullai* blue.
> The wild fowl eats rice, while the domestic
> Eats millet grain. The hillside monkey rolls

[31] This is based on Sivathamby 1974, 29-37; see also Gurukkal 1987, 46-57.
[32] Chelliah 1962, 73-5.

In salty marsh, while cranes that take a bath
in briny sea-waves rest themselves on hills,
Four diverse pleasant regions are thus found
Together in a single realm.

The broad-spectrum cultural differences constituting the profile of early Tamilaham 'subregions' and so subtly articulated in the differential 'patterns of behaviour' (*tinai*) of the *Sangam* poems are not evident in other types of written documents. However, the historical emergence of 'subregions' is visible in documents in different regions of today. To cite one example, Radha, lying to the south and west of Bhagirathi in present-day West Bengal, emerged through the coming together of distinct early 'local' culture zones. The geography of the pre-historic, proto-historic and early historical sites in this subregion shows a distinct shift from one spatial segment to the other,[33] but it is only from the early historic period that Radha, as a subregion, sometimes starts figuring in historical records.[34] The distinctiveness of the different subregions of Bengal (West Bengal and Bangladesh), that is, Radha, Varendra, Vanga and Samatata, has been studied with reference to Sanskrit epigraphy down to the thirteenth century,[35] but it still has to be worked out what ingredients go into the making of a subregional personality. In Bengal, the subregions are distinct geographically, and there are further geographical, and culturally distinct, segments within a subregion with one or several centres in them; but the perception of difference between one subregion and another does not seem to have been derived from their being distinguishable geographical segments alone. Varendra, which was earlier known as Pundravardhana and associated with the Pundras, appears as quite distinct from Radha or Vanga in the records, both inside and outside Bengal. One ingredient may have been political or the way a spatial segment emerged as a politically coherent unit. In both Maurya and Gupta times, Varendra, or more correctly Pundravardhana, figures as a political core area.[36] But the sense of belonging to a subregion or a particular combination of subregions goes far beyond the political. The unique personality of a space may be invoked with reference to its landscape and climate, the way its language is spoken, its style of cooking, its method of house construction and communication, its marriage networks, and so on. In Bengal, again, Bhagirathi is seen as constituting a major cultural divide. The differences between the major segments, east and west of the Bhagirathi, are not essentially political; they are present in the way Bengali is spoken, in styles of cooking and preferences for particular food items, names of favourite rivers, and even in the support of different favourite soccer teams. That marriage networks too,

[33]B.D. Chattopadhyaya (in press).

[34]For the major subregions that came to constitute the region of Bengal, see Ray 1980, Bhattacharya 1977, Morrison 1970.

[35]Morrison 1970.

[36]Ibid.; see also Chattopadhyaya 1990, Chapter 2.

expressed not simply in caste terms, were viewed as sensitive indicators of cultural differences comes out beautifully in two early medieval Buddhist mystic poems in proto-Bengali, which Niharranjan Ray cited in his *History of the Bengali People*.[37] In one, a bridegroom is admonished that he will lose his sense (*vijana*) because he has married a girl from Vanga. In another, Bhusuku, author of one of the poems, is mentioned as having become a true 'Bengali' since he has married a Candali. This may be a typical mystical statement, but Bhusuku's identity as a Bengali does have a veiled reference to the relationship between marriage and identity. Subregion formation too would have to be visible historically, as indeed region formation has to be.

The recognition of regions, subregions and localities as basic sites of elements of diversity (in whatever way we construct these sites) simultaneously demands a search for what may function, and may have functioned, as connecting links between them. These connecting links I have chosen to call 'imitable models'. Although different segments of space do not stand in isolation from one another, and cultural elements that are recognizable across the subcontinent are overwhelmingly present, it is impossible to think of an everlasting cultural pattern engulfing and transforming all the others,[38] given the simultaneous existence of different social formations in India even today. From a historical perspective, it would be preferable to think of 'imitable models' which are not constant, but which nevertheless emerged in the course of history and had varying lives in the process of their circulation. If the patronage of Buddhism, the construction of Buddhist monuments and gifts of land and other resources to monks constituted model acts at some historical stage,[39] the basic 'imitable model' of kingship was Brahmanical, particularly from the Gupta period onward. The vigorous espousal of *varṇāsrama-dharma*, gifts of land (*bhumi-dana*), the creation of *agraharas*, the patronage of temples and monasteries, and projection of the king as someone comparable to an epic hero, all constituted an 'imitable' model of kingship present all over India.[40] Other imitable cultural

[37] Ray 1980, 595.

[38] Concepts such as 'Aryanization' or 'Sanskritization' imply that cultural transformation is a one-way process, in which the agency and medium of change cumulatively represent a diffusionist model. R.K. Mookerji's *The Fundamental Unity of India* thus underlines the role of 'Aryanization', as do many other works, in forging that unity. Mookerji asserts: 'With the gradual extension of Aryan colonization of India beyond the limits of old Aryavarta so as to embrace the whole of Dakshinapatha or southern India, the old Vedic formula of the conception of Indian unity was supplemented by the other appropriate formula to give fitting expression to an expanding geographical consciousness' (Mookerji 2003, 51-2). This completely negates the ingredients of regional personalities in the making of Indian culture.

[39] For an example of the patronage of Buddhism in the early historical period, see Dahejia 1992, Chapter 2; for the ideology of the gift in early historical Buddhism, see Liu 1997, Chapters 4, 5, 6.

[40] See Chattopadhyaya 2004.

models were the Sanskrit language as the medium of elite literary circulation,[41] and major Puranic deities as the representatives of model cults to which local cults could correspond. As a code of social practice, despite the extensive data on non-vegetarian diets, including beef,[42] and the continued practice of eating all varieties of meat among numerous communities, non-vegetarianism was projected and practised as desirable by ideologically active sections of the society.[43] Even when vernacular languages emerged, the major reference points continued to be provided by Sanskrit and the epic-Puranic repertoire of characters, symbols and motifs. For example, the play *Krdabhiramamu*, assigned to the fifteenth century, was written in Telugu.[44] The narrative of the play is similar to that of a *bhana*, a genre of play in Sanskrit, and as a justification for writing it in Telugu, the author asserts:[45]

> They say 'Sanskrit is the mother of all languages,
> but among the languages of the land
> Telugu is the best'. Of course,
> Between the aged mother
> and the ravishing young daughter,
> I'll take the daughter any day!

In addition to the acknowledgement, rightly or wrongly, of Sanskrit as the mother of Telugu, here is the following:[46]

> Vallabharaya composed this play called
> *Ridabhiramamu*: The Joys of Sex, after the model of the
> work know as *Premabhirama*: The Joys of Love, by
> Ravipati Tripurantaka Deva.
> Tripurantaka Deva?
> Not much of a poet, is he?
> And that *Premabhirama*—is it a great book?
> Great enough to be the model for a Telugu play?
> And Vallabharaya thought it was worthy?
> And why make it Telugu?

[41] See Pollock 1996, 197. He writes: 'The spread of Sanskrit in the first millennium as a strikingly homogeneous expressive mode of political power, helped create a new kind of vast zone of cultural interaction, what some might name as ecumene'. Pollock's restriction of Sanskrit to an 'expressive mode of political power' is an inverted perspective that does not do proper justice to the status of Sanskrit as a vehicle of multifaceted expressions, whose political use depended on varying historical contexts.

[42] That beef-eating was prevalent among early Indians and among Indian communities in general is demonstrated from the time of Raja Rajendralal Mitra onward, on the strength of a voluminous corpus of textual and archaeological evidence. For a recent restatement of relevant textual material, see Jha 2001.

[43] Jha 2001, Chapter 4.

[44] Rao and Shulman 2002.

[45] Ibid., 37-8.

[46] Ibid., 47.

At the level of cultic practices too, attempted proximity to what has greater circulation and visibility is very much in evidence. In *Candimangala*, a major vernacular text of sixteenth-century Bengal, the serpent-goddess Manasa, whose cult is at the centre of the text, has to be affiliated to Siva. Kalaketu, a hunter-chief in the text, was originally an earthly incarnation of Indra's son.[47] The evolution of the cult of Jagannatha in Orissa, which grew to be of supra-regional circulation and established in the region a model for the God-King nexus, ensured the multiplication of the model throughout Orissa in contexts in which such a nexus needed to be projected.[48] In other words, 'imitable models' were legitimizers within a complex repertoire of cultural ingredients, the range of which could expand with time. It is the study of the processes and mechanisms of the circulation of such elements, from the diverse sources of their origins, that can provide us with an understanding of the interpenetration between the local, subregional, regional and subcontinental levels.

CONCLUSION

The questioning of 'centre' or 'centrality' as the agency for the making of India and of its structure was undertaken to explore the multiplicity of the sites and sources of ingredients which instead constitute it in kaleidoscopic combination. The exploration will obviously have to continue, but hopefully the perspective of looking at the Indian civilizational entity from above will be turned upside down, and the effort should rather be made to look for the historical processes involved in the making of a large entity rather than for widely distributed sites of diversity as all derived from one tradition. That the perspective of focusing on a centre somehow lingers on seems to be suggested by a recent paper by Ravinder Kumar.[49] Kumar believes that the 'political identity of the Republic of India' ought to be defined in terms of a 'civilization-state' rather than a 'Nation-state'. Kumar also acknowledges 'the . . . great mass of humanity characterized by a striking diversity held together in the cultural unity [emphasis added] which constitutes Indian society'; and further, the 'concept of a subcontinental culture resting upon a multiplicity of religious visions and drawing into its matrix the regional constituents of Indian society'. The use of such expressions as 'held together in the cultural unity' and 'resting upon' lays more emphasis on the agency of some undefined source 'holding' 'the regional constituents' together in the 'cultural unity', while 'resting upon' implies the presence of an immutable superstructure.

[47] See Chattopadhyaya 2004.

[48] Hermann Kulke writes: 'Jagannatha, as the *rastradevata* of Orissa *par excellence*, is directly linked with the deities of the subregional level, most aptly represented by the powerful "Eight Mother Goddesses" (*astamatrka*) of Orissa' (Kulke 1993, 97). At the same time, he stresses the linkage across various levels: local, subregional and other levels.

[49] Kumar 2002.

Since the focus of the present discussion is the notion of the subregion as a 'centre', the question that needs to be raised here is whether one is moving from one type of fixed centre to a multiplicity of centres in isolation. As a research strategy, such a position would be as untenable as the other one in terms of historical evidence. Segments of space are made and unmade, and their constituent cultural ingredients need to be defined and redefined over time. In doing so, one is likely to come across, apart from varieties of ingredient, more than one nodal point and therefore hierarchy. The major nodal point, emerging in a particular context, may function as a political centre and generate cultural novelties which can transcend a delimited space. For example, a style of cooking or singing (*gharana*) associated with a royal court can survive royal space to become a more enduring cultural product and enter into a larger network. Research on the possibility of satisfactorily demarcating a subregion would therefore call for attention to the following:

— Criteria for defining a subregion as a distinct cultural space in a broad sense, with admission of both continuities and shifts over time.
— The need to investigate patterns of interaction with other spaces, keeping in view the emergence of new cultural modes from within and the response to more dominant modes from outside.
— The possibility of the existence of more than one node, which would ensure the coming together of local communities and local cultural forms and which also function as centres of local governance.
— A more comprehensive examination, apart from the major focus on political and cult centres, of craft production, housing types, dialects, styles of cooking,[50] styles of music and so on, in order to construct the personality of a subregion.

To close, I would like to sum up, availing myself of the opportunity given to me here, by suggesting a spatial model for viewing the processes of the making of India. The subcontinent, in this view, represents a space of interlocking regions (and not a given hierarchized combination of them), with the space within each region having to be defined for the time span during which one is investigating it. The space is not simply physical but also cultural in a broad sense, and therefore the spheres of its interaction, dominance, or subordination are also historical and cultural. Space and its historical evolution, therefore, imply hierarchy, but not with one centre forever subordinating the others. The overlapping of regions in this model creates spaces in-between, between points which intersect. They are not peripheral spaces, as they share the cultural ingredients of interlocking regions. In this model, therefore, there is no uniform

[50]For example, a work of posthumous codification such as Kiran Lekha Ray's *Varendra-Randhan* (i.e. Cooking of Varendra) in Bengali, reprinted Calcutta 2000. Material collected for this anthology of recipes was originally a part of a project to amass material on the history and culture of Varendra, a subregion of Bengal.

or homogeneous space, nor a privileged central place, but a multiplicity of spaces and their nodes, with their contours constituting the model being drawn and redrawn to the rhythm of historical movements.[51]

[51] Even as early as the tenth century, Rajasekhara referred to *Audra-Magadhi, Pancala-Madhyama, Avanti, Daksinatya* as different styles of women's dressing; *Kavyamimamsa*, third *adhyaya* called 'Kavya-purusotpatti'.

REFERENCES

Bhattacharya, A. 1977. *Historical Geography of Ancient and Early Medieval Bengal*, Calcutta: Sanskrit Pustak Bhandar.

Brandtner, M. 2001. 'Representations of Kalinga: The Changing Image and Geography of a Historical Region', in H. Kulke and B. Schnepel (eds.), *Jagannath Revisited: Studying Society, Religion and State in Orissa*, Delhi: Manohar, 179-210.

Brumann, C. 1999. 'Writing for Culture: Why a Successful Concept Should not be Discarded', in *Current Anthropology* 40, Supplement 52, 58-66.

Chatterjee, P. 1999. 'Claims on the Past: The Genealogy of Modern Historiography in Bengal', in D. Arnold and D. Hardiman (eds.), *Subaltern Studies* VIII, 3rd impression, Delhi: Oxford University Press, 1-49.

Chattopadhyaya, B.D. 1984. *A Survey of Historical Geography of Ancient India*, Calcutta: Manisha Granthalaya.

———1990. *Aspects of Rural Settlements and Rural Society in Early Medieval India*, Calcutta: K.P. Bagchi.

———2003. *Studying Early India: Archaeology, Texts and Historical Issues*, Delhi: Permanent Black.

———2003a. 'Urban Centres in Early Bengal: Archaeological Perspectives', in idem, 2003, Chapter 5.

———2004. 'State's Perception of the Forest and the Forest as State', in B.B. Chaudhuri and A. Bandopadhyay (eds.), *Tribes, Forest and State Formation in Indian History*, Delhi: Manohar.

———et al. (eds.) 2005. *An Annotated Archaeological Atlas of West Bengal*, vol. 1, Delhi: Manohar.

Chelliah, J.V. 1962. *Pattupattu: Ten Tamil Idylls*. 2nd edn., Tirunelveli/Madras: South India Saiva Siddhanta Works Pub. Society.

Cohn, B. 1998. *An Anthropologist Among the Historians and Other Essays*, Delhi: Oxford University Press.

———1998a. 'Regions Subjective and Objective: The Relation to the Study of Modern Indian History and Society', in Cohn 1998, 100-35.

———1998b. 'Political Systems in Eighteenth Century India: The Benares Region', in Cohn 1998, 483-99.

Crane, R.I. 1967. *Regions and Regionalism in South Asian Studies: An Exploratory Study*, Durham: Duke University Press.

Dehejia, V. 1992. 'The Collective and Popular Basis of Early Buddhist Patronage: Sacred Monuments, 100 B.C.-A.D. 250', in Barbara Stoler-Miller (ed.), *The Powers of Art: Patronage in Indian Culture*, Delhi: Oxford University Press.

Devadhar, C.R. (ed.) 1984. *Works of Kalidasa*, vol. 2, *Poetry*, Delhi: Motilal Banarsidass, 26-86.

Fox, R. (ed.) 1977. *Realm and Region in Traditional India*, Durham: Duke University Press.

Ganguly, D.K. 1975. *Historical Geography and Dynastic History of Orissa (up to the Rise of the Imperial Gangas)*, Calcutta: Punthi Pustak.

Ghosh, A. 1973. *The City in Early Historical India*, Simla: Indian Institute of Advanced Study.

Ghosh, M. 1975. *Glimpses of Sexual Life in Nanda-Maurya India (Translation of the Caturbhani Together with a Critical Edition of the Text)*, Calcutta: Manisha Granthalaya.

Gurukkal, R. 1987. 'Aspects of Early Iron Age Economy: Problems of Agrarian Expansion in Tamilakam', in B.D. Chattopadhyaya (ed.), *Essays in Ancient Indian Economic History*, Delhi: Munshiram Manoharlal, 46-61.

Jha, D.N. 2001. *Holy Cow: Beef in Indian Dietary Traditions*, Delhi: Matrix.

Kulke, H. 1993. 'Legitimation and Town Planning in the Feudatory States of Central Orissa', in idem, *Kings and Cults: State Formation and Legitimation in India and Southeast Asia*, Delhi: Manohar, 93-113.

Kumar, R. 2002. 'India: A "Nation" State or "Civilization State"', in *South Asia: Journal of South Asian Studies* 25, 2, 13-32.

Liu, X. 1997. *Ancient India and Ancient China: Trade and Religious Exchanges A.D. 1-600*, paperback edition, Delhi: Oxford University Press.

Mookerji, R.K. 2003 (1914). *The Fundamental Unity of India*, new edition, Delhi: DC Publishers.

Morrison, B.M. 1970. *Political Centres and Cultural Regions in Early Bengal*, Tucson: University of Arizona Press.

Nagaraju, S. 1995. 'Emergence of Regional Identity and Beginnings of Vernacular Literature: A Case Study of Telugu', in *Social Scientist* 23, 10-12.

Pollock, S. 1996. 'The Sanskrit Cosmopolis, 300-1300: Transculturation, Vernacularization, and the Question of Ideology', in J.E.M. Houben (ed.), *Ideology and Status of Sanskrit: Contributions to the History of the Sanskrit Language*, Leiden: E.J. Brill, 197-247.

Rao, V.N. and D. Shulman 2002 (trsl.). *A Lover's Guide to Warangal: The Kridabhiramamu*, Delhi: Permanent Black.

Ray, N. 1980. *Bangalir Itihas: Adi Parva* (in Bengali), Calcutta, 1949; rev. edn., Calcutta: Paschimbanga Samiti.

Raychaudhuri, H.C. 1958. *Studies in Indian Antiquities*, Calcutta: Calcutta University; 2nd edn., Calcutta: University of Calcutta.

———1997. *Political History of Ancient India*, 6th edition with a commentary by B.N. Mukherjee. Kolkata: Oxford University Press.

Salomon, R. 1998. *Indian Epigraphy*, Indian rpt. Delhi: Munshiram Manoharlal.

Senapati, F. 1977. *Atmacarita, Translated from Oriya into Bengali by Maitri Sukla*, Delhi: Sahitya Akademi.

Sharma, R.S. 1983. *Material Culture and Social Formations in Ancient India*, Delhi: Macmillan.

Sircar, D.C. 1965a. *Indian Epigraphy*, Delhi: Motilal Banarsidass.

———1965b. *Select Inscriptions Bearing on Indian History and Civilization*, vol. 1, rev. 2nd edn., Calcutta: Calcutta University.

Sivathamby, K. 1974. 'Early South Indian Society and Economy: The Tinai Concept', in *Social Scientist* 3, 5, 29-37.

Spate, O.H.K. and A.T.A. Learmonth 1972. *India and Pakistan: A General and Regional Geography*, London: Methuen.

Stein, B. 1980. *Peasant State and Society in Medieval South India*, Delhi: Oxford University Press.

Subbarayalu, Y. 1973. *Political Geography of the Chola Country*, Madras: Madras State Department of Archaeology.

Subbarao, B. 1958. *The Personality of India: Pre- and Protohistoric Foundation of India and Pakistan*, 2nd edn., Baroda: University of Baroda, Chapters 2, 6-8.

Talbot, C. 2001. *Precolonial India in Practice: Society, Region, and Identity in Medieval Andhra*, Delhi: Oxford University Press.

Wagstaff, J.M. 1987. *Landscape and Culture: Geographical and Archaeological Perspectives*, Oxford: Basil Blackwell.

CHAPTER 2

Profiling Dakṣiṇa Kośala: An Early Historical Subregion?*

BHAIRABI PRASAD SAHU

The question of the formation of regional identities, based on a set of region-specific cultural traits, has become a recent concern of historians. This paper attempts to analyse the evolution of Dakṣiṇa Kośala during the early historical and early medieval periods to examine how the socially unified space came to acquire discernible qualities which more or less defined it as a historico-cultural unit. Up to now the region, like most hinterlands, has not been the focus of any sustained historical research, largely owing to the attraction of the coastal belt, which is not entirely unrelated to its alleged historical priority. The area of study is conventionally referred to as western Orissa or Chhattisgarh, neither of which constitutes a historical region on its own. They are rather the products of administrative decision and represent political units. Taken together, however, they manifest commonly shared traits, derived through a long process of historical evolution, and constitute an organic socio-cultural entity. From epicentric perspectives, it is seen as either an extension of coastal Orissa or a buffer or intermediate zone between the coastal tract and northern and central India, and even as a site of contestation between feuding dynasties ranging from the Vākāṭakas and Nalas, through the Kalachuris and Somavaṁśīs, to the Telugu Cōḍas and Chindaka-Nāgas, among others. The question then is, do we continue to perceive it as such or see if it had a personality of its own? In the case of the latter, questions relating to change, agency, cultural forms and their signifiers will have to be addressed. This chapter therefore seeks to understand the trajectory of socio-cultural transformation in the region from an early phase of segmented 'localities' to the constitution of a larger supra-local community identity bound by a commonly shared cultural system, assuming there is one. With reference to regional specifics, it examines whether the movement towards the formation of an agrarian region, a differentiated and hierarchized caste society, larger political enterprises (extending across the region and beyond), and the role of Brahmans, among others, in disseminating

*I am grateful to Professors H. Kulke, B.D. Chattopadhyaya and H. von Stietencron for comments on an earlier draft of this paper. I also thank my younger brother, Shri Lakshmi Narayan Sahu, who facilitated my visit to Sirpur, Rajim, Marguda, Budhikomna and Khariar in the summer of 2001.

cultural forms and the creation of cultic centres, which may have performed a unifying and levelling function, facilitated the creation of a sense of belonging or identity formation. The area is rich in archaeological material and land grant inscriptions, which form the basic evidence in the present case.

Like Vidarbha and Malwa, Dakṣiṇa Kośala is a part of the central Indian Intermediate Zone, which separates the northern plains from Peninsular India. Though communication across this zone was never easy, there have been slow and steady interactions between these subregions, as well as between them and the adjacent and peripheral cultural systems through the ages, which have facilitated the integration of the tribes into the caste-peasant base since the earliest historical phase. Dakṣiṇa Kośala broadly comprised the space between Amarkantak in the north to Kanker (close to the source of the river Mahānadī) in the south, and from the Wen-Gaṅga Valley on the west to the middle valley of the Mahānadī (extending up to Sonpur) in the east.[1] It was bounded by Mekala in the north, Vidarbha in the west, Bastar in the south and Kaliṅga in the south-east. More specifically, this cultural unit is spread over the modern districts of Bilaspur, Raipur, Durg and Raigarh in Chhattisgarh, and Sambalpur, Bolangir and Kalahandi in Orissa.[2] Like other regions, the territorial borders of Dakṣiṇa Kośala were not fixed in the past. The tribal presence in this region was and continues to be strong even today. The tribal situation, together with its physiography, seems to account for the generally late historical transformation of the region. Sites like Malhar (Bilaspur district) and Asurgarh (Kalahandi district) registering early beginnings, instead of disturbing this understanding, point to their favourable geographical location and the uneven patterns of historical growth within the subregion. Notwithstanding the importance of the Mahānadī and its tributaries, the Sheonāth and Tel, for irrigation, paddy cultivation and other activities in the region, this is a land of tanks. The intrinsic importance of both rice and tanks comes through from the early inscriptional references to them in this spatial and cultural segment.[3]

The earliest reference to Kośala as a territorial unit, its location in Dakṣiṇapatha in close proximity to Mahākāntara and Kauraḷa (which comprised parts of Bastar and western Orissa), and indications of its manifest socio-political profile come from the Allahabad *praśasti* of Samudragupta.[4] This is listed among a dozen *aṭavika-rājyas*, which suggests that it was a post-tribal chiefdom or early state. The forest people of central India known as *aṭavi* find mention in the Aśokan edicts, and after a gap of about six hundred years the addition of the suffix *rājya* unmistakably points to the change that had come from within local societies during the intervening period. Vākāṭaka inscriptions

[1]A. Cunningham 2000 (rpt.), 68.

[2]All references in the text are to the undivided districts of western Orissa before 1990. Since then, these districts have been subdivided into many more new districts.

[3]For early references to *dhānya*, see S.P. Tiwari 1985, section on taxes; for tanks, see *ASI-AR* 1930-4, 1936, 140, and K.D. Bajpai and S.K. Pandey 1978, 35.

[4]J.F. Fleet 1970 (3rd edn.), 7.

of the fifth century CE and the Aihole inscription of Pulakeśin II successively record the conquest of Kośala along with contiguous territories such as Mekala, Kaliṅga and Āndhra.[5] Hiuen Tsang provides a good account of the region, its people, their manners and religious beliefs, in the mid-seventh century, among other details.[6] Around the same time the Pāṇḍuvaṁśī king Tīvaradeva is represented in the epigraphical records of the family as the lord of the whole of Kośala.[7] In the land-grant charters of the Somavaṁśīs (ninth to eleventh centuries), who succeeded the Pāṇḍuvaṁśīs, the donated area is usually mentioned as a part of some administrative unit in Kośala desa, their homeland and/or area of control. Continued use of the nomenclature and identification of the region with Kośala is discernible even in a seventeenth-century text, significantly titled *Kośalānanda Kāvya*.[8] It is difficult to pinpoint when and how the territory acquired its name, but the existence of a seal from Malhar (dated to the second century CE) bearing the legend *Gāmasa Kośalīya* may possibly suggest its post-Mauryan origins, especially the early centuries of the Christian Era.[9] It is not certain whether, in using the term Kośala, an already existing name was being appropriated, or whether the process of its continuous usage conferred on the region a discrete identity through imperceptible gradations. It was perhaps a two-way process, involving both the communication and constitution of a spatial cultural image.

The issue of the formation of a subregional identity raises many obvious but interrelated questions—how was it forged, what were its major identifiable constituents, and even, what were the stages, if any, in its creation? Archaeological evidence constitutes the most important source for the reconstruction of the early phase of the history of Dakṣiṇa Kośala. The available evidence suggest that the process of cultural development was mostly dispersed, spread over the river valleys of the Mahānadī, the Tel (which is an important tributary of the Mahānadī) and their tributaries, possibly with interactions of one form or another between clusters of sites and beyond. The reported sites surely did not all share the same history, but rather there were chronological and typological variations across sites.[10] To elaborate, not all known early historical settlements need be perceived as urban centres. It is the cultural assemblage that ultimately determines the character of a site. In introducing these qualified statements, my intention is to make the more general point that not only was the transition

[5]Cited in S.P. Tiwari 1985, 9-10.

[6]Xuanzang 1906, 209-10.

[7]See Adhabhara Plates of Mahā-Nannarāja, in *EI* 31, 1955-6, 220-1, lines 5-9, and Bonda Plates of Tīvaradeva, year 5, in *EI* 34, 1960-1, 115, lines 16-17.

[8]See S.K. Panda in the present volume.

[9]K.D. Bajpai and S.K. Pandey 1978, 21 and 34. It may be mentioned that there is a reference to one Kośala *nagara* in the Malhar Plates of Mahāśivagupta. B. Jain 1977, 52, line 11. Also in A.M. Shastri 1995, 139.

[10]This has been well argued in the case of early Bengal and it is equally true of the other regions. B.D. Chattopadhyaya 2003a, 66-101.

to the historical phase in the region, as elsewhere, a complex phenomenon, but also that there were uneven patterns of growth.

Excavations unveiling the cultural sequence have been carried out at Malhar, Sirpur, Asurgarh, the Mārgudā Valley, Manmuṇḍā and Nehena; and many other sites have been subjected to surveys and explorations. Malhar in Bilaspur district was occupied from the early part of the first millennium BCE to the thirteenth century CE. Periods II and III, which are of immediate concern here, have been dated to *c.* 350 BCE to CE 300 and *c.* CE 300 to 650 respectively.[11] For Period II the mud rampart remains of a fort have been located. This has yielded black-and-red ware, two pieces of northern black polished ware (hereafter NBPW), red slipped ware, stamped pottery and bricks corresponding to the Mauryan and Sātavāhana types. Punch-marked, cast and Sātavāhana coins have also been reported. There is the interesting seal, already mentioned, dated to the second century CE, which reads *Gāmasya Kośalīya*. Black-and-red ware (suggesting its continued use), red polished ware and kaolin pottery have been identified from Period III. The site also yielded a piece of the rim of a large jar, a baked pendant and a clay seal with Gupta Brāhmī characters.[12] The seal is particularly important because it bears the legend Mahārāja Mahendrasya, who has been variously identified with Mahendra of Kośala of the Allahabad inscription of Samudragupta and Mahendrāditya of the Śarabhapurīya dynasty. The remains of Śaivite temples, Buddhist *chaityas* and *vihāras* and bricks used in their construction have also been recovered. A huge tank which now covers an area of about 60 acres is dated to this period. Sirpur or ancient Śrīpura, situated at a distance of 60 km from Raipur, in Raipur district, and associated with the late Śarabhapurīya kings and their successors the Pāṇḍuvaṁśīs, possesses extensive ruins.[13] However, all of it, including the temples, *vihāras*, sculptural remains, and the associated artefacts, belong to the second half of the first millennium CE.

The excavation carried out at Asurgarh, in Kalahandi district, has laid bare a site whose chronology ranges between *c.* the third century BCE and the fifth or sixth centuries CE.[14] From the upper phase of the lowest layer in this fortified settlement, black-and-red ware was found in good numbers, together with black polished ware. A piece of chunar sandstone bearing Mauryan-era polish was also found from this early layer. The second layer contained red glazed pottery, iron objects, and beads of semi-precious stones probably dating to the early centuries CE. Punch-marked coins and a copper coin of Kaniṣka have also been obtained from the site. The top layer contained floors of houses paved with brickbats, and a circular structure between the two trenches was

[11] K.D. Bajpai and S.K. Pandey 1978, 33-5. Megalithic remains have been reported from sites in Raipur and Durg districts. Black-and-red ware (BRW) is a common occurrence at megalithic sites, but it continues well into the early historical period.

[12] K.D. Bajpai and S.K. Pandey 1978, 34-5.

[13] S.L. Katare 1959, 1-8.

[14] *IAR* 1972-3, 29. Also see S.C. Behera 1982, 5-6.

also exposed. It is not certain whether this had anything to do with the autochthonous deity Stambheśvarī mentioned in the Terasinga plates[15] of the Mahārāja Tuṣṭikara, who had acquired a visible political presence around the same area in the same period. Budhigarh in M. Rampur Tehsil, located in the same part of the district as Asurgarh, is marked by an extensive mound (1,000 × 500 metres). This has produced a wide range of antiquities, comprising NBPW, fine black ware, black-and-red ware, punch-marked coins, terracotta figurines, copper and iron objects, two seals and semi-precious beads, among other things.[16] The nature of the evidence alludes to its early historical moorings.

The Mārgudā Valley is situated in Nuapada subdivision of Kalahandi district, bordering Chhattisgarh, on the banks of the Sonk River, which is a tributary of the Mahānadī. The valley is rich in antiquities and monuments. Excavation and explorations have yielded evidence of beads, iron artefacts, sculptural and brick structural remains. The ruins of the settlement, which has a formidable natural fortification, included a Śaivite *vihāra*s complex, a palace complex and a Śaktipitha. An interesting archer image of Durgā has been obtained *in situ* from the single chambered brick temple. The image bears an inscription reading Maheśvarī Bhābadā, which has been ascribed to the fourth century CE.[17] The Amguda copper-plate grant of Jayarāja and the Khariar charter of Sudevarāja (both belonging to the Śarabhapurīya dynasty) have been discovered in the vicinity of the valley. The overall cultural complex suggests that the site can be dated from the fourth or fifth century onward. Nehena, 4 km from Khariar town, in the same subdivision, has produced a cultural sequence ranging from the early historical to the early medieval periods. Material remains unearthed from the trial excavation were black-and-red ware with painting in white, red and brown ware, beads of agate and carnelian, bricks and gold coins of Prasannamitra (of the Śarabhapurīya dynasty). Two cultural phases have been suggested for the site. The earlier period, identified with the early historical phase, yielded much of the pottery mentioned above, which in terms of shape and wares compares well not so much with those from coastal Orissa but with the central and western Indian finds.[18] The early medieval sites had no black-and-red ware with a rough surface but contained iron tools, some iron slags and the gold coins just mentioned.

Kharliagarh, located at the confluence of the Tel and Raul in Bolangir district, is close to the eastern border of Kalahandi district. The mounds inside the fort have yielded evidence of copper punch-marked coins, Kuṣāṇa copper

[15]S.N. Rajaguru 1958, 81-5.

[16]P. Mohanty and B. Mishra 2000, 158-60; B. Mishra and M.P. Singhdeo 2002, 152-5.

[17]C.B. Patel, 'Maraguda Valley Excavations', paper presented to the Seminar on Eastern Indian Archaeology, held at Konark during 5-7 April 2001. Also see J.P. Singh Deo 2000, 418-30.

[18]See M. Brandtner 1993, 101-13.

coins, beads of semi-precious stones, iron implements and metal bangles.[19] These, together with the burnt brick rampart remains of the almost square fort, indicate the early historical origins of the site. Manmuṇḍā, situated at the confluence of the Tel and Mahānadī in Phulbani district, is an early historical site. Black-and-red ware, black polished ware, polished and red slipped ware, iron objects (including a sickle), a silver punch-marked coin, beads of semi-precious stones, lids with knobs in good quantity (reminding one of similar finds on the coastal sites of Orissa) and burnt brick structural remains are among the important finds from the trial excavation at the ancient settlement.[20] Black-and-red ware was totally absent in the upper two layers. At a distance of about 50 km to the east of Manmuṇḍā lies Maryakud, an island in the Mahānadī in the same district of Phulbani, which along with Manmuṇḍā was situated on the eastern frontier of Dakṣiṇa Kośala. Explorations in and around the mound have brought to light sherds of black-and-red ware, black polished ware, red slipped ware, semi-precious stone beads and pieces of iron slag.[21] It may not be out of place to mention that the eastern part of Dakṣiṇa Kośala or what constitutes western Orissa today is rich in precious and semi-precious stones.

Buddhist remains have been reported from the excavations at Ganiapali and Nagraj, on the left bank of the river Oṅg, a tributary of the Mahānadī, in Sambalpur district.[22] The finds comprise sculptures of the Buddha and burnt brick structural remains of a *vihāra* dated to the late fourth and early fifth centuries CE. Carnelian beads, terracotta objects and potsherds were the other miscellaneous finds from these sites.

The provenance of the archaeological data, together with the locations of early numismatic finds and Prakrit inscriptions, seems to suggest a pattern in the evolution of early Dakṣiṇa Kośala. The coin finds—from punch-marked coins through local uninscribed copper coins and inscribed Magha coins to the Kuṣāṇa copper and Roman gold coins—in the western part of the region tend to centre in and around Malhar in Bilaspur district, though with a scattering in the neighbouring districts.[23] The Guñji and the (damaged) Kirāri inscriptions, assigned to the early centuries CE, recording the donation of numerous cows to Brahmans by important state functionaries (like *amātya*, *daṇḍanāyaka* and *balādhikṛta*) and a list of administrative designations (viz., *mahāsenāni*, *pratihāra*, *bhaṇḍāgārika*, *aśvāroha*, *pādamūlika*, *rathika* and *gomaṇḍalika*, among many others) are also located in the same district.[24] Bilaspur thus emerges as a pulsating 'locality', with Malhar as an important node. At the

[19]H.C. Das 1990, 187-8.

[20]S.C. Behera 1982; *IAR*, 1984-5, 58-9; *IAR*, 1989-90, 80-5 and *IAR*, 1991-2, 86.

[21]B. Tripathy 2000, 401-11.

[22]S.C. Panda 1981, 47-52.

[23]This understanding is based on the discussion in Sangeeta Abhay Chandra's 'Transition to Early Historical Phase in Chhattisgarh Region of Madhya Pradesh', unpublished M.Phil. dissertation, Department of History, University of Delhi, 1994, Chapter II.

[24]For details, see N.K. Sahu, 1984, 377-85.

risk of repetition one may reiterate that Malhar has yielded most of the above varieties of coin, as well as other markers of prosperity from Period II (*c.* 350 BCE-CE 300). The site is said to be located on the ancient trade route joining Kausambi with the south-east coast, and that perhaps explains its importance. Influences both from the north and the Deccan and central India, especially under the Sātavāhanas, may account for the long list of official titles in the epigraphic records of the subregion during its formative period. As one moves into the Gupta period, the adjoining districts of Durg and Raipur, to the south, begin to provide material relating to the extension of Gupta influence. In addition to the Gupta coins, there is the Arang fragmentary inscription, assigned to the fourth century, which is perhaps the first Sanskrit inscription in the area, and the copper-plate grant of Bhimasena II, again from Arang, in Raipur district, dated in 182 or 282 in the Gupta Era (CE 502 or 602).[25] The repoussé gold coins of Mahendrāditya and Prasannamātra spread over the districts of Bilaspur, Raipur, Durg and Kalahandi,[26] with the Garuḍa motif and Saṅkha and Chakra to the left and right respectively, bear the unmistakable imprint of the Gupta emblem. Such influences extended to the domains of art, culture and polity as well, and will be discussed later.

On the basis of the combined archaeological and numismatic evidence, it may be surmised that there were mutual interactions and communications between Asurgarh, Budhigarh, Kharliagarh and Manmuṇḍā, cutting across the modern administrative divisions in eastern Dakṣiṇa Kośala, with Asurgarh being in some kind of privileged position. The presence of silver and copper punch-marked coins as well as Kuṣāṇa coins and beads at these sites suggests in that direction. If the alignment of sites is any indication, then the Tel played an important role in the emergence and maintenance of the network of exchange and cultural transactions that contributed to the prosperity of the locality. The river valleys emerge as important factors in the socio-cultural development of and movement towards a complex society in the region.

The trajectory of internal transformation that has been sketched so far demonstrates the formation of localities across variegated spaces. Localities may be taken to approximate to *janapada*s, to use a familiar north Indian term.[27] Development was uneven and segmented, with some areas registering greater visibility than others. But then the question is, how does one explain craft specialization, trade, the money economy and social differentiation, or, to put it simply, the transition from pre-state to state societies? The proliferation of settlements[28] suggests a rise in population and agrarian growth. Change is archaeologically demonstrable during and after the Mauryas. The horizontal

[25] *EI* 9, 342ff.

[26] S.P. Tiwari 1985, 56-7.

[27] For details of this idea, see B.D. Chattopadhyaya 1988, 727-32.

[28] In addition to the sites discussed here, archaeological surveys have identified many ruins and mounds in the region, yielding red ware and burnt brick. For example, see *IAR* 1981-2, 54; *IAR* 1983-4, 61-2; and *IAR* 1995-6, 60-1. Beglar and Cunningham's Reports also provide a list of sites, though mostly belonging to the later centuries.

spread of the Mauryan state and the subsequent ascendancy and expansion of the Sātavāhanas then constitute the background to the early transformation of the region. Flowing from it, it may not be out of place to argue that the transition itself derived, as in the Deccan and Kaliṅga,[29] from a combination of autochthonous forces and the influences emanating from proximate advanced cultural regions through continuous interaction.

A further stage in the transition of Dakṣiṇa Kośala is discernible from the sixth to seventh centuries onward, when the first locally organized subregional state was formed. There was no break but an expansion of and acceleration in the historical processes of change, which continued to influence and impact on each other. For example, the extension of political authority was related to agrarian expansion, the spread of Brahmanical settlements, the dissemination of Śāstric-Purāṇic ideas and the emergence and spread of sacred centres, including Buddhist monasteries. Like Brahmanical ideology and temples, Buddhism seems to have helped in organizing diversity and the process of socio-political integration. The process of state formation shows the phased territorial extension and structural evolution of states from their tentative beginnings to the making of a regional state combining parts of Kośala and central and coastal Orissa.

The stages in the evolution of the structure of the polity can be mapped with reference to the provenance of the land-grant charters, the identification of donated settlements, lists of officials addressed in these records, the privileges and exemptions transferred to the donees, and the titles and epithets borne by the rulers of successive dynasties. The earliest known raja in the region, following those mentioned in the Allahabad *praśasti*, was *Mahārāja Tuṣṭikara*, whose Terasinga plate informs us that he ruled around the fifth to sixth centuries in Kalahandi district, bordering Bolangir. The Śarabhapurīyas were the first local dynasty. They issued most of their land grants from Śarabhapura (not yet satisfactorily identified) and Śrīpura (Sirpur), their successive seats of power.[30] The geographical distribution of the copper-plate grants and the identification of the donated settlements reveal that their dominion roughly comprised the present-day districts of Bilaspur, Raipur and Raigarh in Chhattisgarh and Kalahandi in Orissa.[31] The spatial spread of the gold coins of Mahendrāditya of the same lineage broadly coincides with this political geography. *Bhoga*, *bhukti*, *rāṣṭra* and *āhāra* were the administrative units above rural settlements. The single instance of the term *āhāra* may have been an inheritance from the Sātavāhanas and the Deccan. The taxes included *bhāga*, *bhoga*, *dhānya* and *hiraṇya*. High officials do not seem to have been addressed while making land grants. However, there are references to *bhogapati*s urging them to protect the grants, and such other categories as *dūta*, *adhikaraṇa*, *cāṭa*

[29]S. Seneviratne 1980-1, 54-69; B.D. Chattopadhyaya 1988, and B.P. Sahu 2003a, especially 35-42.

[30]One grant each was issued from Prasannapura and Tilakeswara.

[31]S.P. Tiwari 1985, Chapter 2.

and *bhaṭa*. Towards the end of their reign we come across one *mahāsāmanta sarvādhikṛta* Indrabalarāja. The Śarabhapurīya kings used the title *mahārāja* and at times the suffix *bhaṭṭāraka*, but nothing more grandiose. The construction of a grand genealogy or exaggerated family tradition was conspicuous by its absence. There are several instances of land grants being made by high state functionaries and influential people with the consent of the king.[32] The impression that one is left with is of a state in an early stage of evolution, where power was unobtrusive and the administrative units, taxes and state functionaries were yet to be formally structured.[33]

The Pāṇḍuvaṁśīs, who succeeded the Śarabhapurīyas, made their grants largely from Śrīpura. The provenance of their records and the locations of the place names mentioned in them suggest that their realm broadly coincided with that of their predecessors.[34] While the kingdom was divided into *rāṣṭra*, *bhoga*, *bhukti* and *viṣaya*, the popular revenue terms were *bhaga* and *bhoga*. However, the remissions to the beneficiaries of land grants were more elaborate and included expressions such as *sarva-kara-sameta*, *a-cāṭabhaṭa-praveśa* and *sarva-pīḍa-varjita*. State functionaries were addressed and informed about the grants being made. The list includes *grāmakūṭa*, *droṇagika*, *gaṇḍakanāyaka*, *devavārika* and *cāṭa* and *bhaṭa*. The records of Mahāśivagupta Bālārjuna also informed the *kālādhyasin* (astrologer), *samāhartṛ*, *sannidhātṛ*, *adhikaraṇa* and *sakaraṇa*.[35] The Pāṇḍuvaṁśīs began to appropriate significant titles and symbols of substance such as *Paramamaheśvara*, *Paramavaiṣṇava*, *Parameśvara* and *Kośalādhipati*. Mahāśivagupta Bālārjuna was represented in his records as *dharmāvatāra*, the protector of *varṇa*s and *āśrama*s, and even compared to the epic heroes.[36] Overall it appears that the subregional state had moved forward and that there was a consolidation of royal authority.

The Somavaṁśīs, who were perhaps a collateral branch or junior line of the same family, followed the Pāṇḍuvaṁśīs after a gap of about a century. They were the first to move into central Orissa displacing the Bhañjas of Khiñjali (in the Baudh area) in the later part of the ninth century, and then moved on to occupy coastal Orissa, creating a regional kingdom in the process. Their charters were issued from a number of places like Suvarṇapura (Sonepur), Mūrasīma (near Bolangir town), Vinitapura (Binka, near Sonepur) and Yayātinagara, among others, indicating their eastward expansion. The sites where their charters have been found are spread over the districts of Bolangir, Puri, Cuttack and Balasore, with a conspicuous concentration in the district of Bolangir. Among the settlements identified in the donative records, many

[32]Ibid., 76-7.

[33]The Eastern Vākāṭakas provide a comparable picture. H. Kulke 2004.

[34]See, for example, U. Singh 1994, the discussion on the Śarabhapurīyas and Pāṇḍuvaṁśīs in Chapter 1.

[35]See his Bonda, Bardula, Mallar and Lodhia Plates, in A.M. Shastri 1995.

[36]See 'The Sirpur Stone Inscription of the Time of Mahāśivagupta', *EI* 11, 1911-12, 184-201, verses 12-13, 18-19 and 23-4.

are situated in Bolangir district, especially around Bolangir town and the Bolangir-Baudh area, the Bargarh locality of Sambalpur and Kalahandi districts. *Deśa*, *maṇḍala*, *khaṇḍa*, *bhukti* and *viṣaya* constituted the administrative divisions. The list of privileges of the donees became more detailed, including the transfer of community rights over trees, creepers and forest products. Similarly, the list of functionaries registered a numerical increase, and royal titles were more numerous and pompous.[37] Terms such as *Mahārājādhirāja*, *Paramabhaṭṭāraka* and *Kośalendra*, reflecting the image or self-image of royalty, were in circulation. Through the instrument of land grants and the transfer of rights, pockets of authority were being created, which would have then spread the message of royal power and helped in extending the orbit of state authority.[38] There was an underlying unity in these developments. The rise in the number of possible sources of revenue and the widening political structure were in conformity with the expanding frontiers of the state. That begs the question, what were the forces or conjunction of forces that made such political enterprises possible?

The early medieval centuries were characterized by the growth of a rural economy, burgeoning rural settlements and the emergence of religious centres and towns. Malhar continued to flourish. At Sirpur, Rajim, Tāla and Kharod in present-day Chhattisgarh and the Mārguḍā Valley, Budhikomnā, Belkhaṇḍi and Ranipur-Jharial in western Orissa, for example, there are extant brick temples and their ruins going back to the Gupta and post-Gupta period.[39] Urban centres such as Śarabhapura, Prasannapura and Kośalanagara are also referred to in contemporary dynastic records. Centres like Sirpur and Rajim were multifunctional towns, whereas sites like Tāla and the Ranipur-Jharial complex, with religious activities dominating the scene, may have been largely uni-dimensional in nature. It needs no emphasis that, irrespective of their cultic association and function, temples and towns are markers of agrarian growth. The proliferation of temples thus indicates both the spread of Purāṇic religions and the moving frontier of peasant society. Vaṭapadra, Khadirapadra, Śālagrāma and Kadambapadrullaka, among others, unambiguously suggest that the names of settlements were derived from local flora, and they allude to the rich, thick vegetation in their surroundings. During the Śarabhapurīya period and even later, the evidence of settlements sharing boundaries with other habitations is sparse. Similarly, the four boundaries or *catuḥsīmā* of the donated land are in many cases not specifically defined,[40] implying thinly scattered rural settlements interrupted by intermittent woods and forests. This impression is

[37]U. Singh 1994, Appendixes II and III on 'Official Designations and Fiscal Terms'.

[38]H. Kulke 1995, 243-4.

[39]For details, see J.D. Beglar and A. Cunningham 2000 (rpt.), 4-87, 118ff; K.N. Mahapatra 1947, 167-72; J.P. Singh Deo 2000; D.R. Das 1990; S.S. Panda 1989, 117-26 and 1995, 46-87.

[40]B.P. Sahu 1993, 52.

strengthened by references to trees, plants, animals, forests and forest products in the Somavaṁśī inscriptions,[41] in the general context of remissions to the donees. The evidence for collective grants to several groups of Brahmans throughout the period and the frequency of the occurrence of *padra*s or *padraka*s,[42] not *grāma*s (fully settled villages), as the object of the grants up to the Somavaṁśīs perhaps suggest an early stage in the spread of plough agriculture and the evolution of rural settlements in many parts of the region. Notwithstanding the early patterns of socio-economic transformation, there is a gradual increase in the epigraphic references to rural settlements. The use of the names of rivers, like Oṅg and Tel, in demarcating administrative divisions drives home their importance in these developments. The fact that the land grants of the Śarabhapurīyas and Pāṇḍuvaṁśīs were largely distributed over the districts of Bilaspur and Raipur, while those of the Somavaṁśīs were mostly concentrated in and around Bolangir district, urges the recognition of phased agrarian expansion, with specific localities being the focus of political interest at different points in time.

The Brahmans, with their knowledge of the calendar, agriculture, the Vedas, Śāstras and Purāṇas and, deriving from it their inherent capacity to provide socio-political legitimacy, appear to have played a significant role in the transformation of autochthonous societies. Though they are known to the region since the early centuries CE, they achieved a noticeable presence from the middle of the millennium onward. During this period they were most often the beneficiaries of royal munificence. The Bonda plates of Pāṇḍuvaṁśī Tīvaradeva (seventh century) provide perhaps the earliest allusion to the migration of Brahmans, which in subsequent times became a regular phenomenon.[43] Migrant Brahmans from Rāḍha, Oḍradeśa, Madhyadeśa, Śrāvasti, etc., came in under the Somavaṁśīs. Some more social segments (if not all of them) which emerged in the wider context of social change find mention in the copper-plate inscriptions either as addressees or because of their involvement, in one capacity or the other, in the making of the land-grant charters. Besides the Brahmans, rural society comprised other categories, such as *kuṭumbin*s, *pradhāna-prativāsin*s and *prativāsin*s. While *kuṭumbin* is seen to be the equivalent of the middle peasant,[44] *prativāsin* means inhabitant and, flowing from it, *pradhāna-prativāsins* would then translate as important residents or men of substance. Such esteemed men attained recognition and

[41]Ibid., 51.

[42]*Padra*s, or *padraka*s, in Orissa even today, are settlements with a sprinkling of houses, clearly separated from *grāma*s, which are full-fledged villages. For a good discussion of the typology of rural settlements, see A.K. Choudhary 1971 and B.D. Chattopadhyaya 1990. For collective grants, see, for example, Arang Plates of Sudevarāja, Bonda Plates of Tīvaradeva, Bardula Plates of Mahāśivagupta and Patna Plates of Mahābhavagupta I, in A.M. Shastri 1995, 39-42, 102-6, 119-23 and 172-8.

[43]A.M. Shastri 1995.

[44]R. Chakravarti 1996, 179-98.

visibility from the later part of Pāṇḍuvaṁśī rule.[45] Among the occupational groups, the *sūtradhāra* (architect/master craftsman), *suvarṇakāra* (goldsmith), *vaṇik* (trader), *mālākāra* (garland maker), *gauḍa* (cowherd), *kāyastha* and engravers of records find mention in contemporary sources.[46] The numerous temples and copper-plates, for example, bear testimony to the existence of *ācārya*s, bricklayers, stone-cutters, smiths and composers, among others. Individuals other than royalty were involved in the construction of temples during the early stages,[47] pointing to their accrued economic competence. To make the more general point that there were noticeable disparities, one need not go further than the Brahmans. There were Brahmans enjoying a settlement, others having some shares in a settlement or settlements and still others with only some measures of land.[48] The emergence of new groups helped the transition to a caste society and the unfolding of social complexity, which were gradual, long-term processes. Differential access to economic resources, political power and ritual status contributed to social differentiation and hierarchization within the overarching framework of Brahmanical ideology, and with reference to the dominant schema.

The early medieval period was shaped not just by an expanding agrarian economy and social fluidity, it was equally a period of artistic innovation, cultural growth, and the movement of ideas. The elite showed interest in temple-building activities, and temple towns emerged as important centres of socio-cultural activity. The temple movement can be fully appreciated in the context of the formation of local and subregional agrarian bases and the simultaneous evolution of a complex, hierarchized socio-political structure, where various segments were seeking the confirmation of their assumed or achieved status.[49] Though the construction of temples in South Kośala dates from the late Gupta period onwards, it is only from around the seventh century that there is evidence for royal patronage to temples and Buddhist establishments alike, the reign of Mahāśivagupta Bālārjuna at Sirpur being particularly prominent. Temple rituals became more elaborate, and Brahmans, *ācārya*s

[45] V.V. Mirashi and L.P. Pandeya, 'Mallar Plates of Mahāśivagupta', *EI* 23, 1935-6, 120, lines 6-7; P.B. Desai, 'Bardula plates of Mahāśivagupta: Year 9', *EI* 27, 1947-8, 290, lines 6-8.

[46] See the Gandhareśvara temple inscription from the time of Śivagupta, the fragmentary Gandhareśvara temple inscription and Sonpur Plates of Mahābhavagupta I, in A.M. Shastri 1995, 152 (line 5), 161 (line 8) and 196 (line 19). Also see R.N. Misra 1975, 64-5.

[47] See S.P. Tiwari 1985, chapter on administration; A.M. Shastri 1977, 63-9. See also the Pipardula Plates of Narendra, Arang Plates of Sudevarāja and Senakapat stone inscription in A.M. Shastri 1995.

[48] Inscriptions not only record the grant of a settlement (e.g. *padraka* or *grāma*) to single Brahmanas, but also to more than one Brahmana. The Arang plates of Sudevarāja record a grant to nine Brahmanas, while the Bonda plates of Tīvaradeva mention a grant to twenty-five Brahmanas. As mentioned in the Senkapat stone-slab inscription, some of them received certain *hala* measures of land. See A.M. Shastri 1995.

[49] R. Thapar 1987, 34ff; B.D. Chattopadhyaya 2003b, 153-71.

and local bodies looked after their management.[50] The growing complexity and addition of details is reflected in the introduction of music and dance in these religious institutions.

At Tāla, situated close to the confluence of the Seonāth and Maniarī rivers in Bilaspur district, are preserved the ruins of two temples of remarkable beauty, known as Jiṭhānī and Devarāṇī, the former being relatively older than the latter. They are assigned to the late fifth and early sixth centuries, and the motifs bear affinities with Gupta art, combined with influences from Vidarbha, especially the sculptural idiom. Despite the analogy of sculptural art with Vākāṭaka and Gupta examples, it is said that 'they definitely breathe an atmosphere of their own'.[51] It is further suggested that this art form evolved from an indigenous tradition in wood-carving and laid the foundation of the Kośala style of architecture.[52] There have been efforts to understand the region-specific traits in the sculptures as representing Śaivite affiliation from South Kośala. The integration of animal figures in the main body of sculptures and the carving of the whole body of the deity instead of just the *mukha* on the liṅga in the assemblages at Tāla and Malhar are regarded as the regional characteristics.[53] Under the Pāṇḍuvaṁśīs and later Nalas, a distinct art tradition evolved in the region. Śrīpura and Rajim emerged as important centres with exquisite temples adorning these towns. The Lakṣmaṇa and Rājivlochana temples are fine examples. Malhar and Kharod too illustrate the growth in patronage and the spread of temples. Ranipur-Jharial in Bolangir district, a predominantly Śaivite complex, came to prominence under the Somavaṁśīs. In addition to the numerous temples, the large number of what appear to be votive shrines around Someśvara suggest that it was a *tīrtha* (pilgrimage centre).[54] Kośaleśvara at Baidyanāth, in the same district, and Pātāleśvara at Buḍhikomnā (near Nuapada), in Kalahandi district, among others, are placed in the same time bracket of the mid-ninth to mid-tenth centuries. It appears that under Somavaṁśī rule the tradition of art and architecture in the Upper Mahānadī moved into the Middle Mahānadī Valley and adjoining areas. Some experimentation in art and ground plan were initiated, to which I shall return later. The Kalachuris continued to patronize temples, a large number of which were built between the middle of the eleventh and end of the twelfth centuries. Contemporary records mentioned the presence of artists and craftsmen such as *sūtradhāra*s, *śilpī*s and *rūpakāras*.[55] Under the Kalachuris art assumed a 'provincial' character, and sculptures were marked by excessive standardization, emphasizing an anthropomorphic type in contrast to the earlier elegant

[50] See the Lodhia Plates of Mahāśivagupta, in Shastri 1995, 129, lines 11-12 and 1977.

[51] H. Bakker 1994, 25.

[52] Ibid. 1994, 10, 22.

[53] S.B. Majumdar 2003.

[54] D.R. Das 1990, 49.

[55] R.N. Misra 1987, Appendix I.

simplicity and sensitive rendering of figure work.[56] In the upper Mahānadī Valley the classical tradition faded out by the ninth century. However, it seems later to have influenced art in the middle Mahānadī region, the Somavaṁśīs being its ostensible carriers.

Brick was the popular building material in the temples of Kośala, from Tāla to Buḍhikomnā and from Malhar to Rajim, as was the case with the temples of Vidarbha. As one moves eastwards into coastal Orissa, stone replaces brick as the preferred raw material. Stellate or star-shaped temples, a product of considerable experimentation, were perhaps a typical South Kośala style. They involved the principle of two squares being placed diagonally to one another and intersecting at an angle of 45°. They are known from Kharod, Buḍhikomnā, Kansil (near Ranipur-Jharial), Baudh and other places, and are usually brick temples dedicated to Śiva. While the river goddesses Gaṅgā and Yamunā flank the doorway of the shrine, the Navagrahas with Gajalakṣmī at the centre adorn the lintel.[57] Daśāvatāra images embellish the door-jambs in the Lakṣmaṇa temple at Sirpur and decorate the pillars of the Rajivlochana temple at Rajim. The carving of large figures against the pillars in the temple as at Rajim, Sirpur or Kośaleśvara at Baidyanāth, near Sonepur, appear to be specific to Kośala. Similarly, knotted snakes decorating the doorways of shrines as at Kośaleśvara, for example, were a characteristic feature of the region, not known in the Lower Mahānadī Valley and the plains of Orissa.[58] Some of these traits, which are common occurrences in Dakṣiṇa Kośala, find visible manifestation at places like Baidyanāth and Boudh, largely because they are situated on the border, which helped them to combine influences from both Kośala and Orissa.

The co-existence of multiple forms of religion, beliefs and practices is borne out by the combined evidence of archaeology and inscriptions. Malhar and Sirpur have yielded evidence of both temples and Buddhist *vihāras*. In fact, the *vihāras* at Sirpur were in the vicinity of the Lakṣmaṇa temple. Patronage was broad-based, and the rulers of successive dynasties spent their resources on the temples of Viṣṇu and Śiva as well as Buddhist monasteries. While Bhāvadeva, brother of Nannarāja (a Pāṇḍuvaṁśī king), had a Buddhist *vihāra* repaired, Isāṇadeva, another brother of the same king, built a temple at Kharod.[59] Mahāśivagupta Bālārjuna was equally liberal in his generosity towards Brahmanical shrines and Buddhist establishments. Many rulers, despite their Śaivite affiliations, invoked Vaiṣṇava imageries in their official records. Even Ranipur-Jharial, an ostensibly Śaivite complex, had a Kṛṣṇa temple and at the same site several Vaiṣṇavite figures are present on the walls of Indralath, a

[56]Ibid. 1987, 99.

[57]For the temple art of South Kośala, see R.N. Misra 1987, 99-128; also see J.K. Pattnaik 1999, 236-40.

[58]V. Dehejia 1979, 136-8.

[59]See Arang stone inscription and the inscription in the Lakṣmaṇeśvara temple at Kharod. Also see H. Bakker 1994, 14.

temple dedicated to Śiva.[60] It is thought that at Sirpur the same artists worked at temples and Buddhist sites, a situation akin to what occurred in coastal Orissa.[61]

Narasiṁha and Mahiṣāsuramardinī or Śakti appear to have been popular deities. Images of Mahiṣāsuramardinī are present in Sirpur, at the site museum, and Rajim, and a figure of Durgā has been retrieved from the Mārguḍā Valley, while Stambheśvarī is referred to in the Terasinga plates of Tuṣṭikara. Sculptural representations of Narasiṁha are available at Tāla, Sirpur and Rajim, while the Lakṣmaṇa temple at Sirpur (alluded to in the stone inscription of Vāṣatā) was probably dedicated to Viṣṇu-Narasiṁha. The compulsions of political power or the need to win over one's subjects may explain why royal patronage was inclusive, not sectarian. However, one wonders whether the popularity of Śakti, the man-lion deity and later Śivaism, which unlike Viṣṇuism is kin-based, had anything to do with the autochthonous inheritance of local societies in transition. In the context of adjoining Vidarbha, it has been suggested that the popularity of Narasiṁha rested on his being 'a brave heroic deity'.[62] Even while Buddhist institutions were flourishing and were also the recipients of royal favour, the reformed Brahmanical religion with Viṣṇu and Śiva as its two most important gods seems to have increasingly gained court patronage from around the sixth to seventh centuries onward. The shift mostly in favour of Śivaism is more clearly visible under the Somavaṁśīs and Kalachuris, especially in the artistic record of the times.[63] Whether this shift was a result of a swing in popular support or a change in royal patronage or both warrants careful investigation.

Art and ideas are a product of society and involve particular cultural contexts and specific forms of social organization. The early medieval scene is illuminated by symbols and idioms in contemporary inscriptions, as is temple art, which reflects on these domains. The spread of Vedic, Śāstric, epic and Purāṇic ideas can be gleaned from the images or self-images of royalty as represented in the *praśasti* sections of the copper-plate and stone inscriptions.[64] The influence of the Dharmaśāstras is easily discernible in the benedictory and imprecatory verses in the land grant charters. The *daśāvatāra* images on door-jambs or pillars in temples at Sirpur and Rajim or the story relating to Skanda in the *Mahābhārata* rendered in art at Tāla point in the same direction.[65]

[60]B.C. Chhabra, *EI* 24, 243ff; D.R. Das 1990, 34.

[61]On the basis of the style of carving and treatment of figures, it is suggested that the same artists and craftsmen had been at work at both Ratnagiri and Siśireśvara. See V. Dehejia 1979, 109, 114; S.L. Katare 1959, 7-8.

[62]H. Bakker 1990, 62-85.

[63]See, for example, D.R. Das 1990; R.N. Misra 1987, Appendix II, 139-55. For an analogous situation in Bengal, see R.M. Eaton 1997 (paperback), 12-17.

[64]See the Lakṣmaṇa temple inscription of Vāṣatā at Sirpur and Mahāśivagupta Bālārjuna's Sirpur stone inscription, in A.M. Shastri 1995, 141-7 and 150-1.

[65]For Tāla, see H. Bakker 1994, 27-9.

The significant correspondence between Kośaleśvara, the name of the Śiva temple at Baidyanāth, and the Somavaṁśīs, who constantly projected themselves as the lords of Kośala, cannot be missed. This is just one instance of the ways in which royalty sought to identify with divinity.[66] Understandably the appropriation of divinity was couched in a vocabulary which tried to achieve the desired purpose without doing violence to popular sensibilities. The familiar use of similes, metaphors and double entendre was intended to achieve this. For example, in his charters Mahāśivagupta Bālārjuna described himself as the son of Harṣagupta, just as Kārttikeya was of lord Śiva. Various discursive strategies were employed in the making of dominant ideology and techniques of control. Brāhmaṇas and temples disseminated Śāstric and Purāṇic ideas and values with a view to creating a coherent cultural ethos, a favourable ground for the extension and consolidation of state society.[67] The place of temples as catalysts in this process can be seen from the Senakapat inscription, which besides granting plots of land to a Śiva temple, expected the Śaivite ascetics to arrange for sacrifices (*yāga*) and initiate people into Śivaism.[68] Brāhmaṇa and temple settlements were the 'pillars of the normative order of Hindu Kingdoms',[69] something that explains the grants of land to them as a necessary component of state policy. Whatever may have been its other functions, it surely provided the state with ideological legitimacy.

In the course of their being read out on several occasions, starting with a public proclamation on the occasion of the grant, the copper-plate charters, with their significant use of Śāstric, epic and Purāṇic ideas and symbolisms and focus on legal and moral norms, played an important role in communicating these messages, in the process contributing to the formation of an overarching value system. As public records, the inscriptions on temple walls, such as the Lakṣmaṇa temple stone inscription of Vāsaṭā at Sirpur, among others, were powerful instruments of cultural transmission.[70] The temples and monasteries at Sirpur attracted many devotees of different ideological persuasions, thus investing the stone inscriptions with political meaning.[71] These official records therefore need to be seen not simply as land transaction documents or as being reflective of a cultural milieu, but perhaps as transformatory stimuli in the early medieval social formation of South Kośala, a region which in many areas experienced the transition to historical society largely during the Gupta and

[66]For a general discussion of the issue in the early medieval context, see B.P. Sahu 2003b, 56-64; a good discussion of the situation in adjoining Vidarbha is available in H. Bakker 1992, 83-100.

[67]B.D. Chattopadhyaya 1983, 25-63; H. Kulke 1995, 233-62; and B.P. Sahu 2001, 12-26.

[68]A.M. Shastri 1995, 154-9, verses 15-23.

[69]H. Kulke 1995, 244.

[70]See, for example, the Arang stone inscription, the Sirpur stone inscriptions, Sirpur Gandhareśvara temple inscription and the Senkapat stone slab inscription, in A.M. Shastri 1995, 96-101 and 148-59.

[71]For details of this argument, see H. Kulke 1997, 237-43.

post-Gupta periods. By the time of the Pāṇḍuvaṁśīs, especially Mahāśivagupta Bālārjuna, Śāstric and Purāṇic ideas had been sufficiently internalized by society for artists to express them in stone and poets and scribes to articulate them in their compositions of the drafts of charters so that engravers could transfer these on to copper-plates or stone. By mediating between the local and the pan-Indian, Brahmans, temples, artists and poets helped in the creation of an intermediate level of cultural identity or belonging, which in the long term bound people together through a common way of thinking and believing, leading to the making of an 'experienced region'.[72]

It may be good to remind ourselves at this point that early medieval regimes were neither monolithic nor omnipresent.[73] Similarly, the coherence of Brahmanical enterprises has perhaps been assumed more than is warranted. It may be reasonable to suggest that both agrarian expansion and Brahmanical ideology built on and could not escape opposition and conflict, as such intrusions would have blended coercive and persuasive strategies. At the beginning of the second millennium, then, Brahmanical settlements, temple towns and their influence were not all-pervasive. Agrarian expansion and concomitant developments moved in a phased manner, with unevenness built into the process. On this material and cultural foundation arose the medieval Rajput kingdoms of the region,[74] but that is not within the scope of this discussion.

The chapter started with the premise that socio-cultural transformations are a product of interaction between trans-regional patterns and local initiatives. Viewed from this perspective, many of the developments in South Kośala appear to be universal, yet it marked a distinctiveness in particular cultural forms. The regional autonomy of art forms was a historical reality, though its extent is debatable. At this point one may ask how the Dakṣiṇa Kośala experience differed from the pan-Indian or alternatively geographically proximate Orissan experiences. Notwithstanding influences from the adjoining regions, the cumulative traits of Kośala art and architecture provide a distinctive regional flavour. The important innovations in art forms seem to be an act of self-assurance on the part of the Kośalan people. The projection of the kings as 'Lord of Kośala' (e.g. Kośalādhipati and Kośalendra) and the worship of Śiva as Kośaleśvara (Lord of Kośala) at Baidyanāth perhaps derived from, as well as contributed to, the formation of a Kośala identity. The indigenous people may or may not have comprehended the formation of a subregion, but we can perhaps raise and address the issue by suggesting that it emerged from a shared, common historico-cultural, though not necessarily homogeneous experience, which may have provided the local communities with a spatially distinguishable and culturally identifiable identity. Art and culture would have engendered a sense of affiliation among the people, but how many envisaged it that way is a difficult question to answer.

[72]I have borrowed this expression from K. Chakrabarti 2000, 14.

[73]For a good discussion, see B.D. Chattopadhyaya 1997, 1-14.

[74]For later developments, see C.U. Wills 1919, 197-262; N.K. Sahu 1985, 1-42.

The terms 'regional' and 'subregional' have been used interchangeably throughout, but at this point there is a need for some precision in what is being said. The subregion, like the region, is a category which is easy to understand but rather difficult to define. Like multiple communities, which constitute a plural society with none having a monopoly or privileged position in defining it, subregions are a part of a region but with no single unit constituting it. In other words, they are in it and yet out of it, and in this are embedded the historical roots of contestation and negotiations within regions. In that sense, by the end of the first millennium Dakṣiṇa Kośala was an evolving subregion with features which defined the contours of its personality in the succeeding centuries.[75] Flowing from it, it is necessary to engage in a different evaluation of the subregions than just seeing them as simple extensions and therefore as hierarchically subordinate repetitive images of the epicentre, in this case coastal Orissa. They seem to constitute as much as be impacted by the perceived centre. It appears that both generalizing and essentializing the criteria of the subregion, like the region, have their share of problems. If generalizations subsume subregional historico-cultural specificities, essentializing them tends to ignore the multiple sources of identity formation, as well as the fact that identities in the past, as so often today, were not immutable.

[75] It appears that South Kośala, which, under the later Pāṇḍuvaṁśīs and early Somavaṁśīs, was emerging as a region, became a subregion of Orissa after the Somavaṁśīs' conquest of eastern or coastal Orissa and the forging of a regional or supra-regional kingdom.

REFERENCES

Archaeological Survey of India, *Annual Report, 1930-34*, 1936.

Bajpai, K.D. and S.K. Pandey 1978. *Malhar 1975-78*, Sagar: University of Sagar.

Bakker, H. 1990. 'Ramtek: An Ancient Centre of Vishnu Devotion in Maharashtra', in H. Bakker (ed.), *The History of Sacred Places in India as Reflected in Traditional Literature* (being volume III of Panels of the VII World Sanskrit Conference), Leiden: E.J. Brill, 62-85.

———1992. 'Throne and Temple: Political Power and Religious Prestige in Vidarbha', in H. Bakker (ed.), *The Sacred Centre as the Focus of Political Interest*, Groningen: Forsten, 83-100.

———1994. 'Observations on the History and Culture of Daksina Kosala (5th to 7th centuries A.D.)', in N. Balbir and J.K. Bautze (eds.), *Festschrift Klaus Bruhn*, Reinbek: Verlag für Orientalistische Fachpublikationen, 1-41.

Beglar, J.D. and A. Cunningham. 2000 (rpt.). *Report of Tours in the South-Eastern Provinces, 1874-75 and 1875-76*, vol. 13. Delhi: Archaeological Survey of India.

Behera, S.C. 1982. *Interim Excavation Reports*, Sambalpur: Sambalpur University.

Brandtner, M. 1994. 'Archaeology of Western Orissa: Finds from Nehena', in A. Parpola and P. Koskikallio (eds.), *South Asian Archaeology 1993: Proceedings of the 12th International Conference of the European Association of South Asian Archaeologists held in Helsinki University 5-9 July 1993*, vol. 1, Helsinki: Suomalainen Tiedeakademia (Annales Academiae Scientiarum Fennicae, Ser. B. 271; Suomalaisen Tiedeakatemian toimituksia. Sarja B), 101-14.

Chakrabarti, K. 2000. 'Cult Region: The Puranas and the Making of the Cultural Territory of Bengal', in *Studies in History* 16, 1, 1-16.

Chakravarti, R. 1996. 'Kutumbikas of Early India', in V.K. Thakur and A. Aounshuman (eds.), *Peasants in Indian History*, vol. 1, Patna: Janaki Prakashan, 179-98.

Chandra, S.A. 1994. 'Transition to Early Historical Phase in Chattisgarh Region of Madhya Pradesh', unpublished M.Phil. dissertation, Delhi: University of Delhi, Department of History, 1994.

Chattopadhyaya, B.D. 1983. 'Political Processes and the Structure of Polity in Early Medieval India: Problems of Perspective', Presidential Address, Ancient India Section, *Proceedings of the Indian History Congress, Burdwan Session*, 25-63.

———1988. 'Transition to the Early Historical Phase in the Deccan: A Note', in B.M. Pande and B.D. Chattopadhyaya (eds.), *Archaeology and History*, vol. 2, Delhi: Agamkala Prakashan, 727-32.

———1990. *Aspects of Rural Settlements and Rural Society in Early Medieval India*, Calcutta: K.P. Bagchi.

———1997. 'Autonomous Spaces and the Authority of the State: The Contradiction and its Resolution in Theory and Practice in Early India', in B. Kölver (ed.), *Recht, Staat und Gesellschaft im Klassischen Indien (The Law, the State and Administration in Classical India)*, Munich: Oldenbourg, 1-14.

———2003. *Studying Early India: Archaeology, Texts and Historical Issues*, Delhi: Permanent Black.

———2003a. 'Urban Centres in Early Bengal: Archaeological Perspectives', in B.D. Chattopadhyaya, 2003, 66-101.

———2003b. 'Historical Context of the Early Medieval Temples of North India', in B.D. Chattopadhyaya, 2003, 153-71.

Chhabra, B.C. 1937-8. 'Ranipur-Jharial Inscriptions', *Epigraphia Indica* 24, 239-45.

Choudhary, A.K. 1971. *Early Medieval Village in North Eastern India (A.D. 600-1200)*, Calcutta: Punthi Pustak.

Cunningham, A. 2000 (rpt.). *Report of a Tour in the Central Provinces and Lower Gangetic Doab in 1881-82*, vol. 17, Delhi: Archaeological Survey of India.

Das, D.R. 1990. *Temples of Ranipur-Jharial*, Calcutta: Calcutta University.

Das, H.C. 1990. 'Urban Centres in Ancient Orissa', in Amita Ray and S. Mukherjee (eds.), *Historical Archaeology of India: A Dialogue Between Archaeologists and Historians*, Delhi: Books & Books, 175-93.

Dehejia, V. 1979. *Early Stone Temples of Orissa*, Delhi: Vikas.

Deo, J.P.S. 2000. 'Archaeology of Kalahandi and Nuapada Districts, Orissa', in K.K. Basa and P. Mohanty (eds.), *Archaeology of Orissa*, Delhi: Pratibha Prakashan, 418-30.

Eaton, R.M. 1997 (paperback rpt.). *The Rise of Islam and the Bengal Frontier, 1204-1760*, Delhi: Oxford University Press.

Epigraphia Indica (EI), relevant volumes.

Fleet, J.F. 1970 (3rd edn.). *Inscriptions of the Early Gupta Kings and their Successors*, Corpus Inscriptionum Indicarum, vol. 3, Varanasi: IBH.

Indian Archaeology: A Review (IAR), relevant volumes.

Jain, B. 1977. 'Malhar Plates (second set) of Mahasivagupta', in *Prachya Pratibha* 5, 1, 48-53.

Katare, S.L. 1959. 'Excavations at Sirpur', in *The Indian Historical Quarterly* 35, 1, 1-8.

Kulke, H. 1995. 'The Early and the Imperial Kingdom: A Processual Model of Integrative State Formation in Early Medieval India', in H. Kulke (ed.), *The State in India 1000-1700*, Delhi: Oxford University Press, 233-62.

———1997. 'Some Observations on the Political Function of Copper-plate Grants in Early

Medieval India', in B. Kölver (ed.), *The State, The Law and Administration in Classical India*, Munich: Oldenbourg, 237-43.

———2004. 'Some Thoughts on State and State Formation under the Eastern Vakatakas', in H. Bakker (ed.), *The Vakataka Heritage: Indian Culture at the Crossroads*, Groningen: Egbert Forsten, 1-9.

Mahapatra, K.N. 1947. 'Excavation at Belkhandi in the Kalahandi State', in *Journal of Kalinga Historical Research Society* 2, 167-72.

Majumdar, S.B. 2003. 'Tracing the Region-specific Traits in the Saiva Sculptures of South Kosala', in *Proceedings of the Indian History Congress, Mysore Session*, 277-85.

Mirashi, V.V. and L.P. Pandeya. 1935-6. 'Mallar Plates of Mahasivagupta', *Epigraphia Indica* 23, 113-22.

Mishra, B. and M.P. Singhdeo. 2002. 'A Unique Seal from Budhigarh, Orissa', *Puratattva* 32, 152-5.

Misra, R.N. 1975. *Ancient Artists and Art Activity*, Shimla: Indian Institute of Advanced Studies.

———1987. *Sculptures of Dahala and Dakṣiṇa Kosala and their Background*, Delhi: Agam Prakashan.

Mohanty, P. and B. Mishra, 2000. 'A Note on a Seal Matrix from Budhigarh, District Kalahandi, Orissa', in *Puratattva* 30, 58-60.

Panda, S.C. 1981. 'Buddhist Vestiges at Ganiapali and Nagraj on the Ang Valley', in S.C. Behera (ed.), *New Aspects of History of Orissa*, vol. 3, Sambalpur: Sambalpur University, 47-52.

Panda, S.K. 'Kośalananda Kavyam and the Making of a Rajput Dynasty: A Study on the Chauhans of Western Orissa', in this volume.

Panda, S.S. 1989. 'New Light on the Brick Temples of the Upper Mahanadi Valley of Orissa', in *Orissa Historical Research Journal* 35, 3/4, 117-26.

———1995. 'Some Archaeological Remains of Bolangir District', in *Orissa Historical Research Journal* 40, 1/4, 46-87.

Patel, C.B. (forthcoming), 'Marguda Valley Excavations'. Paper presented at the Seminar on Eastern Indian Archaeology, held at Konark, 5-7 April 2001.

Pattnaik, J.P. 1999. 'Stellate Temples of Orissa', in S. Pradhan (ed.), *Orissan History, Culture and Archaeology*, Delhi: D.K. Printworld, 436-40.

Rajaguru, S.N. 1958. *Inscriptions of Orissa (300-700 A.D.)*, vol. 1, part 2, Berhampur: Orissa Sahitya Akademi.

Sahu, B.P. 1993. 'Aspects of Rural Economy in Early Medieval Orissa', in *Social Scientist*, nos. 236-7, 48-68.

———2001. 'Brahmanical Ideology, Regional Identities and the Construction of Early India', Presidential Address, Ancient Section, *Proceedings of the Punjab History Conference, 33rd Session, Patiala*, 12-26; also in *Social Scientist*, nos. 338-9, 2001, 3-18.

———2003a. 'The Early State in Orissa: From the Perspective of Changing Forms of Patronage and Legitimation', in B. Pati, B.P. Sahu and T.K. Venkatasubramanian (eds.), *Negotiating India's Past: Essays in Memory of Partha Sarathi Gupta*, Delhi: Tulika, 29-51.

———2003b. 'Legitimation, Ideology and State in Early India', Presidential Address, Ancient India Section, *Proceedings of the Indian History Congress, Mysore Session*, 44-76.

Sahu, N.K. 1984. *Kharavela*, Bhubaneswar: Orissa State Museum.

———1985. *Veer Surendra Sai*, Cuttack: Department of Culture, Government of Orissa, 1-42.

Seneviratne, S. 1980-1. 'Kalinga and Andhra: The Process of Secondary State Formation in Early India', in *The Indian Historical Review* 7, 1/2, 54-69.

Shastri, A.M. 1977. 'Temple Administration in Chhattisgarh under the Sarabhapuriyas and Panduvamsis', in *Prachya Pratibha* 5, 2, 63-9.

———1995. *Inscriptions of the Sarabhapurias, Panduvaṁśins and Somavaṁśins*, parts I and II, Delhi: Motilal Banarsidass.

Singh, U. 1994. *Kings, Brahmanas and Temples in Orissa: An Epigraphic Study (300-1147 C.E.)*, Delhi: Munshiram Manoharlal.

Thapar, R. 1987. *Cultural Transaction and Early India: Tradition and Patronage*, Delhi: Oxford University Press.

Tiwari, S.P. 1985. *Comprehensive History of Orissa: Dakṣiṇa Kośala under the Sarabhapuriyas*, Calcutta: Punthi Pustak.

Wills, C.U. 1919. 'The Territorial System of the Rajput Kingdoms of Medieval Chhattisgarh', in *Journal of the Asiatic Society of Bengal* (n.s.) 15, 197-262.

Xuanzang 1906. *Si-yu-ki: Buddhist Records of the Western World: Chinese Accounts of India*, vol. 2, translated from the Chinese of Hiuen Tsiang by Samuel Beal, London: Kegan Paul, Trench, Trübner & Co.

CHAPTER 3

The Feudatory States of Orissa: Centres out There

HERMANN KULKE

The emergence of regional cultures as a major feature of Indian history since the early Middle Ages is well known.[1] Less known but equally remarkable is the fact that late medieval and in particular early modern India is likewise characterized by the shaping and gradual development of subregional and local polities and identities.[2] Colonially enforced processes of modernization further enhanced the development of the Feudatory states and their emergence as Princely States in late nineteenth and early twentieth centuries.[3] But under the impact of the national independence movement and the creation of the States of independent India, they were challenged by and partly submerged into homogenizing processes of emergent regional and national identities.

The former Feudatory states in the predominantly tribal hinterland of Orissa and their development as 'centres out there' *vis-à-vis* the politically and culturally dominant coastal belt depict this development paradigmatically. But surprisingly their emergence in late medieval and early modern Orissa still remains a step child of Orissan historiography. The inscriptions and monuments of their 'classical' predecessors since late first millennium CE are properly studied as is well documented, e.g. by B.P. Sahu's paper in this volume. The same holds good for the history of Orissa's 24 recognized Feudatory or Princely States under colonial rule when most of them had finally emerged as genuine trans-local 'centres out there'.[4] But research on this period focuses primarily on the analysis of their 'feudal' structure and exploitative nature and the collaboration of their rulers with the colonial power on the one hand and on agrarian unrest and political agitation of their people in the wake of Indian

[1] A. Eschmann 1978; B.D. Chattopadhyaya 1994.

[2] K. Chakravarti 2001 and B.K. Mallik 2004.

[3] The Feudatory states of Orissa are known under several names: Their original name was Garhjat (fort-born) Mahals and during Mughal rule they were termed as Zamindaris, under British rule they became first known as Tributary Mahals, then as Feudatory states throughout the later part of the nineteenth and early twentieth centuries and finally as Princely States during the last decades before independence. In this paper they will be usually referred to as 'Feudatory States' (Cobden Ramsay 1910).

[4] The size of Orissa's Feudatory states ranged from 4,243 (Mayurbhanj) to 46 square miles (Tigeria).

freedom movement on the other hand.[5] The inglorious role of rulers of several Feudatory states in the last stage of independence movement finally stigmatized them not only as centres of indirect colonial rule but also as 'centres out there of exploitation' (B. Pati in this volume). The intermediate period, however, between the 'glorious classical' and the 'inglorious colonial' periods still remains outside the mainstream of Orissan historiography. But as also pointed out by A. Tanabe in the present volume, it was exactly this period which was most essential for the emergence of the Feudatory states as 'centres out there' and their till today prevailing trans-local or subregional identities.[6] The present paper intends to highlight few aspects of this development.

THE HISTORY OF THE FEUDATORY STATES OF ORISSA

The history of the Feudatory states of Orissa goes back to the early medieval period when a considerably large number of *mandala* or *samanta* polities surrounded Orissa's coastal kingdoms.[7] Well known among them were the Bhanjas of the Khijjinga and Khinjali Mandalas in modern Mayurbhanj and Baudh respectively[8] and the Sulkis of Kodalaka Mandala in present Dhenkanal. Their political status as *samanta* or 'neighbouring' tributary states was characterized by a strong autonomy. Culturally they competed successfully—as witnessed by the beautiful Buddhist and Hindu art and architecture, e.g. at Kiching, Baudh and Kualo[9]—with the coastal Maharajas. But they were distinguished from the coastal kingdoms by their concomitant patronage of purely tribal goddesses, such as Stambhesvari by the Bhanjas and Sulkis or the powerful Maninagesvari at Ranpur whose first historically known devotee, Raja Lokavigraha, was praised in CE 600 as overlord of eighteen [Gond] chiefdoms.[10]

Little or, in fact, next to nothing is known about these Mandala states during the more than three hundred years of Ganga rule in Orissa.[11] But in the fifteenth century they re-emerged as a strong and increasingly irritating factor in the power struggle of the Gajapati kings of the imperial Suryavamsa dynasty. Kapilendra, its first great ruler, and his son Purushottama were compelled to threaten them in their inscriptions with the wrath of Lord Jagannatha and the confiscation of their wealth if they rebel (*droha*) against his orders.[12] But it

[5]M.M. Mishra 1983; B. Pati 1993; C.P. Nanda 1998.

[6]B. Schnepel 2002 and H. Kulke 1979.

[7]N.K. Sahu 1956, vol. 2, 351-65; K.C. Panigrahi 1981, 134-50; J. Mahapatra 1997 (who was kind enough to reprint map no. 1 of H. Kulke 1979 without reference).

[8]A. Joshi 1983.

[9]T. Donaldson 1985, vol. 1, 111-269.

[10]S.N. Rajaguru 1950; see also Kulke 1977.

[11]S.K. Panda 1986.

[12]A good example is an inscription of Kapilendra at the Jayavijaya doorway of the Jagannatha temple at Puri of the year 1464: 'Oh Jagannatha! Thus prayth Thy servant (*sebaka*). Throughout the kingdom, I maintained from childhood these (feudal) lords

was this great—and in the collective memory of the Oriyas—heroic period to which most of the later Feudatory states and their dynasties trace back their foundation legends. Most popular in this context are the accounts in the local *vamsavali* chronicles about the alleged participation of various dynastic founder kings in the legendary Kanchi Kaberi campaign of the second Gajapati king Purushottama.[13]

Under circumstances which are not yet fully known, the power of at least few of these Garhjat (or fort-born) Mahals apparently had increased tremendously in the sixteenth century as during the decline of the imperial Gajapati kingdom, three scions of the Bhanjas of Mayurbhanj and/or Keonjhar (Raghubhanja, Durgabhanja and Ramachandra Bhanja) were strong enough to play a rather inglorious role in several *coups d'état* against the Gajapatis during the last years before the fall of the Orissa kingdom in 1568.

After their final conquest of Orissa in 1592, the Mughals carried out a settlement which resulted in a tripartite division of Orissa. The coastal region came under the name of Mughalbandi under their direct rule whereas the Garhjat Mahals or Zamindaris, particularly Mayurbhanj and Keonjhar, retained under their indirect rule a strong autonomy. 'These chiefs may be safely considered as *de facto* proprietors of their possession under the native governments, that is, they held them hereditarily, exercised uncontrolled jurisdiction within their limits and appropriated the entire revenues subject to the condition of performing military service'.[14] The newly established Khurda kingdom, as the nominal successor state to the erstwhile imperial Gajapatis, was invested by Akbar's General Mansingh with the fief of the small but important Garhjat Mahals in the lower Mahanadi Valley and the former Ganjam district.[15] The creation of a directly ruled coastal belt under the Mughals, which remained the backbone of foreign dominance in Orissa until 1947, enforced the cultural, social and political division of Orissa which continues till today.[16]

THE GAJAPATIS OF KHURDA AND THEIR FEUDATORY STATES

The dominant position of Khurda as successors of the erstwhile imperial Gajapatis was frequently threatened by Akbar's successors and their Mughal subahdars at Cuttack and after 1751 by the Maratha and temporarily also by

(*samanta*) including the infantry and cavalry and gave them wealth. All of them have forsaken me. I shall deal with them and punish them each according to their desert. Oh Lord! Jagannatha! do Thou judge this fact whether I am right or wrong', K.B. Tripathy 1962, 272; see also H. Kulke 1979, 70-3 and B.K. Mallik 2004.

[13]L.E.B. Cobden Ramsay 1910; G.N. Dash 1979; B. Schnepel 2000 and 2003; M.M. Mishra 2003; Kulke 2004, Berkemer 1993, 234-6.

[14]A. Stirling 1822 (1904), 70.

[15]*A'in-i-Akbari*, vol. 2, 155-7; M.A. Haque 1980, 226-32; H. Kulke 1979, 103-8.

[16]G.N. Dash 2007.

the Parlakhimedi rajas of South Orissa.[17] But due to Khurda's direct access to and control over Puri and its Jagannatha cult and its ritual authority over a large number of small but locally important Garhjat Mahals, it remained the foremost state of Orissa until late eighteenth century.[18] Late N.K. Sahu, the great Sambalpur historian, might have been right when he spoke of Khurda's 'Phantom Gajapatis'.[19] But their kingship and elevated position in the Orissan society was of prime importance for the Jagannatha centred Oriya identity and the emergence of various subregional identities of competing Garhjat chiefs.

The high status of the Khurda rajas is well attested by an unusual witness of mid-seventeenth century. During his campaign in Orissa in 1660-2 the General Khan-i-Dauran sent a report to his imperial master Aurangzeb in which he referred to Raja Mukunda Deva of Khurda as 'the leading zamindar of this country whose orders were obeyed by the other zamindars [and] whom all the other zamindars of this country worship like a god and disobedience of whose order they regard as a great sin'.[20] Khan-i-Dauran's campaign was in fact a reconquest of Orissa after Aurangzeb's war of succession during which more or less all zamindars or chiefs of Orissa had regained their independence. The importance of the Khan's report lies not only in the often quoted reference to the Khurda rajas. Equally revealing are his hints at the formidable resistance offered for several years by various rajas or zamindars of Orissa such as Narsinghpur, Banki, Ranpur, Banpur, Kujang, Kanika, Madhupur, Khallikote and in particular by the Bhanjas of Mayurbhanj and Keonjhar.

Khan-i-Dauran's reports amounts to a 'who is who' of Orissan Garhjat Mahals and Zamindaris in mid-seventeenth century. According to Puri's *Madala Panji* chronicle, the *singha dvara*, the main gate of the Jagannatha temple at Puri, which had been closed for several years by Aurangzeb's order, was again forcefully opened by the Khurda raja with the help of the rulers of the 18 Garhjat Mahals after Aurangzeb's death in 1707.[21]

The short period of Maratha rule in Orissa was of particular importance for the further development of the Feudatory states. As Hindu rulers, the Marathas contested the position of the Khurda rajas as 'sacred and secret rulers' of Orissa and mediatized its Feudatory states and thus 'freed' them from Khurda's overlordship. A short report about this event comes from T. Motte who travelled in 1766 on a mission from Calcutta to Sambalpur:

> When Ragoojee [the Maratha ruler of Nagpur] entered Orissa, he found these parts divided into small zemindaries, dependent on the rajah of Pooree at whose capital is the famous temple of Jeggernaut, near the Chilka lake. This prince was regarded by

[17]H. Kulke 1978.

[18]For Khurda see K.N. Mahapatra 1969; H. Kulke 1979, 80-207; A. Tanabe 2003 and in the present volume; G.N. Dash 2010.

[19]N.K. Sahu 1956, 391.

[20]J.N. Sarkar 1916, 161.

[21]A.B. Mohanty 1969, 70.

his subjects in a religious light also, and appeared formidable to the Mahrattas, who, apprehensive lest he might seize a favourable opportunity to cut off the communication between Nagpoor and Cuttac, resolved to reduce his power by dividing it. He made the petty zemindars independent of him, and formed the chucklas [tax districts] of Dinkanol [Dhenkanal], Bonkey [Banki], Nersingpoor [Narsinghpur], Tigorea [Tigeria], Tolchair [Talcher], Chunda Parra [Khandpara], Dispulla [Daspalla], Hindole [Hindul], Ungool [Angul], and Boad [Baud].[22]

Khurda's feudatories thus came under the sway of the Maratha subahdar at Cuttack to whom they had to pay a light quit rent as was the case with the other Garhjat States of Orissa. But 'being secure in their forts, most of which were surrounded by dense jungles and confident of their strength to resist any attack, many of the feudatory chiefs were often irregular in payment of tribute and occasionally showed a spirit of insubordination'.[23] Apart from a greater reluctance to pay their tribute, the position of the Garhjat rulers under the Marathas seemed to have remained the same as under the Mughals. But there was an essential difference. The dismemberment of 'formidable' Khurda by the Marathas through mediatization of its Garhjat Mahals reduced its political authority to the level of its former feudatories, particularly when the Marathas also began to challenge its ritual hegemony in the Jagannatha cult of Puri.[24] Particularly important in our context is the fact that Khurda's diminution enhanced the position of the Feudatory states and their rulers to a hitherto unknown degree of autonomy. They used their new position to equip their 'capitals' with various paraphernalia of Hindu kingship.

THE RITUAL PRIVILEGES OF FEUDATORY RAJAS IN PURI

An important ingredient of an emerging Hindu kingship ideology of the rulers of the Garhjat Mahals were their ritual privileges in the cult of Jagannatha, granted by the raja of Khurda. Although meant primarily to strengthen Khurda's position, they also validated the rise of the Garhjat rulers to Feudatory rajas. In their desperate struggle against the loss of control over their feudatories, which had already begun during Mughal rule and which culminated in their mediatization under the Marathas, the rajas of Khurda increasingly exerted their ritual authority as 'First Servant' (*adi sevaka*) of Jagannatha. In order to strengthen their own precarious position and to regain the loyalty and support of the feudatory rajas they granted special ritual privileges to them during their visits to Puri and their *darsan* of Jagannatha through 'royal letters' (*chamu citaus*), a policy which they had already begun in periods of crisis under the Mughals.[25]

The archive material of the *Madala Panji* which the first Orissa Research

[22]T. Motte 1930, 27.

[23]B.C. Ray 1960, 129.

[24]H. Kulke 1979, 205-15.

[25]For further details see H. Kulke 1992b and und S.K. Panda 2000.

Project procured from the temple scribe (*deula karana*) of the Jagannatha temple in 1971 contains about 160 *chamu citaus*, most of them being addressed to altogether 32 rajas, princes and zamindars of Orissa during the seventeenth and eighteenth centuries: Ranpur (13), Athgarh (12), Khandpara (10), Dhenkanal (10), Tigeria (9), Nayagarh (6), Baramba (5), Banpur, Khallikote, Sambalpur, Tekkali and Sukinda (each 4), Jeypore, Parlakhimedi and Vijayanagara (each 3), Kanika, Mahuri, Narsinghpur and Patia (each 2), Angul, Badakhemundi, Khemundi, Banki, Baudh, Kujang, Madhupur, Mayurbhanj, Parikud and Sonepur (each 1).[26]

One of the early letters, issued by Raja Mukunda Deva in CE 1662, illustrates the peculiar '*chamu citau* policy' of the Khurda rajas.

> Raja Nilakantha Deva [of Badakhimedi in South Orissa] has gone [to Puri] for *darsan* [of Jagannatha]. We sent Paramananda Patanaik along with him. He will stay with him and make him perform the *darsan*. The palanquin, the royal umbrella, a fan made of peacock feathers and the sword and dagger [of the raja] will be kept at a place near the Lions Gate. He will be allowed to take his big fan and other necessary articles of prestige with him. After being carried over the seven steps of the *batadvara* of the Jagamohana, all this will be kept near the Jaya Vijaya Gate [inside the temple compound]. He will worship at the Jaya Vijaya Gate. Entering [the *sanctum sanctorum*] he will have *darsan*. Then he will perform the golden *camara seva*. After this he will come through the inner southern gate and after having had *darsan* of the 'side deities' (*parsva devata*) he will go out through the Lion's Gate.[27]

As has been shown elsewhere in greater detail,[28] the Khurda rajas had a wide range of different ritual privileges at their disposal, which they granted according to the position of their princely recipients, their loyalty and the support the Khurda rajas received or expected from them. The rajas of neighbouring Ranpur for instance had the privilege of the 'dagger and sword service' (*curi-khanda seva*), carrying these weapons whenever Jagannatha proceeds ritually for hunting. Particularly fascinating is the hierarchy of these privileges. Thus only few princely visitors got the permission to use a *camara* whisk with a golden handle in front of Lord Jagannatha, whereas others had to fan with a silver or only cotton handle. A particular criterion of distinction was the display of one's own 'royal' paraphernalia not only in Puri but also onto the outer Lion's Gate or even onto an inner gate of the temple. Another very rare privilege was the visit together with the womenfolk to the temple after it had been vacated (*sodha*) from pilgrims and priests. Most likely greatest was the privilege to act during the visit of Puri as an administrator (*pariksa*) or even head administrator (*adipariksa*) of the Jagannatha temple.

[26]The complete collection of *Madala Panji* temple archive material of about 15,000 palm-leaves has been donated to the Orissa State Museum in August 1974; see H. Kulke 1987. The edition and translation of its *chamu citaus* is at present prepared jointly with G.N. Dash and S.K. Panda.

[27]Letter MP, 4, 16, 4R.

[28]H. Kulke 1992b.

The grant of these privileges primarily intended to reconfirm and strengthen the precarious position of the Khurda rajas. But, on the other hand, they also enhanced the reputation of their princely recipients. The participation in royal rituals of Jagannatha and the grant of special privileges by the Gajapatis, the highest authorities of Orissan society, elevated their status in their own local society and in the competition with the rulers of other Feudatory states. These ritual privileges enhanced the recognition and validation of their seats as 'centres out there'.

THE 'ROYAL PANTHEON' OF THE FEUDATORY STATES

As shown in greater detail by N. Gutschow and C. Mallebrein in this volume, another essential parameter of a 'centre out there' is its 'royal pantheon'. It forms the kernel of the dynastic ritual policy of the Feudatory states and their identities. It consists of a synthesis of several distinct but closely linked layers of various deities and is the result of a protracted stepwise development of several centuries. Most significant for Orissa's Feudatory states is the elevation and integration of powerful tribal godesses.[29] As has already been pointed out, this process had already begun under the early *samanta* predecessors of the late medieval Garhjat Mahals. It is documented by inscriptions since mid-first millennium CE when Raja Lokavigraha worshipped the 'Lady of the Jewel Serpent' (*maninagesvari*) in the form of a flat round stone (*chata pathara*) on top of the Manigaga hill near Ranpur and when Raja Tustikara in the Sonepur region was praised as a devotee of the 'Lady of the (wooden) Pillar' (*stambhesvari-pada-bhakta*).[30]

The more recent 'royal chronicles' (*rajabamsabali*) of the Feudatory states associate the foundation of the dynasties and their 'capitals' with the integration of three different types of tutelary deities into the royal pantheon.[31] The pristine deity is often of purely local origin and reminds one of the many village goddesses (*grama devata*) of Orissa. Several traditional accounts[32] relate the sacrifice of tribesmen or woman by the legendary founders of their respective dynasties. Their heads were worshipped as 'martyr *istadevatas*' or tutelary deities near the palace gate in the form of an unhewn stone.[33] A good example is the legend of Sabaruni, a pregnant Sabara woman in Baramba. According to the dynastic history of Baramba of the early twentieth century, Sabaruni met Hatakesvara Raut, the legendary founder of Baramba, at the place of his future 'capital'. When she told him about the great miracles of this place,

[29] C. Mallebrein and N. Gutschow in the present volume; for further details see Eschmann 1978; Kulke 1979, 17-26 and 1992a and C. Mallebrein 1999, 2004b and 2007.

[30] S.N. Rajaguru 1950.

[31] For greater detail see Kulke 1992a and C. Mallebrein 2007.

[32] This term was introduced into Orissan studies by G.N. Dash for the various anonymous local accounts.

[33] Kulke 1992, 65-7.

Hatakesvara told her: 'I shall cut off your head and you will become our *thakurani*. We shall keep your head and worship it.'[34] Other examples are Dhenka Sabara whose head (*munda*) is worshipped outside the palace of Dhenkanal as Sabara Dhenka Munda[35] or a *dhobi* (washerman) whose head is worshipped as Dhobei Guru near the old fort of Banki. All legendary accounts report that the victims agreed to be sacrificed under the condition to be worshipped. The irregular rituals of these 'martyr *istadevatas*' are performed not by royal Brahmans but by members of neighbouring tribes and by local low caste Hindus.

At the centre of the royal pantheon of most Feudatory states of Orissa is a *thakurani* of tribal origin, worshipped at her place of origin in an unhewn stone, mostly decorated by some anthropomorphic features like silver eyes and a small sari-like cloth. As the locally most powerful manifestation of divine presence of the state, she represents its veritable overlord and symbolizes the unifying link between the raja and the people, as both are her subjects. Her trans-local power validates the profane and sacred power emanating from the emerging 'centre out there' into its hinterland. Famous examples are Maninagesvari at Ranpur, Bhattarika, the Great Mother (*bada amba*) at Baramba, Charchika at Banki, Hingula at Talcher and Samalai at Sambalpur, all of them belonging to the 'Eight Mothers' (*ashta-matrika*) of Orissa. Although none of them can claim to be as 'old' as Maninagesvari, local traditions relate that they all existed long before the legendary foundation of their respective patron dynasties. In most cases their founders 'discovered' them under miraculous circumstances outside their 'capitals' and acknowledged them as their great tutelary deities. But they were too powerful and obviously also somewhat too dangerous to be fully appropriated by the palace. Usually they remain at their place of origin where they continue to be worshipped by their tribal or low caste priests (e.g. *malik* or gardeners). At the palace they are represented by 'mobile images' (*calanti pratima*), usually in the form of beautiful bronze images of Durga-Mahishasuramardini, worshipped by the royal rajguru.

Local legends explain why such famous tutelary goddesses like Bhattarika of Baramba are worshipped in temples at their places of origin in unhewn pieces of rock whereas in the palaces they are manifested by bronze images of Durga. As in the case of Bhattarika, an often occurring explanation is that their allegedly original bronze idols had once been stolen and, after their miraculous rediscovery, had been 're-installed' in the palaces for safety reasons.[36] During the most important royal festival, the annual Durgapuja, the

[34] *Badamba Rajavamsara Itihasa*, manuscript in possession of K.K. Pattanayak, Cuttack.

[35] R. Nanda 1929, 23.

[36] See B. Schnepel 2003. These legends may be regarded as a kind of Hinduization, of tribal images by explaining and elevating their original stone images. A similar case are the heaps of stones which are worshipped in many places as Sivalinga in the form of 'self-

'mobile images' (*calanti pratima*) are accompanied by the raja and his *rajaguru* to their 'place of origin', transforming their *kshetra* into an arena of royal performance, attended likewise by rulers and the ruled.[37]

As a third category of deities of tribal origin in the royal pantheon 'subsidiary tutelary deities' should be mentioned at least shortly. They are powerful local goddesses in the border regions of these states. These *thakuranis* legitimate the authority of the central rulers over the tribes of these distant regions through their temporary integration into royal rituals. Since their places of origin are often far away from the royal centre they are, usually only once a year during Durgapuja, carried by their local devotees to the royal court where they are well received and treated before they return with presents. Good examples are Khila Munda of Ranpur[38] and Mahakali in Baramba's border region with neighbouring Narsinghpur. A most fascinating recent example of the rise of a formerly subsidiary deity of a Feudatory state is the famous Tarini at Ghatgaon, located in the jungle at the original border of Keonjhar. Her roadside tribal *kshetra* has become a genuine centre out there within the last two decades with hundreds of daily pilgrims, several temples, guest houses and daily markets.[39]

The ritual integration of these powerful *thakuranis* into the royal pantheon, and the network of their ritual relations with the hinterland and the border regions can be regarded as a most essential mode of socio-political integration of the Feudatory states and the emergence of their subregional traditions and identities. As well documented and illustrated in this volume by N. Gutschow this ritual integration with a clear focus on the royal centre is most genuinely performed in Ranpur during Pancadolayatra, when the mobile images of 108 deities from all over the state congregate in small portable shrines on Ranpur's ceremonial ground around its tutelary deity Maninagesvari.

TOWN-PLANNING AND THE 'CAPITALS' OF THE FEUDATORY STATES

Town planning is yet another indicator of the emergence of a 'centre out there'. The rise from the seat of a local, mostly tribal, chief to the 'royal capital' of a Feudatory state was strongly linked with the ritual policy of its rulers. As this aspect the emergence of a 'centre out there' is depicted in detail by the development of Ranpur in N. Gutschow's paper in this volume, only few more

created linga' (*svayambhu linga*), most famous of them being Lingaraja in his monumental temple at Bhubaneswar. The legend of the 'lost' beautiful image of Nilamadhava as the original image of Jagannatha and his miraculous resurrection in a wooden image (*daru devata*) may have to be explained in the same way.

[37]B. Schnepel 2002, particularly Chapter VI, 'Durga and the Dasara Festival', 255-92.

[38]See N. Gutschow's paper in this volume.

[39]C. Mallebrein 2004a; B. Schnepel forthcoming.

general remarks may suffice.[40] In their quest to raise their status and to extend their royal pantheon beyond its tribal heritage, the would-be rajas and maharajas of the Garhjat Mahals began a stepwise policy which has been termed as Ksatriyaization and Hinduization. Ksatriyaization comprises various efforts of the Garhjat rulers to elevate their social position by emulating symbols of Hindu kingship in order to gain the status of Ksatriyas.[41] Hinduization refers in this context primarily to the metamorphosis of tribal *thakuranis* into Hindu deities, as manifested most prominently in the rise of the cult of Jagannatha.[42] In the course of the transformation of Garhjat Mahals into Feudatory states, both processes met in the endeavour of their rulers to create their own veritable 'centres out there' through imitation of or even competition with Khurda and Puri, the seats of the Gajapatis and Jagannatha, Orissa's veritable centres of the profane and sacred domain. This quest lead to the settlement of Brahmans in newly established *sasana* villages,[43] to town planning with an axial road like the *bara danda* at Puri, construction of temples dedicated to their Hinduized *thakuranis*[44] and other Hindu deities, particularly Jagannatha, and, most important, the construction of a palace at the *bara danda* near the Jagannatha temple. The new palace-focused capitals with its temples and *sahi*-quarters of different castes became a microcosm of the States.[45]

This process started after the downfall of the 'Imperial Gajapatis' in 1568 and the temporary destruction of Puri's Jagannatha cult. In competition with the 'local Gajapatis' of Khurda, the rulers of Garhjat Mahals began, in most cases for the first time, to build Hindu temples in their own 'capitals'. Among them were the first Jagannatha temples outside coastal Orissa.[46] The construction of the monumental Balabhadra-Jagannatha temple at Keonjhar in seventeenth century as the greatest temple of late medieval Orissa is particularly impressive and amounted to a ritual declaration of independence from Khurda and the Mughal subahdar at Cuttack.[47] The astonishing proliferation of Jagannatha

[40]See also Kulke 1980 and N. Gutschow forthcoming.

[41]H. Kulke 1976. A special variety of this process in the Hindu-tribal frontier region of Orissa and Chhota Nagpur is 'Rajputization', the attempt to achieve the status of Rajput-Kshatriyas, see S. Sinha 1962.

[42]A. Eschmann 1978.

[43]For the ceremony of the establishment of a *sasana* village according to a manuscript from Keonjhar see G.C. Tripathi 1981 and his paper in this volume. Whereas Puri's *sasana* villages are all situated in its hinterland (see G. Pfeffer 1978), in several Feudatory states, e.g. Ranpur and Keonjhar, *sasana* villages are also integrated into the old township of their capitals.

[44]Examples are the Samalai and Stambhesvari temples at Sambalpur and Sonepur.

[45]L.K. Mahapatra 1997, 902.

[46]K.N. Mahapatra (1971) gives in his short survey mostly much earlier traditional dates, e.g. CE 1485 for Ranpur's undated but supposedly oldest Jagannatha outside Puri and Cuttack which, however, may not be older than seventeenth century; see N. Gutschow in this volume.

[47]See G.C. Tripathi in this volume.

temple construction, particularly in the second half of the eighteenth century, can be directly linked with the 'new age' of the Garhjat Mahals under the Marathas and the increasing weakness of Khurda.[48]

The culmination, followed by the abrupt end, of a new period of palace-centred town-planning in Orissa's Feudatory states or Princely States (as they were then called), were the high-days of British imperialism in late nineteenth and early twentieth centuries. With hitherto unknown means at their disposal the then also imperially acknowledged rajas and maharajas constructed vast palaces in their capitals. Some of them competed with the rajas of Khurda who had their new palace ostentatiously constructed near the Jagannatha temple at Puri's *bara danda* in the seventeenth century,[49] and built their new palaces also near their Jagannatha temples. Ranpur,[50] Khandpara and Tigeria even surpassed Puri as their new palaces were located next to the Jagannatha temple or even in one and the same compound. Jagannatha and his annual car festival (*ratha yatra*) had thus been fully appropriated by the Feudatory rajas, partly side-tracking their great tribal *thakurani*s. After the Great War several Feudatory rajas went a step further and built their 'Little Versailles' outside the old town in the new township which housed also 'the Station' and cantonment of the imperial power in order to validate their new status. Good examples of these, in the context of Orissa, truly monumental palaces were those in Nayagarh, Bolangir and Kalahandi. Due to the 'merger' of the 'Princely States' with the State of Orissa in 1948/9 some of these palaces remained uncompleted (e.g. in Nayagarh) or are now in a dreadful state of dilapidation (e.g. in Keonjhar and Sonepur).

FEUDATORY STATES AS CENTRES OF LEARNING AND LITERATURE

The systematic settlement of Brahmans in *sasana* villages and the construction of Hindu temples near the seats of royal power transformed some of the former Garhjat Mahal into genuine centres of learning and literature of trans-local importance. This development, however, has not yet gained its due share in the history of Orissan literature. In fact, in his standard work on the history of Oriya literature, Mayadhar Mansingh entitles the section of the post-Sarala Das age rightly as 'Literature Goes to Feudal Courts'. But astonishingly he states that 'this age did not produce anything new, but just expanded what had been started earlier'. And then we are even informed by him that 'the voluptuous courts found religious sanction for their bejewelled sensuality in the word-cult of *Gitagovinda* and the decadent Sanskrit *kavya*s and the Krishna-Gopi cult of the Neo-Vaishnavites; and both influences have percolated into the national

[48]For an excellent example of the history of a Jagannatha temple in a 'centre out there' during Maratha period at Dharakote see D. Pathy 2001.

[49]Kulke 1978.

[50]N. Gutschow 2004 and in this volume.

consciousness of Orissa, with disastrous consequences for the national character as well as national literature'.[51]

The present volume contains three case studies which highlight the literary contributions of Keonjhar (by G.C. Tripathi), Ghumsur (by G.N. Dash) and Sambalpur (by S.K. Panda). As they depict in great detail the court culture and royal patronage of Sanskrit and Oriya literature in these three emerging Feudatory states, a more general study of the distribution of poets and manuscripts in the Feudatory states may suffice in the context of this paper.

So far no comprehensive study exists on the rise of the Feudatory states as cultural 'centres out there' *vis-à-vis* the traditional seats of learning in coastal Orissa. But we can derive some revealing information from the manuscript collection of the Orissa State Museum about the various places of origin of its manuscripts and of their authors. Moreover, Kedarnath Mahapatra, the first Curator of Manuscripts of the Orissa State Museum, provides in his *Khurudha Itihasa* detailed surveys of manuscripts and their authors during the reign of each Khurda king which contain so far the most comprehensive history of literature of Orissa during the seventeenth and eighteenth centuries.[52] They are based on a systematic analysis of dated colophons of the palm-leaf manuscripts which were at his disposal when he wrote his descriptive catalogues of the manuscripts of the OSM[53] and the *Khurudha Itihasa.* Although the statistical data derived from the manuscripts of the Orissa State Museum provide only a random sample, they are nevertheless of great significance for our delineations about the rise of the Feudatory states as centres of learning in the eighteenth century, particularly in its second half under the Marathas (1751-1803).

According to Mahapatra altogether 34 Oriya poets were known during the reign of the three Khurda rajas Divyasimha, Harekrishna and Gopinath who ruled for 39 years from CE 1688-1727. Out of them 25 (or 73 per cent) still belonged to the traditional seats of learning in coastal Orissa, whereas only 9 (or 27 per cent) came from the Garhjat Mahals.[54] Their share, however, more than doubled during the following long reign of Virakesari who ruled from 1737-93, thus covering the greater part of the Maratha rule in Orissa. During these years, out of altogether 58 Oriya poets, which Mahapatra was able to trace during this time, 39 (or 68 per cent) belonged the Garhjat Mahals.[55]

During the Maratha period the coastal region with Puri and its famous Brahman *sasana* villages had obviously lost its cultural hegemony as even the

[51]M. Mansinha 1962, 108-9.

[52]K.N. Mahapatra 1969.

[53]K.N. Mahapatra 1958-63.

[54]K.N. Mahapatra 1969, 137-80.

[55]Chikiti (7), Jarada and Jeypore (each 4), Parlakhimedi, Badakhimedi, Dharakote and Baramba (each 3), Ghumsur (2), Nayagarh, Banki, Khallikote, Athgarh, Tarala, Sambalpur, Mayurbhanj, Dhenkanal, Angul and Huma (each 1); see K.N. Mahapatra 1969, 204-47.

places of origin of Sanskrit poets reveal the emergence of the Garhjat Mahals as the new centres of learning. During the reign of Virakesari out of 20 Sanskrit poets, coastal Orissa produced only 6 (or 30 per cent), whereas 14 (or 70 per cent) had their home in the so-called 'tribal hinterland' and its Garhjat Mahals.[56]

Particularly revealing is a comparison of the number of poets (of both Oriya and Sanskrit) from coastal Orissa with those from its hilly hinterland from late seventeenth to late eighteenth centuries. Whereas in the coastal region their number more or less stagnated (increasing only from 25 to 27) during this century, the number of their colleagues in the *vana kshetra*s went up from 9 to 53 poets and thus by more than 500 per cent!

As for the manuscripts collections of the 'centres out there', G.C. Tripathi's detailed description of Keonjhar's 'Royal Manuscript Library' provides in this volume an excellent depiction of their growth and richness. To my knowledge no other such detailed survey exists about other collections of palm-leaf collections in possession of the former Feudatory rajas of Orissa. But a statistical account of the places of origin of Sanskrit manuscripts which the Orissa State Museum collected from various 'centres out there' until the early 1960s may serve as a kind of substitute.[57] But it has to be mentioned again that this 'statistical account' is based on a random sample of the manuscripts which former rulers of the Feudatory states had donated to the Orissa State Museum. This, however, still seems to be the exception rather than the rule. For instance, Keonjhar's valuable collection of about 270 palm-leaf manuscripts is still preserved in the palace and therefore does not figure in the following lists. A catalogue of the still existing manuscripts in the 'royal palaces' of Orissa is therefore a great desideratum. It would throw light on the great contributions of the 'centres out there' to the culture of Orissa before falling into oblivion.

The first volume of the catalogues of Sanskrit manuscripts the Orissa State Museum is particularly revealing.[58] Of its 257 listed Smriti manuscripts the find spots of 17 manuscripts are unknown. Out of the remaining 240 only 115 (or 48 per cent) come from the traditional seats of learning in coastal Orissa, whereas altogether 125 (or 52 per cent) originate from former Feudatory states: Ranpur (60), Khallikota (30), Parlakhimedi (14), Baripada (13) and Athgarh (Ganjam district), Bolangir, Kalahandi and Badakhemundi (each 2).

Taking into account all the 1,105 Sanskrit manuscripts which are listed in the five descriptive catalogues,[59] altogether 424 manuscripts (or 38 per cent) originate from former Feudatory states. Most impressive among them are again

[56]Parlakhimedi (3), Khimedi and Banki (each 2), Athgarh (Cuttack district), Athgarh (Ganjam district), Dharakote, Jeypore, Keonjhar, Baramba, Surangi (each 1); see K.N. Mahapatra 1969, 247-67.

[57]K.N. Mahapatra, 1958-63 and M.P. Das 1965.

[58]K.N. Mahapatra 1958.

[59]K.N. Mahapatra 1958-63 and M.P. Das 1965.

Ranpur (136) and Khallikote (122), followed by Parlakhimedi (63), Mayurbhanj (44), Sana Khimedi (18), Chikiti (13) and Kalahandi (10).[60]

In the seventeenth and eighteenth centuries the Garhjat Mahals and their 'capitals' apparently had become not only important centres of learning, few of them even surpassing the traditional centres in coastal Orissa, but also 'centres of attraction' for learned Brahmans. As shown by S.K. Panda in this volume, a well-known example is Gangadhar Mishra. Born in a *sasana* village near Puri, he was invited to Sambalpur where he wrote his famous *Kosalananda Kavyam* 'to glorify his royal patron Baliar Singh of Sambalpur'. The life story of the famous Vaishnava poet Sadananda Kabisurya Brahma is particularly revealing in this regard. Born in a *sasana* village near Nayagarh in 1737, he spent, except four years in Damodarpur in Cuttack district, all his life at the courts of Ghumsur, Daspalla, Chikiti and Madhupur, where he composed his poems.[61]

No survey exists of the altogether, certainly more than one hundred *sasana* villages, in and around the capitals of the former Feudatory states which were established primarily during the seventeenth and eighteenth centuries.[62] But from the fact that Keonjhar alone claims to have more than thirty of them[63] and from its valuable royal manuscript library, one can easily imagine their significant role in the development of the Feudatory states and their capitals as centres of learning. As shown by S. Arp in this volume, the importance of the *sasana* villages and their learned Brahmans increased further in the late eighteenth century with the creation of the Yayati Kesari legend who allegedly had invited ten thousand Brahmans from Kanauj nearly thousand years ago to perform ten horse sacrifices at Jajpur.[64] Nowadays most Brahmans in Orissa regard themselves as descendants of these Kanauj Brahmans, a claim which seems to be particularly relevant for the court Brahmans in the Feudatory states. On the one hand, it enhanced the status of their royal patrons whose tribal descent was still well remembered and, on the other hand, it distinguished the court Brahmans more clearly from tribal *Dehuri* priests of the powerful tutelary *thakurani*s of the royal pantheon.

FEUDATORY STATES AS CENTRES OF SUBREGIONAL HISTORIES AND IDENTITIES

Another major feature of the princely and Brahmanical centres of the former Feudatory states of Orissa is their 'creative historiographical capacity' and its strong influence on the respective subregional identities. With its two dozen

[60] Moreover Bolangir (5), Bhavanipatna (4), Kalahandi, Athgarh, Badhakhemundi, Aska (each 2) and Nayagarh (1).

[61] K.N. Mahapatra, 1969, 212-13.

[62] For Puri's *sasana* villages see G. Pfeffer 1978.

[63] M.M. Mishra, 2003 and G.C. Tripathi in this volume.

[64] See also S. Arp 2007 and H. Kulke 2008.

States (and several important 'Estates') with their own distinct local traditions, Orissa is particularly rich in traditional local accounts and histories. A major source of inspiration was the *Madala Panji*, Puri's famous temple chronicle, and its legendary accounts of Orissan history.[65] Most common of these traditional local histories are the dynastic or 'royal chronicles' (*rajavamsavali*) which focus on the ruling houses and their tutelary deities. As a pedant to the 'little kings' H. Frese coined the term 'little chronicles' for these *rajavamsavali*s.[66]

Several dynasties of former Feudatory states still have their own unpublished genealogies and 'royal chronicles' in palm-leaf or paper manuscripts in their palaces or with members of their former ruling houses.[67] Only few palm-leaf manuscripts have come to the Orissa State Museum at Bhubaneswar, e.g. from Kalahandi and Ghumsur.[68] But the Orissa State Archives preserves in its District Record Room and the Record Room of the former Board of Revenue a considerably large amount of unprinted paper copies of genealogies and *vamsavali*-like chronicles of Feudatory states, e.g. of Mayurbhanj, Keonjhar, Seraikella, Kanika, Dhenkanal, Daspalla, Baud and Patna. The Oriental Manuscript Library at Chennai possesses a considerable number of genealogies and chronicles (*kaifiat*) of Feudatory states of South Orissa, e.g. Tekkali,[69] Khallikote, Athgarh, Kimedi, Parlakhimedi and Vijayanagara, collected by Telugu Pandits of Colin Mackenzie, the then Surveyor General of the Madras Presidency, in the years 1814-16.[70]

As has been shown in greater detail in the case of the chronicle of Ranpur,[71] the royal chronicles usually consist of three distinct sections, (I) the mythological section which links the foundation of the dynasties and the origin of their tutelary deities with pan-Indian epics and Puranic traditions, (II) the legendary section which associates through 'invented traditions' the history of the ruling houses with regional legendary traditions of the great Gajapati kings and Jagannatha and in several cases also with Rajput heroes of Rajasthan, and (III) the historical section which deals, with a certain historical accuracy, with the local history from the late seventeenth or early eighteenth centuries onwards until the chronicles were finally compiled (usually) in the late nineteenth century. The three sections reflect three distinct but interrelated perceptions

[65] A.B. Mohanty 1969; H. Kulke 1987.

[66] H. Frese 2004, 139.

[67] E.g. the *Bonaigarh Vamsavali* (to be edited by U. Skoda); *Ranapura Rajavamsa Itihasa* (to be edited by B.K. Mallik in N. Gutschow, in preparation), *Sri Jayapura Rajavamsavali* (to be edited by C.P. Nanda and G. Berkemer).

[68] E.g. *Kalahandi Madala* (OSM, No. Or. 123); *Ghumusara Kabya* (OSM, No. Or. 360).

[69] G. Berkemer 1997.

[70] Local Records, Government Oriental Manuscript Library Madras; for details see Kulke 1987.

[71] B.K. Mallik 2008.

of the past: (I) the mythological section, depicting an assumed pan-Indian past, (II) the legendary section, propagating a localized constructed regional past, and (III) the historical section, presenting the remembered local past.[72]

The subregional identities of all important Feudatory states of Orissa are thus a synthesis of local, regional-Orissan and pan-Indian elements. At all these three levels, they are centred around local divine manifestations and their miraculous interference into the profane world of the rulers and the ruled, particularly the tribes. In regard to the emergence of the subregional identities of the Feudatory states, the central sections of their chronicles are most 'productive'. In a process of localization most of them incorporate Jagannatha and the Gajapatis, the supreme sacred and profane Lords of Orissa, into the legendary history of the Feudatory states. The legends of their benevolent interference in the local life became the most important source or point of reference of their still existing subregional identities. Thus, for instance, Jagannatha himself selected Govinda Bhanja of Keonjhar as supreme General of the great Gajapati king Purushottama for his finally victorious Kanchi Kaveri war,[73] whereas he ordered Prataparudra, Purushottama's son, to donate his (Jagannatha's) most sacred Madhava image of Puri to Uddhava, the raja of Ranpur, who then introduced Jagannatha's annual car festival at Ranpur.[74] Similar 'invented traditions' are known from about a dozen other states.[75]

The interest of the Feudatory rajas in their own family histories got a strong impetus in late nineteenth century in the wake of the systematic settlement operations in all states. The Settlement Reports required short introductory historical chapters of the states, usually with genealogies of their ruling dynasties. In many cases these 'histories' and in particular the dates of the royal genealogies appear to have been 'reconstructed' for the first time in a systematic manner for this purpose on the basis of various local, regional Oriya and pan-Indian traditions. The royal chronicles received a kind of imperial sanction by their inclusion into the *Gazetteer of the Feudatory States of Orissa* in 1910 by L.E.B. Cobden Ramsay, the first Political Agent for the Tributary and Feudatory States of Orissa.[76] This was an important step forward for the validation of various local and subregional identities.

But their joint publication also disclosed for the first time various contesting 'historical claims' for superiority among Orissa's leading dynasties. This in turn led to a kind of historiographical contestation among these dynasties, particularly between the Bhanjas of Mayurbhanj and the Chauhans of western Orissa. They invited historians, some of them from Bengal, with the assignment to enhance the greatness of the dynastic history of their royal patrons through a peculiar blending of traditional accounts and 'new histories' based on later

[72]H. Kulke 2004, 48.
[73]M.M. Mishra 2003.
[74]B.K. Mallik 2008.
[75]L.E.B. Cobden Ramsay 1910.
[76]L.E.B. Cobden Ramsay 1910.

discovered inscriptions. A typical outcome of this 'ordered historiography' is B.C. Mazumdar's writing on Sonepur and the Chauhans of western Orissa in his book *Orissa in the Making* published in 1925.[77] The late 1920s and in particular the 1930s witnessed the publication of an astonishingly large number of 'histories' of the Feudatory states, e.g. on Dhenkanal (1929),[78] Keonjhar (1932)[79] and Banki (1934),[80] followed by Jeypore (1938), Nandapur (1939), Baramba (1940), etc. As textbooks of the schools of the Princely States they were primarily *prasasti*-like eulogies of their dynasties. But as they incorporated also all the local legends of rajas, *thakuranis* and their devotees, their influence on the 'constructed identity' of the 'centres out there' on the eve of their merger should not be underestimated.

Modern historians of Orissa usually treat these 'dynastic histories' of Orissa's former Feudatory states according to the verdict of the British government epigraphist J.F. Fleet against the *Madala Panji*, Puri's famous temple chronicle. In 1895 he proclaimed in connection with the legendary Kesari dynasty that 'everything related to ancient times, which has been written on the unsupported authority of these annals, has to be expunged bodily from the pages of history'.[81] This is not the place to examine critically the correctness of Fleet's statement. What matters in our context is the deplorable fact that his historiographically correct verdict as far as 'ancient history' is concerned, 'expunged' also the whole genre of local chronicles of the 'centres out there' from modern Orissan historiography and, what is even worse, rejected them as important sources of local identities.

The same is true in regard to the alleged Rajput origin of about a dozen ruling houses of Orissa.[82] In this case, too, an elaboration of this controversial claim is not required. S.K. Panda is already exemplifying in this volume the Chauhan dynasties of western Orissa, the most prominent 'Rajputs' of Orissa. In the context of our delineations it is relevant that, as shown by S. Sinha in his seminal paper 'State Formation and Rajput Myth in Tribal Central India', Rajputization refers since the sixteenth and seventeenth centuries to widespread social processes of the rise of formerly tribal chiefs through the imitation of the Rajput model of Hindu kinship.[83] A major aim of this endeavour was the creation of valid and socially acceptable stories of their Ksatriya-Rajput origin which in turn became major ingredients of the identities of the 'centres out there'.

[77]B.C. Mazumdar 1925.

[78]R. Nanda 1929.

[79]K.S. Mishra 1932.

[80]N.R. Sarma 1934.

[81]H. Kulke 1993, 137.

[82]According to Cobden Ramsay's *Gazetteer of the Feudatory States of Orissa* of the year 1910, altogether 13 dynasties claimed Rajput origin: Athmallik, Bonai, Kalahandi, Keonjhar, Khandpara, Mayurbhanj, Narsinghpur, Nayagarh, Pal Lahara, Patna, Rairakhol, Sonpur and Talcher.

[83]S. Sinha 1962; see also H. Kulke 1976 and L.K. Mahapatra 1987.

Apart from the creation various kinds of traditional local accounts, it is worth mentioning that the beginnings of genuine historical research in Orissa in the 1940s took its roots not in colonial coastal Orissa, e.g. in the Ravenshaw College at Cuttack, but in the much maligned 'centres out there', the Feudatory states, particularly in Mayurbhanj, Patna and Kalahandi. It was these states where most of the founder fathers of Orissan historiography, like P. Acharya, K.C. Panigrahi, K.N. Mahapatra and S.N. Rajaguru, found their first engagements as historians and archaeologists. Their efforts culminated in the foundation of the Kalinga Historical Research Society under the patronage of the Chauhan Maharajas of Kalahandi and Patna and in the publication of its *Journal of the Kalinga Historical Research Society*, Orissa's first genuine and well-edited historical journal from 1946-50. Its last issue contains a sad story of the difficulties it faced after merger of the states which reminds one of the treatment of Indian scholars during colonial rule.[84] P.C. Rath, the Secretary of the Society and co-editor of the journal, went even a step further when he noted on its last page: 'Such behaviour was not witnessed even during the period of foreign rule.'[85] In 1952 the *Kalinga Historical Research Journal* was succeeded by the *Orissa Historical Research Journal*. Published by the Government of Orissa, it became the genuine organ of Orissan historians. But it left an aching void in the former Feudatory states from which they never recovered.

THE FEUDATORY STATES AS CENTRES OF RESISTANCE?

Let me conclude with a few remarks on the colonial period during which the Garhjat Mahals finally turned into genuine Princely States and became veritable 'centres out there', although in quite different ways. Today many of them are remembered as centres of an autocratic and semi-feudal system of oppression and exploitation. Their image of 'dark zones' in the history of Orissa[86] is based on the collective memory of various kinds of sometimes brutally enacted forced labour (*bheti*) and on the independence movement when the National Congress and its Prajamandal organizations in Orissa fought against the colonially pampered Princely States.[87]

There are, however, a few points which deserve our attention. A major aspect of the history and identity of these 'centres out there' is the continuation of their resistance capacity which we have already come across under Gajapati rule. For a whole century some Feudatory states and their rulers resisted the establishment of colonial rule, beginning with the Ghumsur raja's refusal to pay his tribute to the French in 1757 and ending with Surendra Sai's involvement in the Great Mutiny in 1857-8, India's so-called 'First War of Independence'.

[84] M. Brandtner 1999.

[85] P.C. Rath 1950, 273.

[86] B. Pati in the present volume.

[87] B. Pati 1993; C.P. Nanda 1998.

But when we pass Khurda on the National Highway, we are taught by a sign board that Khurda's *paik bidroha* of 1817 was India's first war of independence.

The post-Mutiny conciliatory policy of the Victorian age towards India's Princely States did not fail to have its effects on Orissa's Feudatory states. It confirmed their rulers in a policy of regulated exploitation and luxury and thus contributed to their final extinction through merger. Their mutation from centres of anti-colonial resistance to centres of feudal or semi-feudal oppression and princely splendour was supplemented by a Curzon-like colonial 'benevolent despotism'. Accordingly the spirit and direction of resistance in the Feudatory states mutated from anti-British to agrarian unrest and anti-feudal and, one should add, anti-modernization revolts which flared up in the second half of the nineteenth century and then again in the 1940s in a large number of Feudatory states.[88] The agency of resistance thus moved from courtly elites to the subalterns of the villages and small towns. The peculiar *meli*-like rural and tribal demonstration and resistance emerged in the Feudatory states decades before similar developments began in coastal Orissa under the impact of the Congress and Gandhi. But even during this time, the subalterns of the Feudatory states bordering British coastal Orissa, such as Nilgiri, Talcher, Dhenkanal and Ranpur, retained their dominant position as centres of resistance in Orissa, a position which more recently tribes of the former 'centres out there' seem to have taken over in their struggle against being opened up for industrialization and globalization.

[88]Athmalik (1863), Mayurbhanj (1866), Narsinghpur (1878), Nayagarh (1849-52 and 1893-4) and Keonjhar (1867-8 and 1891-3), see J. Sengupta 2002, 216 and P.K. Mishra 1983.

REFERENCES

A'in-i-Akbari by Abu'l-Fazl, vol. 2, tr. H.S. Jarrett, Calcutta: Asiatic Society of Bengal, 1948.

Arp, S. 2007. 'In Search of Goddess Viraja', in G. Pfeffer (ed.) 2007, 59-78.

Banerji, R.D. 1928. 'Rajput Origins in Orissa', in *Modern Review* 43, 285-91.

Berkemer, G. 1993. *Little Kingdoms in Kalinga: Ideologie, Legitimation und Politik Regionaler Eliten*, Stuttgart: Steiner-Verlag.

———1997. 'The Chronicle of a Little Kingdom: Reflections on the Tekkali Taluka Jamindarla Vamsavali', in B. Kölver (ed.), *Recht, Staat und Verwaltung im klassischen Indien. The State, the Law and Administration in Classical India*, München: Oldenbourg, 65-96.

———2003 (together with M. Frenz, eds.). *Sharing Sovereignty: The Little Kingdom in South Asia.* Berlin: Klaus Schwarz.

———2004. 'Jaypur Parlakimedi Vizianagaram: The Southern Gajapatis', in A. Malinar, J. Beltz and H. Frese (eds.) 2004, 93-118.

———in preparation (together with H. Kulke). *A Bibliography of the Feudatory States of Orissa.*

Brandtner, M. 1999. 'Koloniale Archäologie: Monopolisierte Vergangenheitsdeutung und Herrschaftslegitimation in Britisch-Indien', in S. Conermann (ed.), *Mythen, Geschichte(n), Identitäten: Der Kampf um die Vergangenheit*, Hamburg: E.B. Verlag.

———2001. 'Representations of Kalinga: The Changing Image and Geography of a Historical Region', in H. Kulke (ed.) 2001, 179-210.

Chakravarti, K. 2001. *Religious Process: The Puranas and the Making of a Regional Tradition*, Delhi: Oxford University Press.

Chattopadhyaya, B.D. 1994. *The Making of Early Medieval India*, Delhi: Oxford University Press.

Cobden Ramsay, L.E.B. 1910. *Feudatory States of Orissa*, Calcutta: The Bengal Secretariat Book Depot (rpt. 1950, 1982).

Das, M.P. 1965. *A Descriptive Catalogue of Sanskrit Manuscripts of Orissa in the Collection of the Orissa State Museum Bhubaneswar*, vol. 5, *Tantra Manuscripts*, Bhubaneswar: Orissa State Museum.

Dash, G.N. 1979. *Janasruti Kanci Kaberi*, Berampore.

———1998. *Hindus and Tribals: Quest for a Co-existence* (*Social Dynamics in Medieval Orissa*), Delhi: Decent Books.

———2007. 'Changing One's Own Identity: The Role of Language in the Transformation of a Subregional Tradition', in A. Malinar (ed.) 2007, 265-86.

———2010. *Jagannatha and the Gajapati Kings of Orissa: A Compendium of Late Medieval Texts* (*Rajabhoga, Sevakarmani, Deshakhanja and Other Minor Texts*), Delhi: Manohar.

Donaldson, T.E. 1985-7. *Hindu Temple Art of Orissa*, 3 vols., Leiden: E.J. Brill.

Eschmann, A., H. Kulke and G.C. Tripathi (eds.), 1978a. *The Cult of Jagannath and the Regional Tradition of Orissa*, Delhi: Manohar.

———1978b. 'Hinduization of Tribal Deities in Orissa: The Sakta and Saiva Typology', in A. Eschmann, H. Kulke and G.C. Tripathy (eds.) 1978a, 79-98.

Frese, H. 2004. 'Anecdotes of Histories: Reflections on Contexts and (Hi)stories', in A. Malinar (ed.) 2004, 119-43.

Gutschow, N. 2003. 'Ranpur—The Centre of a Little Kingdom', in G. Berkemer (ed.) 2003, 137-64.

———2004. 'Ranpur Resolved: Spatial Analysis of a Town in Orissa Based on a Chronicle', in A. Malinar (ed.) 2004, 67-94.

———forthcoming (together with R. Vasavada, B.K. Mallik and H. Kulke). *Ranpur: History and Settlement Patterns of a 'Little Kingdom' of Orissa*, Delhi: Manohar.

Haque, M.A. 1980. *Muslim Administration in Orissa (1568-1751)*, Calcutta: Punthi Pustak.

Joshi, A. 1983. *History and Culture of Khijjingakotta*, Delhi: Vikas.

Kulke, H. 1976. 'Kshatriyaization and Social Change: A Study in Orissa Setting', in S. Devadas Pillai (ed.), *Aspects of Changing India: Studies in Honour of Prof. G.S. Ghurye*, Bombay: Popular Prakashan, 398-409; rpt. in Kulke 1993, 82-93.

———1977. 'Early State Formation and Royal Legitimation in Late Ancient Orissa, in M.N. Das (ed.), *Sidelights on History and Culture of Orissa*, Cuttack: Vidyapuri, 104-21.

———1978. 'The Struggle of the Rajas of Khurda and the Muslim Subahdars of Cuttack for Dominance of the Jagannath Cult', in A. Eschmann, H. Kulke and G.C. Tripathi (eds.) 1978a, 321-44.

———1979. *Jagannatha-Kult und Gajapati-Königtum: Ein Beitrag zur Geschichte religiöser Legitimation hinduistischer Herrschaft*, Wiesbaden: Steiner.

———1980. 'Legitimation and Town-planning in the Feudatory States of Central Orissa', in J. Pieper (ed.), *Ritual Space in India: Studies in Architectural Anthropology*, Art and

Archaeology Research Papers (aarp) 17, London: aarp, 30-40; rpt. in Kulke 1993: 93-113.
———1987. 'The Chronicles and the Temple Records of the Madala Panji of Puri', in *Indian Archives* 36, 1-24; rpt. in Kulke 1993, 137-57.
———1992a. 'Tribal Deities at Princely Courts: The Feudatory Rajas of Central Orissa and Their Tutelary Deities (*ishtadevatas*)', in S. Mahapatra (ed.), *The Realm of the Sacred*, Calcutta: Oxford University Press, 56-78; rpt. in Kulke 1993, 114-36.
———1992b. 'Ksatra and Ksetra: The Cult of Jagannatha of Puri and the "Royal Letters" (*chamu citau*) of the Rajas of Khurda', in H.T. Bakker (ed.), *The Sacred Centre as the Focus of Political Interest*, Groningen: Egbert Forsten, 131-42; rpt. in Kulke 1993, 51-6.
———1993. *Kings and Cults: State Formation and Legitimation in India and Southeast Asia*, Delhi: Manohar.
———2001 (together with B. Schnepel, eds.). *Jagannath Revisited: Studying Society, Religion and the State in Orissa*, Delhi: Manohar.
———2004. 'The Making of a Local Genealogy: The Ranpur Rajavamsa Itihasa', in A. Malinar, J. Beltz and H. Frese (eds.) 2004, 43-66.
———2008. 'Yayati Kesari Revisited: Ramachandra of Khurda and the Yayati Kesari Legend of Puri', in P. Berger, R. Hardenberg, E. Kattner and M. Prager (eds.), *The Anthropology of Values: Festschrift in Honour of Georg Pfeffer*, Delhi: Pearson/ Longman.
Mahapatra, J. 1997. 'The Mandala Kingdoms', in P.K. Mishra (ed.), *Comprehensive History and Culture of Orissa*, vol. 1, Delhi: Kaveri Books, 244-96.
Mahapatra, K.N. 1958-63. *A Descriptive Catalogue of the Sanskrit Manuscripts of Orissa in the Collection of the Orissa State Museum Bhubaneswar*, vol. 1, *Smrti Manuscripts* (1958); vol. 2, *Kavya-Alankara-Sangita* (1960); vol. 3, *Purana Manuscripts* (1962); vol. 4, *Jyotisha and Ganita Manuscripts* (1963), Bhubaneswar: Department of Cultural Affairs.
———1969. *Khurudha Itihasa (1568-1817)*. Bhubaneswar: K.N. Mahapatra.
———1977. *The Jagannatha Temples in Eastern India*, Bhubaneswar: K.N. Mahapatra.
Mahapatra, L.K. 1987. 'Ex-Princely States of Orissa: Mayurbhanj, Keonjhar and Bonai', in S. Sinha (ed.), 1-50.
———1997. 'Ex-Princely States of Orissa: Their Social History', in P.K. Mishra (ed.), *Comprehensive History and Culture of Orissa*, vol. 2, Delhi: Kaveri Books, 897-927.
Malinar, A., J. Beltz and H. Frese (eds.) 2004. *Text and Context in the History, Literature and Religion of Orissa*, Delhi: Manohar.
Malinar, A. 2007 (ed.). *Time in India: Concepts and Practices*, Delhi: Manohar.
Mallebrein, C. 1999. 'Tribal and Local Deities: Assimilations and Transformations', in V. Dehejia (ed.), *Devi: The Great Goddess: Female Divinity in South Asian Art*, Washington, D.C.: A. Sackler Gallery, 137-56.
———2004a. 'Creating a Kshetra: Goddess Tarini of Ghatgaon and Her Development from a Forest Goddess to a Pan-Orissan Deity', in C. Mallebrein and L.J. Guzy (eds.), *Facets of Orissan Studies (Special Issue). Journal of Social Sciences* 8, 2, 155-65.
———2004b. 'Entering the Realm of Durga: Patkhanda, a Hinduized Tribal Deity', in A. Malinar, J. Beltz and H. Frese 2004, 273-306.
———2007. 'Manikesvari and Dokri: Changing Representations of two Tribal Goddesses and the Dynastic Histories of Orissa', in A. Malinar (ed.) 2007, 203-34.
Mallik, B.K. 2004. *Paradigms of Dissent and Protest: Social Movements in Eastern India (c. A.D. 1400-1700)*, Delhi: Manohar.
Mansinha, M. 1962. *History of Oriya Literature*, Delhi: Sahitya Akademi.

Mazumdar, B.C. 1925. *Orissa in the Making*, Calcutta: University of Calcutta.

Mishra, K.S. 1932. *Kendujhar*, Cuttack: Prachi Press.

Mishra, M.M. 2003. 'History of the Royal Dynasties of Keonjhar', manuscript (to be edited by H. Kulke and C.P. Nanda).

Mishra, P.K. 1983. *Political Unrest in Orissa in the 19th Century (Anti-British, Anti-Feudal and Agrarian Risings)*, Calcutta: Punthi Pustak.

Mohanty, A.B. (ed.) 1969. *Madala Panji: Rajabhoga Itihasa*, 2nd edn., Bhubaneswar: Utkal University (1st edn. Cuttack: Prachi Samiti 1940).

Mohanty, N. 2005. *Oriya Nationalism: Quest for a United Orissa 1866-1956*, 2nd rev. edn., Jagatsinghpur: Prafulla.

Motte, T. 1930. 'A Narrative of a Journey to the Diamond Mines at Sumbulpoor, in the Province of Orissa', *Early European Travellers in the Nagpur Territories: Reprinted from Old Records*, Nagpur: Government Press.

Nanda, C.P. 1998. *Towards Swaraj: Nationalist Politics and Popular Movements in Orissa*, Ludhiana: Kalyani.

Nanda, R. 1929. *Dhenkanala Itihasa*, Dhenkanal: The Author.

Panda, S.K. 1986. *Herrschaft und Verwaltung im östlichen Indien unter den Späten Gangas (ca. 1038-1434)*, Stuttgart: Steiner-Verlag; English edition, *The State and the Statecraft in Medieval Orissa under the Later Eastern Gangas (A.D. 1038-1434)*, Calcutta: K.P. Bagchi 1995.

———2000. 'Royal Authority and the Cult of Jagannath: The Politico-Ritual Relation between the Kingdom of Khurda and Sambalpur: A Study Based on Chamu Citau (Royal Letters)', in S.K. Panda (ed.), *New Perspectives on the History and Culture of Orissa*, Calcutta: Punthi Pustak, 90-9.

Pathy, D. 2001. *Art: Regional Traditions: The Temple of Jagannatha: Architecture, Sculpture, Painting, Ritual*, Delhi: Sundeep Prakashan.

Pati, B. 1993. *Resisting Domination: Peasants, Tribals and the National Movement in Orissa 1920-50*, Delhi: Manohar.

———2006. 'Survival as Resistance: Tribal in Colonial India', in *The Indian Historical Review* 33, 175-201.

———2007. 'The Order of Legitimacy: Princely Orissa, 1850-1920', in W. Ernst and B. Pati (eds.), *India's Princely States: People, Princes and Colonialism*, London: Routledge.

Pfeffer, G. 1978. 'Puri's Vedic Brahmans: Continuity and Change in their Traditional Institutions', in A. Eschmann, H. Kulke and G.C. Tripathi (eds.) 1978, 421-38.

———2007 (ed.). *Periphery and Centre: Studies in Orissan History, Religion and Anthropology*, Delhi: Manohar.

Rajaguru, S.N. 1950. 'The Kanas Copper-Plate Grant of Sri Lokavigraha Bhatta Mahasamanta', in *Journal of the Kalinga Historical Research Society* 2, 261-6.

Rath, P.C. 1950. 'Conspectus of Actions of the Kalinga Historical Research Society', in *Journal of the Kalinga Research Society* 3, 271-3.

Ray, B.C. 1960. *Orissa under the Marathas*, Allahabad: Kitab Mahal.

Sahu, N.K. (ed.) 1956. *A History of Orissa by W.W. Hunter, Andrew Stirling, John Beams, N.K. Sahu*, 2 vols., Calcutta: Susil Gupta.

Sarkar, J.N. 1916. 'The History of Orissa in the Seventeenth Century: Reconstructed from Persian Sources', in *Journal of the Bihar and Orissa Research Society* 2, 153-65, 338-49.

Sarma, N.R. 1934. *Banki Itihasa*, Banki: Saraswati Store.

Schnepel, B. 2002. *The Jungle Kings: Ethnohistorical Aspects of Politics and Ritual in Orissa*, Delhi: Manohar.

———2003. 'The Stolen Goddess: Ritual Enactments of Power and Authority in Orissa', in G. Berkemer and M. Frenz (eds.) 2003a, 165-80.

———forthcoming (together with P.K. Nayak, C.P. Nanda, R. Vasavada and H. Kulke). *Keonjhar: Ethnohistory of a Little Kingdom in North Orissa*, Delhi: Manohar.

Sengupta, J. 2002. 'Princes, Prajamandals and Partition: Congress Politics and the Rajas of Orissa, 1937-1947', in S. Settar and I.B. Gupta (eds.), *Pangs of Partition*, vol. 1, *Parting of Ways*, Delhi: Manohar, 213-41.

———2007. 'Imagined Chronologies: Perceptions of "Development" as a Tool in Mapping Oriya Identity', in A. Malinar (ed.) 2007, 287-314.

Singh, D. 1962. 'History of the Dynasties of the Ranpur State' (manuscript) to be published by B.K. Mallik in N. Gutschow, forthcoming.

Sinha, S. 1962. 'State Formation and Rajput Myth in Tribal Central India', in *Man in India* 42, 35-80.

———1987 (ed.). *Tribal Polities and State Systems in Pre-Colonial Eastern and North Eastern India*, Calcutta: K.P. Bagchi.

Skoda, U. forthcoming. *Bansaboli of Bonai Rajfamily: Family Chronicles of the Royal Family of Bonai/Orissa*, Delhi: Manohar.

Stietencron, H. von 2001. 'A Congregation of Gods: The Dolamelana Festival in Orissa', in H. Kulke (ed.) 2001, 363-402.

Stirling, A. 1822. 'An Account, Geographical Statistical, and Historical of Orissa Proper, or Cuttack', in *Asiatic Research* 15, 163-338 (quoted from the rpt. Calcutta 1904).

Tanabe, A. 2003. 'The Sacrificer State and Sacrificial Community: Kingship in Early Modern Khurda, Orissa: Seen Through a Local Ritual', in G. Berkemer and M. Frenz (eds.) 2003, 115-37.

Tripathi, G.C. 1981. *The Rituals of Founding a Brahman Village: A Description of the Ceremony of Establishing a Brahmana-sasana in Orissa on the Basis of an Unpublished Manuscript*, Delhi: GDK.

———1987 (together with H. Kulke). *Katakarajavamsavali: A Traditional History of Orissa with Special Reference to Jagannatha Temple*, Allahabad: Vohra.

Tripathy, K.B. 1962. *The Evolution of Oriya Language and Script*, Cuttack: Utkal University.

Wills, C.U. 1919. 'The Territorial System of the Rajput Kingdoms of Medieval Chhattisgarh', in *Journal of the Asiatic Society of Bengal* 15, 197-262.

CHAPTER 4

The Transformation of a Tribal State into a Centre of Regional Culture: The Case of the Bhañjas of Keonjhar

GAYA CHARAN TRIPATHI

LEGENDARY HISTORY OF THE BHAÑJA FAMILY OF KEONJHAR

According to the traditional records of the history of Keonjhar, the state was founded in the early twelfth century (CE 1128) by a young prince of the Bhañja family called Jyotibhañja, younger brother of Ādibhañja, the ruler of Khijjiṅga-Maṇḍala, whose royal seat is identified with the modern Khijjing in Mayurbhanj district. These two brothers are said to be the sons of Koṭṭa-bhañja, perhaps the first powerful ruler of the Bhañja line of Khijjiṅga, under whom the Bhañjas expanded their territory and rose from an insignificant local power to a strong regional power. All the early copper-plate inscriptions of the rulers of the Khijjiṅgakoṭa line mention Koṭṭa-bhañja as the progenitor of their dynasty, who was born into the family of Vīrabhadra, the founder of the first (i.e. the oldest) family, indeed the very tribe of the Bhañjas. This Vīrabhadra had become a mythical figure in the times of the Bhañja kings and is believed to have been born out of (i.e. 'breaking open' or *bhañj*) the egg of a peahen (*mayūra*) by the grace of Lord Śiva in the penance grove (*āśrama*) of the sage Vasiṣṭha, which was known as Koṭṭāśrama. The child was then reared by the sage Vasiṣṭha.[1] He founded a dynasty which produced rulers of this region, into whose line was born King Koṭṭa-bhañja, who was well known for his might and was a 'firebrand for the forest of his enemies'. He is also glorified with adjectives like 'brave', 'pure' and 'humble' (*śūraḥ*, *śuciḥ*,

[1] Cf. the following traditional verses found at the beginning of a number of copper-plate grants of the Bhañjas, collected and annotated by Snigdha Tripathy as vol. 6 of the *Inscriptions of Orissa* (published by the Orissa State Museum, Bhubaneswar, 1974):

Āsīt koṭyā[koṭṭā] śramamahātapovanādhiṣṭhāne |
māyūrāṇḍaṃ bhittvā gaṇadaṇḍo vīrabhadrākhyaḥ ||
pratipakṣanidhanadakṣo vasiṣṭhamunipālito nṛpatiḥ |

In a number of copper-plate grants, the kings of the Bhañja family, especially Raṇabhañjadeva, describe themselves as *aṇḍajavaṃśaprabhavaḥ*.

vinitaḥ), as well as 'self-respecting', 'generous' and 'compassionate' (*māni, tyāgī, adaṇḍakaḥ*).[2]

However, no mention of Jyotibhañja—who, according to local records, is said to have ruled from 1128 to 1158—as yet been found in any of the copper-plate grants of the Bhañjas. Jyotibhañja is said to have been kidnapped as a small boy from the royal palace of Khijjing by some Bhuiyan chieftains who were finding it too burdensome and tiring to go all the way to Mayūrabhañja—the seat of royal power—crossing the Vaitaraṇī River to hand over their taxes or seek justice. According to the legend, this boy was reared by the Bhuiyan tribals and was left to socialize freely with the young tribal women, from whom a large number of children were subsequently born, who in distinction from others called themselves 'Rājakulī Bhuiyans' (i.e. Bhuiyans belonging to the royal family). Later the Bhuiyan chieftains arranged the marriage of Jyotibhañja with Princess Kṣīrodā of Pallahera. Jyoti's father (Koṭṭabhañja, according to local tradition) was greatly pleased to learn about the safe existence of his son and sent his elder son, Ādibhañja, to meet him. The two brothers greeted each other with great fraternal affection at Vaitaraṇī, where Ādibhañja founded a village named after him (Adipur), on the north-eastern bank of Vaitaraṇī, after which, a few years later, Jyoti also founded a village on the exact opposite (south-west) bank of the river. Adipur has yielded a number of copper-plate grants of the Bhañjas.[3]

The inscriptions of the Bhañjas, however, do not explicitly refer to any 'Ādibhañja' as the proper name of any king. It is, in fact, only the expression 'Ādibhañjavaṃśa' (perhaps to be understood as Ādi-bhañjavaṃśa, i.e. 'the first, original, or oldest line of the Bhañjas' and not as Ādibhañja-vaṃśa, i.e. the family line of [the King] Ādibhañja) which is referred to and in which Koṭṭabhañja is said to have been born later. The mention of an elder brother of Jyotibhañja named 'Ādibhañja' can only be understood as referring vaguely to the first progenitor of the Bhañja dynasty, about whose particular name the later writers of the chronicle of Keonjhar do not seem to have any clear idea. It is probably meant only to emphasize that the Keonjhar dynasty is a genuine offshoot of the original Bhañja line, parallel to that of Mayūrabhañja.

One of the partly mutilated inscriptions of the Bhañjas (i.e. the Kesarī copper-plate of Śatrubhañja),[4] does seem to refer to Koṭṭabhañja as 'Ādibhañja', but if we were to regard him as the elder brother of Jyotibhañja, we would land into great chronological difficulties. The donor of this plate is Śatrubhañja, who called himself a son of Raṇabhañja, the grandson of Durjayabhañja and a great grandson of Koṭṭabhañja. Now, since two of the copper-plate grants

[2] *Tasyādibhañjavaṃśe ripuvanadāvānalaḥ balakhyātaḥ* |
śūraḥ śucir vinītpo jātaḥ śrikoṭṭabhañjākhyaḥ ||
(v. 1. *mānī tyāgī adaṇḍakaḥ khyātaḥ*)

[3] See, for example, Tripathy 1974, Plates 4, 5 and 11 of the *Inscriptions of Orissa*, vol. 6.

[4] Vide Copper-plate Grant No. 6 in the *Inscriptions of Orissa*, vol. 6.

of Raṇabhañja can be dated with certainty to CE 924 and 929 respectively, on account of his mentioning Bhauma Era 188 and 193 as the years in which they were issued, it is certain that Koṭṭabhañja cannot have lived later than the middle of the ninth century (i.e. around CE 850), in which case this would not tally with the dates of the foundation of the city of Keonjhar, which is reported to have taken place in CE 1128.

The only historically important and relevant fact that we can glean from this legend is that the central area of the present Keonjhar state was carved out of the kingdom of Khijjiṅga-Mayūrabhañja in the twelfth century. Whether this was done deliberately by the Imperial Gaṅgas, who had occupied the throne of Orissa a few years earlier (CE 1112), by truncating Khijjiṅga Maṇḍala for strategic reasons, i.e. to create a friendly buffer state towards the north of their empire, or whether it came into being out of its own political dynamics, is not known. But the reason does not seem to be internal feud or enmity between the brothers, given that the political relationship between the two houses of Mayūrabhañja and Keonjhar were always very cordial and on some occasions, when in one of these states a king died without issue, a child from the other state was adopted as the heir to that throne (e.g. Vāmadeva Bhañja of Mayūrabhañja was adopted as heir to the throne of Keonjhar in CE 1246).

In the early nineteenth century, Janārdana Bhañja (1792-1831) of Keonjhar even had to wage three wars against Mayūrabhañja to thrust his younger brother on the throne when the three childless widows of its departed king expressed their reluctance to accept a prince of the Keonjhar line as their successor. Keonjhar also once provided an heir to the state of Ghumsur in the early thirteenth century, this being the same line into which was later born the most illustrious of all Oriya poets of the pre-British period, namely, Upendrabhañjadeva.

EARLY HISTORY OF THE BHAÑJAS

The history of the Bhañja dynasty goes back to the fourth and fifth centuries at least, when we find the image of a Naṭarāja with a three-line Sanskrit inscription donated by one Satrubhañja on its pedestal, discovered at the village Asanpat in Keonjhar, as well as an inscribed painting in a cave called Sitabhinji (Sita Bhenji < Bhañji?), situated on a low-lying hill not far from Keonjhar and depicting Diśābhañja or Digbhañjadeva riding an elephant. The inscription on the painting mentioning the name of the king has been ascribed to a period between the fifth and eighth centuries by different scholars basing their arguments mainly on the palaeography of the script, which appears on the lower right-hand side of the painting. Though paleographic considerations are not absolutely reliable, since a particular archaic mode of writing may retain itself longer in one region than in others, stylistically the painting in Sita Bhenji also appears to belong to the late-Gupta or early post-Gupta period. Thus there may not be any doubt as to the fact that the family of the Bhañjas has been in Orissa since the early centuries of the Christian Era and that remarkably, they have been able to preserve their identity until today. The unusually vast area of their settlement is also amazing. Copper-plate grant No. 1 of this dynasty, issued in CE 924, included in the Inscriptions of Orissa Pt. VI, was discovered in Singhbhum district, Bihar (now Jharkhand), which was situated, according to the statement of the text itself, in the northern part of the Khijjiṅga Maṇḍala. On the one hand, we have inscriptions from Suvarṇapura (Sonepur) issued in the thirteenth to fourteenth centuries,[5] and kings like Raṇabhañjadeva II claim to enjoy the grace of the goddess Stambheśvarī, which connects them unmistakably with the city of Sonepur on the western borders of Orissa. On the other hand, a large number of copper-plate grants still exist, which were issued from Vañjulavāk in the Ganjam region, in the extreme south of Orissa,[6] in the same period. In Copper-plate grant No. 44, issued from Bāṇatumba, Ganjam, by Neṭṭabhañja of the Drumarāja family, the king claims that his dynasty has been on the throne for ninety-nine generations and that his is the one hundredth generation. It is therefore remarkable that such great authorities as D.C. Sircar and S.N. Rajaguru assign the grants of Neṭṭabhañja to the eighth century on paleographic grounds.[7] The same is true of Plate No. 41 of Neṭṭabhañja issued from Navāṅgulakapaṭṭana. Both these plates are composed in excellent Sanskrit. Ganjam district also produced the most prolific and the greatest of all the poets of the Oriya language, namely Upendra Bhañja (first quarter of the eighteenth century). From southern Orissa, the Bhañjas spread westwards and occupied large tracts of the former district of Bastar in Madhya Pradesh (now Chhattisgarh), over which they ruled until almost the present day, the last king, Pravīṇacandra Bhañjadeva, being murdered in the early 1960s by his political adversaries.

The above-noted volume of the Inscriptions of Orissa, compiled by Snigdha Tripathy, contains fifty inscriptions of the Bhañjas from the north, north-west and south of Orissa, starting right from the eighth and ninth centuries up to almost the fourteenth century. It shows that not all Bhañjas belong to the same 'clan' or gotra. Some mention the sage Vasiṣṭha as the first preceptor of their family (vasiṣṭhamunipālitaḥ), while others give this credit to sage Kaśyapa (e.g. the houses of Baudh and Daspalla). Though most Bhañjas claim to be the descendants of Gaṇa Vīrabhadra, the later Bhañjas of Khiñjali Maṇḍala in the Baudh-Sonepur region never mention this. They would rather claim to be Kṣatriyas, descendants of the ancient solar dynasty of Ayodhyā, and for still later Bhañjas, their forefathers allegedly came from Rajasthan like the ancestors of the rulers of Sonepur.[8] King Śatrubhañja, who inscribed a few lines of

[5]Cf. *Inscriptions of Orissa*, vol. 6, Pl. 42.

[6]Cf. *Inscriptions of Orissa*, vol. 6, Pl. 24, 25, 41, 44, etc.

[7]Edited and published by S.N. Rajaguru in vol. 1, 265-70 of the *Orissa Historical Research Journal*. Later included by Snigdha Tripathy in *Inscriptions of Orissa*, vol. 6, no. 44. See also her remarks on p. 249 of her work.

[8]See the opening chapters of the epic work *Kosalānanda-kāvyam* of Gaṅgādhara, published by the Orissa Sahitya Academy, which contains a glorified genealogical history

dedication on the image of Naṭarāja of Asanpat, claims to be a scion of the 'Nāga' family.

The main period of Bhañja rule was from the eighth to the tenth centuries, when they ruled as feudatories of the Bhaumakaras of coastal Orissa, some even having relationships of marriage with the Bhaumas. We know from the Talatali copper-plate grant of Dharma Mahādevī that King Śubhākara Deva V of the Bhaumakara dynasty had two queens, one of whom, Vakula Mahādevī, was the daughter of an unnamed Bhañja ruler. The Bhañjas also used the Bhauma Era of CE 736-7 in their records, the latest date appearing in the copper-plate grant of 'Tribhuvanakalaśa' Neṭṭabhañja of Vañjulavāk, which gives 213 as the year it was issued, meaning some time before CE 950. In using this Saṃvat, they were stressing their allegiance to the Bhaumakaras. It is also possible that the Bhaumas and the Bhuiyans originally belonged to a single clan, as Bhauma seems to be a Sanskritized form of Bhuiyan. This may explain the special regard paid to the Bhaumas by the Bhañjas, who had chiefly Bhuiyans as their subject.

Although, as already mentioned, the traditional account of the ruling dynasty of Keonjhar starts in CE 1128, it is unlikely that Keonjhar was an independent state at this time. It was most probably a town in the Khijjiṅga Maṇḍala of a branch of the Bhañjas that split off and established their capital at Dhṛtipur. Historians have not yet been able to locate this capital precisely, but it must have been situated somewhere in the Baudh-Sonepur region, since a number of copper-plate grants issued by its rulers (especially Raṇabhañjadeva) honour the goddess Stambheśvarī, whose famous temple is located at Sonepur, and refer to the river Mahānadī. Dhṛtipur witnessed the rule of four illustrious Bhañjas of this western line, namely: Śilābhañja (alias Aṅgadi), Śatrubhañja (alias Gandhāṭa), Raṇabhañja I and Digbhañja (alias Diśābhañja),[9] the total period of their rule apparently extending approximately from CE 850 to 975. After this they probably migrated towards the south (i.e. to Vañjulavāk in Ganjam), obviously under the pressure of the inroads of the Somavaṃśīs, who were also called Keśarīs, coming from the west. They probably found it safe and convenient to move towards this hilly tract in the south because there were already a number of Bhañja royal families ruling over this region, as is proved by the Banatumba plate of Neṭṭabhañja, who declares himself to be the hundredth ruler of his dynasty, and also because the rule of the Keśarīs most probably did not extend up to that region but was limited to the western and coastal parts of Orissa.

Even if smaller principalities of the Bhañjas existed here and there in north-west Orissa during the rule of the Keśarīs, they could not have had good relations with the Somavaṃśīs, who had usurped most of their western

of the rulers of Sonepur-Patna. Also S.K. Panda's paper in this volume and Snigdha Tripathy, *Inscriptions of Orissa*, vol. 6, 'Introduction', iii-iv.

[9]These Śatrubhañja and Diśābhañja are not identical with the donors of the Asanpat image or the painting in Sita Bhenji respectively.

territories, as is evident from two copper-plate inscriptions of the first great conqueror of the Somavaṃśī Keśarī, Mahāśivagupta Yayāti. In the first copper-plate, issued in his ninth regnal year, the king records a grant to a Brahman hailing originally from 'Śilābhañjapaṭī in Oḍradeśa'.[10] The second copper-plate grant, belonging to the king's fifteenth regnal year, was issued from a place called 'Gandhapāṭi-maṇḍala, which had been annexed to the country of Kośala (*kośaladeśa-pratibaddhagandhapāṭimaṇḍale*)'.[11]

The Bhañjas who migrated towards the south after the conquest of their territories by the Keśarīs ruled in these hilly and forested tracts without much interference from the latter, apparently peacefully and with absolute authority from Vañjulavāk for more than one hundred years until the arrival of the Gaṅgas from the south (CE 1112). A number of copper-plate grants issued during this period in untainted Sanskrit bear witness to their peaceful and prosperous rule. When the Gaṅgas under Coḍagaṅga conquered coastal Orissa from the northern part of Andhra and ousted the Keśarīs, the Bhañja territory fell between the northern and southern borders of the Gaṅga empire. The only way for the Bhañjas to survive now was to ally themselves with the Gaṅgas, which they promptly did, continuing to rule as their vassals. Their allegiance to the Gaṅgas is indicated by the Kapoteshwar copper-plate of Anaṅgabhīmadeva III (1211-39),[12] which when read together with the Antarigam plates of Yaśobhañja[13] conclusively proves that the latter was a feudatory of the Gaṅga sovereign Anaṅgabhīmadeva, since in these plates both rulers claim to have vanquished King Jagadekamalla (alias Vīrapāṇḍyadeva) of the western Cālukya dynasty, whose capital was at Kalyani.[14] This is taken as proof that Yaśobhañja fought for Anaṅgabhīmadeva as his vassal against the Cālukyas. The attribute of Yaśobhañja 'Samasta-khiñjala-deśādhipati' (sovereign lord of the entire Khiñjala region), expressed in this plate, should therefore be taken with a grain of salt. It is also significant that the donee of both these plates (Jagaddhara Śarman, son of Dharādhara Śarman) is the same person.[15] This Pandit seems to have migrated from the court of Anaṅgabhīmadeva to Khiñjalimaṇḍala and was patronized first by Yaśobhañja and then by his brother Jayabhañja.

After a few futile attempts to assert their suzerainty, the Bhañjas of Keonjhar

[10]Obviously a town founded by the first ruler of Khiñjalimaṇḍala, hence named after him; *Epigraphia Indica* 3, 353; *Inscriptions of Orissa*, vol. 6, xvi.

[11]Named after Gandhapāṭī, the headquarters of the region, founded by Śatrubhañjadeva; *Epigraphia Indica* 11, p. 96.

[12]Published in *Orissa Historical Research Journal* 9, 19-29.

[13]See *Inscriptions of Orissa*, vol. 6, Pl. 38.

[14]*Inscriptions of Orissa*, vol. 6, 37, edited first by Raibahadur Hiralal in *Epigraphia Indica* 18, 298-9. The reference to Jagadekamalla appears in verse 5; cf:
tatsūnurjagadekamallavijayī cāṣṭāṅgalakṣmīyutaḥ ǀ
kṣmābhṛnmaulivibhuṣaṇojjvalamaṇivyagrāṅghripadmadvayaḥ ǁ

[15]Cf. Pl. 38 in the *Inscriptions of Orissa*, vol. 6, 209-14 and *Epigraphia Indica* 19, 41-5.

region similarly allied themselves with the Gaṅgas and were able to come to power again in CE 1128 (as the traditional history tells us) to rule as their feudatories, which gave them freedom regarding the internal affairs of their territory. The Gaṅgas too must have viewed it as an advantage to have them as a buffer state, a sort of protective wall against any hostile attacks from the north and north-west. The possibility of a parallel line of the Bhañjas coming into existence as a breakaway group of the Khijjing royal line at Keonjhar, with the active support and blessing of the Gaṅgas, cannot be precluded since the Gaṅgas must have been interested in splitting up the powerful kingdom of Khijjing for strategic and political reasons. It appears that the relationship between the house of Keonjhar and the Gaṅgas remained, by and large cordial, as is indicated by their uninterrupted and peaceful period of rule. However, the Oriya (Prachi) *Mādalā Pañjī* also records a war between Pratāpa Narasiṃhadeva (1307-27) and the Bhuiyans of Keonjhar, which the latter lost very badly. Since the *Kaṭakarājavaṃśāvalī* (Sanskrit *Mādalā Pañjī*)[16] does not mention this event at all, it is open to some doubt, though we cannot rule out sporadic attempts by the Bhuiyans to regain their freedom from the central power based in Cuttack.

GRADUAL DRIFT OF THE BHAÑJAS TOWARDS THE CLASSICAL TRADITION OF ORISSA

Jyotibhañja, the first ruler of the newly established state of Keonjhar with its capital at Jyotipur, was still deeply embedded in his tribal culture, but he slowly started opening up to the mainstream Brahmanic culture of coastal Orissa and is reported to have invited Brahman and Karaṇa families from outside and settled them in his first capital of Jyotipur. Later, when he shifted his seat of administration to the city of Keonjhar, he took care to settle another group of non-tribal upper-caste people around his newly constructed palace in the city quarter called 'Garh Sāhī'. At the same time he did not give up his tribal beliefs, but created a place of worship for the twelve ancestors of the Bhuiyans[17] and erected shrines to five local tribal goddesses (Andhāri, Tāriṇī, Daṇḍadevī,

[16]See *Kaṭakarājavaṃśāvaliḥ*, Tripathi and Kulke 1986, 22, 78.

[17]The names of these tribal ancestors, who are supposed to have sacrificed their lives to establish an independent state of Keonjhar, are as follows:

Vīr Malāra	Jaya	Rūlā
Jhāḍa	Deṅgā	Jāla
Bhīm Malāra	Andhara	Chora
Jantu	Jhekuā	Kūla

We are also told that they are worshipped everyday by the royal priest in the north-east corner of the royal kitchen before the king is served food. Specific worship is offered on the days of Rākhī Pañcamī (September) and Holi (March). In fact, the occasions are a sort of 'thanksgiving' for the harvest and are called Nuā Khia (eating of new [grain]).

Paṭadevī and Raṅgadevī), of whom the first was the *iṣṭadevī* of most of his tribal subjects. The second settlement of higher caste people in the city was done by his son Udaya Bhañja (1158-73), who on this occasion also invited Khaṇḍāyats (Kṣatriyas), as well as Brahmans and Karaṇas.

After the Gaṅgas had ceased to rule, the Bhañjas seem to have allied themselves firmly with the Sūryavaṃśī Gajapatis (1434-1568). If the personal names of the successors of Jyotibhañja are any indication, the Bhañja family was shifting more and more towards the mainstream of contemporary religious beliefs. Among the successors of Jyotibhañja, after following Jagateśvara, we find in the traditional accounts names like Ananta, Dayānidhi, Narahari, Vāmadeva, Yadunātha, Gaṅgādhara, Jagannātha, Śrīdhara, Śrīkara, Gopīnātha, Candraśekhara and Trilocana, eight of which denote Viṣṇu and four Śiva.

THE HARBINGER OF A NEW ERA: GOVINDADEVA

The great turning point towards classical culture and Hinduism, however, occurred in the reign of Govindabhañja, the son of Trilocana (1461-81), who, because of some differences with his father, left for Aṭhagarh, a dependent state of Keonjhar, recruited young tribals there, gave them intensive training in archery to improve their native skills and created a formidable troop of archers. Making a correct appraisal of the current political situation, he dedicated himself with unflinching loyalty to Gajapati Puruṣottamadeva (1465-97), the most powerful ruler in east India at the time. According to the traditional history of Keonjhar, he even took part as the commander-in-chief of the army of Puruṣottamadeva in his second expedition to Kanchipuram (of the Kanchi-Kaberi episode[18] fame), helped Puruṣottamadeva win the battle, and brought the images of Rāma, Lakṣmaṇa and Vanadurgā from there for his people. His contingent in this expedition consisted mainly of well-trained archers, drawn from the tribal population of the Bhuiyans, who had been especially trained for battle. It is said that these soldiers, elevated to the Khaṇḍāyat caste, fought in the garb of Brahmans, with sacred thread around their shoulders, so as to enjoy maximum protection in the battle and were later called Mastānī Brāhmaṇas (i.e. inebriated or carefree Brahmans; indeed, it is not unlikely that, true to their tribal practices, they really fought under the influence of alcohol!). Of these, Aṭhagarh today has the greatest population. For his timely help and loyalty Govindadeva was awarded rule of the Aṭhagarh state by the Gajapati, and also the position of honorary superintendent (*paricchā/parīkṣaka*) of the Jagannātha temple.

Upon the death of his father Trilocana Bhañja in 1480, Govinda marched towards Keonjhar and occupied its throne, presumably with the blessings and active support of Puruṣottamadeva. This is the greatest landmark in the history of Keonjhar, with which begins a glorious chapter of the transformation of

[18] On the historical validity of this tradition, see G.N. Dash 1979.

this tribal state towards the classical Hindu culture of Orissa. Govinda converted completely to Viṣṇuism and became a staunch devotee—though not exclusively so—of Jagannātha. He caused an image of Madanamohana (i.e. Kṛṣṇa playing on a flute, representative of Lord Jagannātha during anavasara, when the temple is closed for the annual renovation and restoration of the wooden statues) to be fashioned in stone, set it up it in his palace and worshipped it regularly as his *iṣṭadevatā*. The former *rāṣṭradevī* of the state of Keonjhar was the tribal deity Tāriṇī, who was replaced by an image of Vanadurgā. Her shrine was erected in the north-east corner of the palace and she was renamed Tārā, one of the ten Mahāvidyās of Tantric Hinduism. The worship came to be conducted in a double manner—in the tribal manner by a *Dehuri* (tribal priest) and in the classical Hindu manner with Vedic-Tantric *mantra*s being uttered by the royal priest. The worship of Madanmohana also came to be performed in a mode which was a mixture of Śākta and Vaiṣnava practices, much along the lines of the *puja* of Jagannātha.

Govinda Bhañja was the first ruler of Keonjhar to have established two *śāsana* villages (i.e. a village exclusively or primarily established for the settlement of Brahmans), which he called Jayagovindapur and Vīragovindapur, and he invited Brahmans from all over Orissa to settle in these tax-free villages. None of the rulers of the smaller independent states of Orissa had previously done this except the sovereign and the chief ruler of Orissa, who at this time was Gajapati Puruṣottamadeva—the main inspiration for this act and the person whom Govinda wanted to emulate in every respect. He survived his model Puruṣottamadeva and ruled for fifty-four years, until 1534. The previous practice of the Bhañja rulers had been to grant the already existing villages to Brahmans by making them a sort of landlord for collecting and enjoying the proceeds of the revenue, as evidence of which at least fifty copper-plate grants exist. However, the establishment of a *śāsana* village had a particular effect on its environment, helping immensely in spreading the classical Brahmanic culture and learning, which was different in nature from the already inhabited ordinary villages with their mixed populations. It is from these families of *śāsana* Brāhmaṇas that the learning of Sanskrit and important classical literature, i.e. the Dharmaśāstra, etc., spread out to Orissa and even to the outside world. Since the time of Govinda Bhañja it had become a common practice with almost every ruler of Keonjhar to establish Brahman *śāsana*s in his name, some rulers establishing four, five or even six such villages.

One of Govinda's memorable acts was also to accord a sort of Brahmanical status to some of the clans (Chaudhury, Naik, Behera, etc.) of the 'Mastānī Brāhmaṇas', the trusted soldiers of Govinda Bhañja, who were otherwise reckoned as Kṣatriyas. The commanders-in-chief of the army and of the king's personal bodyguard were chosen from among these Mastānīs and were eventually given an important role in the king's coronation. These loyal Brahman-Kṣatriyas became Govinda's greatest supporters and contributed a great deal towards the political strength and stability of Keonjhar.

Govinda Bhañja was not only a brave fighter and a competent ruler but also a man of learning. Besides a few *bhajans*, he is credited with having composed four devotional works in Oriya, namely, *Bhakta-vinoda* (on the *līlās* of Kṛṣṇa), *Rāma-gāthā* (the story of Rāma), *Bāula-carita* (a collection of mystical poems) and *Śrīcaraṇa-sudhānidhi* (spiritual elevation through devotion to one's own Lord).

Vīreśvara Nārāyaṇa, Govinda's son and successor, is also reported to have enjoyed a very long and peaceful rule (1534-91). However, Govinda Bhañja's grandson, Rudranāryaṇa (alias Śiva-Narāyaṇa, 1591-1654), established a *śāsana* in his name for which he brought learned Brahmans from *śāsana* Dāmodarpur near Puri. He appointed one of these learned Brahmans, called Narasiṃha Miśra, as his court Pandit, and the latter repaid this honour by composing an allegorical Sanskrit drama with the philosophical theme of Vedantic Jīvanmukti and called it, after his patron, *Śivanārāyaṇīyam*. This was the first work composed in Sanskrit in the state of Keonjhar. Besides establishing a Brahman *śāsana* called Śivanārāyaṇapur, he also created three new villages in which he settled people from elsewhere, who mainly belonged to the upper castes. The tribal character of Keonjhar was now slowly changing and adopting the mainstream Orissan culture, which flourished mostly in the coastal regions.

THE CLASSICAL REGIONAL CULTURE TAKES DEEPER ROOTS: LAKṢMĪNĀRĀYAṆA AND HIS SUCCESSORS

The next king, Lakṣmīnārāyaṇa Bhañjadeva (1654-88), was one of the greatest and certainly the most powerful Hindu king of his time. He had the courage to challenge the governor (subedār) of Cuttack, although this ultimately harmed the interests of Keonjhar. In his time, the cult of Balabhadra was quite popular in the region watered by the Vaitaraṇī River, using Balabhadra images with quite different features compared to the image of Balabhadra in the Jagannātha temple of Puri. When the most important of all Balabhadra temples, situated in the village of 'Pandra Gacchia', was destroyed by the Mughal subedār, the king constructed a new Balabhadra temple in his capital at a rather exorbitant, not to say prohibitive, cost for a small state like Keonjhar. The construction work of the temple started in 1671 (Śaka 1593) and was finished in 1685. It is the second highest Viṣnu temple in Orissa after the Jagannātha temple and has a height of 90 cubits (*hastas*) or a 135 feet. Though the temple was originally conceived only for the deity Balabhadra, when the construction was already under way, it was thought proper to add the images of Jagannātha (Kṛṣṇa) and Subhadrā, and to make the iconographic features of Balabhadra match these in order to make it a new Puruṣottama temple for the state of Keonjhar which could compete with the temple in Puri. For the consecration of the temple, Brahmans expert in ritual performances were specially invited from Puri. This king also founded another important temple to Dadhivāmana (a single and smaller image of Jagannātha) on the banks of the Vaitaraṇī and with great fanfare instituted the festival of Rathayātrā for both temples, as well as a Candanayātrā in the river Vaitaraṇī for Dadhivāmana. It is clear that his aim was to make Keonjhar a centre of religion and culture to compete with Puri. Indeed, Keonjhar was now competing with Puri in every respect, and the raja had no mind to be subservient and inferior to the raja of Puri.

In order to outdo the contemporary kings of Puri-Khurda, who were weaker by this time, and to attain the status of such famous kings as Yayāti and the Gajapati rulers, Lakṣmīnārāyaṇa invited a number of Brahmans from all over Orissa and further afield and established five *śāsana*s in his territory, all carrying the name of the king, only prefixing adjectives like *vīra* (e.g. Vīra-lakṣmīnarāyaṇapur, two villages of the same name), *śrī*, *vijaya* and *pratāpa*. He also commissioned the writing of the *Mādalā Pāñjī* of his state, to which he gave the new name of *Gaṇasammata* (approved by the people).

Lakṣmīnārāyaṇa Bhañjadeva was also a man of learning. He established a library in his palace and took pains to procure the best works of Sanskrit and Oriya for his collection. The library of palm-leaf manuscripts in the state of Keonjhar was one of the richest royal libraries in Orissa, and there was hardly any work of literary, cultural, or religious importance of that time which was not available in his collection. All the Vedic *Saṁhitā*s and almost all important *kāvya*s and dramas of classical Sanskrit literature, epics and Purāṇas, representative works of the Dharmaśāstra literature, all basic philosophical texts, Āyurveda and veterinary sciences (e.g. *Aśvaśāstra*, *Gajaśāstra*), works on gardening, erotics, astrology/astronomy and all significant Oriya *kāvya*s found a place there, can be seen from a hand-list of some selected important works in his collection, which contains 270 titles and was created by Pandit Madan Mohan Mishra, the present court pandit and librarian, in 1973 for private circulation.[19] Although Lakṣmīnārāyaṇa Bhañjadeva's successors presumably added to this collection, the main collection certainly goes back to his time, and the library itself was also known by his name for a long time (later changed). That the library is really old is also proved by the fact that although it abounds in works that were well known until the time of Lakṣmīnārāyaṇa Bhañjadeva, it lacks many works composed in later times.

It is definitely worth mentioning here that when I was working on the rite of Navakalevara and on the ritual of the consecration of the newly fashioned Jagannātha images, all my sources of information were works procured from this wonderful library of Lakṣmīnārāyaṇa Bhañjadeva. Not a single work of this sort was available in the Pandit Sabhā Library of the Jagannātha temple of Puri. Works like *Netrotsava-vidhi* (on the final painting of the eyes of the statues to bring them to life), *Calaśrīmūrtipratiṣṭhā-vidhi* (containing a very detailed description of the consecration rite of the wooden images of Jagannātha), *Rathapratiṣṭhā-vidhi* (the consecration of the chariots for the car

[19]This list, originally made for the first *Orissa Research Project* (1970-5), is available from the author or Hermann Kulke.

festival) and the rare text of *Hayaśīrṣapāñcarātra*—the basic text for these rituals—all these came from the library of Keonjhar. Lakṣmīnārāyaṇa Bhañjadeva also seems to have had composed or collected from some rare and now unknown sources the mode of worship of Lord Baladeva, his *iṣṭadevatā* and the main deity worshipped in the state temple of Keonjhar. Similarly *Baladevapūjā-vidhi* by Yājñavalkya in this collection is a rare work not found anywhere else and seems to have been composed by some pandit at the behest of the king. The same might be true of the copies of the famous *Gopālārcanapaddhati*, etc., on the worship of Jagannātha, which had been composed, or at least commissioned, by Gajapati Puruṣottamadeva in the second half of the fifteenth century and which was a guide to how the worship should be conducted in his Baladeva temple.

It is clear from the above that Keonjhar emerged as a new centre of Orissan culture during the time of Lakṣmīnārāyaṇa Bhañjadeva and became a hub of religious activities, which were in no way fewer in number or inferior in character to what was taking place in Puri at the same time. There was no looking back for Keonjhar thereafter, and since it was remote from the attention and the evil eye of the Mughal subedārs of Cuttack, which was always directed towards Puri, it could continue its cultural and religious activities without much hindrance or disturbance from outside.

Jagannātha Bhañja (1688-1700), the son and successor of Lakṣmīnārāyaṇa Bhañja, is known for the *Vacanikā* (conversation) between Lakṣmī and Jagannātha after the return of the latter from Gundicā.[20] The *Vacanikā* is still used today in the Rathayātrā festival of Keonjhar. The cult of Jagannātha and the religious practices of the Puri temple now formed a firm part of the Baladeva temple of Keonjhar. Following in the footsteps of his father, Jagannātha Bhañja also established a Brahman *śāsana* called Jagannāthapur.

THE CLASSICAL REGIONAL CULTURE AT KEONJHAR STARTS ABSORBING ELEMENTS OF PAN-INDIAN CULTURE

The next ruler, Raghunātha Bhañja (1700-19), took a special interest in the revitalization of Vedic learning, especially of the *Atharvaveda*, which had declined deplorably in Orissa. There were still some Atharvavedins living in the Ganjam area, whom he respectfully invited and settled in a village founded especially for them, where he built a big water reservoir near Keonjhar. He named the village after himself, as Vīraraghunāthapur or Upādhyāyapur, since most of the Brahmans he invited to settle in the village were teachers of the

[20] In this poetical exchange of verses between the two, recited by their respective priests, Lakṣmī accuses her husband (Jagannātha) of having left her alone in her palace and gone out for a pleasure trip with her brother and sister. She does not let him in until he apologizes and promises not to do it again (only for him to break his promise, of course, the very next year!).

Atharvaveda. From the colophons of a number of palm-leaf manuscripts deposited in the royal library of Keonjhar, we learn that they were either written or copied in Vīraraghunāthapur. With the *Atharvaveda* came also the tradition of the ancillary literature belonging to the *Atharvaveda*, like *Śilpaśāstra*, *Vāstu*, *Tantra* and Ātharvaṇic philosophy, the kinds of works in which Orissa abounds even to this day. Not satisfied with establishing just one *śāsana*, he went on to found another two, called Śrīraghunāthapur and Vijayaraghunāthapur, in later years.

Until his time there was no important temple dedicated to Rāma in Keonjhar, and Rāma *bhakti* was at its lowest ebb. The upsurge of Rāma *bhakti* in north India seems to have spread to Orissa too during his reign, influencing the rulers and the public alike. Realizing this, he took measures to erect a suitable temple for Rāma at Vijayaraghunāthapur and also placed the statue of Hanumān, Rāma's most faithful servant, in front of the temple. He also initiated the celebrations of the festival of Rāmanavamī (the birthday of Rāma), which lasted a week, with great fanfare. It is not impossible that his own name, an appellation of Rāma, might have inspired him to build a temple to this deity.

Raghunātha Bhañja's successor, Gopinātha Bhañja (1719-27), established as many as five *śāsana* villages, and his eldest son, the brave Narasiṃha Nārāyaṇa Bhañja (1727-36), even went a step further: not satisfied with establishing just a village for the Brahmans, he also provided them with well-furnished houses containing all household articles and servants, plus tax-free land for cultivation.[21] The only duty assigned to these Brahmans was to perform *sandhyā* prayers three times a day and to bless the king and thereafter his subjects! Three other *śāsana* villages of normal character were also founded by this king.

The *iṣṭadevī* of the royal family of Keonjhar is Śrīdaṇḍadevī, who is worshipped by the *Dehurī*s with their own specific ritual. She too has a prominent place in the royal palace. Narasiṃha Nārāyaṇa Bhañja changed the practice of worshipping the goddess from the tribal manner to the Hinduistic Śākta manner using Sanskrit *mantra*s. The aniconic form of the goddess was replaced by a *yantra* which became the symbolical 'Image' of the deity. Animal sacrifices to her were stopped and a great festival was introduced for her during the Navarātra of the autumn, in which the tribal Bhuiyans, who had readily accepted the Hinduization of the goddess, also started participating with great enthusiasm. The tribal goddess now entered the Hindu pantheon and became a form of Durgā.

The king was also an avid reader of the Tantric literature. His study of the Tantra told him that the appearance, i.e. the bodily hue of the goddess

[21]This information has its source in the traditional history of Keonjhar based on *Gaṇasammata*, drafted in English by Pt. M.M. Mishra (unpublished manuscript).

Bhuvaneśvarī is red like the rising sun.[22] Now, since Subhadrā is identical in nature and concept to Bhuvaneśvarī and is worshipped using the Bhuvaneśvarī *mantra*, she should logically look like Bhuvaneśvarī. The king therefore changed the colour of Subhadrā's image from yellow to red, as it is still the case in the Balabhadra temple in Keonjhar, in contrast to the image of Subhadrā in the Jagannātha temple, where it is painted yellow. A Brahman *śāsana* called Kamalādevīpur was also established by this king in the name of his wife (Kamalā), or possibly by his wife herself.

Most of Narasiṃha Nārāyaṇa's successors were men of learning and culture. Jagateśvar Bhañja (1758-64) was an erudite scholar of Sanskrit and a good poet of Oriya. He wrote a work in Sanskrit on the 'Science of Horses' (*Aśvaśāstra*), a copy of which is still available in the royal library of Keonjhar. His pathetic poem, a sort of elegy, entitled *Mandodarī Koili* ('Lamentation of Mandodarī', on the death of her husband) is a gem of Oriya literature. The next ruler, Pratāpabalabhadra Nārāyaṇa, was as great a warrior as a scholar and a much more accomplished poet, with a good command of Sanskrit, Oriya and Hindi, and he composed two *kāvya*s in Sanskrit, some intricate *citrakāvyas* and a number of devotional *bhajan*s. As a very devout Vaiṣṇava, he made liberal grants to the temple of Balabhadra, besides establishing three Brahman villages. He is also given credit for having created an island in the middle of a lake for the facilitation of Candanayātrā. We notice that by this time, i.e. the end of the eighteenth century, Viṣṇuism was very firmly established in the Keonjhar state, not only in the royal court but perhaps also among the common people, tribal practices being more and more relegated to the background day by day.

His son, Janārdana Bhañja (1792-1831), is as famous in the annals of Keonjhar for his heroic deeds as for his religious-mindedness. Not only did he annex the territories of Bandhagaḍha Daṇḍapāt and Panduā Daṇḍapāt, to his kingdom, he also waged three wars against the state of Mayurbhanj in order to thrust his younger brother Trivikrama on its throne. It is reported that he was very liberal in his religious policies and never interfered with the religious practices of the territories he annexed (e.g. he did not disturb the worship of the tribal goddess Khandūri in Bandhagaḍha or of a Muslim Pīr in Panduā). He himself was an ardent devotee of Lord Śiva, especially of Viśvanātha of Vārāṇasi, besides having Śrīraghunāthaji (Rāma) and Jayagopāla (Kṛṣṇa) as his *iṣṭadevatā*s, whose temples had been erected by his forefathers. Local chronicles state that whenever he rode out on an elephant, he was preceded by a moving image of Jayagopāla on another elephant. He founded

[22]Cf. (i) *udyad inadyutim indukirīṭāṃ, tuṅgakucāṃ nayanatrayayuktāṃ/*
śmeramukhīṃ varadāṅkuśapāśābhitikarāṃ prabhaje bhuvaneśīm ||
- *Durgāsaptaśatī*, opening verse to *Adhy.* 11

(ii) *bālārkamaṇḍalābhāsām caturbāhuṃ trilocanām* |
pāśāṅkuśavarābhītīr dhārayantīṃ śivāṃ bhaje ||
- ibid., opening verse to *Adhy.* 13

a temple for Kāśī-Viśvanātha in his capital, named his son Viśvanātha and obtained the 'foot water' of Lord Viśvanātha to moisten the hair of his son for his tonsure ceremony. He also sent some of the priests in the Balabhadra temple to Puri to learn the details of the daily *puja* ceremony in the Jagannātha temple and introduced a number of new ceremonies in the Balabhadra temple like *Gītagovinda Sevā* (recitation of *Gītagovinda* at the time of laying the deities to rest), Devadāsī dances and the chanting of *Sāmaveda*. He established four Brahman *śāsana*s, inviting mainly the Brahmans of Vasiṣṭha-gotra to inhabit them, since the Bhañjas have the same *gotra* as them and the Gaṇadaṇḍa Vīrabhadra is said to have been adopted and brought up by Ṛṣi Vasiṣṭha. Like his forefathers, this king was also well versed in Sanskrit and Oriya. He patronized a number of scholars who composed quite a number of works, including *Bhañjamahodayam* (containing the glorified history of the Bhañja family), *Gītasītāvallabham* (an imitation of *Gītagovinda* with Rāma and Sītā as the main characters), both by Nīlakaṇṭha and *Smṛtyarṇava* (a work on the Dharmaśāstra), and himself authored a number of Oriya works, like *bhajan*s and a *kāvya* titled *Līlālatā*. During his reign Orissa was conquered by the British and Keonjhar also had to succumb to British forces, but he saved his rule by entering into a treaty with the British according to which he had to pay them a regular tribute.

Viśveśvara Bhañja (1831-8), Jannārdana Bhañja's son, is reported to have performed a large Vedic sacrifice for the sake of the welfare of his subjects strictly in the manner prescribed in the Vedic texts and observing all the appropriate rites. For the proper performance of the *yajña* he especially invited two families of Agnihotrī Brahmans from Jajpur to carry out the functions of Ācārya and Hotā. The Ācārya who was later offered the post of chief priest of the royal family (Rājapurohita),[23] was also made superintendent of the Balabhadra temple and was given the right to represent the king in a number of religious ceremonies. Viśveśvara's son Gadādhara Bhañja (1838-61) was also a highly devout Vaiṣṇava, on account of which he was made the *Paricchā* of the Jagannātha temple of Puri in an honorary capacity by the raja of Puri, this being a great honour. Having founded a temple of Dadhivāmana at Vaitaraṇī, he also invited 108 Vedic Brahmans from Jajpur, even sending one of them to Varanasi to pursue the intensive study of the Vedas, and upon his return appointing him Brahmā of this temple. Fond of visiting religious places, he died on one of his pilgrimages to Bengal.

Although the subsequent rajas of Keonjhar were educated in English institutions, they remained true to the traditions of their family and took an active interest in maintaining and upholding both the traditions of classical Hinduism and the tribal beliefs. It appears from the life histories and activities of the members of the royal family that, although in their personal lives they

[23]The descendants of this family are still living in Keonjhar and occupy an honourable position in the royal family. Pandit Madan Mohan Mishra is one of them and has been a sort of Guru of the former raja.

were ardent followers of high Hinduism, they were equally devoted and reverential towards their tribal deities and tribal practices. Their adherence to tribal religious practices not only gave them a strong sense of a separate identity, it also strengthened their relationship with their subjects, mainly the tribal population of Bhuiyans and Juangs.

SOME SPECIFIC FEATURES OF THE CULTURAL TRADITION OF KEONJHAR

THE CORONATION PRACTICES OF THE BHAÑJAS

It is obvious that no king can rule over a country without being recognized by the majority of his subjects and without their full support. According to the traditional history of Keonjhar (which is quite similar to the history of the installation of the first royal dynasty in a number of other tribal states), the first king of the state of Keonjhar was a scion of the Khijjing royal dynasty, who according to legend was kidnapped by Bhuiyan tribesmen in order that they might have a king of royal blood for themselves. It is the Bhuiyans who constitute the backbone of support of royal authority. The king worships the ancestors of the Bhuiyans, accepts their gods (especially the goddesses) as his *iṣṭadevatā*s and shows his regard and consideration for them on each occasion, and the Bhuiyans repay the king with their unflinching loyalty to the throne. The Bhuiyans connected with the palace or serving directly under the king are known as 'Rājakulī Bhuiyans' (i.e. belonging to the royal family), and it is they who first of all hold the *daṇḍa* (stick, sceptre) and the *chatra* (umbrella) over the prince when he is declared heir apparent. In fact, they have an important role to play all through the formal coronation of a new king. But since the royal house of Keonjhar has become more and more Hinduized, adopting practices of high Hinduism, an interesting and unique situation has arisen, wherein the coronation ceremony of a crown prince is done twice, first in the traditional manner involving the tribal practices of the Bhuiyans, with their active participation at their earliest convenience, without finding any astrologically auspicious moment, and only thereafter in the Vedic manner as prescribed in the ancient Sanskrit texts, and on a day and time decided by the royal astrologer (*paṭṭajoṣi*). It is interesting to note that during the Bhuiyan ceremony of coronation the tribal chief of the Bhuiyans not only puts the *tilaka* marks on the forehead of the new king but also carries the prince (heir apparent) on his back, assuming the posture of a horse, for quite some distance in the palace. The Bhuiyans also present a long knife to the king, after which the chief of the tribe sits on the ground and bends his neck. The newly coronated king touches his neck seven times with the sharp knife, denoting that the king has full powers to punish erring tribesmen and that they are totally subservient to him. This symbolic rite must have been a part of the original tribal coronation ceremony, but with the royal house inclining more and more towards Vedic practices, an elaborate *Rājyābhiṣeka* is also performed later, on an auspicious day, at an auspicious hour, both having been calculated and determined by astrologers.

It is beyond the scope of this chapter to describe the various rites of the ceremony of Vedic coronation as performed in the state of Keonjhar. I have dealt with this subject extensively elsewhere.[24] It may just be remarked that this elaborate ceremony is minutely described in the work *Rājyābhiṣekavidhi*, the manuscript of which is available only in the Keonjhar Palace Library and which is fairly old (around two hundred and fifty years or so). It appears, therefore, that the ceremony described in it has been performed for many generations.[25] The work is a wonderfully compiled text, which takes into account the whole written and oral tradition of the ceremony of coronation, from Vedic times down to contemporary practices. Its excerpts and quotations are taken from a large number of texts, ranging from the Vedas to the Smṛtis and Purāṇas.[26] This *Paddhati*[27] differs considerably from similar *Paddhati*s available in older Dharmaśāstra texts and appears to have been prepared specially for the coronation of the rajas of Orissa, if not particularly those of Keonjhar, since it prescribes the worship of Kanaka Durgā along with that of Lakṣmīnārāyaṇa before conducting the *abhiṣeka*. The worship of Kanaka Durgā, whose shrine is found in the palaces of a number of Orissan rulers, especially that of the raja of Puri, was a particular phenomenon of Orissa, while the image of Lakṣmīnārāyaṇa, of course, represents Jagannātha and Lakṣmī or Subhadrā.

Further, the instruction that 'after the bathing ceremony (*abhiṣeka*) of the king is over, he should follow the practices of his country, his social group and the customs of his *gotra* and family' is very significant and seems to be an indication of the recognition of the ancestral practices of the family of the king and the customs of the local tribal population.[28]

It is also interesting to note the contrast in the spirit of the ceremony of coronation organized by the tribals (Bhuiyans) a few days earlier and this

[24]See G.C. Tripathi 1991, 73-92.

[25]The Manuscript seems to us to be fairly old and we have the impression that it must have been prepared some time in the first half of the eighteenth century. It is, however, certain that the work *Rājyābhiṣekavidhi* is certainly older than 250 years because it contains such a large number of errors and omissions that it looks probable that the work has undergone a long process of copying and recopying. The Vedic *mantra*s with which the work is full, have suffered the most in the hands of the scribes ...', ibid., 73-4.

[26]The text contains *mantra*s and quotations *inter alia* from: *Ṛgveda*, *Vājasaneyī Saṃhitā* of *Yajurveda* (both Kāṇva and Mādhyandina), *Taittirīya Saṃhitā*, *Maitrāyaṇī Saṃhitā*, *Kaṭha Saṃhitā*, *Śatapatha Brāhmaṇa*, *Viṣṇu-purāṇa*, *Brahmāṇḍa-purāṇa*, *Bhaviṣya-purāṇa*, *Manusmṛti*, *Yājñavalkyasmṛti*, *Bṛhatsaṃhitā* of Varāhamihira and *Śukranīti*.

[27]A text describing the procedure of a particular ritual, with its constituent rites and *mantras*.

[28] *Tataśca kuryān nijajātidharmaṃ* |
deśānuśiṣṭaṃ kuladharmam agryam ||
. . . *svagotradharmaṃ nahi santyajec ca* ||

Vedic one, which is carried out by the Brahmans later. Whereas in the former the leader of the tribe performs the function of a human horse (*narāyāṇa*) for the king and the king touches his neck seven times with a sharp knife in order to demonstrate his absolute authority over his kinsmen, in the latter, it is the Brahmans who lend him authority to rule through their *taporāśi* (*tapas*, i.e. spiritual power) by uttering a particular *mantra* drawn from the *Ṛgveda* (VI. 47.29),[29] but at the same time they raise the horn of a black buck against him in a gesture of intimidation, sounding a warning that he should not misuse his powers or the authority thus bestowed upon him. This is a rite with an old history going back to Vedic times and has been described in the *Śatapatha Brahmaṇa* V.3.4.2.

This second ceremony of coronation along Vedic lines is a proof of its subsequent and secondary introduction. The traditional history of Keonjhar speaks of only one coronation of Jyotibhañja, the founder of the Keonjhar dynasty, by the Bhuiyans in the tribal manner. That ceremony still exists, though considerably shortened, being sandwiched between the other two august ceremonies. They are:

(1) The formal declaration of the abdication of the throne by the king, or the official announcement of his death and the investiture of the crown prince along with the transfer of power, a purely internal, family affair. After receiving the kingship from his father, the prince goes to the family deities, the deities of the tribal folk on which he is ruling, and the 'Rāṣṭradevatā' of his kingdom, i.e. Baladevaji in the great temple and the goddess Daṇḍadevī.

(2) The proper ceremony of coronation according to Vedic-Brahmanical rites, which are usually performed either in the open outside the palace in public view or in the main hall of the palace. This threefold investiture is a good example of a tribal dynasty moving slowly towards the cultural epicentre of a region which was the Puri-Bhubaneswar area and adopting its practices, thus acting more strongly in its attempt to become a part of the mainstream, though at the same time strictly preserving its identity by observing its age-old practices.

It has been mentioned earlier that, from the time of Govinda Bhañja, the Keonjhar Raj family started involving itself more and more in the political affairs of the sovereign rulers of Orissa, which started with him (Govinda) establishing a close friendship with the Gajapati Puruṣottamadeva and taking part in the Kāñcī Kāverī event, as well as participating in religious activities in the Jagannātha temple in Puri. With the passage of time, this led to

[29] *Upa śvāsaya pṛthivīm uta dyāṃ*
purutrā te manutāṃ viṣṭhitaṃ jagat |
sadundubhje sajūrindreṇa devair
dūrād davīyo apa sedha śatrūn ||
iti taporāśī pradānam || (cf. also VS 29.55)

competition with Puri, culminating in the construction of the dynasty's own Jagannātha temple, only a little lower in height than the temple in Puri, and the institution of all the main festivals of Puruṣottama-Jagannātha for the Keonjhar Jagannātha as well. A Gundichā temple was also built and the Rathayātrā was instituted, with Bhuiyans performing the function of the Daitas in Puri. Proper and liberal arrangements were also made for other important 'public' *yātrās*, like *Chandanayātrā* and *Snānayātrā*, etc. However, to have an identity different from that of Puri Jagannātha, the temple of Keonjhar was declared to be a Baladeva temple, and the elder brother was given more prominence. The statues were made of wood, but were intentionally given a slightly different shape, shorter than the Puri images. King Janārdana Bhañja, who ruled in the early nineteenth century, even dedicated his whole kingdom to Lord Baladevaji, thus stepping into the footsteps of the Gaṅga king Anaṅgabhīmadeva and ruling as his deputy.[30] King Gopinātha Bhañja (1905-26) then established a Dharma-nīti-pradāyinī-sabhā, its venue being located inside the Baladeva temple, as an institution parallel to the Muktimaṇḍapa Pandit Sabhā of Puri. This consisted of learned Brahmans drawn from the *śāsana* villages and it gave verdicts on a number of questions pertaining to or connected with controversial religious and social affairs. It is interesting to note that, upon his coronation, every new raja in Keonjhar dedicated the revenue of an additional village to the deity Baladevaji, making the temple better and better endowed over time.

Establishment of Śāsanas by the Bhañjas

The rulers of Keonjhar were very liberal in establishing revenue-free villages for learned Brahmans, who were invited from all over Orissa, though mainly from Jajpur, Puri and Ganjam. There are altogether forty-five Brahman *śāsana*s in the state of Keonjhar, a number exceeding by far what the Sūryavaṃśī Gajapatis of Orissa and the later rulers of the Bhoi dynasty (of Khurda-Puri) did for this community in their states. The practice of establishing *śāsana*s started in the fifteenth century with Govinda Bhañja and continued till the end of nineteenth century up to Dhanañjaya Bhañja. Many rulers created more than one *śāsana*, and Gadādhara Bhañja (1838-61) was so enthusiastic that he founded as many as six for Brahmans he had invited mainly from the Jajpur area.

These *śāsana* villages were established by strictly observing the age-old practice of founding villages. One unique manuscript, the *Śāsanakaraṇam*, on the ritual of founding a Brahman village, is only found in the library of Keonjhar. No other such text is known to exist elsewhere. Internal evidence indicates that it was composed shortly after 1700, but it is based mainly on much older Sanskrit texts on architecture and town-planning, which it quotes. The ritual

[30]See M.M. Mishra n.d. b; with regard to Anaṅgabhīmadeva, see *Mādalā Pāñjī* 1940, 27. Cf. also H. Kulke 1979, 50-1.

it describes is entirely Vedic-Brahmanical in nature, with hardly any trace of tribal practices. This detailed description of the method of founding a new village, its layout, the position of temples and ponds, etc., the situation of the houses of various caste groups and finally the details of the whole ritual which must be performed in establishing a new village, provides an invaluable insight into a domain which is not documented with such precision elsewhere. The *mantras* for performing various rites of the ceremony have been taken almost exclusively from the Vedic *Saṃhitās* of the *Ṛgveda* and the *White Yajurveda* (Kāṇva branch), indicating that the Brahmans of these two branches were most prominently represented in Orissa, and in Keonjhar in particular, at that time. I give here the translation of some of its opening lines, which are quite interesting:

> A settlement of intelligent and noble persons belonging to different jātis is called a grāma, but if the population of the landowners in that settlement solely consists of Brahmans, it is called an Agrahāra [revenue-free]. It may be established with Brahman families numbering as few as twelve or as many as one thousand, depending upon the king's resources. For this purpose one [i.e. the donor] should invite Brahmans endowed with scholarship and noble character, those who are well versed in the Vedas and other branches of learning; who regularly perform their daily Vedic rites after establishing perpetual fire in their homes and, in addition, who are poor and facing hardships due to the high number of children in their families. After inviting them, the Yajamāna [donor king] should honour them in the traditionally prescribed manner in accordance with their seniority. The limits of the village should be clearly and unambiguously marked, and the measurements and location of the land of each individual should be very clearly defined, with detailed descriptions of their boundaries on all the four sides.[31]

We also learn from later in this work that the population of a *śāsana* village—contrary to the popular belief of the scholars—consists primarily but not solely of Brahmans, since they also need the help of members of other social groups and professions in their day-to-day lives, especially to till their land, supply merchandise and do odd jobs in the house. The exact locations for the settlement of the various social groups and the construction of the different temples are described in detail in the work. The foundation stone is dug into the earth in the centre of the village, at the intersection of the two main roads running east-west and north-south, after invoking the deities Viṣṇu and Lakṣmī at it.

[31] *Viprāṇaṃ tu samastāṇaṃ vāso grāma itīritam* ।
anekajātisambandhināvidvajjanair yutam ॥
Sa eva dvijasaṃjñānām agrahāra iti sthitiḥ ।
sahasram uttamaṃ kṣudre [. . .] yathāśakti tu kārayet ।
vidyācāravratair yuktān sāgnikān bahuputrakān ।
daridrān vedaśāstrajñān āhūya cārcayet kramāt ॥
Grāmasīmāṃ viniścitya vayovidyāṃ vicārya tu ।
pramāṇe niścitāṃ bhūmiṃ dadyāc codakapūrvakam ।
Cf. Tripathi 1981, 59.

Most of the *śāsana* villages in Orissa today correspond to the description given in this work.

The work sheds much light on the motives for and purpose of establishing such a settlement, which must obviously have been to introduce classical pan-Indian culture in the region and to acquire a sufficient number of ritual experts to perform the *puja* and the other ceremonies in the temples and the palace. We must feel grateful to the royal house of Keonjhar for having preserved for us a very valuable document on ancient Indian village planning.

The Strengthening of Royal Authority: The Ceremony of Puṣyābhiṣeka

One of the many other very old royal ceremonies of a religious nature going back to the later Vedic period is *Puṣyābhiṣeka*, which has more or less vanished in other parts of India but is still performed in Orissa, especially in the Jagannātha temple and the palace of the Puri raja, but not so ceremoniously or so gorgeously as previously in Keonjhar. There is a text on this ceremony in the personal collection of the raja family—now deposited in its library—which gives details of the ceremony, a close study of which also brings to light the special features of the Keonjhar version.[32]

The term *Puṣyābhiṣeka* simply means 'bathing [the king] on the occasion of the full-moon day of the lunar month Pauṣa [which is conjoined with the constellation Puṣya]'. The aim of this ceremony is to reinforce and strengthen the royal authority of the king year after year. The main part of the ritual consists of a ceremonial bath (or rather the sprinkling of water) given by Vedic Brahmans to the king with holy waters drawn from various *tīrtha*s, while simultaneously uttering the prescribed Vedic and non-Vedic (composed in classical Sanskrit) *mantra*s. It is thus a shortened version of the much larger ceremony of *Rājyābhiṣeka*, in which only the main and substantial part of the ritual (viz., the *abhiṣeka*) is repeated, all the other rites belonging to it being left out.

The first extensive description of the ceremony of *Puṣyābhiṣeka* is found in the *Bṛhatsaṃhitā* of Varāhamihira (Chapter 42), composed towards the end of the sixth century CE. The commentator, Utpala, talking about its origin, remarks that once Indra (the royal power) became very weak and could not conquer the Daityas (the evil forces), whereupon his priest Bṛhaspati (a Brahman) strengthened him by means of his 'spiritual force' (Brahman) uttering the Vedic *mantra*s. It is therefore spiritual authority which strengthens worldly or royal authority. Manu remarks in his *Smṛti* (7.2): 'After receiving the brahmanic Saṃskāra [i.e. having inculcated spiritual refinement in himself] a

[32]For a detailed study of this ceremony with historical and comparative perspectives, see G.C. Tripathi 1996-7, 41-66.

Kṣatriya should provide justice and protection to his subject according to the rules of law.'[33]

The *Puṣyābhiṣeka* ceremony of the ruler of Keonjhar has assumed a distinctly Āgamic character highly influenced by Hindu image worship, except for the rite of *abhiṣeka* proper. For all these Āgamic rites, however, Vedic *mantras* are not only preferred but used almost exclusively. A perusal of the ritual texts composed during the medieval period in Orissa unmistakably points to the fact that there has been a constant and ever-increasing effort on the part of the Brahman priests, right up to the eighteenth century, to lend a Vedic character to their temple and personal rituals.

The most striking feature of the *Puṣyābhiṣeka* of Keonjhar, however, is the inclusion of the worship of the goddess Stambheśvarī in its ritual. As is well known, worship of this goddess is widespread and quite popular in the western part of Orissa, a region which must have been under the sway of the Bhañjas from the tenth to the thirteenth centuries, as a number of kings mention themselves as having received the grace of the goddess Stambheśvarī (*stambheśvarīlabdha-varaprasādaḥ*).[34] The inclusion of this goddess is a unique feature of the *Puṣyābhiṣeka* of Keonjhar. She is not invoked, for example, in the *Paddhati*s describing the ritualistic ceremonies pertaining to the Jagannātha temple or the raja of Puri and is understandably also absent in older works like *Kālikā-purāṇa* and *Bṛhatsaṃhitā*. Stambheśvarī is invoked and honoured as 'Grāmadevatā', i.e. as the tutelary deity of the village or town where the ceremony takes place. She is addressed and praised as the 'bestower of all comforts, one who fulfills all desires and grants all *maṅgala*s (auspiciousness, well being) to the worshippers'.

The *Puṣyābhiṣeka* ceremony of the state of Keonjhar is thus a good example of the acceptance of an age-old ceremony going back to a hoary past by a Hinduized court in a tribal area with proper modifications corresponding to local needs and contemporary practices.

THE INDRADHVAJA FESTIVAL IN KEONJHAR

The last and perhaps most important example of the adoption, assimilation, and celebration of another festival by the Bhañjas of Keonjhar, dealt with here,

[33] Cf. *Brāhmaṃ prāptena saṃskāraṃ kṣatriyeṇa yathāvidhi |*
sarvasyaiva yathānyāyaṃ kartavyaṃ parirakṣaṇam ||

Manusmṛti 7. 2.

The same idea is found in a number of verses in the *Rājadharmaparva* of the *Śānti-parvan* in the *Mahābhārata*. Training in spiritual texts and the Dharmaśāstra was a must for a Kṣatriya.

[34] Among the rulers of the Bhañja dynasty, Rāṇaka Raṇabhañjadeva of Khiñjali-maṇḍala uses this expression very often. He is also the first to use it. Since he also styles himself *ubhyakhiñjalimaṇḍalādhipati* (sovereign ruler of both the Khiñjalis), it appears that this western part of Orissa came under the rule of the Bhañjas for the first time during the reign of Raṇabhañjadeva (with his capital at Dhṛtipur). See Tripathy 1975, 67-100, Plates 14-19, in the *Inscriptions of Orissa*, vol. 6.

related to what is most probably the oldest folk festival in India, going back to Vedic times. Some scholars would like to believe that it even has Indo-European parallels (for example, in the Maypole festival in Europe). This festival was celebrated in honour of the Vedic deity Indra, the most powerful god of the Vedic pantheon, and later the ruler of the gods and of heaven. The festival is variously referred to as Indrotsava, Indradhvaja, Indramahaḥ, etc. It lasts for seven days starting from the twelfth lunar day of the Bhādrapada month (around September) and going beyond the full-moon day. It is celebrated in the open in the middle of pleasant natural surroundings, the centre of the activities being a tall stem of Śāla tree [*Shorea robusta* (Roth)] brought from the forest and erected in the city in a highly decorated form. A number of gods are worshipped in the different parts of this pillar, where they are believed to take up a position after their invocation. After the worship of Indra and the gods is over, merry-making and festivities go on for a full seven days on the occasion of the Indradhvaja. We know from references in the *Nāṭyaśāstra* of Bharata that the first ever Sanskrit drama was also enacted on the occasion of an Indradhvaja festival.

The Indradhvaja festival seems to have survived only in Orissa and—outside India—in Nepal. In Orissa, it is presently celebrated only in the Jagannātha temple in a rather rudimentary form as a temple ritual. As such, it was a pleasant surprise for me to learn that it was celebrated in the state of Keonjhar till very recently, i.e. up to 1963, until the death of the last mahārāja of the 'pre-merger' Keonjhar, Balabhadra Bhañja (1926-63). The significance of this festival can be gauged from the striking fact that the *sūniyā* year (by the Aṅka reckoning) of the rulers of Orissa (now, the raja of Puri) starts from this very day. Elsewhere in India, this day is not important as the beginning of the regional year, but is associated with the birth of the Vāmana incarnation of Viṣṇu and is known as *Vāmana dvādaśī*. The state of Kerala celebrates the festival of Oṇam on this day, when the great and mighty demon king Mahābali is supposed to return to the earth in order to check whether his previous subjects are living happily.

A work in the royal library of Keonjhar, called *Indrotsavavidhi*, describes the festival in detail. A comparison of the details of the festival as it is celebrated in the Jagannātha temple and the town of Keonjhar would show that they each have marked differences and their own older traditions. For example, whereas the pole of the Jagannātha temple has a height of 25 cubits and is made of bamboo, the Keonjhar pole is a Śāla stem, corresponding to age-old tradition, and has a height of 32 cubits with an additional 8 cubits under the ground. It is mentioned in the records of Keonjhar that once, during the time of Balabhadra Bhañja, the stem broke into two pieces when it was being erected with the help of ropes, which did not augur well for virtually the last king of this state.

The stem of the Śāla stands in a hole, which is located at the centre of a Sarvatobhadra Maṇḍala. Two metallic images, of Indra and Viṣṇu, are placed on this Maṇḍala beside this 'standard of Indra' and are worshipped properly.

But before their worship can start, 63 Hindu deities (including planets, mothers, etc.) are invoked in a water pitcher and are honoured. A *homa* (fire sacrifice) then starts in which oblations are dropped while reciting Ṛgvedic hymns to both Indra and Viṣṇu. The standard is considered to be a sort of *axis mundi*, and fourteen *pīṭhaka*s (packets) are suspended from it, symbolizing the fourteen *loka*s (worlds).

The text of the *Indrotsavavidhi* mentions that it is based on the *Bṛhatsaṃhitā* of Varāhamihira. But a close examination of it shows that in the *Bṛhatsaṃhitā* the Indrotsava is a festival meant purely to honour Indra in order to gain the favours of the celestial king for the worldly ruler. However, in the Indra festival of Keonjhar, Viṣṇu has become equally important with Indra, and in the Jagannātha temple much more so.

The worship of minor deities in Keonjhar, like planets, Dikpālas and mothers, in the water jar is purely a later Hindu phenomenon not originally connected with this festival. However, in Keonjhar the god Indra was still important and was accorded proper worship, whereas in the Jagannātha temple he has hardly any significance and the Indradhvaja Yātrā has become a *yātrā* (festival) chiefly in honour of Viṣṇu and Lakṣmī. Lakṣmī does not play any role in the Indrotsava of Keonjhar.[35]

It may thus be seen that, by adopting and upholding a regional tradition, the state of Keonjhar has opted for an older and more pristine version of the tradition, thus not only keeping its separate identity, but also strengthening its links with the older and more classical tradition of Hinduism.

I therefore suggest that Keonjhar is a very significant and powerful centre of culture away from the centre of political power, where we can observe a strong localization of the regional Orissan tradition. Although it certainly absorbed the cultural and religious traditions of coastal Orissa, it also derived inspiration from its local context, left its own imprint on this tradition, and then successfully disseminated it in areas subject to its influence.[36]

[35]For further details, see G.C. Tripathi 1977.

[36]The author is obliged to Pandit Madan Mohan Mishra of Keonjhar for supplying much of the information that has been used in this chapter.

REFERENCES

Dash, G.N. 1979. *Janaśruti Kāñci-kāberi*, Berhampur: Pustaka Bhandara.

Epigraphia Indica 3, 353; 11, 96; 19, 41-5.

Gaṅgādhara, *Kosalānanda-kāvyam*, Bhubaneswar: Orissa Sahitya Academi and Cuttack: Granthamandir.

Hiralal, Raibahadur in *Epigraphia Indica* 18, 298-9.

Kulke, Hermann 1979. *Jagannātha-Kult und Gajapati-Königtum*, Wiesbaden: Steiner.

Mādalā Pāñjī 1940. *Mādaḷā Pāñjī*: *Rājabhoga Itihāsa*, ed. A.B. Mohanty, Cuttack: Praci Samiti (rpt. Bhubaneswar 1969).

Mishra, Madan Mohan n.d. A hand-list of some selected important works in his collection, which contains 270 titles and was created by Pandit Mishra. Orissa Research Project (1970-5), available from the author or Hermann Kulke.

———n.d. *Gaṇasammata*, drafted in English by Pandit M.M. Mishra, unpublished manuscript.

———n.d. *Traditional History of Keonjhar (Based on Local Oriya Sources)*, unpublished manuscript.

Orissa Historical Research Journal 9, 19-29.

Tripathi, Gaya Charan 1977. 'Das Indradhvaja-Fest in Orissa: Überreste der Indra-Verehrung in Ostindien', in Wolfgang Voigt (ed.), *Neunzehnter Deutscher Orientalistentag: vom 28. Sept. bis 4. Okt. 1975 in Freiburg im Breisgau*, Wiesbaden: Steiner, 1977 (*Zeitschrift der Deutschen Morgenländischen Gesellschaft*, Suppl. 3, Teil 2), 1002-14.

———1981. *The Ritual of Founding a Brahman Village: A Description of the Ceremony of Establishing a Brahmana-sasana in Orissa on the Basis of an Unpublished Manuscript*, Delhi: GDK.

———(ed.) 1981a. *The Text of Śāsanakaraṇam*, in G.C. Tripathi, 1981, 59ff.

———1991. 'The Ritual of Royal Consecration in Orissa: Introducing the Manuscript Rājyābhiṣekavidhi', in *Journal of the G.N. Jha Kendriya Sanskrit Vidyapeetha* 47, 73-92; reprinted in B.N. Swain (ed.) 1998, *Dharmaśāstra Paryālocanā*, Puri.

———1996-7. 'The Ceremony of Puṣyābhiṣeka in Orissa', in *Journal of G.N. Jha Kendriya Sanskrit Vidyapeetha* 51-2, 41-66.

Tripathi, Gaya Charan and Hermann Kulke (eds.) 1987. *Kaṭakarājavaṃśāvalih: A Traditional History of Orissa*, Allahabad: Vohra.

Tripathy, Snigdha (ed.) 1974. *Inscriptions of Orissa*, vol. 6, Bhubaneswar: Orissa State Museum.

CHAPTER 5

Jajpur and the Legendary King Yayāti Keśarī*

SUSMITA ARP

A popular Orissan legend relates how King Yayāti Keśarī once invited 10,000 Brahmans from Kanauj in northern India to Jajpur. He had then performed ten horse sacrifices (*aśvamedha*), complex rituals and symbols of powerful kingship since Vedic times. This legend is not unique to Jajpur (Yājpur), where a so-called Daśāśvamedhaghāṭ can be found on the banks of the river Vaitaraṇī, where the sacrifices are supposed to have taken place. It is also widely known among Brahmans in other parts of Orissa, many of whom trace their roots back to the north Indian Brahmans invited by Yayāti Keśarī, who are regarded as particularly pure and learned. King Yayāti is also the subject of another well-known myth which credits him with the revival of the Jagannātha cult in Puri after an invasion by a foreign power.

Many historians believe that the legends have a kernel of truth in them and identify Yayāti Keśarī with a king of the Somavaṃśī dynasty, who is said to have united large parts of contemporary Orissa for the first time. The importance of King Yayāti to Orissan identity is so great that some historians see in him the actual founder of Orissa. Panigrahi points out: 'Yayati I united Koshala and Utkala politically and culturally and can justly be regarded as the father of the modern Orissa.'[1] There were two Somavaṃśī kings called Yayāti; one of them lived in the first half of the tenth, the other at the beginning of the eleventh century. Like so many other details connected with the history of the Somavaṃśī kingdom, the exact chronology of its expansion is unknown. Thus Panigrahi and Sircar are of different opinion[2] as to which of the two Yayātis was the renowned conqueror whose deeds may have sparked off the Yayāti

*This article is a revised translation of the German article 'Jajpur und der legendäre König Yayāti Keśarī', in Conermann and Kusber 2003, 9-22, translated by Nicole Pohland. I am grateful to G.N. Dash, Thomas Oberlies and Stephan Conermann for their advice and valuable information on this subject.

[1]Panigrahi 1981, 106. Similarly Bose 1927, 30: '[Yayati Kesari] is said to have brought ten thousand Brahmans from Kanauj in the United Provinces and they performed a great Vedic fire-sacrifice in the newly founded town of Jajpur. From that time onwards, Orissa has been a land of Hindus. . . . As we have already said, the germs of a separate Orissan culture were laid during the reign of the Kesaris.'

[2]Panigrahi 1961, 13-14; Sircar 1971, 178-9.

Keśarī legends. They do, however, agree that this particular king changed the name of the capital of the Bhaumakaras after its conquest in Yayātinagara and made it his second capital.

Yet whether the Yayāti legends of Orissa can indeed be traced back to the time of the Somavaṃśī seems doubtful. Hermann Kulke has recently shown that the tradition crediting Yayāti Keśarī with the revival of the Jagannātha cult and the construction of Puri's first temple is in all probability a construct of the late sixteenth century. Further, it is directly connected with the legitimization of Rāmacandra of Khurda, who tried to establish himself as local successor of the erstwhile imperial Gajapati kings of Orissa and revived the Jagannātha cult in 1590.[3] According to Kulke, the Yayāti Keśarī myth was created to fashion a heroic king who, in ancient times, triumphantly overcame a disruption of tradition caused by an alleged Muslim rule in the fifth century CE. Kulke arrives at the conclusion that the Yayāti legend of Puri was not, as formerly supposed, modified and adapted to the 'biography' of Rāmacandra at the end of the sixteenth century, but newly created at that time after the 'model' Rāmacandra in order to sanctify his deeds.

In the following I shall take a closer look at the Yayāti legend of Jajpur. I am going to show that it too probably did not originate in the time of the Somavaṃśī, and that it may in fact be even younger than the Yayāti tradition of Puri examined by Kulke.

One of the pivotal lines of reasoning that postulate a former connection between Jajpur and Yayāti, and thus the alleged great age of the Yayāti tradition, is the identification of Yayātinagara with Jajpur. Many of the later documents of the Somavaṃśī dynasty were drawn up in Yayātinagara. This does suggest that Yayātinagara was indeed an important administrative centre, and it may even have been the capital.[4] It does not, however, prove that Yayātinagara is identical with Jajpur. I will therefore begin by closely examining the arguments of Panigrahi and Sircar, the two most prominent defenders of this theory.[5]

Important sources for both authors are the *Mādalā Pāñjī* chronicles, the writing down of which began at the end of the sixteenth century. In connection with the Gaṅga king Anaṅgabhīma, the first *Pāñjī* mentions a place called Abhinava Yayātinagara. Panigrahi states: 'The context in which this place-name has been used leaves no doubt that by Abhinava Yayātinagara the chronicle means modern Jajpur. ...'[6] The particular passage in the text describes how King Anaṅgabhīma visits Puruṣottamakṣetra (Puri) and makes gifts to the Jagannātha temple. Abhinava Yayātinagara seems to be located somewhere within Puri.[7] Also, the remainder of the passage pertaining to the reign of

[3] Kulke (in press).

[4] On the geographical names of the Somavaṃśī inscriptions, see e.g. Rath 1983, 193ff; Sarma 1983, 23ff.

[5] Other authors identifying Yayātinagara with Jajpur more or less repeat the reasons put forth by Panigrahi and Sircar, e.g. Rath 1983, 195-8.

[6] Panigrahi 1961, 14.

[7] *Mādalā Pāñjī* 1940, 28.

Anaṅgabhīma does not indicate that this king had any relationship with Jajpur.

On the contrary: one finds that Anaṅgabhīma resided first in a palace in Chaudwar, and later in Barabati on the other side of the Mahānadī River. The *Mādalā Pāñjī* chronicles do mention Jajpur several times, but the name that is used is always 'Yājpur', not 'Yayātinagara'.[8] In this context, the value of the *Mādalā Pāñjī* seems at least questionable: What was called 'New-Yayātinagara' at the end of the sixteenth century can by no means be identical with the Yayātinagara of the Somavaṃśī inscriptions of the tenth and eleventh centuries.

Panigrahi also follows another important line of reasoning:

> In the Oriya *Mahābhārata* written by Rāja Krishna Simha in the eighteenth century, it is stated that anybody who visits Yayāti-pattana, gets the same merits as accrue from the performance of the Aśvamedha sacrifice. Because of its situation on the river Baitaraṇi, the poet has merely changed Yayātinagara into Yayāti-pattana, but all the same his description of the merits that accrue from a visit to the place, leads to its identification with Jājpur.[9]

Snigdha Tripathy also mentions this passage dating from the eighteenth century. But contrary to Panigrahi, she does not interpret it as proof of a former connection between Jajpur and Yayāti, but sees this late text as the first written evidence for such a tie.[10] Even this is uncertain, since the verse composed by Kṛṣṇa Siṃha in Oriya only rephrases a similar passage from the Sanskrit *Mahābhārata* which obviously does not refer to Orissa.[11] The original Sanskrit text describes a number of different places of pilgrimage along the way between Puṣkara and the Narmadā River, places far away from Orissa. The exact location of most of these sites, including Yayātipatana, is obscure.[12] Nothing, however, suggests that the pilgrimage refers to Orissa. One cannot tell whether Kṛṣṇa Siṃha had Jajpur in mind when he translated the verse in the eighteenth century, but his Oriya version does not contain any modification or amendment that would point in that direction. Several other places of pilgrimage named after a king called Yayāti—for example Yayātitīrtha—are mentioned in the epic and Puranic literature. None of these are located in Orissa, but lie, for example, in Benares or near the Sarasvatī River.[13] Yayāti is one of the great kings of supra-regional Sanskrit mythology, of whom a number of different

[8] *Mādalā Pāñjī* 1940, 22, 34, 52, 77.

[9] Panigrahi 1961, 15.

[10] Tripathy 1998, 42.

[11] The verse from Kṛṣṇa Siṃha's Oriya-*Mahābhārata* reads (cited after Panigrahi 1961, 15):

yayāti-pattanaku yāe yeun naral aśvamedha-phalaṭi huai tāhāra ||
In the Sanskrit *Mahābhārata* 3. 80. 67 the following verse can be found:
pradakṣiṇaṃ tataḥ kṛtvā yayātipatanaṃ vrajet |
hayamedhasya yajñasya phalam prāpnoti tatraiva ||

[12] On the different locations, see Mehendale 1996-7.

[13] See Kane 1973.

myths are told. The many passages alluding to him in epic and puranic literature do not refer to Orissa or contain any hints of the Yayāti Keśarī of Orissan tradition.

The fact that Kṛṣṇa Siṃha, or rather the original Sanskrit text of the *Mahābhārata*, promise those who visit Yayātipatana the same merit as accrues from a horse sacrifice cannot be used to connect the text passage with Jajpur, where, according to regional tradition, Yayāti Keśarī performed a *daśāśvamedha* (sacrifice of ten horses). The promise to achieve for certain pilgrimages the same merit as for a horse sacrifice is one of the most common, almost stereotypical ones in the puranic literature. It can by no means be seen as an exclusive characteristic of Jajpur's mythology. We do not have to discuss two other sources listed by Panigrahi, i.e. Dhoyīs Pavanadūta and some Cola inscriptions.[14] Panigrahi's interpretation of these sources—if they are to be followed[15]—does not prove that Yayātinagara is identical with today's Jajpur; it only confirms that it lay in a coastal area. Many historians who do not identify Yayātinagara with Jajpur are of this opinion, as will be seen in the following.

Sircar's reasons for identifying Jajpur with Yayātinagara differ from those of Panigrahi. He explains that some sources seem to indicate that Yayātinagara is identifiable with Cuttack. This, he argues, is wrong, for: '. . . Jājpur seems to be a corruption of the name Yayātipura which is again practically the same as Yayātinagara, both meaning 'the city of Yayāti'.[16] Sircar even presents the hypothetical linguistic steps that lead from *yayāti-pur* to *yāj-pur*. In fact, the phonetic laws allow for a number of developments, and from time to time an anomalous phonetic process can be detected. However, a shift from *yayāti-* > *yāj-* would entail several anomalous processes[17] and is therefore highly unlikely. Furthermore, anomalous linguistic change usually occurs only in the everyday language, not in proper nouns.[18]

Sircar assumes that not only the Somavaṃśīs, but also the Gaṅgas had their capital in Yayātinagara: 'If the Ganga conquerors of coastal Orissa ruled the country from Yayātinagara or Yayātipura, i.e. modern Jājpur, before the

[14]Panigrahi 1961, 11-14; Panigrahi 1981, 114.

[15]On the question of whether the Cola inscriptions really do read 'Yayātinagara', see Acarya 1969, 90. The Cola inscriptions do not specify clearly the location of this site; see the translation of the inscriptions in Nilakaṇta Sastri 1955, 207. Thus Rath and Panigrahi interpret the Cola inscriptions differently, in spite of the fact that they both identify Yayātinagara with Jajpur. Rath states (1983, 196): 'During the invasion of the Cola army there was only one Yayātinagara located in Kosala.' And Panigrahi 1961, 15: 'There was thus a Yayātinagara in Orissa, now known as Jājpur. Rājendra Cola met Indraratha . . . at this place and defeated him in about 1021 A.D.'

[16]Sircar 1971, 180.

[17]Intervocal *y* would have to become *j*, an entire syllable would have to vanish and the quantity of the vowel would have to move to the front.

[18]Thus the name Yayāti can be found unchanged in later Oriya sources like the *Mādalā Pāñjī* (1940, 5).

transference of its headquarters to the Cuttack region, we can easily explain why the Muslim writers of the thirteenth and fourteenth centuries mentioned the kingdom of the Gaṅgas in Orissa as Jājnagar (Yayātinagara).'[19] Indeed, the name Jājnagar is used in some early Persian sources to denote Orissa. However, the exact region and the origin of the name remain unclear.[20] Apart from the apparent similarity of the Indian toponym Jājpur with the Persian Jājnagar, there are no indications that the Muslim authors might have called the empire thus because they remembered the name of the former capital, Jājpur. Nor do the authors explain the origin of the name, or describe a city of that name. To give an example, no such place is cited in the anonymous *Sīrat-i Fīrūzšāhī*, whose author describes in great detail the route taken by Sultan Fīrūz Šāh in 1361 on his military campaign through Orissa. According to Wali, this is also true of other works.[21] Thus, the author ʿAfīf does not mention anything about an old city or capital called Jājnagar. Instead, he describes Cuttack (Baranasi) as the old residence of the rājas of Jājnagar.[22] Looking at the Persian texts, it cannot be ruled out that the name Jājnagar developed from either Jājpur (Yājpur) or Yayātinagara. However, the sources contain no proof of this derivation, nor do they indicate that Yayātinagara and Jājpur are identical.

To summarize, the arguments for the identification of Yayātinagaras with Jajpur are very weak. Thus, a number of historians reject this theory. One of them is S.N. Rajaguru,[23] whose most important counter-argument—already pointed out earlier by Fleet[24]—is the fact that several Somavaṃśī inscriptions describe Yayātinagara as a city located on the banks of the Mahānadī. Panigrahi and Sircar get round this problem by suggesting that there was initially a Yayātinagara by the river Mahānadī in western Orissa, and later another one in the coastal area, i.e. in Jajpur. There is, however, no convincing proof for the existence of two cities of the same name. The only possible argument would be that Yayātinagara is mentioned in the documents of Yayāti I at a time when the Somavaṃśīs had not yet advanced beyond Koshala. Later documents mentioning Yayātinagara were drawn up by rulers who had by then conquered the Orissan coast, but lost control over Koshala. Accordingly, there must have been a Yayātinagara in Koshala as well as on the coast. Yet this

[19]Sircar 1971, 180.

[20]See, for example, Roy 1942, 61, note 2; Elliot/Dowson 1867-77/1990, 112-13, notes; Wali 1923, 290.

[21]Wali 1923, 289: 'Badayunī commences the description of the expedition as that of Jājnagar, but in the course of the narrative, never once mentions Jājnagar, but other places. Such is also the case with other Persian historians.'

[22]ʿAfīf's *Taʾrīkh-i Fīrūzšāhī*, translated in Elliot/Dowson 1867-77/1990, 312: '. . . Sultan Firoz rested at Baranasi, an ancient residence of the arrogant Rais. At that time the Rai of Jajnagar, by name Adaya, had deemed it expedient to quit Baranasi, and to take up his residence elsewhere; so Sultan Firoz occupied his palace.' See also Desai 1968-9, 43-4.

[23]Rajaguru 1966, 373.

[24]Fleet 1894-5, 355.

argument only makes sense as long as we accept the suppositions about the expansion of the Somavaṃśī kingdom mentioned above. But, as Sircar himself admits, the Somavaṃśī conquest of the coastal area is one of the gaps in Orissan history and has so far been difficult to reconstruct.[25]

Those who disagree with this identification of Yayātinagara suggest several other locations, but list only a few reasons for their choices. Rajaguru speculates that it may have been some city close to Kantilo, or maybe Jagti (near Baudh).[26] Bina Kumari Sarma states that Jajpur must be ruled out and suggests that it may have been Chaudwar.[27] H. von Stietencron and G.N. Dash also favour Chaudwar or Sarangagarh, also situated near Cuttack, and consider possible motivations for the relocation of the capital to this place.[28] P. Acharya, on the other hand, feels certain that Yayātinagara was situated in the west 'on the bank of the Mahānadī somewhere in the Sonpur State or the Sambalpur District'.[29] In the present state of research, any definite identification of Yayātinagara seems to be impossible. However, Jajpur is probably an unlikely candidate—especially because of the Somavaṃśī inscriptions that locate Yayātinagara by the Mahānadī River. For the present question, this means that the allusion to Yayātinagara does not prove any former connection between Jajpur and Yayāti.

The question remains as to when the Yayāti-Keśarī legend of Jajpur originated. A number of different works of supra-regional Sanskrit literature, as well as several Māhātmyas from Orissa, praise Jajpur and its places of pilgrimage, among them the Vaitaraṇī River, diverse Śiva-Liṅgas, the goddess Virajā and Viṣṇu in the form of a boar (*varāha*).[30] According to the *Mahābhārata*,

[25]Sircar 1971, 179: 'The story of the transference of the lordship of that region [the coastal regions of Orissa] from the Bhauma-Karas to the Somavaṃśīs is not clearly known.'

[26]Rajaguru 1966, 373 and 397. Jagti is obviously the place also cited by N.K. Sahu: 'The Capital of the United Kingdom was located at Yayatinagara on the Mahanadi, identified with modern Jagati or Jagatinagar near Baud in Phulvani District'; Sahu/Mishra/Sahu 1979, 29. See also ibid., 179 and Sahu 1977, 41.

[27]Sarma 1983, 25-36.

[28]Stietencron 1978a, 28: '. . . the transfer of his [Coḍaṅgaga's] capital from Kaliṅganagara to the Cuttack area either Sāraṅgagaḍa or Chaudwar after this war may have been caused partly by the need for more direct control of the northern parts of his kingdom, but partly also by the king's wish to supervise the building of the temple in Puri.' See also ibid., 1; Stietencron 1978b, 74, notes; cf. Dash 1978, 161: 'Coḍagaṅga's suspicion of the Śaivas [of Bhubaneswar] seems to be the reason why he shifted the political capital of his empire to Sāraṅgagarh, a few miles north of Bhubaneswar, which was the capital of the later Somavaṃśīs.' Chaudwar is also cited by Kedarnath Mahapatra 1977, 549. The explanations in square brackets are my own.

[29]Acharya 1969, 94. He follows Hiralal 1911-12, 189 and Mishra 1936, 75.

[30]Works are the *Mahābhārata*, a number of different Purāṇas, Nibandhas and Māhātmyas, as well as several Pīṭha lists from Tantric works. These textual references are given in Arp 2006.

Viraja as Jajpur is called here, is a place particularly appropriate for sacrifices.[31] A verse from a ninth-century *Skanda-purāṇa* promises the same gratification as for a horse sacrifice to anyone who visits Śiva here.[32] Much later, probably in the fifteenth or sixteenth century, the *Virajamāhātmya* equates the worship of a certain *liṅga* with the performance of ten horse sacrifices.[33] The story forming the framework of this work, which, like the others, belongs to the category of anonymous literature, tells the tale of how the god Brahmā once performed a great sacrifice in Viraja, during which all the great divinities appeared and settled in Virajakṣetra permanently. As can be seen, several texts mention Jajpur in connection with the performance of sacrifices, sometimes horse sacrifices in particular. If named, however, the sacrificer is the god Brahmā, not Yayāti Keśarī nor, indeed, any other king. In fact, Yayāti Keśarī makes no appearance whatsoever in any of these texts. Even the *Virajamāhātmya*, an entire work concerned solely with the greatness of Jajpur, does not mention him, nor is the place ever called Yayātinagara.

However, several elements of the Yayāti legend can be detected in another source. During a ritual in which rice balls (*piṇḍa*) are offered to the ancestors, the sacrificer retains some of the gifts for the local Brahman and utters the following words: 'I also give a share to the Brahmans, to those dead and to those alive, who were once called from Kanauj by the maker (Brahmā the creator?) in order to perform a ten-horse-sacrifice (*daśāśvamedha*).'[34] The invitation to Brahmans from northern India contained in this verse is an important part of the legend, but again the allusion to Yayāti Keśarī is missing. It is hard to determine the age of the verse since it cannot be found in any written source. The fact that the modern Indian word Kanauj is used instead of the Sanskrit Kānyakubja suggests a more recent origin, as Snigdha Tripathy has already pointed out.[35]

Snigdha Tripathy has found traces of the legendary invitation of north Indian Brahmans in another source which is much easier to date. An inscription on a Bhaumakara copper plate issued in CE 766, and therefore before the time of the Somavaṃśī, mentions 204 Vedic Brahmans who settled in close proximity to Jajpur. Tripathy believes that these Brahmans came from northern India and also performed sacrifices for their patron. According to her, the memory of this was kept alive over the centuries and, together with other legends,

[31]*Mahābhārata* 1927-72, 3.114.4-6 and 13.

[32]Hans Bakker, who along with other authors is editing the *Skanda-purāṇa*, has kindly pointed out this paragraph to me. Verse 167.184 reads:
ekāmre ca vibhoḥ sthānaṃ dṛṣṭvā svargam avāpnuyāt |
virajāyāṃ haraṃ dṛṣṭvā vājimedham avāpnuyāt ||

[33]*Virajamāhātmya* 10.76-7.

[34] *kanaujadeśāt svayamāhūtā ye daśāśvamedhāya purā vidhātrā* |
martyastitāḥ svargagatāś ca viprās tebhya dvijebhyaḥ pradadāmi cārghyam ||
Quoted in Panigrahi 1961, 15, note 44.

[35]Tripathy 1998, 40.

formed the Yayāti tradition.[36] It is indeed plausible that the settlement of such a large number of learned Brahmans by the Bhaumakaras, to which the inscription bears witness, has been linked to Jajpur since that time and later became part of the Yayāti legend. However, it should be noted that the inscription does not reveal the origin of the Brahmans, nor does it mention any rituals.

Thus several sources are the basis for two important components of the Yayāti tradition of Jajpur, i.e. the settlement of learned Brahmans and the performance of great sacrifices. On the other hand, the third important element, King Yayāti Keśarī, is missing. In searching for textual evidence, I only found two works connecting Jajpur with Yayāti,[37] both of which date from the nineteenth century. The Sanskrit chronicle *Kaṭakarājavaṃśāvalī*, written around 1820, notes the following: 'when Yayāti's mother was pregnant with him a voice foretold her that she would bear a great king. Therefore the people took the newborn child to the old capital in Yājapurakṣetra, where the boy, by Śiva's blessing, came to power, thus an old legend tells us.'[38] In another tale about King Yayāti, Jajpur is not mentioned any more. The second text, the *Puruṣottamacandrikā*, is a chronicle of Puri written in Bengali and published in 1844. The author reports what he was told about Yayāti and starts his account with the statement that the king resided in Jajpur.[39] In the following, the story of the re-establishment of the Jagannātha cult by Yayāti Keśarī is told, i.e. the Yayāti legend of Puri, similar to that in the *Kaṭakarājavaṃśavalī*. This story can be found in the *Mādalā Pāñjī* chronicles, which are by far older, whereas the legends about Yayāti's connection to Jajpur are not mentioned there.

As Kulke has pointed out, the *Mādalā Pāñjī* chronicles, written towards the end of the sixteenth century, are the first sources to introduce the figure of Yayāti Keśarī. No older chronicle or inscription alludes to this king. The *Bhaktibhāgavata*, for example, written in 1510, discusses four Orissan dynasties, among them the Somavaṃśa. Obviously taking their title from a number of Somavaṃśī kings, they are called Keśarī in these texts. However, the search for a founder of the dynasty named Yayāti Keśarī remains unsuccessful, as does that for any of the myths associated with him. As mentioned above, Kulke believes that Yayāti Keśarī and the legends about his

[36]Ibid., 42.

[37]The existence of further textual references cannot be ruled out. Since Orissan literature is often hard to access and is not classified and ordered by indices, a systematic search is difficult. However, G.N. Dash, an erudite scholar of Oriya literature, has kindly informed me that he himself knows of no other references.

[38] *Kaṭakarājavaṃśāvalī* 1986, 6:
tatratyalokaiḥ yājapurakṣetrasthapracīnarājadhānīṃ prati nītaḥ |
katikālānantaram īśvaraprasādād ayaṃ rājābhavad iti prācīnā kathā |
yājapurakṣetre yayātike śariṇā rajatvaṃ prāptam |

[39] *Puruṣottamacandrikā* 1844, 27:
likhi tār kichu yāhā śunechi śrabane | *rājā yājpure bās karilen giyā.*

saving the Jagannātha cult were created not until the end of the sixteenth century. After the fall of the powerful Gajapati kingdom and the Muslim rule that followed in Orissa, Ramācandra established himself as the successor of the Gajapatis by re-establishing the Jagannātha cult at the end of the sixteenth century. The Yayāti Keśarī legend records that once before in Orissan history the figure of the 'state god' Jagannātha was hidden from foreign rulers. Only after 144 years was it rediscovered by Yayāti Keśarī, the founder of a new dynasty, and installed in a new temple at Puri. Thus the legend created a historical precedent that showed how a forced disruption of tradition could be successfully overcome.

According to Kulke, the time of Ramācandra was characterized by 'a strong common need to heal the forced break of tradition'.[40] This would have been true for Jajpur, too, which had suffered terrible destruction and had to reassure itself that its current traditions, newly erected temples and re-established cults were firmly rooted in the past. Puri's new myth of the 'old' hero Yayāti Keśarī satisfied the needs of that uncertain period and seems to have been very successful, as can be seen in the wide geographic distribution of the Yayāti legends. It may be that Jajpur's narrators and priests, inspired by the Yayāti legend of Puri's chronicles, also tried to trace their traditions back to Yayāti, and that the Jajpur legend of the settlement of learned Brahmans by Yayāti and his performance of the ten-horse sacrifice arose soon afterwards. Since the only texts connecting Yayāti with Jajpur are from the early nineteenth century, it cannot be ruled out that Jajpur's Yayāti tradition gained fresh popularity only in the late nineteenth century. Then, the healing of a disruption of tradition was no longer at the centre of the legend, but rather Yayāti's role as the 'father of modern Orissa', as Panigrahi later called it.[41] The rule of Yayāti Keśarī, the alleged Somavaṃśī king, became one of the most important historical points of reference. At that time, when the British tried to record the history of the country and Orissa found itself struggling to construct its own identity—not least of all to set itself apart from Bengal—the Yayāti legends emerged almost as an Orissan origin myth.[42] Whether the Yayāti legend of

[40]Kulke 2001, 171.

[41]See above, fn. 2.

[42]This change in the description of Yayāti is foreshadowed in the accounts of the *Puruṣottamacandrikā* and the *Kaṭakarājavaṃśāvalī*. Hunter (1872) also seems convinced of the great importance of Yayāti: 'The history of Lower Bengal starts from an immigration of this sort [migration of north Indian Brahmans], and the same phenomenon looms through the mists of Orissa tradition, which cloud the origin of the Sivaite line of kings. The local legends and the Palm-leaf Records alike relate how about CE 500, the founder of the Long-haired or Lion-line [Keśarīs] imported ten thousand Brahmans from Oudh, and endowed them with lands around Jajpur on the sacred Baitarani river.' Hunter 1872, 238. The 'Palm-leaf Records' refer to the *Mādalā Pāñjī*, which, however, as mentioned above, only cites the Yayāti legend of Puri.

Jajpur originated in this context or already at the end of the sixteenth century soon after the creation of the Yayāti myth cannot be determined on the basis of the few textual references. However, the evidence suggests that it is younger than the Yayāti legend of Puri.

REFERENCES

Acharya, P. 1969. *Studies in Orissan History, Archaeology and Archives*, Cuttack: Cuttack Students' Store.

Arp, S. 2006. 'In Search of Goddess Virajā', in G. Pfeffer (ed.), *Periphery and Centre: Studies in Orissan History, Religion and in Anthropology*, Delhi: Manohar, 59-78.

Bose, N.K. 1927. 'The History of Orissa and Its Lesson', in *The Calcutta Review*, July 1927 [rpt. in ibid., *Culture and Society in India*, London, 1967, 24-31].

Conermann, S. and J. Kusber 2003. *Studia Eurasiatica: Kieler Festschrift für Hermann Kulke*, Hamburg: e.b. Verlag, 9-23.

Das, M.N. 1977 (ed.). *Sidelights on History and Culture of Orissa*, Cuttack: Vidyapuri.

Dash, G.N. 1978. 'The Evolution of Priestly Power: The Gaṅgavaṃśa Period', in A. Eschmann, H. Kulke and G.C. Tripathy, 1978, 157-68.

Desai, Z.A. 1968-9, 'Orissa in the Eyes of Muslim Authors', in *Journal of Ancient Indian History* 2, 39-64.

Elliot, H.M. and J. Dowson 1867-77/1990. *The History of India, as Told by its Own Historians*, vol. 3, London; rpt. Delhi: Low Price.

Eschmann, A., H. Kulke and G.C. Tripathy 1978 (eds.). *The Cult of Jagannath and the Regional Tradition of Orissa*, Delhi: Manohar.

Fleet, J.F. 1894-5. 'Records of the Somavaṃśi Kings of Kaṭak', in *Epigraphia Indica* 3, 323-59.

Hiralal, R.B. 1911-12. 'The Sirpur Stone Inscription of the Time of Mahāśivagupta', in *Epigraphia Indica* 11, 184-201.

Hunter, W.W. 1872. *Orissa, or the Vicissitudes of an Indian Province under Native and British Rule*, in two volumes, vol. 1, London: Smith, Elder & Co.

Kane, P.V. 1973. *History of Dharmaśāstra*, vol. 4 (2nd edn.), Poona: Bhandarkar Oriental Research Institute.

Kaṭakarājavaṃśāvalī 1986. Ed. and trs. G.C. Tripathi and H. Kulke, Allahabad: Vohra.

Kulke, H. 2001, 'Reflections on the Sources of the Temple Chronicles of the Mādalā Pāñjī', in ibid., *Kings and Cults: State Formation and Legitimation in India and Southeast Asia*, Delhi: Manohar, 159-91.

———2008. 'Yayati Kesari Revisited: Ramachandra of Khurda and the Yayati Kesari Legend of Puri', in P. Berger, R. Hardenberg, E. Kattner and M. Prager (eds.), *The Anthropology of Values: Festschrift in Honour of Georg Pfeffer*, Delhi: Pearson/ Longman.

Mādalā Pāñjī 1940. Ed. A.B. Mahanty, Cuttack: Praci Samiti.

Mahābhārata 1927-72. Ed. V.S. Sukthankar et al. Poona, Bhandarkar Oriental Research Institute.

Mahapatra, K. 1977. 'Temples of Bhubaneswar', in M.N. Das (ed.), *Sidelights on History and Culture of Orissa*, Cuttack: Vidyapuri, 542-64.

Mehendale, M.A. 1996-7, *Mahābhārata: Cultural Index*, vols. 3 and 4, Pune: Bhandarkar Oriental Research Institute.

Mishra, B. 1936. *Dynasties of Medieval Orissa*, Calcutta: K.N. Chatterji.

Panigrahi, K.C. 1961. *Chronology of the Bhauma-Karas and the Somavaṃśīs of Orissa*, Madras: M.L.J. Press.

———1981. *History of Orissa*, Cuttack: Kitab Mahal.

Puruṣottamacandrikā Śaka 1766 (CE 1844) [or *Śrīkṣetradhāmer Vivaraṇ*] by Bhavanicaran Bandyopadhyay, Calcutta.

Rajaguru, S.N. 1966. *Inscriptions of Orissa*, vol. 4, Bhubaneswar: State Museum.

Rath, B.K. 1983. *Cultural History of Orissa (A.D. 855-1110)*, Delhi: Sundeep Prakashan.

Roy, N.B. 1942. 'Jajnagar Expedition of Sulṭān Fīrūz Shāh—English Translation and Text of an Extract from Sīrat-i-Fīrūz Shāhī', in *Journal of the Royal Asiatic Society of Bengal, Letters* 8, 57-98.

Sahu, N.K., P.K. Mishra and J.K. Sahu 1979. *History of Orissa*, Cuttack: Nalanda.

Sahu, N.K. 1977. 'Historical Geography', in M.N. Das (ed.), *Sidelights on History and Culture of Orissa*, Cuttack: Vidyapuri, 30-43.

Sarma, B.K. 1983. *The History of Somavaṃśī Rule in Orissa*, Calcutta: Punthi Pustak.

Sircar, D.C. 1971. *Studies in the Geography of Ancient and Medieval India*, 2nd rev. edn., Delhi: Motilal Banarsidass.

Stietencron, H. von 1978a. 'The Advent of Viṣṇuism in Orissa: An Outline of Its History According to Archaeological and Epigraphical Sources from the Gupta Period up to 1135 A.D.', in A. Eschmann, H. Kulke and G.C. Tripathy (eds.) 1978, 1-30.

———1978b. 'Early Temples of Jagannātha in Orissa: The Formative Phase', in A. Eschmann, H. Kulke and G.C. Tripathy (eds.) 1978, 61-74.

Tripathy, S. 1998. 'The Unique Neulpur Charter of Śubhākara II of the Bhauma-Kara Dynasty and a Local Tradition of Virajā-Kshetra', in *Orissa Historical Research Journal* 42, 35-46.

Wali, A. 1923, 'Life and Letters of Malik ʿAynuʾ l-Mulk Māhrū, and Side-lights on Firūz Shāh's Expeditions to Lakhnautī and Jājnagar', in *Journal of the Asiatic Society of Bengal, Letters* 19, 253-90.

CHAPTER 6

Contribution of Sarala Dasa to the Emergence of an 'Oriya Identity' and Its Localization

BASANTA KUMAR MALLIK

Participating in an 'identity discourse' is indeed a significant activity of the intellectual pursuit. Identity of a nation, a region or a community is very often determined by its civilization and culture. Not the concept but identities discriminate between the self and the others in a struggle against 'homogenization'. For minorities the imposition of a national identity is essentially tantamount to a choice between 'survival' through integration and cultural 'extinction'. On the other hand, the construction of one's own identity depends on particular contexts like cultural awakening, resurgence movements or the rise of one's own social group. In these cases the question of cultural identity may become so important that it occupies entirely the cognitive world of the community by edging out other issues. The present paper is an attempt to discuss the construction of an early Oriya cultural identity in Sarala Dasa's *Mahabharata* and its localization.

So far scholars studied the emergence of an Oriya identity mainly in the context of social and cultural movements within the colonial system of the nineteenth and early twentieth centuries. The study of 'Oriya nationalism' and 'Oriya identity' began in the late 1970s with two papers of G.N. Dash and J. Boulton and were followed by the studies of N. Mohanty, B.N. Mohapatra and H. Kulke.[1] A major emphasis of these studies were the literary activities of Oriya poets, the analysis of the Jagannatha temple chronicles and the Oriya language agitation of the Oriya movement in the late nineteenth and early twentieth centuries which finally led to the creation of a separate province of Orissa in 1936. The importance of the late nineteenth century for the emergence of an Oriya identity was again strengthened by B.N. Mohapatra in his study of Orissa's famous Kanchi-Kaveri legend in which he traced the growth and development of an Oriya ethnic and cultural consciousness. But his conclusion that 'no consciousness of cultural identity in the strong sense existed among Oriyas prior to the colonial period',[2] is difficult to accept.

[1]Dash 1978, 359-74; Boulton 1979, 228-60; Mohanty 1982; Mohapatra 1996, 203-4; Kulke 2001, 24-5.

[2]Mohapatra 1996, 206.

In his study on *Jagannatha and Oriya Nationalism* G.N. Dash pointed out that the emergence of an Oriya identity or, as he designated it, the 'formative phase of Oriya Nationalism can already be traced back to the late sixteenth century. In the pre-sixteenth century, however, the Orissan empire of the "imperial Gajapatis" at its best was a mixture of heterogeneous elements, bound together by the person or dynasty of a ruler, where several Aryan and Non-Aryan languages were spoken'. This situation, however, changed considerably in the late sixteenth century.[3] Nivedita Mohanty, in her important work, studied in detail the growth of Oriya language agitations and the Oriya movement in the late nineteenth and early twentieth centuries.[4]

In his paper 'Historiography and Regional Identity', H. Kulke rightly emphasized historiography as another important factor of an emerging Oriya identity. Puri's temple chronicles of the late sixteenth to early nineteenth centuries, generally known as the *Rajabhoga Itihasa* of the *Madala Panji* and related texts have considerably enriched the emerging Oriya identity. Their main contribution was the creation of a hitherto unknown perception of the greatness of Orissan history on the one hand and the universalization of Orissa's regional history in the wider context of India's traditional history on the other. By far the most important influence, however, was exercised by these chronicles by their construction of a Puri and Jagannatha centred perception of Orissa's past.[5] This paper will go even a step further and show that the emergence of an early Oriya identity can be traced back to Sudramuni Sarala Dasa and the efflorescence of the Oriya literature since late fifteenth century.

Regional cultural identities in India emerged in a hierarchically structured society which was characterized by the cultural hegemony of a few over the masses. The specific forms of economic, social and cultural stratification and inequitable access to the means of production and learning were based on the *varna* system. As a system of privileges for a few and deprivation of the many on the basis of birth, the *varna* ideology was contested by the Bhakti movement of medieval India. It endeavoured the shaping of the society, culture, religion and literature and thus regenerated cultural identities. The 'Bhakti reformers' represented a general movement and were by no means confined to their region and language. The painful tenor of their writing and lives testifies their opposition to the social hierarchy and their unwillingness to exercise the art of pleasing the ruling class. The saints of medieval Orissa played a vital role in generating the spirit of equality and human dignity. They undermined the established tradition of writing in Sanskrit and composed their works in the language of the common people, i.e. Oriya. They agitated against superstitions preached by the orthodox priests and propagated that god can be prayed to in their colloquial language and worshipped in their heart and mind filled with *bhakti*.[6]

[3]Dash 1978, 359.

[4]Mohanty 1982.

[5]Kulke 2001, 24-5.

[6]Mallik 2004, 13-16.

Sudramuni Sarala Dasa, a cultivator and poet, composed the Oriya *Mahabharata* in the late fifteenth century in Jhankar, a village in present Jagatsinghpur district, quite far away from the royal court.[7] The orthodox pandits of medieval Orissa did not appreciate the efforts of Sudramunis and saints of the non-Brahman communities to render the main epics and Puranas into the vernacular. As they had to face humiliations from the learned pandits and to protect themselves against hostile criticism, they dedicated their writings to the gods and goddesses they believed in. The anti-caste pronouncement is very conspicuous in their writings and they renounced their original caste surnames and used 'Dasa' after their names, meaning 'servant' to gods and goddesses.[8] In this way they protested against caste surnames and the discriminative character of the Brahmanical order. They were not satisfied only by rendering the Sanskrit works into Oriya, they also attempted to participate in the Veda discussions held in the Jagannatha temple of Puri. The most outspoken and revolutionary amongst them, Balarama Dasa and Achyutananda Dasa, even challenged the authority of the pandits and their prohibition to allow Sudras to study Vedas and Dharmasastras.

The fifteenth century was an era of political and cultural awakening in the history of Orissa. During this time, Gajapati Kapilendra Dev achieved political glory for Orissa by extending the Orissan empire from Ganges to Kaveri and his contemporary poet Sudramuni Sarala Dasa rephrased the great Indian epics in the language of the common people of Orissa. Through them he became the pioneer of a movement protesting against the domination of a section of the people who monopolized learning and education. With this social message in Oriya language Sarala Dasa laid the foundation of an Oriya identity by creating a perennial fountain of literary forms and traditions with distinct characteristics that have come down to posterity as an ever widening stream. Three of his epics, the *Mahabharata*, the *Vichitra Ramayana* and the *Chandi Purana* are so far known, out of which the *Mahabharata* is regarded as his *magnum opus*.

Sarala Dasa was born in an age when in almost every Indian language Puranic literature was composed in the vernacular and when the society and literature of Orissa, too, were taking a new shape. By this time, Oriya literature had attained its fully developed shape and the writers preserved the sacred events of gods and goddesses in the form of their own literature. Sarala Dasa accepted the challenge of the time and played a vital role in this development. The exact date of his birth is unknown but can safely be placed in the second half of the fifteenth century CE. Many scholars confirm the contemporaneity of Sarala Dasa with the reign of Kapilendra Dev, the famous Gajapati king of Orissa, who ruled from CE 1435 to 1467 .[9] The *Adiparva* of Sarala *Mahabharata*

[7]Ibid., 17.

[8]Mohanty 1995, 19.

[9]Mahatab 1959, 263; see also Mansingh 1962, 47-8; Panigrahi 1975, 13; Mukherjee 1981, 7; Das 1982, 59.

opens with a long invocation of Lord Jagannatha of Puri who by then already enjoyed the unquestioned supremacy amongst the Hindu gods and goddesses of Orissa. It describes the manifold powers and qualities of Jagannatha and the innumerable offerings to him which destroyed the sins of the *Kali* age. Since the Brahmans were still adherents of Sanskrit literature and the Brahmanical social order, they had an aversion against the spoken language and a poet from the lower social strata. Sarala Dasa very often tells us that he was an uneducated Sudra cultivator and a man of no importance. But posterity did not accept his low self-estimation, but regarded him as a man of vision who responded to call of the time and initiated hitherto unknown changes in the cultural identity of Orissa.

The Gajapati rulers used to patronize the Sanskrit literature of their court poets. But Sarala Dasa deviated from the tradition of writing religious texts in Sanskrit and therefore did not receive any political patronage. He composed his *Mahabharata*, the *Vichitra Ramayana* and the *Chandi Purana* in his village Jhankar, quite far away from the royal court and the state capital. From a writer of the Oriya *Mahabharata* one would have expected to translate the Sanskrit original or at least to follow it up closely, but he did neither. With innumerable omissions, deviations and creations of his own he borrowed merely the bare outline of the original *Mahabharata*. For example, although Sarala Dasa has accepted the number of eighteen *Parva*s of the Sanskrit *Mahabharata*, he altered and changed the titles of the *Parva*s. In those cases which are largely his own creations he omitted numerous mythological episodes, fables, moral sayings, and philosophical discourses of the original. He even disposed of the entire *Bhagavata Gita* by making only a reference to it in two verses. He seems to have considered the *Gita* as 'an interpolation serving the needs of the upper strata of society'.[10] On the other side, he narrates numerous stories which cannot be traced in the Sanskrit *Mahabharata*. For example, the story of the Jhimiti game as the cause of the Mahabharata war,[11] the story of a jackal and king relating to land grants and wasteland management,[12] the story of King Duryodhana's crossing the river of blood after the war,[13] the story of *Amavasya Kanya* and widow remarriage,[14] the episode of the mango and Draupadi's intense love for Arjuna[15] and particularly the detailed description of the tribal origin of Jagannatha.[16] In this way, Sarala incorporated his own imagination and local Oriya traditions in the pan-Indian *Mahabharata*.

The poets of the pre-Sarala period devoted their writing exclusively to religious themes. Their works never contained the non-religious themes like

[10]Kosambi 1962, 14-18.
[11]*Sarala Mahabharata* (*Adiparva*), I, 443.
[12]Panigrahi 975, 49-50.
[13]Ibid., 56-8.
[14]*Sarala Mahabharata* (*Adiparva*), I, 112-19.
[15]Ibid. (*Vana Parva*) 1, 578-9.
[16]Ibid. (*Musali Parva*), 50-61, 78-86.

state, economy and social problems. Sarala Dasa deviated from this tradition, as his writings contain detailed accounts of the material life of the people and their socio-economic problems. For example, he was sympathetic towards Ekalavya and Karna who were discriminated in the *Mahabharata* because of their different social status based on birth. And his description of the conflict between the Brahmans and Chandalas in the *Adiparva* of his *Mahabharata* depicts caste tensions in medieval Orissa.[17] Moreover, Sarala Dasa did neither believe in rituals, pilgrimages or *yajnas* nor did he advocate the rules of *Sastras* or compromise with the pandits.[18] He criticized and, in his own way, revolted against the exploitative orthodox tradition.

Sarala Dasa's most important contribution to the Oriya identity was his efforts to revive and preserve the original tribal essence of the Jagannatha cult, which faced a serious threat in the process of orthodox Hinduization of the deity and its rituals in his time. He propounded the roots of the Jagannatha cult by strengthening its relations with the tribes of Orissa and protested against the submergence of Jagannatha into the fold of Brahmanism. In his *Musali Parva* Sarala Dasa created new stories by virtue of his poetic imagination and identified Lord Jagannatha as the tribal deity Sabari Narayan. He was worshipped in the form of a tree and, later on, in a piece of a blue stone (*Nila Madhava*) by the tribal chief Jara.[19] In the *Sabha Parva* Sarala described the *pitha* of Sabari Narayan as a great shrine. *Anna* (rice), meat of deer and rhinoceros were offered to the deity by *tantric* rituals and there was no discrimination of caste in the shrine. The *Daitas* or non-Brahman priests of the Jagannatha temple of Puri are believed to be the descendants of Vidyapati, the Brahman minister of King Galamadhava and Lalita, the daughter of the Sabara chief Jara, who got married to each other in the forest before the god Nila Madhava. There is another interesting episode in the famous Indradyumna legend of Sarala *Mahabharata*. In the *Musali Parva* Jagannatha emphatically advocates the cause of the aboriginal Sabaras. Here, the two legends of Nila Madhava and of Jagannatha are combined in a pair of opposing paradigms of negative and positive royal attitudes towards tribes. In the legend of Nila Madhava, King Galamadhava kills the innocent Sabaras, the sons of Krishna and is therefore cursed by the god that his royal line will become extinct. In the legend of Jagannatha, King Indradyumna acknowledges the Sabara chieftain as 'King of the Forest' and as the 'root' (*mula*) of the Jagannatha cult. Hence, Indradyumna is favoured by the god.[20]

The moral of the legend is quite obvious: a king who is harsh to the tribes evokes divine wrath and falls from power. On the other hand, the king who is friendly towards the Sabaras and other tribes wins the favour of Jagannatha and remains in power. Without the cooperation of the Sabaras there is no

[17]Ibid. (*Adi Parva*) II, 693-705.
[18]Ibid. (*Bhisma Parva*), 2, 3, 142.
[19]Ibid. (*Musali Parva*), 38.
[20]Ibid., 147; see Geib 1975, 181.

Jagannatha cult and without Jagannatha there is no kingship. These legendary explanations of the Jagannatha cult embody a unique cultural synthesis of indigenous and pan-Indian traditions in the land of Orissa. Sarala depicted the Jagannatha cult as a form of protest and retrieved its close relation with the neglected tribes and other depressed classes.

Sarala Dasa was also a champion of cultural and social upliftment of women. His contribution to the elimination of superstitions and the elevation of the status of the women had a deep impact on Oriya society. Sarala's deviation from the original *Mahabharata* had obvious social connotations and intended to communicate a clear message to the society. For instance, there was a widespread superstition that a person who weds a girl, born on the *amavasya* day (the last day of the dark fortnight), does not survive. Moreover, prohibition of widow re-marriage prevailed at all levels of the society. Due to the extensive warfare of Gajapati Kapilendra Dev there must have been a large number of widows of soldiers who encountered social indignity and ostracism, besides their personal grief and sufferings. By stating against the original *Mahabharata* that Gandhari (the princess of Gandhara who later became queen of Dhritarashtra of Hastinapura) was born on the *amavasya* day, the poet intended not only to discourage the superstition but also to change the society. Since nobody wanted to marry her, on Vyasa's advice she was first married to a *Sahada* tree (*Streblus asper* Lour.) and then her marriage was solemnized with Dhritarashtra. Sarala Dasa was thus not simply a poet, but also a social reformer conveying his messages through his writing. Besides his endeavour to re-establish the pride and honour of the neglected womenfolk, Sarala Dasa 'empowered' the women characters of his epics and made some of them even superior to their male counterparts. With a remarkable note of dissent he composed his epics almost in opposition to the traditional pattern of patriarchal writings and elevated the status of the female characters of his epics. The role of Sita in killing *Sahasrasira*, the thousand headed Ravana, in his *Vichitra Ramayana*, or of Durga in killing Mahishasura in his *Chandi Purana* and the role of Draupadi in the destruction of the Kauravas in his *Mahabharata* provide an insight into his reformatory quest.[21]

Sarala Dasa is thus known as the pioneer in writing epic texts in Oriya language. He was the poet who laid the foundation stone of regional literature in eastern India. He was a man of the villages to which he owed all his nurture and it was his village where he composed the three major works. It was the goddess of his village who endowed him with the sensibilities of a poet to write the epics as a Sudramuni in Oriya, far away from the traditional centres of learning. To get them recognized by the readers of the contemporary literary taste, was not an easy task but a remarkable contribution to the emergence of an Oriya cultural identity. Through his work Jagannatha became associated with the cultural plurality and people of all denominations of Orissa, from tribal to Brahmanical. The great *bhaktakavi*s of sixteenth and seventeenth

[21] Rath 1997, 533; see also Mallik 2004, 89-91.

centuries accentuated the great tradition inaugurated by Sarala Dasa which envisaged the rise of a strong Oriya consciousness in the pre-colonial Orissa. His writings were a major breakthrough in the history of Oriya language and literature and his literary creations were a challenge against various forms of orthodox hegemony and deprivation.

In the context of this paper it is particularly relevant that Sarala Dasa refers in his poems to a large number of local places in Orissa and narrates various stories of their sacredness thus contributing to the emergence of local and subregional identities. In his *Mahabharata* he described places like Vijayanagar, Mallikarjuna, Gokarneswar, Chilika, Ramachandi, Konarka, Ekamra Kshetra and Kapilasa, to mention only a few. By virtue of his imaginative power, he created and associated stories and cultural attributes with these places. In the *Sabha Parva* he relates the origin of the Vijayanagar kingdom. On his way back to Ayodhya and after having killed Ravana, Rama came to Sri Giri, identified with Sri Sailam which belonged to the Orissan empire during the time of Sarala. When Rama desired to take rest on the hill, Hanuman immediately constructed a fort. Since Rama entered the region or 'appeared' (in Oriya *bije*) there, the name of the place came to be known as Vijayanagar.[22]

Sarala Dasa's account of Sri Sailam shows also interesting similarities of its presiding deity Siva-Mallikarjuna, with the tribal traditions of Puri. The inhabitants of Sri Sailam belong to the Chenchu tribes which believe that Siva once came there for hunting and fell in love with a Chenchu girl and married her. Since then Siva is worshipped by the Chenchus under the name of Mallikarjuna. They observe all his festivals and rituals whereas his priests belong to the Jangamas, a Sudra caste.[23] Sri Sailam thus depicts striking similarities with Puri, its Sabara tradition and the role which the Daita priests play in its rituals.

In the *Adiparva* Sarala Dasa describes the origin of the deity Gokarneswar on the sacred mountain Mahendragiri, which was already well known in Sanskrit sources like the *Mahabharata* and *Raghuvamsa* of Kalidasa.[24] Sarala Dasa relates that Arjuna had climbed up the Mahendragiri to kill a rhinoceros but, by a mistake, killed a holy cow with his arrow. When he carried away its dead body with another arrow, different parts of it fell down on the earth. Wherever these mutilated parts touched the earth, Sivalingas emerged. The place where the head of the sacred cow fell down a most sacred *linga* appeared, popularly known as 'Gokarneswar'. Then all gods and *rishis* assembled on the Mahendra mountain to rescue Arjuna from the sin he committed by killing a cow and performed a *yajna*. When Brahma searched for a person to continue the worship of the Gokarneswar *linga*, Sahadev immediately brought a Sabara who later on came to be known as a Bauri and Kalindi Bipra. After Brahma offered him a sacred thread he settled down with his kith and kin, known as

[22] *Sarala Mohabharata* (*Sabha Parva*), I, 546.
[23] Ibid. (*Vana Parva*), II, 42.
[24] Mishra 2006, 253.

Bauri *sasana*.[25] The Bauris were a tribe in south India and Orissa. In the process of transition from tribe to caste the Bauris seem to have emerged from the Sabara tribe. The episode of killing a sacred cow by Arjuna might have been a brain-child of Sarala Dasa's imagination. But the appointment of the Bauris as the priests of Gokarneswar is socially relevant till today as priests of different scheduled castes are still known as *Kalindi Vaishnavas*.

Sarala Dasa relates also his own story of the origin of the Chilika Lake. In the west of Puri there was a large settlement of Nishadas (hunter tribe) known as Nishadpuri. Participating in a war between the disguised elephant and tortoise, Garuda crashed on Nishadpuri which was completely destroyed. Out of the great hollow which was caused by this occurrence, a great lake emerged that came to be known as Chilika Lake.[26] The interesting information we can derive from this story is that the present Chilika region was once inhabited by tribes.

Sarala Dasa's story of Ramachandi near Konarka contains another important information. It narrates that Rama installed an auspicious pillar on the sea shore at this place for the construction of a bridge to Lanka. But since the place and direction were not suitable to reach Lanka, he moved further to the south. The people, however, started worshipping this pillar as goddess Ramachandi. This tradition is very significant as the cult of Jagannatha, too, is linked with the worship of the pillar goddess Khambeswari or Stambheswari.[27] Today, the goddess Ramchandi is worshipped as ten-handed Mahishasuramardini Durga in her temple, constructed in the nineteenth century. But during the time of Sarala Dasa the goddess was worshipped in form of a pillar[28] which indicates the existence of wooden pillar deities worshipped by tribes in the places near Puri with its famous *daru devatas*.

Sarala Dasa associates several episodes with the Konarka Kshetra. Amongst them, two appear to be particularly important. Firstly, Brahma, the creator of the world and author of the Vedas, kept the Veda manuscripts on the seashore during his bath in the ocean near the sacred Chandrabhaga River. But the demon Sankhasura stole the Vedas and concealed them at a hidden place in the ocean. After bath, when he saw what meanwhile had happened to the Vedas, Brahma was greatly annoyed and worried. He prayed to Vishnu who then, in disguise of a fish, searched around at various places in the Ocean and finally rescued the Vedas from Sankhasura after killing him.[29] Secondly, Sarala Dasa relates the episode of Krishna's son Samba who worshipped the Sun god Surya at Konarka to get cured from leprosy.[30] In addition, the *Kapila Samhita*, composed about hundred fifty years after Sarala's *Mahabharata*, relates that

[25] *Sarala Mahabharata* (*Adiparva*), II, 619-35.
[26] Ibid. (*Vana Parva*), II, 153.
[27] Ibid., 106; see Eschmann 1978, 79-97.
[28] Mishra 2006, 263.
[29] *Sarala Mahabharata* (*Udjoga Parva*), 384-91.
[30] Ibid. (*Vana Parva*), II, 103ff.

Samba was not only cured after worshipping the Surya but also discovered an idol of Surya in the river Chandrabhaga and built a temple for it at Konarka.[31]

These episodes are significant for the socio-cultural traditions of Orissa and the local identity of Konarka. In the first episode Sarala Dasa indicated that the sacred knowledge of the Vedas was exclusively in the possession of a privileged social group and that a militant leader of the deprived section of the society faced punishment of death when he tried to acquire the source of knowledge. The second episode, further elaborated by the *Kapila Samhita*, enhanced the sacredness of the Chandrabhaga where large numbers of people take their holy dip, as once started by Brahma.

The episodes of Ekamra Kshetra (Bhubaneswar) as related by Sarala Dasa have a close similarity with the great myth of killing of Mahishasura by Durga. According to *Vana Parva* and *Swargarohan Parva*, the two demon brothers Kriti and Basan were empowered with blessings of Ekamranath or Siva. In course of time, they became ambitious to rule over the heaven and defeated the gods and plundered the treasury of Kubera, the god of wealth. As the people of Ekamra became frightened Siva persuaded Parvati to kill these two demon brothers. In disguise of a beautiful milkmaid, Parvati offered curd to them. Thereupon the two brothers fell in love and proposed to marry her. Parvati agreed under the condition that Ekamra Kshetra is shown to her by them while standing on their shoulders. Both the brothers immediately agreed. But when Parvati, in her disguise as a milkmaid, climbed on their shoulders they were unable to carry her weight and with her divine power Parvati pressed them into the deepness of the earth.[32]

Kapilas is a famous sacred complex of the Saivism in Orissa. There are three stone inscriptions, inscribed on the Kapilas temple on top of the hill during the reign of the Ganga king Narasimha Deva. One of them, written in CE 1246, states the name of the deity as *Kailasa-Sikharesvara*, whereas the one of the year CE 1253 gives the name as *Kailasa Deva*. Sarala Dasa narrates that Siva gave away all his belonging and that finally he even did not possess a piece of cloth to wear. Siva was then moving with an old bullock on the river bank of Chitrotpala where Sikhara, a member of the Sabara tribe, took care of him. Being satisfied with helpfulness of Sikhara, Siva assumed the name Sikhareswar and retreated to the top of the mountain Kapilasa.[33]

Many of these legends appear to be Sarala Dasa's own creation. But even in those cases where they were already locally prevalent, they received new inspiration through Sarala's imagination. But most important in our context is the fact that Sarala Dasa ascribed the origin of quite a few Orissan deities to a tribal origin, either to have emerged directly from a tribe or to have been

[31] Mishra 2006, 263.

[32] *Sarala Mahabharata* (*Vana Parva*), II, 80ff.; see also (*Swargarohan Parva*), 35ff.

[33] Ibid. (*Vana Parva*), I, 96.

primarily worshipped by Sabaras or other tribes. Examples are the legends of Gokarneswar, of his own village deity Sarala Chandi, of Jagannatha and Sikhareswar. Enriching and creating new traditions in a synthesis of tribal, folk and Brahmanical traditions, Sarala Dasa contributed immensely to the emergence of local and subregional identities. The network of the sacred topography of Orissa in his writings served as a collecting screen for the integration and localization of pan-Indian traditions and thus for a further enrichment of local, subregional and regional traditions of Orissa.

REFERENCES

Boulton, J. 1979. 'Nationalism and Tradition in Orissa, with Special Reference to the Works of Phakirmohana Senapati', in R.J. Moore (ed.), *Tradition and Politics in South Asia*, Delhi: Vikas, 228-60.

Das, C. 1962. *A Glimpse into Oriya Literature*, Bhubaneswar: Orissa Sahitya Akademi.

Dash, G.N. 1978. 'Jagannatha and Oriya Nationalism', in A. Eschmann, H. Kulke and G.C. Tripathi (eds.), *The Cult of Jagannath and the Regional Tradition of Orissa*, Delhi: Manohar.

Eschmann, A. 1978. 'Hinduization of Tribal Deities in Orissa: The Sakta and Saiva Typology, in A. Eschmann, H. Kulke and G.C. Tripathi, op. cit., 79-97.

Geib, R. 1975. *Die Indradyumna-Legende. Ein Beitrag zur Geschichte des Jagannatha-Kultes*, Wiesbaden: Otto Harrassowitz.

Kosambi, D.D. 1962. *Myth and Reality*, Bombay: Popular Prakashan.

Kulke, H. 2001. 'Historiography and Regional Identity: The Case of the Temple Chronicles of Puri', in H. Kulke and B. Schnepel (eds), *Jagannath Revisited: Studying Society, Religion and the State in Orissa*, Delhi: Manohar, 211-26.

Mahatab, H.K. 1959. *History of Orissa*, vol. 1, Cuttack: Prajatantra Prachar Samiti.

Mallik, B.K. 2004. *Paradigms of Dissent and Protest: Social Movements in Eastern India (c. A.D. 1400-1700)*, Delhi: Manohar.

Mansingh, M. 1962. *A History of Oriya Literature*, Delhi: Sahitya Akademi, rpt. 2005.

Mishra, S. 2006. *Sarala Dasa: Eka Adhyayan*, Cuttack: Grantha Mandir.

Mohanty, N. 1982. *Oriya Nationalism: Quest for a United Orissa 1860-1936*, Delhi: Manohar.

Mohanty, S. 1995. *Oriya Sahityar Madhyaparva O Uttar Madhyaparva*, Cuttack: Cuttack Students Store.

Mohapatra, B.N. 1996. 'Ways of Belonging: The Kanchi Kaveri Legend and the Construction of Oriya Identity', in *Studies in History*, 12, 2, 204-21.

Mukherjee, P. 1981. *The History of the Gajapati Kings of Orissa*, Cuttack: Kitab Mahal.

Rath, B. 1997, 'Development of Oriya Literature (*c.* A.D. 1434-1803)', in P.K. Mishra and J.K. Samal (eds), *Comprehensive History and Culture of Orissa*, vol. II, 2, Delhi: Kaveri Books.

Sarala Mahabharata (*Adiparva, Bhisma Parva, Musali Parva, Sabha Parva, Swargarohan Parva, Vana Parva, Udjoga Parva*), ed. A.B. Mohanty, 1965, Bhubaneswar: Department of Cultural Affairs.

CHAPTER 7

Kosalananda Kavyam and the Making of a Rajput Dynasty: A Study of the Chauhans of Western Orissa*

SHISHIR KUMAR PANDA

In an excellent ethno-historical study, 'State Formation and Rajput Myth in Tribal Central India',[1] Surajit Sinha in 1962 demonstrated the emergence of princely states in late-medieval central and eastern India and their alleged Rajput affiliations. He analysed the emergence of the Munda Raj of Chhota Nagpur, the Bhumij state of Barabhum and the Raj Gond kingdom of Gondwana, all based on internal tribal development, 'invented' Rajput affiliation and Brahmanical association. These developments had several parallels in Orissa too, and processes of Rajputization may have been even more evident in western Orissa than in central India. Western Orissa is an excellent example which shows that Rajputization operated not only through ritual and social means, as Sinha shows, but also through the work of court poets who created a new reality of 'invented Rajputization' through literature.

THE PROBLEM

The Chauhan dynasty of South Koshala was an important ruling family of late-medieval Orissa and played a major role in shaping the history and culture of western Orissa. Since its foundation in the first half of the fourteenth century at Patnagarh, it extended its authority to Sambalpur, Sonepur and Khariar, regions where it established separate kingdoms. The claim of the Chauhan kings that they originate from the famous Rajput Chauhans of northern India was for the first time validated in CE 1663 by the court poet of Sambalpur, Gangadhar Mishra, through his Sanskrit work *Kosalananda Kavyam*.[2] Scholars working on the history of the Chauhan dynasty of western Orissa usually

*My thanks are due to Hermann Kulke for his constructive criticism and suggestions on an earlier draft of this chapter. However, I alone am responsible for the facts and opinions stated in it.

[1]Sinha 1962.

[2]Manuscript preserved in the Orissa State Museum, S. No. 43, Cat. No. SMS/12. In the present work I have used the recently published Oriya version of the *Kosalananda Kavyam* (henceforward *KK*); see Sahu Chopdar 2000.

accept the historical authenticity of the *Kosalananda Kavyam* as a reliable source for its descent from the Rajput Chauhans of northern India. In this chapter, I shall attempt to examine its historicity and the alleged Rajput origin of the Chauhans of western Orissa, their lineage and genealogy. A main emphasis will be on contextualizing the *Kosalananda Kavyam* in the history of Orissa and its Chauhan dynasties. Finally, I shall also consider how far its poet contributed to the emergence of a separate identity in western Orissa by designating the land Dakshina Koshala, thus reviving the cultural glory of ancient Koshala under the Chauhans.

ORIGIN OF THE HISTORICAL TRADITION IN SOUTH KOSHALA AND THE POET GANGADHAR MISHRA

The *Kosalananda Kavyam* of Gangadhar Mishra is the earliest historical work on the history of South Koshala in general and the history of its Chauhan dynasties in particular. Prior to this *kavya* no other historical writing on South Koshala is known, though we have a large number of inscriptions from the earlier ruling dynasties. For the first time in Orissan history, the *Kosalananda Kavyam* contains the legendary account of a ruling dynasty tracing its lineage back to a Rajput dynasty of northern India. In order to identify the origin of this tradition, we must examine the poet Gangadhar's own history.

In the last canto of his poem, Gangadhar mentions that he belongs to the Vajpayi family of learned scholars in a Brahman *sasana* village near Purushottamakshetra (Puri). His father Pandit Gopinath and grandfather Vidyakara were scholars and notable Smriti writers.[3] Since Puri was a centre of Sanskrit learning, the Chauhan king of Sambalpur, Baliar Singh, invited the reputed Sanskrit poet and scholar Gangadhar Mishra to his court. He settled him in Sambalpur by granting him land, a common practice among the ruling families since early-medieval times.[4] As a poet and scholar, Gangadhar must have known Puri's chronicle, the *Madala Panji*, and it seems very likely that he was also acquainted with the historical kavyas and Indian bardic literature, like the *Prithviraj Raso*,[5] *Hammira Mahakavya*[6] and *Prithviraj Vijaya*,[7] which glorify the valour and heroism of the Chauhan Rajputs of northern India and trace their Kshatriya ancestry back to the solar dynasty of Vedic fame.

For centuries Puri itself had been recognized as a famous *tirtha* and attracted large numbers of pilgrims, religious preachers and scholars from various parts of India. Inscriptional sources prove that pilgrims from northern India visited Puri as early as the ninth century CE.[8] From the period of Gangadhar, we know

[3]Mahapatra 1960, 'Introduction', p. CXXIX.

[4]Panda 1978-9, 25-35.

[5]Bardai n.d.

[6]Kirtane 1878.

[7]Ojha and Guleri 1941.

[8]Scholars like K.N. Mahapatra and A.K. Rath have suggested that pilgrims visited Puri

from the *chamu citaus* (royal letters) of the Khurda rajas that members of the royal family of Jaipur (Rajasthan) visited Puri in the seventeenth century.[9] By that time the fame of the Rajputs and their bardic literature had already spread to eastern India through Mansingh, Akbar's great General who defeated the Afghans in Bengal and Orissa in 1590 and 1592 and supported the renewal of the Jagannath cult by Ramachandra of Khurda. It is therefore quite likely that Gangadhar was influenced by the 'Rajput myth' and the works of the bards of Rajasthan as well as by the *Madala Panji* tradition of Puri[10] when he wrote the *Kosalananda Kavyam* to glorify his royal patron Baliar Singh of Sambalpur. The purpose of writing this *kavya*, as mentioned by the poet himself, was to obtain a rent-free village from the king: 'By worshipping the Goddess Kali and through her blessings I received patronage from Bali Singh and described his family history. Through the blessings of the mighty destiny, I was able to receive Khandapali (a village). The renowned King Bali Singh was born in the famous royal family. Due to prayer of Gangadhar, he donated a number of villages for his enjoyment of the revenue which also included Khandapali Puri.'[11]

CHANGING FACES OF THE *KOSALANANDA KAVYAM*: TEXTS AND CONTEXTS

The *kavya* was written in CE 1663 in Sanskrit and consisted originally of twenty-one cantos.[12] It describes the history of the Chauhan dynasty of Patnagarh from Ramadeva, its founder, to the rule of King Baliardeva of Sambalpur. The opening canto deals with the political condition of South Koshala before the rule of the Chauhans.[13] It was ruled by Rana Simha, a powerful despotic king who was ousted by the Gajapati king of Orissa. He was succeeded by eight Mallik chiefs who ruled collectively and, in turn, were overthrown by the Chauhan prince Ramadeva.

The second canto desribes the family history and ancestry of Ramadeva,[14] which is traced back to the epic Somavamsa or lunar dynasty. Gangadhar constructed a long genealogy of altogether twenty-four Somavamsi kings

as early as the seventh century CE. (Mahapatra 1954, 17; Rath 1987, 92). But it is more convincing to accept the date suggested by H. von Stietencron (1978).

[9]We have two *chamu citaus* (royal letters) collected from the temple archives of Puri relating to the visit of members of the royal families of Jaipur (Rajasthan) to the Jagannath temple, dated CE 1740 (No. 60, MP 2, 8, 13R and No. 61), *Jagannatha Sthalavrttantam*, translation by S.N. Rajaguru, Orissa Collection in the South Asia Institute, Heidelberg University.

[10]For *Madali Panji* see Kulke 1987, 1-24.

[11]*KK*, 251, verse 3,4.

[12]For details of the text and translation, see *KK*.

[13]Ibid., 1-6.

[14]Ibid., 10-14.

followed by twenty-four Chauhan kings of northern India from Manikya Chauhan to Prithviraj Chauhan, who was killed by the Yavanas. Because of internecine wars, scions of the dynasty migrated to different parts of northern India and established their kingdoms there. Alhanadeva became the founder of the Mainpuri line of the Rajput Chauhans. Visaladeva, the tenth descendant of this line, was killed by a Muslim ruler of Delhi. His wife was at that time pregnant and gave birth to a son named Rama. While on a pilgrimage Rama and his mother reached the Koshala country, where they stayed with a Brahman family at Patnanagara.

From the third to the seventeenth cantos the *kavya* describes at length Ramadeva's youth and his capture of the throne of Patnagarh.[15] We are told that once a white tiger created terror in the Koshala region and the ministers declared that whoever killed the tiger would be made king of Patnagarh. Ramadeva, the valiant Chauhan prince, killed the white tiger, collected its tail, nails, nose and ears, and presented them before the assembly of the people. The assembly was convinced of his heroic act and declared him ruler of Patnagarh. Thereafter, the poet gives a detailed description of the coronation ceremony of Ramadeva, his pilgrimage to Puri, his marriage to a niece of the Gajapati king, his return journey to Patnagarh through Sonepur, and his achievements as a king.

At the end of the seventeenth canto, the genealogy of the nine Chauhan kings of Patnagarh from Ramadeva to Hiradeva is given.[16] The last four cantos, eighteen to twenty-one, narrate the foundation of the Sambalpur kingdom by Balaramadeva and his four successors up to Baliardeva, at whose court Gangadhar wrote his *kavya*.[17]

The original *kavya* of Gangadhar Mishra underwent several changes through interpolations and additions in later days. In 1700 another poet, Gangadhar Guru, added an additional canto, consisting of several hundred *shlokas*.[18] No details about this poet are known, but he mentions in the sixth *shloka* that he composed the additional canto for the presentation of the *kavya* at the court of Gajapati king of Puri, Divyasimhadeva (1688-1716). In this additional canto, he briefly describes again the rule of all the Chauhan kings from Ramadeva to Baliaradeva and adds the story of the succeeding kings of Sambalpur, Ratan Singh and Chhatra Sai. The original *kavya* and Guru's poems are more or less identical, except for a few minor interpolations and the additional canto.[19]

Thereafter, from 1870 to 1945, various copies of *Kosalananda Kavyam* were reproduced by court pandits of Patnagarh, Sonepur, Bolangir and Khariar.[20] Their authors retained the main theme and the Rajput origin of the Chauhans

[15]Ibid., 20-193.
[16]Ibid., 192-3.
[17]Ibid., 200-50.
[18]As mentioned by Sahu and Chopdar 2000, 251-9.
[19]Ibid., 251.
[20]Ibid., 1-11.

but added several additional stories which will be discussed in the following pages. Moreover, one can observe variations in the genealogical lists of different branches of the Chauhan rulers of western Orissa. All this points to a revival and proliferation of the Rajput myth at the courts of western Orissa during the late-colonial period. It flourished not only in Patnagarh and Sambalpur but later on also in Sonepur and Khariar.

Among these versions of *Kosalananda Kavyam*, the largest number of distortions and interpolations are found in the Sonepur Durbar Manuscript. This was prepared by Sri Chintamani Nanda of Sonepur and published in the name of Maharaja Biramitro Singhdeo in 1929.[21] In the original *kavya*, the origin of the dynasty is described in the second canto, whereas in the Sonepur version it has been extended to the third and fourth cantos, thus raising their number from twenty-one to twenty-three cantos. Further, we find some new narratives, for example, about the enmity between Prithviraj and Jayachandra, the Svayamvara ceremony and abduction of Sanjukta and the agnikula theory of the origin of the Rajputs. They seem to have been derived from the bardic literature of Rajasthan like *Prithviraj Vijaya* of Jayanaka.[22] It seems that the Sonepur pandits were well acquainted with these details and interpolated them into the original manuscript in order to validate further the Rajput origin of the Chauhans of western Orissa and of Sonepur in particular. Moreover, we find a different genealogical story in the Sonepur edition. Here, it is mentioned that after the death of Visaladeva, the tenth descendant of the Rajput dynasty of Mainpuri, his pregnant wife fled to Patna kingdom, where she took shelter with a Brahman family and gave birth to Ramadeva, a significant derivation from the original *kavya* regarding the migration of Chauhans to western Orissa.

In the post-independence period the first initiative for re-editing the text was taken by the Sri Jagannatha Sanskrit University, Puri. It was published under the editorship of Niranjan Kar under the title *Kosalananda Mahakavyam* in 1994.[23] The editor produced the full texts of the original manuscript as well as the published Sonepur version in Sanskrit with an English introduction but without translation. More recently, in 2000, J.K. Sahu and D. Chopdar[24] of the Department of History, Sambalpur University, again published the *Kosalananda Kavyam*. They undertook the painstaking work of compiling the Sanskrit texts from all the available versions of the manuscripts and of providing an Oriya translation. Further, they wrote a detailed historical note on the history of the manuscripts, the historical geography of South Koshala, the origin of the Chauhan dynasty and their history at Patna and Sambalpur. This is the most exhaustive and detailed reproduction of all the manuscripts available so far.

[21] Singhdeo 1929.

[22] Sahu and Chopdar, op. cit.

[23] Kar 1994.

[24] Sahu and Chopdar 2000.

KOSALANANDA KAVYAM AS A SOURCE FOR THE RAJPUT ORIGIN OF THE CHAUHANS: A SURVEY

Apart from the *Kosalananda Kavyam*, the earliest reference to the history of the ruling family of Patna-Sambalpur is to be found in the narrative account of T. Motte who visited Sambalpur in 1766.[25] He stated that a group of Hindus from Sambhar in the province of Ajmer went on a pilgrimage to Jagannath at Puri. On their return journey the whole party was murdered except for a pregnant woman who escaped to Sambalpur. She supported herself by begging and subsequently gave birth to a son. He grew up, and since he showed all the qualities of a prince, the king adopted him as his successor. When he came to the throne, he built a palace and called it Sambalpur after the home of his father in Rajputana. Motte may have collected his information from the court pandits. But since he did not mention the *Kosalananda Kavyam* and its historical narrations, it is more likely that his writing was based on oral information which he collected during his stay at Sambalpur.

Subsequently, we find a version of the *Kosalananda Kavyam* in a Hindi work, *Jaya Chandrika*, written in 1782 by Prahllad Dubey, a Brahman court poet of the Sarangagarh zamindar.[26] The main aim of his *kavya* was to highlight and glorify his masters, the chiefs of Sarangagarh who had helped the Sambalpur kings Chhatra Sai and Jayant Singh to regain their throne. Regarding the ancestry of the Chauhans of Sambalpur, his story is similar to that of Gangadhar Mishra. He designated Ramadeva as 'Ramaideva' (the term in the local dialect for Ramadeva), a scion of the Chauhan dynasty of Garh Sambar. However, regarding the accession of Ramadeva to the Patnagarh throne, he gave a completely different story. Ramadeva is said to have captured the throne by killing seven Malliks except his mentor Chakradhar Panigrahi, the chief Mallik. Further, Prahllad Dubey's work contains a rather confusing and defective genealogy of the Chauhans. As a result, modern scholars have generally rejected his *Jaya Chandrika* as a genuine source of Chauhan history.[27]

But Charles Grant in 1870, in the *Central Provinces Gazetteer*,[28] and Major H.B. Impey in 1863, in his 'Notes on Gurhjat State of Patnagarh'[29] repeated this new story of 'Ramadeva's rise to power'. They mention that the pregnant wife of Hitambar Singh, the Rajput king of Sambhar, fled to Patnagarh, where she gave birth to Ramadeva, who later captured its throne by killing eight Malliks. They seem to have collected their information from the *Jaya Chandrika* of Prahllad Dubey.

A different origin for the Chauhans is referred to in a report of Sir Richard Temple from 1863.[30] He states that 'the Sambalpur and Patna rajas are

[25]Motte 1953.

[26]S.P. Dash 1969, 189-95.

[27]Sahu 1953, Appendix I, 14.

[28]Grant 1870, 393-4.

[29]Impey 1953.

[30]Temple 1863.

sometimes said to have descended from or related to the royal or independent Haihayavamsi dynasty of Ratanpur, which was formerly the capital of Chhattisgarh'.[31] Sir Richard may have collected this information from the Ratanpur durbar of the Haihayavamsi kings, who also claim Rajput origins, although not through the Chauhans.

The British Gazetteers of L.S.S. O'Malley (1909)[32] and L.E.B. Cobden Ramsay in 1910[33] also mention that the Chauhans came from Sambar. It seems that they followed the writings of Charles Grant and Major Impey and that they too had no access to the original *Kosalananda Kavyam*. In all versions of the original *kavya* it is mentioned that the widowed queen was given shelter by a Brahman, but in these colonial writings it is always a Binjhal tribal. Moreover, Cobden Ramsay reports yet another new story of Ramadeva's birth.[34] He states that Hamiradeva fled from Garh Sambhar and established himself at Manikgarh fort near Khariar. But from other sources it is known that Hamiradeva, a scion of Prithviraj from a separate branch of the Rajput dynasty at Ranthambor, committed suicide after being defeated by Alaud-din Khalji in CE 1301.[35] Before going into battle Hamiradeva took leave of his seven queens and told them that if his messenger pigeons returned without him, they should acknowledge his death on the battlefield. When the pigeons returned without him, six of his queens committed suicide by drowning themselves in the Ramadraha (lake) near Narsimhanath temple to the north of Patnagarh. The remaining pregnant queen was found wandering in the jungles on the border between Patna and Khariar. She was cared for by a Binjhal and in due course gave birth to Ramadeva. Ramadeva put an end to the rule of the eight Malliks by killing them and establishing his supremacy over eighteen forts (garhs) and thus expanded the Patna kingdom. The thrust of the story is that the Khariar kingdom was founded by Ramadeva's father, Hamiradeva, which indicates that Cobden Ramsay most likely collected his information from Khariar sources.

Apart from Khariar's claim that the Chauhans founded their first kingdom in its territory, the Chauhan family of Sonepur also tried to legitimize their Rajput origins through an invented family history. They even engaged B.C. Mazumdar, an advocate and historian from Calcutta, to write their history in 1911. He tells us that 'the legendary account of Chauhan rajas is that one Humeru of the family of Prithviraj of Delhi, having lost his position at Mainpuri in upper India during the time of Mohammedan rulers, came with his queens to the borders of Patna state and established a little principality of his own in that locality'.[36] Although he 'reconfirmed' the Rajput origin of the Chauhans

[31] Ibid., 8.
[32] O'Malley 1909, 21-3.
[33] Cobden Ramsay 1910.
[34] Ibid., 284-5.
[35] Sharma 1959, 131-2.
[36] Mazumdar 1911, 44-5.

from north India, he rightly raised a question: 'how this Rajput adventurer came upon this far off tract after travelling many hundred miles through rugged hills and dense forests is not easy to ascertain'.[37]

In 1925, Mazumdar, in his work *Orissa in the Making*,[38] accepted without any objections O'Malley's and Cobden Ramsay's versions of the Rajput origin of the Chauhans of Sonepur. He stated again, 'so early as the twelfth or thirteenth A.D. one Humeru of the family of the Chauhan Rajputs of Mainpuri in the United Provinces came to Patna with his wife'.[39] Regarding the foundation of Chauhan rule in Patna, he followed the story of Prahllad Dubey of the year 1782: 'The son of Humeru born in Patna State became by his mythical powers the chief of the eight Malliks who had the government of Patna and Sambalpur in their hands and thus established the Chohan rule in the Koshala country.'[40]

It is interesting to note that although Mazumdar was writing about the Rajput origins of the Chauhans, he spoke of 'legendary accounts'. This shows his reluctance to accept them as historical facts, but obviously he followed the writings of Major Impey in order to satisfy his patrons at the Sonepur durbar. However, at the height of the national independence movement he obviously avoided linking the rise of the Chauhans with the killing of eight indigenous local leaders and spoke instead of Ramadeva's 'mythical power' which brought him to power.

In 1928, R.D. Banerji, one of the earliest scholars of Orissan history to pursue a scientific method and analysis, for the first time raised doubts about the Rajput origins of the Chauhan dynasty of Sambalpur and Patna. In his seminal article, 'Rajput Origin in Orissa',[41] he pointed out the parallels with an alleged Rajput claim of the Vizianagaram ruling family and the Bhanjas of Mayurbhanj and Keonjhar. He wrote his article at a time when he was just completing the manuscript of his monumental *History of Orissa*,[42] which was published in two volumes in 1930-1. On the basis of his thorough study of inscriptional sources, he unveiled the indigenous tribal origin of many ruling dynasties of early Orissa, particularly of the various Bhanja dynasties. Of the alleged Rajput origin of the Chauhans, he remarked: 'The chiefs of the Patna-Sambalpur-Sonepur group were descended from a pilgrim of some unknown caste who came on pilgrimage from Sambhar to Jagannath in the earlier part of the sixteenth century, founded a kingdom which later on became powerful and began to claim Rajput origin and who, with the help of British Gazetteer writers, have now become the agents of Prithiviraj II of Delhi and Ajmer.'[43]

[37] Ibid.
[38] Mazumdar 1925.
[39] Ibid., 219.
[40] Ibid., 220.
[41] Banerji 1928, 285-91.
[42] Banerji 1930-1.
[43] Banerji 1928, 290.

Banerji thus rejected the Rajput claim of Orissa's Chauhan dynasty but accepted the 'pilgrim theory' as known since T. Motte. In this context it is interesting to note that neither Mazumdar nor Banerji mention the *Kosalananda Kavyam*. They seem to have used exclusively the Gazetteers compiled by Grant, Impey, O'Malley and Cobden Ramsay.

Rama Chandra Mallick's *Samkshipta Kosala Itihasa*,[44] published in 1931, contains again a different genealogical list of the Chauhan kings from Ramaideva (Ramadeva) to Narasimha, which also does not tally with the original manuscript of *Kosalananda Kavyam*. Regarding the ancestry of Ramadeva, he seems to have followed Cobden Ramsay. But he invented new place names, names of queens and details of the tribal people who took care of Ramadeva. As he called Khariar the first kingdom of the Chauhans in South Koshala, it is very likely that he too used the Khariar version of *Kosalananda Kavyam* without, however, referring to it. Regarding the ancestry of Ramadeva,[45] we are told that a Chauhan prince from Mainpuri founded the Khariar kingdom. The thirtieth ruler of this dynasty, Hamiradeva, was a feudatory of the Gangas and had four queens. He founded the Hamirgarh (fort) on the hills of Gandhamardan. The king once took part in a war between the Ganga and Kalachuri dynasties. As his two messenger pigeons did not return from the battlefield, his queens, except the youngest one, assuming that he had been killed, committed *sati* by drowning themselves in a lake. The youngest queen, Jayantidevi, was pregnant and fled to the jungle and, after crossing the Patpani hill, delivered her son Ramadeva with the help of a tribal priest (*jhankar*) and his wife. The local Binjhal zamindar, Ramod Bariha, took care of mother and son. Later on, Chakradhar Panigrahi, one of the Malliks, reared Ramadeva as his own son. Finally Ramadeva overthrew the rule of the eight Malliks and became king.

In 1962 Siba Prasad Dash wrote his *Sambalpur Itihasa*,[46] which is still regarded today as the major work on the history of Sambalpur. In it he referred in detail to the accounts of *Kosalananda Kavyam*, the *Jaya Chandrika* of Prahllad Dubey and the *Samkshipta Kosala Itihasa* of Rama Chandra Mallick in order to prove the Rajput origins of the Chauhans of western Orissa in a comparative study. He also provided the different genealogical lists of all these works.

J.K. Sahu[47] was the first scholar to take up a serious study in his Ph.D. thesis 'The Chauhan Rule in Orissa' at Utkal University in 1968. It is based mainly on the *Kosalananda Kavyam*. He too accepted the Rajput origins of Orissa's Chauhan dynasties, the main aim of his work being to study their achievements as kings of Patna and Sambalpur. In a 1971 article he again mentions that the

[44]Mallick 1931.
[45]Ibid., 87-8.
[46]S.P. Dash 1969.
[47]Sahu 1969.

Kosalananda Kavyam preserves an 'accurate and authentic genealogy'.[48] However, he has now discarded the story of Ramadeva killing a white tiger as mentioned in the Sonepur version of the *kavya*. In his opinion, 'the account of the *kavya* is a symbolical one, the white tiger being a representation of the government which Ramai Deva overthrew'.[49]

In the most recent edition of *Kosalananda Kavyam*, the joint editors J.K. Sahu and D. Chopdar of Sambalpur University raise several interesting and relevant questions about its authenticity.[50] Earlier Sahu had accepted that the *Kosalananda Kavyam* was genuine and authentic work, but in this recent work the editors agree that it contains a considerably large number of interpolations by the durbar pandits of Sonepur. They reject the stories of the pregnant queen of Visaladeva, the killing of a white tiger by Ramadeva and the genealogical list of the early Chauhan kings of Garhsambhar and Mainpuri as imaginary creations. However, in spite of their objections, they finally subscribe to the Rajput origins of the Chauhans of western Orissa as depicted in the *Kosalananda Kavyam*.[51]

Their most important contribution is that for the first time they take up the challenging theory of R.D. Banerji[52] that the Chauhans of western Orissa were not genuinely Chauhan Rajputs of northern India. They put forth a number of arguments in favour of the Rajput origin theory, which I shall try to evaluate critically. To prove the Rajput Chauhan origin, the editors cite the earlier work *Prabodha Chandrika*, composed by Vaijaladeva II (*c.* 1510-40), in which he proclaimed himself Chauhanavamsa-tilaka Patnadhinatha (Lord of Patna and the Glory of Chauhan Dynasty).

But we must also take into consideration that nowhere does this royal poet care to mention any details of the origin of his ancestors, and in particular any relationships with the Chauhan Rajputs of Garh Sambhar. On the one hand, the *Prabodha Chandrika* confirms that there existed some vague earlier tradition of Rajput origins which then might have been taken up by Gangadhar Mishra in the seventeenth century. But the fact that King Vaijaladeva claims Chauhan origins in his poem without, however, giving any further reference to his ancestry makes it more likely that it was just an invention in support of the claim to Kshatriya status of the indigenous rulers of Patnagarh. He seems to have followed the example of many ruling dynasties of tribal origin in eastern India who later claimed Kshatriya status with the help of their Brahman court priests and poets.[53] The *Prabodha Chandrika* appears to belong to this tradition.

So far, the Narasimhanath temple inscription is taken to be the first epigraphic

[48]Sahu 1971, 31.
[49]Ibid., 32.
[50]Sahu and Chopdar 2000.
[51]Ibid., 35-50.
[52]Banerji 1928.
[53]Panda 2004.

record of the 'future' Chauhans in western Orissa.[54] It mentions that the temple was constructed by King Vaijaladeva I, son of Vatsarajadeva of Patna in CE 1413.

This inscription, however, does not say anything about his dynasty or ancestors, which was the general practice of the ruling kings, although certainly not a rule. But in the case of the Chauhans, later so proud of their Rajput origins, it is certainly strange that Vaijaladeva I did not care to mention it in his inscription, whereas Vaijaladeva II referred to it in his *Prabodha Chandrika*. This makes it very likely that Vaijaladeva II's reference to an alleged Chauhan origin was just to claim 'Kshatriyahood', without any concrete genealogical significance. The full story of their Rajput origins from Garh Sambhar was a later invention by Gangadhar Mishra. In this context the editors argue that since the early rulers of Patnagarh did not claim any ancestry from or relationship with any other dynasty, their Rajput origins cannot be ruled out using a negative approach.

Finally, they argued in favour of a Rajput origin on the basis of Ramadeva's marriage to the daughter of Gajapati's brother Samar Singh. In their opinion the Gajapati king would not have given his niece in marriage to a non-Rajput or non-Kshatriya ruler of Patnagarh.

I have strong doubts about Samar Singh being a brother of the Gajapati king, as the name Singh never appears as the family title of the imperial Gajapatis of the fifteenth and sixteenth centuries. Moreover, the Gajapatis of the succeeding Khurda dynasty were originally from the Bhoi or writers' caste, and were not Kshatriyas.[55] Therefore I am convinced that the poet has 'invented' this imaginative matrimonial relationship with the erstwhile imperial Gajapatis of Orissa in order to strengthen the Rajput-Kshatriya status of the rulers of Sambalpur.

In the different versions of *Kosalananda Kavyam*, one finds mainly two theories about the Rajput origins of the Chauhan rulers: (1) the pilgrimage theory; and (2) the migration of the pregnant queen. The story of a Rajput prince travelling with his pregnant wife on a pilgrimage to Puri is a common legend about the origin of ruling dynasties in central and eastern India. As an example, the legendary origin of the Barbhum Raj family may be cited here. According to the legend, a prince of Rajputana was once going on a pilgrimage to Puri. He was accompanied by his pregnant wife who gave birth to a pair of twins without his knowledge. She left her newborn babies in the forest, where they were reared by a pig. The Bhumijs rescued the babies and killed the pig. When the twins grew up with superior mental and physical qualities, the Bhumijs were convinced of their Kshatriya origin and took them to the royal court. The king was impressed by the brothers and allocated them a part of

[54] Dash 1969, 212.

[55] The Srijanga Inscription of Achyuta Bahar Singh Mahapatra (1598) mentions Ramachandradeva of Khurda even as 'Sudra Gajapati', Patnaik 1940, 25; the *Madala Panji* designates Ramachandradeva as Ramai Routray of Bhoi family, see Mohanty 1969, 64.

his kingdom, which later became known as Birbhum.[56] Such legends in different versions are prevalent among many of the ruling feudatory families of Orissa, such as in the Athamallik, Bonai, Keonjhar, Mayurbhanj, Khandpara, Nayagarh, Talcher and Tigiria.[57]

The main lacuna in the editors' arguments is the fact that they do not take into consideration research on either the bardic traditions of Rajasthan[58] or the social processes in eastern India that have been called Rajputization by Surajit Sinha[59] and Kshatriyaization by H. Kulke.[60] S. Sinha pointed out four essential measures adopted by ruling families to be recognized as Rajputs, which we observe also in the case of the Chauhans of western Orissa:

— Inviting Brahmans from distant lands and patronizing them by means of land grants. The poet Gangadhar Mishra was also invited to come as a court poet from Puri and received a grant of a village.
— A major duty of these Brahmans was to write the royal genealogies to establish a legendary connection with an illustrious Rajput clan of northern India. The *Kosalananda Kavyam* was a typical outcome of this endeavour.
— Ritual display by the kings through the observence of Brahmanical rites, and in particular, by patronizing local cults and festivals. After coming to power, the Chauhans of western Orissa continued to interact with local tribals by patronizing their goddesses, such as Patneswari at Patna, Samaleswari or Samalai at Sambalpur and Khambeswari at Sonepur.
— Entering into marriage alliances with already recognized Rajput or Kshatriya families. The poet Gangadhar Mishra described the supposed marriage alliance of Ramadeva, the founder of the dynasty, with the imperial Gajapatis.

This analysis shows that claims to Rajput origins were prevalent among many of the ruling families of central and eastern India, and that the Chauhans of western Orissa were no exception to this 'rule'. In view of this situation, the question arises, who were the Chauhans if not Rajput Kshatriyas? To answer this question, the dynastic history of the ruling families of early medieval Orissa must be taken into account. Elsewhere I have shown, on the basis of epigraphical evidence, that some of the ruling families were of tribal origin who later claimed the status of the Kshatriyas.[61] The Sailodbhavas, Bhaumakaras, Nalas, Bhanjas, Sulkis and Varahas were originally of tribal stock and were elevated to the status of Kshatriyas through the process of Hinduization. This process was strongly influenced by Brahmans who were invited in from outside

[56]Dalton 1969, 154.
[57]Cobden Ramsay 1910, 114-15, 143, 213, 239, 262-3, 329, 335.
[58]Fürer-Heimendorf 1961.
[59]Sinha 1962, 1987.
[60]Kulke 1976, 398-409; 1993, 82-92.
[61]Panda 2004, 83-4.

by the ruling families in the tribal belts of Orissa. The most significant result of this development was the emergence of a number of princely states and small kingdoms which became the 'nuclear areas' of diffusion of the 'great tradition' of Brahmanical culture and thus of chronicles, too. When composing the royal prasastis of land grant charters, the court pandits would link the origin of the donor, the ruling king, with some ancient Kshatriya clan through an invented genealogy. In my opinion, the court poet Gangadhar Mishra continued this tradition in his *Kosalananda Kavyam* by linking, in a sophisticated and elaborate way, the ruling dynasty of Sambalpur with the Rajput Chauhans of north India, who meanwhile had emerged as the imagined ideal Hindu kings of late-medieval India. Hence, we come to the conclusion that the Chauhans of western Orissa were indigenous people of the locality, neither outsiders nor linked with the Rajput-Kshatriyas of the Chauhan dynasty of Rajputana, as claimed by Gangadhar Mishra.

KOSALANANDA KAVYAM AND THE SEPARATE IDENTITY OF WESTERN ORISSA

Gangadhar Mishra and his *kavya* doubtlessly contributed to the emergence of a separate identity in western Orissa. By calling his poem 'Kosalananda', which means 'Koshala [the land of] happiness', he wanted to eulogize the prosperity of the land. By associating it with Koshala of Puranic fame, he not only depicted the land as a separate geographical entity, but also glorified the Chauhan kings for their royal and cultural revival of western Orissa. As coastal Orissa was identified with the cult of Jagannatha and the Gajapati kings, Gangadhar tried to equate or even to supersede the humble origin of the Gajapati kings of Khurda by proclaiming a Rajput origin and the marriage of his royal patron with the erstwhile imperial Gajapatis. Furthermore, the poet praised the Chauhans of western Orissa as the revivers of the ancient cultural glory of Koshala, as a new era started with the foundation of their rule. Therefore the poet called the first canto of his *kavya* 'Kosaladesa Svarupa Nirupanam'.[62] The founder of the Sambalpur Raj, Balaramadeva, constructed the two imposing temples of Samaleswari and Pataneswari at his new capital. He and his successors patronized a new culture, combining Brahmanic and folk and tribal traditions. The new religious cult centring around the goddess Samalai and the Kosali language has had a deep influence on the life and society of western Orissa right up to the present time.

Summarizing this argument, therefore, one may come to the following conclusions. The Sambalpur court poet Gangadhar Mishra was well acquainted with the historical tradition of Puri and most probably was also familiar with the bardic literature of Rajasthan. In order to glorify his royal patron, Raja Baliardeva of Sambalpur, and to win his favour, he composed the *Kosalananda Kavyam* on the model of the *Prithiviraj Vijaya* of Jayanaka and *Prithiviraj*

[62] *KK*, Text, 6.

Raso of Chand Bardai, combining it with Puri's local historical tradition.

The fame of the Rajput tradition reached Orissa fairly late. Its impact was felt only under the impression of the conquest of Orissa by the great Mughal Rajput General Man Singh. Since the seventeeth century the concept of the Rajput origins of the local ruling families had spread to the 'capitals' of the emerging Garhjat Mahals of northern and western Orissa. It seems that Gangadhar's *Kosalananda Kavyam* was an outcome of this 'Rajputization process'. Gangadhar created a consistent and fascinating story, combining Rajput traditions with local legends and imaginations, in order to establish a Chauhan Rajput origin for the Sambalpur rajas and even to link them to the Puranic Somavamsa of pan-Indian tradition. In a later process, the original *kavya* was extended by the court pandits of the Sonepur, Patna and Khariar durbars to satisfy the ambitions of their ruling families, thus popularizing the 'Rajput myth' even more through the invention of new imaginary stories. While writing the history of the region, the authors of the British gazetteers depended on information provided by these court pandits. By referring again and again in their gazetteers to similar 'Rajput stories' of other princely states, they strengthened and validated the 'Rajput myth' of the ruling families of western Orissa through its official proliferation.

Geographical separation, the evolution of a synthesis of tribal and Brahmanic cultures, the emergence of new cults centring around tribal goddesses, the Kosali language and the Chauhan myth became identity markers of the people of western Orissa, as they still are up to the present. Members of the ex-ruling families are not only revered by the people as Chauhan Rajputs but have also been elected by them to various official positions, from Members of the Legislative Assembly to Chief Minister, in spite of their affiliations with different political parties. Western Orissa has been represented repeatedly by these ruling families in the government. The leaders and the educated elite of the former royal families often play the card of a separate identity to arouse public sentiment whenever they feel that their interests and 'legitimate demands' are being neglected or suppressed by the coastal leadership. The present Koshala movement for a separate state of western Orissa has its roots in these processes.[63]

[63]G.N. Dash 2006.

REFERENCES

Banerji, R.D. 1928. 'Rajput Origin in Orissa', in *Modern Review* 43, 285-91.

———1930. *History of Orissa*, 2 vols, Calcutta: R. Chatterjee.

Bardai, Chand n.d. *Prithviraj Raso*, Nagaripracarini Granthamala Series, Varanasi: Nagaripracarini Sabha.

Cobden Ramsay, L.E.B. 1910. *Feudatory States of Orissa*, Calcutta: The Bengal Secretariat Book Depot (rpt. 1950, 1982).

Dalton, E.T. 1969. *Descriptive Ethnology of Bengal*, Calcutta: Firma K.L. Mukhopadhyay.

Dash, G.N. 2006. 'Changing One's Own Identity: The Role of Language in the Transformation of a Subregional Tradition', in A. Malinar (ed.), *Time in India: Concepts and Practices*, Delhi: Manohar, 272-91.

Dash, S.P. 1969. *Sambalpur Itihasa*, 2nd edn., Sambalpur: Visva-Bharati Press.

Fürer-Heimendorf, C. von. 1961. 'The Historical Value of Indian Bardic Literature', in C.H. Philips (ed.), *Historians of India, Pakistan and Ceylon*, London: Oxford University Press, 87-93.

Grant, Charles 1870. *The Gazetteer of the Central Provinces of India*, 2nd edn., Nagpur: Education Society Press Bombay.

Impey, H.B. 1953. 'Notes on Gurhjat State of Patna', in *Orissa Historical Research Journal* 2, 2, Appendix II (rpt.).

Kar, Niranjan (ed.) 1994. *Kosalananda Mahakavyam*, Puri: Samskrtagavesanakendram, Sri Jagannathasamskrtavisvavidyalayah.

Kirtane, N.J. (ed.) 1878. *Hammira Mahakavya of Nayachandra*, Bombay: Education Society's Press.

Kulke, H. 1976. 'Kshatriyaization and Social Change: A Study in the Orissa Setting', in S. Devadas Pillai (ed.), *Aspects of Changing India: Studies in Honour of Prof. G.S. Ghurye*, Bombay: Popular Prakashan, 398-409, rpt. in idem, *Kings and Cults: State Formation and Legitimation in India and Southeast Asia*, Delhi: Manohar 1993, 82-92.

———1987. 'The Chronicle and the Temple Records of the Madala Panji of Puri: A Reassessment of the Evidence', in *The Indian Archives* 36, 1, 1-24; rpt. in *Kings and Cults*, 137-58.

Mahapatra, K.N. 1954. 'Antiquity of Jagannatha Puri as a Place of Pilgrimage', in *Orissa Historical Research Journal* 3, 1, 6-21.

———1960. *A Descriptive Catalogue of Sanskrit Manuscripts of Orissa*, vol. 2, Bhubaneswar: Orissa State Museum.

Mallick, R.C. 1931. *Samkhipta Kosala or Sambalpur Itihasa* (in Oriya), Sambalpur.

Mazumdar, B.C. 1911. *Sonepur in the Sambalpur Tract*, Calcutta: Brahmo Mission.

———1925. *Orissa in the Making*, Calcutta: University of Calcutta.

Mohanty, A.B. (ed.). 1969. *Madala Panji* (in Oriya), Bhubaneswar: Utkal University.

Motte, T. 1953. 'A Narrative of a Journey to the Diamond Mines at Sombhulpur', in *Orissa Historical Research Journal* 1, 3, Appendix II, 1-48 (rpt.).

O'Malley, L.S.S. 1909. *Bengal District Gazetteer: Sambalpur*, Calcutta: The Bengal Secretariat Book Depot.

Ojha, G.H. and C. Guleri (eds.) 1940. *Prithviraj Vijaya of Jayanaka*, Ajmer: Vaidikayantralaya.

Panda, S.K. 1978-9. 'Brahmanas in Medieval Orissa, Cir. A.D. 1000-1600', in *Journal of Ancient Indian History* 12, 25-35.

———2004. 'Situating Tribals in Early History of Orissa', in B.B. Chaudhuri and A. Bandopadhyaya (eds.), *Tribes, Forest and Social Formation in Indian History*, Delhi: Manohar, 81-8.

Patnaik, Sudhakar 1940. 'The Srijang Inscription of Achyuta Bahar Singh Mahapatra (1598)', in *Journal of the Orissa Academy* 3, 1, 21-32.

Rath, A.K. 1987. 'Jagannatha-Puri as a Place of Pilgrimage in the Early Medieval Period (*c.* AD 700-1200): A Study Based on Epigraphical and Literary Sources', in idem, *Studies on Some Aspects of the History and Culture of Orissa*, Calcutta: Punthi Pustak, 90-100.

Sahu, J.K. 1953. 'Historical Value of Jaya Chandrika', in *Orissa Historical Research Journal* 2, 2, Appendix I (rpt.).

———1969. 'The Chauhan Rule in Orissa', Ph.D. thesis, Utkal University, Bhubaneswar.

———1971. 'Chauhan Rule in Western Orissa', in N.K. Sahu (ed.), *New Aspects of the History of Orissa*, Sambalpur: Sambalpur University.

Sahu, J.K. and D. Chopdar (eds.) 2000. *Kosalananda Kavyam*, Sambalpur: Sambalpur University.

Sharma, D. 1959. *Early Chauhan Dynasties*, Delhi: Chand.

Singhdeo, Biramitradaya (ed.) 1929. *Kosalananda Kavyam*, Sonepur.

Sinha, Surajit 1962. 'State Formation and Rajput Myth in Tribal Central India', in *Man in India* 42, 1, 35-80.

———(ed.) 1987. *Tribal Polities and State Systems in Pre-Colonial Eastern and North Eastern India*, Calcutta: K.P. Bagchi.

Stietencron, H. von 1978. 'The Advent of Viṣṇuism in Orissa: An Outline of its History According to Archaeological and Epigraphical Sources from the Gupta Period up to 1135 A.D.', in A. Eschmann, H. Kulke and G.C. Tripathy (eds.) 1978. *The Cult of Jagannath and the Regional Tradition of Orissa*, Delhi: Manohar, 1-30.

Temple, Sir Richard 1863. *Report on the Zamindaries and Other Petty Chieftaincies in the Central Provinces*, Nagpur: Govt. Press (rpt. 1923).

CHAPTER 8

Between Narratives and Silence: Centring Gangpur State*

CHANDI PRASAD NANDA

This chapter seeks to contest the 'centre-periphery' binary opposition in the study of the politico-cultural history of Orissa by proposing a shift in the prevailing historiographic paradigms.[1] As part of a larger research project exploring the social history of colonial and pre-colonial Orissa, and in particular the creation of diverse cultural specificities and attendant subregional or local identities in the Orissan hinterland, the present chapter attempts to examine the socio-cultural history of a former princely state of Orissa, namely, Gangpur, which was administratively incorporated into Sundargarh district in post-colonial Orissa. It may not be out of place to suggest here that, having the distinction of being the main steel manufacturing city in India, Sundargarh paradoxically symbolizes the 'march of modernity' against the backdrop of a predominantly tribal population and their associated cultural values and traditions. By 'centring Gangpur', as the title of the paper suggests, on the basis of the hitherto perceived, unchallenged and generally claimed centrality

*I am indebted to Hermann Kulke and Georg Berkemer for generating the desire in me to study the *vamsavali*s as part of my overall interest in exploring the social history of pre-colonial and colonial Orissa. For this specific study on the erstwhile State of Gangpur of Orissa, the generous support extended by Bhawani Singh, Biswajit Pradhan (Sambalpur University), Kasinath Sekhar Deo, Rabinarayan Thakur and Gouri Patel (Sundargarh) is noteworthy. During the tedious fieldwork at Sundargarh in piecing together the varieties of information concerning its local history, they have remained both as my informants and as my critics consistently. Though it has not been possible to fully negotiate all the questions raised in the study, still it can be seen as a preliminary draft of a larger exploration into the world of western Orissa including its cultural boundary in order to probe the nature and ramifications of the idea of subregional identities of the region.

[1]In the specific context of undertaking a systematic research on the hinterland of Orissa, focusing on the numerous ex-feudatory states of Orissa as a contrast to historically well-researched coastal plains of Orissa, I have argued elsewhere that the existing historiographic traditions ranging from Orientalist perspective to Colonial, Nationalist and Marxist perspectives have more or less delimited the possibility of exploring the varied yet integrally complex relationship existing between the domains of politics, religion and culture in the context of these princely states. Therefore, it has been suggested alternatively, to look into the Orissan hinterland by engineering a shift in the historiographic paradigm itself. Nanda 2003, 205-20.

of Puri and the Jagannath cult, the main attempt of the paper is to subvert the 'centre-periphery' binary opposition by shifting the historian's gaze to one of the ex-feudatory states of the Orissan hinterland.

By looking beyond the existing historiographic narratives based on Orientalist, Colonial, Nationalist and Marxist perspectives, the paper attempts to tap unexplored literary and oral traditions in the shape of *vamsavali*s, myths, legends, etc., relating to the cultural and social practices of such regions. These unexplored aspects may be seen as the 'voices of silence' in the prevailing historiographic traditions, which await vocalization so that the collective memories relating to the Orissan hinterland may be brought to life. In the final analysis, as can be seen, so-called 'peripheral zones' like Gangpur assume 'centrality' and 'focus' in terms of both mental and geographical aspects. Such 'strategic shifts' in existing historiographic traditions, in my view, pave the way for understanding the process of the crystallization of the 'multi-layered identities' grounded in subregional contexts. Moreover, this aids significantly in critiquing and contesting the hegemonic 'centre-periphery' discourse.

My field studies and research in the last two years or so in certain ex-princely states of Orissa have revealed at least one important and inescapable reality, namely, documenting local historical traditions by examining the royal palace, its library (though it is currently in a deplorably dilapidated state) and temple archives alongside locating or re-reading the *vamsavali*s of such states at one end and the folk traditions and cultures of the locality at the other in order to form a comprehensive picture of the region under study. This, I suggest, may pave the way for methodological shifts in terms of historical research to overcome the 'silence' in the sphere of collective memory pertaining to Orissa.

Horizontally, Gangpur State can be viewed as lying on the margins when compared to the coastal tracts of Orissa, the so-called 'centre'. Similarly in a vertical sense, the exploration of the demographic, socio-political nature of the state yields much information on the marginalized social strata of the region. For instance, the very attempt in this chapter to map the social history of Gangpur State significantly reminds one to examine the historical trajectory of tribal resistance in the tract (namely, the Bhuyan and Munda rebellions), apart from understanding the several complex issues with regard to the social stratifications of this former princely state.

For the 'silence' part of the present study, I have mainly tried to locate and analyse a few of the *vamsavali*s pertaining to Gangpur State as well as certain hitherto unexplored documents unearthed from the Sundargarh District Records Collections as preserved in the Orissa State Archives, Bhubaneswar. The *vamsavali*s, which often highlight political, dynastic and regal details and were invariably written to valorize the particular deeds of the kings, also contain significant insights into the interwoven aspects of culture, religion and society. In other words, the twin interrelated processes of 'Hinduization' and 'tribalization' are indirectly and tacitly suggested in the body of the *vamsavali* texts.

It is similarly the case with the archival records mentioned above, which have yet to be fully tapped and which provide a plethora of information for the study of the culture, history and society of such states. Although it has not been possible to utilize fully all these highly relevant source materials to reconstruct the history of Gangpur State, the present chapter is a modest attempt in this direction.

The aim of the chapter as a whole is to study the origin of Gangpur State by examining its many genealogical traditions alongside its myths and legends. Secondly, the chapter seeks to bring into sharper focus the voices of the subalterns who sought to resist and subvert domination from any centre and thus positioned themselves as virtual centres of authority. Importantly too, the chapter attempts, from the horizontal point of view, to show how—despite an apparently dichotomous 'centre-periphery' relationship between the 'Hindu kingdom' of coastal Orissa and a predominantly tribal tract such as Gangpur State—certain tribal cultural practices underwent a process of gradual transformation in terms of 'Hinduization' and, vice versa, 'in between'. The chapter begins with the origin and rule of the Kesari and Sekhar dynasties in the Gangpur region on the basis of some of the local traditions, including genealogical accounts. Furthermore, it also aims to show how the tribal people of this region sought to relate themselves to these two dynasties. By specifically examining the 'moments of resistance' and 'mentality of reverence' on the part of the tribal people of the region *vis-à-vis* the state or centre, the chapter aims to demonstrate the fragile basis of a constructed conceptual binary opposition in terms of 'centre and periphery'.

The main idea in pursuing such a study of one of the ex-feudatory states is to indicate the 'possible nature of polycentric, multilayered and dynamical quality' so far as the pre-modern state in India is concerned. This view is appropriately corroborated when it is argued that the state 'is an idea and a system of symbols which can be more or less deeply rooted in the social norms and values of a society (where "the state" is given in people's view of the world, there is a state)'.[2]

The present district of Sundargarh or the former Princely State of Gangpur formed a part of South Koshala and was ruled by the Somavamsis from the first half of the sixth century CE.[3] During the rule of the Somavamsi king, Udyotakesari Mahabhavagupta, the Somavamsi dominion was not only consolidated but became divided into the two main political units of the Koshala and Utkal regions. The former chief, Abhimanyu, who was the grandfather of Udyotakesari, was made ruler of the Koshala division, which was sometimes referred to as 'Paschima Lanka' or 'Paschima Kalinga'.[4] Suvarnapura or modern Sonepur was the capital of the Koshala division. The reference to the early origin of the Kesari dynasty in the Gangpur region around the eleventh and

[2]Berkemer 2003, 2.
[3]Sahu 1971, 16.
[4]Ibid., 20; Rajaguru 1971, 49.

twelfth centuries CE in some of the genealogical accounts may have certain links with the Somavamsis, who are also known as the Kesari dynasty.

However, later on, the Kalachuris seem to have occupied the territory during the early part of the twelfth century. The Ganga rulers subsequently contemplated the conquest of Koshala following the occupation of Utkal by Chodaganga, the Ganga king. However, the conquest of Koshala succeeded when Anangabhima III (CE 1211-38) fought and defeated the Kalachuris, thus wresting South Koshala from them. This is the time when the Ganga rulers came to control the region of the erstwhile Gangpur state or the modern Sundargarh region. Given the paucity of historical evidence as far as this part of Orissa during the period of Ganga supremacy is concerned, one has to take note of local traditional accounts which point to rule over Gangpur by a number of kings with Kesari titles. Even though the exact relationship between these Kesari kings and the Gangas cannot be determined, it seems probable that all these rulers with the Kesari epithet were feudatories of the Gangas of Utkal.[5] It was probably during the time of the Gangas that Gangpur was consolidated as a separate political unit and thus thrived as a feudal state.[6]

In this context, it is pertinent to note that the local traditions of Gangpur point to the existence of a Kesari line with sixteen kings who ruled over Gangpur. It is also said that they had their capital at various places, like Masabiragarh, Sukhabandha, Hemagir, Belsaragarh, Keshargarh and Karamgarh. The names of Kesari kings vary in different local traditions and seem to be imaginary. However, based on traditions, it appears that a local dynasty using the epithet 'Kesari' ruled over the region from about the twelfth century onward. Much later, official colonial writings also mention the rule of this dynasty in the region.[7]

As one tradition relates:

> Some of the scions of the Somavamsis (famous as Kesari kings in the tradition), on their defeat by the Gangas, migrated to Gangpur region and established their authority. These Kesari rulers were apparently allowed to carve out a self-contained principality in the Gangpur region and continued as vassals of the imperial Gangas. The last of these Kesari rulers, called Raja Deo Kesari, was an oppressive ruler and was therefore eventually murdered together with members of his family by a powerful Bhuiyan leader, Madan Pradhan. The consequent political confusion that prevailed offered the opportunity for the progenitor of the Paramara-Sekhara family to seize the land.[8]

The veracity of this tradition concerning local Kesari rule in Gangpur may be judged against the backdrop of Chatesvara inscriptions, pointing to a decisive victory by Anangabhima III's General Vishnu over the Kalachuri king of

[5]Behera 1971, 53.

[6]*Orissa District Gazettear: Sundargarh* 1971, 54 (hereafter, *ODG*).

[7]References can be made to the writings of Colonel Dalton, C.W.E. Connolly (*Settlement Report of 1911*) cited in *ODG* 84, 54 respectively; Hunter 1877, 189-95.

[8]*ODG*, 54.

Tumana in a battle fought on the banks of the Bhima, the edges of the Vindhyas, and the shore, and resulting in the Gangas taking possession of a vast stretch of land in western Orissa. Furthermore, findings from certain *maufi* grants indicate that Anangabhima visited the Sambalpur region. Also, the Khambesvari temple inscription bears testimony to the fact that the Sonepur region was under the control of the imperial Gangas during the time of Bhanudeva (1264-79), which had been placed under the charge of a governor.[9]

Yet another tradition relates that the Kesari family of Gangpur owed its origin to Puri, where two brothers named Ratan Kesari and his younger brother, Kapila Kesari, 'having title to the royal stock left Puri in order to find out places where they might be rulers'. Accordingly, 'the elder brother, Ratan Kesari, succeeded to the *gaddi* of Keshargarh whereas the younger, Kapila Kesari, succeeded to the *gaddi* of Karamgarh'. They and their descendants began to rule over these two places, which were two separate states at that time.[10]

In addition, a local genealogical tradition corroborates the suggestion that two brothers, namely, Kapila Kesari and Ratan Kesari, who hailed from the country of 'Puri and Cuttack' of Aitreya gotra, settled in the village of Masabira in the Gangaimati region. Once, while Kapila Kesari was asleep, the presiding deity of Gangpur (Kashari, perhaps a tribal deity, who used to be worshipped every Tuesday through the offerings of the usual sacrifices) appeared to him in a dream and told him that a bamboo tree would bear flowers in the Masabira hillock and he would be the king of that region. The deity disappeared after asking him to organize worship for the 'god Narasimha Garuda, Dharmaketu Khanda (the sword protecting Dharma), the Ashtabhuji Khanda (a sword with eight handles), Bijekarna Katari (a victory axe?), Chhatrabauti (a bamboo tree in the shape of canopy) and Dwarasini (the guards at the temple entrance)'. Then Kapila Kesari narrated the dream to his brother Ratan Kesari. Afterwards, he not only founded the village at Masabira by making people settle there, but also made Masabira a fort. In the *gaddi* of Masabira, he installed the above-mentioned god and became king in CE 1135.[11]

Ratan Kesari established his rule at Keshargarh in the border region around present-day Orissa and Chhattisgarh. Similarly, Kapila Kesari 'sat on the *gaddi* [throne]' of Karamgarh. Afterwards, he relocated Karamgarh around Hemgir Sukhabandh and ultimately founded his capital on the site of the fort of Belsaragarh. In another account, it is pointed out that Kapila Kesari kept shifting his capital from 'Karmaga to Sukhabandha before finally opting for Belsaragarh as the appropriate place for the capital site from the standpoint of defence'.[12] The two brothers continued to maintain amicable relations, even though they exercised different territorial jurisdictions from the twin centres

[9] Ibid., 53-4.
[10] Pandey 2003; *Private Loose Records ACC No. 700*; *ACC No. 677* (hereafter *PR*).
[11] *PR*, 677.
[12] Pandey 2003.

of Kesharagarh and Belsaragarh. Ratan Kesari was succeeded by Birata Kesari and Bikram Kesari. As Bikram Kesari died without issue, the queen bequeathed the state to a member of a certain Behera family, namely, Jayadev Behera, along with five diamonds. Tradition has it that the queen committed *sati*.

Meanwhile, at Balsargarh, Kapila Kesari was succeeded by his sons and grandsons. The last king of this line was Deo Kesari, who had three queens. While the two eldest queens stayed at Belsargarh, the youngest, who belonged to the 'stock of the Ho family' of Ratanpur in Bilaspur, lived at Hemgir near Sukhabandh. Deo Kesari appointed Madan Pradhan diwan of the state and continued to manage 'the state together with him'. The raja used to perform the sacrifice to propitiate the goddess Kusari every Tuesday.[13] In another account, it is told that the king used to offer human sacrifice to the *istadevata* Kesar Mati every Tuesday.[14]

In course of time, the king and the diwan fell out. Consequently, Deo Kesari divested Madan Pradhan of the diwanship and appointed him a mere zamindar, granting only two villages in his favour. Humiliated, Madan Pradhan vowed to destroy the Kesari dynasty and sought to mobilize 'all the Bhuiyans and the Khandayat Bhuiyans of twenty-two zamindaris'.[15] He also sought the support of the king of Pallikote of Nagpur in his 'war' against Deo Kesori. In return, he handed over a tract of land of around 28 miles (14 *kos*) to the raja of Nagpur. The land that was exchanged at this time is still known as Kesalpur. Similarly, in exchange for granting the parganas Ganjagiri or Jagyangiri and Karmagarh to the king of Raigarh, he secured his military support. The two kings mentioned above helped Madan Pradhan by providing soldiers. Thus emboldened, Madan was able to defeat King Deo Sekhar.

Not only was the king brutally murdered at Belsaragarh, his pregnant queen was also beheaded. According to the popular memory, the lower portion of her body came to be worshipped at Belsaragarh in the form of the goddess Rani Aai, a practice that still exists today. The other queen of the king at Belsaragarh jumped into the water out of panic upon learning about the dreadful attack on the royal family. This place is known as Rani Buda. The youngest queen, who was living at Hemgir, was also murdered, later emerging in Hemgir in the form of the goddess Manikeswari.[16] In the popular perception, the goddess of Belsaragarh attained more prominence than the goddess of Hemgir.[17]

Yet another tradition suggests that one queen fled to her father at Ratanpur in Chhattisgarh. According to this tradition, the last ruler of the Kesari dynasty,

[13]*PR*, 700.

[14]Pandey 2003.

[15]Ibid.; *PR* 677; 700. The account contained in these sources refers to the '*bloody massacre*' (emphasis added) of the royal family with subtle variations in terms of narratives.

[16]The tradition relating to the accounts of local deities can be gleaned from the following sources; *PR*, 700, 677; Pandey 2003.

[17]Pandey 2003.

Manabhanja Kesari, was murdered at Hemgir while he was with the youngest queen. This incident is dated to CE 1597.[18] This tradition also adds that the splash of blood that oozed out upon the brutal murder of Manabhanja Kesari ultimately flowered into a Sivalinga. Siva is still worshipped at Hemgir under the name of the god Manikeswar. The variation in these accounts as to the difference in the gender of the 'local' deity is interesting.

As the tradition continues, Madan Pradhan took possession of the sword, a symbol of the god Garuda Devata Bada Deo, the state deity, the palm-leaf book (the book containing the history of the four *garh*s) and the vermilion case to Indrapur. He also reorganized the 'due worship' of the local goddess.[19] All the wealth belonging to the raja, including the horses, elephants and other domestic animals, was 'plundered' and 'fairly and proportionately' divided amongst his followers.[20] The iron wristlets (*kural khada*) and the chains of the elephant were also removed to Belsaragarh. This tradition has been maintained here down the generations.[21] It is still possible that, as this account points out, initially Madan Pradhan preserved the 'sword with eight handles and a big iron chain' in the cave at Hemgir mountain and that these articles were worshipped by the *garotia* (the military fief-holder) at Hemgir. Moreover, after his supposed victory, Madan Pradhan distributed all the booty looted from the royal household, including cattle, elephants and horses, proportionately among the zamindars who had stood by him during the 'war' against the king.

From the preceding accounts, it appears that, during his rule in the tract, the Kesari king, Kapila Kesari, may have used Gangaimati, Masabira, Karamgarh, Sukhabandh or Hemgir, and finally Belsargarh as his capital fort. The very process of shifting the capital leads the social historian to consider the idea of shifting boundaries and centres. The other interesting references are to the act of *sati* allegedly committed by the queen of Bikram Kesari at Keshargarh and the subsequent abdication of the throne in favour of Jayadev Behera, who did not belong to the Kesari line. These point first, to the due observance of 'Hindu practices' on the part of the royal family, including the act of *sati* by the queen. Secondly, it seems probable that the death of King Bikram Kesari was followed by the rule of a 'powerful local chief' who may have been a vassal of the king. Given the association of the Gaudas (milkmen), to which Behera may have belonged, with the royal history of Gangpur, it is also possible that Bikram Kesari took a wife from a non-Kshatriya community.

[18]The peculiarity with the Oriya version of the genealogical account, of Gangpur state is twofold. First, it ascribes CE 1135 as the year of accession of Ratan Kesari, the founder-ruler of local Kesari/Kesori dynasty. Second, it talks of the local god of Gangpur, i.e. Manikeswar (Lord Siva) as the emerging presiding deity of Hemgir instead of the local goddess, as evident in other accounts.

[19]*PR*, 700.

[20]Ibid.

[21]Pandey 2003.

As he died without issue, the state lapsed into the control of one of his powerful 'vassals' or 'chiefs'.

A critical reading of all these accounts alerts the historian to take note of the following issues and ideas.

(a) The meticulous attempt of the authors of these local genealogical traditions of Gangpur state to ascribe its 'legend of origin' to the Puri and Kesari dynastic traditions may be a much later 'imagined or invented' tradition. As has been pointed out, the Yayati Kesari tradition was transformed into a foundation myth of early Orissa by modern historians based on the typical combination of history and legend and flavored with the argument that Yayati I (*c.* 922-53) was the first to establish a regional kingdom in Orissa, uniting both Koshala and Utkal politically and culturally and thus emerging as the father of modern Orissa.[22] It is further argued that, 'despite some possibly genuine historical allusions to the tenth century, Puri's Yayati Kesari legend has to be regarded primarily as a construct of [the] late sixteenth century of Orissa for validation and legitimization of priestly and royal authority after the downfall of the imperial Gajapatis'.
In this context, what merits consideration is that the 'foundation legend' of Gangpur is one of the typical legends of the Garhjat (ex-feudatory) states, which most likely emerged during the Khurda Period (and certainly not during the Ganga period) as part of the project of the 'revival of Yayati Kesari tradition' of late-sixteenth-century Orissa.

(b) The reference to the story of the two brothers in the local traditions venturing out to places where they might be rulers apparently has close parallels in the 'origin legend' of certain other ex-feudatory states such as Keonjhar, which merely points to similar narratives being composed in favour of the 'origin' of such princely states pushing their antiquities back into the 'hoary past' at a much later historical period. In addition, such stories also highlight the contestation and reconciliation between two or several contenders for power and political control.

(c) Similarly, the reference to the names of Kesari, Kesuri and Kesar Mati as the presiding local goddess of Gangpur in the local traditions may have contributed to the texturing of the legend of the Kesari dynasty ruling over Gangpur State. However, the reference to the god Manikeswar as the presiding local god (Lord Siva) in other accounts indicates the possible impact of the Brahmanical tradition and a conscious attempt by the chronicler of such a tradition to distance his material from the overwhelmingly tribal religious traditions of the region. Furthermore, the dominance of Madan Pradhan as the Bhuiyan leader during the period concerned also reminds us that the Bhuiyans were the *mulavasis*

[22]For detailed reference, see Kulke (forthcoming); Panigrahi 1961.

(the original inhabitants) of the region, the 'Kesari' being a much later 'invented' dynasty of Gangpur.

In addition, the 'foundational myth' in terms of pregnant women being killed and later being transformed into istadevi as seen in the local tradition of Gangpur is also evident in the context of other princely states of coastal Orissa, such as Nayagarh, Baramba and Banki. The association of such legends with the 'royal tradition' of the states may imply a certain amount of space being allocated by royalty in favour of (or to accommodate) tribal religious traditions in terms of mother worship.

(d) The vernacular genealogical account of Gangpur State makes specific mention of 1135 as the year of the inception of the Kesari dynasty in Gangpur, with Kapila Kesari mounting the throne at Masabira. It further mentions the name of Manabhanja Kesari as the thirteenth successor king in the line of Kapila Kesari, who assumed the throne in 1548 and was killed by the Bhuiyan leader Madan Pradhan in 1597. The supposed variation in the name of the king killed by Madan Pradhan, Sri Deo Kesari and Manabhanja Kesari, in two local traditions minimally but clearly shows that the 'Kesari tradition' was invented during the late-sixteenth century in the 'Khurda Period' of Orissan history.

In the final analysis, what merits attention in these accounts is that the foundation of a 'Hindu' state in this region was marked by both a process of attempting to 'control and integrate' the tribal and other communities of the region, and valiant efforts from 'below' to arrest such processes at certain times. However, such alleged 'resistance' from the indigenous communities was also associated with the idea of the emulation of values, as we have been told, with the continuation of the religious traditions of the Kesari dynasty by Madan Pradhan or the 'smooth succession' to the *gaddi* of Kesharagarh after Bikram Kesari, someone who belonged to the non-Kshatriya community. In the latter case, it was suggestive of the fact that someone who belongs to a non-Kshatriya community could only be made king after he had been 'rightfully nominated and acknowledged' by the previous king, who himself was a Kshatriya.

Similarly, the 'divine dream' in which Kapila Kesari was asked to organize worship for certain gods and goddesses of both Hindu and tribal origin along with a bamboo parasol and 'typical swords' central to tribal religious practices perhaps indicates the idea of reconciling the Hindu with the dominant tribal religious practices on the part of a Kshatriya king who was seeking to control and integrate the region under his authority. However, as these accounts suggest, the alleged oppression and misrule of the Kshatriya ruler evoked mass mobilization and solidarity on the part of the indigenous tribal communities under Bhuiyan leadership.

The alleged 'resistance' of the tribals to Kshatriya and Hindu domination, as seen in the context of Madan Pradhan's 'war' against Manabhanja Kesari or Sri Deo Kesari, has conversely been integrated into popular memory and local traditions by investing the persons or places that bore the burnt of the murderous assault on Madan Pradhan with an aura of religious sanctity. As has been shown above, the places of Rani Aai, Rani Buda at Belsaragarh or the goddess or god Manikeswar in the form of Sivalinga at Hemgir retain this legacy and have become part of the collective memory and local subregional identity.

It might also be argued that the attainment of divinity on the part of the king or queen following their murder not only implies the 'divine wrath' expressed against the indigenous tribal population through the mere fact that the miracles happened: it also implies the so-called 'invincible prowess' of the Kshatriyas *vis-à-vis* the tribal chiefs. All these components have obviously been tailored and stitched into a dominant discourse revolving around the Hinduization or Kshatriyaization process. Naturally, therefore, the genealogical accounts, local historical traditions and popular memory integrally share and supplement such a discourse through their own narratives.

The tradition of a wholesale massacre of the local Kesari royal family by Madan Pradhan was followed by the rule of the Bhuiyans, who had grouped themselves into several principalities. Madan Pradhan seems to have been succeeded by his son and grandson Medini Pradhan and Betal Pradhan respectively. With the death of Betal Pradhan, who died without issue, one of his kith and kin, Panu Pradhan, continued to maintain the tradition of worshipping the sword symbolizing the god 'Garuda Debata Bada Deo'. This 'sword was preserved at Pradhan Pat and was removed to Samleswari temple by the late Tikait'. The tradition of worship of the sword by the Bhuiyans is suggestive of the tribal origin of the sword itself having religious significance. As the priests of the 'aboriginal deity', the Bhuiyans continued to worship their traditional god or goddess and the symbols associated with such deities. However, the sword as an alleged marker of the Hindu and Kshatriya ritual order, or for that matter in the context of the religious practice of local Kesari rule, including its link with the sword, may have been a later 'invented tradition'.

Perhaps, after the death of Betal Pradhan the region of Gangpur continued to be controlled by several Bhuiyan leaders. We come across quite a few names of Bhuiyan zamindars who belonged to this phase and wielded considerable 'power and authority' in different tracts of this region. These were Mansingh Majhi/Bharathi Majhi of Sargipalli; Bimbadhar Singh/Madan Mohan Singh (Hemgir), Jagat Singh Mohapatra (Nagra), Madan Pradhan (Kirma Danda), Charusingha Dansana and Prahallad Gartia (Sarpagarh or Sarapgarh).[23] Of all these chiefs, it seems that the Majhi of Sargipalli managed to secure the largest tracts of land.[24] The continuous conflicts among the Bhuiyan chiefs to rule over larger tracts of land often led to attempts to obtain external support from the rajas of Raigarh and Palikot.

[23] *ODG*, 69; *PR*, 677.
[24] *PR*, 700.

It was in this context that the Majhi of Sargipalli, who had by now emerged as the most powerful Bhuiyan leader, may have sought the help of a wandering Kshatriya called Parikhit Sekhar, alias Gangadhar Sekhar Deo, in subjugating his rivals who were contesting his authority.[25] The Majhi of Sargipalli thus invited Gangadhar Sekhar Deo to help defeat his rivals and subsequently put 'vermilion on his forehead' and made him the king of this region. Gangadhar's reign signalled the advent of the so-called 'Kshatriya rule' in Gangpur.

Let us now pause to examine the nature of social stratification in this region and the probable explanations for the emergence of a so-called Kshatriya dynasty under the name of 'Sekhar' in the Gangpur region. Writing his impressions of the 'most numerous' and 'dominant' Bhuiyan tribe of Gangpur, W.W. Hunter, the colonial administrator, noted that the Bhuiyans held not only 'fiefs in most parts of Gangpur' under the raja but were also regarded as the 'especial priests of the aboriginal gods'.[26] Referring to the 'current belief' among the tribals, he also noted that the 'local divinities are most readily propitiated by the tribe which has had the longest acquaintance with them; that is, who first claimed the county'. Elaborating on the hierarchy existing within this tribal group, Hunter mentioned Bhagwan Manjhi of Tilla (an estate situated in the north-west corner of Gangpur) as the chief of the Bhuiyan vassals having the 'sole right of conferring *tilaka* or token of investiture on the raja of the state' (a 'custom' which he realized, was on the wane with the structuring of 'Hindu ideas' in the region). The next Bhuiyan feudatory in order of importance was Balki Mahapatra, who controlled the estate of Nagra in the south-east of Gangpur. Apart from rendering military service to the king when required, in the form of 'a contingent of armed followers or naiks', he used to pay annually for his land four hundred rupees, of which half consisted of rent and the other half of *magan* or cess (the feudal levies). On the other hand, the Naiks who were themselves Bhuiyans held land in his estate as feudal sub-tenures on a par with the position of the Mahapatra himself.

Similarly, 'Sibnath, the *garhotia* or military fief holder' controlled the estate of Hemgir, which had eighty-four villages. Interestingly, he would boast that 'he can travel 24 miles in a direct line over his own land without seeing a single house', perhaps an indication of the vast stretch of forest land under his control. Similarly, Balram was the *garhotia* of Erga. The *garhotia*s of Hemgir and Erga were 'bound to render military service' to the king, but their tenures were 'more like ordinary zamindaris than those of the Manjhi and Mahapatra'. Hunter grouped them into the category of ordinary zamindars along with five other Bhuiyan feudatories who were distinctly less socially privileged and whose 'estates are small and need no special notice', as in the case of Maneswar Singh, the *garhotia* of Sarapagarh.

Further, Dalton, in his 'Report on the Tour in Bonai and Gangpur during

[25] *ODG*, 69.

[26] Hunter 1877, 192-3.

1863-64', observed that the 'Bhooyas' were 'no doubt' the 'first settlers' of the region and formed the 'majority of the population'.[27] He further notes significantly that

all the zamindars under the Rajah are of that race, and hold their estates as fiefs at low fixed rates and terms of service. Consequently, the Rajah is under the necessity of adopting a conciliatory policy towards some of them at least. There are generally one or two in opposition, but fortunately for the Lord Paramount the great vassals are too jealous of each other readily to combine. The largest estate is held by the vassal who bears the title of Mahapater. . . .

Dalton further states that 'the chiefs' of Gangpur, Bonai, Keonjhar and Bamra States 'now call themselves Rajputs; if they be so, they are strangely isolated families of Rajputs'.[28] In this connection, he points out,

the country for the most part belongs to the Bhuiyan sub-proprietors, they are a privileged class, holding as hereditaments the principal offices of the State, and are organized as a body of militia. The chiefs have no right to exercise any authority till they have received the tilak or token of investiture from their powerful Bhuiya vassals. Their position altogether renders their claim to be considered Rajputs extremely doubtful, and the stories told to account for their acquisition of the dignity are palpable fables. They were no doubt all Bhuiyas originally; they certainly do not look like Rajputs.

Refuting the theory of the Kshatriya origins of Gangpur state and the expulsion of the 'Kaiserbuns', the Kesari dynasty of Rajput-Kshatriya lineage from Gangpur, Dalton reasons that the ruling family descended from the 'original Bhooya chiefs'.[29] He goes on to stress that the 'traditions' of 'assigning' the ruling chiefs 'a nobler birth' are founded

on the supposition that the Rajpoots or Cshetryas were the only class qualified to rule, that where there was no one of this class over a nation or a people, 'the Gudee' was vacant, and a Cshetrya, had only to step in and take it. The Cshetryas must have wandered about like knights-errant of old, in search of these vacant Guddee, as we do not find in the country any descendants of the followers whom they must have had, if they came in other fashion to oust the native chiefs and seize the country.

Dalton's equation of the sons of the soil theory (bhumi, earth) with the Bhuiyans finds an echo in Hunter.[30] Hunter considers the legend of 'stealing a child of Sikhar family from Sikharbhum or Panchet', who was subsequently 'elected as the chief', as 'one form of the Brahmanical doctrine that all rulers should be Kshatriyas, and the wide prevalence of similar stories, together with the dark complexion and non-Aryan features of the raja, make it far more

[27]Report on Lt. Colonel T. Dalton's Tour in Bonai and Gangpur during 1863-64 cited in *ODG* 84 (hereafter, *Dalton Report . . .*).

[28]Dalton 1973, 140; Russel and Hira Lal 1975, 306-7.

[29]*Dalton Report*, 84-5.

[30]Hunter 1877, 195; Bhuiyan may also stand for 'Lord of the soil' or 'Belonging to the soil' and is a Sanskrit derivative. Russel and Hiralal 1975, 305.

probable that he is, like most of his fief-holders, a Bhuiya'. However, in this connection, what needs to be ascertained is the specific equation between this so-called 'outsider' and the indigenous Bhuiyan community of the region. The Bhuiyans could have either collaborated with the 'chief from outside' to defeat their rivals or accepted him as the new ruler or been entirely subjugated by this chief.

The accounts of Hunter and Dalton remind us interestingly about a similar development in the Keonjhar state and its 'foundational legend' when one takes into account the ceremonial practice of royal investiture as organized by Bhuiyan chiefs or the story of a child of the royal lineage being stolen by the Bhuiyans and subsequently being groomed to be the king of the region.

Moreover, the legendary foundational Rajput origin of some of the ruling dynasties of central and eastern India as has been exemplified by Surajit Sinha in the context of the Barbhum Raj family,[31] or in the case of the Chauhans of western Orissa as pointed out by Shishir Kumar Panda,[32] reinforces the above arguments.

Against the backdrop of these possible scenarios, however, the fact remains that the Bhuiyans traditionally asserted their rights over the land as well as over the 'kingdom in the making' [emphasis added]. It was in this context that the 'primordial right' to participate in the rituals of royal investiture on the part of the Bhuiyans assumes critical significance, at least clearly symbolizing that royalty in the region was to be validated by the Bhuiyans in the last analysis.[33]

Apart from the Bhuiyans (24,000), other tribes such as the Oraons (47,000), Gonds (37,000), Kharias (26,000) and Mundas (19,000) along with the Agharias (7,000), a cultivating caste, were the other significant social constituents of this region.[34] Given the nature of the social composition, what needs to be stressed further is the distinct initial resistance of the Bhuiyans, under Madan Pradhan's 'bloody move' to extinguish the local Kesari dynasty, or, as may be seen in the revolt of Madri Kalo in 1897 (the aboriginal Gauntia and a Bhuiyan) *vis-à-vis* the Agharia (belonging to the dominant and prosperous agrarian class and non-tribal in origin), which also assumed the shape of 'social banditry' [emphasis added].[35] Finally, viewed against the backdrop of the peak of nationalist politics and popular mobilization all over Orissa during late 1930s, the Munda rebellion against the 'colonial and feudal order' in Gangpur in 1939 can be seen as emanating from the highly subjectively structured perceptions of the tribals of the region in terms of the 'original authority over their land'.[36]

[31] Sinha 1962.

[32] See Panda in this volume.

[33] One comes across similar patterns in the context of Keonjhar State so far as the notion of 'primordial right' of the Bhuiyan is concerned; Nanda 2003.

[34] Cobden Ramsay 1910, 178-9; P.P. Mishra 2002, 4.

[35] Cobden Ramsay 1910, ibid.; *ODG*, 84.

[36] Hunter 1877, 192-3 . . .'The current belief is that these local divinities are most readily

It is crucial to note here that the tribal rebellion led by Madri Kalo in 1897 was a reaction to the policy of introducing a new Revenue Settlement in 1874 by Raja Raghunath Sekhar Deo, backed by the overall colonial land revenue policies.[37] The very introduction of the settlement resulted in the transfer of some villages to the highest bidders in the neighbouring states. As a result, quite a number of tribal chiefs lost their earlier privileges to people of other castes, mostly 'Agharias and rich people from Sambalpur'.[38] The colonial administration interestingly characterized the nature of the rebellion as follows:[39]

> The discontent had been smouldering for some years until in February 1897, it took the shape of open revolt by the malcontents, which culminated in a series of more or less serious dacoities and a general blackmailing of the villages in the disturbed tracts. It was at length found necessary to depute the Deputy Commissioner of Singhbhum with an armed body of British police to assist the chief in restoring order and in arresting the insurgent leaders.

The Agharias, who in the words of Cobden Ramsay were the 'most thriving cultivators' in the state, in the course of time emerged as a threat to the indigenous tribal communities by vigorously taking up the profession of agriculture and thus becoming wealthy and influential. As a new-rich class, they sought to threaten the privileged social status hitherto enjoyed by the Bhuiyan and other tribal communities. In this connection, Dalton's note on the Agharia caste assumes significance.[40]

> According to their own tradition, they are called Agrahia [*sic*] from having come from Agra. They were there, they say, Kshatriyas; but having been subjected to some persecution by the ruler of the State, they left it, and taking up new lands in a new country, cast aside their sacred thread, the badge of twice-born, with all its privileges and obligations, and took to the plough. Their appearance favours their pretensions to be of good blood. Tall, well-made with high Aryan features and tawny complexions, they look like Rajputs; but they are more industrious and intelligent than the generality of the warrior caste.

Under these circumstances, it may be argued, the gradual dominance of the community as the new successful class of agriculturists in the region threatened the privileged positions of the indigenous castes and communities. The resultant social tension may have expressed itself in the shape of a tribal reaction to non-tribals under the leadership of Madri Kalo.

The continuing discontent among tribals was increased further around 1939, when the durbar administration in Gangpur sought to increase the demand for

---

propitiated by the tribe which has had the longest acquaintance with them; that is, who first colonised the country'.

[37]P.P. Mishra 2002, 5-7.

[38]*ODG*, 75.

[39]Ibid., 75-6.

[40]Cobden Ramsay 1910, 180.

land revenue. On this occasion the tribals resisted the attempt under the leadership of Nirmal Munda, a converted Christian, and demanded a revision of the rent structure. The movement gathered momentum and resulted in the firing on the tribal people of Simko village on 25 August 1939, during which a number of tribal people were killed.[41]

We now shift our focus to explore briefly the history of the Sekhar dynasty of Gangpur, which was supposed to have originated with the rule of Gangadhar Sekhar Deo, who assumed the *gaddi* of Gangpur a little later, after the end of the local Kesari rule. However, what needs to be emphasized is that any attempt to explore the social history of a region during the pre-colonial and colonial periods on the basis of genealogical and local traditions needs to be critically reconstructed and informed of varieties of processes at work, given the complexities associated with the nature of social stratification and the 'notion of rights, privileges, along with the idea of the state', as perceived by the indigenous communities of the region.

Here I shall probe the origin of the Sekhar dynasty and some of the socio-cultural aspects pertaining to this royal lineage on the basis of a few genealogical accounts, including an account of the history of the ex-princely family of Gangpur by one of the relatives of the present raja called Kasinath Sekhar Deo.[42]

All these accounts mention the infighting among several Bhuiyan chiefs soon after the decline of the local Kesari dynasty. This infighting ultimately resulted in growing 'political anarchy and confusion' in the region. It led to such a situation that a group of Bhuiyan chiefs got together under the leadership of the zamindar of Sargipalli and decided to search for a Kshatriya king to be installed on the throne of Gangpur. As mentioned in Kasinath's account, before the advent of the Sekhar dynasty, the Bhuiyans used to choose their leader by placing a lemon before potential candidates. The person towards whom the lemon rolled was chosen as the king. In any case, it seems that continuous conflict among the Bhuiyan chiefs to arrogate power and authority to themselves created an opportunity in which a Kshatriya and Hindu king from 'outside the region' was sought by preference by the Bhuiyans at large.

In one account, it is said that the Bhuiyan chiefs stole a child from Sikharbhum or Panchet and elected him as their chief.[43] It is worth pointing out that in Keonjhar State, we have similar references to two brothers, Adi Bhanja and Jyoti Bhanja, who originally belonged to the Khijjing Kota or Khijjinga Mandala (ex-feudatory state of Mayurbhanj). The younger brother Jyoti Bhanja was kidnapped by the Bhuiyans of Keonjhar and subsequently groomed to be the king of Keonjhar. In fact, the Bhuiyans, the original inhabitants of Keonjhar, had long felt the acute need for a Kshatriya king who

[41] P.P. Mishra 2002, 10.
[42] *PR* 677, 700; Sekhar Deo 2003.
[43] Hunter 1877, 195.

would rule their 'territories' instead of being ruled and controlled by the remote political authority located at Khijjinga Mandala.[44] However, in all these genealogical and local traditions, a detailed reference can be gleaned as to how a Kshatriya ruler of the Paramara clan who originally belonged to Dhar in Ujjain and a branch of that family had migrated to Panchet or Sikharbhum or Panchakot Kashipur in Dhalbhum or to the Manbhum region of West Bengal. The sovereign family deity of this royal line was Sekhar Basini, and a member of this royal family occupied the *gaddi* of Kesaripur, named after the former king of the Kesari line, and subsequently went on to rule Gangpur State. For instance, the genealogical traditions pertaining to Gangpur maintain that:

Gangadhar Sekhar alias Parikshit Sekhar, the younger brother of the king at Sikharbhum in Manbhum, fell out with the latter and thus left his home in search of 'some other country where he might be the ruler'. Seeking permission of his mother, he set out on his journey without letting others know about his mission. Being only 22 years old, he started his journey 'on Saturday, the seventh day of Kanya of 407 Hindu era of Delhi emperor'. On the way, he met a born-blind Brahman performing his morning ablutions in a river. The shadow of the prince, his galloping horse, and the goddess Sekhar Basini fell on the Brahman. Upon this, the Brahman predicted that 'he who was riding by him would become a raja in no time and further advised him to proceed in Northward direction'. As a result, Parikshit Sekhar instantly alighted from the horse and promised the Brahman that he would make him and his successor not only his family priest but also the raja for two hours on Vijayadashami day. The old Brahman agreed to the proposal and warned Parikshit Sekher that 'he should not astray from the path of virtues' and assured him that he would be a nice ruler if he adhered to his instructions. Encouraged by the blessings of the old Brahman, Parikshit Sekhar proceeded further and on the way reached Kesaripur. In fact, Kesaripur provided an opportunity to Parikshit Sekhar to realize his dream of becoming a king there. He witnessed the continuous infighting amongst the Bhuiyan zamindars and chiefs. With the arrival of Parikshit, a realignment of forces amongst the Bhuiyan chiefs took place. Parikshit sided with the supposedly dominant Bhuiyan chiefs like the Majhi or zamindar of Sargipalli and waged war against the other chiefs. He emerged triumphant in the war and finally received the vermilion mark, the sign of royalty on his forehead from the hands of Majhi of Sargipalli and Madan Pradhan, 'on the eighteenth day of kanya 408 Delhi era'. Later on, Parikshit was taken to Masabira, where the royal umbrella had been preserved. He continued to rule from Masabira for sometime afterwards. . . . Parikshit's elder brother from Panchakot Kashipur came down to Masabira region in search of the former. However, he couldn't find him there as the Bhuiyan kept him concealed in a manchan (a platform) made in the midst of a stream. However, his elder brother assured the Bhuiyans that he would not take away his brother and they should properly inform him whether he was alive or not. Upon this, the Bhuiyan leaders produced him and renamed Parikshit as Jalandhar as he had been kept in the manchan inside water (jala). Finally, his elder brother left for Panchkot Kashipur, thereby leaving the younger one to rule the State of Kesaripur which was subsequently named as Gangpur.[45]

[44]M.M. Mishra n.d.
[45]*PR, 700*; Sekhar Deo n.d.

This account is really one of the fascinating examples of a legend of Rajputization, most likely of the same period, as has appropriately been described in the context of the Chauhans of western Orissa.[46] Needless to say, such narratives associated with the Rajputization model are typical of the period dating back to the seventeenth and eighteenth centuries.

As Masabira was not placed at the 'centre' of his domain, Jalandhar decided to shift his capital to Patnagarh, later called Gangpurgarh. What is more significant is that Jalandhar or Gangadhar also granted two villages, namely, Masabira and Laikera, 'free of rent in perpetuity' to the Kalo, an influential Bhuiyan family of the locality. He further ordered that the Kalo should supply only two *chhatra dandas* (bamboo for Chhatra) at the time of the accession of a new raja to the *gaddi*. He also resolved that 'no Paramara ruler will overlook the practice and collect rent from these villages and if any one goes beyond it [*sic*], he will meet with premature death'. The Kalos seem to have accepted the new king and become reconciled to the new Kshatriya regime in the region by making a declarative oath inscribed on a piece of stone called the Gadha Sila. The oath reads as follows:

> We the Kalos, priest gar-majhi and all the zamindars do hereby promise to have perfect amity among ourselves and shall have no hostile attitude against each other and the raja on any account.[47]

Yet another account mentions that:

> Gangadhar alias Parikhita Sekhar is referred to as Hatihambar Sekhar who was crowned at Masabira 'seated on a platform (mancha) inside a stream'. As his coronation took place in the pool of water, he came to be called as Jalandhar Sekhar Deo. . . . With the coronation of the king, the zamindars became powerful. The king could never object to whatever the zamindars wished to do. As per the account, the Bhuiyan zamindars gave Jalandhar Sekhar Deo, a few praganas and distributed the rest amongst themselves. Accordingly, the zamindar of Sargipalli received seventeen praganas in the relatively plain areas of the region, while the zamindars of Sargipalli, Hemagir, Nagra, Saraphgarh, Erga, Laikera, Pithabhuin, Giringkela, Mahulgaon, Nuagada, Bauseni, Baghabandha, Kukurdiha and Lurkidihi received 17 praganas, 84 praganas, 30 kos (of land), 14 kos, 42 praganas, 24 praganas, 12 praganas, 15 praganas, 5 praganas, 12 praganas, 12 praganas, 5 praganas, 5 praganas and 5 praganas respectively. Further this account mentions that 'all the zamindars got together and convinced Jalandhar Sekhar to return the lands which originally belonged to Madan Pradhan'. Thus, Madan Pradhan got back his dewanhuda. Finally, after giving a few praganas to the king Jalandhar Sekhar Deo, the zamindars distributed the rest of the praganas amongst themselves. Afterwards, both the 'zamindar and the Raja Dewan' got united to rule over the region. The period from 1597 to 1618 A.D. is ascribed to the reign of Jalandhar Sekhar Deo.[48]

The narrative is perhaps suggestive of the fact that, leaving aside the most

[46]For detailed references, see Panda in this volume.

[47]*PR* 700.

[48]*PR* 677.

likely late 'invented' Kesari dynasty [my emphasis], there was always the dominance or rule of the various Bhuiyan chiefs, only once interrupted by the 'unsuccessful' attempt of Madan Pradhan, one of the powerful Bhuiyan chiefs, to establish something like a kingdom. Once he and his weak successors were dead, his 'land' was redistributed among the Bhuiyan chiefs. This seems to be a typical case of tribal resistance, 'however not by the tribal subalterns but by the tribal chiefs'. The real 'tribal subalterns' rose in revolt only when, under colonialism, the chiefs and kings attempted or had to exploit the people more because of new settlement regulations and so on.[49]

What is more interesting in this account is the reference to the continuous 'disturbances' that the kings of Sekhar had to face subsequently in the form of the threats posed by the 'tigers' of the region, the 'poor health' of subjects or the 'divine wrath' caused by the discontent of the presiding deity of Gangaimati. The account goes on to suggest that,

> on account of these (above said) reasons, the *gaddi* didn't suit Jalandhar Sekhar for long as a result of which Jalandhar relinquished the throne and lived in the fort of Gangpur on the bank of river Ib. Similarly, Hamir Sekhar Deo (1635-1698) also faced the same kind of crisis. The 'divine wrath' caused by the presiding deity of Gangaimati was so terrible that the tigers infested the region. Hence, the former asked Betala Pradhan to propitiate the presiding deity by 'preparing a kite'. But however, the Pradhan family got wiped out in two months time while performing the *puja* to propitiate the deity.
>
> . . . The phase of crisis persisted till Gaikan Sekhar Deo (1698-1737). During his reign, the 'threat of the tigers, sickness of the people and wrath of the presiding deity all combined to disrupt the peace and security of the region. The only solution for the state appeared to be the propitiation of the state deity who was seen as the 'creator of all these problems'. It was in this context, the Bhuiyan zamindars attributed the reasons for such disturbances to the murder of Manbhanjakesari, the last ruler of Kesari dynasty. They further reasoned that the son of the youngest queen of Manbhanjakesari who had been pregnant and fled from Hemagir to her father's place at Ratanpur in Bilaspur to escape death after knowing about the brutal murder of the king, should be brought back to the Gangapur kingdom with honour. The son of the queen, Bharata Kesari had married in the Chauhan family. The Bhuiyans were convinced that if he was brought back to the kingdom, then the presiding deity of the state could be conciliated and the problems of the kingdom would be eased out. The king of Ratanpur agreed to the proposal and ordered the zamindars to fetch Bharata Kesari.
>
> Thus, Anand Singh Majhi, Sansadhar Majhi, Tetiasingh Dansana, the Zamindars of Sargipalli, Hemagir and Sarapagarh respectively went and met the Ho king of Ratanpur and appealed to him to return Bharathi Kesari to Gangpur. Initially, the Ratanpur king hesitated and reminded the zamindars that they had killed the Kesari king in the past. Upon this, the Bhuiyan zamindars en masse vowed to protect the surviving scion of ex-local Kesari rule with due honour. Finally, the Ho king conceded and agreed to send Bhrarathi Kesari to Gangpur. On return, the Bhuiyans pleaded with

[49]I am grateful to Kulke for his valuable comments on this aspect of 'Subaltern resistance'.

the Sekhar king to install Bharathi Kesari on the Gangpur throne, which was unacceptable to the king. On the other hand, Bharathi Kesari, as the scion of ex-royal rule was provided with 20 lakhraj villages and assumed the title of Bada Kuanar, a zamindar. As Bada Kuanar, he was supposed to offer worship to the presiding deity of the state. The deity was finally satisfied and the problems of the 'kingdom' were surmounted. Bharathi Kesari continued to remain as the zamindar of Kopasingha.[50]

This story is yet another symbolic example of 'tribal resistance' in the shape of a presiding tribal deity who stood opposed to a non-Bhuiyan king. It was only after a person of tribal origin became a zamindar that the deity was pacified. The account further points out that, during the reign of Brajanath Sekhar Deo (1795-1822), the zamindar of Sargipalli sought to contest the authority of the king. The latter 'killed (?)' the Sargipalli zamindar at Kopasingha. Under these circumstances, the king had to shift his capital to Kopasingha for five years. However, in all probability,

> Indra Sekhar Deo had his capital at Gangpurgarh but he subsequently removed his capital to Raibogagarh when Pratap Majhi, the zamindar of Sargipalli defied his authority and made preparation to attack Gangapurgarh. After Indra Sekhar Deo, his son Parsuram Sekhar Deo became the ruler. He received the first Sanad from the British Govt. in CE 1827. He had his capital at Nabrangpur, near modern Rajgangpur. He was a powerful king and attacked Sargipalli to take revenge on Pratap Majhi who had been a bitter enemy of his father. Pratap Majhi escaped but later on when he was found addressing a meeting at Kupsingha, he was dramatically stabbed to death with a spear by Raja Parsuram Sekhar Deo from horse back.[51]

The history of Gangpur State as furnished by Kasinath Sekhar Deo, with certain twists in the narratives, presents almost the same story as mentioned above.[52] This account runs as follows:

> Gangadhar, accompanied by one of his brothers who fell out with the eldest brother at Panchakot Kashipur, set out on a hunting expedition in a northern direction. On this expedition, he was accompanied by the family deity Sekhar Basini. On the way, Gangadhar left behind his middle brother and met a blind Brahman while proceeding by the side of river Brahmani. The Brahman who was moved by the shadow of Gangadhar and the deity Sekhar Basini predicted that if Gangadhar moved in the northern direction, he would definitely be a king. Gangadhar thus promised the Brahman that if his prediction went right he would make him the king for an hour during the day of Vijayadashami by offering him royal canopy and parasol. After this, Gangadhar proceeded in the north-ward direction and met a group of people at Mandiakudar who were herding buffaloes. These people served Gangadhar with cheese and curd as the latter was feeling hungry. Finally, Gangadhar crossed the Ib river and reached Patnagarh. Herein, he came in contact with the Bhuiyans and cultivated relationship with them. Afterwards, the Bhuiyans expressed their desire to install him in the *gaddi*. But, Gangadhar told them that his middle brother who was following him would not allow

[50] *PR* 677.
[51] *ODG* 70.
[52] Sekhar Deo n.d.

him to be the king there and instead would prefer to take him back. Then, the Bhuiyans concealed Gangadhar in the place called Rajaluka of Masabira by erecting a platform (*mancha*) inside a stream. After some time, Gangadhar's brother reached Masabira and enquired about him. But the Bhuiyans didn't divulge any information about Gangadhar and on the other hand, argued that Gangadhar might have been killed by the animals on the way. But, Gangadhar's brother was not prepared to accept this and instead argued that Gangadhar could never have been killed as he was a great warrior. Rather, he suspected that the Bhuiyans had kept him secretly. But, the Bhuiyans pleaded their innocence. Finally however, the brother returned to Kashipur Sikhar Bhuiyan.

. . . Then the Bhuiyans persuaded Gangadhar to be the king. But, Gangadhar wanted to ensure the blessing of the local deity (who would reside in the royal canopy) before becoming the king. Thus, he planted a dried bamboo on the soil and branches came out of the plant overnight. This finally made him accept the *gaddi* of Gangpur, whereupon, the zamindar of Sargipalli coronated him to the throne by putting vermilion on his forehead. The king further made arrangements for the worship of the bamboo tree at Masabira.

Thus, the bamboo umbrella came to assume critical significance in the coronation rituals of the king. The account goes on to state:

If at any point of time, a bamboo tree in Masabira bore flowers at the top like an umbrella, then it was a sure signal for the death of the king. Accordingly, the dehuri was supposed to inform the king about this development. After the death of the king, the bamboo was cut off into three pieces, and brought back to the royal palace with a procession. Two pieces of this bamboo were placed by the side of goddess Samalai and Kali in the Samleswari temple, situated inside the palace of Sundargarh. The other piece was placed in the royal canopy. Gangadhar also made the blind Brahman who had done the authentic prediction for his kingship, the royal priest and donated him the village of Ekma. The Bhuiyan zamindars who had helped him to be the king were also considerably rewarded by granting them large tracts of land. These zamindars afterwards helped Gangadhar in consolidating his authority over the region. Later on, Gangadhar also brought back his middle brother and gave him Hatibari or Kinjiri State by way of Kharposh (maintenance) grant. Gangadhar also tried to compensate the help rendered to him by the people belonging to gauda caste of Mandiakudar by granting them the said village. This caste was importantly integrated to the royal ceremony and royalty subsequently. They were assigned the task of beating drums by using the horns of buffaloes during the day of Vijayadashami and used to accompany the king in the latter's inspection of the township during this auspicious day. As the beating of drums with the horns of buffaloes required tremendous energy, castor oil used to be applied on their heads at regular intervals.

. . . afterwards, Gangadhar shifted his capital to Patnagarh from Masabari. It is only after the death of Gangadhar, his son Jagannath and grandson that Jalandhar renamed their state as Gangpur in the name of the late king. Jalandhar who was a powerful king fought against the raja of Raigarh over the issue of the Gangpur boundary.

During the rule of Indra Sekhar Deo, the capital of Gangpur was shifted to Raibogagarh to counter the resistance of Pratap Majhi, the zamindar of Sargipalli. However, the latter was killed by Raja Parsuram Sekhar Deo, the son of Indra Sekhar, at Kopsingha. Thus, both Indra Sekhar and Parsuram largely succeeded in removing the threat posed by the Bhuiyan zamindars. The son of Parsuram Sekhar Deo, Jagadev Sekhar Deo, was in all probability the same person as Indra Sekhar Deo.[53] Jagadev Sekhar Deo had shifted his capital to Jagatgarh. As Jagadev Sekhar Deo did not have a son, his brother's son, Janardan Sekhar Deo, became the king after his rule. Danardan or Janardan Sekhar Deo had established his capital at Suadihi near the river Ib. One day, while he was on his way to Ranchi to attend the durbar, the family priest killed him near Ekma village.[54]

The reason for the alleged murder, as the popular memory recounts, is attributed to the anger of the Brahman, who had been humiliated by a joke against him made by the king. While travelling on the back of an elephant himself, the king had seen the royal priest being carried in a *palki* by the servants. The king made a disparaging remark, enquiring where the dead body was being taken,[55] which greatly offended the Brahman. However, the incident goes on to suggest that a Kshatriya ruler was bound to respect the Brahmans. It was, after all, the old blind Brahman who had rightly predicted that Gangadhar would become a king. He had also warned him 'not to go astray'. It may also be suggested here that the king in question may have tried to deviate from the custom of having the Brahman perform the role of a king during the Vijayadashami function, or else he wanted to divest the Brahman of the traditional privileges enjoyed by the latter. The story also reinforces the belief that Brahmanical support was essential and indeed a precondition for the Kshatriya to be a king, particularly if the latter's Kshatriya status was not fully authenticated. What further needs to be emphasized here is that the constant relocations of the so-called 'capitals' implies that these were neither 'capitals' nor ruled by 'kings' with so-called kingdoms, but only refer to certain territorial boundaries containing forts that were controlled by the tribal zamindars.

Kasinath's account also provides certain other fascinating details regarding the kings of Gangpur State and the rituals they observed. For instance:

> As the son of Danardan/Janardhan Sekhar, Pitambar Sekhar didn't have a son, his brother's son, Raghunath Sekhar Deo, became the ruler of Gangpur during 1858-1917. It is worth noting that Raghunath Sekhar Deo succeeded to the throne when he was a minor. However, he took over the charge of the state from 27 January 1871. He renamed Suadihi as Sundargarh. Raghunath was a Ramanujaite and established the temple of Jagannath in 1916. The rituals as followed in the temple of Jagannath in Puri came to be emulated here. He also built the temple for Sikharbasini, i.e. Rajeswari Durga, the presiding deity of the state. Twice in a year, once on the day of Nuakhai and the other on the day of Ambagundi of Phaguna Purnami, the deity used to be offered *puja*. The Samaleswari temple was constructed by his grandson.
>
> The two other goddesses Kali and Durga were seated in the left and right side of Samaleswari goddess. Besides, the bamboo sticks collected from Masabira were also

[53] *ODG* 70-1; Sekhar Deo, n.d.
[54] *ODG* 71; Sekhar Deo, n.d.
[55] Sekhar Deo, n.d.

kept by the side of goddess Samleswari on both sides. The Bhuiyans have been offering worship in this temple since its inception.

. . . During the Dushera festival, sixteen swords are usually worshipped from the day of Amabasya to the day of Vijayadashami. And in each of these days, a he-goat used to be sacrificed which stands for one of the sixteen swords. The royal guns, swords as well as the royal books and royal canopy are also worshipped during this period in the temple of Samaleswari. In the eighth day, ashtabali was offered to the goddess which included—black hen, black swan, black pigeon, black she-goat, pumpkin, black fish, etc. The practice of human sacrifice before the goddess Kali in every three years duration as supposedly practiced in the state came to be substituted by the above form of sacrifice afterwards.

. . . The day of Vijayadashami marked the apex of royal festivities and glamour. It started with the coronation process of the king amidst the placing of thirty two golden chairs. In this specific day, all the zamindars including the members of Royal family in all the villages came down to greet the king. The zamindar of Sargipali, the traditionally influential Bhuiyan, not only offered the king the right of investiture by gifting the royal turban but importantly also paid the annual dues on the same day. It was during this occasion the king in fact, sought to implement his promise made to the Brahman by making the latter the king at least for two hours. The royal priest had to hold the royal sword and the bamboo canopy and being seated on the back of the elephant, he was driven to the place of target-shooting. After performing the *puja*, the royal priest returned to the king his sword and canopy. The priest who had killed Danardan Sekhar Deo/Janardan Sekhar Deo was dismissed and instead, another Brahman was brought from Sonepur and thus made the royal priest.

. . . The king used to move around the royal capital accompanied by the zamindars and the royal army including elephants and horses and moved on to the place of target shooting. This was followed by a grand feast wherein the general populace of the city partook and dancing performance and music concerts took place at night.

. . . At the lion's gate of the palace, the goddess Kanaka Durga used to be worshipped as the protector of the palace, by a Bhuiyan dehuri. In this temple, the royal sword (Patta Khanda) was also worshipped. Inside the palace, there is a place called Chattra ghara (room containing the royal canopy). A piece of bamboo brought from Masabira was kept inside the royal canopy. In order to protect the fort, usually a he-goat sacrifice was made in the northern end of the palace. The sacrifice was made in the name of Brahmarakhysa.[56]

What emerges clearly from these local genealogical accounts of Gangpur state is their focus on what may be called the 'constructed regional and remembered local past'.[57] The regional past to which these accounts draw our attention seems like a world of legendary traditions of regional heroes and gods and their constructed relations with the respective localities. Similarly, the remembered past of the accounts consists of a barrage of information narrating local events, including references to earlier dynastic genealogies. What is more evident in these accounts is the authors' predilection for exploring and forging links on behalf of the local dynasty with the Kshatriya tradition as a whole and the north Indian Kshatriya tradition in particular.

[56] Ibid.

[57] Kulke 2004.

The so-called triumph of Kshatriyaization in the region, despite temporary setbacks (as in the case of the decline of local Kesari dynasty), as vindicated by these accounts, really consists of stories punctuated with moments of assertion, resistance and subversion by the indigenous communities of the locality *vis-à-vis* outsiders who belonged to the Brahmanical order. Furthermore, what is equally critically discernible in these accounts is the marginal triumph of Kshatriya rule associated with its precarious and ambivalent positions with continuous contestations and negotiations.[58] The periodic resistance of the Bhuiyan zamindars or the Munda rebellion in the region over a prolonged historical period illustrates this. What is more crucial to point out in this context is the subtly 'muted valorization' (emphasis added) of the advent of Kshatriya rule over the region. In contrast, the indigenous communities, and the Bhuiyan zamindars in particular, are shown to have played a decisive role in determining the nature and extent of Kshatriya rule.

The 'declarative oath' of one of the Bhuiyan chiefs, i.e. the Kalos, inscribed on the rock, regarding the 'primordial right' of the Bhuiyans to legitimize the coronation of the king by putting vermilion on the forehead or handing over the royal turban to the king or the conciliatory policies adopted by the king *vis-à-vis* the Bhuiyan chiefs with regard to land distribution as reflected in these accounts, all point to a not so dominant position of authority for the Kshatriya kings. In a way, the Bhuiyans sought to assign the king a position of centrality without marginalizing their own positions. The Bhuiyans were always zealous in guarding their 'traditional and time honoured privileges', and any infringement of such freedom bred tension and resistance.

Similarly, the stories of Brahmanical support of Kshatriya rule in terms of Brahmanical prophecy for the king or the revenge unleashed by the royal priest on the king through murder or elevating the Brahman to the position of the king in the royal rituals are suggestive of the ambiguity of the Kshatriya-Brahman combination on the Hindu-tribal frontier in ensuring the subjugation of the indigenous communities.

More important, however, are the host of repeated references in the accounts to local deities, gods and goddesses and the ways they sought to relate themselves to the local dynasties. The story of the *chattra bauti* (bamboo canopy), with its 'highly venerated' implications for royalty and its association with the rituals of the presiding deity of the state invariably indicates the stronger hold of indigenous religious practices which impacted on the Kshatriya religious order.

The history of the *chattra bauti*, starting with its origin in the fort of Masabira to its subsequent link with the state capital of Gangpur, and mediated by a long process of transformation 'in between', in a way implies a reconciliation

[58] Kulke 1993, 85. As has been aptly pointed out by Kulke, Kshatriyaization in its functional sense, refers to a social change 'from above' which was initiated in tribal areas by the Kshatriyas, i.e. zamindars, chiefs or rajas in order to strengthen their legitimation as Hindu rajas in their own society and broaden the basis of their economy and political power.

of the 'Hindu' and 'tribal' religious perceptions. As stated earlier, the processes of the 'Hinduization' of tribal gods, goddesses, rituals and religious practices and of the 'tribalization' of kingship not only co-existed but characterized the socio-cultural space of the region.

The other significant aspect of the accounts is the attempt to forge links with the earlier local Kesari dynasty and thus ensure an 'imagined' continuity of Kshatriya rule in the region by 'incorporating' the surviving members of the erstwhile royal lineage to the 'present ruling dynasty'.

As the story tells us, the surviving member of local Kesari rule, who was residing at Ratanpur and belonged to the Ho tribe, was invited to settle down in the Sekhar kingdom. The Bhuiyan zamindars had realized that the adversities through which their region was passing could only be warded off if they repented for their crime of brutally murdering the last local Kesari king, Manabhanjakesari. The Bhuiyans thus 'repented' by appealing to the father of the Kesari queen at Ratanpur in Bilaspur and successfully persuading the latter to 'return' the surviving scion of the former Kesari rule to the fort of the Sekhar royal family. A member of the Kesari family was therefore not only invited, accommodated and granted a 'prestigious position' in the social hierarchy, but also the Bhuiyans had done sufficiently to atone for their brutal crime of killing the so-called Kshatriya rulers. One can therefore understand the strategy adopted by the authors of such accounts, which were mainly narratives drawn up by the Brahmans of the royal court to validate and legitimize the hegemonic position of the Kshatriyas over the region, particularly the tribal communities in general.

REFERENCES

Banerji, R.D. 1928. 'Rajput Origins in Orissa', in *Modern Review* 43, 285-91.

Berkemer, G. 2003. 'The Centers Out There: Facets Subregional Identity', Call for Papers, Salzau Conference, Germany.

Behera, K.S. 1971. 'Barapati Copper Plate of Hambhir Deva', in N.K. Sahu (ed.), *New Aspects of History of Orissa*, vol. 1, Sambalpur: Sambalpur University, 52-4.

Cobden Ramsay, L.E.B. 1910. *Feudatory States of Orissa*, Calcutta: The Bengal Secretariat Book Depot (rpt. 1950, 1982).

Dalton, E.T. 1973. *Tribal History of India*, Delhi: Cosmo.

Hunter, W.W. 1877. *Statistical Accounts of Bengal: Singhbhum District, Tributary States of Chota Nagpur and Manbhum*, vol. 17, London: Trübner & Co.

Kulke, H. 1993. 'Ksatriyaization and Social Change: A Study in the Orissa Setting', in H. Kulke (ed.), *Kings and Cults: State Formation and Legitimation in India and Southeast Asia*, Delhi: Manohar, 82-93 (1st pub. 1976).

———2004. 'The Making of a Local Chronicle: The Ranapur Rajavamsa Itihasa', in Angelika Malinar, Johannes Beltz and Heiko Frese (eds.), *Text and Context in the History, Literature and Religion of Orissa*, Delhi: Manohar, 43-66.

———2008. 'Yayati Kesari Revisited: Ramachandra of Khurda and the Yayati Kesari Legend of Puri', in P. Berger, R. Hardenberg, E. Kattner and M. Prager (eds.), *The Anthropology of Values: Festschrift in Honour of Georg Pfeffer*, Delhi: Pearson/Longman.

Mishra, M.M. n.d. 'Keonjhar Rajavamsavali', unpublished manuscript.

Mishra, P.P. 2002. 'The Hillsmen of Gangpur: Social Stratification and Resistance Movement', paper presented at Modern South Asian Conference, Edinburgh (unpublished).

Nanda, C.P. 2003. 'Validating "Tradition": Revisiting Keonjhar and Bhuyan Insurgency in Colonial Orissa', in G. Berkemer and M. Frenz (eds.), *Sharing Sovereignty: The Little Kingdom in South Asia*, Berlin: Klaus Schwarz.

———2008. *Vocalising Silence: Political Protests in Orissa 1930-42*, Delhi: Sage Publications.

Orissa District Gazetter: Sundargarh, 1971, Cuttack: Govt. Press.

Panigrahi, K.C. 1961. *Chronology of the Bhauma-Karas and the Somavamsis of Orissa*, Madras: M.L.J. Press.

Pandey, S. 2003. 'Belsaragarh: Eka Anudhyana' (Oriya), in *Mukta Kalam*, vol. 7-13, Bhubaneswar/Sundargarh.

Pati, B. 1993. *Resisting Domination: Peasants, Tribals and the National Movement in Orissa 1920-50*, Delhi: Manohar.

Private Loose Records: 'Traditional Note of Gangpur Raj Family (Kesari and Sekhar Raj Families)', ACC. No. 700, Orissa State Archives, Bhubaneswar. 'Genealogy of the Ruling Chief of Gangpur State (Oriya)', ACC. No. 677. Orissa State Archives, Bhubaneswar.

Rajaguru, S.N. 1971. 'Somavamsi Kings of Kosala', in N.K. Sahu (ed.), *New Aspects of History of Orissa*, vol. 1, Sambalpur: Sambalpur University, 49-51.

Russel, R.V. and R.B. Hira Lal 1975. *Tribes and Castes of the Central Provinces of India*, vol. 2, Delhi: Cosmo (rpt.).

Sahu, B. 2010. 'Profiling Dakṣiṇa Kośala: An Early Historical Subregion?', in Hermann Kulke and Georg Berkemer (eds.), *Centres Out There? Facets of Subregional Identities in Orissa*, Delhi: Manohar.

Sahu, N.K. 1971. 'A Survey of the History of South Kosala', in N.K. Sahu (ed.), *New Aspects of History of Orissa*, vol. 1, Sambalpur: Sambalpur University, 9-24.

Sekhar Deo, K. n.d. 'Gangpur Itihasa' (Oriya), unpublished manuscript.

Sinha, S. 1962. 'State Formation and Rajput Myth in Tribal Central India', in *Man in India* 42, 35-80.

Skoda, Uwe 2005. *The Aghriā: A Peasant Caste on a Tribal Frontier*, Delhi: Manohar.

CHAPTER 9

The Centre Was Out There in the South, in Ghumsar

GAGANENDRA NATH DASH

> I would suggest rather, let them take a chasa[1] of Dacca and a chasa of Ghumsar and see how much they understand of one another's talk.
>
> JOHN BEAMES 1870[2]

Beames, Collector of Balasore in 1870, made this remark to disprove the contention that mutual intelligibility between Bengali and Oriya is very high, as was claimed by Kantichandra Bhattacharya and supported by R.L. Mitra.[3] It was part of a larger thesis Beames put forward, that Oriya was not merely a dialect of Bengali, as Mitra and others claimed, but an independent language. This was again in the context of a controversial debate on the question of introducing Bengali instead of Oriya as the medium of instruction in schools in Orissa.

My main aim in referring to this remark and the context in which it was made is to show that, in the second half of the nineteenth century, the language spoken in and around Ghumsar appeared to an outsider like Beames to be a specimen of the 'true' Oriya language. Ghumsar was a small and former princely state in the south, which had been annexed to the British territory of the Madras Presidency and was therefore out of 'Orissa Proper', which consisted of the three coastal districts of Cuttack, Puri and Balasore. However, it must also be emphasized here that Beames, who was then working on the northern frontier of Orissa, in Balasore, never had the occasion to visit any place, let alone Ghumsar, in the southern region of the Oriya-speaking tracts when he made this observation.

Although this observation might have been based, at least partially, on public perception, it should not be dismissed as a casual and careless remark by an ordinary and not so knowledgeable British administrator. On the contrary, it was a well-considered opinion by a serious scholar. Beames was an Orientalist and philologist in his own right, who made this observation in all seriousness

[1] In Orissa the cultivator caste is known as *chasa*.

[2] Beames 1870.

[3] For more information on the views and arguments of Kantichandra Bhattacharya and R.L. Mitra; see Dash 1993.

in a paper presented to a session of the Asiatic Society of Bengal, later to be published in the proceedings of the Society.[4] Furthermore, about two years later, in the first volume of his famous work, *A Comparative Grammar of the Modern Aryan Languages of India*, Beames was even more forthright when he stated, 'Oriya literature begins with Upendra Bhanja, who was a brother of the raja of Ghumsar, a petty hill-state in the south of Orissa, which even to the present day is celebrated as the home of the *purest form* of the language'.[5] Beames further noted: 'It is said by the Oriyas themselves that the language is spoken in its greatest purity in the hill-state of Ghumsar, the birthplace of the first national poet, Upendra Bhanja.'[6] Therefore Beames' opinion was based, at least to a certain extent, on the public perception, 'said by the Oriyas themselves'. But Beames did not accept that opinion blindly and without careful consideration. He even tended to doubt the veracity of this view when he said: 'As, however, Ghumsar is very to the south, closely adjoining areas peopled by Dravidians and Kols, this assertion seems rather doubtful.'[7] But finally he came to the conclusion that 'The poems of Upendra Bhanja and his contemporaries are written in a language, which hardly differs in a single word or inflection from the vernacular of today, and every word of which is distinctly intelligible to the meanest labourer. These poems, written three hundred years ago, exhibit a perfectly settled modern language. . . .'[8] In other words, to Beames, if not the language of Ghumsar, certainly the language used by Upendra Bhanja, the prince of Ghumsar, represents standard Oriya or 'the purest form' of the speech. Therefore his opinion was based not only on public perceptions but also on his own careful considerations.

At about the same time, in 1872, W.W. Hunter similarly regarded Upendra Bhanja as 'the most eminent of all the Oriya poets',[9] a statement which also reflects the prestige and celebrity that Upendra Bhanja and Ghumsar enjoyed. Another British official, T.J. Maltby of the Madras Civil Service, also observed that '[t]he purest Uriya is spoken in Gumsur, and north of Rushikulia river as owing to Bengali being the official language in Orissa, and its having a considerable affinity to Uriya, the latter seems to have assimilated to it more than to Telugu in the south'.[10] Moreover, in 1864, in one of his essays a Bengali intellectual, Rangalal Bandyopadhyay, who first came to Orissa in 1863 as a government official, had accorded Upendra Bhanja at any rate the second position among the celebrated poets of Orissa,[11] crediting him with fifty-two

[4]Beames 1870.

[5]Beames 1872, 88 [emphasis added].

[6]Ibid., 105.

[7]Ibid., 119.

[8]Ibid.

[9]Hunter et al. 1956, 220.

[10]Maltby 1874: Preface, VI. The preface was written in October 1873.

[11]Bandyopadhyay 1864. In first position he placed Dinakrushna Das, author of *Rasa Kallola*.

famous literary works. As in the case of Beames, the opinions expressed by Hunter and Rangalal appear to have been based both on public perceptions and on their own judgements.

It is not my intention to either accept or examine critically the truth of the judgements of these three administrators-cum-scholars. What I want to emphasize is that, in the second half of the nineteenth century, to Oriyas, knowledgeable outsiders like Beames, Hunter and Maltby, and even Bengali intellectuals like Rangalal,[12] the linguistic and literary centre of the Oriya-speaking tracts was in the south, in and around Ghumsar, beyond the then political boundaries of Orissa.

This high estimate of Ghumsar and Upendra Bhanja among the Oriyas in the second half of the nineteenth century seems to have existed continuously since the eighteenth century, the time of Upendra Bhanja (*c.* 1685-1735), the great late-medieval Oriya poet. This is indirectly confirmed from another, rather unusual source, namely, public interest in the Ghumsar Raj family, which manifests itself in a large number of *vamsavali pothi*s, or family genealogies, both in Sanskrit and in Oriya (in Oriya prose and verse), by different authors,[13] although the rajas of Ghumsar reigned only until 1835. No such other large numbers of genealogical texts are known from any other Raj family of Orissa (including the Feudatory states), although these rajas continued to reign until 1948-9. This is indicative of the high public esteem and importance of the Ghumsar Raj family.

II

In order to understand the rise of Ghumsar to this high position, we must go back more than three hundred years, to when Dhananjaya Bhanja (*c.* 1637-1701) was the raja of Ghumsar. He set certain literary trends, which matured in the hands of his grandson Upendra Bhanja (*c.* 1685-1735) and made Ghumsar famous throughout the Oriya-speaking tracts. In addition, Ghana Bhanja (1707-54)[14] and Trivikrama Bhanja (1773-80)[15] of the same Ghumsar Raj family are also known for their important literary contributions. Suryamani Chyau Pattanayak (1773-1828), who translated the Sanskrit *Adhytma Ramayana* into Oriya and wrote *Ghumusar Bhanja Vamsavali* also belonged to Ghumsar.

Dhananjaya has several works to his credit. He exhibited great interest and talent in writing long narrative *kavya* poems, divided into several cantos based

[12]It is also said that a little later, in 1879, another Bengali intellectual, Bhudev Mukhopadhyay, also praised Upendra Bhanja's poetic talents. See Durgacharan Ray 1998, 103-4, 112-14.

[13]At least seven such *vamsavali* texts have been identified up till now. See 'Ghumsar *Bhanja Vamsavali* Texts' in the references.

[14]K.N. Mahapatra 1969, 215-16. Ghana Bhanja has written two kavyas called *Trailokyamohini* and *Rasanidhi*.

[15]Trivikrama Bhanja has written a *kavya* called *Kanakalata*.

on either Puranic (mythical) or imaginary stories. Besides *Raghunatha Bilasa*, the story of *Ramayana* in the form of a *kavya*, he wrote at least four more imaginary kavyas such as *Icchabati*, based partly on a folk tale, the *Tripuramohini*, *Madanamanjari*, *Anangarekha* and some songs. Dhananjaya's chief merit lies in his thematic and stylistic innovations in late medieval *kavya* literature. For the theme of his kavyas, he preferred imaginary stories[16] to mythological or Puranic ones and introduced rhetorical subtleties and eroticism into the realm of Oriya narrative poetry. He allowed his imagination free reign in using similes, metaphors and other figures of speech. For him, poetry was not merely to be read or recited but also to be sung, as was expected at princely courts in those days.[17] Therefore these long narrative poems could very well be sung, as their cantos were written in different metrical arrangements, or *chhanda*s as they are called. This led to experimentation in the making of *chhanda*s. Because of this, the medieval Oriya kavyas are known as *chhanda pothi*s or *chhanda* texts.

All these developments came to full maturity in the hands of Upendra Bhanja, Dhananjaya's grandson. Although Upendra's father Nilakantha was king for a short while after Dhananjaya was murdered in a palace conspiracy, Upendra was not destined to be king and lived most of his adult life in exile, away from his kingdom. Nonetheless he became and remained the uncrowned king of the Oriya literary world for more than a hundred and fifty years. He was the author of more than forty texts of different kinds, including a verse lexicon, a translation of *Purushottama Mahatmya* and a treatise on poetics.[18] As far as the themes of his kavyas are concerned, he had nothing really new to offer, but he was a 'master of rhetorical excellence' and 'knew intimately the Sanskrit rules of elegance'.[19] Moreover, he was extremely fond of playing on sounds, of which he was a master, and therefore developed an exceptional control over items of vocabulary of every kind: *tatsama*, *tadbhava* and *desaja*. 'Sometimes he wrote poems with only vowel "a" added to consonants; at other times he retained a particular sound as the initial sound of each lines, even of the title, of a *kavya*.' For example, in *Baidehisha Bilasa* and *Subhadra Parinaya*, two of his kavyas, he retains the consonant sounds '*b*' and '*s*' respectively as the initial sound of each line. Similarly, in *Kalakautuka*, another of his kavyas, he retains the consonant sound '*k*' at both the beginning and the end of each line.[20] He was a learned man and showed off his learning at every opportunity.

[16]In Orissa, in the context of Oriya literature, such imaginary stories are classified as 'secular themes', in contrast to Puranic stories, which are classified as 'religious themes'.

[17]The singing of *Gitagovinda* by Jayadeva, especially in the Jagannath temple, Puri, was extremely popular in Orissa. See Dash 1976 and 2004 for more information.

[18]See Surendra Mohanty 1992, 403-7; Binayak Mishra 1962, 146-7.

[19]Chakravarti 1898, 367.

[20]When retained at the end of the lines, '*k*', of course, is invariably followed by an '*a*' vowel, as Oriya syllables are invariably open and end with a vowel.

In one of his kavyas he even boasts that he 'has crossed the ocean of words'.[21] He was, in fact, a juggler of words. But, 'in spite of the innumerable lines of unequal merits, due to his constant attempt to play on sounds and with words and show off his learning, a large number of passages contain poetical excellence, fit to stand the fierce light of modern criticism'.[22] To quote Mayadhar Mansinha:

> It has to be admitted, however, that, in spite of the artificialities and all the pretentious pedantries, Upendra sweeps his readers off their feet by the deep subtle rhythm of the lines, by his superb metrical success and last, but not the least in importance, by the enchanted world of love, beauty and youth into which he ushers his readers or audience the moment his lines are sung or read. Unrivalled in the power of manipulating words most dexterously according to their own laws of beauty, unmatched in the art of painting sensuous, youthful love and unique in the total grand music of his lines, Upendra Bhanja dominates Oriya poetry with an influence that has almost been totalitarian for nearly two centuries.[23]

For at least a hundred and fifty years after him, most Oriya poets fell more or less under his influence and tried to imitate his ornate, pedantic and even erotic court poetry and songs throughout the Oriya-speaking tracts. Even those who attempted to move away from him and make innovations or experiments had to imitate him to start with, perhaps for their own legitimation as poets. As mentioned earlier, Ghana Bhanja and Trivikrama Bhanja of the Ghumsar Raj family, following Dhananjaya also wrote kavyas. Again, many of the most eminent Oriya poets of the early nineteenth century, such as Kavisurya Baladeva Rath (1789-1845), Jadumani Mahapatra (1781-1866) and Gopal Krishna Pattanayak (1785-1862), were from the south of Orissa, where Ghumsar is situated. They too appear to have dominated the scene.[24] Besides them, there were a host of authors, both in Oriya and in Sanskrit, who belonged to southern Orissa, for whom Ghumsar and their princes were always a source of inspiration.

The late medieval Oriya *kavya* literature became very popular among both the educated people and the illiterates throughout Orissa. While only a few could read the palm-leaf manuscripts, innumerable copies of which were made, both the educated and the illiterates listened to them because of their musical qualities. In coastal Orissa, Oriya *kavya* literature became popular through the media of Pala and Dasakathia, semi-musical theatrical performances, the kavyas of Upendra being immensely popular. The educated and the illiterate knew many *chhanda*s of his kavyas by heart, even though they did not understand them properly. They were so popular that Utkalamani Gopabandhu wrote in August 1906, in a poem on Upendra Bhanja:

[21] *Koti Brahmanda Sundari*, 14/38.

[22] Chakravarti 1898, 367.

[23] Mansinha 1962, 11.

[24] A large number of late medieval Oriya poets and authors of religious and other treatises in Sanskrit were from southern Orissa.

Oh Upendra,
Your lines are recited by the learned ones in assemblies,
And sung by the travelers on the road during
long and tedious trekking,
By the peasants working in the fields,
By the ladies within the confines of inner
apartments of the households,
And by the courtesans too, while dancing.[25]

The popularity of this literature helped in bringing about some kind of uniformity in the use of the Oriya language, a development which had already begun with the Oriya rendering of *Bhagavata-purana* in Oriya by the saint-poet Jagannath Das in the sixteenth century, as Beames had already acknowledged indirectly.[26] Because of their popularity and prestige, the poets of southern Orissa, led by the prince of Ghumsar, deeply influenced the poets of other parts of Orissa. Thus, the impression gradually gained acceptance that the language of the southern area was the purest form of Oriya.

Apart from this, Dhananjaya of Ghumsar may be credited with the pioneering attempt to write Chaupadi[27] or Odissi songs, which nowadays often accompany Odissi dance. Of course, some earlier attempts to write such songs were made. But they were numerically few and were mostly confined to Sanskrit plays written by Oriya authors[28] or were referred to in Sanskrit treatises on music.[29] But it was only Dhananjaya who accorded an independent status to them.[30] Upendra Bhanja, closely following his grandfather also showed exceptional talent and interest in composing a large number of such songs. Other poet-composers of such songs from southern Orissa include Kishorachandra Rajendra and Krushnachandra Rajendra, kings of Chikiti; Dinabandhuraj Harichandan, the king of Manjusha (Mandasa), Gobinda Rayaguru of Pittala and Jadumani Mahapatra.[31] This trend culminated in the late eighteenth and early nineteenth centuries in the works of Kavisurya Baladeva Rath, who was associated with several princely courts of southern Orissa and Gopalakrushna of Parlakhimedi.

A little more than half a century ago, the dance form today popularly known

[25]The poem was first published in a literary periodical, *Mukura* (I/5), and later, after Gopabandhu's death, was included in an anthology of his poems, *Abakashachinta*. See *Pandit Gopabandhu Granthabali* 2004, 170-1 for the poem and 13-14, 25, for further information.

[26]See Beames 1872, 119.

[27]These songs do not necessarily consist of four *padas* or couplets as the name indicates. See J.B. Mohanty 1976, 51f. and 1982, 3-18 for more information.

[28]For such a song written in Oriya, see *Parasurama Vijaya*, a Sanskrit play, the authorship of which is attributed to Gajapati Kapilendra Dev. See *The Prachi* 2, 3/4, 115.

[29]Such songs are to be found in *Sangita Muktavali* by Srichandan and *Sangita Narayana* by Gajapati Jagannath Narayan Dev of Parlakhimedi. See J.B. Mohanty 1982, 9-10.

[30]Dhananjaya's available work is *Chaupadi Bhusana*, in which 34 such songs have been compiled, though he may have written many other songs too.

[31]For more information, see J.B. Mohanty 1976, 1982.

as Odissi dance took the important step of being 'reconstructed' by a fusion of two still living but distinct dance forms: Gotipua dance[32] and the Mahari (or Devadasi) dance of the Jagannath temple at Puri. Their synthesis was refined on the basis of some medieval Orissan dance treatise and temple sculpture of Orissa[33] in order to have it recognized as a margi (in the terminology of medieval texts) or classical dance form, a project very dear to Oriya nationalists.[34] It appears that instead of being a decadent or corrupted version of an originally *margi* or classical dance form, the Gotipua dance was from the very beginning a *desi* or regional dance form from southern Orissa. It consisted mainly of two components: (i) *bandha* or *nritta*, i.e. rhythmic dance accompanied by *bol* and *tala*, played on drum, and (ii) *abhinaya*,[35] based on Chaupadis or Odissi songs that were strongly influenced by the Ghumsar tradition.[36] It contained no other components of what today is known as Odissi dance.[37] The very name Odissi also appears to be not very old.[38] The trend to trace artificially the origin of Gotipua dance in temple sculptures, in the Mahari dance of the Jagannath temple,[39] and in some medieval texts is also recent.

When female dancers were not available to dance in public places, especially in princely courts (the Maharis of the Jagannath temple of Puri were a rare exception), male dancers, mostly adolescent boys, took their place and played the female roles. That is how the Gotipua dance originated. In connection with the subject of this paper, it is worth mentioning that the adolescent boys used to be called Dakshini pila (the southern children), which indicates that in former days the Gotipua dancers came from southern Orissa. Moreover, the Gotipua dance appears to be intimately related to the Sakhi Nacha, which was

[32] See D.N. Patnaik 1990, 73-9.

[33] The Gotipua dance was exclusively male in contrast to the Mahari dance, which was exclusively female. There were other distinctions. Gotipua dancers used to sing mostly the Chaupadis or Odissi songs, whereas the Maharis sang mainly the songs of *Gitagovinda*.

[34] *Dasarupakam* I/9. See Vatsyayan 1987 for a theoretical discussion of the concepts of *margi* and *desi*.

[35] According to *Dasarupakam* by Dhananjaya, *nritta* is based on *tala* and *laya* and is different from *nrittya*, which consists of *abhinaya* or 'acting'. See *Dasarupakam* I/9.

[36] In *Prayaschitta*, a novel by Fakir Mohan Senapati published in 1915, the term *chaupadi* is qualified significantly by the term *Dakshini*, i.e. 'the southern'.

[37] This is the style of Gotipua dance that I saw in my childhood days, more than fifty years ago.

[38] Kalicharan Pattanaik seems to have only slightly hinted, but not explicitly claimed, that the term *Odisi* occurs in an old proverb, *utha, baitha, thia, chali*; *buda, bhasa, bhaunri, pali*; *Odisi natara atha beli*, which he came to know from one Somanath Mahapatra of the village Ardia (Pattanaik 1975, 204). However, this proverb, which has not been noted by any other folklorist, seems to be modern. Somanath Mahapatra might even have created it himself. Of course, the *Oudra* or *Oudra-Magadhi* dance forms are mentioned in the treatise on music.

[39] In contrast to the Gotipua dance, the Mahari dance might have originated from a classical, that is, Margi dance.

also prevalent in southern Orissa.[40] Thus it seems quite likely that both Odissi songs and Gotipua dance originated in the princely courts of southern Orissa, and Ghumsar in particular, from where it spread to the whole of coastal Orissa, where it was much in demand during Dola and Jhulana festivals. In the course of this development Puri and its adjoining area became another centre of Gotipua dance.[41]

As pointed out by Eberhard Fischer, illustrated palm-leaf manuscripts of outstanding artistic quality are generally found in the south, but rarely in the Puri area.[42] This is another indication of the rich cultural and artistic tradition of the south, which has, at least indirectly, a lot to do with literature, as illustrated by these palm-leaf manuscripts. It seems that works in the Oriya *kavya* literature, such as the *Labanyabati*[43] and *Rasikaharabali* of Upendra Bhanja and the romantic kavyas of other poets of southern Orissa, were a major source of inspiration for the production of such illustrated palm-leaf manuscripts.

The importance of the Ghumsar Raj family in the Oriya literary and cultural traditions has now become well established and recognized. Thus Mansinha aptly observes: 'In the midst of murders, frauds, intrigues, and unspeakable immoralities, the ruling Bhanjas of Ghumsar kept up a living tradition of literary culture in the family.'[44] Gopabandhu too, at the end of the poem on Upendra Bhanja, already referred to, says that in the future, Oriyas, especially those interested in literature, would regard Ghumsar as a holy place, a *tirtha*, and would pay homage to it. No wonder, then, for Beames and Hunter, as well as for Oriya-speakers in general, the linguistic, literary and cultural centre of the Oriya-speaking tracts was to be located in Ghumsar in the age of Upendra Bhanja.

[40]D.N. Patnaik 1990, 77. Dinanath Pathy, although he does not say so explicitly, gives a broad hint that the Gotipua dance form might have evolved from Sakhi Nacha when he says, 'The *sakhinata* slowly moved from the religious enclosures and was performed for the king and the palace. Could the source of *rajanrtya* be traced in the *sakhinata* of south Orissa?' (Pathy 2003, 41).

[41]There is a tradition that Ray Ramananda, an Oriya associate of Sri Chaitanya, was the creator of this dance form, which thus would have originated from Puri. But this tradition is highly doubtful, as from the *Chaitanya Charitamrita* we know that Ray Ramananda was staging dramas with the maharis or devadasis, i.e. female actors, playing different roles. See *Chaitanya Charitamrita*, *Antya*, 5,10-24, 36-9. At best he might have been the creator of the Puri school. Kelucharan Mohapatra, the famous Guru of Odissi, is a product of the Puri centre. See Citaristi 2001.

[42]Eberhard Fischer, unpublished paper entitled 'Painting in Southern Orissa in nineteenth and early twentieth centuries: Regional Styles, Workshop Styles or Individual Styles?' delivered as keynote address in the Annual Conference of the Orissa Research Project at Salzau, Germany, May 2003; see particularly the famous palm-leaf illustration of Upendra Bhanja's *Rasika Haravali*, jointly published by Fischer and Dinanath Pathy (1990).

[43]See Williams and Das 1988.

[44]Mansinha 1962, 116.

Modern Oriya literature had yet to emerge when Beames and Hunter made their observations as mentioned earlier. But even after its emergence in the late-nineteenth century, it still took a long time to be firmly established in the public mind and to compete with the prestige that Upendra Bhanja's works, and all those later works that came under his influence, had once enjoyed. As is known from the literary controversy of *Indradhanu* vs. *Bijuli* (The Rainbow *vs*. The Lightning)[45] in the last decade of the nineteenth century, the popularity of the Oriya literature represented by Upendra Bhanja initially appears to have successfully withstood the challenge of the newly emerging Oriya literature represented mainly by Radhanath Ray. At the height of the controversy, Radhanath himself in a letter published in a periodical admitted the poetic talent and greatness of Upendra Bhanja and even called him one of his poetic gurus,[46] after which the controversy gradually subsided. The debate in fact had started when a supporter of Radhanath vehemently attacked Upendra Bhanja and his works. Thus the supporters of Upendra Bhanja and the genre of literature he represented appear to have emerged victorious out of the controversy. But ironically though, since this controversy, and especially since the beginning of the twentieth century, the genre of literature Upendra Bhanja represented gradually lost its influence and foundations to the emerging modern Oriya literature, although it continues to have its admirers and imitators and to generate academic and scholarly interest.[47] It was certainly not just sheer coincidence that Gourishankar Ray, the celebrated editor of *Utkal Dipika*, actively and ardently supported Upendra Bhanja and the genre of literature he represented in the *Indradhanu* vs. *Bijuli* literary controversy and debate, because by that time he had already played a crucial and pivotal role in the Oriya language agitation and in the construction of an Oriya identity, the implications of which will be explained below.

[45] After this debate was taken up in other periodicals, it gradually became very personal, involving the respective supporters of Upendra Bhanja and Radhanath Ray. Once the personal insinuations and accusations had reached a new low, it was considered inadvisable to publish such writings in prestigious periodicals. Therefore two special periodicals, *Indradhanu* (The Rainbow) and *Bijuli* (The Lightning), came into being. *Indradhanu* supported Upendra Bhanja and was anti-Radhanath, whereas *Bijuli* supported Radhanath and was anti-Upendra Bhanja. For more information, see Samantaray 1981, 54-66, 78-83; 1960, 118-20; *Indradhanu*, Introduction, 1-49; and P.C. Mishra 1996, 2002.

[46] For this letter, published on 14 March 1894, see Samantaray 1981, 54-66. It may be further noted that at the start of his literary career Radhanath paid homage to Upendra Bhanja in a poem titled *Kabibar Upendra Bhanja*, which was written in Bengali and published in 1868 in *Kabitabali*, an anthology of his Bengali poems. For this poem, see Durgacharan Ray 1998, 67.

[47] Besides books, popular articles and research papers on Upendra Bhanja and the genre of his literature, a number of Ph.D. and D.Litt. dissertations have been submitted to different universities in Orissa. In the Oriya-medium M.A. curriculum, Upendra Bhanja and the related literature he represents always occupy a vital place.

Furthermore, it may be pointed out that even in the nineteenth and twentieth centuries, although the literary and cultural centre had shifted to central coastal Orissa, especially to the Cuttack-Puri region, the rich literary and scholarly heritage of southern Orissa did not just die out. Southern Orissa still produced a number of important scholars who continued to make contributions to the culture of Orissa. This continuity, though in a somewhat less forceful and influential manner, indicates that once, and in the not too distant past, the literary and to a large extent the cultural centre also had indeed been located in southern Orissa.

III

Upendra Bhanja and the genre of literature he represented might have lost its influence and foundations to modern Oriya literature, but he continued to remain extremely popular among the common people. And what impresses most, apart from the musical quality of his poetry, is the way he played with sounds and words. Upendra Bhanja, like the Sun temple of Konarka, gradually became a symbol of Oriya pride and a marker of Oriya identity.[48] This is partly because to the Oriyas the Bengalis, who were specifically seen as 'the political other'—Telugu- and Hindi-speakers, and even the British, were much less so—do not have any such medieval poet or temple to be proud of. Another reason for the continuous popularity of Upendra Bhanja is the musical aspects of his literary works. They are often sung in small or large gatherings, in radio and television broadcasts, and accompanying Odissi dance performances. The popular admiration for Upendra Bhanja has found expression in a total of seven different plays on his life,[49] mostly based on traditional popular accounts. No other medieval or modern author or individual in Orissa has been honoured in such a way. Besides the host of literature that has sprung up around the Bhanjas of Ghumsar, such as *Upendra Bhanja* (1895), a poem by Gopalaballav Das; the *Ghumsar Itihas* (1912) by Tarini Charan Rath; or the *Ghumusar Kavya* (1936) by Chintamani Mahanty, the ordinary people were so impressed by Upendra's skill of playing on sounds and words that a popular saying in verse was created, running as follows:[50]

> Raising both of his arms (in defiance) announces Upendra Bhanja,
> He does count anybody as poet under the Sun.

[48] See below for further discussion of the subject.

[49] These plays are (i) *Rajakabi Upendra* (1928) by Mayadhar Mansinha; (ii) *Kabisamrat Upendra Bhanja* (1947) by Manoranjan Das; (iii) *Bhanjakabi* (1948/50) by Debendra Kumar Singh; (iv) *Kabisamrat* (1953) by Rajat Kumar Kar; (v) *Sisira Sikta Kabi* (1972) by Raghunath Mishra; (vi) *Kalinga Kabi* (1977) by Pitambar Pradhan; and (vii) *Upendra Bhanja* (1984) by Saileswar Nanda. A film has also been made on the life of Upendra Bhanja.

[50] Some people attribute the authorship of this verse to Upendra Bhanja, which is extremely doubtful.

He only takes shelter at the feet of Jayadeva and Dinakrishna;[51]
(But) he puts his left foot on the heads of other poets.[52]

The popularity of Upendra Bhanja finds expression even today in many different ways. Several literary organizations have been established throughout Orissa, with the aim of popularizing Upendra Bhanja and his literature.[53] At Berhampur, Bhanjanagar, one of the seven university campuses in Orissa is named after him. The only other individual who was—though much later—distinguished by such an honour is Fakir Mohan Senapati at Balasore. It is significant that in competition with the Rabindra Jayanti, the week-long Tagore festival that used to be held by the Bengalis of Cuttack, a Bhanja Jayanti or week-long Upendra Bhanja festival was started in Cuttack in 1944, and continues under the aupices of ardent Oriya nationalist, Bichhanda Charan Pattanayak.[54] It is significant that Bhanja Jayanti is also celebrated in the month of May. Whereas Tagore was born on 7 May, nothing is known about Upendra's birthday. But Bhanja Jayanti almost became a movement, and nowadays it is held throughout Orissa with much ceremony. Similarly, after an auditorium called Rabindra Mandap was constructed in Bhubaneswar during the celebrations of Tagore's centenary (1961), the name of another already existing government auditorium was changed in the 1970s under public pressure from Kala Mandap to Bhanja Kala Mandap. In the same way, a town in the former kingdom of Ghumsar, which was called Russelkonda during the British period, was renamed Bhanjanagar after Independence. All this indicates that Ghumsar and Upendra Bhanja, its famous prince, not only formerly occupied a central position in the sphere of literature and culture, but also that they continue to occupy an important place in the public mind in present-day Orissa.

IV

From the time when Upendra dominated the Oriya literary scene, Ghumsar also played a significant role in Orissan politics. Some of the available *Ghumsar Raj vamsavali*s maintain that Ramachandra II, the raja of Khurda (1727-36), his queen, and his son and successor, Birakesari (1737-93), had something to do with Ghumsar, although the precise nature of this relationship remains unclear due to the differences among the *vamsavali* texts.

But a study of these *vamsavali*s reveals that, in spite of the differences among them, there are also many similarities which make it amply clear that Ghumsar and its monarch played an important role in the lives of Ramachandra

[51] Dinakrushna Das might have been a senior contemporary of Upendra Bhanja. He is the author of *Rasakallola*, a *kavya* dealing with Krishna's life and famous for its lyrical beauty.

[52] Translated from Oriya by the present author.

[53] Kainga Bharati, established by Bichhanda Charan Pattanayak, is the most prominent and famous among them; see Rajalaxmi Mohanty 2002, 46-9.

[54] *Bhanja Vamsanucharita*, ed. Maguni Das 1977, 30-2.

Dev II, the raja of Khurda who became a Muslim, and of his queen and his son, Birakesari Dev.[55] Besides, there is some corroborative evidence to prove some of the claims contained in the *vamsavali* texts. First, Ghana Bhanja, raja of Ghumsar (1707-54), in both of his kavyas (*Trailokyamohini* and *Rasanidhi*) held the title of *ksatriyabara*, which, according to the *vamsavali* texts, was conferred on him by the raja of Khurda. Secondly, Ghana Bhanja established a Brahman *Sasana* called Ksatriyabarapur near his capital of Kulada. Finally, one Brundaban Kuanar Guru Mahapatra, who is mentioned in the *Ghumsar Raj vamsavali*s, is also known from a bilingual copper-plate inscription which was issued by Birakesari Dev in his fifth *Anka* year. According to this inscription, Brundaban Kuanar Guru Mahapatra, the *Parichha* (*pariksa*) of the western door, had helped the *Mahasrama* (i.e. the Gajapati king) on his flight to Chakapadumal in Ghumsar and to Angul and was rewarded accordingly.[56] Moreover, Brundaban Kuanar Guru Mahapatra is also mentioned in the *rajabhoga* section of the *Madala Panji*.[57] From this corroborative evidence it is clear that the events recorded in the *Ghumsar Raj vamsavali*s are more or less based on historical facts. Ghumsar and its king played an important role in eighteenth-century Orissan politics, as he provided shelter to Ramachandra Dev II's queen and to Birakesari, and most likely also to Ramachandra II, the Gajapati of Orissa.

Occupation by the colonial powers was also not plain sailing. After the French invasion of 1757, the British invaded Ghumsar in 1768, 1778, 1799, 1801, 1815 and 1835.[58] Even after its annexation to British territory in 1835, its continued resistance to colonial administration required further military operations. The resistance offered by its people, especially the Konds led by Dora Bisoyi and then Chakra Bisoyi, gradually spread to other areas and was directly responsible for the annexation of the Kandhmal region of the Kingdom of Baud (1855-6)[59] and indirectly for the annexation of Angul in 1847.[60] In this connection it is worth mentioning that the Paik rebellion only broke out openly in Khurda in 1817 after a sizeable number of Konds from Ghumsar appeared on the scene.[61] After a gap of about half a century, in the later part

[55]These *vamsavali* texts have not yet been fully utilized by scholars in writing the history of the Khurda rajas.

[56]See K.N. Mahapatra 1958, 131-4 and 1969, 268-70. According to K.N. Mahapatra, the date of the inscription is 6 October 1739.

[57]*Madala Panji* 1940, 78.

[58]Padel 2000, 329 (note 5 of Chapter 2).

[59]Ramsay 1910, 24. But on another page (136) of the same book it is mentioned that the Khondmals were taken over by the British in 1835. For more information, see Padel 2000.

[60]Ramsay 1910, 24. For further information, see Padel 2000, Sudhakar Patnaik 1956 (Introduction) and De 1957, 90-4, 159-95.

[61]G. Toynbee writes: 'In March 1817 a body of Gumsur Khunds, 400 strong, crossed over into the Khurda territory and openly unfurled the banner of revolt.' Toynbee 1960, 15. See also B.C. Ray 1960, 268.

of the nineteenth and early twentieth centuries, the Oriyas of Ganjam, including Parlakhimedi and particularly Ghumsar, again played a significant role in the construction of an Oriya identity. In 1870, for example, the very year when Beames made his observation quoted at the beginning of this paper, representatives of Oriya-speakers in Ganjam held a large meeting in Russelkonda. In view of their sorry plight in the Madras Presidency, they made an appeal to the Oriyas of the districts of Cuttack and Puri in the Bengal Presidency to make sincere efforts to bring all the Oriya-speaking tracts under one administration, with Oriya as the official language.[62] Even though this was not the first time a demand had been made for the unification of the Oriya-speaking tracts,[63] it was certainly the first time that such a demand was made to a large public meeting. It is significant that the meeting was held in Russelkonda (which was renamed Bhanjanagar after independence) in Ghumsar taluk.

Since the middle of the nineteenth century, Upendra Bhanja has often been cited as a witness to the glorious past of the Oriyas, and especially of Oriya literature. He became, at least indirectly, a source of inspiration for those who played leading roles in the construction of an Oriya identity in the nineteenth and early twentieth centuries. As pointed out earlier, Beames, Rangalal, and other non-Oriya administrators of the nineteenth century, in whose perception the linguistic and literary centre of the Oriya-speaking tracts lay in Ghumsar, made very definite and positive contributions to the emergence of an Oriya identity,[64] the imagined community of Oriya-speakers.

In this connection, Gourishankar Ray in particular, the editor of *Utkal Dipika*, should be mentioned.[65] He was an admirer of Oriya literature, especially of Upendra Bhanja and the genre of literature he represented, and he took an

[62]This is known from a letter to the editor by one Janarddan Das, published in the 22 October 1870 issue of the *Utkal Dipika*. See S. Patnaik 1972, 172-6.

[63]The demand for the unification of the Oriya-speaking tracts under one administration was made for first time in the pages of *Utkala Dipika* by Gourishankar Ray in March 1869. See S. Patnaik 1972, 531-6.

[64]During the Oriya-language agitation, in the seventh decade of the nineteenth century, Beames supported the Oriya language, forcefully claiming that it was an independent language. Besides, he asserted that '[a]t a period when Oriya was already a fixed and settled language Bengali did not exist; the inhabitants of Bengal spoke a vast variety of corrupt forms of eastern Hindi' (Beames 1872, 119). The claim made by Beames was a great source of inspiration in the construction of an Oriya-language identity. Furthermore, it may be recalled here that Beames accorded Upendra Bhanja the position of 'the first national poet' (see ibid., 105). For more information on Beames' role here, see Dash 1983, 49-53, 67-73; 1993, 17, 23-4, 170-204. The important role played by Bengali intellectuals like Rangalal Bandyopadhyay and Bhudev Mukhopadhyay in the Oriya-language agitation and the construction of an Oriya identity should not be underestimated. For Rangalal's role, see Dash 1978, 368-9, fn. 45; 1979, 74-7, 83-104.

[65]The Oriya-language agitation in the seventh decade of the nineteenth century, championed by Gourishankar Ray, was the very first important step in the construction of an Oriya identity. See Dash 1991, 1993.

active interest in its publication.[66] As early as 1866, *Premasudhanidhi*, a *kavya* by Upendra Bhanja, was published by the Cuttack Printing Company over which Gourishankar Ray presided. This was the first 'medieval' literary Oriya text to appear in printed form since a translation of the *Gitagovinda* by Dharanidhar was published along with the Sanskrit text in 1840. Between 1866 and 1875 as many as nine other works by Upendra Bhanja were published, some of them more than once, and in most cases edited by Gourishankar Ray.[67] Therefore, in the very early phase of the construction of an Oriya identity, this prince of Ghumsar, 'the centre out there', played an important indirect role when, with the arrival of printing machines, his works were made available to a steadily growing readership. They contributed to the emergence and consolidation of what Benedict Anderson calls a 'national print language' in Orissa.[68] Thus Gourishankar Ray took a major step, which was followed by others, in making Upendra Bhanja popular among the people of Orissa and, finally, turning him into an icon of Oriya identity.

At a still later period, in the first decades of the twentieth century, Utkalamani (the jewel of Utkal) Gopabandhu, along with his colleagues Pandit Nilakantha Das and Pandit Godabarish Mishra, the famous trio of the Satyabadi School and ardent nationalists, followed Gourishankar Ray in their admiration for Upendra Bhanja. Gopabandhu's much quoted lines in his poem on Upendra Bhanja have already been referred to.[69] In it he lamented that Ghumsar was beyond the then political boundaries of Orissa. This indicates how Ghumsar and Upendra Bhanja had become markers of the emerging Oriya identity. Pandit Nilakantha Das also admired Upendra Bhanja and his literature, but for a slightly different reason. According to him, the literature of Upendra Bhanja was a reflection of true Oriya culture.[70] Following him, nationalist critics of Oriya literature admired Upendra Bhanja and his literature not only for purely literary reasons, but for nationalistic ones as well. Pandit Godabarish Mishra, who was also a poet, admired Upendra Bhanja and his poetic talent, as is known from one of his poems on Upendra.[71] But Upendra Bhanja was certainly also a source of inspiration for Mishra's political activities. Another ardent admirer of Upendra Bhanja was Bichhanda Charan Pattanayak, who, as mentioned earlier, increased Upendra's popularity through the Bhanja Jayanti celebration.

[66]Moreover, he was an active and ardent supporter of his in the famous *Indradhanu* vs. *Bijuli* debate, mentioned earlier.

[67]All this information has been extracted from Shridhar Mahapatro Sarma 1986.

[68]See Anderson 1991, 67.

[69]See *Pandit Gopabandhu Granthabali* 2004, 170-1, and also 13-14, 25.

[70]According to Pt. Nilakantha Das, the mutual loyalty of husband and wife (*svakiya priti*), which he considered a characteristic feature of Oriya culture, was emphasized in the literary works of Upendra Bhanja, in contrast to the permissiveness and licentiousness (*parakiya priti*) of Krishna as reflected in the works of the Vaisnava poets of Bengal and their Oriya followers. See Nilakanth Das 1953, 484-8.

[71]See Godabarish Mishra 1946, 48.

V

It can therefore be claimed that from a linguistic and literary point of view, Ghumsar was the most important of a number of centres in the Oriya-speaking tracts, prior to and during the early modern period. As the 'centre out there' in the south, it had a strong impact on the emergence of an Oriya identity in the late nineteenth and early twentieth centuries. But recent events—such as establishing the political as well as literary and cultural capitals in central coastal Orissa in Cuttack and Bhubaneswar, as well as the histories written by some of our colonial masters and then by Oriya nationalists mostly from central Orissa—have successfully clouded our perception to such an extent that it is often mistakenly taken for granted that the literary and cultural centre has always been located in central Orissa, around Cuttack and Puri. The rediscovery of the 'southern centre out there' is therefore now long overdue.

REFERENCES

Anderson, Benedict 1991. *Imagined Communities*, London, New York: Verso.

Bandyopadhyay, Rangalal 1864. 'Upendra Bhanja', in *Rahasya Sandarbha*, 2/16; rpt. in *Rangalal Rachanavali* of the year 1381 (=1974). Calcutta: Datta Chowdhury, 108-11.

Beames, John 1870. 'On the Relation of the Uriya to the Other Modern Aryan Languages', in *Proceedings of the Asiatic Society*, June 1870, 192-216.

———1872. *Comparative Grammar of the Modern Aryan Languages of India*, vol. 1, London: Trübner & Beames (rpt. 1970, Delhi).

Chaitanya Charitamrta by Krishnadas Kaviraj, edited with *Gaurakripa-tarangini*, Commentary by Radhagobinda Nath, 6 vols., Calcutta: Sadhana Prakashani, 1947-53.

Chakravarti, M.M. 1898. 'Notes on the Language and Literature of Orissa, Parts III and IV', *Journal of the Asiatic Society of Bengal* 67, 332-86.

Citaristi, Ileana 2001. *The Making of a Guru: Kelucharan Mohapatra: His Life and Time*, Delhi: Manohar.

Cobden Ramsay, L.E.B. 1910. *Feudatory States of Orissa*, Calcutta: The Bengal Secretariat Book Depot (rpt. 1950, 1982).

Das, Pt. Nilakantha 1953. *Odia Sahityara Kramaparinama*, vol. 2, Cuttack: Nababharata Granthalaya (rpt. in Das, Nilakantha, *Nilakantha Granthabali*, vol. 3, 1967), Cuttack: Cuttack Students' Store.

Dash, G.N. 1976. 'The King and the Priests: An Analysis of a Gita-Govinda Tradition', *Visva Bharati Quarterly* 40, 227-46.

———1978. 'Jagannatha and Oriya Nationalism', in A. Eschmann, H. Kulke and G.C. Tripathi (eds.), *The Cult of Jagannath and the Regional Tradition of Orissa*, Delhi: Manohar, 359-74.

———1979. *Janasruti Kanchi Kaveri*, Berhampur: Pustak Bhandar.

———1983. *Odia Bhasacharchara Parampara*, Cuttack: Institute of Oriya Studies.

———1991. 'Gourishankar O Odia Bhasa Suraksha Andolana', in Mohanty, Sricharan (ed.), *Satabdinayak: Gourishankar*, Rourkela: Pragati Utkala Sangha.

———1993. *Odia Bhasa Suraksha Andolana*, Cuttack: Cuttack Students' Store.

———2004. 'Gita-Govinda Traditions: A Medieval Debate and Its Impact on Modern Oriya Identity', in A. Malinar, J. Beltz and H. Frese (eds.), *Text and Context in the History, Literature and Religion of Orissa*, Delhi: Manohar, 331-60.

Dasarupakam by Dhananjaya. Ed. K.P. Parab. Bombay: Sagar Press, 1941.

De, Sushil Chandra 1957. *History of the Freedom Movement of Orissa*, vol. 1 (*1757-1856*). Cuttack: State Committee for the Compilation of History of the Freedom Movement.

Fischer, Eberhard and Dinanath Pathy 1990. *Die Perlenkette dem Geliebten: Elf illustrierte Palmblätter zur Rasika Havavali-Romanze des Dichters Upendra Bhanja von Orissa, Indien, aus der Sammlung Alice Boner im Museum Rietberg Zürich*, Zürich: Museum Rietberg.

Ghumsar Bhanja Vamsavali Texts

(i) *Bhanja Vamsanucarita* (Oriya verse), ed. Maguni Das (1951, 1977 Bhanjanagar).

(ii) *Bhanja Vamsa O' Gumusara Bidroha* (Oriya verse), by Gangapani Mahapatra, ed. Maguni Das, Berhampur, 1978.

(iii) *Bhanja Vamsavali* (Oriya prose), ed. Maguni Das, Bhanjanagar: Kavisamrat Book Store, 1982.

(iv) *Bhanja Vamsavali* (Sanskrit verse), ed. S.N. Rajaguru, 1932/3. See 'The Chronological Account of the Bhanjas of Gumsur', in *Prachi* 2, 3/4, 2-17, rpt. in *Bhanja Smaranika*, 22 (1991), 10-17. Rourkela: Adarsha Pathagara.

(v) *Gumusara Bamsabali* (Oriya prose), an extract is given by M.M. Chakravarti; see M.M. Chakravarti 1898.

(vi) *Gumusar Bhanja Vamsavali* (Oriya verse), by Suryamani Chyau Pattanayak; ed. Durgamadhab Nanda, Berhampur: Orissa Book House, 1973.

(vii) *Historical Narrative of the Rajahs of Goomsor*. English translation of a text in Oriya by Rama Chandra Gura. Translated from Oriya first into Telugu and then into English. See Revd. W. Taylor, 'Some Additional Notes on the Hill Inhabitants of Goomsoor Mountains', with the translation of a Telugu paper, containing an Historical Narrative of Bhonju Family, Feudal Chieftains of Gumsara', in *Madras Journal of Literature and Science* 18, January 1838.

Hunter, W.W., A. Stirling, J. Beames and N.K. Sahu 1956. *A History of Orissa, by W.W. Hunter, Andrew Stirling, John Beames, N.K. Sahu*, vol. 1. Ed. N.K. Sahu. (A reprint from the selected works of Stirling, Hunter and Beames.) [With new material by N.K. Sahu.] Calcutta: Susil Gupta.

Indradhanu. Ed. Sudarsana Acharya. Berhampur: Berhampur University, 1991.

Kotibrahmnada Sundari by Upendra Bhanja. Cuttack: A.K. Ghose, 1924.

Madala Panji. Ed. Arttaballav Mohanty. Cuttack: Prachi Samiti, 1940.

Mahapatra, K.N. 1958. 'Gajapati Birakesari Dev', *Jhankar* 10, 1, 131-4.

———1969. *Khurudha Itihasa*, Bhubaneswar: Government of Orissa.

Mahapatro Sarma, Shridhar 1986. *Odia Prakasana O Prasaranara Itihasa*, Cuttack: Grantha Mandir.

Maltby, T.J. 1874. *A Handbook of Uriya or Odiya Language*, Calcutta: Wyman & Co.; rpt. as *A Practical Handbook of Uriya or Odiya Language*, Cuttack: Orissa Govt. Press, 1945.

Mansinha, Mayadhar 1962. *History of Oriya Literature*, Delhi: Sahitya Akademi.

Mishra, Binayak 1962. *Odia Sahityara Itihasa*, Cuttack: Rastrabhasa Pustak Bhandar.

Mishra, Godabarish 1946. *Stor Odia Patha*, 5th edn., Berhampur and Cuttack: The Students' Store.

Mishra, Purna Chandra 1996. *Utkala Dipikare Bhanja Prasanga*, Berhampur: Royal Book House.

———2002. *Bitarka Balayare Bhanja*, Berhampur: Jayanti Mishra.

Mohanty, J.B. 1976. *Odia Giti Kabya*, Cuttack: Grantha Mandira.

———1982. *Odia Chaupadi Sahitya*, Bhubaneswar: Orissa Sahitya Akademi.

Mohanty, Rajalaxmi 2002. *Mo Smrutire/Drustire Bapa Bichhanda Charan Pattanayak*, Cuttack: Shankar.

Mohanty, Surendra 1992. *Odiya Sahityara Madhya Parva O Uttara Madhya Parva*, Cuttack: Cuttack Students' Store.

Padel, Felix 2000. *Sacrifice of Human Being: British Rule and the Konds of Orissa*, Delhi: Oxford University Press.

Pandita Gopabandhu Granthabali. Ed. Smaran Kumar Nayak. Cuttack: Jagannatha Ratha, 2004.

Parasurama Vijaya by Gajapati Kapilendra Dev. Ed. K. Kar and T.B. Patnaik, in *Prachi* 2, 3/4, 97-121.

Pathy, Dinanath 2003. *Beyond the Canvas: Critical Vision of an Indian Painter*, Delhi: Harman.

Patnaik, D.N. 1990. *Odissi Dance*, Bhubaneswar: Orissa Sangeet Natak Akademi.

Patnaik, Sudhakar 1956. *Raja Somanatha Singh Jagaddeba*, Cuttack: S. Patnaik.

———1972. *Sambadapatraru Odisara Katha*, Cuttack: Grantha Mandir.

Pattanaik, Kalicharan 1975. *Kumbhara Chaka*, Cuttack: Cuttack Students' Store.

Prayaschitta by Fakir Mohan Senapati. Cuttack: Friends' Publishers, 2003.

Ray, B.C. 1960. *Foundations of British Orissa*, Cuttack: New Students Store.

Ray, Durgacharan 1998. *Radhanath Jibani*, Cuttack: Friends' Publishers.

Samantaray, Natabar 1960. *Jugaprabarttaka Srasta Radhanath*, Cuttack: Rajahamsa Sahitya Mandir.

———1981. *Adhunika Odia Sahityara Bhittibhumi*, Bhubaneswar.

Toynbee, G. 1873. 'A Sketch of the History of Orissa (From 1803 to 1828)'; rpt. in *The Orissa Historical Research Journal* 9, 1/2, 1960, 1-67.

Vatsyayan, Kapila. 1987. 'Sastra and Prayoga: Marga and Desi: On Conceptual Frameworks of Indian Culture', in G.C. Tripathi and H. Kulke (eds.), *Religion and Society in Eastern India* (*Eschmann Memorial Lectures*), Delhi: Manohar, 15-48.

Williams, Joanna and J.P. Das. 1988. 'Raghunatha Prusti: An Oriya Artist', *Artibus Asiae* 48, 131-59.

CHAPTER 10

The Formation of a Centre Out There: The Case of Ranpur

NIELS GUTSCHOW

INTRODUCTION: HISTORICAL AND SPATIAL BACKGROUND

THE EMERGENCE OF THE GARHJAT STATES

Almost fifteen hundred years ago, eighteen 'jungle states' were first mentioned in the hinterland of coastal Orissa. At that time Maṇināgeśvarī appeared as a Hinduized tribal deity, worshipped on a hill some 50 km south-east of the capital of earlier dynasties near Bhubaneswar. Hermann Kulke has described the later process of the formation of feudatory states (or 'Little Kingdoms') west, south-west and north-west of Bhubaneswar (Fig. 10.1):

> The Gajapatis encircled their fertile coastal granary and their political and religious centers, Cuttack and Puri, by a large number of feudatory states which bore the name gaḍajāta, meaning 'born from the fort' (gaḍa). Several decades after the downfall of the Gajapatis in the year 1568, the Moghuls assigned the small Garhjat (Gaḍajata) states of central Orissa to the rājās of Khurda who had meanwhile become local successors to the imperial Gajapatis. Under the Khurda rājās, the Garhjat states achieved a semi-autonomous status which they retained even when the Marathas conquered Orissa in 1751. When the British conquered Orissa in 1803, the autonomy of the Garhjat states even received imperial sanction when the East India Company acknowledged them for a quit-rent as their allied feudatories.[1]

TRIBAL GODDESS AND STATE DEITY: AN ASSOCIATION IN CONFLICT OR IN PACIFICATION?

From the start, political power needed legitimation: rituals connected to an expanding religious infrastructure offered a platform to celebrate the king's divine affiliation. The seat of power in the shape of an urban settlement served as an arena in which to place symbols of Hindu royalty, namely, temples and palaces. However, a settlement of Brahmans, around these symbols served to legitimize an emerging power in a tribal territory.

In the case of Ranpur, the development of a settlement at the foot of a power place of tribal origin certainly offered an immense strategic advantage. A

[1]Kulke 1980, 30-1.

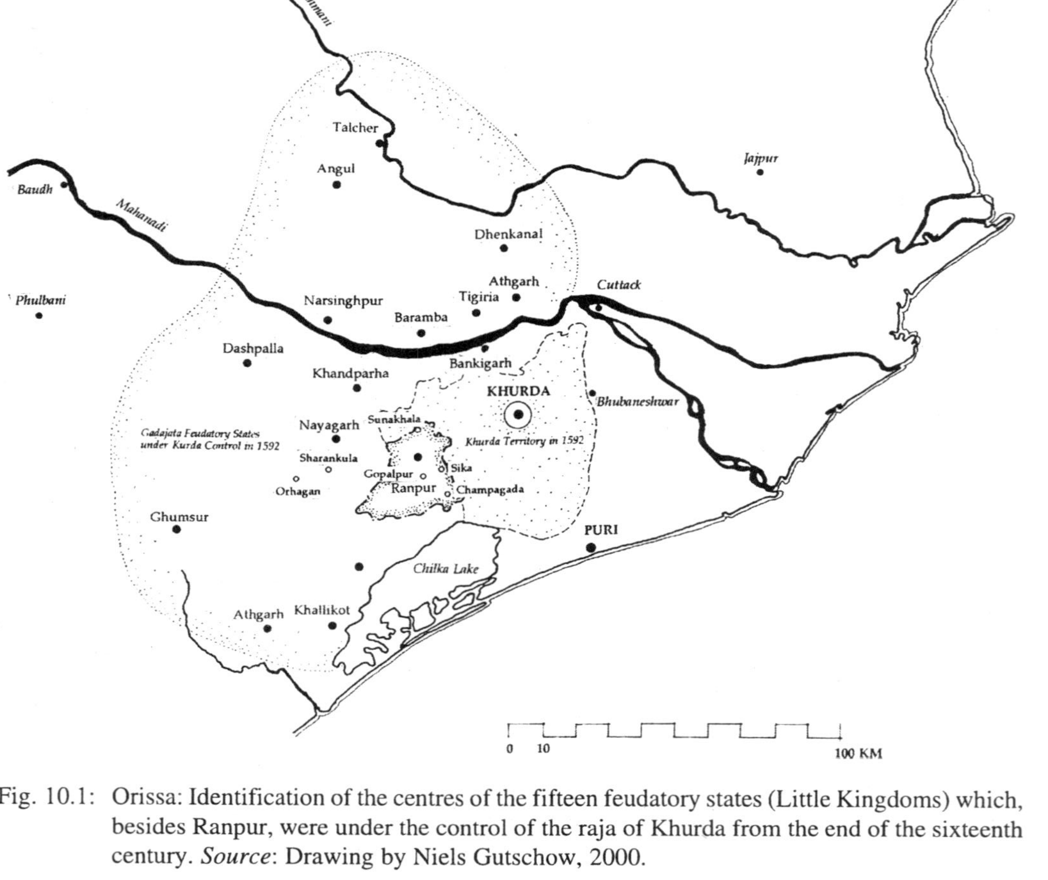

Fig. 10.1: Orissa: Identification of the centres of the fifteen feudatory states (Little Kingdoms) which, besides Ranpur, were under the control of the raja of Khurda from the end of the sixteenth century. *Source*: Drawing by Niels Gutschow, 2000.

variety of associations were tied to Maṇināgeśvarī, one of the eight Mother Goddesses (*Aṣṭamātṛkā*) who exerted power at a subregional level. During ritual events (see the Pañcadoḷayātrā below), her association with tribal cults overruled the role of Jagannātha as the state deity (*rāṣṭradevatā*), a role that Jagannātha (The Lord of the Universe) had already attained under the Gajapati kings. While accepting the sovereignty of the tribal goddess over a restricted realm, the king of Ranpur ruled simultaneously as the son of the supreme overlord. Represented in a non-iconic, chthonic fashion, the goddess represented 'place', being immovable and thus unique. Jagannātha, however, had to be brought from the centre: a replica served as a kind of governor on local level, mirroring regional power on the subregional level of a feudatory state.

A local chronicle (*Rāṇapura Rājavaṃśa Itihāsa*), basically a nineteenth-century compilation,[2] reflects the hierarchy between the tribal goddess and the imported governor. It tells us that in 1727 BCE 'God' ordered a local chief to establish Maṇināga, the Jewel Serpent, as an act with rich cosmogonic associations. The goddess demonstrates the origin of place and territory. In a second step, the chronicle constructs a suitable past for the kings of Ranpur to legitimize their power: in the fifteenth century CE the king secured the necessary paraphernalia of Hindu kingship in Puri and returned with an image of Mādhava as a representation of Jagannātha and subsequently constructed a temple. Soon afterwards he moved his fort from its probable location on the hilltop to the foot of the hill, thus taking the first step towards a permanent settlement.

Some time later, a conflict with the central power in Puri created a peculiar discontinuity in Ranpur's development. In the early eighteenth century the king had to include in the royal pantheon what Kulke has called a 'subsidiary ishtadevata'.[3] It was only with the support of a jungle goddess (Khiḷāmuṇḍa) and her tribe that he was able to re-establish his local power. This goddess remained in the jungle, but appears annually with great pomp in the centre of the Little Kingdom on the occasion of Durgāpūjā, the autumnal ritual of renewal *par excellence.*

The following events in the eighteenth century may already belong to what Kulke has called the 'remembered past',[4] as the chronicle continues by saying that one raja established seven main roads and forty-two small streets and built a new temple—again royal actions with cosmogonic claims.

By the middle of the eighteenth century, when the Marathas conquered Orissa, Ranpur's religious infrastructure must have been fully established. It was probably at this time that the present temple of Jagannātha was constructed, while the king established his new quarters in a large compound adjoining the temple. To complete the new set-up, the tribal goddess was replicated in iconic form and housed in a temple at the foot of the hill. As Taḷamaṇināga (literally

[2]See Gutschow 2004, Kulke 2004.
[3]Kulke 1980, 32.
[4]Kulke 2004, 62.

'the lower jewel serpent'), the goddess was now easily accessible and probably tamed. One more movable representation was kept in the palace to be paraded in a portable shrine on the occasion of the vernal ritual of renewal.

The chronicle tells us that the 'twelve festivals/rituals' tied to Jagannātha were introduced as early as the sixteenth century. These significant rituals established a strong ritual tie between a peripheral kingdom in the jungle and the centre. As this notion is clearly part of a 'constructed past', we must assume that these rituals had been introduced or re-introduced by the middle of the eighteenth century.

Not much later, the Doḷameḷaṇa festival must have been established to celebrate a vernal ritual of renewal on the occasion of the full moon in March, close to the spring equinox. The sequence of this development already reveals a hierarchy. On the regional level the jungle king demonstrated his loyalty to the state deity Jagannātha. On the subregional level the king renewed his ties with the jungle goddess who had been instrumental in renewing his kingship. And on a third level, that of the tutelary goddess of the king and protective power of his territory, the Jewel Serpent (Maṇināga) called for a demonstration of loyalty from all (in reality a hundred and eight) the village gods, including those from Ranpur.

The Urban Fabric

An immaterial axis dominates the urban site in an east-west direction. To the west, Maṇināga is located high above the settlement and the surrounding fields. The powerful tribal goddess ultimately represents the sense of place and territory (*kṣetra*). From the hilltop she graces her divine realm in an otherwise unprotected and potentially chaotic landscape. In this capacity she cannot be moved, transferred, or otherwise manipulated. From her hilltop the Jewel Serpent looks down on the temple of Jagannātha, together with the neighbouring compound of the palace, to which three imposing structures were added in around 1910 in what one could call Orissan baroque with a vernacular touch.

The temple turns strictly east towards the main street of a settlement which was established in the late seventeenth century. This main road (called Samukhasahi) runs along an s-shaped curve before it reaches one of Jagannātha's five 'ministers', Svapneśvara, who presides over the eastern direction. The bends are smooth enough not to obscure the dominant axis: at a certain point in the approach to the abode of Jagannātha, the goddess Maṇināga appears almost as a crown high above the temple. Perpendicular to this main axis, which also divides the town in two halves consisting of six neighbourhoods (*sahi*) each, runs the ritual axis of the settlement, appropriately called *baḍa daṇḍa*, literally the 'main stick'. This originates at the main gate of Jagannātha's compound and ends at the gate of Guṇḍīcā, the summer residence of Jagannātha at a distance of some seven hundred metres. Opposite the gate of the summer residence, the ritual axis opens up to form a large square or field (*padiā*) to accommodate the needs of two major urban rituals. In this spatial constellation Ranpur mirrors Puri, where the commanding main axis extends in an east-west direction in a prolongation of the temple's axis. The opposition of temple and summer residence (Guṇḍicā) in Puri served as a prototype which guided every other urban development in Orissa. It would be misleading to call the result a 'replica', because neither the scale nor the design and its traces in the urban plan recalls the 'original'. It is rather the 'idea' and the programme that is realized in a new configuration, adapted to the local conditions.

In early July, the three chariots of Jagannātha, Subhadrā and Balabhadra are placed here for a period of five days in a waiting position until the Triad returns 'home', and on the occasion of Pañcadoḷayātrā a hundred and eight gods convene here to demonstrate their loyalty to the great goddess, Maṇināgeśvarī. Thus, this ritual space is created as a stage for the performance of the two main events in the calendar of the Little Kingdom: the chariot festival in honour of the Lord of the World 'legitimises the Hindu kingship'[5] of the Little King, while Doḷameḷaṇa secures territorial integrity.

The shift of the royal residence documents a decisive change from fortress to settlement, traces of which can still be seen. The first kings must have ruled from a fort on top of the hill, close to a shrine with the non-iconic representation of Maṇināga. The chronicle tells us that in the early-sixteenth century the king moved his residence to a plateau below the hill and slightly above the later settlement. Before the middle of the eighteenth century, Rāmachandra Narendra—who had regained the kingship with the help of the jungle goddess Khiḷamuṇḍa—moved his 'palace' (in reality nothing more than a one-storey structure around a large square courtyard) further down, close to the Lord of the World, whose temple must have been rebuilt at the same time on a much grander scale. With the establishment of a new proximity between, if not unity of, palace and temple, a powerful symbol of Hindu kingship evolved as the centre of a complex urban configuration which defined the centre of an expanding territory, often in conflict with neighbouring entities of a similar type.

Other temples dedicated to Kṛṣṇa and Lakṣmī were built in the nineteenth century. The construction of yet another new palace in the early twentieth century adjacent to the wall of the temple compound only accentuated the already existing pattern. A gate now provided direct access from the palace courtyard to the temple.

In imitation of patterns known from Puri, the Lord of the World is encircled by five 'ministers': Harihareśvara within the deity's compound (the centre), Svapneśvara to the east, Daṇḍabaluṅkeśvara to the south, Candeśvara to the north and Baluṅkeśvara far beyond the limits of the settlement to the west. Eight monastic institutions (*maṭha*) are scattered across the twelve neighbour-

[5]Kulke 1980, 36.

hoods, one other being located in the village of Purnavasanta, close to the temple of Baluṅkeśvara. A temple dedicated to Baḍibaluṅkeśvara was added recently at the ritual square and in 1998 a temple dedicated to Gaṇeśa was constructed close by. Besides these, a temple dedicated to Nārāyaṇī and eleven shrines to Maṅgala (often represented in non-iconic form by a pair of reeds) are found, as well as temples dedicated to Brāhmaṇīdevī (in Nuagaon), Bhuvaneśvarī and Habudasinghī.

A simple second shrine to Nārāyaṇī was constructed in 1996, and next to her a small shrine dedicated to Tariṇī, the popular goddess of north-east Orissa, was added in 2002. New shrines dedicated to this goddess mushroomed all over Orissa in the 1990s. The latest development is characterized by the construction of a Hanumān temple on the slope between Taḷamaṇināga and the temple of the tribal goddess on top of the hill. A crude concrete structure was provided on the initiative of a group of young men from Ranpur. Slogans like 'Jay Hanumān, Śrī Rām; Hare Kṛṣṇa, Hare, Hare' are painted on to the rocks flanking the structure. An additional notice excludes non-vegetarians from visiting the shrine. With these latest additions, the former Little Kingdom has successfully been integrated into what, on a higher level in scale, is called 'globalization', in the light of the growing influence of the pan-Indian Hindutva movement. All-Indian and all-Orissan trends have arrived, if only on a modest scale. The original urge to replicate the spatial and ritual model of the centre has been considerably widened to bind Ranpur to the wider world, in which Tāriṇī will overrule and even replace Maṇināga, while Rāma appears as the rival of Jagannātha. Seven Bhagavatamaṇḍapas, small buildings in which the *Bhagavata* is read out in the evening, add to the religious infrastructure, as do Bibahamaṇḍapas and two Kamanaghars, towards which the competing groups in the Dance of Punishment (Daṇḍayātrā) are oriented.

To sum up, the centre of the urban landscape is occupied by a double representation of divine and profane kingship. The division of the settlement by means of an east-west axis and the placement of the five 'ministers' stresses the cosmic orientation towards the four directions, although the cross appears to have been truncated. The duality of the two halves of the settlement surfaces again with the existence of two Kamanaghars and two Bibahamaṇḍapas. This is indeed a well-known pattern that may allow competition and even aggression to arise in the course of urban rituals in times of crisis.

Similarly, the social topography adds to this spatial duality. Clearly 'beyond' the northern end of the ritual axis, the Untouchable quarter unites lumbermen, bamboo-workers, sweepers, cobblers, fishermen and watchmen, while at the southern end a less distinct quarter unites fishermen, washermen, the tribal priest (*Jani*) and the (landless) Muslim community as butchers, who also acted as the care-givers of elephants and horses in the days of the Little Kingdom. Originally the tribal community of Behera, whose members produce items made of reed like the ritual stick needed for the Daṇḍayātrā, also settled here.

In contrast to what is known of *śāsana* villages in Orissa, in which it was planned to settle exclusively Brahmans, the social topography of Ranpur appears mixed. Along the east-west axis, for example, a number of *sevaka*s (Brahmans who serve Jagannātha) settle, but side by side with blacksmiths and carpenters and the *diwān*, the minister of the Little King, as well as the *karaṇa*, the temple accountant. The ritual axis or *baḍa daṇḍa* originally had only a small row of houses on the eastern side, as the opposite side belonged to the royal family. This pattern had changed already by the 1920s, when a Marwari trader occupied a plot on the western side and constructed a pretentious building which imitated the palace of the king. Since then the *baḍadaṇḍa* has turned into a market street, with old houses with thatched roofs being replaced by multi-storeyed reinforced concrete structures.

The north-south orientation of the settlement is even reflected in the location of the cremation grounds. About 2 km north of Ranpur, the cremation ground for commoners and members of the Scheduled Castes is located on the banks of the Mandākinī. The royal cremation ground remained near the site of the former fort in the south, Upargaḍa. The Muslim cemetery (Mosani Padiā) is found at the southern end of the axis, which is not straight as it tends to follow the slope of the hill. Not surprisingly, the inhabitants of Nuagaon, the 'model village' that was planned after the great fire of 1943, have a separate cremation ground even beyond the Muslim cemetery. Ritually speaking, Nuagaon is treated as a separate entity which cannot be absorbed by the original settlement.

The Urban Pattern

The spatial pattern of Ranpur (Fig. 10.2) reveals the realization of a preconceived plan, the basic element of which is a neighbourhood (*sahi*) that differs considerably in size from case to case.[6] Two rows of houses face a broad road similar to what in English is called a common. This is clearly a rural element which is replicated in order to shape a more complex settlement as the centre of a Little Kingdom. The surrounding villages demonstrate this organization of space more clearly because a large open space in front of the house legally belongs to the plot. This means that the actual 'public' space is much narrower than can be visually perceived. The house itself extends over two or three courtyards in depth and marks the centre between the forecourt and a long backyard which is accessible from behind along a narrow service lane. Half of Ranpur's quarters are laid out in an east-west direction, the other

[6]The field survey conducted in July 1999 counted altogether 1,299 households, nearly agreeing with the census of 1981, which counted 1,308 households with 6,894 inhabitants. In 1981, 1,140 'houses' were counted, a number which reflects the survey made in July 1999. Houses are not easily defined, as quite often more than one household resides below one long roof. Only after some time does a household become identical with a house, when repairs result in a clear definition of what constitutes a single entity.

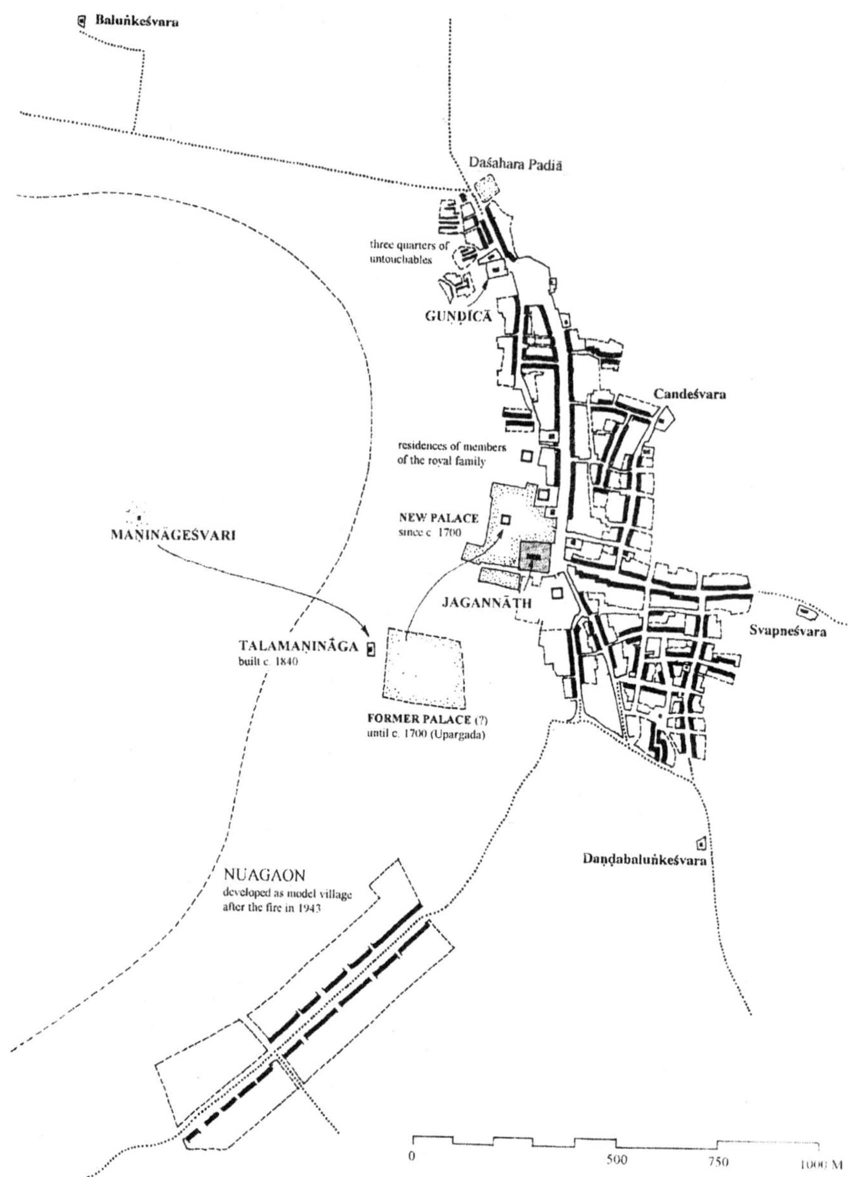

Fig. 10.2: Ranpur: Development of the sacred landscape from the seventeenth century to the establishment of a model village following a devastating fire in 1943. Chronicles mention the establishment of the first temple dedicated to Mādhava and a fort (Upargada) in the first half of the sixteenth century. By 1700 the settlement is said to have developed along the main ritual axis, the *bada daṇḍa*, stretching from the temple towards Guṇḍicā. At that time a new phase began with the relocation of the palace to the ritual axis and probably the replacement of a simple temple by a grander scheme. Transformed into an iconographic representation, the tutelary deity Maṇināgeśvarī was installed at the foot of the hill by about 1840.

half in a north-south direction. This change in direction produces a T-shaped pattern which makes small connecting lanes obligatory. The original fabric has been greatly obscured by changes that were made following the fire in 1943, which devastated most of the town. Long rows of houses were reduced to small rows, creating additional access lanes which changed the basic linear system into a grid pattern.

Every settlement in the coastal belt of Orissa needs ponds to bridge the dry season. Some are architecturally framed, with steps leading down from an artificial dam. Sixteen such ponds surround the settlement. The chronicle of Ranpur mentions the 'digging of a tank' called Baḍa Sāmukā, and at the end of the nineteenth century two ponds were united and named pretentiously 'Sagara' (ocean).

THE JAGANNĀTHA TEMPLE OF RANPUR: A REPLICA NEEDED TO DEMONSTRATE ROYALTY?

THE TEMPLE IN PURI

Concerning the origins of the Jagannātha temple in Puri, 'nothing definite can be said about the early history of Puri until proper excavations . . . under the main temple reveal the hidden past of this place'.[7] The earliest possible temple on the site had a shrine to Nīlamādhava in the tenth century. The present structure, however, was built only after CE 1135. In a long process, but not before the beginning of the fourteenth century, Jagannātha has acquired the status of the uncontested imperial deity of the Gaṅgā dynasty, and it took another two hundred years before the deity fulfilled a similar legitimatory task for a number of feudatory states in the hinterland of Puri and Bhubaneswar, one of which was Ranpur.

Likewise, little is known about the architectural development of the Puri temple. The deul tower and the adjoining assembly hall (*jagamohana*) of the present temple must have been completed by the beginning of the thirteenth century. The adjoining festival hall (*nātamaṇḍapa*) was probably added in the fourteenth century, and the westernmost hall of offering (*bhogamaṇḍapa*) in the fifteenth. The entire architectural configuration of the temple, with the subsidiary temples of the inner enclosure, was walled less than a hundred years before the Ranpur chronicle talks about the establishment of the first temple. Hundreds of years later, the outer enclosure with the 'graveyard' of Koili Baikuṇṭha and the bathing platform attained its present shape (Fig. 10.3).

THE TEMPLE IN RANPUR

The Ranpur chronicle tells us that one King Uddhava Singh received an image of Mādhava in Puri, brought it to Ranpur, and established a temple there in CE 1530 (4632 Kaliyuga). No trace remains of such an early temple structure,

[7] Stietencron 1978, 62.

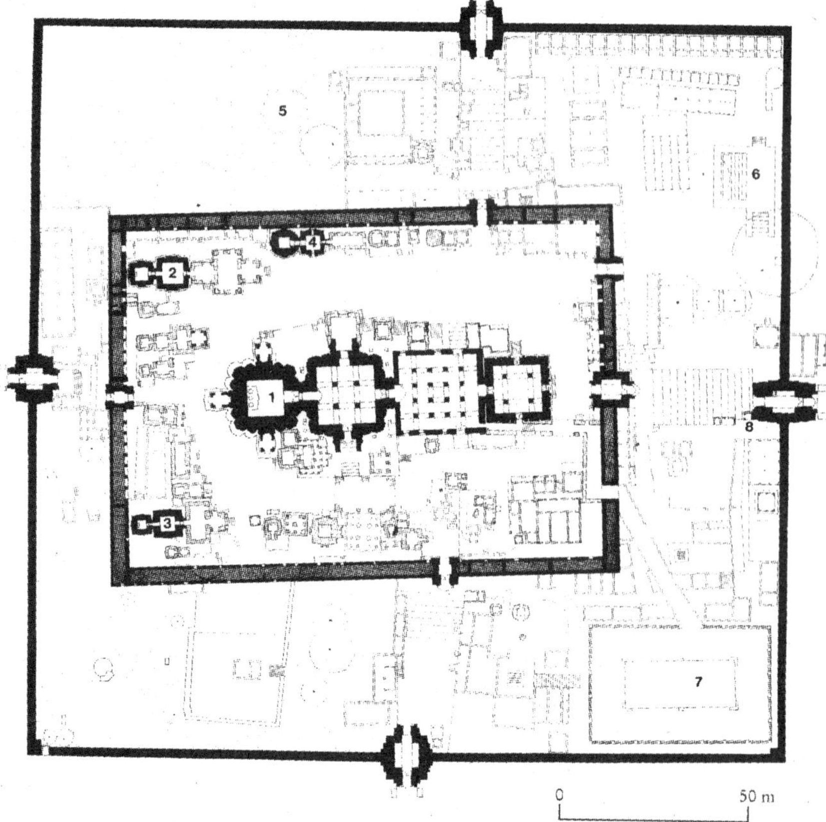

Fig. 10.3: Puri: Jagannātha Temple compound, drawing by Bijay Basukala, 2000. The outline of the main temple is based on measurements taken by R.J. Vasavada, N. Verma and H. Pandya in December 1999. All the structures of the inner compound are based on measurements taken by A. and B. Basukala, while the structures of the outer compound are based on the Settlement Map of 1987-8 on a scale of 1 : 990.

1. Jagannātha Temple;
2. Mahālakṣmī Temple;
3. Vimalā Temple;
4. Sūrya Temple;
5. Koili Baikuntha, the 'graveyard' of the old deities;
6. Snānamaṇḍapa, the bathing platform;
7. Central kitchen for the preparation of *bhoga*;
8. Kāśīviśvanātha, representation of the Lord of All (of Vārāṇasī).

and we doubt whether the deul tower of the present temple is the one the chronicle talks about when it mentions the installation of three large deities by King Sarangadhara, who also is said to have established the chariot festival, in the middle of the eighteenth century. As not a single reliable date is available in Orissa for temple structures of the eighteenth century, we must accept this information for the time being. But we must also assume that the chronicle, whose origins date to the middle of the nineteenth century, would have mentioned the building of a large temple at a later stage, as such an event would have constituted a well-remembered past. The assembly hall can be seen as belonging to the early eighteenth century period, while the elaborately crafted hall of offering must have followed a few decades later. The dancing hall between them represents a later addition.

The comparative presentation of the ground plans of the temples in Puri and Ranpur (Fig. 10.4) demonstrates a typological identity which seems striking. The difference in size—Ranpur's temple covers little more than one third of the grand imperial scheme in Puri—clearly demonstrates the restricted resources of a Little Kingdom in the jungle. Relocating an earlier Mādhava, installing a replica of the powerful triad of Puri, and initiating the annual ritual journey of the gods in chariots contributed to shaping Ranpur in imitation of the centre. In ritual terms, the kings of Ranpur turned into the sons of the Lord of the Universe. Cleaning the chariots with a broom under the eyes of his former subjects still bears witness of the king's role today.

The moment the new temple was built, the king moved his palace to the north of it, establishing a unity of the two structures, which was further strengthened when in 1910 the new ambitious palace touched the compound wall of the temple (see the site plan, Figs. 10.5 and 10.6). By establishing and further reinforcing this constellation, the king legitimized his power. Initiating annual rituals to incorporate powerful tribal deities like Maṇināga and Khilamuṇḍa subsequently became instrumental in meeting their claims to precedence and power. A well-balanced designation of roles must have created a solid base at the beginning of the nineteenth century which lasts until today.

THE LEGITIMATION OF POWER THROUGH RITUAL PERFORMANCES

Of the annual calendar of festive events, every urban ritual of Ranpur is performed along models developed in Puri, the uncontested ritual centre of the entire region. Considered to be one of the Four Corners (*cārdhām*) of the subcontinent, the Indian universe, Puri grew to become a major pilgrimage centre from the ninth century. The rituals observed in Puri largely reflected the agricultural cycle, which governs life in the fertile valleys of the major rivers of Orissa.

RATHAYĀTRĀ: CONFIRMING THE PRESENCE OF THE IMPERIAL DEITY ON THE PERIPHERY

As was noted earlier, the Ranpur chronicle mentions the early establishment of a temple in Ranpur in CE 1530 by King Uddhava Singh. The chronicle does not fail to mention that Jagannātha ordered in a dream the performance of the twelve festivals (*dvādaśayātrā*) that mark the annual cycle of rituals tied to the Lord of the Universe. The shaping of a new centre in the jungle obviously also needed a framing in time. The cycle starts with the bathing of Jagannātha on the day of the full moon in the month of Jyeṣṭha (June). During a critical

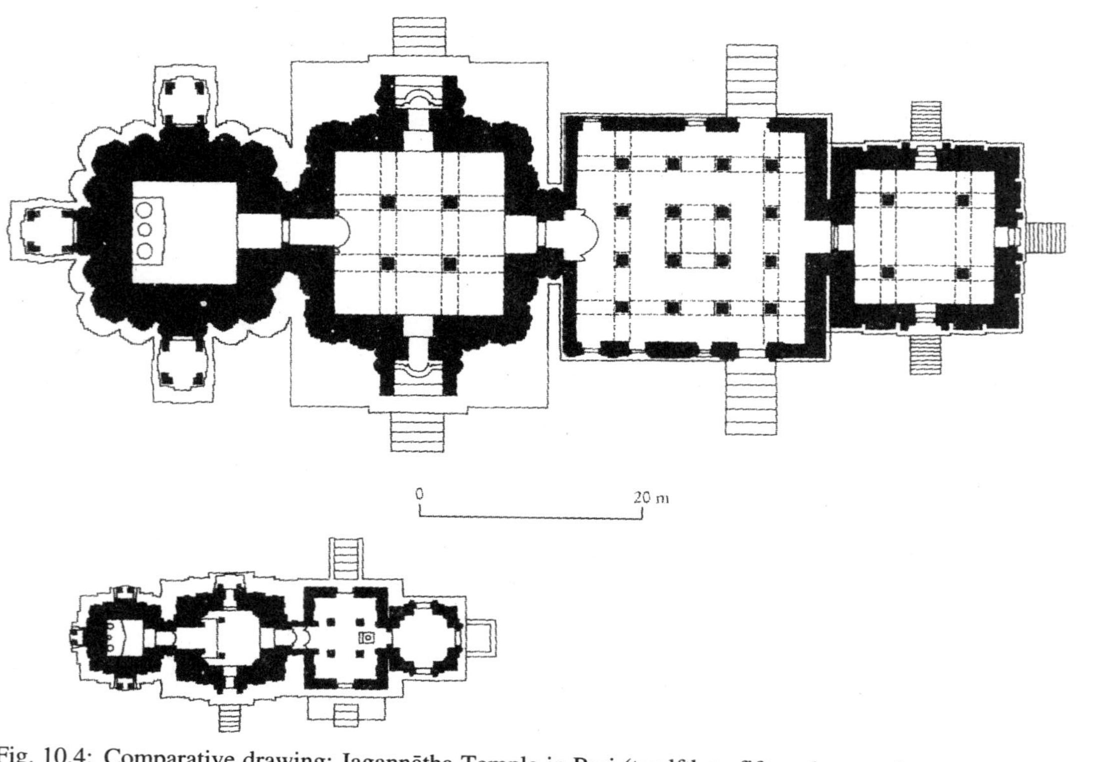

Fig. 10.4: Comparative drawing: Jagannātha Temple in Puri (twelfth to fifteenth centuries), drawing by B. Basukala, based on measurements by R.J. Vasavada (in May 2000) and R.P. Mukharji (in 1872); Jagannātha Temple in Ranpur (eighteenth-nineteenth centuries), survey and drawing by R.J. Vasavada, July 1999.

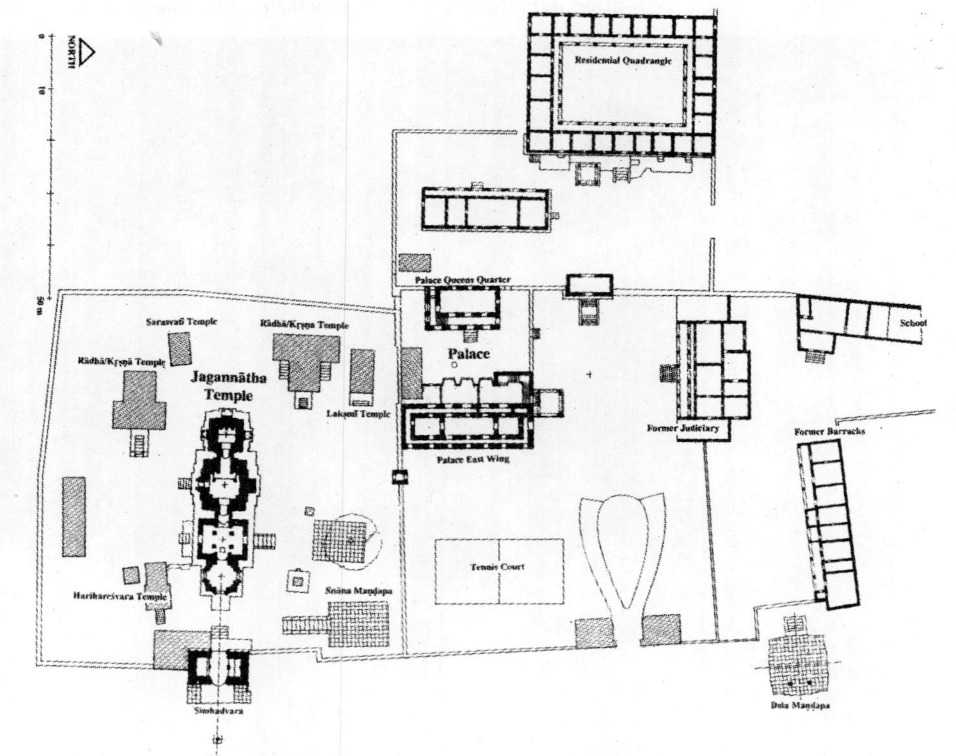

Fig. 10.5: Ranpur: Jagannātha Temple compound and adjoining palaces. Survey and drawing by R.J. Vasavada, with M. Jain, M. Patel and R. Mehta, July 1999 and H. Pandya and N. Verma, December 1999.

Fig. 10.6: Ranpur: The temple of Jagannātha as seen from the north-east. Photo, Niels Gutschow, 13 July 1999.

period of fever, the surface of the wooden deities are renewed and finally painted on the first day after the new moon. On the following day the three deities are placed in three ceremonial chariots which have been under construction over a period of fifty-eight days since the 'indestructible third' (*akṣaya tṛtīyā*). The three chariots are paraded along the main ritual axis, which covers less than one third of that in Puri. The deities retire to their temporary abode of Guṇḍicā for seven days. In the company of the five ministers of her husband, Lakṣmī pays Jagannātha a visit and returns home through the darkness of the back lanes (Fig. 10.7). With the return of the three deities to the temple on the eleventh day (Fig. 10.8), one of the main events of the year is over. In a renewed form, the greatest regional deity has graced his urban territory with his retinue. Striding through this space, he confirms the existing order, which, ritually speaking, is identical to that in the centre, in Puri.

DURGĀPŪJĀ: PAYING TRIBUTE TO THE TRIBAL GODDESS KHILAMUṆḌA

Nine days before the day of the new moon in October a Brahman priest accompanies a long bamboo pole (in 2002 this measured 632 cm) carried in procession to the shrine of a jungle goddess (Khilamuṇḍa) about 15 km south-west of Ranpur. Until recently, her non-iconic representation in the shape of a simple stone was kept in a wooden hut and attended to regularly by a tribal priest, a *Jani*. The goddess is invited once a year to attend the great ritual of renewal in Ranpur in a tribute to her decisive role in re-establishing the power of the Ranpur dynasty of kings, an event which is stated by the local chronicle to have happened in the early eighteenth century in order to add a new layer to the process of appropriating the tribal territory and turning it into a Little Kingdom.

The goddess enters the bamboo pole to attain another non-iconic form, probably a rare case of a non-iconic deity remaining in a non-iconic state as her portable representation. The newly coloured pole is carried in a procession to Ranpur (Fig. 10.9) to be kept in the palace compound for sixteen days (*sorapūjā*). On the Victorious Tenth (*Vijayadaśamī*) or Daśaharā festival, the pole is carried to the festival ground (*Daśaharā Padiā*) beyond the northern edge of the settlement. Flower garlands and saris are offered to the goddess while she is paraded along the ritual axis, accompanied by a frantic crowd. The king follows with the representation of Maṇināga from his palace under a ceremonial umbrella, accompanied by the *diwān*, who carries the ceremonial sword, and his preceptor, the *rājaguru*. Upon the completion of the ritual, the bamboo pole returns to the palace, where it is kept in a state of slumber. The essence of the goddess returns to Ukutukumei in the form of a pigeon.

Khilamuṇḍa only enters the bamboo pole for a period of sixteen days. The pole itself is renewed annually as long as the king is in power. At this level of understanding, the pole represents royalty and merges with the generative forces of the tribal goddess for a limited period which precedes her victory over her enemies. In this event, Maṇināga, the primary manifestation of place,

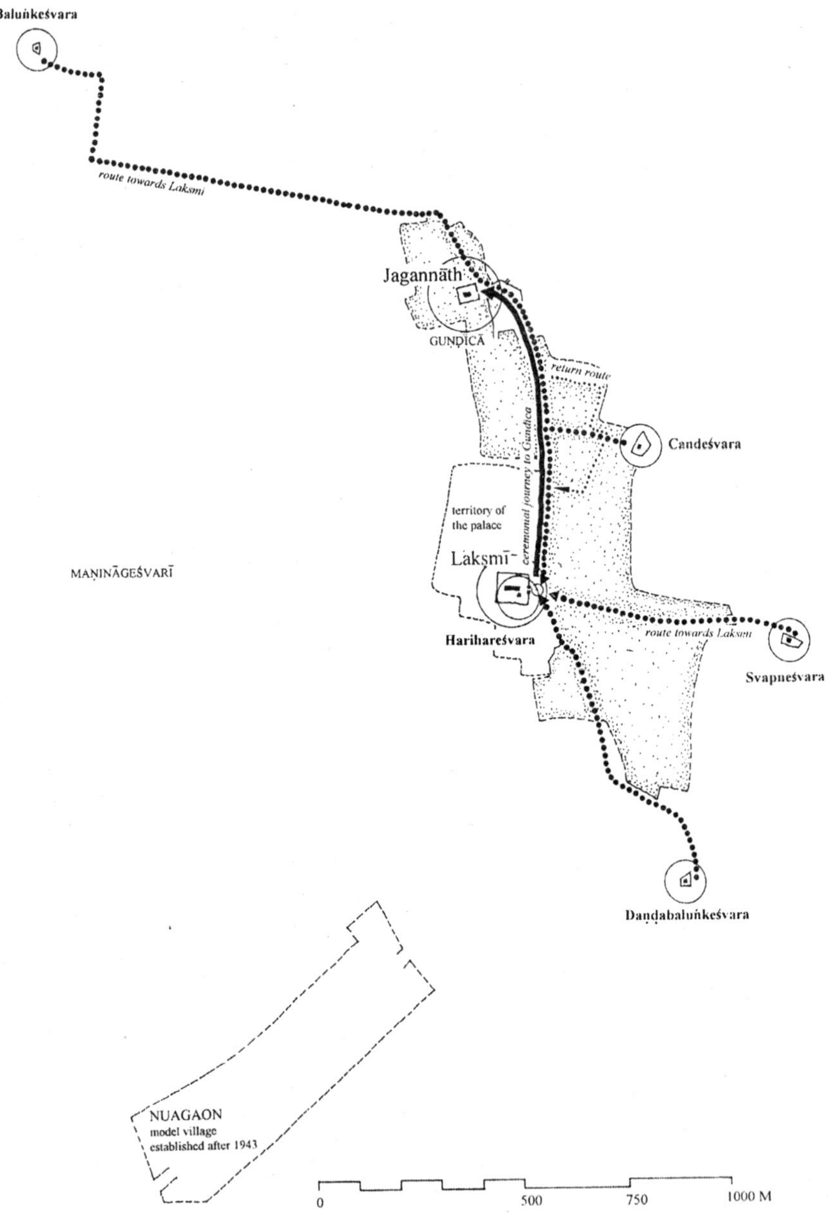

Fig. 10.7: Ranpur Rathayātrā: the trinity of Jagannātha, Balabhadra and Subhadrā embark upon their ritual journey in chariots on the second day after new moon in July and reach Guṇḍicā the same day. On the fifth day, Lakṣmī visits the three deities in the company of the 'Five Ministers of Jagannātha' and returns through back lanes 'unseen' the same day. On the tenth day the three deities mount their chariots, but only Balabhadra returns to the starting point. On the eleventh day Subhadra returns, followed by Jagannātha on the twelfth day. Jointly they return into the sanctum of the temple.

Fig. 10.8: Ranpur: Rathayātrā, the return of the chariot of Subhadrā to the temple on the eleventh day of the bright moon in July. For the first time the chariot is pulled by women. Photo 23 July 1999.

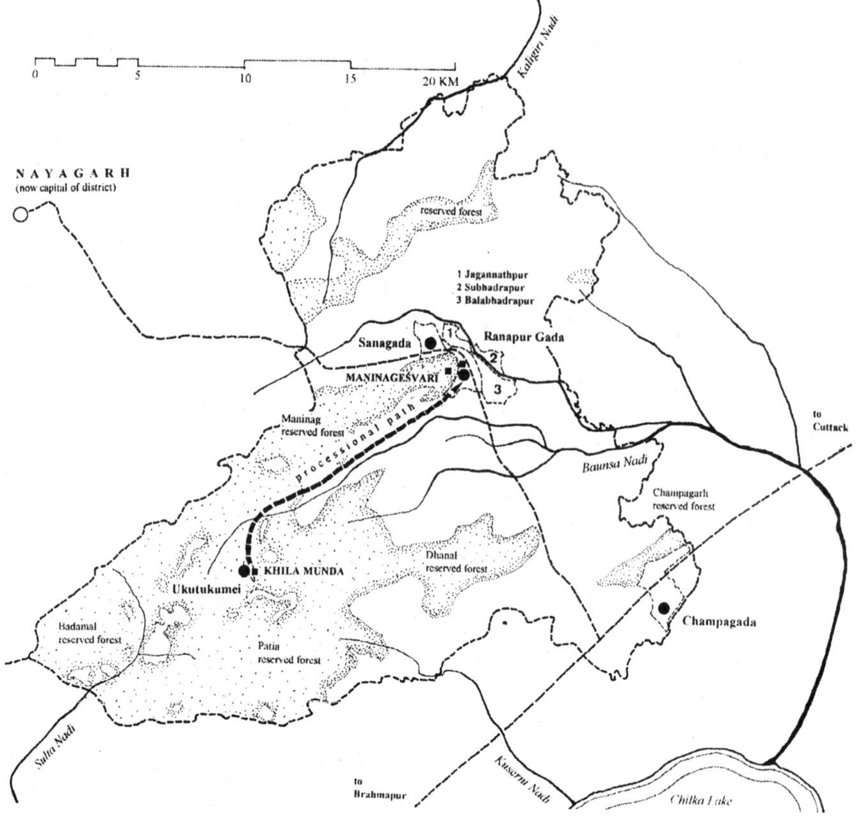

Fig. 10.9: Ranpur: The tribal goddess Khilamuṇḍa is brought from Ukutukumei to Ranpur once a year on the occasion of Durgā Pūjā in October. Besides Sanagada and Champagada, Ukutukumei was one of the three forts that guarded the periphery of the king's territory.

merely witnesses the renewal of the tribute which the king owes to the goddess of the jungle. On yet another level, a more Brahmanical goddess, Nārāyaṇī, is present at the ritual ground in the shape of a pot, the *ghaṭa*.

DAṆḌAYĀTRĀ: LIFE AND DEATH AS THEMES OF THE 'FESTIVAL OF PUNISHMENT'

The following brief account focuses on notions of time and space in a complex ritual. It is not the motives or social dramas that are of interest here, but the territorial aspects.[8]

[8]Burkhard Schnepel has focused in a couple of accounts on what in South Orissa is known as *daṇḍo nato*. He covers the performative aspect of 'quite rustic and comic theatrical interludes' and elements of 'love of and devotion to the goddess, Kālī'. See Schnepel 2000.

Like the slightly earlier Pañcaḍoḷayātrā, the Daṇḍayātrā is tied to a highly symbolic moment in the calendar. It does not reflect the movement of the moon, but of the sun. The first day of the month Vaiśākha (14 April) is not only the day that recalls the mythic event of Gaṅgā touching the earth. According to the solar calendar it also heralds the beginning of a new year. In Orissa this day is called *panāsaṃkrānti*.

The festival lasts for twenty-three days. During the twenty-one days preceding the advent of the New Year, twelve young men (called *bagata*), exclusively from those sub-castes that have a tribal origin, make their rounds through town with performances of penance. The prominent figure of the group carries a pair of cane sticks which represent the divine couple, Śiva and Kālī. In a singular term, the sticks are also called *Gaurībeta*, arousing associations with Gaurī, Śiva's spouse, who symbolizes the oceans or fertilizing rains which flow down from her.

On the twenty-first day, Caitra maśanta or New Year's Eve, the groups turn to Kamanāghar, a small temple along the main ritual axis which houses Kālī. All participants are ordered by their teacher, the guru, to perform in the name of Maṇiāmā, the protective mother goddess of Ranpur's territory. Finally, the guru, who appears to represent the goddess, is carried away, covered with white cloth to signal his death. Late at night, the pair of cane sticks also die symbolically as they are clandestinely carried away to the sound of a drum usually struck in cases of death.

On the twenty-second day, the first day of the new solar cycle, the participants complete their performance with fire-walking in front of the Kamanāghar—in a way in the presence and in honour of Kālī. Three pits have to be crossed: the first is filled with milk, the second with glowing charcoal, and the third with water. Within the temple, a jar is opened in which rice has been sprouting over the period of twenty-one days. Such a demonstration of growth within the sanctum adds another notion of far-reaching renewal. The entire ritual celebrates death and subsequent renewal at a critical point in time. On the twenty-second day the participants undergo purificatory rituals before being reintegrated into society.

The territorial aspect of the entire exercise is equally overwhelming in its complexity. Every group of participants is organized around a *kothi*, a 'small house' that is identified with an unassuming temple dedicated to Kālī, who in Ranpur is identical with Maṇiāmā, the primeval goddess of place. Within the present-day territory of Ranpur district, people share the notion that a hundred and eight such *kothi*s were formerly established within a realm that is specified as *caudakośa*, with a radius of 14 *kośa* or a little over 47 km around the centre, marked by the palace of the king (Fig. 10.10). When it comes to naming the location of these *kothi*s, never more than thirty-six, exactly one third of the auspicious number one hundred and eight, can be counted. The notion of a circle, a maṇḍala of *caudakośa*, recalls a territorial extent that can be attributed to the constructed past. Only a faint idea survives that it covers religious

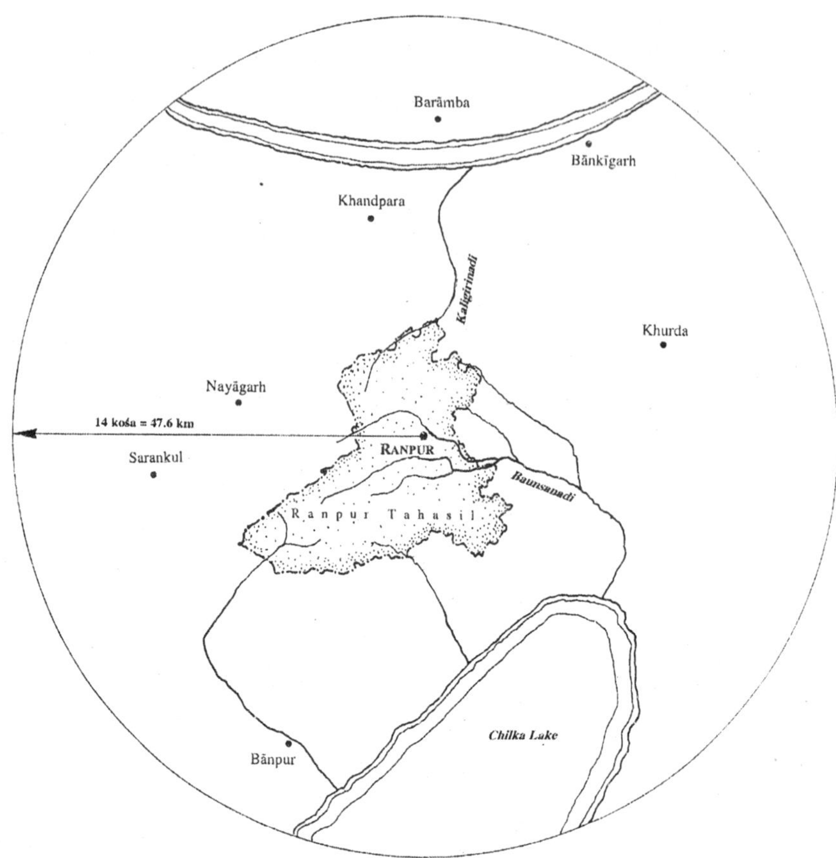

Fig. 10.10: Ranpur: Map demonstrating the idea of the *caudakośa* maṇḍala, a realm that is delineated by a radius of 14 *kośa*, which is equal to 47.6 km. Although the present Ranpur tahsil and the former princely state (until 1948) covers a much smaller area, it is said that originally there were 108 congregations for the Daṇḍajātrā (the festival of 'punishment') prior to the Vaiśākhi, the first month of the solar year.

endowments made by the king of Ranpur in neighbouring areas. The number of acting *kothi* varies. While some are desperately seeking participants, others have been recently established after receiving the necessary stick deities from Ranpur.

The tribal associations with the event are not only demonstrated by the social status of the participants. Brahmans are not only strictly excluded; they make sure that groups do not enter their villages. Daṇḍayatrā indeed splits the society of Ranpur: Brahmans, who once migrated here from the centre, represent the elite, being engaged in reading, teaching and administering; farmers and gardeners are inevitably tied to the agricultural calendar and depend on the grace of Gaurī. A generation or two ago all groups had to convene in Ranpur to demonstrate loyalty in front of the king. A first offering of fire was made to Jagannātha as the representation of the imperial power, a second to the king. All the participants joined in a chorus wishing well-being.

THE ULTIMATE RECONFIRMATION OF THE DIVINE AND ROYAL TERRITORY IN SPRING: PAÑCADOḶAYĀTRĀ

THE URBAN RITUAL ARENA

The Doḷameḷana festival, literally 'the meeting of swings', is widely celebrated around the full moon in the month of Phālguṇa (February/March), which in Orissa is known as Doḷapūrṇimā. This is the day of the lunar calendar that precedes the spring equinox, which in the northern hemisphere marks the advent of renewal. In Orissa this has many profane consequences: budgets are prepared and land lease contracts renewed.

In Ranpur the entire festival lasts for eleven days and is called 'Pañcadoḷayātrā' (literally 'the procession of swings or palanquins on the fifth day'), after the final event on the fifth day after the full moon. On that day all swings from the former princely state of Ranpur are carried in procession (*yātrā*) to the central ritual ground to pay homage to the presiding royal deity. Such swing festivals are commonly enacted for the divine couple Kṛṣṇa/Rādhā in many parts of India, but only in Orissa does the gentle swinging of the couple transcend the narrow confines of a Vaiṣṇava event to turn into a powerful manifestation of territorial integration.

Neither in Ranpur nor in the surrounding villages are swings made for the sole purpose of rocking the deities. Rather, the swing is a portable shrine which houses the movable images of deities for a certain time, rarely longer than a day. The deity 'leaves' the temple to undertake a journey and returns to its original place after its completion. Often the deity represents a copy of the presiding deity of the sanctuary or a variation that suits the purpose of the journey. On such occasions, the deities grace and validate the protective quality of the quarters of the settlement and turn to individual households upon their invitations. On such occasions, the deity is praised and receives offerings in exchange for granting 'the eye contact or vision that confers divine blessing' (Skt. *darśana*).[9]

These small shrines are shaped like a real temple with an open platform, complete with four or even twelve elaborately carved columns. The roof is often two-tiered, complete with a vase (*kalaśa*) at the pinnacle and, if the shrine carries a manifestation of Śiva, a trident and a snake-hood or, if the shrine houses a form of Viṣṇu, his disk. Iron rings on the side permit the entire

[9]Stietencron 2001, 365.

structure to be slung between two pillars to be rocked. However, this is rarely done as the shrine is there to undertake a pre-designed journey. Two poles of bamboo are fixed below the shrine or to the sides, thus converting the swing into a palanquin. It is carried by four helpers from its temple, while a member of the Mali sub-caste of gardeners heads the procession banging on a metal plate. A second Mali follows with a ceremonial umbrella, the usual symbol of royal or divine presence.

Until recently, the ritual ground was amorphous in shape, without any architectural framework. However, at ground level, a hundred and eight platforms can be seen framing and surrounding a space measuring roughly 100 × 70 metres. Throughout the year, most of these platforms are covered with food stalls. But for the occasion of the grand urban ritual the stalls have to be moved for a fortnight, the platforms repaired and painted light blue.

Three phases of the ritual can be identified, which form a symmetry in time. The full moon day is preceded by five days of local significance and succeeded by five more days culminating in a grand gathering of the deities, representing the state of Ranpur.

First Phase: The Divine Couple, Viṣṇu/Lakṣmī Graces the Urban Territory in the Company of His Five Ministers, Manifestations of Śiva

On the first five evenings, the ritual journey starts in front of the temple of Jagannātha (Fig. 10.11). The five representations of Śiva in Ranpur are considered to act as 'ministers' of Jagannātha, and as such they accompany the divine couple, Doḷagovinda and Lakṣmī, on the journey (Fig. 10.12). Their manifestation in the shape of a *liṅga* is kept at temples which mark the boundary of the urban territory.

On the night preceding the full moon the final event is announced. Jagannātha appears in his manifestation as Doḷagovinda and in the shape of a four-armed Viṣṇu with his usual attributes. He is accompanied by his consort Lakṣmī as well as by Kṛṣṇa in his form as a child (Bālakṛṣṇa). As soon as they leave the temple compound, the troupe of deities are accompanied by their 'ministers'. Five temple servants head the procession: a barber with a torch, followed by a musician with a conch shell, and three members of the sub-caste of gardeners with a ceremonial umbrella and metal plates, the sound of which announces the coming of the deities. The group heads immediately northwards towards the ritual ground, *pañcadoḷa padiā*. The procession stops a few times to pay its respects to deities enshrined in temples facing the *baḍa daṇḍa*, the main ritual axis of the town. At these halts the four carriers from the sub-caste of farmers do not place their palanquins on the ground but support the carrying poles with sticks of equal length. The palanquins remain floating in mid-air. At the ritual ground the three palanquins are lined up facing the east to attend a purification ritual to the continuous sound of the metal plates, which prepares

Fig. 10.11: Ranpur, Pañcadoḷayātrā: Preceding Doḷapūrṇimā, full moon in March, the divine couple Madanmohana and Lakṣmī are carried in a portable shrine from the temple of Jagannātha, to be paraded in the company of the five ministers in two more shrines along the *bada daṇḍa*, the main ritual axis, to the ceremonial ground. The procession stops wherever offerings are presented from houses nearby. Photo 8 March 2001.

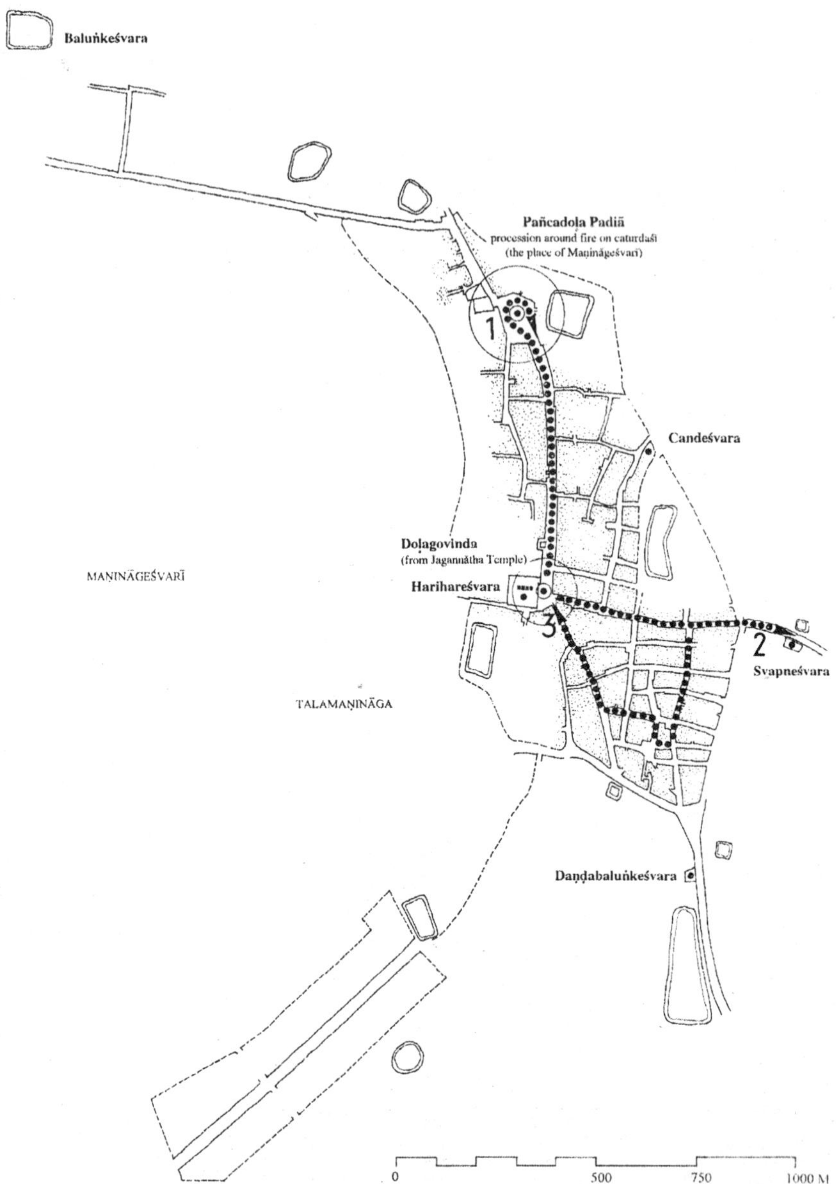

Fig. 10.12: Ranpur, Pañcadoḷayātrā: For a period of seven days five movable representations of Mahādeva who act as the 'ministers' of Jagannātha, convene at the temple gate to accompany the divine couple Doḷagovinda and Lakṣmī on a nocturnal journey through the lanes of the twelve quarters. The night preceding the full moon, the troupe carrying the portable shrines turns to the *pañcadoḷa padiā*, the festive ground (1), to witness a fire in honour of Maṇināgeśvarī, the tutelary goddess of the king. On the way back the procession first turns east to the temple of Svapneśvara (2) and then returns after a circuit through the southern quarters.

the ground for the final event. A fire of straw is lit to purify the place where Maṇināgeśvarī, the tutelary goddess of the 'Little King' and his kingdom, will be seated six days later to accept the submission of the hundred and eight territorial deities of the kingdom.

The three palanquins return in a formal procession along the ritual axis towards the temple of Jagannātha, then turn east to the temple of Svapneśvara, add a detour through the southern quarters of the town, and then return to the point of origin a few hours after midnight.

SECOND PHASE: DOḶAPŪRṆIMĀ, OR FULL MOON, THE ADVENT OF SPRING

In the morning of the day of the full moon, a palanquin carrying the divine couple (Ḍoḷagovinda-Lakṣmī) leaves the temple and is placed on a large platform with a carved plinth, the doḷavedi, in front of the palace and facing the ritual axis. As the posts from which the shrine was originally suspended to form a swing have broken, the palanquin is simply placed on the ground. Two ceremonial umbrellas are placed on either side, while a large canopy covers almost the entire platform. The son of the last acting king, who survives in poverty in his ruined palace, worships the divine couple. The offering of green mango fruits and a large jackfruit mark the beginning of spring, the renewal of the world.

On the same day, the one hundred and eight deities within the territory of Ranpur leave their temples and are placed in their portable shrines, which are put to rest for a few hours on the swing platform within the temple compound. In Ranpur itself, the five 'ministers' mentioned above and the deities of the nine *maṭha*s and the Nṛsingha temple appear to be worshipped by the people of the respective quarters of the city. In these cases the *maṭha*s represent a manifestation of the divine couple, mostly Rādhā/Kṛṣṇa. On that day and the day following, the 'ministers' accompany the divine couple again on their nocturnal journey through the lanes of the city.

The following day, Holipūrṇima, is dedicated to a violent celebration of the change of the seasons. All the shops along the ritual axis are barricaded and women seek to hide themselves as young men go round throwing coloured powder not only at each other but at anybody who happens to come into sight. Obscene slogans fill the air of the main street, which turns into an arena of violence for about two hours. Although the crisis is intentionally created, it is experienced as a spontaneous outburst ignoring accepted social behaviour and hierarchy. The day of Holi has the quality of a liminal event. It is neither here nor there in time, but in between. The crisis or chaos that is produced is meant to dissolve the accepted order. Dissolution embraces the germ of renewal, and the vernal equinox or the full moon preceding indeed provides perfect timing for this process. In the case of Ranpur, the dissolution is the inevitable precondition for the concluding event which celebrates the reconfirmation of the territorial order of the Little Kingdom.

Third Phase: The Convention of the One Hundred and Eight Deities of the Territory

The administrative servant of the Jagannātha temple sends invitations to the deities of the former kingdom's territory well in advance. The caretakers of fifteen temples and *maṭha*s of Ranpur and ninety-two temples of villages which dot the agricultural land of the former kingdom need this invitation as a gesture of belonging (Fig. 10.13). Only one deity is invited from beyond the nineteenth-century territorial boundaries, from the village of Siko. From there a representation of Śiva appeared in mythic times to reconfirm Ranpur as a place of kingship. The ritual seems to 'remember' this relationship.

The hundred and eight deities leave their abode on the fifth day after the full moon in the palanquin that had been used on the day of the full moon and arrive in Ranpur after midnight. The majority of palanquins originate from the southern villages, seven alone from Gopalpur. Four come from the south-west, where reclaimed land stretches like a finger into the forest, five from the west

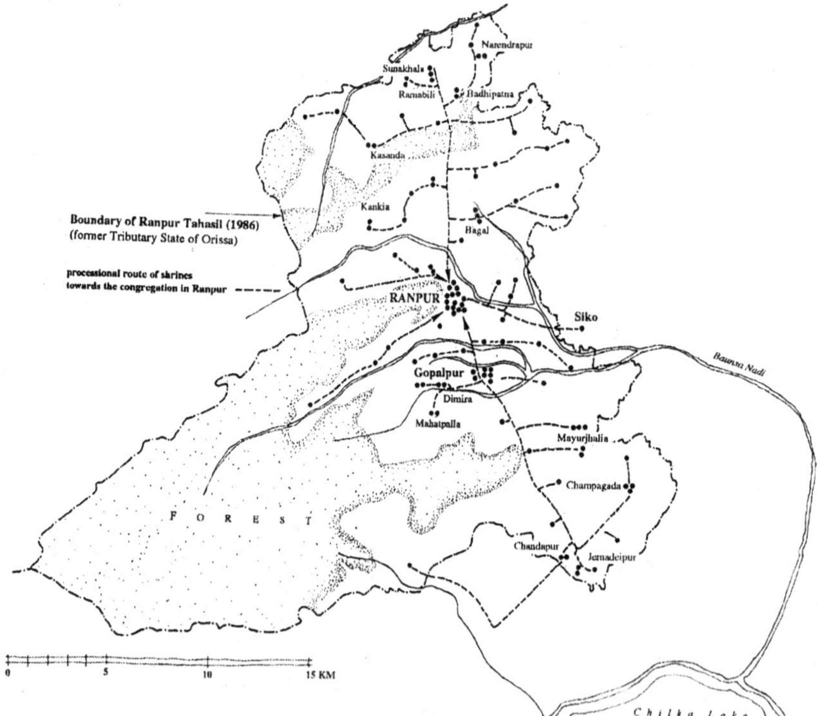

Fig. 10.13: Ranpur, Pañcadoḷayātrā: On the fifth day after the full moon in March the movable representations (*calanti pratima*) from villages of the former State of Ranpur (including one from neighbouring Siko) are carried in festive processions towards the festival ground at the northern end of the ritual axis of Ranpur. From the north 39 and from the south 34 portable shrines join those from Ranpur itself.

and five from the east. The remaining thirty-six palanquins originate from the northern villages, three alone from Sunakhala, an important marketplace on the border with the former neighbouring state of Khandpara.

The palanquins are paraded with great pomp towards the designated ritual ground, which is encircled by one hundred and eight platforms. Colourful animals in bizarre shapes are brought on cycle rickshaws, and the night is passed in dancing and singing songs in praise of the gods. Collective excitement fills the access roads towards Ranpur.

The assembly of the deities on the ritual ground is strictly organized (Fig. 10.14). This means that every shrine has its predetermined place, one of the platforms that form a modified circle along the edge of the ground. The spatial order of the territory is reflected in the order of sequence, which is divided by an invisible axis. The host or rather the 'master of the place' (*thānapati*, Skt. *sthānapati*), namely, Jagannātha in the form of Doḷagovinda, presides over the congregation at the top of this axis, facing south. The western part of the circle is reserved for representations of Viṣṇu (in the form of Jagannātha, Kṛṣṇa or Rādhā/Kṛṣṇa), the eastern part for representations of Śiva. The configuration of the congregation suggests a strong element of what has been described as the meeting of Viṣṇu and Śiva (*hari-hara-bheṭa*).[10] In contrast to similar meetings elsewhere in Orissa, the śaiva element dominates the scene. Altogether sixty-four representations of Śiva are placed to the left of the presiding deity and forty-three representations of Viṣṇu to his right. One more form of Kṛṣṇa, the Brajavihari from the Brajavihari maṭh in Purnavasanta (the village north of Ranpur), is placed between Doḷagovinda and his five śaiva ministers to avoid what could be seen as an unwanted confrontation. Brajavihari is needed to mediate the hierarchy or make it obscure. The dividing line between the two groups thus becomes less decisive: Jagannātha's (or Doḷagovinda's) role becomes less assuming, the hierarchy more ambivalent.

The division of the circle clearly reflects an opposition between Śaiva and Vaiṣṇava without aiming at symmetry. The question of superiority does not surface, because all the deities are arranged around the centre, which is occupied by the most powerful territorial deity, Maṇināgeśvarī. Whether Vaiṣṇava or Śaiva, on this occasion all one hundred and eight deities are subsidiary territorial deities. They have assembled to pay their respects to and be reconfirmed by the primeval protective goddess. She is the territorial goddess par excellence, representing the origin of the place, and she once witnessed the clearing of the forest. All the other deities stand for the settlements that participate in her protective powers. Literally 'the jewel serpent' (*maṇi nāga*), the goddess ensures water and fertility. Seen as a meaningful event of renewal, one could argue that the one hundred and eight territorial deities merge with the ultimate deity of place. Their concentric movement could be seen as a march of death, one that ends in a circular fashion to overcome any hierarchy. The return to

[10]See Stietencron 2002, 379.

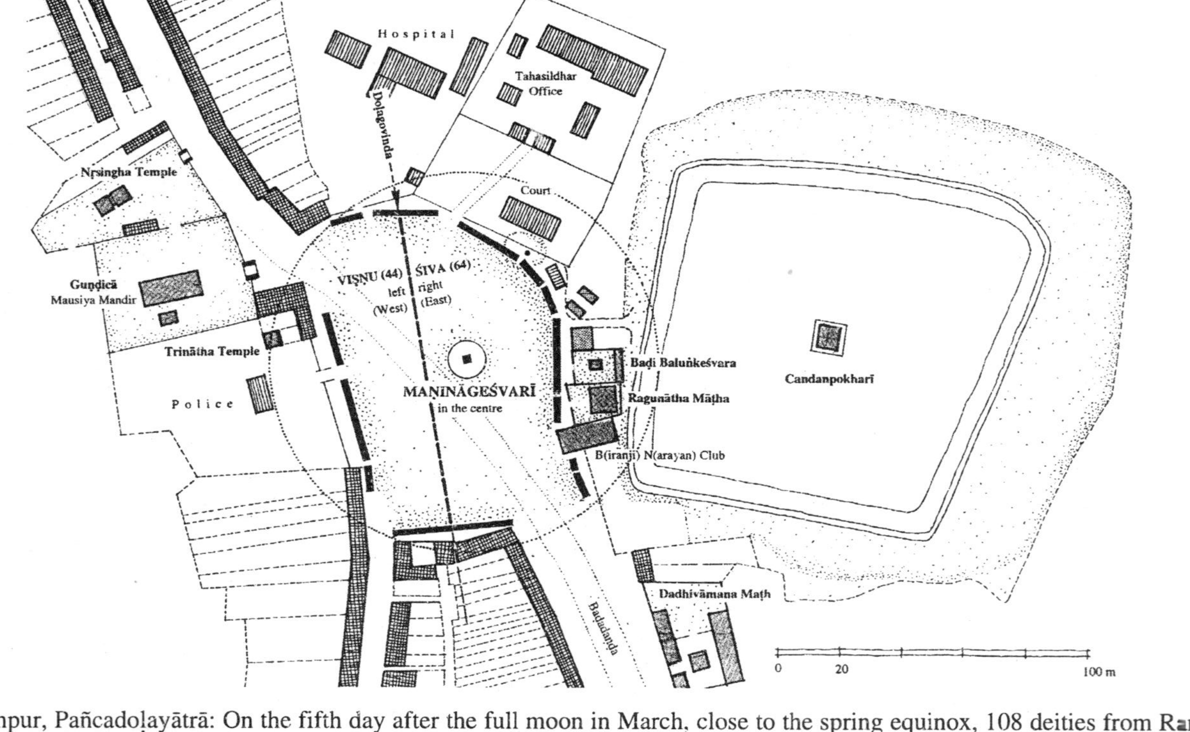

Fig. 10.14: Ranpur, Pañcadoḷayātrā: On the fifth day after the full moon in March, close to the spring equinox, 108 deities from Ranpur and the surrounding villages, representing the territory of the former princely state, are brought to the ritual ground, *pañcadoḷa padiā*. They convene in a circular manner to pay their respects to the original goddess of place, the tutelary goddess of the king, Maṇināgeśvarī. The goddess occupies the dominant central position. The circular configuration is divided by a north-south axis: 64 representations of Śiva are positioned on the eastern side and 44 representations of Viṣṇu towards the west. The unnumbered position presiding over the axis is occupied by Jagannātha in the form of Doḷagovinda, with one form of Kṛṣṇa towards his right to avoid direct contact with his five Śaiva ministers.

the villages equals a rebirth on the occasion of the vernal equinox. One hundred and eight deities fan out from a centre to reclaim the cultivated land of their villages and to reoccupy their position as the Lord of Place.

THE SYMBOLISM OF SPACE AND TIME

The spring equinox is a perfect occasion for rituals of renewal throughout the northern hemisphere. Calendrical diversity, however, allows this day to be fixed at different times. In the Gregorian solar calendar this day is 21 March. The incorrect calculations of Brahmanical astronomers have caused a gradual shifting of it towards 14 April, the first day of the month of Vaiśākha, which in many subcultures of the subcontinent is still celebrated as New Year. In Orissa, Dolāpurṇimā, the full moon in March, represents the alternative according to the lunar calendar.

New Year by definition calls for a ritual of renewal to ensure the continuity of time and space, as well as the continuity of individual and collective life, human beings, and even gods in a given territorial situation, whether a temple compound, a village, an imperial city, or a royal or divine territory. In Ranpur, the ritual addresses the territory of the Little King which, on that occasion, is identified as a divine territory over which Maṇināgeśvarī presides. Her presence in the centre of a circle of a meaningful number of gods ensures and confirms the territorial set-up. Taking into account similar ritual events, one could even talk of a rebirth. In this context, the fire made on the site of the congregation the night before the full moon probably indicates death, or at least a far-reaching cleansing of evil influences from the site.

To return to Ranpur, the mobile representation of Maṇināgeśvarī, the *iṣṭadevatā* of the Little King and thus the tutelary deity of his territory, leaves her shrine within the palace for what I would call a demonstration of loyalty by all the village gods, and above all by Jagannātha and his 'ministers'. At this moment the notion of the Little Kingdom turns into a 'divine kingdom'. It is Maṇināgeśvarī who rules the divine kingdom, while in profane matters the Little King becomes her tool. Kulke has referred to the annual coronation ceremony of Jagannātha, during which he is visited by the subregional deities, Maṇināgeśvarī among others. This act has been translated into the image of a tent, with the eight Mother Goddesses forming the pegs of the tent and Jagannātha representing the supporting central pole.[11] This idea is certainly applicable to Ranpur, where the one hundred and eight gods represent the pegs of the tent, with Maṇināgeśvarī representing the centre. This is probably truer than anywhere else, because the congregation of gods on the occasion of Pañcadoḷa forms a circle around the tutelary goddess.

The number one hundred and eight fits into this model of interpretation, as it is the most perfect number in combining spatial and temporal symbolism:

[11] Kulke 1980, 31.

nine represents space and twelve represents time. Most often, the number is tied to a processional route which opposes a meaningful, protective inside to a potentially unordered outside.[12] The case of Ranpur is unique as a hundred and eight sites dot the entire territory without an inherent order. Only once a year does this territory assume the shape of a circle to create an order that can be experienced visually. The circle is formed to acknowledge the superiority of the centre. Individually, the a hundred and eight territorial deities represent fractions of a whole. The number and the ritual convention only tie each part to a cosmic and eternal model.

THE COLONIZATION OF THE TERRITORY: *ŚĀSANA* VILLAGES

The people of Ranpur insist that the former state had nine *śāsana* villages (see Fig. 10.15), thus associating them with a significant number: nine is the perfect number, which provides the symbolism of time and space to any spatial entity, be it a single temple, a village, or a larger territory. The Ranpur chronicle refers to only eight gifts of land settling Brahmans in such villages, excluding the establishment of *Samukhāsahi*, the east-west axis of the city, along which today many Brahmans and the *diwān* of the former kingdom are settled. The chronicle says nothing about specific motifs such as vows for the establishment of the villages. Nothing is known beyond what Pfeffer has referred to as a process of immortalizing the king's or queen's name and 'appeasing an extremely influential elite of ideologists',[13] who are settled in some thirty villages in the vicinity of the Jagannātha temple of Puri, where a universe with a strong numerical symbolism has been created around the seat of the Lord of the Universe. In the centre, four so-called 'seed' villages, where the *rājagurus*, the royal preceptors of the kings, settled, established the apex of the hierarchy. Sixteen *śāsana* villages followed, thirty-two villages were founded for queens and other dignitaries and thirty-two villages for menial workers. The first wave of immigrants were allegedly summoned from Kannauj, the legendary heartland of Brahmanism, to emphasize their civilizing ability. These Brahmans were assigned the mission to shape the administrative and political framework of 'an "underdeveloped" politically insignificant region'.[14]

The Brahmans who were called to colonize the jungle of the Little Kingdom of Ranpur had to fulfil similar expectations. The establishment of the eight *śāsana* villages belongs to the period of the 'remembered past'. The pattern of civilization claimed by the political and ritual centre of Orissa reached the periphery by the beginning of the eighteenth century. Puri now attained the role that was earlier reserved for Kannauj, the imperial centre of Harsha. However, only faint notions of their origin survive among the Brahmans of Ranpur. The Ratha Brahmans of Brundabanpur, established by King Brundaban

[12] Gutschow 1994, 201.
[13] Pfeffer 1978, 423.
[14] Ibid., 426.

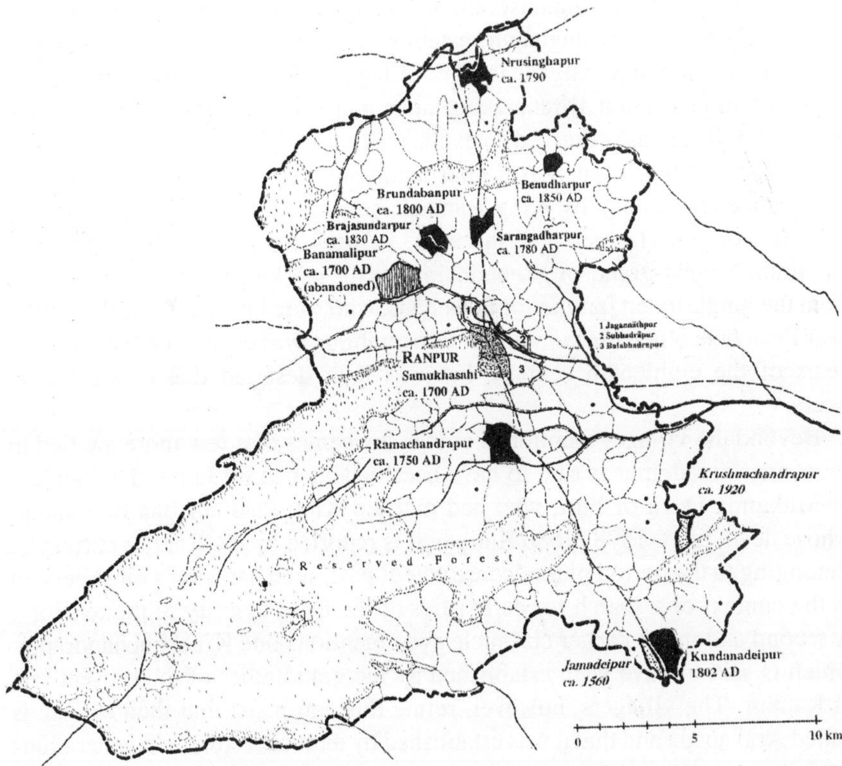

Fig. 10.15: Ranpur: Location of nine *śāsana* villages with the territory of the former princely state of Ranpur. According to the chronicle, these were established between 1560 and 1850 by the kings and queens of Ranpur. Two more villages, Jamadeipur and Krushnachandrapur (indicated in italics on the map), bear witness to a royal deed, but are settled not by Brahmans but by oil pressers and farmers. East of Ranpur, a belt of three 'revenue villages' (fields without any settlement) are dedicated to the temple of Jagannātha and named after the Trinity: (1) Jagannāthpur, (2) Subhadrāpur, (3) Balabhadrapur.

in the early years of the nineteenth century, recall that their ancestors were ordered to migrate from Balabhadrapur and Parvatipur by the king of Puri. Two or three decades later, King Brajasunda ordered Brahmans from Ranpur itself to establish Brajasundarpur in an area adjoining the earlier settlement. King Sarangadhara, who was mentioned earlier as the king who first established a replica of the Puri triad of deities in a new temple, settled Mahāpātra Brahmans from Balapur near Puri in a village named after him, Sarangadharpur. Unusually, even the name of the first Mahāpātra, Grameshvar, is remembered by the villagers, who belong to some thirty Mahāpātra families and a few named Nanda and Miśra. For Kundanadeipur at the southern edge of Ranpur's territory, even the exact date of the establishment, the fourth year of the reign of King Mukunda Deva of Puri (1802), is mentioned by the chronicle, which is based on a now lost palm-leaf manuscript, written in the 1830s. A second chronicle also mentions one Nrusinghapur, established by King Bajradhara Nrusimha Narendra, the son of Sarangadhara. The villagers remember that their ancestors were summoned from Biranarasinghapur and Lalitapatapur near Puri. Till today the village has preserved an exclusive population of Brahmans, whereas other *śāsana* villages, such as Ramachandrapur, established in the middle of the eighteenth century by King Ramachandra, include satellite clusters for menial workers (farmers, washermen, barbers, fishermen and weavers). Nrusimha's great-grandson, Benudhara, was the last king to offer land claimed from the jungle to ten families of Brahmans, who were brought from Parvatipur near Puri. One other *śāsana* village, Banamalipur, was established in the early years of the eighteenth century, but was later deserted due to attacks by tigers.

Beyond the villages mentioned above, the names of a few more are tied to sponsors. Jamadeipur is said to have been established by Jama, the daughter of Mukunda Deva of Puri, who had married King Padmanabha of Ranpur, whose death in CE 1578 (4680 Kaliyuga) is reported by the Ranpur chronicle. Belonging to the period of the 'constructed' past, such narratives must be seen in the context of a search for earlier ties of the local dynasty to the territory. A second and much earlier chronicle even mentions one Krushnachandrapur, which is said to have been established by the grandfather of the present raja of Ranpur. The villagers, however, refute this and insist that their village is called Arakapada and that it was established by their ancestors 'ten generations ago'.

To sum up, human resources seem to have been drained away from the centre since the early eighteenth century to shape the territory of the jungle king. Around such early core villages, a few settlements of farmers were established to claim more fields from the virgin jungle. Even more than these, eighty-five villages, which represent the territory in the context of the Pañcadoḷa festival, were established in the course of the twentieth century. Following a devastating fire in 1943, as mentioned earlier the establishment of Nuagaon on the southern periphery of Ranpur as a 'model village' served as a prototype. Up until today, such settlements have been developed along existing roads in a bid to provide land for the landless.

SUMMARY: HOW A NEW CENTRE RECALLS THE IDEA OF THE ORIGINAL

It would be misleading to characterize the establishment of a new centre in the jungle of the Orissan hinterland as a 'replica' or 'copy'. In referring to an urban configuration and to architectural features, both terms indicate identity with the original, or at least a high degree of likeness. As neither the urban fabric nor the built form of temples in Ranpur bear any visual likeness to the originals, the process of transferring an idea into a new spatial context needs to be described along different lines. It would be rather like sound being echoed or contours and colours being vaguely reflected in a new environment. It would be better to say that an idea or a cluster of constituent ideas is put into a new form.

In the case of Ranpur, the seat of the Lord of the World, Jagannātha, and his ritual requirements at the place of origin, in Puri, constitute the prevailing idea, which is transported into the hinterland to be reshaped in a local context. A tower indicates the location of the sanctum as the house of the deities who look towards the rising sun—which is not in any way a specific idea. It is rather the definition of ritual space between the permanent abode of the deity and his summer residence that shapes the capitals of Little Kingdoms. Beyond the reflection of a spatial configuration, it is the enactment of the 'twelve festivals' that ties time to the cosmic calendar. Realizing or re-enacting the parameters of the original in space and time imbues the new place with the qualities that are needed to legitimize royal power.

The establishment of Jagannātha as a replica of the greatest regional deity certainly represents a constituent act of appropriation. The deity is truly a replica or duplicate. His presence is replicated in order to occupy 'foreign' territory symbolically and to attach what is a process of colonization with cosmic significance. With the regional deity came a retinue of settlers to receive royal grants. The *śāsana* villages were standardized and served as the models for every other settlement in the region.

This process of territorial appropriation was never intended to uproot or replace an existing subregional identity. Local deities like Maṇināgeśvarī in Ranpur were never overpowered but rather incorporated into the ritual of Jagannātha. As she presides over the congregation of all territorial deities on a calendrically significant day, she celebrates her partial superiority. Similarly, she emphasizes this supremacy on a second vernal event, *Daṇḍayātrā*. The exclusion of Brahman (or 'foreign') participants stresses the subregional territorial aspects.

The centres of the Little Kingdoms managed to establish an equilibrium between the aspirations to reflect cosmic claims and standards and the urge to respond to the needs of the chthonic deities of tribal origin.

REFERENCES

Gutschow, Niels 1994. 'Vārānasī/Benares: The Centre of Hinduism?', in *Erdkunde* 48, 194-209.

———2003. 'Ranpur: The Centre of a Little Kingdom', in G. Berkemer and M. Franz (eds.), *Sharing Sovereignty: The Little Kingdom in South Asia*, Berlin: Klaus Schwarz, 137-64.

———2004. 'Ranpur Resolved: Spatial Analysis of a Town in Orissa Based on a Chronicle', in A. Malinar, J. Beltz and H. Frese (eds.), *Text and Context in the History, Literature and Religion of Orissa*, Delhi: Manohar, 67-92.

Gutschow, Niels and Rabindra J. Vasavada. 2001. 'Temples of Jagannāth in Puri and

Ranpur—Orissa, India: A Preliminary Typological Comparison', in *Beiträge zur Allgemeinen und Vergleichenden Archäologie*, vol. 21, Mainz: Philipp von Zabern, 59-74.

Kulke, Hermann 1980. 'Legitimation and Town Planning in the Feudatory States of Central Orissa', in J. Pieper (ed.), *Ritual Space in India: Studies in Architectural Anthropology*, Art and Archaeology Research Papers (aarp) 17, London: Aarp, 30-40.

———2004. 'The Making of a Local Chronicle: The Raṇapur Rājavaṃśa Itihāsa', in A. Malinar, J. Beltz and H. Freese (eds.), *Text and Context in the History, Literature and Religion of Orissa*, Delhi: Manohar, 43-66.

Pfeffer, Georg 1978. 'Puri's Vedic Brahmans: Continuity and Change in Their Traditional Institutions', in A. Eschmann, H. Kulke and G.C. Tripathi (eds.), *The Cult of Jagannath and the Regional Tradition of Orissa*, Delhi: Manohar, 421-38.

Schnepel, Burkhard 1997. *Die Dschungelkönige. Ethnohistorische Aspekte von Politik und Ritual in Südorissa, Indien*, Stuttgart: Franz Steiner Verlag.

———2000. 'Der Körper im 'Tanz der Strafe' in Orissa', in Klaus-Peter Köpping and Ursula Rao (eds.), *Im Rausch des Rituals: Gestaltung und Transformation der Wirklichkeit in körperlicher Performanz*, Berlin: LIT, 156-71.

Singh Deo, Damodhar 1962. *History of the Dynasties of the Ranpur State*, Ranpur: Manuscript (translation by A. Das, Orissa Research Project Library Ms 688).

Stietencron, Heinrich von 1978. 'Early Temples of Jagannātha in Orissa: The Formative Phase, in A. Eschmann, H. Kulke and G.C. Tripathi (eds.), *The Cult of Jagannath and the Regional Tradition of Orissa*, Delhi: Manohar, 61-77.

———2001. 'A Congregation of Gods: The Dolamelaṇa Festival in Orissa', in Hermann Kulke and Burkhard Schnepel (eds.), *Jagannath Revisited: Studying Society, Religion and the State in Orissa*, Delhi: Manohar, 363-401.

CHAPTER 11

King, Goddesses and Jagannatha: Regional Patriotism and Subregional and Local Identities in Early Modern Orissa

AKIO TANABE

INTRODUCTION

This chapter examines the topic of regional patriotism and subregional and local identities in the context of late pre-colonial, early modern Orissa. It will look at the historical development of regional patriotism in early modern Orissa and try to understand its mechanism and structure, also taking into account how it was possible for different groups of people, embedded in different local and subregional socio-political units, to have a sense of belonging to and love for the then politically non-existent state of Orissa.

Before I proceed to my discussion of these issues, I would like to contextualize this chapter in respect of the theme of this conference and the research framework of the German Orissa Research Project (hereafter ORP). A great contribution was made by the former ORP in pointing out the existence of a regional culture, in contradiction to the more usual dichotomy between a pan-Indian great tradition and a series of local little traditions.[1] This chapter certainly owes a great deal to the former ORP for the attention it gave to the significance of the regional level. In discussing regional identity in Orissa, however, the danger of privileging the regional culture of the Jagannatha cult has been correctly pointed out by the members of the present ORP, who are making efforts to shift attention to subregional identities or little kingdoms. The present ORP reconsiders and problematizes the centrality of the Jagannatha cult, at the same time aiming to understand its historical and socio-cultural complexities by positing multiple centres in Orissa.[2]

I agree that any claim regarding the existence of a culture in a given territorial space—such as that being made in this case that the Jagannatha cult is a national or rather regional culture of Orissa—often leads to the conceptual imposition of a dominant culture of the centre that is supposedly shared by all members

[1]The best products of the former ORP are represented in Eschmann, Kulke and Tripathi 1978.

[2]Peabody also stresses the need to pay attention to multiple centres in opposition to the 'monocentric view' represented by Dirks (Peabody 2003, 82; Dirks 1987).

of the region in question. By positing a centre, we should not privilege a dominant culture as an essence representing the territory as a whole, thus imposing the modern idea of a 'bounded' space with a homogenous culture.[3] In this sense, I agree with the idea of deconstructing the supposed essence of a monocentre and thus seeing Jagannatha and the Gajapati in their socio-historical contexts, instead of taking their privileged positions within Oriya culture for granted. However, I am also opposed to the other extreme: the post-modernist, deconstructionist idea that everything depends on viewpoints and that there are only fragments which represent multiple centres. Regional integration is a reality, and although subregional units are indeed important as multi-centres, they cannot have their own viewpoints and agency independently of the larger politico-cultural structure. An extreme post-modernist framework not only loses sight of actual political dominance and the question of cultural hegemony, it also fails to see the overall politico-cultural framework without which contestations and communication would not be possible in the first place.

In my view, it is not the positing of a centre that is the problem. Indeed, I think we can safely say that certain centres existed in precolonial Orissa and that there was a sense of regional territoriality deriving from them and defined through exchanges and networks. In this sense, pre-colonial Orissa can indeed be said to have been a centre-oriented territory, where regional integration existed through networks connecting multiple spaces with a core centre (Tambiah 1985).[4] It should be noted that this idea of a centre-oriented territory is not the same as assuming cultural homogeneity in a presupposed 'bounded' space. What leads to the imposition of an essentialized dominant culture is the obsession that the culture or cosmology of the centre must be shared homogeneously within a bounded space for a particular territory to be called a nation or cultural region. In this kind of representation, there is little scope for explaining the existence of the diversity of cultures that characterizes regional societies and communities, not only in Orissa, but anywhere else in India.[5]

What is necessary here, in fact, is to think carefully and seriously about the relationships between the different nodal points in the network. In the words of Berkemer, one of the organizers of the conference on which the present

[3]Tambiah 1985.

[4]See Berkemer (2002) on the transformation of the 'traditional border regions (*sīma* in Oriya) into border lines (*sīmānta*)'.

[5]A related difficulty applies to the conundrum of the 'great' and 'little' traditions. It is not the analytical assumption of great tradition *versus* little tradition that is the problem. In fact, the problem begins when the great and little traditions are somehow defined in a substantive manner, with the little tradition being seen as a residue which does not fit into the great tradition. In this kind of schema, the little tradition is defined negatively as mere deviation from the unity represented by the great tradition. Thus the little tradition is considered to have little importance for national integrity.

volume is based, attention should be drawn to areas, institutions and phenomena 'in between' as a way out of centrist and dichotomous paradigms.[6] Previous arguments on culture and identity have tended to ask what the common feature is, or what is the key to integration? They have therefore focused on describing and explaining the essence of a nation or a region, be it caste, kingship, or religion. The problem with trying to identify the essence of national or regional integration is that it posits a dominant culture or institution as a common feature and thus essentializes national or regional cultures and identities at the cost of ignoring diversity and complexity in the nation or region. As a way out of this problem, I propose that we examine the interrelationships between the various levels of polities and institutions within the region and consider what kind of integration, contestation and diversity these entailed.

In this chapter, I would like to concentrate on the relationships between the regional, subregional and micro-regional (local) spaces, each of which seems to have great significance in the understanding of identities in early modern Orissa.[7] It is my contention that there came into being a new kind of relationship between the three levels—regional, subregional and microregional—in the early modern period, from which a sense of patriotism emerged. This sense of patriotism connected the people's feelings of attachment to land, which were until then confined to the micro-regional locality, with the cultural design of sovereignty and political legitimacy at the regional level in Orissa. The workings of little kings and the great little king of Khurda at the subregional level were pivotal here.[8] By looking at the transformation of the relationships between the Khurda king, other little kings and the people in the local society, I would like to show how the early modern development of state formation and social change connected the people in the locality not only to the subregional kingdom, but also to the patria of Orissa as a sphere of shared political legitimacy and ethics.

Recent research on patriotism in late pre-colonial India[9] has demonstrated its non-exclusive characteristics, which permitted the co-existence of multiple and heterogeneous identities, along with a sense of belonging to the same country. We can more or less safely state that the key to regional patriotism in early modern Orissa lay in the institutions of the Jagannatha cult and Gajapati

[6]Berkemer 2003.

[7]This can be said, from another point of view, to be an attempt to contribute an answer to the problem as regards the nature of the Indian state as put forward succinctly by Chattopadhyaya as follows: 'In trying to understand the presence of autonomous spaces of authority within the structure of a State it is . . . necessary to understand how sources of authority were perceived and how they were sought to be related to the authority of the State' (Chattopadhyaya 1997, 8).

[8]The Khurda king was 'great' in its authority as Gajapati, but 'little' in terms of its territorial size and because it was under suzerainty of the Mughals and later the Marathas. Hence I call the Khurda king a 'great little king'.

[9]Bayly 1998, Ray 2003.

kingship. A notable feature of Oriya patriotism was that the network of exchanges centring around the Jagannatha cult and Gajapati kingship succeeded in connecting the people's sense of self, which was embedded in particular localities and subregions, with regional level ideas and institutions regarding sovereignty and political legitimacy, without imposing homogeneity. It integrated people of the region who associated themselves with Jagannatha through different channels, at the same time permitting a continuity of subregional and micro-regional identities, which were often associated with particular polities and communities—little kingdoms, chieftaincies, micro-regions and castes—and correspondingly diverse forms of cultural and religious practices, including various goddess cults rooted in localities and clans.

In the following, I focus first on the structure of the micro-regional community and its system of patrimonial entitlements, which I believe was the basis for people-embodied personhood and attachment to land. Next, I examine the relationships between the micro-regional and subregional levels. I argue that there was an important transformation in the relationships from the medieval to early modern periods, which transformation involved the permeation of the royal power of the subregional kings (i.e. little kings) down to local levels. In the process, the little king came to be established as the source of authority for the local system of entitlements. The importance of subregional identities among the people seems to have increased with this early modern application of royal power, which connected embodied personhood with its attachments to land and people embedded in micro-regional localities with the authority of the subregional level kingship. Then, I consider the relationships between the subregional and regional level. I look at the changes in the network of relationships between the subregional little kings, Gajapati and Jagannatha. The little kings came to be more intimately related with Jagannatha, so to speak, as some of them began to participate in the regional system of honour and privileges centring around Jagannatha and Gajapati, as Kulke has pointed out.[10]

Thus, in sum, closer interaction and exchange developed between the regional, subregional and micro-regional levels during this period. This made it possible for people living in particular localities to connect and reflexively define their selves *vis-à-vis* the universal politico-religious values represented by the Jagannatha cult and Gajapati kingship through the mediatory channel of the subregional kingship. In this way, they came to identify themselves in relation to the country of Jagannatha and Gajapati, that is, Orissa. What I shall argue in the following, in other words, is that the channelizing or mediating power of the Gajapati Khurda king and other little kings worked to connect idiosyncratic groups of people belonging to various castes, religions and localities under an emotional-ideational unit of the Jagannatha country having a common framework of politico-cultural ethics regarding power and sovereignty in seventeenth- and eighteenth-century Orissa.

[10]Kulke 1978b, 1993a.

THE BASIS OF PATRIOTISM: MODES OF FORMATION OF PERSONHOOD AND IDENTITY IN ORISSA

I now turn to the level of the micro-regional community, which I suggest provided the basis for a kind of primordial patriotism. To understand the popular sense of attachment to and love for the local land, I suggest that we start by considering how personhood and identity are formed. In the following, I first look at the basic mechanism of the formation of body-personhood in Orissa, and then discuss how this is related to the system of entitlements in micro-regions.

In understanding personhood and identity in India, it is necessary to look at how humoral and fluid bio-moral[11] interactions, involving an exchange of code-substance[12] materials that carry cultural meanings and values, constitute and determine the position and identity of a body-person. The term 'body-person' is used here to indicate how the body as a corporeal substance and personhood as a social role and position are inseparable. This is because bio-moral exchanges form a body in a given social network, and the kind of code-substance that constitutes the body carries socio-cultural meanings and values.

According to this bio-moral definition of identity of a body-person, interactions between land, food and human bodies—the aggregate of which makes up the basic network of eco-society—are particularly important. A body-person is constructed from the corporeal code-substance made through the marriages he concludes and food he ingests. Since the food is produced on a plot of land, the moral nature of that particular earth-substance is also taken into the body-person.[13] The socio-political position, titles and ritual privileges that are granted to someone also constitute his or her personhood, as they carry certain code-substances as well. Similarly, actions influence a body-person, since they involve an exchange of bio-moral substance. In this regard, gift exchanges are extremely important in determining personhood, since the moral nature of the giver is contained in the gift of women, food, land and other ritual-economic resources, and influences the personhood of the receiver. Anthropological studies of India in the 1960s and 1970s have described in detail the kind of care and attention Indians pay regarding from whom to accept water, food and women. These matters are related to concerns about maintaining their proper body-personhood, and previous studies considered them to represent the norms of Indian society.[14]

However, I would argue instead that we can also see this phenomenon the other way around. That is to say, instead of starting with the existence of a society where there are norms prescribing exchanges, we can see how the

[11] Bayly 1998.
[12] Marriot 1976, Daniel 1984.
[13] Daniel 1984.
[14] Classic examples of these works include Mayer 1960 and Parry 1979.

politico-cultural acts of exchange determine relationships of sociality between various body-persons and their relationships with the land. In other words, it is the aggregate of these bio-moral exchanges that forms a body-person, and their networks that make up the society and polity. A body-person can be seen as a knot in the overlapping and multi-layered networks of exchanges that constitute group and territorial formations.

According to a common folk discourse in Orissa, a human body is formed when the man's seminal fluid (*birja*) mixes with the woman's sexual secretion (*raja*) during intercourse. The man's sperm is referred to as the seed and the woman's womb as the field. It is not only the seed that determines the character of the body, since seeds grow through bio-moral exchange with the field.[15] It is considered important that the right kind of seed should be planted in the right field, so that the result will be a suitable body-person who befits the duties of the particular family and caste.[16] Right from conception to death and subsequent incorporation as an ancestor, a person is involved in interactions and exchanges of code-substances, which embed him or her in the society and locality.[17]

The body that is produced as a result of an appropriate combination of seed and field takes in food which is produced on a particular piece of land which has been passed down over the generations. Ingesting food produced on the land is one of the most important ways in which code-substances affect the body constitution of a person.[18] Food is produced on land allocated to a family as part of the patrimonial entitlements attached to the office the family holds. More precisely, a family holds entitlements over a certain proportion of products on a particular piece of land.

There is a telling expression about the nurturing of the body through land. When a man occupies a service land, he is said to eat the land (*jami khāibā*).

[15]This is not only in relation to human reproduction: the same kind of discourse can be found in relation to agricultural production (cf. Daniel 1984, Gupta 1998).

[16]The territorial sphere of marriage alliances was also connected with territorial identities in an important way. There are several marriage alliance networks. The immediate sphere consists of direct 'relatives by marriage alliance', called *bandhu*, that is, the family of one's spouse. Then comes the network of the *bandhus* of one's own family, and then that of the *bandhus* of one's lineage. Thereafter, there comes the network of *bandhus* of *bandhus*. Lastly, there is a network of potential *bandhus*, which is same as the endogamous caste group or *jati*. In the context of pre-colonial Orissa, the territorial sphere of a *jati* as an alliance network often corresponded to the unit of subregional kingdoms. For example, in Khurda the peasant militias were called 'Oriya' by caste name and formed a marriage alliance network within the Khurda kingdom: they did not form marriage alliances with peasant militias belonging to other kingdoms. (Other *jatis* had their own territorial networks.) In this way, it was partly the *jati* or networks of marriage alliances that endorsed the importance of the subregional unit in little kingdoms.

[17]Tokita-Tanabe forthcoming.

[18]Since the bio-moral substance of whoever cooks also affects the eater, care is taken regarding 'from whose hand one eats' (*kāhāra hātru khāiba*).

This means that the entitlement holder is eating and nurturing his body from the product of the allocated land. The organic and humoral relationship between personhood and land is strengthened by the fact that a particular piece of land allocated to a family often has a proper name suggestive of the owner's identity. For example, there are plots of land called *Khumbāra hetā* (potter's service land), *Pradhān hetā* (village head's service land), and *Rāmacaṇḍiṅka bhogo khañjā jami* (land as offerings to the goddess Ramachandi, this being the Khond priest's land). Thus we see that there is a parallel conception here between the body, personhood and the allocated land.

Land was allocated as part of patrimonial rights in the 'system of entitlements' that defined the socio-political structure of local communities in Khurda.[19] It is therefore natural that, in order for a person to occupy a certain office and thus the land that has been allocated to him, it is considered necessary for him to have a body-personhood to suit the office. In other words, there is an idea that a person should live on and at the land which is appropriate to his body-personhood. Just as it is important for the seed to match the earth, the sperm the womb and the food the body, it is also important for the body to match the family, with its prescribed entitlements to land and office. The question, 'Does that person suit the land?' (*se loka se jamiku sohibạ ki?*) arises especially in the case of an adoption, when someone is brought from the outside to inherit the office. Let me give an example here by way of illustration. The chief of Garh Manitri today was adopted by the family from an affinal relative, after the original chief emigrated to England. His elder brother was brought in first but returned to his natal home, as he was said not to have matched the chief's family land and had caught leprosy. The present chief was then brought in but also caught leprosy. It is said, however, that he was cured after he prayed to Ramachandi, the tutelary goddess of the region, so that he might be accepted. He remains in the office today.

The system of entitlements defined rights to shares of the products of the land, salary, privileges and the duties of the office. This system defined people's identity in the locality and the kingdom, since it decided where a person lived (residential land was also provided tax-free to entitlement holders), how much land he was given and where he was given it. It also defined the person's role and privileges in the local community and the state. The entitlement holders included the chief, warriors, priests, scribes, accountants, barbers, potters, carpenters, musicians, labourers, etc., each of whom was provided with particular patrimonial duties and entitlements.

The local community or the micro-regional unit, which was the basis of the system of entitlements, had a tutelary deity, usually a goddess, who protected the fort and its community. At Khurda fort there were the sister goddesses, Barunai and Karunai, at Garh Manitri there was Ramachandi, at Tapang there was Hastesvari, etc. People in the locality ascribed their fortune and well-being

[19]Tanabe 1998, forthcoming.

to the protection of the goddess in all kinds of matters, ranging from agricultural fertility to military success. The land on which they lived and the rice they ate were all seen as manifestations of the goddess herself. It was through the goddess's acceptance and protection, as well as bio-moral exchange with the goddess as the manifestation of nature in the locality, that the people could eat the land they lived on and come to suit it. There was thus an intimate relationship between the people's attachment to the locality and their devotion towards the local goddess. The system of entitlements also worked as a sacrificial organization for the tutelary goddess.

I would like to emphasize the importance of the unit of the local community as the basis of people's identity, with its patrimonial lands, houses and offices, sacred groves and local shrines,[20] neighbourhood and community, all of which bio-morally formed one's body-personhood. The importance of the local community or fort area in the hilly tracts of Orissa as the unit of the system of entitlements and the basis of identity is perhaps comparable to the importance of the unit of the *nāḍu* in south India. It has been pointed out in studies of south Indian history that this was significant in establishing ritual, social and political identities.[21] According to Srinivas, like the village, the *nāḍu* is a unit which corresponds to the sentiments of the people, and not merely an administrative division imposed by the rajas.[22] He also adds that man has a great love for his *nāḍu* and points out that patriotism for one's *nāḍu* was widespread and deep.[23] It is notable that Srinivas used the word patriotism to describe the people's sense of love and attachment to the locality. As Schaar points out, to be a patriot is to have a patrimony, or to be grateful for a legacy and to recognize that this makes him a debtor.[24] The local community in Orissa contained not only familiar surroundings and people, but also the system of entitlements defining patrimonial rights to the products of the land and duties in the community. Thus these might have indeed led to feelings of indebtedness and a moral bond towards the local community, which can be called patriotism in a primordial sense.

In this way we can see that the territorial and moral basis of people's identity was embedded in the exchange relationships of code-substances involving body, food and land that were defined by the system of entitlements which intimately connected people to the local community and land. This may be seen as the basis of a primordial sense of patriotism which brought about a bio-moral bond within the micro-regional territory. How did this local sense of patriotism extend to patriotism for the country? For this feeling to develop, it required a further step.

I argue that for the locally embedded patriotism to be cultivated into love for one's country and a sense of indebtedness towards it required a particular

[20]Schaar 1981, 309.

[21]Bhatt 1980, 55; see also Subbarayalu 1973; Stein 1977; Beck 1972.

[22]Srinivas 1952, 57.

[23]Ibid., 66, 69.

[24]Schaar 1981, 288.

working of kingship at the subregional level. It was through politico-ritual exchanges with royalty that local body-persons came to be linked beyond the locality to the larger referential spaces of the subregional kingdom and regional country. I further argue that it was through such a process that regional patriotism developed in early modern Orissa. The important point about this particular development of regional patriotism was not how people imagined their country.[25] Instead of an abstract and mental construction of a sphere filled with discrete literate persons sharing information and imagination, as I describe below, what constituted patriotism in early modern Orissa was the ways in which the body-persons of people of diverse groups connected through bio-moral exchanges in local communities were linked, via the little kings, with the Gajapati king and with Jagannatha, who represented the centres of Orissa. In other words, one of the important aspects of patriotism in early modern Orissa consisted of how people embodied their relationships with these centres. A reflexive and ideational sense of love for the country was consistent only with this kind of embodied feeling.

In the following section, I deal with the history of how this might have occurred, taking the Khurda kingdom as an example of early modern subregional kingdom.

STATE FORMATION AND THE TRANSFORMATION OF A LOCAL COMMUNITY

The medieval Orissan empire came to an end in 1568, and the Khurda kingdom was established as the major subregional polity with an all-Orissa level authority in about 1570, later being acknowledged by Akbar in 1592.[26] Before the establishment of the Khurda kingdom, there were many autonomous mini-chieftaincies in the region which usually consisted of a (few) fort(s) and surrounding villages. Numerous chieftaincies seem to have existed throughout the hilly jungle areas, as well as in some parts of the coastal area, in pre-colonial Orissa, even on the eve of colonialism. W. Ewer, a British Commissioner, observed that, besides the countries occupied by the present Gurjat (*garhjat*) tributaries (feudatory chiefs in the hilly tracts), there were numerous smaller estates called *guṛh*s or *killah*s (forts), situated chiefly on the sea coast between Coojung (Kujang) and Juggernaut (Puri), which were held at a quit rent by chiefs called *Khundait*s or *Gurjat Khundait*s.[27] Ewer says that there were fifty small chieftaincies with forts on the coast at the time of the British conquest.[28]

[25]Anderson's notion (1991) of an 'imagined community', which rests on the idea that there is a literary and mental imagination of a nation, cannot take into account the kind of embodied emotions dealt with in this paper.

[26]Kulke 1978b.

[27]Ewer Report, para. 11, *Selections* I, 5. The word in brackets have been added by the author.

[28]Ibid., para. 228, *Selections I*, 86.

These local chieftaincies enjoyed considerable autonomy in medieval times (till the sixteenth century), as the chief, the *khaṇḍāyat-rāja*, along with his *iṣṭadebatā* (often a goddess), were regarded as the central figures responsible for the overall welfare of the chieftaincy. The Gajapati emperor-king did not play any integral role in the internal organization of the chieftaincy. In this medieval political scheme, there were distinct differences in levels between the chieftaincies and the regional empire. At the level of the regional empire, the tutelary god (*rāṣṭradebatā*) and the real ruler of Orissa was Lord Jagannatha, the emperor-king being seen as Jagannatha's deputy on earth.[29] The latter conducted rituals of worship (*pūjā*) to Lord Jagannatha in Puri and dealt with the military and administrative affairs of the state from Cuttack. At the level of the chieftaincy, the chief worshipped his tutelary goddess, who was also the tutelary deity of the chieftaincy, and managed everyday affairs within the micro-region. The local goddesses often had tribal priests (Khond or Saora in case of Khurda region), though many later also acquired Brahman priests in the course of Hinduization or Kshatriyaization.[30] The imperial regional kingdom in medieval Orissa was established by integrating the surrounding chiefs and kings in such a way as to maintain their autonomy at the lower levels. This situation is described aptly by Kulke: local autonomous corporate institutions continued to exist within and autonomous tributary kingdoms outside these enlarged imperial core areas.[31] Tributary and indirect administrative relationships were established with the existing institutions without interfering directly in internal matters. There was thus a multilayered state structure of regional-imperial, subregional and local level polities, in which the lower level of local chieftaincies was encompassed by the higher level of the imperial kingdom. This medieval arrangement of encompassment with autonomy was to be irreversibly transformed through the development of early modern sub-regional kingdoms, where the autonomy of local institutions was increasingly eroded.

The indigenous sources say that the Khurda king obtained his territory from the king of Buddha Saori (a pure Saora who had originally ruled the region). Ramachandra Deva, the first Khurda king, is said to have sacrificed the latter and buried his head under a tree.[32] There are several instances where an indigenous tribal is said to have been sacrificed at the moment of the integration of tribal chieftaincies into a kingdom. They often became the tutelary deity (*iṣṭadebatā*) of the fort or the local chieftaincy. Kulke mentions instances of these as martyr *iṣṭadebatās*.[33] Cited here is one example I collected from Manika Garh, a fort under the Khurda king:

[29] On the idea of the Gajapati being the deputy of Jagannatha, see Kulke 1978a.

[30] Kulke 1976; Eschmann 1978.

[31] Kulke 1985, 114 (quoted in Kulke 2006, 65).

[32] Pattanaik 1959, 6; Kulke 1978a, 325.

[33] Kulke 1993; 100-1.

A brother of the maharaja of Orissa came to this place to live. He tried to construct a fort here around the shrine of the indigenous goddess Bunya, but the wall of the fort never held up. He had a dream in which the goddess told him that if he wanted to construct a wall he had to sacrifice a human being and bury the head. The king's brother told the villagers about the dream. The Khond chief was in distress. The daughter of the Khond chief, seeing her father's condition, asked what the problem was. The chief told her the situation. The girl offered herself to be sacrificed on the condition that her name would be attached to the goddess. The girl, whose name was Manika, was sacrificed and the fort was built. Today the sacrificed girl is worshipped as Manikibunya, who is said to be a Khond goddess (Khond *thākuraṇī*) and considered the *iṣṭadebatā* (tutelary goddess) of the fort. Manika Garh (Fort of Manika) is also named after the sacrificed Khond girl.

I would like to offer one perspective for interpreting these myths of martyr *iṣṭadebatā*s where a tribal chief (or his representative, the Khond chief's daughter, as in the above case) is sacrificed by the king (or his representative, the king's brother, as in the above case) and becomes the tutelary deity. It seems to me that, in a symbolic manner, these mythical oral histories indicate an important historical shift in the agency of the sacrificer for the goddess. The tutelary goddesses of the localities had special relationships with the indigenous tribal populations. The tribal chief was the main worshipper and sacrificer of the indigenous goddess. The king making a sacrifice of a tribal chief is a symbolic act which represents the fact that it is now the king who has become the sacrificer and is responsible for the welfare of the population. The tribal chief is transformed from the sacrificer to the sacrificed with this shift in the agency of the sacrifice. Interestingly, however, the sacrificed tribal becomes symbolically one with the goddess. The indigenous tribal special relationship with the goddess had to be recognized when the king became the sacrificer. The early modern characteristic of royal integration, which can be seen from this myth, is the irreversible loss of autonomy of the micro-regional polity or chieftaincy. The chief no longer held the seat of the sacrificer for the local tutelary goddess but became dependent on the king's politico-ritual authority as a sacrificer. Thus the autonomy of the encompassed micro-regional polity was irrevocably lost, and the king came to be established as the sole sacrificer for both Jagannatha and the local fort goddesses. I suggest that the oral histories of martyr *iṣṭadebatā*s symbolize this important historical transformation in politico-ritual authority. By becoming a sacrificer for the local goddesses, the king also came to occupy the central place in the local sacrificial organization that made up the micro-regional socio-political structure. Needless to say, the infiltration of royal authority into the locality and the removal of the autonomy of the local polity correspond to the early modern penetration of royal governmental power into the local level, which worked to monitor and control local resources.[34]

[34]Tanabe 1999a, 2000. The position of the king as the sacrificer for the local goddess is also represented in local rituals I have described elsewhere (Tanabe 1999b, in press).

At the time the Khurda kingdom was established, there are said to have been numerous Saori *khaṇḍāyat*s, apart from the Saori chief who had been sacrificed.[35] Besides the territories of these chiefs, there were also many other autonomous chieftaincies, such as Atri, Kalupareh, Murdeswara, Banpur and Haldia, in the Khurda region. The Khurda king had initially probably allowed the indigenous chiefs considerable autonomy, while he himself ruled from above as the encompassing power over them. However, in the course of the seventeenth and eighteenth centuries these chiefs were gradually driven out and replaced by the chiefs of the fort areas, called *bisoi* and/or *daḷabeherā*,[36] who were more directly under the king's command. The number of independent Saori chiefs was reduced to thirteen, and hence came to be called *tera Saori khaṇḍāyat* (*tera* means thirteen), and this title can still be found in oral history today.[37] Besides these, there were four *śuddhi khaṇḍāyat* (purified Khandayats), who were autonomous (tribal but purified) chiefs in the Khurda kings' time.[38] The number of these autonomous chiefs further decreased, and only two *śuddhi khaṇḍāyat*s and four *Saori khaṇḍāyat*s remained at the time of the advent of the British. Meanwhile, Atri, Kalupareh and Murdeswara became forts under *daḷabeherā*s in the Khurda kingdom. Banpur became a district in

[35]Ewer Report, para 35, *Selections* I, 109. It should be noted here that *khaṇḍāyat* refers not to the caste name but to the 'autonomous chief'. The Saori *khaṇḍāyat*s tell us an interesting oral history regarding their origin: 'One day, the king of Khurda came to the jungle for hunting. There he saw a *sari* hanging to which bees were attracted because of its sweet fragrance. The king asked to see the owner of this *sari*, who was an extremely beautiful Saora girl. The king had a relationship with her and she gave birth to thirteen sons. The king granted thirteen territories for the sons to rule as *khaṇḍāyat*s (autonomous chiefs). Since they were born of a Saora mother, they came to be called Saori *khaṇḍāyat*s' (oral information collected in a Saori *khaṇḍāyat* village by Tanabe). Thus the Saori *khaṇḍāyat*s claim that their ancestors were in fact the sons of the king, though they acknowledge their Saora origin by admitting that their mother was a Saora. This is another example of the legitimation of one's position and rights in relation to kingship. The Saori *khaṇḍāyat*s have the following legend regarding their ritual status as 'water untouchables' (those who cannot give water to caste Hindus): 'Village people [implying caste Hindus] visited a Saori *khaṇḍāyat*'s house for a meeting. The Saori *khaṇḍāyat*, however, did not even offer them water out of pride that 'I am the king's son'. When the king heard this, he became angry and prohibited Saori *khaṇḍāyat*s from giving water to people. Since then they have become 'water untouchable' (collected in a Saori *khaṇḍāyat* village by Tanabe). In this legend, their ritually inferior status is ascribed to an incident rather than to their origin. According to this, it is by the king's order that they became 'water untouchable' and not their Saora origin. Thus they explain the discrepancy between their political strength and ritual inferiority. These legends can be seen as the attempts by Saori *khaṇḍāyat*s to reinstate their position as legitimate Kshatriya rulers, claiming that only incidental and peripheral factors mark them in name and ritual position.

[36]Bisoi refers to the head of a *bisi* (county, Skt. *viṣya*). *Daḷabeherā* refers to the leader (*beherā*) of a regiment (*daḷa*). *Bisoi* and *daḷabeherā* were usually the same person.

[37]Forrester Report, para 35, *Selections I*, 109.

[38]Ibid., para 33, *Selections* I, 108; Srichandan 1989.

the Khurda kingdom,[39] while Haldia remained autonomous till the British period.[40]

Thus, in seventeenth- and eighteenth-century Orissa, there was a process of depriving small chieftaincies of autonomy and incorporating them into the kingdom, as autonomous chiefs were replaced by chiefs subordinate to the king.[41] It should be noted that the *daḷabeherā*s or military chiefs, who replaced the autonomous chiefs in Khurda, never had independent authority. They were given the king's sword as the symbol of royal authority and could command power in the localities only as partial representatives of the sovereign king.[42] In other words, even the *daḷabeherā* was just one among the many office-bearers in the local system of entitlements. It was the king and not the *daḷabeherā* who occupied the central place as the source of authority.

The extension of the king's control over the micro-regional polity-society, however, did not mean centralization in the sense of the modern state, where bureaucrats and armies are dispatched from the central government and the structure of command is unified. Although the chiefs, scribes, accountants, soldiers, etc., who provided military-administrative functions for the state were indeed stationed in the micro-regional forts, where they became hereditary office-bearers in the locality and lived as members of the micro-regional community, they were guaranteed not only economic bases but also administrative and military power as well as ritual capacity from the king, which they enjoyed in the locality. In other words, while the command came from the king, the military-administrative functionaries became embedded within the local system of entitlements. In this sense, it can be said that the process by which the state took control over a micro-region paradoxically involved decentralization and a sharing of sovereignty with the localities. Therefore, it can be said that centralization had a distinctly decentralized character[43] in pre-colonial Indian kingdoms.

[39] Ibid., para 23, *Selections* I, 107; Sterling 1904, 44-5.

[40] Ewer Report, paras 26-32, *Selections* I, 108.

[41] The fate of small chieftaincies outside Khurda was very similar. Although the Marathas retained the Khurda king and other principal chiefs, it was their 'policy to destroy as far as practicable the community and institutions of the smaller gurhs (forts)'. The *khaṇḍāyat-rājas* of '50 small killahs (forts) on the seacoast' previously mentioned were reduced to common zamindars by the Marathas. Ewer also says that, among these, 'not one was admitted by the Revenue authorities as entitled to hold a peshcush on the first settlement of the province, and the very name of paik, kundait, and peshcush would appear to have been altogether lost in many'(Ewer Report, para. 232, *Selections* I, 87).

[42] This does not mean that the chiefs were totally dependent on the king for the legitimacy of their rule. The chiefs also attempted to establish their own authority in the locality by claiming that they acquired the territory through their own actions in conquering the place. This corresponds to proving their body-person's worth as the ruler of the locality. Peabody notes that Rajputs forged special links with the conquered land by offering *pinda*, a ball made from land sustenance or land itself, that is offered to ancestors who conquered the land, thus creating bio-moral bonds with the territory (Peabody 2003, 90).

[43] Perlin 1985, 475.

While the socio-political structure of the local system of entitlements was largely maintained in spite of the penetration of royal power, the important aspect of change in the relationship between the state and the community was the transformation in the source of legitimacy and authority of the system of entitlements. It was not the local chief but the king who came to be seen as the giver of these entitlements and the central sacrificer for the local tutelary goddess. Each entitlement was classified, enumerated and recorded on palm-leaf manuscripts by the royal government scribes and accountants who were stationed in these forts. These records not only legitimized each entitlement, but also functioned to demonstrate clearly that all the resources originally belonged to the king and that he was the giver of these entitlements. It is no coincidence that these palm-leaf manuscripts are worshipped alongside the royal swords that are said to be filled with the local goddess's power during her autumn festival in Garh Manitri.[44] The manuscripts were and still are a ritual representation of the royal authority and royal legitimation of the local system of entitlements.

Many families claim that they were called by the king to take up their present positions and live in the particular micro-region. Some of the land also has names which are related to oral histories which tell us how the land and other entitlements were presented by the king to their family. It is important to note that the stories concerning the acquiring of land are invariably related to the king as the donor of the land.[45] The king was the centre of authority for the distribution of land, honour and positions, through which the recipient came to acquire his specific identity supported by the sanction of the king and by implication of the divine ruler, Jagannatha. For example, we find the name 'rice water land' (*tu niā nāla*) held by the Pujāri Brāhmaṇa family.[46] When I asked the priest how he acquired the land and how the land came to have that particular name, he said:

Once the king of Khurda, under the attack by the Mughals, escaped to Garh Manitri.[47] He did not have anything to eat from the morning. The king asked the Pujāri for some

[44]Tanabe 1999b.

[45]Cf. Tanabe 2000.

[46]*Tuḷani* refers to the liquid that goes with *pakhāḷa* (water rice). *Pakhāḷa* is made by mixing rice with water and *torāṇi* is that water taken along with *pakhāḷa* rice. *Pakhāḷa* is typical Oriya food, which is also offered to Lord Jagannatha. Villagers often comment that drinking *torāṇi* after eating *pakhāḷa* rice gives them satisfaction. The name *torāṇia nāla* thus contains a certain humorous touch.

[47]This seems to reflect certain historical facts. In 1617, King Purushottama Dev of Khurda fled with his family to Garh Manitri 'near the border of Ranpur and made it (a provisional) capital' after being attacked by Mukarram Khan, the new subahdar of Orissa, under the Mughals (Mahapatra 1969, 61). According to K.N. Mahapatra, Purushottama Dev hid Jagannatha in Garh Manitri in 1619-20 in fear of a Mughal attack on the temple in Puri. The king had to flee again and go to Garh Manitri after being defeated by Ahmed Beg Khan, the subahdar of the Mughals, in 1621, and he stayed there till his death in 1621 (ibid., 62; P.K. Pattanaik 1979, 32). The next king, Narasinha Dev, again secretly brought

food. The Pujāri had just finished offering pakhāḷa (rice in water) bhoga (offering) to Tṛtīyā Deba.[48] He offered the pakhāḷa praśād to the king. The king had pakhāḷa to his hearts content and, finally drinking up the remaining torāṇi (rice water), became very satisfied. Thereupon, the king granted the Pujāri a piece of land called 'torāṇia nāla', which was added to the Pujāris khañjā land for the service of Tṛtīyā Deba.

In another example, there is a piece of land called 'clarified butter-eater' (*ghia khiā*), which is held by the chief's family.[49] The following is one story about how the chief obtained this land.

The chief of Manitri fort area was one of the selected few persons who had the privilege of free entrance into the royal palace. One day, the chief saw cooks in distress and asked them the reason. The cooks answered, 'The king has ordered fried spinach as one of the dishes for lunch today, but we have put salt in it twice by mistake. It has become too salty. There is no more spinach in the kitchen and the king is waiting for lunch right now.' The chief told them, 'Do not worry. Just do what I tell you.' He told them to put a large amount of clarified butter into the fried spinach. The cooks served the king lunch including the fried spinach with plenty of clarified butter. The king tasted the spinach and liked it very much. The king summoned the cooks and asked them where they got the idea, as the spinach tasted much better than usual. The cooks told the king what had happened with the promise that their heads will be saved. The king became very pleased with the chief and presented land to him saying, 'You will need more land since you know how to eat clarified butter.'

Ownership of a particular piece of land, combined with the discourses regarding how the land was obtained from the king, serves to legitimize the landowning family's position in the micro-region and their right to consume the fruits of the land and to reconfirm their unique identity based on history. Notably, their position and entitlements were invariably related to the king as the bestower of all resources. The king was the centre of authority for the distribution of land, honour and positions, through which the recipient came to acquire his specific identity supported by the sanction of the king. The king as the giver of the land had particular importance, as the land was the basis of the identity of the body-person who ate the land. By eating the king's land, the body-person of the entitlement holder acquired a particular bio-morality that represented a certain aspect of sovereignty.

Moreover, the link between the king and the entitlement-holders was reinforced through gift exchanges between them. The king bestowed gifts on some of the prestigious office-bearers at festivals, and the latter gave gifts to the king on such occasions as the annual celebration of his enthronement

---

Puri Jagannatha's *brahma*—the divine essence of the deity—to Garh Manitri, hid it and built a Jagannatha temple there to house it (K.N. Mahapatra 1969, 65). The king also constructed his palace in the village (Tripathi and Kulke 1987, 103), the Jagannatha temple (temple for Tṛtīyā Deba) being placed in front of the gate of the palace.

[48] Tṛtīyā Deba is another name for Jagannatha.

[49] It is commonly known that clarified butter is rare and expensive.

(*suniā*).[50] Through these gift exchanges, a hierarchy was created among the various entitlement- and office-bearers in relation to the king.

Thus, through gifts of land, honour and positions, each entitlement-holder came to acquire a bio-moral connection with the king as the source of legitimacy for his role in the local system of entitlements. Dirks's argument about caste being centred around the king is relevant here,[51] but we should also remember that the king's position in relation to the entitlement-holders in the locality must be seen in the context of historical transformation. The centrality of the king's authority in the caste system may be an early modern or late medieval development, rather than being the essence of caste, as Dirks seems to suggest.[52] The sacrificial organization of the local community came to be incomplete in itself, so to speak, and came to require the presence of the king as the sacrificer who had central authority in the local system of entitlements in this early modern development. So, while the system of entitlements as the basis of the caste division of labour remained in principle the same throughout the pre-colonial period, the penetration of the king's authority and the royal legitimation of individual entitlements were added as new characteristics of the early modern period.

In this way, complementary and more intimate relationships were established between the sacrificer king and the sacrificial community in early modern Orissa. The penetration of royal authority into the locality came to connect the people, who were embedded in the locality, with the king. This connection worked not only at the level of body-personhood, but also at the level of the people's sense of self. The latter, which had strong links with the local patrimony, came to be connected with the idea of the sovereignty of the king as the source of position, honour and titles. The people's sense of attachment to the patrimony thus came to be connected with kingship, as it was the king who was seen as the giver of patrimonial entitlements. The people's body-personhood, which was closely linked to patrimonial lands, came to acquire a new sense of self, by which the people reflexively saw the basis of their personhood as being linked with the king. The old kind of medieval patriotism, which hitherto had been largely confined to micro-regional territoriality, at least in the Khurda region, thus came to acquire a broader territorial reference of subregional kingship. This must have helped in strengthening the people's sense of subregional identity during the late-pre-colonial period, when there was a rise in the politico-administrative importance of the subregional kingdoms.

The development of a sacrificer state and sacrificial community in the late sixteenth to eighteenth centuries in Khurda can therefore be seen as an irreversible process of change in the relationship between the micro-regional

[50]See Tanabe 1999a for details of the gift exchanges between the Khurda king and the local office-bearers.

[51]Dirks 1987.

[52]Also see Peabody for criticism of Dirks' model (Peabody 2003, 5-9; Dirks 1987).

unit and the subregional little king.[53] The king as the head of the state came to occupy the seat of the sacrificer for the local and subregional goddesses too, and the local sacrificial community came to depend on the royal authority for the legitimation of the system of entitlements. This development was concomitant with important transformations in the people's sense of self, as well as in aspects of the political-economy. The permeation of the king's authority as the sacrificer into the locality entailed the penetration of the early modern state's administrative technology and power of surveillance into the locality, without, however, breaking up the integrity and basic mechanism of the system of entitlements of the local community. The entitlement holders thus came to acquire a patriotic sense of belonging in relation to the subregional king, while still being embedded in the locality.

PATRIOTISM AND FOUR MODES OF INTEGRATION OF THE LITTLE KINGS IN ORISSA

Although the examples I have given here are limited to the Khurda area, it would not be unreasonable to assume that there were parallel phenomena in many subregional kingdoms in Orissa, though this remains a subject for further research. I would like to present a general hypothesis here (for future research), namely, that the importance of subregional little kingdoms as a focus of people identity increased as the administrative workings and ritual authority of subregional royal government penetrated into micro-regional localities in seventeenth- and eighteenth-century Orissa. The subregional king was established as the centre of authority even for the local socio-political system of patrimonial entitlements, which provided the most primordial basis for people-embodied personhood and identity. This contributed towards connecting the people's sense of attachment to the local patrimony to the larger sphere of the subregional kingdom, thus generating subregional level patriotism. Subregional kings, in their turn, were integrated into the region of Orissa in various ways, as described in this section. We may say that the people's sense of self and patriotism was connected indirectly with the regional unit of Orissa via subregional kings, there being a common source of sovereignty and political legitimacy. If this was indeed the case, we may find here the mechanism of regional patriotism in early modern Orissa.

Let us now see how the different subregions in Orissa were connected with Jagannatha and the Gajapati kings. I suggest here as a hypothesis that there were four main modes of integration that connected subregional and micro-regional units to Jagannatha and the Gajapati kings in early modern Orissa. They are conceptual integration centring around Jagannatha as the sovereign; ritual integration centring around the Khurda king as Gajapati; feudatory integration centring around the Khurda king as the feudatory lord; and direct

[53] See Tanabe 1999a, in press, for the notions of 'sacrificer state and sacrificial community'.

political dominance by the Khurda king. These four main modes of integration can be seen as constituting four overlapping concentric spheres and can be represented in a model map of integration of early modern Orissa. In this map, the Khurda king is placed at the centre, though alternative maps can be drawn from different viewpoints with other powerful kings as the centres. However, historically the Khurda king does seem to have exercised the most influential authority as the Gajapati. Therefore, the map drawn here should have some relevance for understanding Orissan integration of the period, though it should not be taken as the only possible one.

The largest sphere of integration in Orissa is represented by the shared conception of political legitimacy centring around Jagannatha as the real ruler of Orissa. It would be difficult to ascertain the extent of the territory in which Jagannatha was recognized as the sovereign ruler of Orissa. However, we can assume that there was such recognition in much of what constituted the former Orissan medieval empire.[54] There were kingdoms, like Parlakhemundi, which fought for the position of Gajapati against the Khurda king as the representative of Jagannatha and did not recognize the former's supremacy. These kingdoms were peripheral from the point of view of the Khurda king, but also were the most important alternative centres of integration that attempted to extend their authority.[55] This sphere of a shared sense of political legitimacy centring around Jagannatha represented the extent of what could be called Jagannatha country, which more or less corresponded to the early modern Orissan *patria*. There were indeed contestations over who represented Jagannatha on earth, but it should be noted that these contestations were possible precisely because there was a shared understanding regarding political legitimacy which provided a common field of contestation. The sharing of the sense of political legitimacy without actual political dominance seems to be a characteristic of the situation in seventeenth- and eighteenth-century Orissa.[56]

Encompassed within this sphere of the Orissan country was the second largest sphere of integration centring around the Khurda king as the Gajapati. As stated, there were other alternative centres for the position of Gajapati, but it is a historical fact that it was the Khurda king's authority that was recognized most extensively in seventeenth- and eighteenth-century Orissa. Within this sphere were included little kings and chiefs of areas such as Kujang and Kanika,

[54]'[M]any of the former feudatory rajas have introduced Jagannatha temples in their capitals' (Stietencron 1978, 473).

[55]Cf. Berkemer 2006.

[56]In medieval Orissa, the Jagannatha cult was monopolized and used as a religio-ritual resource by the regional emperor-king to legitimize his political power. By the late sixteenth century, however, the tables had been turned, and it was the Jagannatha cult which defined political legitimacy in Orissa. This meant that there came to be a shared sense of political legitimacy centring around Jagannatha, which provided the basis for territory of Orissa, with a particular cultural design of power within which contestations over political authority could take place.

who were politically under Mughal (and later Maratha) overlordship, but recognized the ritual sovereignty of the Khurda king as the Gajapati. These little kings and chiefs received gifts, titles, ritual roles and privileges from the Khurda king as the centre of authority.[57] There were such interpenetrations and overlaps of sovereignties of various kinds among many polities in late-pre-colonial Orissa.[58] A semi-regional system of honour and privilege and a sharing of ritual sovereignty[59] was constructed around the Khurda king, which extended beyond the sphere of his political dominance. Here, one can see that the ritual resource of Jagannatha was no longer monopolized by the Gajapati king, as had been the case in medieval times, but shared out among the little kings. Kulke explains this as an aspect of ritual politics on the part of the Khurda king to compensate him for his weakened political power.[60] However, I would argue that this was not simply about the politics of a weakened king. As Kulke noted in his earlier work, what seems to have been more important for the integration of the semi-region was the ritual bond between the feudatories and the state deity (*rāṣṭradebatā*), which was under the control of the central raja.[61] The establishment of the semi-regional system of sharing honours and privileges centred around Jagannatha contributed to forming a common field of service for the sovereign God and thus a sphere of ritual bonding among the feudatories. Jagannatha was no longer just an imperial God but a shared focus of identity and activity in the region. Whereas under the medieval Orissan empire, the Gajapati king monopolized relations with Jagannatha, the little kings and chiefs having their own relationships with local goddesses, the little kings and chiefs came to participate in the system of sharing a common source of legitimacy and honour in the early modern period.[62]

[57]Cf. Kulke 1978b. See the important map drawn by Steitencron and Kulke in 'Feudal Ties in Late Mediaeval Orissa' (Eschmann, Kulke and Tripathi 1978).

[58]The overlapping and interpenetrating character of sovereignties is pointed out by Wink (1986) in his study of the eighteenth-century Maratha and is also highlighted in the description of late-pre-colonial Rajasthan polities by Peabody (2003), who says, '[K]ings were implicated in multiple hierarchies of authority that intersected not only with the hierarchies of sectarian organizations . . . but also with the hierarchies of rival kings' (ibid., 83).

[59]The theory of the 'segmentary state' argues in effect that the king has only ritual authority and that political power lies in the local societies within a state. Here, I am referring to the situation in which there were different modes of integration involving different levels of polities. I am aware that no straightforward dichotomy can be drawn between the ritual and the political, but I use the terms here to describe different modes of integration.

[60]Kulke 1993.

[61]Kulke 1978a, 342.

[62]The ritual sovereignty of the Khurda kings seems to have continued even after considerable reduction in their political power under the Marathas in 1760-1, as they continued to have 'their regnal years (*aṅka*) and they were allowed to send "royal letters" (*chāmu ciṭhāu*) to the rajas and chiefs of Orissa' (Kulke 1978a, 338). Ewer also notes: 'Even in the fallen condition of Rajahs of Khoordah, they continued to exercise the regal privilege of conferring titles on the inhabitants of the Mogulbundee and the Gurjhat countries,

Next, this sphere of the ritual sovereignty of the Gajapati also came to include the sphere of feudatory relationships. The feudatory rajas paid *peshkash* and provided military service to the Khurda king. These feudatory rajas included those of Banki, Dhenkanal, Athgarh and Ranpur, among others. In 1592, the Mughal emperor Akbar acknowledged the Khurda king's authority over thirty-one feudatory rajas. These in their turn recognized the political overlordship of the Khurda king as the Gajapati and also participated in the semi-regional system of honour and privileges centring around Jagannatha.[63]

Lastly, there was the Khurda kingdom itself, which was under the direct political dominance of the Khurda king. Here it is very easy to see how the notion of one's self being embedded in the local system of entitlement was linked to regional patriotism.[64] I have already discussed how the Khurda king was established as the central sacrificer and the source of authority even for the local micro-regional units, thus linking the people's sense of self with the subregional Khurda kingship. In Khurda, as the king was the Gajapati himself, the channellization of the body-persons in the locality with royalty meant that their sense of self was also linked with Jagannatha, who defined the centre of the Orissan *patria*. Thus, the local entitlements and duties also had ritual-spiritual importance as service for Jagannatha. The people self-reflexively considered their positionality *vis-à-vis* Jagannatha as the representative of the universal value as well as the sovereign of Orissa. This may be related to the popular development of the bhakti cult in Orissa during this period, where devotion to Jagannatha as oneself was emphasized. Here perhaps one can see a development of patriotism, where the sense of selfhood embedded in the local patrimony was connected to the wider sense of country, with a common source of political legitimacy and authority.

In this way, the various subregional and micro-regional units in Orissa were connected to the regional unit of Orissa through one of the four forms of integration. Although there was indeed no 'country' in early modern Orissa in the political sense, there was a shared sense of the sovereignty of Jagannatha and the political legitimacy of the Gajapati institution among the subregional units that constituted the Orissan *patria* at the level of political morality and political theology.[65] This shared sense of a political morality and a love for

---

which was never objected to by the Mahratta. I am informed, indeed, that no title granted by the Mahratta Government was considered to confer any distinction in Orissa, until confirmed by the Rajahs of Khoordah' (Ewer Report, para. 187, *Selections* I, 65).

[63]The number of feudatory rajas under the Khurda king declined to seventeen after the Maratha intervention in 1759 (Kulke 1978a, 337-8).

[64]Khurda is referred to as 'Orissa' and the peasant warriors of Khurda refer to themselves as 'Oriyas'. Khurda is often seen as the centre of Jagannatha's country by the people of Khurda and *garhjat* areas.

[65]The term 'political theology' is borrowed from Kantorowicz 1957. See also Schnepel 1995.

the Jagannatha country must indeed have had some part to play in the later formation of Orissan nationalism.[66]

CONCLUSION

In this chapter, I have tried to show how micro-regional, subregional and regional identities were inter-related to form regional patriotism in early modern Orissa. First, it should be pointed out that identity formation in the micro-region was based on intimate connections between the body, food and land. Identity formation in this case was not about people's ideational attachment to an imagined community, but about their embodied organic relationships with the land through bio-moral exchanges of code-substances. These exchanges took place primarily in the context of the local system of patrimonial entitlements, which defined rights to shares of products of the land, as well as the salaries, privileges and duties of the offices of people in the micro-region. The system of entitlements also constituted a sacrificial organization in which each person with an entitlement participated in the functioning of the community, usually with a goddess as the tutelary deity. However, with the replacement of indigenous chiefs by the subordinated chiefs in the forts of micro-regions and the permeation of the subregional king's surveillance over each entitlement in early modern Orissa, due to improved technologies of administration the

[66]The two symbols of the Jagannatha cult and Gajapati kingship, which were the centres of politico-morality and Orissan regional identity, played an important part in the Oriya nationalist movements in the later colonial period, especially during times of popular participation (Mohanty 1982; Dash 1978; Das 1992; Bayly 1998, 73-4). The Paik Rebellion in 1817 induced the Khurda king to accept leadership as the representative of Jagannatha. The insurgent *pāika*s and Jagabandhu marched towards Puri, which was the abode of Lord Jagannatha, 'the true ruler of Orissa'. It was also the place where Jagannatha's representative on earth, the king of Khurda—their former ruler, who was reduced to being the superintendent of the temple—resided. On 14 April 1817, Jagabandhu and *pāika*s entered Puri, the aim of the insurgents being to restore the king's sovereignty in Khurda. According to the petition of the raja of Puri dated 6 March 1818, 'Jagabandhu . . . tried to take him [the Khurda king] and his family to Khurda with the intention of installing him on the throne there as the Raja of Khurda' (De 1962, 20; Ewer Report, paras 14-22, *Selections* I, 7-11; Pattanaik 1978; Mohanty 1982, 11-12; Mishra 1983). In 1880, the Oriya nationalist movement gained popular impetus when protests surged against an attempt by the British to increase their control over the management of the Jagannnath temple and reduce the role of the Gajapati through the Puri Temple Act (Mohanty 1982, 44-5; Dash 1978; Das 1992; Bayly 1998, 73-4). Jagannatha and Gajapati are still very important in shaping Oriya identity even today. I have described elsewhere how the sense of identity and politico-morality related to Jagannatha and Gajapati can lead to political repercussions for the present Orissa state government (Tanabe 1995). The sense of self and identity related to regional patriotism centring around the Gajapati and Jagannatha seem to have played an important role as the central symbol in shaping conceptions of popular Oriya nationalism and nationality into the nineteenth and twentieth centuries (Dash 1978; Mohapatra 1996).

king came to be seen as the bestower of entitlements as well as the sacrificer for the local goddesses. Each entitlement-holder embedded in the micro-regional system of entitlements came to have exchange relations with the king who represented the focus of subregional identity. The entitlement-holders came to eat the king's land and embody their relationships with the king. This must have certainly contributed to the strengthening of subregional identities in early modern Orissa.

In Khurda, since the subregional king was also the Gajapati, further association was established with Jagannatha, the supreme ruler of Orissa, through the mediation of the Khurda king. With the popularization of the bhakti cult, people began to consider their duty, prescribed by the system of entitlements and sanctioned by the king, to be service for the king and for Jagannatha. This linked the people's attachment to patrimony to a sense of love for the country.

The other subregional kings in Orissa also accepted the supreme sovereignty of Jagannatha. Many of them also accepted the ritual sovereignty if not political overlordship of the Khurda king as the Gajapati. The shared political theology regarding the sovereignty of Jagannatha and the institution of the Gajapati thus linked up subregional kings in Orissa to form an emotional-ideational territory of the Orissan country.

In this way, we can see that patriotism in the early modern period was based on a multilayered territoriality consisting of micro-regional, subregional and regional levels. The people related to the land through bio-moral exchanges at the micro-regional level came to be connected with the subregional king, whose authority increasingly penetrated into the locality. These subregional kings were further integrated into the Jagannatha country through a shared political theology and institutions. Thus the multi-layered territoriality of micro-regional, subregional and regional levels was reciprocally connected to form the Orissa *patria* without imposing a homogeneous culture, and it managed to maintain subregional and micro-regional idiosyncrasies.

Lastly, I suggest that a study of regional patriotism in early modern Orissa may throw light upon an understanding of the development of regional identity and nationalism in Orissa in the (post-)colonial period. Although the idea of nationalism in the language of the modern politics of liberalism and self-determination indeed came to India from Europe, it would be wrong to see nationalism in nineteenth- and early twentieth-century India as a totally derivative discourse.[67] Territorial identities and popular ideas of political morality and good governance also developed in pre-colonial India, which influenced the sense of belonging to India and the perception of Indian nationalities in the nineteenth century, as Bayly argues.[68] Between the imported

[67] Cf. Chatterjee (1986), who also sees the importance of indigenous ideas of nationalism, but seems to regard 'derivative' and 'indigenous' ideas and discourses on nationalism too much in a dichotomous manner. See note 69 below.

[68] Bayly 1998, 14. The problem with Bayly, however, is that he does not pay enough

idea and institution of nationalism on the one hand and the indigenous sense of politico-moral goodness and rightness on the other, there have been many serious attempts to articulate the two to create an Indian form of good government and democracy in colonial and post-colonial India.[69] These attempts to bridge derived and indigenous political ideas were also an endeavour to reconcile the concepts of nationality held by the elite and the popular masses respectively. It might be said that nationalist struggles won popular participation only when they were successful in bridging the popular sense of politico-morality with the anti-colonial nationalist movement.[70] Even today in the post-colonial period, the need to integrate the popular sense of politico-morality with the institution of the nation-state is arguably one of the most important political agendas of Indian democracy.[71] In order to fully understand the development of Indian nationalism and democracy in the colonial and post-colonial periods, then, it is necessary to pay attention to indigenous and popular ideas of politico-morality, as well as to how they manifested themselves

---

attention to the effect of colonialism when he says, for example, 'What modernity did was to transform and redirect these emergent identities [from the pre-colonial period] rather than to invent them *ex nihilo*' (Bayly 1998, 3). It is important to acknowledge that the idea of liberal democracy as a universal political ideal upon which nationalism was based was indeed imported to India from outside, and that it was institutionally and politically monopolized by the British while being denied to the Indian people. Thus, it would be necessary to consider the effect of the 'colonial rule of difference' (Chatterjee 1993) between the colonizer and the colonized upon the form of Indian nationalism more than Bayly seems to allow. This does not mean, however, that we should be content with simply pointing out the division between imported ideas and indigenous ones and analysing the duality of nationalism in India. Such an approach is taken by Partha Chatterjee (1993), who points out the existence of two spheres of nationalism: while nationalists admitted the superiority of the West in the material 'outer' sphere, they insisted on their spiritual superiority and the bases of the cultural sovereignty of India in the 'inner' sphere. However, granted that there was indeed a division between the inner and outer spheres of nationalism under colonialism, we should not forget that many efforts have also been made to create an Indian form of nationalism by integrating the two spheres.

[69]The various strands in nationalist movements—including those of Tagore, Gandhi, Nehru, Iqbal and Jinnah—can be said to have been different attempts to create a form of nationalism which could appeal to both modern and indigenous ideas of nationalities. They attempted to command legitimacy and support from people with different ideas about nationality.

[70]The Gandhian movement in its successful periods is a prime but short-lived example of such bridging and articulation between the elite and the popular masses, as well as between nationalism as a derivative discourse and an indigenous politico-moral sense (Haynes 1992). Kaviraj says, [Gandhi] managed to bridge the gulf between the two sides [the Indian elite and the lower orders], and keep the values, objectives and conception of the world of the two sides intelligible to each other (Kaviraj 1991, 85).

[71]I have suggested elsewhere (Tanabe 2002) that we need to pay attention to the sphere of 'moral society', as distinct from 'civil society' and 'political society' (Chatterjee 2000), where attempts have been made by the people to articulate an indigenous sense of rightness and goodness with contemporary liberal-democratic ideas and institutions.

historically in different periods of time in conjunction with political and institutional arrangements. The present chapter is therefore intended as a step towards understanding popular ideas and the sense of politico-morality, as well as how they manifested themselves in the form of regional patriotism under the particular historical and political contexts of seventeenth- to eighteenth-century Orissa.

ABBREVIATIONS

Ewer Report: From W. Ewer to W.B. Bayley, Calcutta, 13 May 1818, in *Selections from the Correspondence on the Settlement of Khoorda Estate in the District of Pooree*, vol. 1.

Forrester Report: From W. Forrester to the Secretary to the Commissioner of Cuttack, 17 October 1819, in *Selections from the Correspondence on the Settlement of Khoorda Estate in the District of Pooree*, vol. 1.

Selections I: *Selections from the Correspondence on the Settlement of Khoorda Estate in the District of Pooree*, vol. 1.

REFERENCES

Anderson, Benedict 1991. *Imagined Communities: Reflections on the Origin and Spread of Nationalism*, London and New York: Verso.

Bayly, Chris A. 1998. *Origins of Nationality in South Asia: Patriotism and Ethical Government in the Making of Modern India*, Delhi: Oxford University Press.

Beck, Brenda E.F. 1972. *Peasant Society in Konku: A Study of Right and Left Subcastes in South India*, Vancouver: University of British Columbia Press.

Berkemer, G. 2002. 'Borders, Lines and Cases: From Sīma to Sīmānta in South Orissa and Beyond', K.C. Panigrahi Lecture, Ravenshaw College, February 2002 (publ. in *Ravenshaw Historical Journal* 2003).

———2003. 'Call for Papers' for Annual Conference of the Orissa Research Project, at Salzau, 13-17 May 2003. 'Centres Out There? Facets of Subregional Identities'.

———2006. 'The King's Two Kingdoms, or: How the Maharaja of Parlakimedi Became the Ruler of Orissa', in G. Pfeffer (ed.), *Periphery and Centre: Studies in Orissan History, Religion and in Anthropology*, Delhi: Manohar, 341-60.

Bhatt, Bharat L. 1980. 'India and Indian Regions: A Critical Overview', in David E. Sopher (ed.), *An Exploration of India: Geographical Perspectives on Society and Culture*, Ithaca: Cornell University Press, 35-61.

Chatterjee, Partha 1986. *Nationalist Thought and the Colonial World: A Derivative Discourse*? London: Zed Books.

———1993. *The Nation and its Fragments: Colonial and Postcolonial Histories*, Princeton: Princeton University Press.

———2000. 'Two Poets and Death: On Civil and Political Society in the Non-Christian World', in Timothy Mitchell (ed.), *Questions of Modernity*, Minneapolis and London: University of Minnesota Press, 35-48.

Chattopadhyaya, Brajadulal 1997. '"Autonomous Spaces" and the Authority of the State: The Contradiction and its Resolution in Theory and Practice in Early India', in Bernhard Kölver (ed.), *Recht, Staat und Verwaltung im klassischen Indien*, Munich: Oldenbourg, 1-14.

Daniel, V.E. 1984. *Fluid Signs: Being a Person the Tamil Way*, Berkeley: University of California Press.

Das, Jagannatha P. 1992. *Desa Kala Patra*, Bhubaneswar and Delhi: Prachi Prakashan.

Dash, G.N. 1978. 'Jagannatha and Oriya Nationalism', in A. Eschmann, H. Kulke and G.C. Tripathi (eds.), *The Cult of Jagannath and the Regional Tradition of Orissa*, Delhi: Manohar, 359-74.

De, S.C. (ed.) 1962. *Guide to Orissan Records*, vol. 3, Bhubaneswar: Orissa State Archives.

Dirks, Nicholas B. 1987. *The Hollow Crown: Ethnohistory of an Indian Little Kingdom*, Cambridge: Cambridge University Press.

Eschmann, A., H. Kulke and G.C. Tripathi (eds.) 1978a. *The Cult of Jagannath and the Regional Tradition of Orissa*, Delhi: Manohar.

———1978b. 'Hinduization of Tribal Goddesses in Orissa: The Śākta and Śaiva Typology', in A. Eschmann, H. Kulke and G.C. Tripathi (eds.) 1978a, 79-97.

Gupta, Akhil 1998. *Postcolonial Developments: Agriculture in the Making of Modern India*, Durham: Duke University Press.

Haynes, D.E. 1992. *Rhetoric and Ritual in Colonial India: The Shaping of a Public Culture in Surat City, 1852-1928*, Delhi: Oxford University Press.

Kantorowicz, Ernst H. 1957. *The King's Two Bodies: A Study in Mediaeval Political Theology*, Princeton: Princeton University Press.

Kaviraj, Sudipta 1991. 'On State, Society and Discourse in India', in J. Manor (ed.), *Rethinking Third World Politics*, Delhi: Oxford University Press, 72-99.

Kulke, Hermann 1976. 'Kshatriyaization and Social Change: A Study in Orissa Setting', in S.D. Pillai (ed.), *Studies in Honour of Prof. G.S. Ghurye*, Bombay: Popular Prakashan, 398-409.

———1978a. 'Jagannāth as the State Deity under the Gajapatis of Orissa', in A. Eschmann, A., H. Kulke and G.C. Tripathi (eds.) 1978a. 199-208.

———1978b. 'The Struggle between the Rājāṣ of Khurda and the Muslim Subahdārs of Cuttack for Dominance of the Jagannāth Cult', in A. Eschmann, H. Kulke and G.C. Tripathi (eds.) 1978a, 321-42.

———1993. 'Legitimation and Town-planning in the Feudatory States of Central Orissa', in H. Kulke, *Kings and Cults: State Formation and Legitimation in India and Southeast Asia*, Delhi: Manohar, 93-112.

———1993a. 'Ksetra and Ksatra: The Cult of Jagannatha of Puri and the Royal Letters of the Rajas of Khurda', in H. Kulke, *Kings and Cults: State Formation and Legitimation in India and Southeast Asia*, Delhi: Manohar, 51-65.

———2006. 'The Integrative Model of State Formation in Early Medieval India: Some Historiographic Remarks', in M. Kimura and A. Tanabe (eds.), *The State in India: Past and Present*, Delhi: Oxford University Press, 59-81.

Mahapatra, K.N. 1969. *Khurudhā Itihasā*, Cuttack: Granthamandir.

Marriot, M. 1955. *Village India*, Chicago: University of Chicago Press.

Mayer, Adrian C. 1960. *Caste and Kinship in Central India: A Village and its Region*, London: Routledge & Kegan Paul.

Mishra, P.K. 1983. *Political Unrest in Orissa in the 19th Century*: Calcutta: Punthi Pustak.

Mohanty, Nivedita 1982. *Oriya Nationalism: Quest for a United Orissa 1866-1936*, Delhi: Manohar.

Mohapatra, Bishnu N. 1996. 'Ways of "Belonging": The Kanchi Kaveri Legend and the Construction of Oriya Identity', *Studies in History* (n.s.) 12, 2, 203-21.

Parry, Jonathan P. 1979. *Caste and Kinship in Kangra*, London: Routledge & Kegan Paul.

Pattanaik, P.K. 1979. *A Forgotten Chapter of Orissan History (with special reference to the Rajas of Khurda and Puri) 1568-1828*, Calcutta: Punthi Pustak.

Pattanaik, S. (ed.) 1959. *Cakaḍā Pothi o Cakadā Basāṇa bā Cāyini Cakaḍā*, Cuttack: Friends' Publishers.

Peabody, N. 2003. *Hindu Kingship and Polity in Precolonial India*, Cambridge: Cambridge University Press.

Perlin, F. 1985. 'State Formation Reconsidered, Part Two', in *Modern Asian Studies* 19, 415 80.

Ray, Rajat K. 2003. *The Felt Community: Commonalty and Mentality before the Emergence of Indian Nationalism*, Delhi: Oxford University Press.

Schaar, John H. 1981. *Legitimacy in the Modern State*, New Brunswick and London: Transaction Books.

Schnepel, B. 1995. *Twinned Beings: Kings and Effigies in Southern Sudan, East India and Renaissance France*, Göteborg: Institute for Advanced Studies in Social Anthropology at Göteborg University (Sweden).

Srichandan, D. 1989. *Khuradhā Darpaṇa (second and third part)*, Khurda.

Srinivas, M.N. 1952. *Religion and Society among the Coorgs of South India*, Oxford: Clarendon Press.

Stein, Burton 1977. 'Circulation and the Historical Geography of Tamil Country', in *Journal of Asian Studies* 3, 1, 7-16.

Stietencron, H. von 1978. 'The Jagannāth Temples in Contemporary Orissa', in A. Eschmann, H. Kulke and G.C. Tripathi (eds.) 1978a, 460-75.

Sterling, A. 1904. *An Account (Geographical, Statistical, and Historical) of Orissa Proper or Cuttack with Appendices*, Calcutta: Bengal Secretariat Press.

Subbarayalu, Y. 1973. *Political Geography of the Chola Country*, Madras: State Department of Archaeology, Government of Tamil Nadu.

Tambiah, Stanley J. 1985. *Culture, Thought, and Social Action: An Anthropological Perspective*, Cambridge: Cambridge University Press.

Tanabe, A. 1995. 'Remaking Tradition: Martial Arts Competition and State Government in Orissa, India', in *Journal of Asian and African Studies* 48-9 (Thirtieth Anniversary Commemorative Issue 2), Institute for the Study of Languages and Cultures of Asia and Africa (ILCAA), Tokyo University of Foreign Studies, 221-41.

———1998. 'Ethnohistory of Land and Identity in Khurda, Orissa: From Pre-colonial Past to Post-colonial Present', in *Journal of Asian and African Studies* 56, ILCAA, Tokyo University of Foreign Studies, 75-112.

———1999a. 'Kingship, Community and Commerce in Late Pre-colonial Khurda', in N. Karashima (ed.), *Kingship in Indian History*, Delhi: Manohar, 195-236.

———1999b. 'The Transformation of Śakti: Gender and Sexuality in the Festival of Goddess Ramachandi', in M. Tanaka and M. Tachikawa (eds.), *Living with Śakti: Gender, Sexuality and Religion in South Asia*, Osaka: National Museum of Ethnology, Senri Ethnological Studies, 137-68.

———2000. *Early Modernity and Colonial Transformation: Rethinking the Role of the Little King in Eighteenth and Nineteenth Century Orissa*, ASAFAS Special Paper, Graduate School of Asian and African Area Studies, Kyoto: Kyoto University.

———2002. 'Moral Society, Political Society and Civil Society in Post-colonial India: A View from Orissan Locality', in *Journal of the Japanese Association for South Asian Studies* 14, 40-67.

———2003. 'The Sacrificer State and Sacrificial Community: Kingship in Early Modern Khurda—Orissa Seen Through a Local Ritual', in G. Berkemer and M. Frenz (eds.), *Sharing Sovereignty: The Little Kingdom in South Asia*, Berlin: Klaus Schwarz, 115-35.

———forthcoming. 'The Structure of Local Community in Pre-colonial Khurda: The Case of the System of Entitlements in Garh Manitri', in P.K. Nayak and R. Parkin (eds.),

Rethinking Orissa: Society, Culture and History (provisional title), Delhi: Manohar.

Tokita-Tanabe, Y. forthcoming. 'Women's Life Style, Women's Life Course: Ritual, Cosmology and Social Interaction in Village Orissa', in P.K. Nayak and R. Parkin (eds.), *Rethinking Orissa: Society, Culture and History* (provisional title), Delhi: Manohar.

Tripathi, G. and H. Kulke. 1987. *Katakarājavamsāvaliḥ: A Traditional History of Orissa*, Allahabad: Vohra.

Wink, A. 1986. *Land and Sovereignty in India: Agrarian Society and Politics under the Eighteenth Century Maratha Svarajya*, Cambridge: Cambridge University Press.

CHAPTER 12

Tutelary Deities at Royal Courts in Orissa

CORNELIA MALLEBREIN

The religious ideas, concepts and traditions of the numerous tribal communities in Orissa have exercised an important formative influence on the religious landscape of this state.[1] Numerous prominent deities here have a tribal background, among the best known being the god Jagannāth from Puri.[2] But in most cases it was a goddess from the forest, the realm of the tribes, who rose to regional prominence.

One of the most famous forest deities is the goddess Tāriṇī from Ghatgaon, a rapidly growing religious centre in Keonjhar district.[3] Up until thirty years ago, this goddess was worshipped in a sacred grove in the form of a simple stone at the foot of a tree surrounded by clay horses. Her devotees feared this lonely place, thinking that her mount, a tiger, roamed in the dense woods. Rarely did anyone dare to go there alone. Today the situation is strikingly different: instead of a forest path, a wide road flanked on both sides by numerous souvenir shops and food stalls leads to the impressive temple compound. Cars, buses and trucks take pilgrims to the temple of Mā Tāriṇī. A huge, recently constructed enclosure wall shields the inner sphere of the temple from the noise and bustle of the outside world. Inside, the goddess Tāriṇī is worshipped within an open enclosure, still in the form of a simple stone, her original cult image. According to the priest it was her wish to be worshipped in the open air, so that no roof should restrict her view of the sky. Thousands of coconuts, her favourite offering, are donated to her everyday. Devotees name their shops, companies, restaurants, even vehicles after her. All over Orissa, small shrines have been built in her name in thanksgiving for her help. On the Internet, she has her own website.[4] Her rapid growth is paradigmatic of the increase in goddess worship, not only in Orissa, but all over India as well.[5]

[1] The present chapter forms one part of a wider study of the Hinduized tribal deities at royal courts in Orissa, which is being supported by the German Research Council (DFG) within the Orissa Research Programme (ORP). I would like to thank the DFG for making this research possible. I am grateful to Dillip Sethi for his assistance during my fieldwork in Orissa.

[2] Kulke 1978 b.

[3] For a detailed study of the goddess Tāriṇī of Ghatgaon, see Mallebrein 2004b.

[4] www.maatarini.com (greatness of Maa).

[5] The website of Mā Tāriṇī provides further links (*arati links*) to the websites of famous goddesses like Vaiṣṇodevī and Naina Devī.

Goddess Tāriṇī's fame starts with her being the tutelary goddess of the royal family of Keonjhar, who fostered her cult and worship and who had a shrine constructed for her, as their family goddess, within their palace compound in Keonjhar.[6]

The former rulers of Orissa played an important role in the growth and development of the worship of goddesses.[7] In order to establish and strengthen their power as local rulers, they depended on the assistance and protection of the main local goddess, who was in most cases a tribal deity. Owing to a strong belief in her power, she received the status of a tutelary deity of the royal family, and as such she was also considered to be a protective goddess of the territory. Since the rulers promoted her cult and worship, she often acquired supra-regional recognition. These tutelary deities of the former royal families of Orissa form a specific group of deities, many of whom have their roots in the tribal fold.[8]

I have tried to document these deities by collecting data in the royal courts of the former feudatory states and raja-zamindaris of Orissa (the Bengal Presidency, Central Provinces and Madras Presidency). I have also taken into account the deities of the border regions of Andhra Pradesh, Chhattisgarh, Bihar and Jharkhand, to determine whether they too might be linked to the royal families of Orissa, as is Danteśvarī, the family deity of the royal house of Jagdalpur.[9]

This research attempts to show their ability to create a sense of identity and loyalty between the various social groups and royal families, as well as to discuss their integrative function with respect to a larger region.

The present chapter focuses on five topics: first, the interrelationship and links between profane and sacred centres on the secular and political as well as religious levels; second, different forms of secular and sacred legitimation, such as festivals and rituals, but also chronicles and local legends; third, traditional factors in securing and defining regional identity; fourth, the development of and changes in sacred centres in recent times as a result of shifts in patronage since independence; and fifth, the importance of historical photography as documents of the former days of royalty.

THE RELATIONSHIP BETWEEN PROFANE OR SACRED CENTRES AND THE PERIPHERY

The territory of a ruler and its periphery are interconnected by a network of relationships on different levels.

[6]Cf. Cobden Ramsay 1910, 212-31; Mishra 1974.

[7]On this topic, see Berkemer 1993, Schnepel 2002, Kulke 1992.

[8]Cf. Schnepel 1993.

[9]For more information on Danteśvarī, see Mallebrein 1996, Sundar 1997.

The Secular and Political Levels

This level is marked by various interrelations between the local rulers and the supra-regional rajas, as well as between the rajas and their subordinate local authorities, like the zamindars and gauntias.[10] To a great extent the latter relationship is based on economic exchange in the form of tribute. In addition, there is another exchange on the religious level. Often the zamindars, but also the gauntias, acknowledge the tutelary goddess of the ruler as their own family deity; as such she is given the status of the protective goddess of their administrative villages. This results in the fame of the royal tutelary goddess spreading all over the ruler's territory.

The rulers maintain a specific network of relationships between their own tutelary goddesses in their capitals—in most cases within the palace compounds—and the numerous shrines and temples donated to them on the village level. During the annual main festival of the goddess, which in most cases was integrated into the Daśaharā festival, the respective local priests and the subregional authorities—the zamindars, gauntias and other dignitaries—assemble during the durbar, which is performed in a lavish style by the raja.[11] Due to her close proximity to the royal family, the deity of tribal origin was finally incorporated into the fold of Hinduism.[12] As a royal goddess she was looked after by the court Brahmans, who were entrusted with her worship at the main temple within the palace compound. Due to her power and strength, they linked her with the goddess Durgā, in which role she acquired further respect and honour. Although her main annual festival was incorporated into the Daśaharā festival, she often managed to remain independent and to maintain her wild tribal character. Many of these family deities are considered tantric and thus demand tantric worship, which includes animal sacrifices.[13] Rarely did her identification with Durgā obliterate her tribal origin and character. In adopting the tutelary deity of the raja as their own family goddess, the local subordinate authorities obtained access to a divine power in whose strength and efficiency the raja had full trust. For the local population, this divine power caused a feeling of security, and at the same time the royal goddess reminded the villagers of their manifold obligations towards the raja. The raja in his turn showed his respect towards the royal goddess in the villages by presenting her with sacrificial offerings and donations during her main annual festival. To a large extent this network of worldly economic and religious exchanges bound to a ritual context has contributed to the spread of the tutelary goddesses, most prominently Maṇikeśvarī,[14] who is worshipped widely in Kalahandi, Rayagada

[10]Skoda 2003, 2005.

[11]On the importance of the Daśaharā festival, see Schnepel 2002.

[12]Cf. Mallebrein 1999, 137-56; Eschmann 1978a.

[13]Cf. Singh Deo 2001.

[14]For a detailed discussion of Maṇikeśvarī, see Mallebrein 2006.

and Ganjam districts, and the goddess Sāmleśvarī,[15] who is known in the Bolangir and Sundergarh areas. They exert a strong integrative influence in these particular regions.

Another network is kept alive between the various tutelary goddesses of the royal families. This may be the result of an inter-family-marriage relationship. As a token of memory towards her own family goddess, the new wife may take a figurine or photograph to her new home, where it is worshipped daily within the private sphere. But this outside goddess may also be given her own temple within the palace compound, so that she may look after the well-being of the people.

Family deities are also interlinked by well-planned marriage policies which bring the territories of dynasties closer and thus enhance their influence and importance. As a result, various forms of ritual partnership on a worldly and other-worldly level are observed. Likewise, the adoption of a ruler from another royal family can cause a shift in the family deity. A newly adopted son from another dynasty introduces his own family deity into his new realm as a protective goddess.

Another shift in tutelary deities is caused by the auction of a territory, a custom which was quite prominent in British times. The tutelary goddess of the former dynasty enters the court of the new owner, where she is given a place as the younger sister of the family goddess.

A network of relationships may also result from a family splitting up, as was the case within the Kimedi raja family. The royal families of Parlakimedi, Badakimedi and Sanakimedi join in worshipping the goddess Maṇikeśvarī.

Over time, the tutelary goddesses of various royal families developed a certain sisterly relationship among themselves, which reflects actual profane relations and dependencies among the rulers concerned. Striking examples are the 'seven sisters' surrounding the goddess Bhagavatī of Banpur.[16] The image of the seven sisters is widely known all over Orissa, but in contrast to south India, in Orissa they do not generally consist of disease goddesses. The number seven has a connotation of completeness, and on the lowest level the seven sisters may control seven villages or hamlets. The seven sisters surrounding the goddess Bhagavatī mark the territory of a group of local rajas who had close relations.[17] Bhagavatī of Banpur is considered the most important of the sisters. The Gajapati of Puri is her main patron. Within her temple compound, two of the seven sisters, the goddesses Bīrajāi and Phūlkāsinī, are present in a shrine. Of all the sisters, the goddess Bīrajāi is the oldest. Her place of origin is a small, barely accessible temple in the dense forest near Bankada. Her priest is a member of the Kondh tribe. The stone image depicts her as dangerous, with Cāmuṇḍā chewing on the little finger of one of her left hands. Hence she

[15]On Samleśvarī, see Pasayat 1997, 1998.

[16]For information on Banpur and connected deities, see Das 1999, 136-41.

[17]The goddess Bhagavatī protects the west, Siddheśvarī the north, Narāyaṇī the south, and Kālījāi the east.

is referred to as Carccikā.[18] The figure can be dated to the seventh and eighth centuries. Within the group of seven mothers (*saptamātṛkā*), Cāmuṇḍā is usually shown as the last. In contrast to the other mothers, she has no partner, although she is associated with Śiva, who has his own impressive temple close to Bīrajāi's jungle abode. The Sopneśvar temple of Bankada used to be a centre of the Śailodbhava dynasty.[19] After the extinction of the Śailodbhava power in this region, the centre of Bīrajāi worship was shifted to Banpur. As the most senior of all the sisters, she enjoys the privilege of a movable image (*calantī pratimā*), the Kāṭhithākurāṇī, a long wooden pole, being placed inside the main temple, in front of Bhagavatī's sanctuary. Phūlkāsinī, who is the lowest sister in the hierarchy and who lives with Bīrajāi and Bhagavatī, no longer has a special relationship with any king. The fourth sister in the hierarchy is the goddess Kanaka Durgā, represented by a metal statue of Durgā Mahiṣāsuramardinī, which is kept within the Dakṣaprajāpati temple in Banpur. Dakṣaprajāpati is considered the male companion of the seven goddesses, or rather their father.[20] The Kāṭhithākurāṇī of Bhagavatī has its place in his temple. The fifth among the sisters is Siddheśvarī, the family goddess of the royal house of Bhatapada Garh, a small village near Banpur. Rajasaheb Dulal Manabendra Moharatha of Bhatapada Garh still plays an important role in the various festivals in Banpur today. During the *rathayātrā* of the god Jagannāth, he performs the *cherāpāhārā* ritual in Banpur. The sixth among the sisters is the goddess Narāyaṇī, the tutelary goddess of the royal family of Khallikot.[21] The last in the series is the goddess Kālījāi, whose temple is situated on an island in the Chilika Lake. She is the family goddess of the royal family of Parikud.

When all the local rulers were still in power, the seven sisters enjoyed an elaborate system of mutual recognition and honours. Today only a few of the once highly differentiated and hierarchically structured sister rituals are kept alive, but, transposed on to a religious and supra-mundane level, they still reflect the actual political and hierarchical structures of the past. It is still a tradition for the sisters Narāyaṇī, Kālījāi and Siddheśvarī to take part in the Daśaharā festival of the goddess Bhagavatī at Banpur in the form of a flower chain (*ājñāmālā*). Once a year, in the month of Caitra, the Kāṭhithākurāṇī of Bhagavatī visits her sister Siddheśvarī in Bhatapada Garh. The movable image, the Kāṭhithākurāṇī, is a huge wooden pole, wrapped in numerous saris on ritual occasions. The trunk recalls her origin in the forest. The saris are wrapped in such a way that the whole arrangement resembles a magnificent umbrella. Out of joy at being together with her sister Siddheśvarī, the Kāṭhithākurāṇī of Bhagavatī dances through the village street of Bhatapada Garh. The devotees

[18]On Cāmuṇḍā as Carccikā, see Donaldson 1985-7, vol. 3, 1077-8.

[19]On Bankada/Punjiyama and the Śiva temple, see Donaldson 1985-7, vol. 1, 132ff.

[20]For more information on the Dakṣaprajāpati Śiva temple, which can be dated to the second half of the thirteenth century, cf. Donaldson 1985-7, vol. 2, 635ff.

[21]Cf. Das 1999, 179.

are convinced that it is only because Bhagavatī endows those who carry this trunk, the priests of the Banpur temple, with divine power that they can carry such an enormous weight. Bhagavatī is given splendid food and spends the night in the temple of her sister Siddheśvarī. The whole village stays awake till the early morning, when Bhagavatī, after a lavish feast, returns to Banpur.

A further network of relationships is formed on the political and secular level between the local ruler and the clan sections of different tribes. In their migration myth, it is told that a clan group once left its former settlement in the mountains to move towards the plains. This movement is clearly expressed in the migration myth of the goddess Pāṭkhaṇḍā.[22] Her main temple is in Jarasingha, Bolangir district. In the territory of the new ruler the clan members play a double role: as a protecting power—*pāika* soldiers and *khaṇḍāiat*—for the raja; and as farmers who clear the forest in the name of the raja to introduce the cultivation of profitable crops like rice.[23] Pāṭkhaṇḍā is a clan deity of the Muṭkīā Kondh. Her place of origin lies in a dense forest grove near Mahasinghi, a village about 7 km south-east of Balliguda, a subdivision of Kondhmal district. According to the legend, Pāṭkhaṇḍā stayed in the house of a Kondh in the form of a powerful and magical vegetable chopper (*paniki*), which automatically cut the objects placed on it. Once this Kondh took a loan from a Brahman. As he could not pay it back, the Brahman stole the magic chopper. Pāṭkhaṇḍā showed her anger by breaking it into three pieces, then she decided to leave the place and, together with her brother Birpāni and her adoptive brother Jenābuḍhā, she left the jungle region and wandered to the plains of Jarasingha. She asked permission from the god of the local hill of Buḍhādaṅgar to stay there, and he advised her to contact the family deities of the Patnagarh Chauhan king, the goddesses Pāṭaṇeśvarī and Samleśvarī, to permit her to stay. They agreed under the condition that Pāṭkhaṇḍā assisted the Chauhan king, Vatsarājādeva of Patnagarh, in a battle against the king of Bastar. Eventually, it was only due to Pāṭkhaṇḍā's help that the Chauhan king won the war. Pāṭkhaṇḍā realized that Bastaren, the family deity of the king of Bastar, had dressed as a woman and sold poisoned food to the Chauhan king's soldiers in order to weaken his army. Pāṭkhaṇḍā caught Bastaren, and she surrendered. Pāṭkhaṇḍā received the territory of Jarasingha from the grateful Chauhan king as her new region to rule. Bastaren acknowledged the supreme power of Pāṭkhaṇḍā and went with her to Jarasingha, where she was granted the right to be worshipped as a village deity. This myth tells how the Muṭkīā Kondh settled in the area of Jarasingha, and it testifies to their importance as soldiers in the service of the Chauhan rulers. Pāṭkhaṇḍā is the tutelary deity of the raja-zamindar of Jarasingha. Today a sword and shield represent her in the temple. Although she is a tribal deity, her annual festival is integrated into

[22]For a detailed study of Pāṭkhaṇḍā, see Mallebrein 2004c.
[23]On the theme of Kṣatriyaization, see Kulke 1993b.

Daśaharā. Pāṭaṇeśvarī and Samleśvarī still send offerings (*pāṭsindūr*) to her today at the beginning of the Pāṭkhaṇḍā festival.[24]

However, some of the clan deities have retained their former tribal identities. The most prominent of these are Śūliā, the clan god of the Māuñsia Kondh, and Śikerpāṭ, the clan god of the Khadaṅgiā Kondh, who is widely worshipped in Bolangir District.[25] Their migration myths reflect the movement of the clan section from the mountains to the plains. In both cases the clan gods were first worshipped on top of a hill. One day, the priest forgot his ritual water pot and left it at the site of the sacrifice, so he climbed back up to get it. When he reached the top, he saw the gods sharing the animal sacrifices, but always leaving one share. They looked around and found the priest hiding. When they saw him they became very angry, and Śūliā and Śikerpāṭ threw the sacrificial pot down the hill towards the plain. There they continue to be worshipped, and every year the Kondhs celebrate a great festival (*yātrā*) at these places. Śikerpāṭ's main site is near the village of Ghuna, and Śāliā's is near the village of Khairaguda. Huge numbers of buffalo and goats are offered as sacrifices. Their main festival is performed in the month of Pauṣa, the traditional month for tribal festivals.

The Network on the Religious Level

On the religious level, a network between the palace and the place of origin of the family deity (*mūlpīṭha*) is maintained. This place is often quite a distance away from the capital, in an area mostly inhabited by tribes. One reason for this distance is the tradition of the constant moving of forts in dynastic histories. The old fort was abandoned, and only the fort deities remained, being silent testimonies to the former rulers. They mark the various migrations in the history of their former rulers and reflect former geographical and historical connections.

Rulers began to establish their power on a great scale mainly under British supremacy in the nineteenth century.[26] A new representative capital was planned with a huge palace, various government buildings and new temples. The tutelary goddess was also given her impressive temple within the palace compound, and court Brahmans took over her cult and rituals. In the course of time the Brahmans acquired enormous importance as being responsible for the ritual care of a multitude of deities within the territory. Integrative festivals like Daśaharā are supervised by them.

Although the Brahmanical influence grew, the traditional relationship between the king and the tribal communities in his realm was kept alive. The close links became most visible in the coronation ritual. The seal (*sindūr ṭikkā*)

[24]For a detailed study of Pāṭkhaṇḍā and the Pāṭkhaṇḍā *yātrā*, see Mallebrein 2004c.

[25]For a detailed study of Śūliā and Śikerpāṭ, see Mallebrein 2004a.

[26]On early state formation, royal legitimation and the new town planning of royal families, see Kulke 1978a, 1993a.

of legitimation of rule over a certain region, was in most cases taken from the original cult image (*mūrti*) of the tutelary goddess. This close bond between the tribes and the raja is made very clear in the coronation rituals of the royal families of Keonjhar, Pallahara, Bonai, Sundergarh and Kalahandi, in whose territories the major part of the population once belonged to a tribal community. It is a senior chief of the major tribe of the area who invests the future ruler with the right to rule. During the coronation ritual, the future king sits in the lap of the tribal chief, who places the *ṭikkā*, the sign of rule, on his forehead, thus endowing the ruler with the power to rule over the tribal region.[27]

THE MECHANISM OF WORLDLY OR SACRED LEGITIMATION

In this section, some aspects of constructing collective identities are discussed. I shall examine further the relationship between political and religious power, which strives for legitimation. In constructing an identity, different kinds of texts and their interpretations play an important role. Among them are 'stories' and 'legends' about the first encounter of the founder of a dynasty with his future tutelary deity of tribal origin. She suddenly appears to the homeless and wandering Rajput prince in a dream and shows him the way to his new realm, or else she helps him in a miraculous way to conquer a new territory.[28] Quite often, the self-sacrifice of a tribal chief is mentioned.[29] Through his sacrifice, the tribal victim paves the way to power for the Kṣatriya prince. These texts contain valuable information on historical changes in a region, the expansion of the territory by a dynasty, or, alternatively, the loss of a region, and they allow an insight into the historical movements of various dynasties.

Another important function is connected with festivals and rituals. They strengthen the ties between the ruler and his family deity and thus legitimate his worldly rule. It is the medium (Dehuri, Sirhā, Kālisī) who plays a leading role as a 'living god on earth' within these festivals, visibly confirming the

[27]For the tradition in Kalahandi, see Cobden Ramsay 1910, 202 (citing a Lieutenant Elliot); also P.K. Deo 2000, 51. As the Kondh consider the raja from Kalahandi to be a member of their community, it was customary till recently for the Kalahandi raja to take a Kondh girl as his first wife (*paṭrāṇī*). It was also a custom in the Kalahandi royal family for the coronation of a new king to take place in the lap of the Kondh Pāṭmāji of Merkul. This custom was still followed by P.K. Deo, the father of the present Maharaja, Udit Pratāp Deo, in Jugsaipatna, who mentions in his biography that before his official investiture ceremony was celebrated on 16 March 1940, his *rājyābhiṣeka* was conducted on an auspicious day at the ancestral stone in Jugsaipatna. While he was sitting in the Pāṭmāji's lap, his turban was tied by the zamindar of Lanjigarh. He also gave the *tilaka* with *sindūr* taken from the Maṇikeśvarī stones inside the temple.

[28]On this topic, see Schnepel 2002, 147, fn. 30: 'The widespread production of *vaṃśāvalīs* and genealogies proclaiming Rajput descent is probably to be dated to the period between 1770 and 1820, when early colonial interests provided a stimulus to such productions.' See also Schnepel 2002, 155-7; Sinha 1962; Banerji 1928.

[29]Cf. Kulke 1992.

right of the raja to rule to everyone present. The importance of this divine legitimation becomes manifest during the annual festival in honour of the goddess Hiṅgulā in Gopalprasad near Talcher. Hiṅgulā is the protective goddess of the royal family of Talcher.[30] Every year through her medium, she answers three questions asked on behalf of the raja, in which she assures the royal family and all the inhabitants of the region of her support and protection. The climax of the last main day of the festival is the transformation of the Dehuri into the goddess Hiṅgulā inside the temple.[31] The Dehuri, her medium, is worshipped in an elaborate ritual similar to a cult image, with leaves, flowers, bananas and puff rice. A huge potful of nectar (*pañcāmṛta*) and molasses is poured over his head. While he is being worshipped this way, the Dehuri starts trembling, a sign that Hiṅgulā has started to enter his body. Suddenly he takes Hiṅgulā's sword and, possessed by divine power, runs towards a spot where Hiṅgulā appeared at the beginning of the festival in the form of a flame. The self-created flame symbolizes her power and energy. In the eyes of her believers, the land around Talcher belongs to the body of the goddess. This area is exceptionally rich in coal, so much so that earth gas spontaneously ignites on the surface. The mining of coal is experienced by the local people as a painful encroachment of 'mother' Hiṅgulā's body. During the Hiṅgulā yātrā, vast amounts of sacrificial offerings, saris, butter fat and flowers are thrown into the growing fire, whose colossal flames climb up to the sky. The festival ends after the Rajasaheb of Talcher and his wife have offered their oblations to the fire the night following the main day, after the transformation of the Dehuri into the goddess Hiṅgulā.

The medium also plays an important role within the tradition of offering animal sacrifices to the tutelary goddesses. However, this tradition is highly controversial, and it has been changed considerably. At many temples animal sacrifices have been replaced with vegetarian offerings, often due to pressure from the government. This 'vegetarization' of deities is creating numerous changes.[32] For example, the institution of the medium, in most cases a male, who represents the deity on earth, is gradually disappearing, as one major task of the medium was to drink the blood of the sacrificial animal in the sight of all the participants as proof that the deity had accepted the sacrifice. For the temple the prohibition of animal sacrifices also has economic implications, as the sale of animals to be offered as *mahāprasāda* was an important source of income. The task of the medium in being the mouthpiece of the deity has shifted to the domestic arena. The number of women who are becoming possessed by a goddess is growing. In an altered state of consciousness, and possessed by divine power, they can respond to believers' questions and also heal afflictions. The medium, in his role as the deity on earth, has an important

[30]Cf. Eschmann 1978b.

[31]For more information on the Hiṅgulā yātrā, see Eschmann 1978b, 277-8; Hiṅgulā Pītha Unnayan Pariṣad (ed.) 1998.

[32]On this topic, see Mallebrein 2007.

integrative function within his village. Social conflicts can be resolved by the pronouncements of the medium, which are accepted as coming from the deity. On the occasion of great celebrations in honour of the deity, mediums embodying deities from villages all over the area come together to celebrate the feast, thus strengthening the social ties of the region, whose major divinities they represent. The tradition of the Sirhās (medium) is particularly alive in the border area of Orissa and Bastar (Chhattisgarh). The Sirhās of different gods and goddesses meet annually in large numbers during the Mondai festivals, which are performed in several villages, primarily in the Nawrangpur region. Being clothed in ritual dress and decorated with cowries, the Sirhās are led in a trance around the village in a great procession. Often hundreds of local divinities take part, represented either by their Sirhā or by bamboo bars with conical metal tops. The festival ends in the Sirhās' ecstatic dances. Once again the deities show all their power and ecstatic wildness before they leave the body of their Sirhā. The Sirhā, in his manifestation as a 'living god on earth', serves as a further source of inspiration for the metalcasters in the Bastar Orissa border regions, who have been inspired by the performances of the Sirhās as the representatives of a deity in creating the metal figurines of gods and goddesses.[33]

The family history of the dynasties justifies their legitimatory claim to rule over a specific territory. It is often reported that an assembly of tribes asked the future raja to rule over them and that they gave their goddess to him as the tutelary deity of his family and state.

TRADITIONAL FACTORS IN SECURING AND DEFINING REGIONAL IDENTITY

Since the foundation of new capitals in the nineteenth century, an ever-increasing number of new temples have been erected for major Hindu gods and goddesses, as numerous social groups have migrated from the hinterland to the capital. They all demanded a temple in which to worship their specific deities. Parallel to this, numerous monasteries (*maṭha*) were founded. With the extension of the palace, a great number of Hindu deities entered into the private temple sphere of the palace compound. The palace of the ruler became a microcosm, tied to a sacred geography. A close association developed between the deities of the palace area and those beyond it. The performance of festivals in honour of all these various deities created a feeling of identity, and the relationship between the ruler and his subjects was strengthened and defined. The celebration of festivals thus played a major part in local power struggles. The splendid performance and arrangement of the Daśaharā festival became an important aspect of these. Every ruling family arranged their Daśaharā differently, but they all stressed that as part of Daśaharā the ruler receives the permission of his tutelary goddess to rule over her territory.

[33]On this topic, see Mallebrein 1993, 1998.

Daśaharā is still the most important of festivals within the annual festival calendar of the royal families. The relationship between the raja and his family goddess as a tantric goddess who demands animal sacrifices is particularly close. Every year the royal family of Kalahandi offers animal sacrifices to the goddess Maṇikeśvarī, who is believed to have such enormous power that she appears to the devotees only in a darkened sanctuary, where she can only dimly be seen.[34] As a Kondh deity, she is linked to the Buḍhā Rājā, her male companion, whose shrine is to the right side of her temple. Like Pāṭkhaṇḍā, she is also linked to Jen, whose place of worship (*Jenā-khālo*) lies approximately 3 km from the temple. During Daśaharā, in the night from Mahāṣṭamī to Navamī, countless animal sacrifices are offered at this spot. Jenā is also called Bali-Rājā and is regarded as Yama's assistant. He demands blood. Maṇikeśvarī's movable image (*calanti pratimā*) is a huge umbrella, similar to Bhagavatī's. During Daśaharā it is brought outside the temple to receive the animal offerings.

The institution of ritual service holders (*sevaka*), who take an active part in the performance of the festivals, is another factor that creates a feeling of collective identity. The members of various castes and tribal groups promise to perform certain duties within the festival, thus strengthening the relationships of the various social groups.

THE DEVELOPMENT OF SACRED CENTRES IN RECENT TIMES

With the Independence of India in 1947, radical changes took place in traditional power structures and in other ways. The abolition of the royal privileges (privy purses) in 1971 meant another serious cut in the patronage of divinities and temples.[35] The documentation of tutelary deities at royal centres takes note of changes such as the weakening of the palaces as worldly and sacred centres. Members of the royal family still take part today in the rituals for their tutelary goddess, mainly during the Daśaharā celebrations, but they are no longer her representatives on earth and main sponsors. Due to outside influences, the former structure of the Daśaharā festival is changing in the direction of a generalized Bengali form of the Durgā *pūjā*. Nevertheless, at some places the association of the goddess with her tribal origins is maintained.

This lack of patronage has resulted in the neglect of many small local temples, shrines and monasteries, many of which have already been given up. However, new temples are being built, mainly in the name of Rāma and Hanumān, but also for goddesses who have attained supra-regional fame. This is the result of a new temple policy on the part of the temple trusts, to attract huge crowds of devotees and thus increase the income of the temple. The former temple compounds are being extended, and numerous new temples for other deities and huge wedding halls and rest houses are being added. Thus

[34]For a discussion of the origins of Maṇikeśvarī and Ḍokrī, see Mallebrein 2006.

[35]On the princely states of Orissa before Independence, see Samal 1988.

the temple is becoming a well-organized, multifunctional, religious centre. The various religious events are splendidly performed. Since the goddess now requires male protection, Śiva has moved in, and a temple has been constructed in his name. To expand the sacred area on the divine level too, the goddess is linked to other deities, such as Jagannātha/Kṛṣṇa, who is given a place of worship close by. The new sponsors of these multiple religious centres are a financially strong clientele, often actively engaged in politics. Thanks to their generous patronage, Orissa is experiencing a boom in the construction of new temples and the enlargement of existing ones. The increased number of devotees is leading to an expansion of their cults, and new shrines and temples are being set up all over Orissa, side by side with the traditional local divinities. The *yātrās* of these popular deities are becoming events of interest to religious tourism and are carried out on a large scale on festival days.

HISTORICAL DOCUMENTATION

Modern life in India is producing such changes that it is not always easy to imagine the influence and power of the former rulers and their way of life. Documentation of that period is not easy to come by. I have therefore created an extensive documentation of early photographs which can serve as historical documents. Only a few people remember earlier times, when the raja attended the Daśaharā procession in his howdah on the state elephant. Therefore the historical photographs provide a valuable insight into earlier ways of life at the royal capitals and religious events like rituals in honour of the tutelary deity or the Daśaharā festival.[36] Thus they represent a valuable historical source of data for the history of religion.

The aim of the documentation is to demonstrate the socio-political dynamics of the religious worship of tutelary deities at royal capitals in Orissa. Related to local royal cults and patronage, the worship of female deities combines the power of royalty with the power of the ritual ecstatic performance. The ritual worship of goddesses links the experience of a spiritual power with the experience of the secular power of ritual patronage. The history of the goddesses and their popularity reflects the history of local chiefs and the expansion of their political influence right up to the present time.

[36]The historical photography of India has received great attention in recent years; see Dehejia 2000.

REFERENCES

Banerji, R.D. 1928. 'Rajput Origins of Western Orissa', in *Modern Review* 43, 285-329.

Berkemer, G. 1993. *Little Kingdoms in Kalinga: Ideologie, Legitimation und Politik Regionaler Eliten*, Stuttgart: Franz Steiner Verlag.

Cobden Ramsay, L.E.B. 1910. *Feudatory States of Orissa*, Calcutta: The Bengal Secretariat Book Depot (rpt. 1950, 1982).

Das, H.C. 1999. *Sākta Pithas: A Study*, Bhubaneswar: Bharati Prakashan.

Dehejia, Vidya (ed.). 2000. *India Through the Lens: Photography 1840-1911*, Ahmedabad: Mapin and Munich: Prestel.

Deo, P.K. 2000. *Memoirs of a Bygone Era*, Delhi: Minerva Press.

Donaldson, T.E. 1985-7. *Hindu Temple Art of Orissa*, 3 vols., Leiden: E.J. Brill.

Eschmann, A. 1978a. 'Hinduization of Tribal Deities in Orissa: The Śakta and Śaiva Typology', in A. Eschmann, H. Kulke and G.C. Tripathi (eds.), *The Cult of Jagannath and the Regional Tradition of Orissa*, Delhi: Manohar, 79-97.

———1978b. 'Prototypes of the Navakalevara Ritual and Their Relation to the Jagannātha Cult', in A. Eschmann, H. Kulke and G.C. Tripathi (eds.), *The Cult of Jagannath and the Regional Tradition of Orissa*, Delhi: Manohar, 265-83.

Hiṅguḷā Pīṭha Unnayan Pariṣad (ed.). 1998. *Talcher Mā Hiṅguḷā*, Talcher: Gītā Offset Press.

Kulke, H. 1978a. 'Early State Formation and Royal Legitimation in Tribal Areas of Eastern India', in R. Moser and M.K. Gautam (eds.), *Aspects of Tribal Life in South Asia I: Strategy and Survival*, Berne: The University of Berne, Institute of Ethnology, 29-37.

———1978b. 'Jagannātha as the State Deity under the Gajapatis of Orissa', in A. Eschmann, H. Kulke and G.C. Tripathi (eds.), *The Cult of Jagannath and the Regional Tradition of Orissa*, Delhi: Manohar, 199-208.

———1992. 'Tribal Deities at Princely Courts: The Feudatory Rajas of Central Orissa and their Tutelary Deities', in S. Mahapatra (ed.), *The Realm of the Sacred: Verbal Symbolism and Ritual Structures*, Calcutta: Oxford University Press, 56-78.

———1993a. 'Legitimation and Town Planning in the Feudatory States of Central Orissa', in H. Kulke, *Kings and Cults*, Delhi: Manohar, 93-113.

———1993b. 'Kṣatriyaization and Social Change: A Study in the Orissa Setting', in idem, *Kings and Cults*, Delhi: Manohar, 82-92.

Mallebrein, C. 1993. *Die Anderen Götter: Volks- und Stammesbronzen aus Indien*, Cologne: Rautenstrauch-Joest-Museum and Heidelberg: Edition Braus.

———1996. 'Danteśvarī, the Family Goddess (kulasvāminī) of the Rājas of Bastar, and the Daśaharā Festival of Jagdalpur', in A. Michaels, C. Vogelsanger and A. Wilke (eds.), *Wild Goddesses in India and Nepal*, Berne: Peter Lang, 483-511.

———1998. *Darshan: Blickkontakte mit indischen Göttern: Die ländliche und tribale Tradition*, Berlin: State Museum of Ethnography.

———1999. 'Tribal and Local Deities: Assimilations and Transformations', in V. Dehejia (ed.), *Devi: The Great Goddess: Female Divinity in South Asian Art*, Washington: A. Sackler Gallery, 137-56.

———2004a. 'Ruler, Protector and Healer: The Clan Gods Sulia, Patkhanda and Sikerpat of the Kondh Tribe', in C. Mallebrein and L.J. Guzy (eds.), *Facets of Orissan Studies*. Special Issue of *Journal of Social Sciences* 8, 2, 143-53.

———2004b. 'Creating a Kshetra: Goddess Tarini of Ghatgaon and her Development from a Forest Goddess to a Pan-Orissan Deity', in idem, *Facets of Orissan Studies*, Special Issue of *Journal of Social Sciences* 8, 2, 155-65.

———2004c. 'Entering the Realm of Durgā: Pāṭkhaṇḍā, a Hinduized Tribal Deity', in A. Malinar, J. Beltz and H. Frese (eds.), *Text and Context in the History, Literature and Religion of Orissa*, Delhi: Manohar, 273-305.

———2006. 'Maṇikeśvarī and Ḍokrī: Changing Representations of two Tribal Goddesses and the Dynastic Histories of Orissa', in A. Malinar (ed.), *Time in India: Concepts and Practices*, Delhi: Manohar, 209-41.

———2007. 'When the Buffalo Becomes a Pumpkin: The Animal Sacrifice Contested', in

G. Pfeffer (ed.), *Periphery and Centre: Groups, Categories and Values*, Delhi: Manohar, 443-72.

Mishra, Madan Mohan 1974. 'Data on the Ex-State of Keonjhar: Its History, Religious Institutions, Legends, and Rituals Performed in the Royal Palace', Keonjhar (manuscript).

Pasayat, C. 1997. 'Tribal-Non-Tribal Interaction in Orissa: A Study of Samalei/Samaleswari Devi in Sambalpur', in G. Pfeffer and D.K. Behera (eds.), *Contemporary Society: Tribal Studies*, vol. 2, Delhi: Concept, 304-16.

———1998. *Tribe, Caste and Folk Culture*, Jaipur/Delhi: Rawat.

Samal, J.K. 1988. *Princely States of Orissa (1905-1947)*, Allahabad: Vohra.

Singh Deo, J.P. 2001. *Tantric Art of Orissa*, Delhi: Kalpaz.

Sinha, S. 1962. 'State Formation and Rajput Myth in Tribal Central India', in *Man in India*, 42, 1, 35-80.

Skoda, U. 2003. 'On a Tribal Frontier: Aghria-Gauntia as Village Kings', in G. Berkemer and M. Frenz (eds.), *Sharing Sovereignty: The Little Kingdom in South Asia*, Berlin: Klaus Schwarz.

———2005. *The Aghria: A Peasant Caste on a Tribal Frontier*, Delhi: Manohar.

Schnepel, B. 1993. 'Die Schutzgöttinnen: Tribale Gottheiten in Südorissa (Indien) und ihre Patronage durch hinduistische Kleinkönige', in *Anthropos* 88, 337-50.

———2002. *The Jungle Kings: Ethnohistorical Aspects of Politics and Ritual in Orissa*, Delhi: Manohar.

Sundar, N. 1997. *Subalterns and Sovereigns: An Anthropological History of Bastar, 1854-1996*, Delhi: Oxford University Press.

Fig. 12.1: The Chattra of Bhagavati at Banpur

Fig. 12.2: Dokri-Manikesvari of Rampur

Fig. 12.3: Birijal Birajalmala

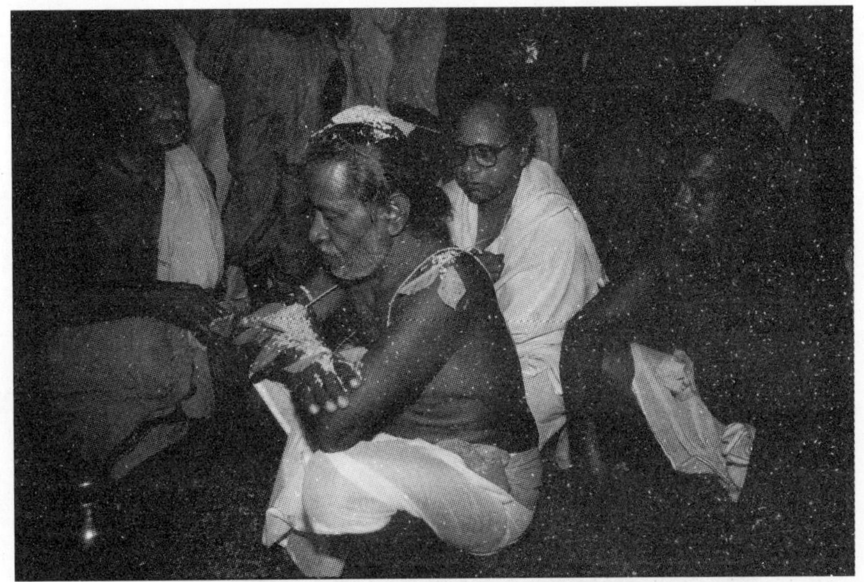

Fig. 12.4: Dehuri of Hingula-Talcher

Fig. 12.5: Manikaesvari in Parlakhemundi Palace

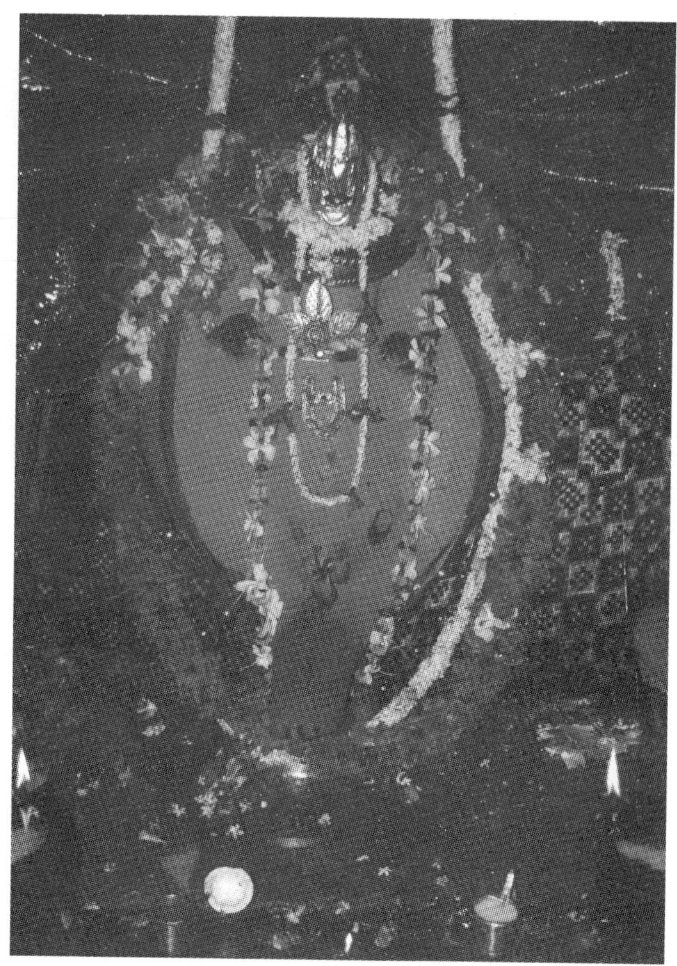

Fig. 12.6: Samalesvari at Sambalpur

Fig. 12.7: Raja's Palace at Kalahandi

CHAPTER 13

Sitting on the Tribal Chief's Lap: Coronation Rituals in Ex-Princely States of Orissa

CORNELIA MALLEBREIN

The peculiar coronation tradition of a future raja sitting on the lap of a tribal chief who is installing him as a ruler attracted the attention of British colonial writers from the nineteenth and early twentieth centuries,[1] such as Elliot, Dalton, Roy and Cobden Ramsay,[2] and found a place in their reports on the royal families of these former feudatory states.[3] In searching for the real origins of Indian rulers, this ritual stimulated their interest. They read it in two ways. One was as a visible demonstration of the power of the dominant tribes, who in these states were the real owners of the land,[4] and as demonstrating the interdependence between the raja and the tribal chiefs. Secondly, it was seen as indicating the possible tribal origin of the kings themselves.[5]

The rajas on their side tried to eradicate any indication of a possible tribal origin by demonstrating excessive pomp and splendour and maintaining glorious genealogies. Referring to their genealogical narrative texts (*rājavaṃśāvalī*), they claimed to be the legitimate rulers and descendants of famous and powerful Rajput clans, originally descended from either the sun or the moon.[6] In their

[1]The present chapter forms part of a wider study of Hinduized tribal deities at royal courts in Orissa, which is being supported by the German Research Council (DFG) within the Orissa Research Programme (ORP). I would like to thank the DFG for making this research possible.

[2]Elliot 1856, 479; Dalton 1872, 145ff; Roy 1935, 199ff; Cobden Ramsay 1950, 45.

[3]On the history of the princely states in Orissa, see Sahu 1993, Patnaik 1988.

[4]See Dalton 1872, 140: 'They [Bhuiya] are the earliest known settlers in parts of Singhbhum, Ganpur, Bonai, Keonjhar and Bamra. The chiefs of these estates now call themselves Rajputs. . . . The country for the most part belongs to the Bhuiya sub-proprietors. They are a privileged class, holding as hereditaments the principal offices of the state and are organized as a body of militia. The chiefs have no right to exercise any authority till they have received the "*tilak*" or token of investiture, from their powerful Bhuiya vassals. Their position altogether renders their claim to be considered Rajputs extremely doubtful. . . . They were no doubt all Bhuiya originally; they certainly do not look like Rajputs.'

[5]See Roy 1935, 6: 'But the physical characteristics are all alike Dravidian, and in Captain Brown's time (1772-8) the Chiefs never thought of claiming to be other than Bhuiya.'

[6]Cf. Inden 1998, 46, on this idea. Schnepel (2002, 155-7) discusses the term 'Rajput'

family histories, their relationship with the tribes was clearly defined. They were not intruders from outside who captured rule by force; on the contrary, the different tribal clans were not in a position to govern themselves, so, being in need of a strong hand, they sought a future king from among the Kshatriya caste. To obtain such a powerful ruler, they did not hesitate to steal a child from a Kshatriya family. In proclaiming the need of the tribes for a strong ruler from outside, the kings received support from the Brahmanical court historians, who defined a kingdom, the duties of a king (*rājadharma*),[7] and his relationship to his subjects in accordance with the old Hindu scriptures on royal kingship like the Dharmaśāstra.[8] They took the view that the egalitarian tribal society and its traditional tribal chieftainship represented nothing less than anarchy, leading to chaos and constant fighting.[9] Only a Hindu king with Kshatriya blood, it was claimed, could protect the people by maintaining the moral order or *dharma*, as well as the order of the world and even the whole universe. In short, he represents the *rājadharma*.[10] It was at the coronation ritual, the *rājyābhiṣeka* performed by the Brahmans, that this idea of a king as a god—as a microcosm of the Cosmic Man and thus the *axis mundi*, the centre of his kingdom and the microcosm of the world—received its visible expression.[11] This Brahmanical view of the king as the 'lord' or 'master' of the earth, with his people being his 'dependents', and the Brahmanical self-perception that the Brahmans are the 'gods' on earth (*bhū-deva*) elicited a response from the tribes, who, to counterbalance this view, insisted on the performance of their own installation ritual in their own traditional tribal manner. They made it clear that only after legitimation of the king by themselves could the royal accession be completed. The rajas, however, were ambivalent about being crowned in this way by a tribal chief. They were aware that the intention of this ritual was a visible demonstration of the real power in the state, which was actually still a tribal state.

This unique part of the coronation ceremony, when the future raja sits on the lap of a tribal chief, is known from the ex-feudatory states of Kalahandi, Gangpur (Sundergarh), Bonai, Pallahara and Keonjhar, which are dominated by the strong and powerful Kondh, Bhuiyan and Saora tribes, but not from Bamra (Deogarh). The reason is said to have been that the present royal family was brought to the area by two tribal chiefs, one each from the Bhuiyan and Kondh tribes, and he can sit only on one lap.

---

in connection with the Jeypore royal family. According to him the question is not whether the Jeypore kings were 'true' or 'pseudo' Rajputs, but whether their 'Rajputish-ness' was based on 'blood' or merit. 'Rajput' was a generic title for a number of relatively open groups originating in military service (and reputation). Cf. also Banerjee 1928.

[7]Cf. Derrett 1976.

[8]Kane 1946, vol. 3, 1-103 (*Rājadharma*); Kotani 1999, 239.

[9]On the traditional Bhuiyan form of chieftainship, the role of the headmen and the great meetings of tribal chiefs (*gāddi*), cf. Roy 1935, 101.

[10]On this topic, cf. Heesterman 1998.

[11]Cf. Inden 1998.

In the context of my research project on Hinduized tribal deities at royal centres in Orissa, I carried out fieldwork between 2002 and 2004 in Sundergarh, Bonai, Deogarh, Pallahara, Kalahandi and Keonjhar. Members of the present royal families kindly described to me their past and present coronation traditions. To provide additional information, members of those tribal chief families who traditionally perform the coronation ritual at the royal court were also interviewed. In this way, I collected a body of quite heterogeneous information on the meaning and importance of this ritual, both formerly and today. It has to be borne in mind, however, that in most cases, the people I questioned had never personally witnessed a coronation ritual, but referred instead to what they had heard about this tradition as performed in the times of their fathers or grandfathers. The only informant who personally underwent a consecration ritual was Rajasaheb Kadamba Keshari Chandra Deo Deb of Bonai, whose installation ritual took place in 1949. Besides this field data, various reports from the British period and by modern historians like Madan Mohan Mishra have also contributed to this chapter.

The Bhuiyan, who still today are the most powerful and the dominant tribal community in Sundergarh, Deogarh, Bonai, Pallahara and Keonjhar districts, consider themselves to be the original owners of the land, despite having handed it over to the newly selected leader on the condition that 'he look after land and people'. In their eyes, it is only through his legitimation by the tribal chief in a proper coronation ritual that the raja is entitled to rule. Otherwise the Bhuiyan are prepared to fight for their rights, as with the disturbances in Keonjhar in 1868, when the British Government tried to install a new king without the consent of the Bhuiyan leaders.[12]

Although Independence has dissolved the former relationship between the tribes and the raja, the installation ritual is still performed today, though in a changed and very much reduced form, and in private rather than in public. Deprived of its legitimizing function, it is now more of religious and symbolic importance: the rajas' may be struggling for survival and their former splendid palaces are being left to fall into ruin, but even without a kingdom they still enjoy a high social status within local society, being called *rajasaheb* by the people.

[12]The Keonjhar chief Rai Bahadur died without legitimate issue. Dhanurjay, one of his two illegitimate sons by a *phulbihai* (concubine), was placed on the *gaddi* by the *diwan*. The rani of Keonjhar secretly installed the grandson of the raja of Mayurbhanj on the *gaddi*, in which she was supported by the principal leader of the Bhuiyan Ratna Naik. The British Government, however, decided to install Dhanurjay formally on the throne. A dispute arose between the supporters of the rani and the government, culminating in an insurrection by the Bhuiyan and Juang tribes, which was finally suppressed by the aid of British troops and the troops of neighbouring rajas of Bonai, Pal Lahara, Dhenkanal and Mayurbhanj. The installation ceremony of Raja Dhanurjay by the Bhuiyans on 13 February 1868 is reported at length by Dalton, who was present (cf. Dalton 1872, 144-7). On the rebellion in Keonjhar by the hill tribes, see Hunter 1872, vol. 1, 115ff.; Cobden Ramsay 1910, 216-22.

What keeps the coronation tradition alive is the strong relationship between the royal families and the tribal deities, which is based on a deep belief in the power of the latter. As rulers who came from the outside, they accepted the autochthonous tribal deities such as *iṣṭadevatā* and patronized their worship and cult.[13] Indeed, they still believe in the deities' protective power, which they need in their present-day lives and struggles for survival, as well as for their activities in the field of politics, a domain followed by many members of the royal families.

The *iṣṭadevī* of the leader of the major tribal group plays a central role in the coronation ritual. After the future raja has taken his seat on the chief's lap, he marks a sign (*ṭikkā*) on his forehead with *sindūr* taken from the mūrti of the *iṣṭadevī*'s main temple (*mūlpiṭh*); the *ṭikkā* thus stands for the divine seal of legitimation. The autochthonous deity of the dominant tribal group invests the new king with the power to rule over her country and her people. Therefore, even today the representatives of the tribes insist on their inherited right to perform this part of the coronation, which demonstrates the raja's acceptance by their goddess, while at the same time recalling their own high status as the former landowners. Thus, the Kondh Pāṭmāji of Merkul reminded the present maharaja of Kalahandi, Udit Pratap Deo, that since the recent death of his father, Pratap Keshari Deo, he has not performed this part of the installation ritual, that is, the official sanction to rule granted by Maṇikeśvarī, the *iṣṭadevī* of the royal family of Kalahandi, as well as by the Kondh Pāṭmāji of Merkul. The rite performed by the tribal chief concluded the coronation. By that time the king had already been installed and crowned in the prestigious Vedic form, and therefore in an elaborate and solemn manner, by the Brahmans.[14]

The photograph albums kept by the royal families also speak to us in a clear language, since they show us what they considered to be important events. Whereas weddings are documented in all their splendour, photographs of coronations are rare, and none of the rituals performed by tribal chiefs have been discovered so far in these albums. Only Bhanga Tribhuvan Deo, the young raja of Bamra, asked a professional photographer to document his pompous investiture durbar in Deogarh in 1936 and its huge gathering of 'Who's Who' in the state.

The representatives of the dominant tribes were perpetually engaged in a struggle with the raja for their recognition and acknowledgement. They considered themselves the real, original owners of the land, and that only their priests 'were able to control the divine power of the powerful and dangerous autochthonous deities'.[15] But the pressure of competition increased with the

[13]Cf. Kulke 1993a, 1992, on this topic.

[14]For a description of the traditional ritual of royal consecration in Orissa, cf. Tripathi 1998.

[15]Still today, in most temples dedicated to a royal *iṣṭadevī* of tribal origins, tribal priests perform the daily rituals. Only during Daśaharā the Brahmans, the Rājpurohits of the raja, are in charge of special rituals. According to Mahapatra (1997, 901-3), the palace fort

great number of immigrant castes and tribes invited into the country by the rajas. Now Brahmans were not only engaged in the important rituals of the palace, the royal court, but they also looked after the numerous newly constructed temples of pan-Indian Hindu deities.[16]

This intermingling of various castes and tribes was an aim of the rajas. In promoting people from outside, the rajas sought to counter the claims to power of the dominant tribes. The deities of the newcomers also acquired their own specific places of worship within the palace grounds, which thus represented a microcosm of the state. The superior power of the autochthonous tribal deities was thus controlled and restricted. Going a step further, the rajas allowed the Brahmans to install their Hindu gods in the temples of the tribal deities, and now Hindu as well as tribal deities are worshipped side by side.[17]

The various and quite heterogeneous family histories and myths of the ex-princely states mirror the political, social and religious roles played by various subregional identities. Within this power play, the decisive role is played by the Brahman genealogists and their capacity for never-ending invention. Tracing this process will form part of this chapter.

THE GENEALOGIES OF THE ROYAL FAMILIES

As already mentioned, the genealogies of the royal families of Bonai, Bamra, Gangpur, Pallahara, Keonjhar and Kalahandi purport to confirm the assumption that, since the tribes are divided among themselves, they are not in any position to rule. Therefore tribal chiefs start searching for a strong ruler, a king, to put an end to the anarchy. This idea of searching for a king from the outside follows

---

housed all the important deities of the state and was guarded by all the important tribes of the state and the royal *iṣṭadevatā* and *rāṣṭradevatā*. All the subdivisions or older chiefdoms and tribes are represented through their deities. 'The primordial sentiments and moral bindings of various chiefdoms, regions, tribes and castes in a princely state were sought to be centred round the royal dynasty, its seat in the palace-fort and in the person of the raja and rani, through the assemblage of gods and goddesses, even aniconic tribal deities, and observances of rituals, cults, and ceremonies. . . .'

[16]On this topic, cf. Mahapatra (1997, 911): 'Induction of several Hindu castes and especially the Brahman priest and pandits along with other service castes like barber, cowherd, watermen and washermen, was necessary to make the princely state function like a Hindu rashtra, and not as a tribal kingdom of the ancient past. If the ruling family was actually derived from some tribal group and if the royal family or the palace rituals depended on the tribal priests, this came in direct conflict with the royal ambitions for Kshatriya status or Rajput affiliation. Hence, the founding of numerous Brahman shasans or agrahar villages, Brahmanization of the deities and goddesses from tribal into shastric, building of temples with Brahmanic rituals and Brahman priests. . . . Sanskritization of their family customs and rituals. . . . The processes aimed at raising the social status of the raja, his family, and other royal descendants much higher above the lowly status of the common subjects and of course, above the "primitive" adivasi subjects.'

[17]Cf. Kulke 1993.

the Hindu model in similar situations:[18] the 'characteristics' (*lakṣaṇa*) of a proper king are then recounted and the 'dignitaries of the country' (*rāṣṭra-mukhya*) enjoined to select and welcome (*varaṇa*) a man who appears to have these characteristics.

That a kingless country (*arājaka*) comes to ruin is an old belief, which was already expressed in the *Mahābhārata*,[19] and one may assume that the genealogists at the royal court were well acquainted with it. Indeed, this statement might have been a source of inspiration for them in composing it. It is significant that the different versions of the migration myths of the royal family's legends of migration resemble one another. According to the *Mahābhārata*, the most desirable thing for a state is to crown a king, for in a kingless country there is no *dharma*, nor any security of life or property. A state is not a state without a king, and only anarchy will result if it does not have one. People living in the *arājaka*[20] fall into ruin by attacking each other because they lack a king. Therefore they seek a king for their own protection, as well as to create the state and its welfare. They appeal to Brahmā, the creator, to appoint a ruler whom they will all honour and who will protect them. Manu is selected as the king, though he only agrees after a lot of persuasion.

This story therefore proclaims the first kingship to have been a divine institution created by the god Brahmā himself and asserts the necessity of a mutual agreement between king and people—the king had to be persuaded to accept to rule, but finally agreed. This seems to be an ideal concept which ambitious 'jungle kings' used to legitimize their rule, not only towards their subjects, who were mainly members of different tribes, but also towards the new colonial power intruding from the outside, since it justified their existence.

How the court poets formulated these migration myths by blending together local tribal ideas with Hindu concepts can be seen by examining the origin myth of the royal family of Bonai. This family has until today maintained a very close relationship with the Bhuiyan tribe, the main tribe of their area, and it is still the Bhuiyan Sāmanto from Kaleiposh who traditionally performs the coronation ritual of the future king. I shall now examine more closely two of the traditional Bhuiyan myths that explain the origin of the close relationship between the Bhuiyan, the peacock and the Kadamba tree,[21] the royal symbols of the present royal family.[22]

According to Bhuiyan myths, the Bhuiyan were originally all of royal blood.

[18] *Viṣṇudharmottara-purāṇa* (VDhP); cf. Inden 1998, 59.

[19] For an examination of the theories of origin of kingship in the *Mahābhārata*, *Śānti Parva*, Chaps. 59 and 67, cf. Kane 1946, vol. 3 (*Rājadharma*), 33-4.

[20] On the term *arājaka*, cf. Kane 1946, vol. 3, 30; it means a situation in which there is no king and no ruler.

[21] *Neolamarckia cadamba* (ex *Nauclea cadamba*, Roxb. = *Anthocephalus cadamba*, Miq.), a very large flowering tree [add. the editors].

[22] On the Pauri Bhuiyan and their legends, see Patnaik (et al.) 1979-80, 2-5.

However, thanks to an asura's seven clever daughters, they became polluted. While out hunting one day, the seven royal brothers saw beautiful naked girls and were attracted to them not realizing that they were the daughters of a demon. Until then, the Bhuiyan brothers had followed strict rules of austerity, refraining from drinking any liquor or eating fowl or pork. The girls' aim was to pollute the brothers, thus degrading them from their social status and then being able to marry them. They served them cooked rice which concealed chicken curry, thus making the brothers impure. Only the younger brother, who arrived a little later, tried to escape, but the demon girls followed the hoof prints of his horse. To save him, a peacock wiped out the hoof marks with its legs. The six Bhuiyan brothers married the girls but, being impure, they had to remain in the hills and forests. The pure younger brother was installed as the Bhuiyan's king, and because his life was saved by a peacock, he ordered that no one should kill it.

The next myth explains the close relationship between the Bhuiyan and the Kadamba tree. The seven brothers once quarrelled about who should sit on the throne, finally deciding that it should be the brother who could shoot an owl sitting on a Kadamba tree with a single shot. The first six brothers all missed, but the youngest was successful. Now king, he called himself 'Kadam Kesari' after the tree, while the six other brothers continued to call themselves 'Bhuiyan'. The name 'Kadam Kesari' is still used within the royal family, and the name of the present raja of Bonai is 'Kadam Kesari Deo'.

The compositions of the royal family's genealogists also include the peacock and the Kadamba tree in their story of migration, but in a quite different way. Several versions exist. According to Cobden Ramsay,[23] the Bonai family came from Sakaldwip or Ceylon; the founder of the family was abandoned by his mother under a Kadamba tree and was on the point of falling into the hands of the enemy when a peacock rescued him by swallowing him and keeping him in its craw until the danger had passed. In gratitude for this service, the boy, who later became king, adopted the peacock as his family's emblem. Referring to the Kadamba tree, the chiefs describe themselves as 'Kadamba-Vaṇśī Rajputs'.

In another version, the first king came voluntarily, by chance, and the local god Baneśvar predicted supremacy for him if he joined up with a local chief.[24] According to this story, the previous name of Bonaigarh was Shronitanagar. The first Kshatriya king was Pratap Deo from the island of Singhal.[25] With his seven brothers, he went to Orissa to visit Lord Jagannāth. To save having to pay the usual fee for visiting the temple, they tried to enter it forcibly. But the Gajapati of Puri placed a sharp-edged saw blade (*karata*) across the way

[23] Cf. Cobden Ramsay 1910, 143-4.

[24] I am grateful to Uwe Skoda, who is writing a monograph on the royal family of Bonai, for his valuable information. The present version is only a summary of the family history.

[25] Identified as Sri Lanka.

to the sanctum. Four brothers were killed while trying to cross this blade. Of the three remaining, two went to Singhbhum, while Pratap Deo came to the deeply forested Bonai region. He was told that the state belonged to the Banāsura demon who worshipped Baneśvar Śiva near the Brahmani River. Pratap Deo went to worship him. The local chiefs, Mahabira, Bira, Hamira, Necha Keuta and Leda Kamar, who came to know about the foreigner, decided to kill him. When Pratap Deo came out of Baneśvar's temple next morning, he saw them ready with their weapons. He escaped and found refuge in a hollow Kadamba tree. To save his life, a peacock wiped out his footprints with its tail. The same night Baneśvar appeared to Pratap Deo in a dream and told him that he would become king of the area. He was told that he should join up with the first person he met next morning, and together they were to kill all the local rulers. Next morning Kalei Kisan, the Bhuiyan ruler of Kaleiposh, sent a member of his family, called Lechada, to visit Baneśvar's temple. On his way he met Pratap Deo bathing in the Brahmani River. They became friends and together decided to kill the local chiefs Hamira, Mahabir, Bira, Lecha Keuta, Leda Kamar and Kahiru. After having killed them, Kalei Kisan of Kaleiposh performed the royal consecration (*rājābhiṣeka*) of Pratap Deo. An umbrella (*chhatā*) was offered to Baneśvar, and the new Raja Pratap Deo made the Bhuiyan Lechada his Sāmanta.

A further variation of the mythical story concerns the present raja of Bonai. It differs in some points, but here too Baneśvar orders the first ruler to join with a local person and to kill the other chiefs.[26] According to the raja, his family is descended from a Rajput family in Rajasthan. The seven brothers went to Puri. On their way back they parted, three of them passing through the Bonai area. They took refuge in a Kadamba tree from dangerous enemies who tried to kill them. One brother, Pratap Varaha, was advised by Baneśvar to make friends with everyone who came into his temple in order to make himself a ruler. Accordingly he met the chief of a Bhuiyan clan, Indra Sāmanto, from Kaleiposh village. During that time, the area was divided into seven small chiefdoms and split into two warring groups. The Bhuiyan Indra Sāmanto asked Pratap Varaha to help him subdue the chiefs of the two groups, whose leaders belonged to various other tribes (Ho, Kolha, Kisan) and castes (potter, fisherman, blacksmith). But this war was not without its consequences, because the chiefs uttered a curse on the later royal family, which has remained in force until today. In the meantime, the other brothers left to look for Brahmans. As this took a very long time, the Bhuiyan chief installed Pratap Varaha as raja, with the blessing of Lord Baneśvar Śiva. Later the brothers returned with the Brahmans and were asked to remain in the country. Because they had taken refuge in a Kadamba tree, the dynasty was called 'Kadamba'. Thanks to the

[26]I would like to thank Rajasaheb Kadam Keshari Chandra Deo Deb of Bonai and his son Bir Keshari for their support in obtaining information about the coronation ritual in Bonai.

peacock's help, their throne became Mayursiṃhāsan, and the peacock became the state symbol.

In former times the Sāmanto from Kaleiposh, whose ancestors once joined hands with Pratap Varaha to kill all their rivals, played the central role in the coronation ritual. The future king sat on his lap, as will be discussed in the next section.

These examples show how the court genealogists use parts of tribal myths, like those relating to the Kadamba tree and the peacock, to create their own myth of legitimacy justifying the rule of the present king. The idea that the various tribal clans are unable to rule and therefore need the strong hand of a Kshatriya, if possible one from Rajasthan, is also the basic message in the origin myth of the royal family of Bamra.

THE ORAL HISTORY OF THE ROYAL FAMILY OF BAMRA

In contrast to Bonai, no local god is involved in the selection of the new ruler in Bamra. According to local oral history, the dominant tribes of this area, the Kondh, Bhuiyan and Gond, had no proper leader and constantly quarrelled among themselves.[27] Finally, Kanto Bhuiyan and Suna Kondh went in search of a strong ruler. They came to Patnagarh, once the stronghold of the powerful Gaṅga kings, but at that time the Chauhan Ramai Deo had had all the members of the former Gaṅga dynasty killed. Kanto Bhuiyan and Suna Kondh stole the child of the murdered Gaṅga king from the main wife, the *pāṭrāṇī*.[28] But the treacherous Chauhan followed them, so to save the child's life they hid him on top of a Char tree (*Buchanania lanzan*). The Chauhan questioned the Bhuiyan and Kondh about his whereabouts, but being quite bright, they answered: 'He is not with us either in the sky, in heaven or on the ground', thus not disobeying the tribal prescription not to tell lies. After reaching the village of Titlipada, they went to a rock on which was a wonderful Sar tree (*Saraca indica*, the Asoka tree). Under this tree the Gaṅga prince was crowned, in whose memory he received the name Saraju Dev. Because the Bamra were tribes living wild in nature, they had only the bark of a tree to bind around the prince's head like a turban. Being poor, they had nothing more to offer than the soil of Bamra, which they gave him, saying: 'From now on you shall be our leader'. Until recently they brought a handful of Bamra soil to the king during Daśaharā as an offering.[29]

One difference in this story from other examples is that the ritual of sitting on the lap of a tribal chief is not performed in Bamra, as the raja cannot sit on

[27] I am grateful to Kesri Gang Deb, Prasun Gang Deb and Nitish Gang Deb for their valuable information on the royal family of Bamra.

[28] According to one tradition, the boy escaped and wandered homeless. He voluntarily went with the Bhuiyan and Kondh chiefs to the Bamra area.

[29] To make an oath with earth or by touching earth is an old tribal tradition; cf. Roy 1935, 87.

the laps of two tribal chiefs simultaneously. Today the *rajaguru* plays the main role in the coronation ritual.

THE COURT HISTORY OF THE ROYAL FAMILY OF GANGPUR

In Gangpur, it is a blind Brahman who prophesies supremacy and a deity who confirms this in a miracle. The family chronicle of the Gangpur royal family also states, like the previous ones, that, since the various tribal groups were once unable to rule the country and the different Bhuiyan clans were constantly fighting, a new form of rule was needed.

As the history of the Sundergarh region and the rulers of the Kesari and Śekhar dynasties are discussed in detail by C.P. Nanda,[30] I shall merely summarize the history of the Gangpur Śekhar family given to me by Kashinath Sekhar Deo.[31] The family claims descent from the Parmar clans of the Rajputs of Ujjain, whose founder, Vikramaditya, also founded the Samvat Era.[32] The present line of chiefs belongs to the Parmar Kshatriya branch of Dhar in Ujjain.[33] Two brothers once migrated to Panchakot Kashipur in Manbhum (West Bengal). There the younger, Gangadhar, fought with his brother, left home, and went towards Suruguja in search of a country to rule. There he met a blind Brahman, who prophesied that he would be a raja. Gangadhar told the Brahman that if he became a raja, he would allow the Brahman and his descendants to sit on his *gaddi* (throne) for two hours every year.[34] The Brahman accompanied the raja. When they arrived, the powerful and very influential Bhuiyan leader, Madan Pradhan had the family of the previous Kesari rulers killed. Thus the Bhuiyan leaders of various principalities were involved in constant fights. One reason for this was their traditional system of choosing a ruler, who was not selected according to his ability but through the actions of a lemon placed in the middle of the group of clan leaders: the lemon moved among them, and the one it touched was chosen as the new king. Therefore a new form of rule was needed. The Rajput Gangadhar joined hands with the dominant Bhuiyan chief of Sargipalli, and they started to subdue the others. They won the struggle and the outsider Gangadhar became their king. The Māji of Sargipalli placed the vermilion mark, the sign of royalty, on his forehead. In the meantime, the elder brother came from Panchkot in search of

[30]Cf. Nanda in the present volume.

[31]I would like to thank Kashinath Sekhar Deo for his information on the history of the Sekhar family.

[32]Some historical data is mixed up in this genealogy. Vikramaditya of Ujjain is said to have founded the Vikrama Era of 58 BCE. The Samvat Era refers to the Śaka Era of CE 78.

[33]An ancient town called Dhar served between the ninth and fourteenth centuries as the capital of the Paramāra Rājputs.

[34]This ritual function was observed by the royal family on the Vijayadaśamī day. The blind Brahman received the village of Ekma for his maintenance. His descendants are still the Rājpurohits of the royal family.

Gangadhar. The Bhuiyan zamindars of Sargipalli concealed Gangadhar on a platform floating in the middle of a tank near Masabira village. When they were asked by Gangadhar's brother where he was, they answered obliquely, 'We have not kept him in the air, heaven or earth', again in order not to lie. Then the delegation left and the Bhuiyan decided to make Gangadhar their king, but he refused, saying, 'It is god's wish whether I shall be your king'. He placed a bamboo stick, which he had brought along with him, in the earth, saying: 'If this bamboo grows branches by tomorrow, I shall be your king'. The next morning the bamboo had reached a height of 21 feet and had grown like a *chhatā*, thus providing the future king with shade.[35] He was installed as king by the Māji of Sargipalli, who placed the *ṭikkā*, the vermilion mark, on his forehead as sign of royalty. All the villages were given to him. The Bhuiyan zamindars received several parganas in return. Masabira became the first capital of Gangpur State. It is the Sargipalli zamindar who takes the future raja on his lap and places the *sindūr ṭikkā* on his forehead.

THE COURT HISTORY OF THE ROYAL FAMILY OF PALLAHARA

In Pallahara, as in Bamra, no god is involved in the selection of the ruler. Here too one can discern the imaginative abilities of the court genealogists, who use the motif of a kidnapped child.[36] According to this history, the family came from north India and trace their origin back to the famous dynasty of Anang Pal, the last king of Delhi. He had no male issue, so his nephew forcibly assumed rule. The former king went to Puri on a pilgrimage. Two of his five wives accompanied him, and on the way they both became pregnant and gave birth to sons. During this period the Savaras (Sora) were ruling the area of Pallahara State, but they were in constant conflict with each other. Traditionally there was no ruler over all the clan leaders, so for some years they declared a wooden pole to be their leader. After some more years they gathered to renew the wooden pole as ruler. But one day they decided to cut the pole down as

[35]The bamboo is worshipped as *Chhatāpati* (*Chhatā Bautī*) in the Bhuiyan village of Demul, where this goddess has a shrine. Her worship takes place in the month of Caitra. It is said that before the approaching death of a raja, a miracle appears in Masabira. People see a bamboo whose twigs are growing in the shape of an umbrella. This miracle happened in 1967, before the death of the late Udit Pratap Sekhar Deo. The bamboo was then cut into three pieces, two parts being used to hold the *chhatā* for Kālī and Saṃleī. The remaining part was used to hold the *chhatā* of the new ruler. According to C.P. Nanda, Kapila Keshari, a king belonging to the dynasty that ruled this area before the Sekhar Rajputs, had already had a dream in which the presiding deity of Gangpur told him that a bamboo would bear flowers in the Masabira hillock and he would be the king of that region. He became king in CE 1135.

[36]I am grateful to Rajasaheb Ram Chandra Pal of Pallahara, who provided me with this information about the history of his family, and Guru Charan Boita, from the village of Tambur, the present Savara raja, for his valuable information. On Pal Lahara, cf. Cobden Ramsay 1910, 275ff.

there was no peace. This was done by a Savara, who cut the pole into several pieces, which resulted in streams of blood flowing out. So the people demanded a new, strong ruler, and they ordered the Savara to search for one. During the search, in one village they found Sulepal, a small boy, sleeping on a heap of straw. His mother was wandering around with a group of village actors. They realized that she was a princess and one of the wives of King Anang Pal, who had taken refuge with the Gypsy people to save her son's life. The younger wife who had also given birth to a son and demanded of her husband that her son should become king. In pursuit of this plan, she tried to kill the son of her older rival. To get hold of Sulepal, the Savaras decided to poison the wandering troupe, in this way managing to kidnap him. In memory of the fact that he was found sleeping on a heap of straw, the dynasty received the title 'Pala'.

THE COURT HISTORY OF KEONJHAR

According to local tradition, the Bhuiyan of the region of Keonjhar decided to have their own ruler, who would remain in their area. They stole Jyoti Bhanja, one of the two sons of King Jai Singh, the ruling family of Mayurbhanj, and made him their king. The Bhuiyan still play a central role in the coronation ritual today.[37]

THE COURT HISTORY OF KALAHANDI

According to the family tradition, the dependency of Kalahandi formerly belonged to a family of Gaṅgavaṃśī Rajputs. Here no tribes are involved; the selection goes back to an internal family decision. The last member of this royal line, Jagannath Deva, had no male issue. In CE 1008 he gave his daughter in marriage to Raghunath Sai Deva, the younger brother of the then raja of Shatranjigarh in Chhota Nagpur. Raghunath Sai Deva was a Nāgvaṃśī Rajput; he started the line of the present family.[38]

However, the Kondh Pāṭmāji of Merkul has his own tribal Kondh version, one which makes the tribes responsible for the selection. According to him, a long time ago the different Kondh clans were quarrelling among themselves. They decided to have their own ruler,[39] and they chose an ancestor of the present royal family of Kalahandi as their first king. The first fort of their new ruler was located high up in the mountains, at a place called Salapgarh. Later the ruler moved his fort down to the plains, to Jugsaipatna, where a temple

[37]For a discussion of the early history of Keonjhar, cf. Cobden Ramsay 1910, 212-14; Senapati 1986 (Kendujhar), 44-5.

[38]I am grateful to the present maharaja, Udit Pratap Deo, for his information on his family's traditions and his support in my fieldwork in his area; cf. also Mahapatra 1982.

[39]There are various opinions about the origin of the first ruler of the present royal family. Some Kondh informants are of the opinion that the first ruler was a member of the Kondh tribe who belonged to one Nāga (*Nāgvaṃśī*) clan, while others say that he was a wandering strong hero, a Kshatriya, whom they had chosen as their leader.

was constructed for Maṇikeśvarī, the tutelary goddess of the Kondh Pāṭmāji and the royal family. At Jugsaipatna there is also the ancestor stone, where the installation rituals were performed. Since the Kondh played a dominant role, the new raja also has to marry a Kondh girl.

THE CORONATION RITUALS OF VARIOUS ROYAL FAMILIES

The following section examines the installation ceremonies of the ex-feudatory states of Bonai, Bamra, Gangpur, Keonjhar, Kalahandi and Pallahara. How is the coronation ritual of sitting on a tribal chief's lap related to the family histories (*rājavaṃśāvalī*) discussed earlier?

All these histories contain one crucial aspect: the ruler did not forcibly take over rule, but came as the saviour of quarrelling tribes, thus bringing unity and peace to the area. The court histories of these royal families deny the tribes any ability to rule their own country, even though it is where they claim ownership rights. It may be assumed that this ascribed incompetence is not easy to accept for freedom-loving, proud tribal groups, which the Kondh and Bhuiyan are considered to be. Thus one may conclude that their role in the coronation ritual was a sort of concession made to give them particular importance and to acknowledge their traditional place as the original owners of the land. Thus the coronation ritual was a balancing act between, on the one hand the raja, who claimed to be the ruler of the area and its people, and on the other the various tribal groups and clans, who were well aware of the real ownership of the country and of their own power. Accordingly the raja tried to minimize their role in the coronation rituals, as was already observed by British writers of the early-nineteenth century. Today this tradition has been given up or is simply retained as a sort of reminiscence of the good old days.

There are only a few old reports about the coronation rituals in Bonai, Keonjhar and Kalahandi, provided by Elliot (1856), Dalton (1872) and Roy (1935) respectively. It is the ritual of sitting on a tribal chief's lap that attracted their attention. The *rajaguru* of Keonjhar, Madan Mohan Mishra (1974), describes the coronation ritual in Keonjhar of the last king Nrusingha Narayan Bhanj, the son of Raja Balabhadra Narayan Bhanja. P.K. Deo, the late maharaja of Kalahandi, refers in a short chapter to his investiture ceremony at Jugasaipatnam on 16 March 1940.

THE BRAHMANICAL VERSION OF THE CORONATION

The various rituals of royal consecration and enthronement differ with the various royal families,[40] each of which has its own traditions. But they agree

[40]The present-day rituals performed by Brahmans in Orissa are short versions of the elaborate descriptions given in the traditional literature. On the various coronation rituals, see Drekmeier 1962, Gonda 1966, Kane 1946, vol. 3, 73, Heesterman 1957, Schlerath 1960, Inden 1998.

on one point, that sitting on a tribal chief's lap follows the royal *abhiṣeka* performed by the court Brahmans.

One example of a Brahmanical royal consecration once performed in Orissa is described in the old palm-leaf manuscript, *Rājyābhiṣekavidhi*, which is presented here in abridged form in order to provide an insight into a traditional accession ritual.[41] The coronation of a king should take place in the open, in full view of the people. A pavilion (*maṇḍapa*) is erected. First the metal statues of the deities are worshipped. Then the king expresses his desire to perform the religious rite of *abhiṣeka* through the ācārya and the priests. This is followed by the elaborate worship of Lakṣmī and Nārāyaṇa. To the figure of Lakṣmī-Nārāyaṇa is added an image of the Goddess Durgā, made of solid gold (Kanaka Durgā), who is worshipped to ward off and conquer the king's enemies. This is followed by the actual bathing ceremony: the royal couple is bathed eight times, with eight different varieties of water. The first bathing is performed with the water containing some soil of the land on which the king has to rule. After the ceremonial bath, the king and his consort change their clothes, put on new silken garments, and crowns are placed on their heads. These golden crowns are wrapped in a garland of flowers. Then the priest starts the rite of the *siṃhāsana pūjā*, that is, the worship of royal throne, which consists of making obeisance to the lowest base of the throne, which is also the base of the earth. Then the ācārya worships the earth as a goddess. After reciting a *mantra* on Viṣṇu, the king steps on to the throne with the queen at his side. The *mantra*s are recited for the purpose of infusing the king with the holy splendour of Brahman (spirituality). Now endowed with Brahmanic spirituality, he is finally able to rule his kingdom properly. He is then endowed with the royal insignia and the 'attributes', of which six are most important, namely, the *chatra* (umbrella), *cāmara* (chowrie whisk), *khaḍga* (sword), *carma* (shield), *dhanu* (bow) and *śaras* (arrows). The king also receives the particular emblem of his family and the flag of his state, after which he should be addressed as a raja or 'His Highness' as a full-fledged king.

The aim of the next part of the ceremony is to impart the character of Viṣṇu to the newly consecrated king. This is followed by a 'mantric' *abhiṣeka* with sanctified sacrificial water, with which the king and the queen are sprinkled with the help of a bunch of *kuśa* grass, while uttering Vedic *mantra*s. This turns the king into a *calanti* Viṣṇu. His right arm is separately sprinkled with holy water, and the royal authority (*sāmrājyam*) is transferred to the right hand of the king. Finally the king puts on the royal robe. After this ceremony in the open, the king goes for *darśana* (sight) of the deities in the main temple of his capital. Finally he comes back to the palace, where ladies greet him with a *tilaka*.

According to Inden,[42] the *rājyābhiṣeka* itself is binary in its structure. The first half, the *abhiṣeka* proper, consists of a series of baths in which the king

[41]According to G.C. Tripathi (1998) the manuscript is older than 250 years. He has translated this important work and provided a commentary.

[42]Inden 1998, 61.

is the passive recipient. The second half, which is often referred to as the *paṭṭa-bandha*, that is, the 'fixing' or 'tying on' (*bandha*) of the 'headband' or 'crown' (*paṭṭa*), consists of the crowning, enthronement, and a series of other rites by which the king acts out his royal role.

THE TRIBAL VERSION OF THE CORONATION

The unusual ritual of the future king sitting on the lap of a tribal chief is supplementary to the Brahmanical version described above and is added to the second half of *rājyābhiṣeka*; it therefore takes place in the afternoon and completes the installation ceremonies, which last a whole day.

This rite reflects the claim of the tribes to the inherited right to install the designated raja, just as they did hundreds of years ago during the time of the first ruler.[43] Their former living conditions are reflected in the performance: at that time they lived in the deep jungle. Instead of a wooden throne, and in order to show honour and respect to their chosen king, the tribal chief offered his own body as a throne. From the outset, therefore, the Kshatriya prince is symbolically elevated and endowed with the power to rule. At that time they had nothing more than a tree creeper to bind around their new ruler's head like a crown,[44] and to seal this contract, they made a *tilaka* on his forehead with the soil from their land and another with *sindūr* or blood from the temple of the main local goddess. To enhance his royal status, they endowed him with the insignia of royalty made out of perishable materials. By claiming this right, the tribes made the king understand that he could only be the ruler if he was acknowledged as such by the tribal chiefs, otherwise they would rebel.[45]

How seriously they took their claim is reflected in the fact that only they had the right to bestow the *rājtilaka*, the seal of mutual agreement that empowers the raja to rule, on the new king. In the ex-feudatory state of Kalahandi, this role was that of the Kondh headman (*Pāṭmāji*) of the village of Merkul, as the Kondh formed the strongest tribal group; in Gangpur, Bonai and Keonjhar, it was a headman of the Bhuiyan tribe; in Bamra a Bhuiyan and a Kondh, later replaced by the *rajaguru*; and in Pallahar a Savara (Sora). In Bamra the tribal ritual is no longer performed.

The *sindūr tilaka*, which the tribal chief places on the forehead of the future king, who is sitting on his lap, is of particular importance. It is taken from the *mūrti* of the *iṣṭadevī* of the dominant tribal group, who is often considered tantric. This immense power, which transcends all worldly forms of rule, whether local or from the outside, is still controlled by tribal priests. In Kalahandi the *iṣṭadevī* is Maṇikeśvarī from Jugsaipatna; in Gangpur it is Saṃleī, the *iṣṭadevī* of the Bhuiyan zamindar from Sargipalli; in Bonai it is

[43]Cf. Roy 1935, 119, on the coronation tradition in Keonjhar.

[44]This tradition was alive till recently only in Bonai, Pallahara and Keonjhar. In Kalahandi, Bamra, and Gangpur a silk turban was wrapped around the head of the raja. The members of the other major tribal groups hold royal insignia like *pāṭchhatā* and *cāmara*.

[45]In Kalahandi the new ruler also had to marry a girl from the Kondh tribe.

Kālapāṭ, the *iṣṭadevī* of the Bhuiyan samantā from Kaleiposh; and in Pallahara it is Durgā (Grāmśrī)[46] from Sulepal, the *iṣṭadevī* of the Sawar raja. The royal families of Bamra and Keonjhar are strong followers of Vaishnavism. The *sindūr* of the *tilaka* does not come from the *iṣṭadevī* temple of the tribal chief, but from the shrine of the family goddesses. In Bamra this is Kanaka Durgā, in Keonjhar most probably the shrine of Tāriṇī.

The place where the tribal coronation rituals are performed may be the ancestor stone or throne[47] or the durbar hall of the Rajmahal (Bamra, Gangpur), a hall within the guest house (Bonai), or the Rānī-Mahal (Pallahara, Keonjhar).

Common to all royal families, not only in Orissa but all over India, is the strong belief that the throne should not be vacant even for a minute. As soon as the death of a raja is confirmed, his successor must be installed on the throne. It is a tradition that a future raja is never made impure by the death of his father. The new raja gives the order for the dead body to be removed from the palace through a special gate.[48] The moment the new raja is installed, the late raja's rani becomes a widow. In Bamra, Gangpur and Keonjhar, this installation ritual is performed immediately after the death of the raja; in Bonai and Pallahara conversely, the empty throne is guarded by Bhuiyan soldiers (Bonai) or the soldiers of the Sawar raja (Pallahara).

THE CORONATION RITUAL IN BONAI

In this section, a summarized account of the coronation ritual of Bonaigarh is given. The ritual was performed for the present, fifty-eighth ruler of Bonai.[49]

In Bonai, the *rājtilaka* ceremony takes place on the twelfth day[50] after the former raja has passed away.[51] In the meantime, the throne is guarded by the

[46]Roy (1935) calls her Gāi-śrī. On her importance as a village goddess, cf. 221-4.

[47]In Kalahandi the ritual is performed on the ancestor stone in Jugsaipatna, where the first coronation took place. In Keonjhar the raja takes a seat on the ancestor throne, which is said to contain a *śālagrāma* of the god Viṣṇu.

[48]S.N. Roy (1929) writes a short note on the raja's funeral in the Feudatory State of Orissa.

[49]I would like to thank the present rajasaheb of Bonai, Kadam Keshari Chandra Deo Deb, the Sāmanto of Kaleiposh and Uwe Skoda for their valuable information on these traditions in Bonai.

[50]According to S.C. Roy (1935, 129), the ritual takes place on the sixteenth day.

[51]S.C. Roy (1935, 128-9), who describes the installation ceremony of a raja of Bonai, adds that a new silk turban is placed on the head of the corpse of the deceased raja and than the new raja is crowned with this turban. The ancient sword known as the 'Kumāri Prasād' is also placed in the hands of the new raja. While he is sitting on the throne (*gaddi*), he orders that the corpse be removed. Between the day of the demise of the former raja and the formal *abhiṣeka*, the new raja must live in seclusion, all the time holding a sword in his hand.

Bhuiyan soldiers of the Bhuiyan Sāmanto from Kaleiposh, the only zamindar in the Bonai area, and the first among the tribal leaders.[52]

In the early morning of the twelfth day, the designated raja is carried in a palanquin to the temple of Siva Baneśvar, where he is received with great honours.[53] In the ritual that follows, the god Baneśvar hands over his realm to the new king. The new raja sits opposite Baneśvar, flanked on both sides by a Rājpurohit. Two Bhuiyan Dehuri are also present.[54] Now the new raja is identified with Baneśvar and is therefore addressed as Baneśvar-agrya. At first the offerings are given to Baneśvar and then in the same way to the new raja, and the Rājpurohit ties a turban first on Baneśvar and later the same one on the new raja. The last item that the raja receives from Baneśvar is the white royal umbrella (*pāṭ-chhatā*), which is kept behind Baneśvar. The Bhuiyans have the honour decorating the umbrella with a new layer of white cloth. Now the ceremonial umbrella is held over the king, and everyone stands up. The king addresses the god Baneśvar with the following words: 'By your order the universe functions; please give me your blessings. I swear, O God, that I will administer and look after the people of Bonai on your behalf. Bonai is your country.' This is a clear sign to the Bhuiyan that Baneśvar is handing over his rule to the new king, therefore the Bhuiyan must accept him. Accompanied by music, the raja returns to his palace in a palanquin.

Before the ritual of sitting on the lap of a tribal chief takes place, the Brahmanical *purohit* performs the official *rājā-abhiṣeka* in the jaj mahal.[55] As part of the ritual, the royal sword Pāṭkhaṇḍa is handed to the raja. The Pāṭkhaṇḍa is worshipped only during the *rājā-abhiṣeka* and twice a year on the raja's *pauspūrṇimā-abhiṣeka* and *śrāvaṇa-abhiṣeka*.[56] A sword called Mohana Khaṇḍa is also brought from her shrine, only being worshipped during *rājā-abhiṣeka*. The royal umbrella (*pāṭ-chhatā*) is brought from the Baneśvar temple, and a

[52]The Sāmanto belongs to the Pañcasahakhaṇḍa Bhuiyan, who served as the militia to the king. It is said that the king gave them five hundred swords to assist him in his wars. The Sāmanto belongs to this group. The *iṣṭadevī* is Kālapāṭ. The Sāmanto family gave five hundred villages to the king to rule.

[53]It is said that the Bonai area was ruled by Banāsura, a giant. Everyday he went to Varanasi to worship Kāśī Viśvanāth. When he was old and no longer able to go to Varanasi, he asked Kāśī Viśvanāth to come to his kingdom. The latter agreed to come with Banāsura to the Bonai region, but Banāsura must not look back. Suddenly Banāsura could not hear the sound of the god Śiva any more. He turned back to look, and Kāśī Viśvanāth told him that he would henceforward remain in this place and be worshipped by the name of Baneśvar.

[54]The priests of this temple are still members of the Bhuiyan tribe.

[55]According to Roy (1935, 130), the raja remains all the time seated during the *Hōm* ceremony, armed with five kinds of weapons: the Kumāri Prasād sword, one dagger, one knife, a bow and three arrows.

[56]According to Roy (1935, 130), this is the Pāṭkhaṇḍa, which is said to be the sword with which the first Kadam Bāmṣi raja conquered the country.

small black stone representing the god Rāmchandra, the *iṣṭadeva* of the family, is placed close by.[57]

In the late afternoon, the ritual of sitting on the lap of a tribal chief takes place in the big hall of the guest-house, marking the end of the ceremony. In the centre of the hall a big wooden throne, richly decorated with red velvet and flowers, is set up, and the floor is covered with carpets. Seats are arranged for the Sāmanto of Kaleiposh and the Gond jagirdārs, called Daṇḍapāṭ and Mahāpāṭ. When the raja is led into the hall, everyone stands up; only the Sāmanto remains sitting with a group of Bhuiyan warriors (*pāika*) with their weapons ranged behind him. Then the Sāmanto asks the new raja to sit on his lap.[58] He hands the raja some soil in a leaf, and places a *tilaka* of the soil on the his forehead, followed by a *tilaka* of *sindūr* brought from the temple of Kālapāṭ, the *iṣṭadevī* of the Sāmanto.[59] In this way Kālapāṭ, the real ruler of this region, sanctions the rule of the new king.

After the raja has sat on the lap of the Bhuiyan Sāmanto, the latter guides the new raja to his official throne and addresses him with the following words: 'You are the raja of Bonai from this day onwards'. The raja answers: 'From this day onwards you are my zamindar. I shall give you around thirty villages.' During this ritual conversation, the raja is accompanied on his left by the Pāṭāyat and on his right by the Ṭikkāyat. Then the chief of the Pahudi Bhuiyan takes a holy thread made of a Siali creeper [*Pueraria tuberosa* (Roxb. ex Willd.)] and presents it to the raja. Out of joy, the tribal musicians begin to play their horns and drums, and start moving around the town. After the Sāmanto has declared the new raja the ruler of Bonai region, all the important state officials, like the chief minister of Orissa and the collector, are informed, as is the Government of India in Delhi.

THE CORONATION RITUAL IN KEONJHAR

Of all the coronation rituals of royal families being considered here, it is that of Keonjhar which has attracted the most attention. Information on it comes from Roy, Dalton and M.M. Mishra. By way of a short introduction, Roy's description will be summarized here.[60] A special aspect of the ceremony in Keonjhar is the tradition that a Bhuiyan carries the raja on his shoulders, like a horse. Also at the end of the ceremony, a Bhuiyan symbolically dies as if in a human sacrifice (*meṛiāh*).

After the Bhuiyan receive the permission of the designated raja to perform the ceremonies identical to those with which they are reputed to have installed

[57]Roy (1935, 130-1) mentions that after this ritual the new king visits all the important temples of the town.

[58]Roy (1935, 131) does not mention the ritual of sitting on the tribal chief's lap.

[59]He is worshipped in the villages of Ladam and Anga. In the early morning of the *rājtilak* ceremony, the Sāmanto goes to the Kālapāṭ temple in the village of Anga to take the soil for the *ṭikkā*.

[60]Roy 1935, 119-23.

the first Bhanja raja of Keonjhar, a Bhuiyan with the title of *mahānāyak* carries the raja on his back, like a horse, to the *siṃhāsan melā* or throne room, where another Bhuiyan official called *kāṭoi* is sitting on a cotton quilt. The *mahānāyak*, in the guise of a horse, seats the raja on a new cloth spread over the knees of the *kāṭoi*, while another Bhuiyan (*rōṛā*) sprinkles sanctified water on him. The *mahānāyak* then places a crown, made of a long flexible creeper (*suālatā*), on the raja's head, invests him with a sacred thread (*poitā*) made of the same creeper, and marks a *rāj-ṭika* or mark of royalty on the raja's forehead with vermilion and sandalwood paste. The headman of the Sanoti tribe (probably a subtribe of the Bhuiyan), who is styled *berājal mahāpātra*, then ties a silk turban (*pagṛi*) on the raja's head, while another headman of the same tribe, who is called *Gharpo*, stands by the raja's side, fanning him with a bunch of *sīāṛi* fibres [*Pueraria tuberosa* (Roxb. ex Willd.)] fastened together in the shape of a *chāmar* or whisk, and the headman (*Kabāṭ*) of the Khond tribe holds an umbrella made of *sīāṛi* leaves over the raja's head. A number of Bhuiyan stand round the raja, holding in their hands clubs made of tree-branches, with the leaves and bark still attached, to represent maces of gold and silver and other symbols of the insignia of royalty, such as flags and banners, canopies and *chāmar*s or fanning whisks, royal umbrellas, etc.

After the tribes have demonstrated their power by installing and legitimizing the new king through the seal of their *iṣṭadevī*, the ritual that follows brings back the power to the king from the divine to the profane, worldly level. Now the king demonstrates who is in charge of the executive power over life and death.

The headman of the Rājkuli Bhuiyan, who bears the title of *Daṇḍa-Sena*, sounds a gong, and the *Mahāpātra* of the Sanoti tribe marks the raja's forehead with a mark of *dahi* (curded milk). Then the *Kabāṭ* of the Khond tribe gives the royal umbrella to a Bhuiyan to hold it over the head of the raja, and the Bhuiyan lies down with his face to the ground before the raja, impersonating a *meṛiāh* (or victim for human sacrifice). The Bhuiyan (the headman of the village of Bargōṛā), who bears the designation *Roṇā*, hands a sword to the raja, telling him: 'I invest thee with the right of beheading people. Do thou thy will.' The raja touches the neck of the *meṛiāh* with the sword twice and hands the sword back to the *Roṇā*. The *Roṇā*, in his turn, similarly touches the neck of the mock *meṛiāh* with the sword, and then puts it back. Then the Khond *meṛiāh* gets up and runs away, after three days reappearing before the raja, as if restored to life by a miracle.

In his description of the coronation in Keonjhar, M.M. Mishra refers only briefly to the ritual of sitting on the tribal chief's lap, since he concentrates on the Brahmanical ritual that precedes the short tribal rite. He mentions that on the coronation day of Raja Nrusingha Narayan Bhanja the raja was led to the *Muguni Mela*, that is, the hall where the ancient coronation stone seat lies. It is said that inside the stone there is a *śālagrāma*. The raja took a seat on the coronation stone, and eight eminent Brahmans performed the *abhiṣeka pūjā*. After visiting the shrine of several deities, he went to the *Bhula Mandei*, part of the royal harem, where the Bhuiyan performed their traditional rites for the raja's coronation. A Bhuiyan *sirdar* called Makhamal of Daumla sat on the ground. He held the raja who was seated on the ground just close to his lap in front. A white umbrella (*śvetachhattra*) was placed on the head of the raja. The Bhuiyans admitted to him being a raja and did *namaskār*. After this the new raja ordered that the dead body of the late raja be taken to the cremation ground for cremation and went to his royal quarters.

From M.M. Mishra's description, one receives the impression that this ritual lost its former wild character and became just an integral part of the coronation ritual. This contrasts with the lively and slightly amused report given in 1872 by Dalton,[61] who witnessed the coronation ritual of Dhanurjay Bhanj. According to Dalton, after the rituals performed by the Brahmans, the tribal rite took place, but not in the palace:

> A large shed attached to the raja's palace and ordinarily used as lumber room, was cleared out, swept and garnished, spread with carpets, and otherwise prepared for the occasion. A number of Brahmans were in attendance in sacerdotal costume, seated amidst the sacred vessels and implements, and articles for offerings used in the consecration of rajas, according to the ceremonies described in the Veda. Beyond the circle of the brahmanical preparations a group of the principal Bhuiyans were seated, cleanly robed for the occasion and garlanded . . . [there] was heard a great crash of discordant but wild, deep-toned instruments and drums of the Bhuiyan and other tribes, and the raja entered mounted on the back of a strongly built Bhuiyan chief, who plunged and pawed and snorted under him like a fiery steed. Moving to the opposite side of the brahmanical sacred circle, followed by a host of the tribe, one of them placed himself on a low platform covered with red cloth, and with his body and limbs formed the back and arms of the throne on which the raja, dismounting from his biped steed, was placed. Then the attendant Bhuiyan each received from the raja's usual servants extemporised imitations of the insignia of royalty—banners, standards, pankhas, chaurs, chhattars, canopies—and 36 of the tribe as hereditary office-bearers, each with his symbol, arranged themselves round their chief.

COMPARISON OF THE RITUALS IN GANGPUR, BAMRA, PALLAHARA AND KALAHANDI

In Gangpur, the coronation ritual takes place immediately after the death of the raja: the throne should not be vacant for a moment. A sardār, a high Rājput official, informs the zamindar of Sargipalli about the incident. Then all the zamindars proceed to the palace to be present at the *rājtilaka* ceremony. The coronation ritual takes place in the new palace, in the main hall of the *raja-mahal*. Along with the zamindars, the Rājpurohit and Brahmans are present. The ritual starts with the *abhiṣeka pūjā* performed by the Brahmans. Then the new raja takes a seat on the decorated floor along with the Sargipalli zamindar. For a brief moment the Sargipalli zamindar takes him on the right thigh and

[61] Dalton 1872, 145-7.

places the *candana* and *sindūr tilaka* on his forehead, saying, 'From this day onwards you are our king'. Then the raja sits in front of him. The Sargipalli zamindar binds the silk turban, places the crown on the raja's head, and then hands him the king's sword (*pāṭkhaṇḍa*) taken from the Kanaka Durgā shrine. Then all the other Bhuiyan zamindar give him a *candana* and *sindūr tilaka*. A Rajput holds the *chhatā*, made from the bamboo of Masabira. After the *rājtilaka* is presented by the Sargipalli Māji, they proceed to the Saṃleī temple near the palace for *darśana*. On the twelfth day after the former raja's funeral, the guests come to greet the new raja, but the great festival for the new king takes place during Daśaharā, when all his officials and the members of his family come together.

In Pallahara, on the day of the coronation, the Savara raja takes his seat on a small decorated platform in front of the royal throne. Then he asks the raja to sit on his lap. Behind him the representative of the Kondh holds the *pāṭchhattar*, while the Bhuiyan holds the *cāmar*. Now they place a golden crown on his head, and a Savara binds a creeper (*simba*), made by the Savara, around the crown as a sign that they are poor and therefore cannot offer anything else. Then the Savara raja puts a *tilaka* on the raja's forehead with soil from Sulepal and addresses him, saying 'From today you receive the State; take care of it and its people'. The soil for the *rājtilaka* comes from the shrine of the goddess Durgā, also called Grāmśrī of Sulepal, the *iṣṭadevī* of the Savara raja (in former times the Savara raja had his royal *gaddi* in Sulepal). To arrange the coronation *gaddi* for the new raja in Pallahara, they bring some soil from the former Savara *gaddi* in Sulepal.[62] After the new raja sits for a brief moment on the Savara's lap, he is guided to his official royal throne.

As mentioned earlier, in Bamra, there is no tradition of sitting on the lap of a tribal chief. Here the *rajaguru* plays the main role. Immediately after the death of the old raja, the *rajaguru* performs the *rājtilaka* and binds the turban around the new raja's head. The king sits on the *siṃhāsan* (*gaddi*) and then gives the order to start the cremation rituals. Members of the families of Kanto Bhuiyan and Suna Kondh still live in the Deogarh area today, but they play no part in the coronation ritual; only during Daśaharā do the Bhuiyan and Kondh come to present some soil from Bamra as a gift to the ruler.

In Kalahandi, P.K. Deo had his *rājyābhiṣeka* ritual performed on 16 March 1940, at the ancestral stone in Jugsaipatna. While sitting in the Pāṭmāji's lap, his turban was tied by the zamindar of Lanjigarh who also gave the *tilaka* with *sindūr* taken from the Maṇikeśvarī[63] stones inside the temple. As the Kondh consider the raja of Kalahandi to be a member of their community, it was

[62]The king and the earth are apparently regarded as husband and wife. Elsewhere in India, Galey (1990, 153), for instance, says that the king is married to the throne as he is to the queen, and that he is considered the masculine protector of the earth and the Goddess; cf. also Inden 1998, 44, 62.

[63]On Maṇikeśvarī, cf. Mallebrein 2006.

customary until recently for the Kalahandi raja to take a Kondh girl as his first wife (*pāṭrāṇī*).[64]

CONCLUSION

All the coronation rituals presented in this paper demonstrate the crucial historical link between local royal dynasties in Orissa and local tribes, as represented by their tribal chiefs. My data on the coronation rituals and the oral histories about them, including myths, stories and interviews with members of the families involved, indicates the highly intensive and symbolic importance of this ritual for the region. Obviously the tribal rite within the coronation ritual is crucial for the maintenance of peace between local ethnic groups like the Gond, Kondh, Bhuiyan and Sora tribes. The performance of the coronation ritual creates a single cultural identity among diverse ethnic groups, integrates diverse local cultures, and thus generates a communal feeling within the kingdom.

It is significant that this tradition of sitting on the lap of a tribal chief at a royal coronation is mainly found in those royal families who claim their ancestors were brought to the area by tribes, often forcibly, in order to make them their kings and assume rule. This assertion is found in the histories of those the families who rule over an area mainly inhabited by the Bhuiyan and Kondh tribes, who have a reputation as very powerful and freedom-loving communities.

For the tribes, the Brahmanical rite of coronation was a mystery, consisting of an endless number of elaborate *abhiṣeka* rituals, using symbolic gestures and a language only understandable to the small elitist Brahmanical circle. Conversely, the tribal form of coronation had a clear message: it is the goddess, the *iṣṭadevī* of the dominant tribe, who installs the ruler as king over the area, just as it is the tribal chief, her representative on earth, who places the *sindūr tilaka*, the seal of mutual agreement, on the king's forehead. It is the country of the tribes that holds and maintains the king. Moreover, it is represented by the throne consisting of the body of the tribal chief, who, like the throne itself, personifies the kingdom. Finally, this kingdom is actually ruled and under the protection of the main goddess of the dominant tribes. The king's contract is with the local goddess. In Kalahandi, this contract becomes even clearer: the raja must marry a Kondh girl before his official marriage with a Kshatriya girl, thus establishing a close family bond between the raja and the tribe, however, symbolic (this first marriage is dissolved as soon as it has been carried out).

On the one hand, the coronation ritual reveals the valorization of the tribal communities as important parts in the formation of the body of the local kingdom. On the other hand, the tribal ritual actors are subordinated in the

[64]For the tradition in Kalahandi, cf. Cobden Ramsay 1910, 202 (citing a Lieutenant Elliot); also P.K. Deo 2000, 51.

TABLE 13.1: SYNOPTIC TABLE OF CORONATION RITUALS AT VARIOUS ROYAL COURTS

Feudatory States	*Kalahandi*	*Bamra*	*Gangpur*	*Bonai*	*Pallahara*	*Keonjhar*
Tradition of sitting on the lap.	Yes	No, as two tribes are involved.	Yes	Yes	Yes	Yes
Which tribal chief performs the *rāj-tilaka* ritual?	The Kondh Pāṭmāji from village Merkul. The Raja sits on his lap	Formerly Kanto Bhuiya, Suna Kondh. Today no role in the ritual. Rājguru is important.	Bhuiya Zamindār of Sargipalli. The Rājā sits on his lap.	Bhuiya Samanta from Kaleiposh. Rājā sits on his lap.	Sawar Rājā from village Tampur, place of the first fort. Rājā sits on his lap.	A Bhuiya called Katoi. Rājā sits on his lap.
Name of the tribal chief's *iṣṭadevī* and her main place of worship.	Maṇikeśvarī from Jugsaipatna.	No relation to a tribal goddess within the ritual.	Saṃleī from Sargipalli.	Kālapāṭ from the villages Ladam and Anga.	Durgā (Grāmśrī) from Sulepal, the place of the old Sawar Rājā *gaddi*.	Not mentioned.
Name of the Rājā's *iṣṭadevī/iṣṭadeva.*	*Iṣṭadevī*: Maṇikeśvarī *iṣṭadeva*: Buḍā Rājā.	*Iṣṭadevī*: Kanakadurgā, Baṇadurgā. Came with the Gaṅgā dynasty to Bamra. No tribal goddesses	*Iṣṭadevī*: Shekharbāsinī Fort goddess: Saṃleī Palace goddess: Kanakdurgā.	*Iṣṭadevī*: Mā Kuāñrī *Iṣṭadeva*: Baneśvar plays central role.	*Iṣṭadevī*: Mahāpāṭ. Bhuiya goddess.	*Iṣṭadevī*: Tāriṇī *Kuladevī*: Danda Devī *Iṣṭadeva*: Joy Gopal. Important in the ritual.
Does the tradition of binding a *siali*-creeper around the head of the Rājā still exists?	Not mentioned. Zamindār of Lanjigarh binds the turban, assisted by all the five Zamindārs.	Not performed. According to tradition, the prince was crowned with a bark of a tree. A silk turban is wrapped today by Rājguru.	Not performed. The Sargipalli Zamindār binds a silk turban around his head. On top he places the crown.	Not performed. Later, when he sits on the real throne, a Pahudi Bhuiya hands over a thread made of *siali* creeper.	Performed: a Sawar binds the *samba* creeper around the crown.	Performed: a Bhuiya places a crown made of flexible creeper (*suālatā*) on the Rājā's head. Headman of Saonti tribe ties silk turban on Rājās head.
From where comes the *rājtilaka*?	From the temple of Maṇikeśvarī, given by Pāṭmāji.	Most probably Kanakadurgā, Banadurgā. *Rājtilaka* given by Rājguru.	From the shrine of Saṃleī in Sargipalli. Donated by Zamindār of Sargipalli.	From Kālapāṭ temple. Donated by Sāmanta of Kaleiposh.	From Mahapat shrine. Donated by Sawar Rājā.	Not known.

(Contd.)

TABLE 13.1 *(Contd.)*

Feudatory States	*Kalahandi*	*Bamra*	*Gangpur*	*Bonai*	*Pallahara*	*Keonjhar*
Does the tradition of giving an earth *tilaka* exist?	Not mentioned.	Not tradition. The Bhuiya and Kondh offer soil of Bamra during Daśaharā.	Not mentioned.	Bhuiya Samant gives an earth *tilaka* from Kālapāṭ.	Sawar Rājā gives a soil *tilaka* from Durgā temple of Sulepal, the old Sawar *gaddi* ruled in Sulepal.	Not mentioned.
Time the royal coronation ritual.	At an auspicious day. In case of P.K. Deo in 1940 before the investiture Durbar ceremony.	Performed immediately after the death of a Rājā. Throne should not be empty.	Performed immediately after the death of the Rājā. First *pūjā* by Brahmans, then *rājtilaka.*	On the 12th day after the death. Till then throne is guarded by the Bhuiya soldiers of the Sāmanto.	*Rājtilaka* on the 11th day after the death. Till then throne is guarded by the Sawar Rājā and his men.	Immediately after death. First the Brahmans perform the *abhiṣeka* ritual, then the *rājtilaka* ritual by the Bhuiya.
Where is the ritual of sitting on the tribal chief's lap performed?	In Jugsaipatna, at the ancestor stone, the first capital of the new ruler after Salapgarh.	According to the history, the first coronation took place in Titlipada, on a rock under a Sar tree. Today in the palace.	In the main hall of Rajamahal (new palace).	Hall of the Guesthouse	In the Rani Mahal of Pallahara palace.	Siṃhāsan Mela, or throne room (Roy). M. Mishra: Phula Mandei portion of the royal harem.
Marriage to tribal girl?	Marries a girl from Paki village.	Not this tradition.	No tradition.	No tradition.	No tradition.	No tradition.
Tribe who brought king.	Kondh made him king under the condition that he marries a Kondh girl.	Kanto Bhuiya and Suna Kondh went to Patnagarh, stole a child from Pāṭrānī, other story, they found a homeless boy.	The Bhuiyas selected the first ruler.	The Bhuiya Sāmanto from Kaleiposh helped Pratap Deo kill all other local chiefs.	Sawaras saw the child in a Kela family. They poisoned the family members and took away the child.	Bhuiyas stole the child Jyoti Bhanj.

succeeding ritual sequences featuring a human sacrifice, thus being placed correctly in the correct hierarchy (holy order) of the local kingdom.

By examining the coronation rituals of local dynasties in Orissa, their ritual symbols and their actors, the performative power of rituals is revealed to us. Through the symbolic ritual performance of a new king sitting on the lap of a tribal chief, a sense of unity is created for the local kingdom and its diverse local ethnic cultures.

REFERENCES

Banerjee, R.D. 1928. 'Rajput Origins in Orissa', in *Modern Review* 43, 285-329.

Cobden Ramsay, L.E.B. 1910. Feudatory States of Orissa, Calcutta: The Bengal Secretariat Book Depot (rpt. 1950, 1982).

Dalton, Edward Tuite 1872. 'Descriptive Ethnology of Bengal' Illustrated by Lithograph Portraits Copied from Photographs, Calcutta: Office of the Superintendent of Government (rpt. under the title: *Tribal History of Eastern India*, Delhi: Cosmos, 1978).

Deo, P.K. 2000. *Memoirs of a Bygone Era*, Delhi: Minerva Press.

Derrett, J.M. Duncan. 1976. 'Rājadharma', in *Journal of Asian Studies* 35, 4, 597-609.

Drekmeier, Charles 1962. *Kingship and Community in Early India*, Stanford: Stanford University Press.

Elliot, C. 1986 (1856). 'Report on Kalahadi State', in N. Senapati and D.C. Kuanr (eds.), *Orissa District Gazetteers (Kalahandi): Supplement*, Cuttack: Orissa Government Press, 457-2.

Galey, J.C. 1990. 'Reconsidering Kingship in India: An Ethnological Perspective', in J.C. Galey (ed.), *Kingship and the Kings*, Chur: Harwood Academic Publishers.

Gonda, J. 1966. *Ancient Indian Kingship from the Religious Point of View*, rpt. from *Numen* 3 and 4 with Addenda and Index, Leiden: E.J. Brill.

Heesterman, J.C. 1957. *The Ancient Indian Royal Consecration*, The Hague: Mouton.

———1998. 'The Conundrum of the King's Authority', in J.F. Richards (ed.), *Kingship and Authority in South Asia*, Delhi: Oxford University Press, 13-40.

Hunter, W.W. 1872. *Orissa, or the Vicissitudes of an Indian Province Under Native and British Rule: Being the Second and Third Volumes of the Annals of Rural Bengal*, London: Smith, Elder & Co.

Inden, Ronald 1998. 'Ritual, Authority, and Cyclic Time in Hindu Kingship', in J.F. Richards (ed.), *Kingship and Authority in South Asia*, Delhi: Oxford University Press, 41-91.

Kane, M.P.V. 1946. *History of Dharmaśāstra (Ancient and Medieval Religious and Civil Law)*, vol. 3, Chaps. 1-10, 'Rājadharma', Poona: Bhandarkar Oriental Research Institute, 1-103.

Kotani, Hiroyuki 1999. 'Kingship, State and Local Society in the Seventeenth to Nineteenth Century Deccan with Special Reference to Ritual Functions', in Noburu Karashima (ed.), *Kingship in Indian History*, Delhi: Manohar, 237-71.

Kulke, H. 1992. 'Tribal Deities at Princely Courts: The Feudatory Rajas of Central Orissa and their Tutelary Deities', in S. Mahapatra (ed.), *The Realm of the Sacred: Verbal Symbolism and Ritual Structures*, Calcutta: Oxford University Press, 56-78.

———1993a. 'Royal Temple Policy and the Structure of Medieval Hindu Kingdoms', in H. Kulke, *Kings and Cults*, Delhi: Manohar, 1-16.

———1993b. 'Legitimation and Townplanning in the Feudatory States of Central Orissa', in idem, *Kings and Cults*, Delhi: Manohar, 93-113.

Mahapatra, K.N. 1982. 'Kalahandi Under the Gangas and the Nāga Kings', in H.K. Mahtab (chief ed.), *The Orissa Historical Research Journal* 23, 1/4, *Special Volume, Dedicated to the Memory of Late K.N. Mahapatra*, Bhubaneswar: Orissa State Museum, 1-13.

Mahapatra, L.K. 1997. 'Ex-Princely States of Orissa: Their Social History', in P.K. Mishra (ed.), *Comprehensive History and Culture of Orissa*, vol. 2, Delhi: Kaveri Books, 896-927.

Mallebrein, C. 2006. 'Maṇikeśvarī and Dokrī: Changing Representations of Two Tribal Goddesses and the Dynastic Histories of Orissa', in A. Malinar (ed.), *Time in India: Concepts and Practices*, Delhi: Manohar, 209-41.

Mishra, Madan Mohan 1974. 'Data on the Ex-State of Keonjhar: Its History, Religious Institutions, Legends and Rituals Performed in the Royal Palace', Keonjhar (manuscript).

Nanda, Chandi Prasad 2003. 'Between Narratives and Silence: Centring Gangpur State', in this volume.

Patnaik, Jagannath 1988. *Feudatory States of Orissa (1803-1857)*, Allahabad: Vohra.

Patnaik, N. (ed.) 1979-80. *Handbook on the Pauri Bhuinya*, Bhubaneswar: Tribal and Harijan Research-Cum-Training Institute.

Roy, Sarat Chandra 1935. *The Hill Bhũiyās of Ōṛissā*, Ranchi: Man in India Office.

Roy, Satindra Narayan 1929. 'A Raja's Funeral in the Feudatory States of Orissa', in *Man in India* 9, 1, 7-9.

Sahu, Bhagabana 1993. *Princely States of Orissa Under the British Crown (1858-1905)*, Cuttack: Vidyapuri.

Schlerath, B. 1960. *Das Königtum im Rig- und Atharvaveda*, Wiesbaden: Franz Steiner.

Schnepel, B. 2002. *The Jungle Kings: Ethnohistorical Aspects of Politics and Ritual in Orissa*, Delhi: Manohar.

Senapati, N. and D.C. Kuanr 1980. *Orissa District Gazetteers (Kalahandi)*, vol. 6, Bhubaneswar: Gazetteer Unit, Department of Revenue, Government of Orissa.

———1986. *Orissa District Gazetteers (Kendujhar)*, Bhubaneswar: Gazetteer Unit, Department of Revenue, Government of Orissa.

Fig. 13.1: Manikesvari at Jogsahipatna

Fig. 13.2: Kali Samalei at Sundergarh

Fig. 13.3: The Palace of Bamra 1937

Fig. 13.4: Royal Investiture at Bamra, 17 January 1935

CHAPTER 14

The Aghriā and Their Mythology: In Between Politico-Religious Centres and Hierarchical Antipodes

UWE SKODA

In north-west Orissa, particularly in Sambalpur District, a mixed tribal and caste society has emerged through migration of peasant castes such as the Aghriā into predominantly tribal areas in the second half of the nineteenth and first half of the twentieth centuries. During these periods, Aghriā peasants started to clear a large part of the forests, became revenue collectors for various little kings, managed to establish themselves as village kings, and were influential in integrating the tribal population into the little kingdoms.

In this chapter I shall explore how the Aghriā locate themselves in this peripheral mixed tribal and caste society and how they conceptualize their origins, status and links to religious and political centres. It will be argued that, claiming to be Kshatriya and descendants of Bidur, place themselves mythologically in between in terms of status, but also geographically. They situate themselves between Agra, the Muslim centre they left behind, and Puri, the Hindu centre and their destination. Furthermore, on the one hand mythological links are constructed with the Brahmans, or rather Tihāris, their own Brahmanical priests, and on the other hand with the low-caste Chamār, in other words, to both ends, or complementary antipodes, of the caste hierarchy, while their tribal neighbours are not mentioned at all.

Thus the Aghriā firmly locate themselves within caste society. In addition, the central but irresolvable conundrum of caste society, the relationship between the Brahman or priest and the king, appears as a prominent theme of the myth in the form of the relationship between the Aghriā as holders of the plough (Fig. 14.1) and the Disandhrī (Fig. 14.2)[1] as their younger brothers guarding the sacred thread. The Disandhrī became the bards of the Aghriā, thus

[1] There are various ways of spelling the name of the bards of the Aghriā such as *Disandhrī* (see below), but also *Disondhi*, *Diśondhi* or *Dossondhi* (see e.g. publication of Bolangir *Aghriā samāj* 1993) or even *Bisandhi* in Chhattisgarh area. I use the former version in the text.

Fig. 14.1: Plow-*puja*

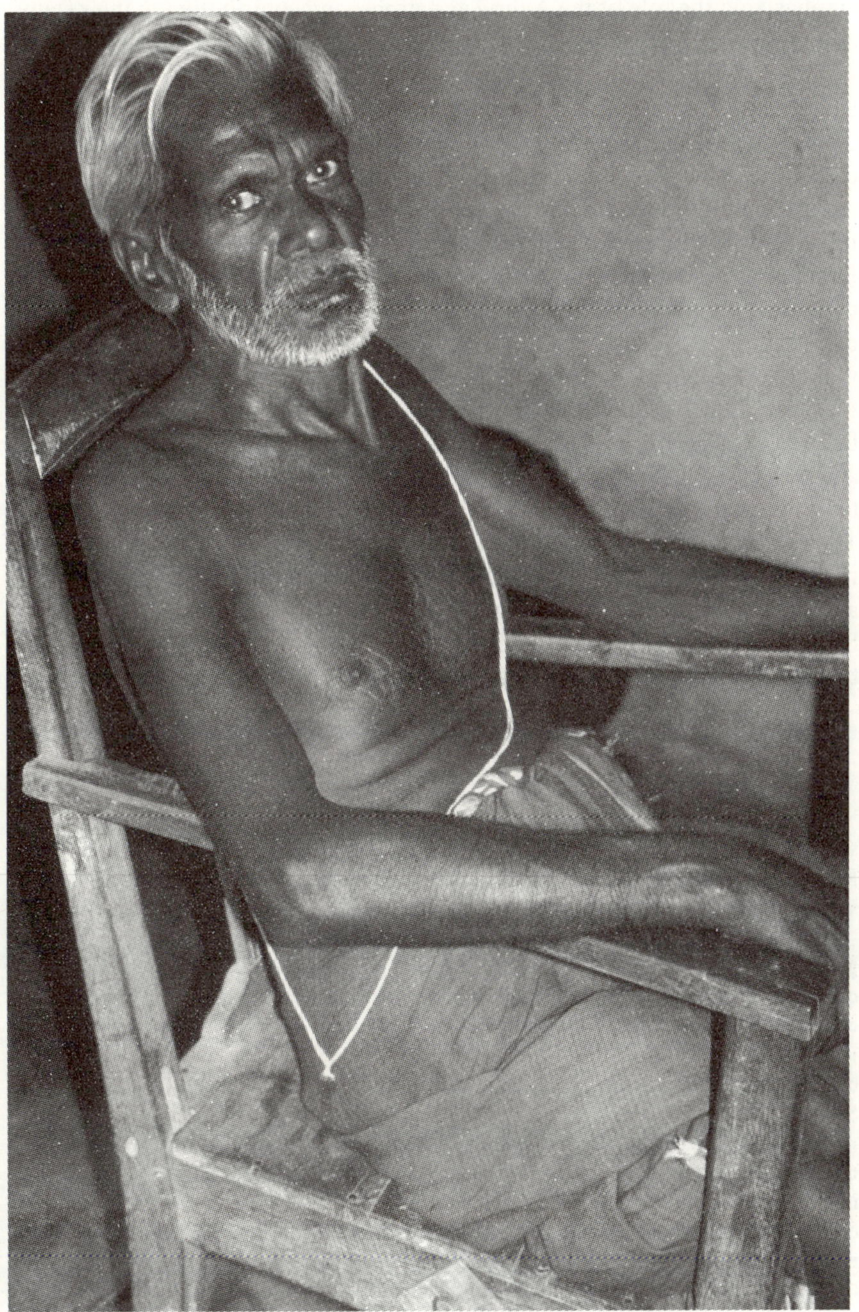

Fig. 14.2: Disandhrī

emphasizing the role of the Aghriā as patrons[2] and contributing to their status as 'village kings', as I have elaborated elsewhere.[3]

Since myths are an essential part of political discourses in which claims and counterclaims are being put forward, this myth might well be related to the rise of the Aghriā to the position of 'village kings' in a mixed tribal and caste society, as well as to a subsequent process of 'Kshatriyaization'.[4] In this regard, and in order to legitimize their place and rank, Aghriā myths seem to fulfil a similar function as the *vaṃśāvali* literature or the chronicles of royal families.[5] Nor, within this political arena, is the existence of different versions contesting their origins and their Kshatriya status at all surprising. Thus, other explanations and ideas about the origins of the Aghriā and their place in society will also be highlighted here.

These days Aghriā mythology[6] is generally transmitted in two ways. On the one hand myths are passed on by Disandhrī acting as the Aghriās' bards and reciting mythological stories known as *maṇḍlā*[7] on special occasions. For their performance the Disandhrī were entitled to a gift of a cow or a buffalo. The relationship between Aghriā and Disandhrī is an essential aspect of the myths and will be discussed below. On the other hand, there are published accounts of the origins of the Aghriā. The Aghriā caste organization (Aghriā Samāj), which was founded in 1904,[8] has published Aghriā myths since the beginning of the twentieth century and has been particularly influential in

[2]For the role of bards in a kingdom in western India see Basu (2000).

[3]Skoda 2005.

[4]The term is borrowed from Kulke (2001 [1976]). For further examples of the widespread phenomena of caste mobility and castes aspiring a higher status by adopting a Kshatriya model see also Rowe (1968a, 1968b). For social mobility in the wider perspective see also Dumont (1980 [1966]: 196).

[5]Kulke 2001b, 2001c; Berkemer 1993; Schnepel 2002. *Vaṃśāvalīs* or family chronicles gained particular importance during British rule in late eighteenth and early nineteenth centuries at a time of a routinization of the colonial administration, i.e. the records were consulted by British officers and became a tool of Indian rulers to legitimize themselves *vis-à-vis* the British. Therefore the chronicles of Puri were 'systemized' in early nineteenth century or even fabricated in feudatory states at the time (see Kulke 2001 [1987a]: 140ff; Schnepel 2002: 139ff).

[6]I use the term mythology here in the sense of myths as sacred narratives (Leach 1991: 66), since it is said that the *Disandhrī* as bard traditionally used to tell these stories only in a ceremonial context and were entitled to gifts afterwards (for the sacred character of oral tradition in orthodox Brahmanism see also Gough 1986 [1968]: 135). However, there is no clear-cut distinction between mythology and history—myths may well contain a 'historical core', which might be termed historical if it can be cross-checked with other independent sources (Leach 1991: 66; for the relation between myth and history see also Basu 2000: 15).

[7]On the term '*maṇḍlā*' and its use in Puri see Kulke (2001 [1987a]: 154). He states two possible explanations of the term: either as 'beginning'/'first' or as 'king'/'chief'.

[8]Compare *Gazetteers of India, Orissa, Sundargarh Districts*, ed. by N. Senapati/D.C. Kuanr, 1971 (1975).

propagating certain versions. Thus one finds oral and written accounts not only co-existing, possibly even merging in a process of canonization, but also occasionally deviating in certain details. This double transmission of mythology itself, of both written and oral versions, may lead, or may have led, to contradictions in the texts, or, rather, as Goody and Watt have remarked, express existing conflicts.[9] For these authors, while the emergence of a literate tradition is often related to the realization of contradictions between various texts, an oral tradition might be more easily adaptable to changing conditions within society. Different accounts from both oral and written sources have been recorded and will be presented here in an attempt to reveal a dominant Aghriā myth. However, no homogenization or reduction of mythological narratives to a singular standard version[10] is intended, but merely a description of the discursive field. Subsequently, the myths will be interpreted by exploring etymologies put forward by the Aghriā before turning to radically different accounts which may question their status and origins.

Let us now turn to the Aghriā myths themselves. Most accounts distinguish two phases of the origins of the Aghriā: a very early period is differentiated from a much later period with dated events, specifically migration into Orissa. In the following description, I follow this emic order and distinction.

EARLY ORIGINS

One Disandhrī related the earliest part of Aghriā mythology in the following manner:

The wife of Atriya Rushi [= a sage] is Anusuyā. Chandra [= the Moon God] had an affair with the Goddess Tārā [= star]. The name of the Moon's son is Budha. Puraraba was his son. Puraraba's son is King Prabira. His son was Mata Sananta. His son was born as Raibira. Raibira's son is Dusmanta.

This is to note that Bharata is the son of Dusmanta. The son of Bharata is Abhimanyu and his [Abhimanyu's] son; Biratha—a great hero—is as powerful as Indra. The son of Biratha is King Sambhurana. He has five sons of the name of 'Kuru'. The son of the eldest Kuru is Karaka. The son of Karaka is the King Shantanu Mahadev. The sons of Shantanu were Chitra and Bichitra Birja. They died without sons due to bad blessing. This is the result of sin. His [Shantanu's] wife is Satyabadi and her son is Vyasa Mahajati. The sons of Vyasa Deba, the great Saint (Mahajati), are Pandu and Dhrutarastra. The son of Pandu is the great King Jujesth.

There was a king named Hath Keshab. His caste is Shudra. His daughter gave king Padmanava birth to Ambhu, Ambhika, Ambalika and Ambabati. The son of Ambhu is Dhrutarastra. The son of Ambhika is King Pandu. The son of Ambhubati is Bidur. Gandhari got married to Dhrutarastra. King Gainta offered his daughter to King Pandu named Bhojraj.

The marriages of those ancient kings are the same as that of the marriage of eighty-one kings. His daughter, called Punchho, has a son Bhanu Chandra. Bhanu is a very powerful

[9] Goody and Watts 1986, 93.

[10] On the heterogeneity of myths see Lévi-Strauss (1996 [1980]: 171).

miraculous king of Kuru family. Satyabati the king's mother saw the annihilation of the Bhanu Chandra bansa after the death of Bichitra Birja, without any son. The strong desire as per the instruction of King Bhisma, she remembered Vyasa Deba (Mahajati) and requested for the remedy and for the ability to produce a son. By obeying the order of his mother Satyabati Vyasa Deba (Mahajati), through his miraculous power, created the conception of legitimate offspring Dhrutarastra and Pandu and through servant (dasi) Vaishnabi Sanjay of Sujani caste, Umabati and Bidur are born.

From his childhood Bidur in the best family tradition was a prophet of the *Bhagbat Gita*. He got married to the daughter of the Shudra King Kesab of Hathkesar near Kashi. To his legitimate two sons were born Prīya Bhānu and Sūra Bhānu.

In this account the statuses of Bidur's mother and wife are given as Śudra, though in the case of his wife this is a reference to a Śudra royal family. Bidur is presented as the son of a maidservant as well as of Queen Ambhubati, which, of course, contains an inherent contradiction. Such ambiguities are also expressed in a variety of other Aghriā texts. For example:

The great King Bichitra Birja of Chandra bansa died without having a son. When the king's mother Satyabatdebi saw the annihilation of the Somabansa [= Chandra bansa] with strong desire as per the instruction of magnanimous King Bhisma, she has requested the great Saint Vyasadev, who had the ability to see the past and to predict the future, to beget sons. The sage, through his own power, begot Dhrutarashtra and Pandu, and from the uterus of Vaishnabinavī Dāsi [dāsi = maidservant] Sanjay and from the womb of Shudra dāsi Bidur were born.

From childhood Bidur was too much attached to God, and good in behaviour. He was a man of justice and ascertainment. The great King Dhrutarastra took advice from him. Bidur got married to the daughter of Keshab Das, Shudra king of Hatakeshwar near Kashi. The name of the mother of Bidur is in the list of Shudras, but that is not the fact. She is Ambubati, daughter of King Harikeshwar of Surya bansa and the second queen of the great King Bichitra Birja.[11]

Thus in the latter version, which is more or less exactly reproduced in more recent publications of the *Aghriā Samāj*, for example, in 1983, it is emphasized that Bidur was the son of Queen Ambhubati. In other words, it is asserted that he was apparently of Kshatriya origin, while in the Disandhrī version and the Gazetteers[12] he is said to be of Śudra status. This corresponds to north Indian versions of the *Mahābhārata*, for example Sörensen, in which Vidura (Bidur), also called 'Kshattr' and seen as an incarnation 'of a portion of Dharma', is described as the son of Vyāsa and a Śudra woman who was a maid of Queen Ambikā.[13] However, according to one version of the *Mahābhārata*, which I

[11] 'History of the society of eighty-four houses Agaria and a list of Regulations, written from the ancient palm leaf manuscript, True Copy.' Original Author: Late Balunkeshwar Pandey, Jharsuguda. Compiler: Sri Rajendra Patel, M.A., B.Ed., Rastravasha Ratnaa (Researcher), Village/P.O. Darlipalli, Dist. Sundargarh; Dr. Bishwambhar Patel (Lecturer—L.N. College, Jharsuguda).

[12] The same is also mentioned in the *Gazetteer of India* 1971 (1975), Orissa-Sundargarh District, ed. N. Senapati and D.C. Kuanr, p. 113.

[13] Sörensen 1978, 733.

came across in an Aghriā household and which was supposed to have been written by Sarala Das, Bidur apparently married the daughter of a Vaiṣya king. In this book it is noted (the poem-like structure has been maintained as far as possible):

The king of Harikesh is in the state of Harikesh. He is the king, born in the family of Rudra [Śiva], his daughter's name is Ambhubatee. The great king Bichitra Birja got married to her. Amba and Ambalika are blessed with sons, but Ambhubatee is deprived of it. You are my son, who is very great in wisdom. You arrange it to give birth to a son through Ambhubatee. The excellent wise person Vyāsa, went by the order of mother, and entered the womb of Ambhubatee. The wife, Ambhubatee, got herself dressed the same as, Amba and Ambalika used to dress themselves. The emotional meeting was with great joy and pleasure, she became fortunate in copulating with Vyāsa. . . . A son fair face like moon, was born at once. The son was born in an auspicious moment of immorality, Vyāsa saw that he is too much learned. That son was born from the leg side, Again there were signs of lotus and the conch shells in both legs. He makes sound in the divine speech in words of the learned, The name Bidur is given by the great ascetic Vyāsa. By holding him on the lap, Vyāsa gave him kisses on his lips, Vyāsa told, 'Let him be very expert and intelligent'. 'You be rich in all qualities, always riches and beauty will not break from your shoulder. In enlarged knowledge let all your activities be seen, In wisdom and righteousness let all your days be spent.' The excellent ascetic Vyāsa after giving such a boon, has handed over the son on the lap of 'Satyabatee' [name of Vyāsa's mother].[14]

Of Bidur's marriage, the following is said:

A king named Kasheeshawar was there in the State of Kashee, he has a daughter named as Vandanabatee. He has given Vandanabatee as a gift to Bidur. The King of Kasheeshwar belonged to Vaishya.[15]

Thus in this version of the *Mahābhārata*, Bidur is apparently born to a queen and married to a Vaiṣya. In other words, Bidur's mother and wife are described in the texts mentioned above either as Śudra, Vaiṣya or Kshatriya. This makes Bidur's Kshatriya origins as the ultimate forefather of the Aghriā, on whom a descent model of origin is focused, somewhat ambiguous, although Bidur is closely associated with the royal family of Dhrutarashtra and with a sage called Vyāsa, who is said to have begot Bidur. However, although the Aghriā believe themselves to be the descendants of Bidur, to whom Krishna once promised that his descendants would never be poor, Bidur does not play any role in the ritual cycle of the Aghriā.

MIGRATION

In a second, clearly marked, even more common part of the myth, a process of migration is described. Once again, a version told by a Disandhrī will be presented first:

[14]Das 1983, 32-3.
[15]Ibid., 44.

In the name of Shri Vishnu pay respect: The Soma-bansa Rajputs were the inhabitants of Agra. When the emperor (badshah) told them to pay respect, then the Aghriā Rajput replied that the Aghriā are bold heroes (bīra) and they are very strong, and that is why they should not bow down in front of the emperor. After receiving this answer from the Rajputs the emperor became angry. He consulted his courtiers and decided to tie a sword (karat batā) in the middle of the court.

When the Aghriā will come to the court keeping the heads up high, they will be cut off. When the Rajputs will learn about this, they will be frightened and will have to bow their heads down. Near the entrance the emperor watches what the Aghriā will do. When the Aghriā came around ten to twenty heads were cut off. Most of the Aghriā died, but they never bowed down their heads. When the Aghriā came to know about this conspiracy they decided to leave Delhi and Agra, and even vowed not to take water any more in the absence of a cosmic order (*pane pine ka dharam nahi*). They left Agra and Delhi, and came to the Gajapati Maharaja [i.e. 'to Puri']. They requested the Maharaja to allow them some occupation. 'If you do not allow us any occupation, what will we do? We have come under the foot of the King [i.e. 'under your jurisdiction'].' After listening to them the Gajapati Maharaja replied: 'I will allow you some occupation.'

He constructed two sword sheathes (*dhāl*).[16] One sword (*khandā*) was made of iron, but its handle was of silver. Instead of constructing a second sword, he just kept a stick to drive the bullocks (*pāchen bāḍi*) with a golden handle. He kept them in front of Parmeshwar [i.e. 'Lord Jagannātha']. The Gajapati said: 'You have to choose one among these two. Whatever is in your fate, that will be your occupation.' After listening to this, Uros Raut said [implicitly: 'to the Aghriā']: 'If you permit me to lift one sword, I will do it, otherwise I will not do it.' All the Aghriā agreed and allowed him to choose one. After being permitted he lifted the sword with the golden handle. They brought out the sword [i.e. 'from its cover'].

Bām and Jatām, two brothers (*bhāi*), handed over their axe (*kathār*) to Ram Singh and then they started to take care of the land [i.e. 'started cultivation']. They made ten shares, and one share will go for the Dissondhi. That's the order of the Gajapati.

In one written account,[17] the migration of the Aghriā is described in the following manner:

The Bidur Kshatriya continued to live in Agra in Rajputana and in its nearby areas. The Muslim king Adilshaha sat on the king's throne in the year CE 1550 at Delhi. During his reign the Hindu tenants were in much oppression. The Kshatriya born in the family of Bidur did not even salute the king by bowing their heads. After having been informed about it the king introduced a new formula to receive salutations. If anyone salutes without bowing his head, while standing on the line drawn by the king

[16]*Dhāl* literally means shield rather than sword. However, in other versions *Ḍhār* is given in this passage indicating cover or sword cover.

[17]The text is a translation of 'History of the Society of Eighty-four Houses Agaria and a List of Regulations, Written from the Ancient Palm Leaf Manuscript, True Copy.' Original Author: Late Balunkeshwar Pandey, Jharsuguda. Compiler: Sri Rajendra Patel, M.A., B.Ed., Rastravasha Ratnaa (Researcher), Village/P.O. Darlipalli, Dist. Sundargarh; Dr. Bishwambhar Patel (Lecturer—L.N. College, Jharsuguda). An almost identical text has been published by the Aghriā samāj in their yearly publication 1983.

on the floor of the house, he will be very certain to get his throat cut by the very sharp, prickly iron saw hung on the top. But the Kshatriya born in the family of Bidur got wounded by the saw . . . , even then they did not bow down their heads.

The king proposed and announced order for sending them to Kandhar war after seeing their determination and moral courage. Those who were reluctant to go for war, will have to accept the Islam religion or else will be convicted with capital punishment. When the announcement of this strict order was known, the 44 houses out of 84 houses (*chaurāsia ghar*) of Kshatriya with their families fled to Orissa State. They took refuge in Utkal (Orissa) in the year CE 1550, ruled by the Gajapati, the Maharaja Mukundadeba. The king of Orissa had made arrangements for the maintenance of the newcomers (*āgantuka*) of those 84 houses. Two sword covers were kept on the back side of the king's throne Sri Jagannātha—one made of gold with a stick to drive the bullocks (*pāchen bāḍi*) inside and a silver one with an iron sword inside, only the covers being visible, while the remaining part were covered with a silk cloth. The Maharaja called the 84 houses and said, 'Let the eldest person among you hold the hilt of any of the two weapons kept under the throne and bring it when lifted up'. Uros Rout, the senior in age present among the 84 houses, was selected for the accomplishment of that work. When he got tempted, he lifted the weapon hilted with gold and brought it. The Maharaja, seeing this, ordered farming to be their livelihood from that day.

From that day Uros Rout and rest of them started the work of cultivation in their own hand, after having abandoned the sacred thread. Only the youngest brother of Uros took the sign of Kshatriya, the sacred thread and axe (*kaṛār*). They were known by the title Disandhrī. The Disandhrī have continued to keep the past symbol in their successive generations. They did not do the work of cultivation in their own hand, same as that of Brahman and Kshatriya. They were ordered by Uros in the past to attend the priestly work (*jāchakatā*)[18] in the 84 households as their main part of their livelihood.

The 44 households Kshatriya of Bidur descendants, that had come from Orissa, at first established in a colony at Patna State. . . . The contemporary emperor of Patna, after seeing their skills in cultivation, donated large lands and villages for the excellent prosperity of the State. Few households from them came out of Patna when supported by the clever Emperor Madhukar Sai of newly formed Sambalpur State in order to place a colony in the village of Laida at the beginning. Even now the people of that caste say that the village Laida is inherited land of their family. This is called as the place of 'Jhāmpi Peḍi Utra'.[19]

According to the increase of their number of families, they started to live at Patna, Phuljhara, Bilaspur, Sambalpur, Gangapur, Bamanda, etc. They are called as the Agrihā caste as they have come from Āgrā. In due course of time the word āgruā changed to āgriā and further to Agriā. The Āgriā caste (*jāti*) was divided into three parts: Choudhary, Nayak and Patel. Out of 84 households, 6 are Choudhary, 18 households are Nayak, and 60 households are Patel. All are Kshatriya. 'Koili kattar' [kattar = dagger] belongs to Choudhary households. 'Jama dadha kattar' belongs to Nayak households. 'Meghanada kattar' belongs to Patel households.

[18]The work for a *jājmān*.

[19]*Jhāmpi* designates a basket, while *peḍi* signifies a precious box. *Utrā* means 'to get down'. Thus literally it might be translated as: to get down with all their belonging.

The various myths I have collected differ to some extent. Occasionally, for example, Agra is replaced by Delhi or Rajputana. Also, both the period and the Mughul emperor who was reigning at the time are disputed. Most Aghriā, however, say that Adil Shah was ruling at that time, though historically he does not seem to fit the context of the myth. No Mughal emperor of that name is known to have ruled in Delhi or Agra within the time frame mentioned in the myth.[20] Nor is there unanimity over the date of migration or the ruler of Puri. However, in most versions like the one above, Mukuṇda Deb is mentioned as the ruler of Utkal (Orissa), possibly a reference to the historical figure of Mukunda Harichandana.[21]

THE MYTHOLOGICAL LINK WITH THE CHAMĀR

In some versions of the dominant myth, particularly in the accounts narrated by members of the Leuniā clan of the Aghriā, one finds as subsidiary element a peculiar link to the Chamār who were instrumental in the Aghriā's survival. Strikingly similar stories are also remembered, as well as emphasized, by the Chamār themselves.

The most common version told by the Leuniā runs as follows:

> The Aghriā were called to the Moghul court in order to decide whether to bow down their heads or to have their heads cut off by the hanging sword. All the Aghriā refused to bow down their heads in front of the Moghul emperor until only two or three were left, who searched for ways to escape. They called some Chamār standing next to them and asked them for help. The Chamār knew that they would die by the hanging sword

[20] Adil Shah neither ruled Agra nor Delhi in the fifteenth or sixteenth century as suggested by the myth (compare H. Kulke/ D. Rothermund, 1999 [1986]). However, the name Adil Shah appears as a historical figure in various epochs and regions (see *Cambridge History of India 1958*, vol. III: 148-50, 193, 300, 313-4, 425ff, 439ff). Firstly, an Adil Shah established and ruled the kingdom of Madura in fourteenth century (1356-69) after having been a governor of Muhammad Tughlaq. Secondly, a dynasty known as Adil Shahi is mentioned in Bijapur as one of the Deccan kingdoms of fifteenth and sixteenth centuries. This dynasty was founded by Adil Shah, also known as Yusuf Adil Shah or Yusuf Adil Khan, in 1490, who was succeeded by Ismael Adil Shah (1510-34), Ibrahim Adil Shah (1534-58), Ali Adil Shah (1558-80) and Ibrahim Adil Shah II. It seems that each of them were involved in constant feuds with their neighbours, e.g. the Hindu kingdom of Vijayanagar, for which they may have hired and dismissed foreign troops, e.g. Maratha, as well as killed courtiers suspected of conspiring against them. Thirdly, a dynasty founded by Adil Khan (1435-41) and succeeded by Adil Khan II (1457-1501) and Adil Khan III (1501-20), etc., ruled over the Khāndesh kingdom neighbouring Gujarat, whose influence is said to have reached even Jharkhand. Fourthly, an Adil Khan is mentioned as Governor of Lahore under Nasir ud din Mahmud in the late fourteenth century. Thus, though all of them were Muslims (Sunni and Shia), none of them has ever ruled Delhi or Agra.

[21] According to Panda (1999: 241ff) King Mukunda Harichandana or Mukunda Deb of Chalukya family is said to have ruled Orissa from 1560 to 1568. He became involved in conflicts between Mughals and Afghans, which ultimately led to the fall of the Orissan Kingdom.

if they replaced the Aghriā. They told the Aghriā: 'When we will die, who will perform the obituary rites (*śrāddha*)?' The Aghriā promised to perform all rituals necessary.

Other versions highlight the struggles of the Aghriā against the Mughals, in which they are said to have been supported by the Chamār. A father-son-relationship or link between ancestors and descendants, usually expressed by offering *piṇḍa*, is stressed even more explicitly in the following version, this time told by a Chamār:

Most Aghriā were hanged by the Moghul emperor . . . , but one Aghriā managed to escape. The emperor's guards followed him. The Aghriā took refuge in the house of an old Chamār, who was hanging pieces of leather on a rope and was pouring some water over it [the traditional work of a Chamār]. The Aghriā pleaded with the Chamār: 'Please, save me, otherwise I will be hanged.' The Chamār replied: 'You will do my work, while I will sit next to the door.' When the emperor's guard, searching for the Aghriā, reached the house of the Chamār and asked, 'Have you seen the Aghriā?', the old Chamār replied. 'Look for yourself: only my son is working here, nobody else.' The guard left and the Aghriā was saved. Later the Aghriā offered a cake (*piṇḍa*)[22] with some water to the Chamār on Nuā Khāi, subsequently repeating this every year.

In some narratives, not only is a relationship with the Chamār as the lowest stratum of caste society emphasized, but also links between the Aghriā and their Brahman priests, known as Tihāri are stressed.

RELATIONS WITH THE TIHĀRIS AND BRAHMANS

Significantly, the Aghriā are served by priests who are supposed to work exclusively for them. These ritual specialists are known as Tihāri or Tiwāri and claim to be Kānya Kubja Brahmans, a claim which links them to the Vedic Brahmans of coastal Orissa. However, other Brahmans contest the status of the Tihāri and doubt their Brahmanical credentials.

Occasionally the Tihāri are also called the *kul purohit* of the Aghriā. The origin of the peculiar relation between the Aghriā and the Tihāri as their own priests is explained in the following quotation from an undated pamphlet—probably an early publication of the *Aghriā Samāj*—entitled 'Why Aghriā do not accept food from Brāhman?' It also highlights a certain tension between the Aghriā and high-status Brahmans in general:

In former times Aghriā were Kshatriya serving the King as warriors. Once there was a war against Kandahar, and the Aghriā were fighting bravely for the King. The Aghriā asked the Brahmans for help in the war, but the Brahmans refused, saying they do not want to die in this war. Therefore the Aghriā vowed not to accept food from the hand of a Brāhman any more. Due to these difficulties with the Brāhmans, the Aghriā decided to leave the place. On their way to Puri they met a Brāhman from Kānya Kubja, who

[22]The Chamār might have mixed *piṇḍā* (cake) and *piṇḍa* (rice balls offered for the ancestors) here.

was a Tiwāri. The Tiwāri saw that the Aghriā did not even accept water from a Brāhman. The Aghriā, being happy to have met the Tiwāri, promised that the Tiwāri could perform all their rituals.

This statement is confirmed by various Aghriā publications,[23] for example, one containing a description of the Aghriā of 1925, according to which the priestly acts of the Aghriā are conducted by *Tihāri*.[24]

However, some Aghriā asserted that they only started accepting food from Brahmans about thirty years ago, prior to which they used to cook for themselves. Although the rule not to accept food from Brahmans is still maintained during caste feasts (*bhoji*), a Brahman may be hired to cook for the guests during larger functions.

INTERPRETATION

The origins of the Aghriā are obviously remembered in two phases: a very distant and undated mythical past, and a more recent historical past conceptionalized as being linked to precise dates, for example, the year of leaving Agra (though the dates vary from version to version). The former contains a long list of mythical kings, starting from the union between the moon and a star as the 'point of commencement'.[25] Thus the Aghriā are directly linked to the moon and claim to be of Chandra bansa origin (one of the two important lines of Kshatriya descent),[26] which might also help legitimize the present position of the Aghriā as a dominant caste. From there the line of ancestors leads to Bidur, a character in the *Mahābhārata* epic, who is asserted to be the forefather of all Aghriā. His credentials as a Kshatriya are somewhat ambiguous, however, since in some versions (many of them put forward by the Aghriā or the Disandhrī themselves), his mother and wife are said to be of Śudra or Vaiṣya origins.

The second phase, which asserts a more recent migration, is metaphorically richer in the sense of containing more oppositions. It places the Aghriā somewhere in the periphery between two centres and seems to offer an explanation for their place and occupation in Orissa. Apparently there are two

[23] See 'Description of Aghriā bansa', published by B. Pandey, Sambalpur 1925 [the title might be an indicator that the author was an Aghriā himself—US] or 'History of the Society of Eighty-four Houses Agaria and a List of Regulations, Written from the Ancient Palm Leaf Manuscript, True Copy.' Original Author: Late Balunkeshwar Pandey, Jharsuguda. Compiler: Sri Rajendra Patel, M.A., B.Ed. Undated manuscript.

[24] In case there was a scarcity of Tihāri or Kānya Kubja Brāhman, Aghriā may have managed with Utkalīya (Oriya) Brāhman or Araṇyaka Brāhman (Jungle Brāhman). The same system is currently practised: Every Aghriā family should call the Tihāri when a family priest (*purohit*) is needed, but if he is already engaged by another family any other Brāhman might be called for urgent rituals.

[25] Thapar 2000a, 758.

[26] For the *Mahābharāta* as epic of the Candravaṃśa see Thapar (2002 [1992]: 788).

centres opposed to each other. On the one hand, one finds Agra (or Delhi) as centre of the Mughal empire ruled by a Muslim dynasty, which the Aghriā leave behind. Agra, as the myth says, is a place where you can neither drink nor eat, thus implying that it is without *dharma* (religious or cosmic order). The departure of the Aghriā is due to a trick at the ruler's court to force them to bow down their heads. Such a ploy is obviously incompatible with the *kṣatra-dharma*, which prescribes conquest, warfare, and duels on the battlefield instead of the playing of tricks.[27] On the other hand, Puri in the text is ruled by the Gajapati, a Hindu dynasty and associated with Lord Jagannātha, and therefore a place of *dharma*. Thus apparently the Aghriā migration is based on oppositions, as seen in the table, the journey or migration itself being a medium of transformation,[28] which may also be indicated by the decapitation of the Aghriā at the Mughal court:

Agra (Delhi)	*Puri*
Mughal	Gajapati
west (north-west)	east (south-east)
Muslim	Hindu
absence of Gods/dharma (cosmic order)	presence of Gods/dharma (cosmic order)
centre left behind	centre of destination
autochthonous	immigrants (newcomers)
rebellion against orders	obeying orders
negative centre	positive centre

Thus on the one hand, one finds Puri, ruled by the Gajapati as a Hindu king and situated in the east, the direction generally associated with Hindu gods, including Lord Jagannātha. On the other hand, there is Agra, the western centre left behind, where there are no gods or rightful cosmic order (*dharma*). While the Aghriā have to leave their place of origin after rebelling against the orders to bow down, they readily accepted the divine order of Lord Jagannātha. Keeping in mind that there are virtually no Muslims in north-west Orissa, the construction of Muslim rule in opposition to Hindu kings may be surprising, but it may also refer implicitly to their tribal neighbours, who are otherwise conspicuously absent in the myth. As in the case of hierarchy, certain relationships are hardly expressed verbally, but nonetheless taken for granted or explained by reference to other communities. Therefore tribals and Muslims might be implicitly identified as the 'Others'. This, though in reversed form, may correspond to the opposition between autochthonous and immigrant, the tribal population being imagined in opposition to the Aghriā as newcomers. In contrast to this interpretation, however, a reference to Muslims might also

[27]For *kṣatra-dharma,* see e.g. Zimmermann (1987: 184).

[28]In the way that Lévi-Strauss described cooking, etc., as medium of transformation in myths.

replicate the chronicles of royal families in which a victory over Muslims is sometimes mentioned.[29]

In the final part of their migration, the Aghriā obey an order by Lord Jagannātha conveyed by the Gajapati as a Hindu king. Similar myths of divine interventions in order to legitimize rulers coming from outside—or 'intruders'—are also found in other parts of Orissa, and the *vaṃśāvali* or chronicles of the royal family of Jeypore may serve as an example here.[30] Without wishing to over-interpret the myth, it can be said that in this way the Aghriā rationalize their share in consolidating the rule and increasing the revenue of Hindu kings in tribal areas, which they may also have started to imitate, as well as being agents of an ongoing process of Hinduization and peasantizations.

It is also significant to note that the Aghriā are placed in between two centres. They also have to leave Puri, after they have been assigned a new occupation. This time, however, they do not escape, but are given a command by Lord Jagannātha, and thus leave in obedience to a divine decision. It is this divine order—combined with a fault of their own, their greed—which justifies their reduction in status: warriors turn into peasants; the stick replaces the sword.

warrior	peasant
sword	stick

However, the Aghriā's myths are not just apparently simple and straightforward stories, which reflect only past 'grand events',[31] and provide an explanation for a perceived fall.[32] They are not simply representations of empirical facts, but are rather characterized by various inversions.[33] In my view, a central paradox of the myths concerns the relationship between the Aghriā and the Disandhrī, their bards. On the one hand, the Aghriā are regarded as the elder brothers of the Disandhrī. However, the distinction between elder and younger found here, and known from various parts of Orissa and Middle India, is not only related to the domain of kinship and biological age but also to a difference in status, the elder being in a hierarchically superior position.[34] This seems to be reflected occasionally in local characterizations of the Disandhrī as *sān* (small, 'junior') in relation to the Aghriā, on whom they are dependent and who are *baḍ* (big, 'senior'). The superior Aghriā provide their younger brothers with their means of survival, offering ideally a tenth of their harvest to them as their share (*bhāg*;[35] hence the

[29] For the Jaipur dynasty see Berkemer (1993: 212).

[30] Schnepel 2002, 148f.

[31] Thapar 2000a, 755.

[32] The theme of decline in low caste myths is quite frequent and occasionally combined with one's own decisions leading to the fall (see also O'Flaherty (1988 [1976]: 19-21).

[33] See Lévi-Strauss (1992 [1973]).

[34] Pfeffer 2000, 342.

[35] Similar traditions of offering $\frac{1}{10}$ known as *bhāg* during feasts are found as well among Rona in Koraput indicating that such a tradition might be common in tribal society too (L. Guzy: personal communication).

name 'Disandhrī' is derived from ten, *dis* 'ten', via *dos*, = 'ten').[36] Thus a material dependence is clearly expressed in the myth and related to the elder-younger distinction. On the other hand, the Disandhrī are ascribed the task of guarding the sacred thread (*paitā*), which the Aghriā had to remove in order to turn to agriculture and start ploughing. Obviously ploughing cannot be combined with the standards of purity required for wearing the sacred thread, which the Disandhrī still wear today. This differentiation of status, related to the use of ploughs, is found among Brahmans in Orissa as well, the Vedic or Śāsana Brahmans, who are only engaged in their ritual functions, claiming superiority over the Oriya or 'plough' Brahmans, who have been influential in introducing the plough to the 'tribal frontier'.[37] Thus a second conflicting hierarchy of purity is contained within the myth: the Disandhrī as the younger brothers being relatively purer, but materially dependent on their elder brothers, the Aghriā, as shown here.[38]

higher	lower
elder	younger
Aghriā (eB)	Disandhrī (yB)
materially independent	materially dependent
higher	lower
purer	more polluted
Disandhrī	Aghriā
sacred thread	plough

The ambivalent relationship between the Aghriā and the Disandhrī is expressed in terms of the acceptance of food as well. Although the Disandhrī, who claim a higher status than the Aghriā because they wear the sacred thread,[39] should not, according to their own standards, accept cooked food from the Aghriā, in practice they do. To some extent, the ambiguous position of the Disandhrī in relation to their patrons mirrors the role of the Chāraṇ as opposed to the Rajput. The Chāraṇ, as royal bards in western India, are conceptionalized as the ritual sisters of their Rajput patrons.[40] This implies on the one hand an inferior status

[36]In Chhattisgarh I heard the name *Bisandhi* indicating a share of $\frac{1}{20}$ (*bis* = 20) for the bards. The name *Disandhrī* in its 'avatar' *daśondi* seems to be common in Gujarat as well. Basu (2000: 49, 62) translates it as 'poet' or 'bard'. However, it is apparently not related to the number ten there.

[37]Pfeffer 1978, 425-6.

[38]For the Brahmanical ideal of non-dependence at which the entire ideal-typical life of a Brāhman is aimed see van der Veen (1973: 47ff).

[39]According to some Aghriā they might be allowed to accept food from a *Disandhrī*, but in practice there is hardly any opportunity, because it is the *Disandhrī* coming to the Aghriā also seen as his patron (*jājmān*—see Chap. 4.4.) demanding his share (*bhāg*) and not the other way round. Other Aghriā told that it was strictly forbidden to accept food from a *Disandhrī* in former times, but a *Disandhrī* was allowed to enter the kitchen of his Aghriā patrons. However, though conceptionalized as brothers every community practices endogamy.

[40]Basu 2000, 119.

for the Chāraṇ within the gender hierarchy, while on the other hand the Chāraṇ, as sisters, are the recipients of gifts (*dān*), just like the Brahmans and ascetics, which indicates a higher status. Thus, like Chāraṇ bards in western India, the Disandhrī seem to stand in a similar structural position to their 'patron-kin', though the ritual idiom in which the relationship is expressed is completely different.

Without stretching my interpretation of the myth too far, the Aghriā-Disandhrī relation resembles the Kshatriya-Brahman pair or king-priest in a wider sense.[41] This seems to be confirmed by the fact that priestly functions are assigned to the Disandhrī in the myth—even though the Disandhrī do not fulfil them in reality—while the Aghriā receive a stick by order of Lord Jagannātha, which itself is a symbol of rule over the world and of royalty.[42] Therefore, the Aghriā appear as relatively impure givers in relation to the Disandhrī as purer receivers. Thus, like the Asdiwal myth studied by Lévi-Strauss,[43] the Aghriā myth seems to deal with a more general societal paradox, one which Trautmann once called 'the central conundrum of Indian social ideology'.[44] In the myth one finds a contradiction between two conflicting patterns of ordering society or two hierarchies, one from the perspective of the king as universal giver, the other from that of the relatively purer priest. The myth reveals this paradox, though in a disguised form, and thus, following Lévi-Strauss, one might argue that one function of the myth might well be to acknowledge the existence of an irresolvable paradox, the admission of a practical antinomy.[45]

This might be further substantiated by another inversion of the myth. In most versions it is the eldest among the Aghriā who is described as greedy and who commits a serious mistake by choosing the golden sword handle instead of the silver one, a mistake which proves to be so fatal to the Aghriā. Keeping this in mind, it seems that the status as Kshatriya is being opposed to greed here. At the very moment in which the oldest Aghriā is tempted and overwhelmed by his greed, Kshatriya status in the sense of the Aghriā being warriors is lost, and a decline sets in. Thus this part of the myth might represent a symbolic reminder of the close link between Kshatriya status and generosity, not greed. Only by generosity, by giving, can a Kshatriya status be maintained and the *kṣatra-dharma*

[41]For critical remarks on the structural interpretation of myths see e.g. Douglas (1988 [1968]: 61ff) who warns particularly of reductions of meanings by imposing binary oppositions, or Burridge (1988 [1968]: 109) additionally advocating a meaningful dialogue between culture and myth.

[42]For the stick as royal symbol see Hardenberg (2000: 21)

[43]Lévi-Strauss 1992, 197ff.

[44]Trautmann 1995, 285; Trautmann related the conundrum to two types of exchange: sacred *versus* profane and noble *versus* ignoble. For multiple hierarchies resulting from these overlapping pattern of classification see also Basu (2000: 45f).

[45]Lévi-Strauss 1992, 197ff; Lévi-Strauss (1985: 239ff) also argued—perhaps in contrast to the rather pessimistic Asdiwal myth—that myths may express or 'communicate' options, theoretical solutions or models for certain societal problems out of which one may be chosen by the society.

be fulfilled—a point which seems to reflect the position of the Aghriā as 'village kings' and givers at the centre of a redistributive system[46] rather than as warriors.

Now let us turn to the peculiar link between the Chamār and the Aghriā mentioned in various versions, and stressed particularly by the Chamār, for whom it is clearly a matter of prestige to be able to link themselves to the dominant caste. However, this relationship is also acknowledged by the Aghriā, particularly of the Leuniā clan.[47] One might argue, as some Aghriā do, that the Chamārs—who share their language, Laria, with the Aghriā—may have migrated from the same area or at the same time as the Aghriā. This quite close relationship might also be explained through the fact that in former times the Chamār used to produce special leather pots known as *puhurā*, which were required to lift water and carry it to the fields. Since such pots were essential for agriculture,[48] the Aghriā were, to some extent, dependent on the Chamār for their production. In contrast, however, another opposition seems to be expressed here, one related to the relative impurity with which the Chamār are associated throughout India. In the myth the Aghriā are endangered by the Mughal, but they find safety in the house of a Chamār. While the Chamār are usually associated with death, specifically of cattle, in this myth they appear as the protectors of life from the perspective of the Aghriā, though they may also have to sacrifice their own lives.

Thus one finds the following oppositions:

Kṣatriya	Chamār
pure	impure
high	low
needing help	offering help
endangered	safe/surviving
status temporarily given up	status temporarily sought

Being a Chamār, or having an impure status in a wider sense, may offer protection against life-threatening forces. Interestingly this story is recalled specifically in the case of death: some Aghriā acknowledge that until recently their forefathers had offered a *piṇḍa* during their *śrāddha*, although nowadays most Aghriā reject this practice, which they probably conceive as degrading.[49]

In addition, the Aghriā are not the only peasant caste claiming Kshatriya descent who are, at the same time, associated with the 'Untouchables'

[46] Skoda 2005.

[47] Some Leunia rationalize the peculiar custom of their clan by stating that they were the leaders of the Aghriā trying to escape, but other Aghriā do not agree.

[48] It is not quite clear, if such pots were used for drinking too, but it is likely that they were used in ancestor rituals (*śrāddha*) for the Chamār as well.

[49] I heard that in some cases children of communities like the Gaṇḍ occasionally teased their Aghriā classmates by calling them Chamār or even beef-eater if they were quarrelling. The Aghriā used to explain it as envy.

mythologically. In an apparently very similar case of the Noniya of north India, to which I shall return later, one finds a related myth: the escaping warrior-heroes are saved by 'Untouchables', but at the price of eating the latters' defiling food.[50]

The very same idea seems to be expressed in the custom of selling sick or endangered children to lower-status communities in the hope for their survival. A temporarily impure state or an association with the Chamār in particular is considered life-protecting.[51]

VARIANTS OF THE MYTH

Though not in itself fully coherent, the mythology presented above might be called the dominant myth transmitted orally as well as in written form. Apart from these 'official' and 'public' versions—myths circulated by bards or caste organization—there are various other ideas and deviating legends about the origins of the Aghriā and their name which contest the dominant myth and place it in perspective.

The existing variety of competing versions might best be demonstrated with reference to explanations for the caste name. According to the myth already mentioned, the Aghriā fled from Agra, hence their name 'Aghriā'. However, different spellings and intonations of the caste name leave room for divergent interpretations. In written sources the name is spelt 'Āgriha, Agria, Agriha', and 'Āgria' (see the mythical accounts above), but also 'Āgrihā' and Agharia' or 'Aghariā'. The spelling 'Aghariā', as in publications of the Bolangir *Aghriā Samāj*,[52] is obviously not fully identical with Agra and exhibits inconsistencies. Spellings such as these ('Aghariā') may have led some non-Aghriā—for example, members of the royal family of little kingdoms—to argue that 'Aghriā' is derived rather from a-ghar-iā (ghar = house/home; a- = without), which implies that the Aghriā were either homeless after coming to Orissa, or that they had a low status and were not allowed to enter the houses of others. Some Aghriā accept the former explanation and say that they camped under a Mahuā tree first, which offered them some protection and has been highly respected in the community ever since. It is further argued that this special relationship is expressed in the fact that the Aghriā place Mahuā trees at the centre of their

[50]According to Rowe (1968a: 73) a subsidiary element of the Noniya myth describes the escape from the battle against Muslims. Being chased by Muslim armies the Noniya take refuge in the house of an 'Untouchable'. The Muslim officer demands a proof, that the Noniya Cauhān are indeed kinsmen of the 'Untouchables' as they claim. In order to prove it the Noniya have to eat the impure food of the 'Untouchables'—being thus saved, but defiled. The similarity to the Aghriā myth is striking.

[51]O'Flaherty (1988 [1976]: 21) mentions interesting cases in which some 'Untouchable' communities argue that they were Kshatriya pretending to be Untouchables while fighting Muslims, but were cursed later on and, therefore, remained 'Untouchable'.

[52]See for example a publication of the Bolangir *samāj* 1976. In more recent publications of the same *samāj* the spelling has changed to Āg(a)riā.

wedding altars, and that they are also highly venerated among the tribal communities of the region.[53]

Other explanations have also been put forward. The Aghriā are sometimes apparently confused with the Aghori or Agnori, a Śaiva sect supposed 'to feed on human corpses',[54] which, however, is not the case. In a publication by the Aghriā Samāj of 1983, the name is derived from *agra* (front, first row) and *hiya* (chest), an allusion to the Aghriā as brave warriors always fighting in the front lines of the battle. Similarly, as one elderly Aghriā told me, the name is based on *ag* (front) and *rahi* (to march) thus implying that the Aghriā were the 'front-runners' who led the 'Aryan' to central India. Some Aghriā[55] are convinced that their forefathers were iron-smelters and that their name is logically derived from *āg* (fire), though this may represent confusion with a tribal community of Madhya Pradesh and Chhattisgarh,[56] which has a similar name.[57] Still others believe the Aghriā to have been salt-makers, the name in this version being based on *agar*, the salt-makers' sallow pan.[58] These sallow pans, Nanda argues, are used in Rajputana and Punjab.[59] This theory may derive substantiation from the fact that some Aghriā or Tihāri argue that the Aghriā caste is in fact a mixture of various different castes that migrated to Orissa together.

This theory may be linked to the possibility that one of the Aghriā's most important clans, the Leunia, may be related to a caste of traditional salt-makers turned peasants called the Loniya, Luniya or Noniya, who are found in Uttar Pradesh, Madhya Pradesh, Bihar,[60] Punjab and Sindh,[61] and perhaps other parts

[53]For the importance of Mahuā (*Madhuca longifolia* (J. Konig) J.F. Macbr., syn. *Bassia latifolia* (Roxb.).) among tribal communities of the region, e.g. among Gaṇḍ see Elwin (2000 [1936]: 13).

[54]Russell and Lal 1975, 13; see also Risley 1981, 10.

[55]Patel (1995).

[56]Elwin (1991 [1942]: 73) considers at least some segments of the Agaria as sub-tribes of the Gond.

[57]In one case an Aghriā believed that their name was created under British influence. According to this line Aghriā originally comes from *agrarian*—the British knowing the Aghriā as good peasants or agrarians. In Raigarh I was told a new way of explaining the name Aghariya: A(gility) G(anga) H(oly) A(ffability) R(egularity) I(ngenious) Y(eomanly) A(uthentic).

[58]For example Nanda 1994, citing Elwin.

[59]Apart from that I also heard Aghriā say, that there are *Agaria* salt makers in Gujarat and that they saw a TV documentary about them. However, I could not gather any further information. Additionally, many Aghriā have heard that the title Patel used by most Aghriā is very common in Gujarat. Though the title Patel is indeed frequently used in Gujarat, e.g. by Patidar (see Pocock 1972), there is neither another hint at a common origin nor any other common features, the title being most likely only a superficial common characteristic. Apart from that other titles used by the Aghriā, e.g. Naik, are also widely used among Gaṇḍ and no Aghriā sees that as sufficient proof of a common origin.

[60]Rowe 1968a, 1968b.

[61]Kurin 1990.

of India as well. As Rowe mentions of the Loniya residing in Uttar Pradesh,[62] these salt-makers are also undergoing a process of upward social mobility and claiming to be of Kshatriya or Cauhān status. There is also a myth which links the Loniya to the struggle against Muslim rulers and which 'explains' their subsequent loss of status after their escape from the Muslim armies, which is almost identical with the Aghriā case.[63] In addition, Kurin describes how, in Punjab, Nunari—or Nuniya, Luniya, among other spellings—turned from salt-making to agriculture under British influence at the end of the nineteenth century and were consequently even included in the category of 'notified' agriculturist castes.[64]

Caste brethren from neighbouring Chhattisgarh do not share the dominant Aghriā myth from Orissa that has been discussed here. During a short survey among the Aghriā of Chhattisgarh (Raigarh and Sarangarh areas), some significant differences emerged, particularly regarding the link with Puri as the religious centre of Orissa. Here another point of reference for the migration—Alkatara, a place in Chhattisgarh—figures prominently, which is not very well known among the Aghriā of Orissa. Asked whether the Aghriā[65] had gone to Puri, the president of the Aghriā Samāj of Raigarh, a frequent visitor to meetings of the Aghriā Samāj of Sambalpur and Sundargarh and therefore certainly aware of the dominant myth in that area, replied that the traditional Alkatara Aghriā did not go to Puri, but that others went. Other Aghriā of the region confirmed the change in perspective by claiming that the Aghriā had come from Agra to Bilaspur and other parts of Chhattisgarh, but had not gone on to Puri, while yet others said that the Aghriā had come via Sundargarh to Puri

[62]Rowe 1968a, 98ff.

[63]Rowe (1968a: 68ff) analysed the process of upward mobility among the Noniya/Loniya, arguing that they are originally of Śūdra descent, but have acquired wealth by doing contract work in late nineteenth and twentieth century and claiming Kshatriya/Cauhān status. Subsequently they started to enhance their status by wearing the sacred thread and by creating 'a body of literature which functionally served as a social charter to authenticate the claims' (Rowe 1968a: 71). In their myth published by the influential caste organization from early twentieth century onwards, it is said that in the twelfth century under the Hindu king Prithviraj of Delhi they defended the kingdom as brave warriors, but were defeated and had to escape. Now landless they were forced to turn to salt-making. The process parallelled by an improving economic position is conceived as having reclaimed a rightful status.

[64]Kurin 1990, 989ff; Kurin further describes the different developments of Hindu and Muslim segments of the community—the former sticking to their traditional occupation of salt-making, while the latter turned to agriculture using opportunities to acquire land under canal irrigation schemes. In order to be eligible under and to benefit from such schemes Nunari successfully followed a strategy of being included in the Jat category. In addition, Kurin analyses various folk models that Nunari employ to conceptionalize their own community. Though it is highly speculative, one can certainly not exclude the possibility of an Aghriā origin as salt makers who turned to agriculture as described by Kurin (1990) or as indicated by Rowe (1968a, 1968b).

[65]Unfortunately I could not meet and communicate with these Alkatara Aghriā.

and spread over Orissa subsequently. Still others argued that there might have been different waves of immigration and that although some Aghriā might have gone to Puri, not all of them did so. Thus the link between the Aghriā in Chhattisgarh and Puri as centre of the Jagannātha cult—a connection so prominent in Orissa itself—is rather weak in Chhattisgarh. Some Aghriā in Chhattisgarh whom I questioned had no idea whatever about any mythological link between the Aghriā and Puri or Jagannātha, which is not surprising given their greater geographical distance from the coast of Orissa.[66] However, as far as I know no other religious centres feature in Aghriā myths from Chhattisgarh. Instead, here, links with other communities are mentioned, such as the Kurmi, although their proposals for marriages with the Aghriā have been rejected by the latter.

CONCLUSION

Beginning with the long genealogy given in the first part of a dominant myth, the Aghriā highlight their descent from the moon and later from Bidur as a leading mythical figure in the *Mahābhārata*. Subsequently a change in profession is described in the second part, linked to migration from one political centre, namely, Agra, to another, politico-religious centre, namely, Puri, the two locations being sharply contrasted. Through the combination of a divine order from Lord Jagannātha and a fault of their own, the Aghriā are forced to move into a peripheral region between these centres. However, the myths presented here correspond only very loosely at best to historical facts, as the case of Adil Shah documents.

The Aghriā perceive of their position as being in between, not only in the geographical sense, but also in terms of status. Their mythical migration as a transformative process expresses a perceived decline in status, from warriors to peasants. Similarly the Kshatriya status they lay claim to is not unambiguous in their own stories and is contested by others. Given the history of the Aghriā from the end of the nineteenth century on the village level, they established themselves fairly successfully as landowners and 'village kings', as has been discussed elsewhere.[67] One might argue that the rise of the Aghriā in the late-nineteenth and early-twentieth centuries might be related to a concurring myth describing a great past. The cases of the Noniya in north India and of other communities have shown that a process of upward mobility is quite often reflected in an elaborated 'caste history' published by an influential caste organization.[68] Thus a process of Kshatriyaization might be discovered among the Aghriā, who share many features with the Noniya. In contrast to the Noniya, however, the Aghriā have not only an influential caste council trying to enhance

[66]That does not mean, however, that Jagannath is not worshipped in many parts of Chhattisgarh (see also Babb 1975: 144).

[67]Skoda 2005.

[68]Rowe 1968a.

their caste status by publishing a 'caste history'. They also have their traditional bards who narrate their myths and in turn may be considered important for status as well.

In addition, the Aghriā myths of which written sources exist from the early twentieth century onwards appear to reflect and perhaps imitate earlier *vaṃśāvalī* or chronicles of the ruling families of the feudatory states of Orissa. These family chronicles and the Aghriā myths have certain features in common, such as conflicts with Muslims or a divine intervention determining the fate of the protagonists. Therefore, the existence of such myths among the Aghriā, seen as peasants-turned-village kings in predominantly tribal areas, may indicate the spread of the ideas and structures of kingship on this tribal frontier.

Finally, what Aghriā mythology does not express is also significant. In the myths discussed here, the Aghriā are linked to Brahmans on the one hand and to Chamār on the other, that is, to the extreme poles of caste society. However, no direct reference is made to tribal society, to their immediate neighbouring communities. This link is completely absent, suggesting that the Aghriā firmly perceive and maintain their roots in caste society, though these are simultaneously extended into tribal society.

REFERENCES

Babb, L.A. 1975. *The Divine Hierarchy: Popular Hinduism in Central India*, New York: Columbia University Press.

Basu, H. 2000. 'Die Göttin und die Chāraṇ: das Gedächtnis des Königtums, Verwandtschaft und Askese in Kacch (westl. Indien)', unpublished habilitation thesis. Berlin: Free University of Berlin.

Berkemer, G. 1993. *Little Kingdoms in Kalinga: Ideologie, Legitimation und Politik regionaler Eliten*, Stuttgart: Steiner.

Burridge, K.O.L. 1988 [1968]. 'Lévi-Strauss and Myth', in E. Leach, 91-118.

Haig, W. 1958 [1928]. *Cambridge History of India*, vol. 3: *Turks and Afghans*, Delhi: S. Chand.

Das, Sudramuni Sarala 1983. *Sāralā Mahābhārata: Caritrara Citraśālā*, ed. Sarala Sahitya Samsad, Cuttack: Grantha Mandir.

Doniger, W. 2002. *Splitting the Difference: Gender and Myth in Ancient Greece and India*, Delhi: Oxford University Press.

Douglas, M. 1988 [1968]. 'The Meaning of Myth, with Special Reference to "La Geste d' Asdiwal"', in E. Leach (ed.), *The Structure of Myth and Totemism*, London: Tavistock, 49-70.

Dumont, L. 1980 [1966]. *Homo Hierarchicus: The Caste System and its Implications*, Chicago: The University of Chicago Press.

Elwin, V. 1939. *The Baiga*, London: John Murray.

———1991 [1942]. *The Agaria*, Bhopal: Vanya Prakashan.

———2000 [1936]. *Leaves from the Jungle: Life in a Gond Village*, Delhi: Oxford University Press.

Goody, J. and I. Watt. 1986 [1968]. 'Konsequenzen der Literalität', in J. Goody, I. Watt and K. Gough (eds.), *Entstehung und Folgen der Schriftkultur*, Frankfurt am Main: Suhrkamp, 45-104.

Hardenberg, R. 2000. *Die Ideologie eines Hindu-Königtums: Struktur und Bedeutung der Rituale des Königs von Puri, Orissa/Indien*, Berlin: Das Arabische Buch.

Kulke, H. and D. Rothermund 1999 [1986]. *A History of India*, London: Routledge.

Kulke, H. 2001. *Kings and Cults: State Formation and Legitimation in India and Southeast Asia*, Delhi: Manohar (rpt.).

———2001a [1976]. 'Kshatriyaization and Social Change: A Study in Orissan Setting', in Kulke 2001, 82-92.

———2001b [1987a]. 'The Chronicles and the Temple Records of the Mādaḷā Pāñji of Puri: A Reassessment of the Evidence', in Kulke 2001, 137-58.

———2001c [1987b]. 'Reflections on the Sources of the Temple Chronicles of the Mādaḷā Pāñji of Puri', in Kulke 2001, 159-91.

Kurin, R. 1990. 'Turbans, Skirts and Spirit: Folk Models of a Punjabi Muslim Brotherhood', in *Social Analysis* 28, 97-113.

Leach, E. (ed.). 1988. *The Structural Study of Myth and Totemism*, London: Tavistock.

———1991. *Lévi-Strauss: Zur Einführung*, Hamburg: Junius.

Lévi-Strauss, C. 1992 [1973]. 'Die Geschichte des Asdiwal', in C. Lévi-Strauss, *Strukturale Anthropologie II*, Frankfurt am Main: Suhrkamp, 169-224.

———1996 [1980]. *Mythos und Bedeutung*, Frankfurt am Main: Suhrkamp.

———1985. *Der Blick aus der Ferne*, Munich: Fink.

Nanda, S. 1994. 'Study on Secular Growth Trend in Orissa', unpublished Ph.D. thesis. Sambalpur: Sambalpur University.

O'Flaherty, W.D. 1988 [1976]. *The Origins of Evil in Hindu Mythology*, Delhi: Motilal Banarsidass.

Panda, S.K. 1999. *Political and Cultural History of Orissa*, Delhi: New Age International.

Patel, S.K. 1995. 'Origin of the Agarias', in *Orissa History Congress, Proceedings of 1995 Session*, 103-5.

Pfeffer, G. 1978. 'Puri's Vedic Brahmans: Continuity and Change in their Traditional Institutions', in A. Eschmann, H. Kulke, and G.C. Tripathi (eds.), *The Cult of Jagannath and the Regional Tradition of Orissa*, Delhi: Manohar, 421-37.

———2000. 'Tribal Ideas', in *Journal of Social Sciences* 4, 4, 331-46. (Special Issue: Roland Hardenberg (ed.), *Asian World Views: Context and Structure*, Sambalpur, Deparment of Anthropology.)

Pocock, D.F. 1972. *Kanbi and Patidar*, Oxford: Clarendon Press.

Risley, H.H. 1981 [1891]. *Tribes and Castes of Bengal: Ethnographic Glossary*, Vol. 1, Calcutta: Firma K.L. Mukhopadhyay.

Rowe, W.L. 1968a. 'The New Cauhāns: A Caste Mobility Movement in North India', in J. Silverberg (ed.), *Social Mobility in the Caste System in India*, The Hague: Mouton.

———1968b. 'Mobility in the Nineteenth Century Caste System', in M. Singer and B. Cohn (eds.), *Structure and Change in Indian Society*, Chicago: Aldine, 201-7.

Russell, R.V. and R.B. Hira Lal. 1975 [1916]. *Tribes and Castes of the Central Provinces of India*, vol. 2, Delhi: Cosmo (rpt.).

Schnepel, B. 2002. *The Jungle Kings: Ethnohistorical Aspects of Politics and Ritual in Orissa*, Delhi: Manohar.

Skoda, U. 2005. *The Aghria: A Peasant Caste on a Tribal Frontier*, Delhi: Manohar.

Sörensen, S. 1978 [1904]. *An Index to the Names in the Mahabharata*, Delhi: Motilal Banarsidass.

Thapar, R. 2000a [1978]. 'Origin Myths and the Early Indian Historical Tradition', in R. Thapar, *Cultural Pasts*, Delhi: Oxford University Press, 754-81.

———2000b [1992]. 'Clan, Caste and Origin Myths in Early India', in R. Thapar, *Cultural Pasts*, Delhi: Oxford University Press, 782-96.

Trautmann, T.R. 1995 [1981]. *Dravidian Kinship*, Delhi: Vistaar.

Tripathi, B. (ed.). 1972. *Census of India 1971, Series 16 - Orissa, Part IX-A*, Delhi, Govt. of India: Manager of Publications.

van der Veen, K. 1973. 'Marriage and Hierarchy among Anavil Brahmans of South Gujarat', in *Contributions to Indian Sociology*, n.s., 7, 36-52.

Zimmermann, F. 1987. *The Jungle and the Aroma of Meats: An Ecological Theme in Hindu Medicine*, Berkeley: University of California Press.

CHAPTER 15

Interrogating Stereotypes: Exploring the Princely States in Colonial Orissa*

BISWAMOY PATI

> Whilst in ordinary life every shopkeeper is very well able to distinguish between what somebody professes to be and what he really is, our historiography has not yet won this trivial insight. It takes every epoch at its word and believes that everything that it says and imagines about itself is true.
>
> MARX and ENGELS, *The German Ideology*

INTRODUCTION

This paper examines the historical basis of labels attributed to the *andharua mulakas* or 'dark zones' of Orissa. While popular memory remembers the people in the princely states as *garhjatias* who accepted and tolerated their despotic chiefs and were *Dhenkanalias* (a term used disparagingly to describe the people of the state of Dhenkanal), the question of whether the terror struck by these despots has any empirical historical basis or is a part of a fantasized nationalist construction needs to be examined. This becomes necessary in a climate in which there seems to be some re-thinking of the magnitude of the problems in the former princely states or zamindaris in colonial India.[1] Yet another stereotype relates to the personal world of the princes, namely, their education, exposure to the West and interest in reforms, which needs to be contextualized within the real world in which the bulk of the people in the state lived.[2]

Outlining the details of some of the princely states of Orissa, this chapter examines the problems posed by a feudal system that rested in the lap of

*I would like to thank the participants in the Orissa Research Programme conclave at Salzau (13-18 May 2003) on 'Centres out There? Facets of Subregional Identities' for their suggestions and comments. I would like to dedicate this paper to Prof. Hermann Kulke.

[1]It would not be possible to distinguish rigidly the princely states from the zamindaris or even so-called British Orissa without being trapped by the classification strategies of colonial discourse. In factual terms, Orissa had 24 princely states that were incorporated into the province in 1947-8.

[2]B. Ramusack, 1996, refers to reformatory health initiatives, without any reference to the basic questions related to the resources that were utilized in these projects and the problems they posed. As I. Copland (1997, 5), puts it, truly vicious rulers were rare; he points to how some of them were educated at Aligarh, Oxford, etc.

colonialism and how this impacted upon the day-to-day lives of the common people. Colonial and nationalist sources, as well as those of the Prajamandal movement and oral evidence collected from interviews, have been explored for this chapter. Some of the typical points of argumentation are described in order to interrogate constructions of post-Orientalist Orientalism that tend to romanticize the princely rulers and in turn gloss over the despotic order in these enclaves.[3]

THE SETTING

The princely states of Orissa were created on the permanent settlement model. Let us begin by examining the agrarian and social structure in the seven princely states that form the focus of this study, and start with Dhenkanal. In 1804 the state of Dhenkanal entered into an agreement with the British. In 1849 it had its first revenue settlement. The gross rental (land) of the state increased from Rs. 63,316 in 1846 to Rs. 2,39,347 in 1923. Interestingly, the *peshkush* paid by the state to the colonial government was only Rs. 5,099. At the top was the 'invisible' colonial government, followed by the raja. This state had no zamindars. The dominant section of the state comprised people holding *khanja* (charitable) and *lakhiraj* (rent-free) tenures as well as holders of *brahmottar*, *debottar* and *paikan jagir* lands. These were land grants to Brahmans, specific idols to facilitate worship and the 'martial' Paika caste, respectively. They were held chiefly by Brahmans and Kshatriyas. Rarely did they cultivate their own lands but got others to do it for them. The state depended on the *sarbarkar*s (revenue officers enjoying privileges) to collect land revenue and other cesses as well as help out in the administration. They received commissions of 12.8 per cent for the land revenue and 6.4 per cent for the forest cess. Their posts were hereditary, but they could be removed by the state.

The *raiyati* tenures comprised *thani* (resident), *pahi* (non-resident), *chandna* (a non-agricultural homestead) and *paikali*. The *paikali* tenures, which were originally tax-free, came to be taxed under the 1923 Settlement. These *paikali* tenures were held by Paikas (feudal warriors). The *thani raiyat*s were mostly Chasas, the largest caste group in the state. There were some *raiyat*s who held the lands of occupancy. These *raiyat*s were purely tenants-at-will and had no occupancy rights. Some *adivasis* (like Savaras, Gonds, and Kandhas) and some

[3]Most of the princely rulers of Orissa invented their past through their *rajabansabalis* (i.e. accounts of their family histories). This was a process that saw a virtual competition among the princely rulers to prove their 'ancientness' and in many cases establish links with the martial 'Rajput' tradition of north India, being prompted by colonialism's desire to classify the states; 'Brief Histories of Each of the 24 Feudatory States (1909)', can be cited as a classic example to prove the point being made here. The trend to play down the oppressive component has its origins in some of the earlier works on the subject, like Ramusack (1978) and Copland (1997). Bhagavan (2003) is deeply influenced by a spirit of romanticism and is a victim of 'modernity' in his examination of the princely states of Baroda and Mysore. I am using the term 'feudal' here in a loose sense.

Untouchables (like Panas, Bauris, and Dombs) held lands which they were not supposed to sell to non-*adivasis* or upper castes, respectively. At the bottom were the agricultural labourers, mostly Panas and most probably some *adivasis*, invisible in the settlement reports. These agricultural labourers were called *haliyas* and were recruited around March for one year. They were paid a loan in cash and paddy by their employers, which formed the basis of an 'agreement' for them to work. They were also paid three *manas* of paddy per day and were given a small plot of land (about a quarter of an acre) or something in kind, in lieu of the plot. The female agricultural labourers or *kamtunis* were not given these plots of land. There is evidence of *bethi*, *begar* (both forms of forced labour) and *rasad* (free supply of provisions).[4]

As for Talcher, this state made a treaty with the British government in 1848. The state paid a tribute of about Rs. 1,040, though its land revenue collection rose from Rs. 21,290 in 1846 to Rs. 58,971 by 1913. As in Dhenkanal, the colonial establishment was at the top, but in real and visible terms since the state had coal deposits which were mined. The chief controlled the state, which had no zamindars in the state. Land grants were held by the dominant castes. The *sarbarkars* collected the land revenue as well as other levies and managed the administration. Their position was similar to that of their Dhenkanal counterparts. The *raiyati* tenures comprised the *thani*, *pahi*, and *chandna*. The Chasas, who were the dominant agricultural caste, constituted nearly 37 per cent of the state's population. The majority of the *raiyats* were 'average' (middle peasants), very few well-to-do ('rich' peasants). Most of the agricultural work was done by the members of the peasant family themselves. There were few under-*raiyats* and some of them had *raiyats* under them, who were tenants-at-will. Their rents were paid in cash or kind (*sanja/bhag*). The agricultural labourers were composed of Panas and some *adivasis* like Savaras, Gonds and Kandhas. Male agricultural labourers were paid 4 annas and females 1 anna per working day. Some of the Panas settled down as peasants on small plots ('poor' peasants). The state extracted *bethi* and *begar*. Besides, the chief boasted of the *kankar* collection during the Naanka (1866) famine, which he expected would yield a great profit.

The state had some workers in the coal mines and the railway system, who came mostly from the de-peasantized section of the state's population and people from outside. Coal was an important resource from the point of view of the colonial establishment throughout the nineteenth and the twentieth centuries.[5] What needs to be borne in mind is that the existence of coal mines

[4] *Final Report on the Settlement of the Dhenkanal Feudatory State*, 1966, 11-14; 24-8; 40. *Memoranda on the Indian States, 1930* (1931, 222-3) gives us the amount of the *peshkush*; R.K. Ramdhyani, n.d., 77-82.

[5] *Report on the Land Revenue Settlement 1911-1912 Talcher State*, 1963, 13, 21-2, 31-5, 43, and *Completion Report of the Talcher State Revision Settlement Season 1928-9*, n.d., 13-14, 19; Ramdhyani, n.d., 280-6; 'Confidential History of Talcher State (1926)'. The details of the *kankar* tax are not known. It seems to be derived from *kankar*, which means

explains both the visible presence of colonialism and the importance attached to Talcher by it.

Ranpur state had almost the same agrarian structure as the two other states just studied. The first Settlement of 1877-9 was followed by the 1880-1 Settlement, which expected the peasants to pay three-quarters of the assessed *jama* in cash and the remaining quarter in kind. This was followed by the 1899 Settlement, which formally abolished the system of grain rent and saw the intervention of the colonial government in a big way, leading to the appointment of a diwan. There were no zamindaris in the state, and the land grants were roughly similar to those of Dhenkanal and Talcher.

What, perhaps, ought to be mentioned here is the existence of a set of *khanjadar*s who were of the Kshatriya caste and descendants of the chief's family. Their *khanja*s (land grants) were privileged enclaves where they wielded power and authority. They collected taxes through their agents, paying a quarter to the chief. The *sarbarkar*s under them were paid a commission of 5 per cent and some of the *khanjadar*s performed this role. The *raiyati* tenures were of similar categories and the *raiyat*s were mostly Chasas. The *raiyat*s of *khanjadar*s, however, had no permanent rights over their land, i.e. they could not sell it. We have no evidence of the caste composition of the under-*raiyat*s, and we only know that they had no rights and could be ejected. It is possible that some adivasis, like the Lodhas, Kandhas and Savaras, held some of these tenures. The agricultural labourers were composed chiefly of Panas, although other Untouchables like the Dombs, Chamars, Bauris and Hadis perhaps also performed this role. Some adivasis were most probably agricultural labourers. Along with several levies, the state extracted *bethi*, *begar*, *magan* (forced contributions) and *rasad* (forced supply of various items).[6]

The first reference to the joint drive to appropriate resources was premised on the colonial administration's demand for wood needed to manufacture salt in the 1850s. In 1855 the durbar, we are told, demanded a high price for supplying this. In 1877 its diwan admitted to some of the oppressive levies, including *hooba* and *sadabart*, two taxes that amounted to 17½ seers of paddy per *bigha* of land owned, the reason for which was 'not known'. In addition, *basanel* was collected on the basis of each plough owned. Levies like *toila* (at 5 annas per head), 5 seers of oil per mill from Telis (oilmen), 2 annas from each house for the *rathajatra*, along with fees on the remarriage of widows, were also imposed. The inhabitants of the state were expected to offer *bheti*, *sunia* and *ank*. Each village had to provide three cartloads of vegetables on certain Hindu festivals like Dutiya Ausa and Charkhai, along with a general

---

a long-handled spade. Perhaps it was a form of forced labour which was extracted during the 1866 famine, since we are told how the chief 'had got Villiers & Co. to agree use it in their works', p. 10. The *Report on the General Administration of the Tributary Mahals of Orissa for the Year 1890-1*, 9, mentions that Talcher had large deposits of coal.

[6]G.N. Singh, 1963, 10, 32-6, 61-71; it was mentioned that the land revenue had gone up by 40.5 per cent over the 1899 Settlement (ibid. 57); Ramdhyani, n.d., 82-92.

levy on Shree Panchami (a religious festival of the Hindus). By 1894 the durbar sought to impose further restrictions on the use of the forests by the inhabitants of the state, a point that indicates the massive profits extracted from this sector. In addition, efforts were made to increase rent collection above the fixed amount (viz., a quarter of all produce in kind).[7]

As for Nilgiri, in 1809 its chief agreed to pay an annual tribute of Rs. 2,108 to the British government. The proceeds of the land revenue increased fivefold between 1850 and 1920. The agrarian structure of Nilgiri was almost similar to the other states under discussion. There was a marked absence of big landlords. The state had a similar pattern of land grants and *raiyati* tenures. The subtenants had the same position. Some jagirs were held by adivasis, in exchange for which they were expected to contribute unpaid labour to the state. These adivasis were mostly Bhumij, Bhuiyans, Kols and Santals. The agricultural labour force of the state was composed of these adivasis and Panas. Their wages were mostly in kind. Besides *begar*, a number of cesses were imposed.[8]

Mayurbhanj, the next state to be considered, was the largest princely state in Orissa. Its alliance with the British had been tested by confrontations between the East India Company and the ruler of Nagpur. This formed the basis of a relationship that was formalized in 1912, when the durbar agreed to pay a *peshkush* of Rs. 1,001 per year. Mayurbhanj had plenty of resources and had the largest income among Orissa's princely states, which stood at Rs. 29,41,000 in the 1930s. It had a zamindari, Kaptipada, which had been under it since 1890.[9]

Mayurbhanj poses serious problems for historians, especially due to the lack of sources, the settlement reports for this state not being available. Along with this, several factors conceal the internal order of exploitation.[10] I will try to discuss some typical aspects of exploitation on the basis of the empirical evidence available. It can perhaps be mentioned here that one of Mayurbhanj's chiefs, Sri Ramachandra Bhanja, was the first president of the Orissa Sammilani (who delivered the first presidential address in the Cuttack session in 1903), which championed the cause of the unification of the Oriya-speaking tracts.[11] This body was a congregation of the Oriya middle class, which joined the

[7]'Confidential History of Ranpur State', R/2-306/13.

[8]*Final Report on the Nilgiri Settlement 1917-22*, 1922, 34-41; 51; Ramdhyani, n.d., 195-200. B. Das pointed to the absence of 'big' landlordism in the state and characterized it as a 'small peasant' economy (interview 1982).

[9]Senapati and Sahu 1967, 72-5, 84; *Memoranda on the Indian States, 1932* (1933) puts the average annual revenue at Rs. 28,20,000; the payment to the government was Rs. 1,068, an increase of Rs. 67 over what had been paid in 1812, as mentioned earlier (ibid., 222-3). Mahtab et al. 1939, 218.

[10]In fact, it is worth pondering whether the omission of Mayurbhanj from Ramdhyani (undated) which examines almost all the princely states of Orissa, is a mere coincidence or a result of this process.

[11]Senapati and Sahu 1967, 81.

princes and the zamindars of Orissa. Alongside, the post-colonial middle class and bureaucrats like Nilamani Senapati, the pioneer who compiled the data relating to the *District Gazetteers of Orissa*, hardly spoke of there being any unpleasant features in Mayurbhanj. After all, many like him were part of an order that had been patronized by the durbar and its educational intervention.[12] These sections have contributed significantly to concealing the structure of oppression and virtually legitimizing it. These two features need to be borne in mind while exploring the structure of exploitation at Mayurbhanj.

That everything was not going well for the people becomes clear from their anger in the context of the settlement operations in early 1866, when the Naanka famine hit Orissa, especially the coastal tract. The people of Bamanghatty and Uparbhag were particularly affected by the harassment of the settlement officials. The anger of the adivasi population, comprising Santals, Bhumijs, Kols and Hos, was also directed against the Hindu population of Gaudas, Chasas and Mahantis who had taken over their lands. While the officiating superintendent of the feudatory states, T.E. Ravenshaw, is accused of being 'unwilling to see starvation' (due to the famine), it is vital to see this discontent as a result of the settlement operations in the volatile context of the famine, which polarized the anger of the state's population. Moreover, it also needs to be emphasized that various institutions created during the rule of Krushna Chandra Bhanja (1867-82), like the jail and hajat system, the charitable dispensary and the postal system, also created new burdens on the people.[13]

The laudatory references to Sri Ramachandra Bhanja increasing the forest revenuc from Rs. 30,000 to 1,50,000 per year can similarly be taken as illustrating the mechanism of exploitation that troubled the adivasis. After all, the adivasi rebellion that shook the state in May 1917 had a pre-history of economic hardship to which the adivasi population of the state was exposed—increasing pressures, alienation of land and the loss of forest rights—which was triggered by forced recruitment for the First World War. Even after being assured about the recruiting operations, the Santals continued to hold mass meetings. These gatherings 'discuss[ed] sundry grievances with regards to some features of the administration', a point which illustrates the pressures on the people of the state. The context had a special significance with regard to the colonial presence in Mayurbhanj. Thus, the sudden death of Sri Ramachandra Bhanja in 1912 led to a minority, and the state came directly under the colonial establishment till 1920.[14]

[12]Ibid., 80-1. Thus we are told that the Maharaja improved the school which produced, among others, three Indian Civil Service officers, viz., Nilamani Senapati, Rabindranath Bannerjee and Satyendra Mohan Dhar, and one Indian Education Service officer.

[13]Ibid., 338-9.

[14]Ibid., 79-82; *Report of the Indian States Committee 1928-29*, 1929. During this time the state was under the Court of Wards. The *Report on the General Administration of the Tributary Mahals of Orissa for the Year 1890-91*, 9, refers to the presence of iron ore; this undoubtedly made Mayurbhanj important from the point of view of colonialism.

Gangpur, however, had a structure that was quite different from all the states we have discussed so far. Gangpur received a *sanad* from the British government in 1827. The relationship between the colonial government and the chief was regulated by the *sanad* granted in 1889, which was renewed in 1905 when it was transferred from the Central Provinces to Orissa, and a political agent was appointed to assist the chief, this indicating the direct presence of colonialism. The state paid Rs. 10,000 to the colonial government. Nevertheless, the land revenue tapped by the state can be judged from the following table:

Name of area under the chief	*Land revenue demand before the 1929-36 settlement in Rs. (appx.)*	*Land revenue demand after settlement in Rs. (appx.)*	*Percentage increase (appx.)*
Khalsa	110,257	149,861	36 %
Zamindaris:			
Nagra	27,116	38,538	42 %
Hemgir	11,371	18,786	65 %
Sargipali	4,691	6,962	48 %
Sarapgarh	1,855	2,583	39 %
Hathibari	5,889	8,956	52 %
Total	161,179	225,686	(avg.) 47 %

Moreover, by the 1940s the total revenue of the state was Rs. 8.22 lakh. The raja of Gangpur had the Khalsa land directly under him. These were originally leased out to *gountia*s for five years in lieu of cash. These *gountia*s had taken over villages reclaimed by the adivasis, and it appears that they were mostly the affluent section of the adivasis. However, by the 1890s the preference for such leases was being given to Aghrias and Telis (non-adivasis) of Sambalpur. Given the logic of the system, the *gountia*s enjoyed privileges in terms of lands (*bhogra*), and there were no limits on how much they could collect from the peasants. Then there were the customary land grants as in any other state. The state had five zamindaris: Nagra, Hemgir, Sargipalli, Sarapgarh and Hathibari. These were privileged landed elements, who did not have to encounter problems like the 'sunset law'. They paid *tekauli* to the chief, which amounted to only 5 per cent of the amount they collected; this was raised to 10 per cent in the 1936 Settlement. The zamindars had various privileges and enjoyed a number of rights. They were originally Bhuiyans, but distinguished themselves from their tribesmen by calling themselves Khandayat Bhuiyans. Below them were the *ganjhu*s or village headmen, whose ancestors had cleared the forests and who were the patriarchal heads of families. The fact that most of them were Bhuiyans implies the possibility that they had received land grants. There were two main kinds of *ganjhu*: *khuntkalti* and *thica*. These headmen were the intermediaries between the zamindars and the tenants. They were given 45 per cent of the collection as their commission and had some privileges in land too. Below them were the sub-*ganjhus* and *sikmi gountias*, who assisted the head *ganjhus*. The chief also had three *parganadars* under him: Raiboga, Erga and Daldali. Raiboga paid 50 per cent of the collection to the chief, while the *parganadars* of Erga and Daldali themselves decided the amount they had to pay. These *parganadars* had a large number of villages under them; they had absolute rights like the zamindars and enjoyed rent-free lands. They either collected taxes directly or used the services of *gountias*. The evidence available is extremely meagre, but one can perhaps deduce that these *parganadars* were also adivasis. There was no distinction between the *thani* and *pahi raiyats*. There were *chandna raiyats* as well. The Aghrias were the chief cultivators of the state. They had occupancy rights but could be removed by the *gountias* or *ganjhus* for failing to pay rent. Some peasants who tilled the *bhogra* or *nijchas* lands were tenants-at-will, as were those under-*raiyats* who held the lands of others. Along with a host of cesses, the state extracted *bethi* and *begar*.

The agricultural labourers came mostly from the adivasi population and were composed of Mundas, Bhuiyans, Oraons, Gandas and Kisans. Their wages varied from 3 annas a day for men to 2 annas a day for women. Some of the adivasis resorted to rice cultivation. It is interesting to note that as late as 1911 there is evidence of Karuwas, who were food-gatherers and hunters, bartering forest products for food.[15]

Kalahandi, the next princely state under discussion, had five zamindaris: Karlapat, Mahulpatana, Madanpur-Rampur, Lanjigarh and Kashipur. Interestingly adivasi rebellions and their 'management' provided the starting point for the links with colonialism. Kalahandi came directly under colonial rule in 1863, and this was formalized by the *sanad* of 1867 and complemented by the two summary settlements of 1883 and 1888 under the direct supervision of the colonial establishment, which had taken over Kalahandi's administration in 1882. Incidentally the railway line linking Kalahandi with Rajnandgaon was inaugurated in 1883. Kalahandi seems to have been a prize catch for the Empire, given that it was the only Orissan princely state to be granted a nine-gun salute in the nineteenth century.[16]

The power structure was dominated by the not so visible colonial administration, except during the 1880s, when the state was taken over by the

[15] I. Mukherjee 1938, 17-19, 29, 33, 41-6; and Ramdhyani, n.d., 82-92. There were 907 *ganjhus* and *gountias* in the state; 19 per cent of them were Bhuiyans and 15 per cent were Agharias. Besides upper castes (Brahmans and Kshatriyas) there were low castes and Untouchable *ganjhus* and *gountias* (ibid., 18-19). *Memoranda on Indian States*, 1931, 222-3, mentions the amount paid by the state to the British.

[16] J. Das 1962, iii; *The Imperial Gazetteer*, 1908, 293; Thus, *Memoranda on the Indian States, 1932* (1933, 232) informs us that Mayurbhanj was granted a nine-gun salute status for services in connection with the First World War on 1 January 1918; Land takeovers without payments continued; thus Ramdhayani, n.d., 112, cites a 1928 case, when land was acquired to build a railway line without any compensation being paid.

colonial administration at the top, followed by the chief who had five or six zamindars (who were members of the ruling family) under him. The raja held the Khalsa land directly under him and granted *maufi* tenures to gods and Brahmans. The state paid a paltry *peshkush* to the British, which amounted to Rs. 16,000 in 1938. However, the resources siphoned off were massive. Thus, in 1894 the total income of the state was Rs. 1,11,000. In 1933-4 its total land revenue alone was about Rs. 2,12,698. And, by 1938 its total income stood at Rs. 6,25,000. Consequently, in a period of forty-four years, viz., 1894-1938, the total income of the state increased more than five times.

The magnitude of the problem can also be judged from the level of enhancement after the settlements. Thus, the 1911 Settlement led to a 30 per cent enhancement for the villages, with a 50 per cent increase for individual peasants. Similarly, the 1922 Settlement was marked by a 60 per cent increase for the villages and 100 per cent rise in the tax paid by the *raiyat*s. Also, the land tax in Kalahandi was higher than in the neighbouring states.[17] The exploitative system was also perfected by the zamindars, who had sub-zamindars under them. The zamindars were quite powerful and levied their own tolls and taxes. The colonial administration was closely aligned with the zamindars, whose presence by the twentieth century was felt in the remotest corners of the state.[18]

At the village level, the Brahmans and the Kulta *gountia*s dominated the power structure. These were the landed elements who also dominated moneylending and the grain trade. There was only one type of *ryotwari* tenure in the state. One should mention here the indigenous internal exploiters within adivasi society, who either sought upward social mobility and became integrated into the caste system, or else continued to identify themselves as adivasis.[19]

The *gountia*s were landed elements. Every village was held by a *gountia*, and the *maufi* villages had *sikmi gountia*s. The built-in logic of parasitism can be grasped if one keeps in mind the fact that *gounti* rights were frequently auctioned off to the highest bidder. The power of these *gountia*s pivoted around their tax-collecting role, with which came vital privileges. They owned the best land (*bhogra*). They could reclaim wasteland and take over land surrendered by ejected peasants. They were supposed to construct water sources, and

[17]J. Das 1962, 12, 16; Ramdhyani, n.d., 112, 115. It should be noted that Mahtab et al. (1939, 195) refer specifically to the high rents collected at Kalahandi compared to the other Western Orissan states like Patana. Thus, the highest rent collected at Patana was Rs. 1-8-0, whereas at Kalahandi it was Rs. 6-11-0.

[18]Ramdhyani, n.d., 110-11; *The Imperial Gazetteer*, 294; out of the total of 69,194 holdings in 1946-50, Brahmans had 2,461, Kultas had 2,196, Gonds had 13,725, Kandhas had 11,910 and Dombs had 12,350. Although the Brahmans and Kultas together had 4,657 holdings, land was heavily concentrated in their hands, with the others having smaller holdings. Interestingly, as mentioned by R.K. Ramdhyani, n.d., some of the settlement reports of the zamindaris were not available (ibid., 110).

[19]J. Das 1962, 3; Senapati and Kuanr 1980, 99; Ramdhyani, n.d., 112.

originally were rewarded by the durbar for these. However, although the water systems were built by forced labour, these were 'stolen' from the people subsequently. The *gountias*' power stretched, without any legal basis, into the *dongarla* area. They tapped the *dongarchasis* and appropriated the resources that were thus obtained.[20]

Large parts of Kalahandi were not surveyed even up to the 1940s. Most of the *dongarla* area was part of this unsurveyed region. Although not assessed systematically, the adivasi inhabiting them were sometimes taxed on the seed capacity of the strips they had cleared for cultivation or the number of ploughs and axes they owned. In the twentieth century, settlements were made quite frequently (every six to twenty years) with these people. The mode of assessment and the regularity of the settlements, coupled with the nature of cultivation, made things extremely difficult for the people in *dongarla* areas.

The villages had some officials such as the *jhankar*, *chaukidar* and *nariah*, and washermen and barbers held service tenures. The occupancy tenants had no rights. Some of them leased out portions of their land to others in return for paddy or cash rents. The *sukhabasi* were those who held homesteads not above 0.25 decimals. Together with the agricultural labourers, they worked for others. The normal working day was eleven hours, for which men got 3 *seers* of paddy and women half of this in the early part of the twentieth century. This became 25 paise in 1942 and 37 paise in 1945 for males. The forced labourers were recruited from among the occupancy tenants, the *sukhabasis* and the agricultural labourers.[21]

Conventional practices included the recruitment of forced labour. This was supposedly abolished in 1923 and a cess imposed in lieu. Nevertheless the practice continued, and what was witnessed was the co-existence of monetization and feudal exploitation, which crippled the people. Then there was *rasad*. Given the fact that the state had monopoly rights on almost everything, anything ranging from forest products to grain was 'bought' for paltry amounts from the people. Among the other ways adopted for extracting money, we should mention the innumerable cesses, which assumed alarming proportions between the 1880s and 1940s. The concept of compensation to those whose lands were taken over or of remissions and suspensions in years of crisis was not known.[22]

Thus what can be seen in the case of the princely states that we have examined so far is the emergence of a system which was a virtual re-creation of a dead European feudal model, with a colonial aspect. In fact, it is very striking that colonial reports and printed materials project these enclaves along the lines of Europe's past. Although the princely rulers paid token amounts to the colonial government, which were almost fixed amounts, they had access

[20] J. Das 1962, 3; Senapati and Kuanr 1980, 99.

[21] Ramdhyani, n.d., 109, 115; J. Das 1962, 10; Senapati and Kuanr 1980, 234, 269, 274; J. Das (1962, 11-13) refers to land revenue settlements in 1904-5, 1911-12 and 1922-3.

[22] Ramdhyani, n.d., 112-16; Mahtab et al. 1939, 195.

to massive resources which increased with the passage of time. In addition, most of the exploitative practices—such forced labour, forced supply of items, rents which were increased with every land settlement, lack of land rights for the bulk of the peasantry, innumerable levies, low wages, which were even lower for women, and the enforcement of a monopoly system are sharply visible. Nevertheless, features like large-scale transfers of lands belonging to the adivasis, which they made cultivable, are not easily visible.

The existence of the monopoly system, coupled with market fluctuations and their associated problems like the debt structure, needs further elaboration. Thus, the debt structure was linked to an extremely vicious network, which was based on an understanding of prices, and seasons from which recovery was impossible. The case of Kalahandi can be cited here as an example. Thus, food grain prices were lowest immediately after the harvest, and dearest immediately before it. For example, the price of rice fluctuated between 12,130 and 16,800 kg per rupee and that of *mandia* (millet) between 20,527 and 29,857 kg per rupee in 1912. Similarly, the price of rice rose from 18,660 kg per rupee in September 1918 to 8,864 kg per rupee in March 1919, while that of *mandia* rose from 23,325 kg per rupee in April 1918 to 11,662 kg per rupee in March 1919. In 1933-4 the price of rice was 31 *seers* per rupee in December, but 20 *seers* per rupee between July and September. In the same period, the price of *mandia* was 40 *seers* per rupee in April, May, January and February and 32 *seers* per rupee from July to November and in March. Local factors like rumours about impending scarcities as well as general features affecting the colonial economy (viz., the First World War and the 'Great Depression') also exacerbated the situation. And, given these, a harvest 'boom' was actually followed by scarcities, given the hoarding of grain by traders.[23] Consequently, it is important to understand that a level of monetization and of associated capitalist 'development', irrespective of how distorted they were, co-existed with the feudal order, thus making it highly predatory and making life extremely difficult for the people of the state.

It should also be emphasized that some features, like the preservation of social hierarchies, though considered very vital, were nevertheless 'invisible'. This was because they were rooted in social and cultural practices that were intrinsically associated with the caste system itself. One should also refer to patriarchal practices like dowry, which was legitimized by some chiefs. Thus, by demanding 2 lakhs of rupees for the marriage of his son, the Talcher chief was legitimizing a practice which was an integral part of the caste system, and which was a burden for the people of the state.[24]

In discussing this point, one should refer to customs that 'integrated' the adivasis into the brahmanical order through the Jagannatha cult.[25] This proved

[23]Senapati and Kuanr 1980, 229-31; J. Das 1962, 3; *Report on the Administration of Kalahandi for 1933-4*, n.d., 16.

[24]'Confidential History of Talcher State (1926)'.

[25]See, for example, H. Kulke 1993, 93-113.

to be colonialism's greatest legitimizer[26] and was championed by the feudal chiefs since it served to 'disguise' the levies collected during the *rathayatra*. It was through features like the Brahmanical order that a system of exploitation was created. It comprised the chiefs and their 'martial' kinsmen (technically Kshatriyas), along with upper-caste collaborators ranging from Brahmans and Paikas to Kultas and Chasas (as well as privileged sections from among the adivasis like the Khandayats) and state officials who exploited the adivasis and Untouchables. This needs to be linked to restrictions on the use of forests, grazing, the manufacture of liquor, low wages, a crippling debt structure, and land transfers in order to grasp the magnitude of the problems faced by these sections.

It should also be emphasized that the system in the princely states was designed, preserved, and reinforced by colonialism with the active collaboration of the feudal chiefs as its junior partners throughout the nineteenth century. Both were actively involved in siphoning off resources. The system of *peshkush*, which formed the basis of the formal links with the princely states, was only the tip of the iceberg when it came to the question of the 'external' draining away of resources. Colonialism's looting and plunder included diverse features that ranged from building railway lines, mining resources like coal to recruitments made and resources obtained for the First World War.[27]

The Oriya middle class provided this structure with administrative inputs and legitimacy in the early years, even though the situation changed dramatically in the post-1920s, with the rise of the mass movements, including the Prajamandal movement, and the rise of a middle class in the princely states, which questioned the existing order, including the inhuman practices that existed.[28] This explains why features like civil rights, which figured in the demands of the Prajamandal movement in the 1930s, are invisible in what we have seen.

THE PROBLEMS

This section examines the typical features taken up by the Prajamandal movement—not the actual forms of struggle that developed—in the late 1930s in the princely states that I have examined in this chapter. This will serve to historicize the magnitude of these problems and show what the people of the state had to live with.

The Dhenkanal Prajamandal was set up in June 1938. Interestingly, the first

[26] Ibid., 108-10.

[27] Here I am not mentioning the Second World War, in which many of the princes and zamindars of Orissa provided resources, ranging from those collected as 'War Contributions' to aircraft.

[28] This was an all-India body with a presence in the Orissan states. It was associated with the struggles of the states' people against the princes and colonialism; see B. Pati (1993) for details related to the Prajamandal movement in Orissa.

major issue that was taken up by the Prajamandal was related to the question of state monopolies. Thus, its first formal decision was to oppose the high price of *pana* (betel leaf), which was a popular commodity and a monopoly item. The formal decision to boycott *pana* was taken on 2 July 1938. The Prajamandal finalized its demands very soon after this. These included demands for civil liberties and representative government, the abolition of *bethi*, *magan*, the monopoly system for certain commodities and the re-structuring of the forest and tenancy laws. What followed was the stopping of *suniya vethi* (New Year's gift) from 6 September 1938.[29]

The Prajamandal movement united people from different sections, which was naturally perceived as a threat by the durbar. Since the state attached a great deal of importance to the preservation of social hierarchies, it invoked the caste system to disrupt the peoples' struggle. Thus, a typical method adopted by the durbar to counter the Prajamandal movement in 1938 was to divide the unity of the people by employing Untouchables to beat and arrest people of high caste.[30] This trend was seriously resurrected in post-August 1946 as well. Thus, while Brahmans who held *brahmottar* land grants were promised that these would be made permanent, simultaneously landless outcastes were promised lands and were also mobilized to cut the standing crops of Prajamandal activists and sympathizers from the upper castes.[31]

In Talcher, the starting point of the Prajamandal movement was also provided by the hated system of monopolies. In an attempt to promote the sales of a cloth store owned by the raja's brother, khaki uniforms were made compulsory for students in January 1938. This led to a student's strike.[32] The Talcher Prajamandal was formed on 6 September 1938, and its demands included the right to form associations, hold meetings, the abolition of *bethi*, *magan* and *vethi*, modifications of the tenancy and forest laws, and better working conditions in the collieries. From the early phase of the movement, the direct presence of colonialism caused the Prajamandal to appeal to the people not to recognize the durbar and the British authorities. Subsequently, it also set up small shops to sell those commodities that were declared to be under the monopoly system.[33]

The Ranpur Prajamandal's starting point was devoted to a demand for its recognition. Subsequently its demands included the recognition of civil, democratic and social rights, and the abolition of *bethi* and customary feudal levies. What needs to be emphasized is that its basic problem was one of mere survival. The level of intolerance on the part of the durbar, cradled by

[29] All India Congress Committee Papers (hereafter AICC), file no. G-35, Part 1, 1938, Statement of Sarangadhar Das, 27 November 1938; S. Pradhan 1986, 99; *National Front*, 25 September 1938; interview: B. Patnaik 1985.

[30] AICC, Statement of S. Das, 27 November 1938.

[31] All India State People's Conference (hereafter AISPC), file no. 127.

[32] S. Pradhan 1986, 113.

[33] AISPC, file no. 164; *National Front*, 4 June 1939.

colonialism, exploded when Bazellgate, the political agent, was murdered in the state in January 1939.[34]

Nilgiri was perhaps the only state where the divisive politics of caste perpetuated by the durbar were challenged in the course of a process which saw the formation of the Prajamandal itself. Thus, in line with Gandhian ideals of social reform and Harijan uplift, the practice of organizing an annual dinner where people of different castes, including Untouchables, sat and ate together had originated in 1932 in Ajodhya in Nilgiri. The number of people participating in this contributory dinner had increased to two thousand by 1937, and Congressmen like Kailash Chandra Mohanty were addressing the gatherings.[35]

Since this common feasting undermined the basic principle underpinning the order of caste, which operated on the basic principle of preserving its associated hierarchies and, in turn, served to preserve the social order, the durbar decided to act in November 1937. Some of the sponsors of the subversive dinner were asked to explain why they should not be excommunicated. This, along with attempts to prevent meetings, the circulation of radical newspapers like *Krushak* and the arrests of left-wing student activists associated with literacy campaigns, provided the initial spark that led to the foundation of the Prajamandal.[36] What can be seen most clearly in all of this is the feudal order attempting to assert itself against anything that created possibilities for the people to unite and question its authority.

Regarding the demands of the Prajamandal more specifically, it should first of all be mentioned that its list of thirty-one demands included the abolition of all kinds of *bethi*, the lowering of rents (to the level of neighbouring Balasore, which was in British Orissa) and forest rights. It also included the abolition of restrictions on the manufacture of *handia* (rice liquor) and the standardization of rent assessments for adivasis as well as caste Hindus. Subsequently, the Nilgiri Prajamandal incorporated demands which included the abolition of forced levies by *sahukar*s, limiting the maximum interest on loans to 25 per cent, a standardization of measurements for the whole state, and the fixing of a minimum wage at 5 *seer*s of paddy per day.[37]

Mayurbhanj also had a Prajamandal, even though it was largely free of any major struggles in the explosive phase. Interestingly, the Orissa State Peoples' Conference named it as one of the best-administered states, though by 1940

[34]Interview: K. Misra 1984; R. Ram 1986, 113-16. Bazellgate, the political agent of the Orissa states, was murdered in the state by a crowd. He had panicked, shot at and killed someone, after which he was disarmed and beaten to death; for details, see B. Pati 1993, 125-6.

[35]*Nilgiri Praja Andolanara Itihasa*, 1981, 64; *Krushak*, 3 January 1938.

[36]*National Front*, 19 June 1938; Home Political Fortnightly Report, file no. 4/4/1938; *Nilgiri Praja Andolanara Itihasa*, 1981, 74.

[37]According to B. Das (interview 1982), the *sahukar*s gave grain loans in small, Laxman *gaunis* and took back repayments in big, Ram *gaunis*, seeking to justify this on the basis that Ram was Laxman's elder brother.

it was being admitted that civil liberties had been conceded only after the Prajamandal movement developed in the princely states.[38] In 1938, when the Prajamandal movement developed in Orissa and efforts were being made to enquire into the conditions of the people in the states, it was admitted that the adivasi population, which comprised 70 per cent of the people, 'have real grievances'. As reported, adivasis like Kols and Bathudis went to meet the Enquiry Committee at Balasore to express their grievances. These included *bethi* extracted to build schools and state bungalows and repair roads; *rasad* paid to state officials and during *shikar* (i.e. hunting expeditions); a road cess (which was 1 anna per rupee of rent paid), though carts were not allowed to use main roads (which were only for motor cars); 4 annas per month per family as fuel fee; 2 annas per head of cow for grazing cattle in villages outside their own settlement; a fee of 4 annas per yoke of oxen for obtaining Sal wood for agricultural implements; a 12 anna cess for *tassar* (i.e. silk) cultivation; and a *chaukidari* tax of between 2 and 5 annas.[39]

Another point requiring emphasis is the superficiality of the reforms, with criticism being directed against the monarchical and autocratic rule which was marked by a sharp contrast between the capital Baripada, where the 'administration was polished', and the other outlying areas. The lack of irrigation facilities and high land rents—which were not proportionate to the average produce and much beyond the capacity of the people to pay—caused serious indebtedness and undermined the stamina of the people. Sardars or revenue collecting agents used their offices as positions from which to make profits. When the durbar set up representative institutions called *praja sabha*s in 1938 to counter the Prajamandal movement that had swept the princely states, it was dominated by *padhan*s and *mahajan*s, money- and/or paddy-lending exploiters, their emergence in the arena of the state-sponsored public domain illustrating the close links they had with the durbar.[40]

Finally, the 'Resolution of the Prajamandal' in its third Annual Session (14-15 May 1947) under the presidency of Sarat Chandra Das at Pratappur—which was attended by about 20,000 people, including 1,500 women—offers us more clues to understanding the problems faced by the people. Besides thanking the maharaja for joining the Constituent Assembly as it matched the expectations of the Prajamandal, it also outlined some of the grievances of the people. Among the important points, the meeting articulated a demand to do away with all kinds of privileged jagirs and *lakhiraj* tenures, condemned the policy of exporting wood—even though the people of the state faced problems

[38] AISPC, file no. 127, letter of S. Das, Secretary, Orissa State Peoples' Conference, 16 March 1940.

[39] As Mahtab et al. (1939, 218-19) put it: 'Evidently the 24 per cent of the Oriya population in Mayurbhanj who are vocal, are quite satisfied with the administration, though at the cost of their much less advanced aboriginal brethren. Humanity requires that much more attention should be given to improve the lot of the aborigines'.

[40] AISPC, file no. 112, 'Reforms in Mayurbhanj in Their True Colour', undated, perhaps written in 1945-6.

in obtaining firewood—and called for the immediate enforcement of the Trade Union Act in the state, since labourers were being exploited. The demand to allow more than one person to operate transport buses, which carried people like gunny bags, illustrates the problems associated with the existing system of monopolies.[41]

At Gangpur the immediate issue that precipitated the anger of the people of the state was the sudden increase in the rate of rent. The revision settlement that had started in 1928 and was completed in 1936 raised the rent by 100 to 150 per cent above the 1910 Settlement. The main feature of this settlement was that the whole state was surveyed and all lands assessed. This settlement hit the Munda adivasis the hardest, since they were 'irregular', i.e. shifting cultivators. Although there was no Prajamandal, the state people submitted a petition to the rani, the diwan and the tahsildar. The petition demanded the abolition of *bethi* and forced levies (which were also hated, since on occasion people were beaten for failure to provide these), restrictions on land transfers, the use of the forests and selling of forest products, abolition of the export cess, the right to use the roads, improvements in irrigation and employment facilities, and doing away with the income tax (this was the only state which levied such a tax). A representative government was also demanded. The demand to sell *mahua* (an intoxicating drink) indicates not only an attempt to interfere with a customary adivasi practice, but possibly also anger against the monopoly system.[42]

As for Kalahandi, it was in virtual isolation from the nationalist movement and the Prajamandal-inspired struggles that swept many of the Orissan princely states. Apudu Sahoo's attempt to establish an adivasi sevamandal at the Kashipur zamindari in November 1947 is the only reference to the attempts to mobilize the people of the state. This effort was directed towards educating the Kandhas and Dombs and the campaign against *begari* and the forced supply of items. The Adivasi Sevamandal was outlawed and the 4 anna Kandha and Domb recruits of the Congress arrested and beaten.[43] This implies that these exploitative practices were not only present, but continued even after Independence.

CONCLUSION

This paper illustrates that 'the centres out there' were indeed centres of exploitation. The situation was compounded in the case of states like

[41] AISPC, file no. 112; as reported, distinguished Congressmen from neighbouring states attended this meeting, where messages from the prime minister of Orissa and the Socialist leader, Surendranath Dwivedy, were read out.

[42] Ramdhyani, n.d., 82-92; Home Political Fortnightly Reports, file nos. 18/2/1939; 18/3/1939; AICC, G-12, 1937-9; AISPC, file no. 127, 'Orissa State News Bulletin', a note prepared by S. Das, 27 April 1939.

[43] S. Das, file nos. 129-30, 27 November, 1947. One needs to add here that most of the princely states of Orissa did not experience any major upheavals associated with the Prajamandal movement.

Mayurbhanj, Gangpur or Kalahandi, which had zamindaris. This intensified the scale of the oppression. Our discussion demonstrates how the internal order of the princely states was closely integrated with the colonial system and the process of colonial underdevelopment. That both sought to tap resources, drain the states and exploit the people is quite obvious. What remains disguised, and hence not so clear, is the manner in which social practices associated with caste and patriarchy were preserved and reinforced in order to maintain the social hierarchies, acquire legitimacy and thus obtain access to resources. The role of the Utkala Sammilani, which united a section of the middle class with the feudal chiefs and the colonial and post-colonial bureaucrats to conceal this exploitative order in some of the princely states, needs to be emphasized. Similarly, another aspect that lies hidden is the distinctly anti-adivasi and anti-Untouchable orientation of this order. Features like restrictions on the use of forests as well as the contrasts between these sections and the non-adivasis and upper castes need to be grasped. Until this happens, historians will be blind to the hardships faced by these marginalized people, who formed the dominant section, in terms of population, in all the princely states.

What is apparent here is the drive by the chiefs and colonialism to introduce aspects of modernity in their states. These efforts were much more nuanced than they are made out to be and need to be located within the paradigm of colonial modernity. And, in the context of what has been discussed in this paper, it would be unhistorical to talk of colonial modernity abstracted from the phenomenon of oppression—the hallmark of the states examined. Consequently, this reformatory exercise saw the creation of railway lines, mines, educational institutions and hospitals, for which land was taken over without any compensation, along with the extraction of forced labour and levies.[44] Besides, one should not lose sight of the fact that this project of modernity was in many ways aimed at concealing the oppressive aspects of the princely states and at securing legitimacy from both colonialism and a section of the people of the state. At the same time, this project legitimized the colonial presence in the states. In this sense, my examination of the princely states of Orissa demonstrates the hollowness of some scholars who appear as apologists for both the feudal enclaves and their colonial associates.[45]

Although it would go beyond the scope of this chapter, it should be emphasized that the situation was hardly any different in the zamindaris of

[44]It should be mentioned that Mayurbhanj had a railway line that connected its capital Baripada to the Bengal-Nagpur Railway.

[45]I. Copland (1997, 6) individualizes the issue by talking of the abilities of the chiefs. As he asserts, the princes could not rule autocratically since the job was simply too big for any one person, and it was the 'quality of the bureaucracy that really mattered—in particular the calibre of the princes' ministers'. J. Manor (1978, 14) projects the princes and their advisors as people 'buffeted by circumstances, people whose plans were often formulated on the run, or in the dark because of lack of knowledge, people struggling valiantly to "muddle through"'. Besides being too simplistic, such assessments do not grasp the broader links between these enclaves and the process of colonial under-development. Bhagawan (2003) and Ramusack (2004) are also affected by the same problem.

British Orissa. Any difference can perhaps be explained by the depth of the pre-colonial economic interventions in the coastal tract and colonialism's interaction with this region since the eighteenth century, which undoubtedly served to 'disguise' the process, making everything appear to be relatively smooth and less traumatic. One can end by saying that it is not enough to criticize the exploiters of the colonial past, since many of these practices haunt the people in many parts of Orissa even in this post-modern twenty-first century.

REFERENCES

All India Congress Committee Papers, Private Papers, file no. G-35, Part 1, 1938; G-12, 1937-9, Nehru Memorial Museum & Library, New Delhi.

All India State Peoples' Conference, Private Papers, file nos. 112; 127; 164, Nehru Memorial Museum & Library, New Delhi.

Bhagavan, M. 2003. *Sovereign Spheres: Princes, Education and Empire in Colonial India*, Delhi: Oxford University Press.

Completion Report of the Talcher State Revision Settlement Season 1928-29, n.d. Cuttack: Orissa Government Press.

'Confidential History of Talcher State (1926)', *Crown Representative Papers* R/2-306/134, India Office Records, British Library, London.

Copland, I. 1997. *The Princes of India and the Endgame of Empire*, Cambridge: Cambridge University Press.

Das, J. 1962. *Final Report of the Land Revenue Settlement in Kalahandi District Ex-State Khalsa Area 1945-56*, Berhampur: India Law Publication Press.

Das, Sarangadhar n.d. *Private Papers*, file nos. 129-30, New Delhi: Nehru Memorial Museum & Library.

Final Report on the Nilgiri Settlement 1917-22, 1922. Berhampur: Sarada Press.

Final Report on the Settlement of the Dhenkanal Feudatory State Orissa 1923-24, vol. 1, 1966. Berhampur: Swadheen Press.

Home Political Fortnightly Reports, file nos. 4/4/1938; 18/2/1939; 18/3/1939, Delhi: National Archives of India.

Interviews: Banamali Das, Nilgiri, May 1982; Krupasindhu Misra, Ranpur, June 1984; Baishnab Patnaik, Dhenkanal, June 1985.

Krushak. 3 January 1938.

Kulke, H. 1993. 'Legitimation and Town Planning in the Feudatory States of Central Orissa', in H. Kulke, *Kings and Cults: State Formation and Legitimation in India and South-East Asia*, Delhi: Manohar, 93-113.

Mahtab, H.K. et al. 1939. *Report of the Enquiry Committee: Orissa States*, Cuttack: Orissa Mission Press.

Manor, J. 1978. 'The Demise of the Princely Order: A Re-assessment', in R. Jeffrey (ed.), *People, Princes and Paramount Power*, Delhi: Oxford University Press.

Memoranda on the Indian States 1930, 1931, 1932, 1933. Calcutta: Central Publication Branch, Government of India.

Mukherjee, I. 1938. *Final Report on the Land Revenue Settlement of the Gangpur State 1929-1936*, Berhampur: Indian Law Publication Press.

National Front. 19 June 1938; 25 September 1938; 4 June 1939.

Nilgiri Praja Andolanara Itihasa (Oriya; 'The History of the Nilgiri Prajamandal') 1981. Balasore: Nilgiri Prajamandal Compilation Committee.

Pati, B. 1993. *Resisting Domination: Peasants, Tribals and the National Movement in Orissa 1920-50*, Delhi: Manohar.

Pradhan, S. 1986. *Agrarian and Political Movements: States of Orissa, 1931-1949*, Delhi: Inter-India.

Ram, R. 1986. *Sangrami* ('Freedom Fighter'; Oriya), Cuttack: Nabajuga Granthalaya.

Ramdhyani, R.K. n.d. *Report on the Land Tenures and the Revenue System of the Orissa and Chattisgarh States*, vol. 3, Berhampur: Indian Law Publication Press.

Ramusack, B. 1978. *The Princes of India in the Twilight of Empire*, Columbus: Ohio State University.

———1996. 'Maternal and Child Health Initiatives: Madras and Mysore, 1880-1947', presented at a conference, 'Medicine and the Colonies' (Oxford, England, 19-21 July).

———2004. *The New Cambridge History of India*, III 6: *The Indian Princes and Their States*, Cambridge: Cambridge University Press.

Report of the Indian States Committee 1928-29, 1929. Calcutta: Government of India, Central Publication Branch.

Report on the Administration of Kalahandi for 1933-34, undated. Kalahandi: Kalahandi State Press.

Report on the General Administration of the Tributary Mahals of Orissa for the Year 1890-91, 1891, Calcutta: Bengal Secretariat Press.

Report on the Land Revenue Settlement 1911-1912 Talcher State, 1963. Cuttack: Orissa Government Press.

Senapati, N. and Nabin K. Sahu 1967. *Orissa District Gazetteers: Mayurbhanj*, Cuttack: Orissa Government Press.

Senapati, N. and D.C. Kuanr, 1980. *Orissa District Gazetteers: Kalahandi*, Cuttack: Orissa Government Press.

Singh, G.N. 1963. *Final Report on the Original Survey and Settlement Operations of the Ranpur Ex-State Area in the District of Puri 1943-1952*, Berhampur: Sarada Press.

The Imperial Gazetteer, vol. 14, 1908. Oxford: Clarendon Press.

CHAPTER 16

Divine Possession as a Religious Idiom: Considering Female Ritual Practice in Orissa

BEATRIX HAUSER

In academic discourse, people who experience spirit possession are commonly regarded as having weak personalities vulnerable to exterior forces. They appear to be under some kind of external control, not only when their body is taken over by a non-human agent, but also in their daily lives, a feature that is often identified as a precondition for their possession. This is particularly so in the case of women, who are considered as the favourite gender of demonic and divine powers. The at times violent and desperate behaviour while possessed is interpreted as a reaction to a woman's lack of recognition in and exclusion from many spheres of life.[1] The academic discourse on South Asia is no exception to this: the cultural phenomenon of spirit possession is overwhelmingly seen as involving women who are distressed in some way.[2]

My aim in this article is to question the usual assumption that Hindu women are purely the passive victims of possession and highlight instead the religious dimension of these events. I argue that women in southern Orissa consider divine possession as essentially religious act that shapes and explains their engagement in rituals, as well as their perspective on Hinduism.[3] This argument

[1]For a review of the anthropological discourse on spirit possession see Boddy (1994), who largely questions the instrumentality of these events and hence its character as an oblique strategy of protest. Behrend and Luig (1999) as well as Mageo and Howard (1996) reflect this debate on the basis of ethnographic examples from Africa and the Pacific respectively. For a feminist critique on the deprivation theory in the academic discourse on possession see Sered (1994).

[2]Fortunately, some recent research provides more nuanced forms of understanding. For an overview of the present South Asian discourse on possession see the compilations of essays edited by Assayag and Tarabout (1999) and also by Carrin (1999); cf. Smith (2006, Chapter 2) for a brief survey of ethnographic studies on deity and spirit possession.

[3]Since my research focus was on the negotiation of female identity in and through cultural performances, I began to look at how this practice may influence the women's self-definitions and self-images (see Hauser, forthcoming a). Initially the project was part of the Orissa Research Programme and I am grateful to the editors for their invitation to present my results in this volume. I owe even more thanks to Burkhard Schnepel who together with others encouraged me to continue with this project in another institutional

is not entirely new. Elisabeth Schömbucher had already pointed out that in the academic discourse on South Asia there is a tendency to ignore the reality of possession as a religious experience.[4] Recently, Frederick Smith argued on the basis of Indian literature from different ages that ecstatic possession is the most common form of spiritual expression in India.[5] His argument certainly is a challenge to historians of religion, given the fact that several introductions and general books on Hinduism simply skip the subject of possession.[6] However, even Smith's criticism of academic scholars—who obviously have difficulties acknowledging the religious potential of possession[7]—does not explore the issue of gender differences. It is understood that '[p]ossession more often than not involves the feminine—either women are possessed or men are possessed by a form of the goddess.'[8] From a gendered perspective on religion and identity, this preponderance of women in (some of the) contemporary traditions of possession in South Asia indeed calls for further investigation.

Focusing on southern Orissa, more precisely the town Berhampur and its rural surroundings, I shall evaluate a variety of private and public rituals that *may* include deity possession.[9] It will be shown that from the perspective of women, possession is a rather common religious idiom that is limited neither to a specific ritual event nor to a particular class of persons. Although possession episodes are fairly patterned and also predictable, they create extraordinary experiences for those overwhelmed as well as for onlookers. Moreover, they contribute towards a discourse on the power of deities and the necessity of women's religious commitment and activities to appease them.[10]

The significance of deity possession to women's religious experiences in southern Orissa differs from and partly contradicts the notion of female victims in the academic discourse on possession in South Asia. Taking a close look at the ways scholars have represented possessed women and evaluated gender

---

framework. For the presentation of an earlier version of this paper my thanks go to the Max Planck Institute for Anthropology in Halle, and to Bettina Schmidt for her valuable critique on this article.

[4]Schömbucher 2003, 261.

[5]Smith 2006.

[6]See, for instance, Michaels (1998), an otherwise very recommendable introduction to Hinduism.

[7]Although Social Anthropologists in general classify spirit possession within the religious realm, they are also likely to focus on its social context rather than considering it as embodied knowledge by itself. Hence Lambek (1989) calls for a change in the perspective 'from disease to discourse'.

[8]Smith 2006, 153.

[9]The database for this article derives from participant observation and narrative interviews during sixteen months of anthropological fieldwork in and around the city of Berhampur, Ganjam District (five periods in 1999, 2000-1, 2003).

[10]Elsewhere I had explored how individuals actually perceive deity possession, how they sense their bodies being overpowered by an exterior force, and in what ways they personify the divine presence (Hauser 2004b).

differences concerning the experiential states of those possessed, I shall argue that the contrast emerging in comparison with accounts of possession from other parts of the Indian subcontinent is in some degree due to the dynamics of academic knowledge production itself. Whereas the psycho-medical and also the sociological 'explanations' of possession each have their local counterpart in folk theory, the religious relevance of possession is a matter of social contestation. From a 'high-caste, educated male' perspective (which of course is a label which summarizes a variety of views) possession is denied the status of a religious idiom in its own right. Thus, the apparent importance given to possession in Orissa may reflect women's religious practices even beyond this region, assuming there is a similar emphasis on devotionalism (*bhakti*) and the worship of goddesses (Shaktism).

Before I introduce some exemplary possession episodes, some remarks are in order concerning terminology and classification. As in other languages of the Indian subcontinent, there is no Oriya term for spirit or deity possession.[11] Instead people speak of a supernatural being who is likely to 'dance' (*nācibā*) and 'play' (*kheḷibā*), to 'catch' (*dharibā*), 'jump upon' (*ḍeĩki yibā*) or to 'come to the body' (*dehaku āsibā*), regardless of whether or not the human host is prepared for such an encounter or whether the possessing power is identified as an ancestral spirit, ghost, demon or deity.[12] Although people distinguish between forms of possession that are beneficial (anticipated by ritual preparations) or unwanted (spontaneous, but also explained with calculable circumstances), this does not allow any conclusions to be drawn regarding the nature of a particular entity. Rather, the cosmos is characterized as having a continuum of supernatural powers of higher and lower order, some of whom appear to be rather fierce. Non-human beings may also change in status over time. An ancestor who had suffered an inauspicious death might be appeased by rituals and gradually gain a reputation as a powerful guardian, before later being identified with a well-known Hindu deity. Hence disturbing and harmful forms of possession (rather than creatures) are removed or banished.[13] At times, this process may also address a particular type of goddess, known by the generic term *thākurāṇī* (literally: mistress, lady). Even what might be labelled

[11]The terms for possession in South Asian languages have been rendered by Smith (2006, Chapter 4). He proposes to identify most of these experiential states with the Sanskrit concept *āveśa*, literally 'entrance into', here taken as an umbrella term for 'positive oracular possession'. However, the semantic meaning of this word varies historically and in the Indian languages, as Smith (2006, 14, 119) has pointed out. Similarly, the Oriya term *ābeśa* translates into English as 'attention'.

[12]In Oriya, the terms *mahāpuru* (Lord), *mā* (mother), *ṭhākura* or *ṭhākurāṇī* (master/mistress, lord/lady) are used to address a possessing deity; ancestral spirits are referred to as *sajība debatā* (enlivened god) and as *ātmā* (spirit, soul); overwhelmingly fierce entities are classified as *bhūta* (ghost, spirit), as *ḍāhāṇī* (demoness/female ghost) or as *ḍākiṇī* (demoness, witch).

[13]The very notion of 'evil spirits' is, according to Smith (2006, 116), a Western construction imposed on the ethnographic and textual descriptions from South Asia.

'exorcism' serves to re-situate a non-human being within his or her own realm, a process performed by those ritual specialists well versed in magical techniques (and addressed as *tāntrika*). Yet any spontaneous and involuntary possession conveys the potential to develop divinatory skills, and most mediums initially underwent a similar ordeal.

In other words, the classification of an event as either 'divine' or 'demonic' possession is partly a matter of context and perspective, as some deities are known for their disturbing powers.[14] Thus it is difficult to find an appropriate English term that embraces this ambivalence (and goes beyond the Christian connotations of 'devil possession'). Whereas the anthropological term 'spirit possession' generally includes divine beings, several scholars working on South Asia employ this term to specify malevolent and unwanted forms.[15] In the latter case, the positive dimension of possession is recognized by a variety of expressions, such as 'spirit mediumship', 'possession mediumship', 'oracular possession' or 'ecstatic possession'. Considering the subject position of possessed persons, scholars speak of 'mediums' or, to acknowledge their competence, of 'shamans'.[16] With respect to Orissa, however, the term 'shamanism' alludes to 'tribal' religions and influences rather than normative or popular Hindu practices, although these forms certainly may overlap and influence each other.[17] Since the majority of possession episodes I encountered during fieldwork were identified with the agency of a goddess, and since the behaviour of female hosts did not suggest any consistent markers to distinguish novices from specialists, I alternately use the terms 'divine possession' and 'deity possession'; the possessed (Hindu) woman is referred to as a 'medium'.

FEMALE POSSESSION: CASE STUDIES FROM ORISSA

At the beginning of my fieldwork, I was not looking specifically for incidents of possession. While watching women's rituals, time after time one of the

[14]On the dark qualities of a *thākurāṇī*, see Hauser 2005.

[15]See Gold 1988, Mayaram 1999, cf. Claus 1975 and Smith 2006.

[16]The problem with these terminological distinctions is that they are based on the assumption that possession is an altered state of *consciousness* rather than an embodied practice. As Mary Keller (2002) rightly pointed out, scholars tend to conceive of religion as a mental activity (a modern Christian concept) and therefore, while discussing possession, repeatedly get stuck at the question of awareness—in Western discourse the means of human agency.

[17]The distinction between 'shamanism' (referring to spirit journeys while the body remains unconscious) and 'possession mediumship' (the inhabitation of the body by another spirit) goes back to Mircea Eliade. With respect to South Asian ethnography, the usage of these terms—as of 'trance' and 'exorcism'—is rather arbitrary and there is little evidence to support the necessity of these conceptual distinctions (see Tarabout 1999, 10-12). Moreover, to link possession solely to Hinduism is no less problematic since similar forms occur among South Asian Muslims, Sikhs, Buddhists and Christians. Sometimes, the possessing entity and its medium belong to different religions altogether (Mayaram 1999).

participants' behaviour changed radically, so that her body was regarded as taken over by a deity. Some of the possessed trembled, jumped wildly or painfully twisted their faces; others had their eyes closed, walked calmly and responded to questions. On the one hand, I had severe doubts about what was happening and therefore shared the uncertainty of several onlookers. On the other hand, I could sense the tension that the incident gave rise to through my own body. I watched the scene full of excitement, at times slightly worried, and more than once I forgot to take any notes. Women encouraged me to tell them what I had experienced and also to test an oracle. Some of them regularly learned that their own and other's behaviour was being driven by a goddess. This divine presence was not at all an unusual topic of conversation. On certain ritual occasions, young girls were encouraged to interpret some of their bodily reactions in terms of non-human agency. The respective female host, her family and others appreciated this kind of divine encounter. Although it constituted an extremely exhausting physical experience, it also contributed towards the self-esteem of the possessed woman. Later, when I began systematically attending rituals to witness manifestations of the divine, one of my research assistants left because she could not bear the, on some occasions, intense drumming and its psychophysical effects. She feared becoming possessed herself. (As a graduate in journalism, she finally joined a private TV channel.)

In the following paragraphs, I give a variety of examples that show when and how women in southern Orissa recognize divine possession, as well as how they conceive of this embodied state and social practice. The descriptions are largely based on women's personal memories and thus also reflect common ways of talking about possession. My compilation is not exhaustive but rather tries to cover different ritual settings (private, public, spontaneous, institutionalized, individual, and collective).[18]

When I devote myself very much to worship (*pūjā*), then the Lord (*mahāpuru*) enters my body. (Basanti, 37 years, tea-stall owner)

It is the duty of a Hindu wife to take care of the family deity. Thus most married women devote some time of the day to pray at the house altar, i.e. a place attached to the kitchen or located in a separate *pūjā* room. During this form of solitary worship, some women face possession. This may happen particularly on those weekdays on which it is particularly auspicious to worship a *ṭhākurāṇī* (i.e. on Tuesdays) or the divine man-lion Narasiṃha (on Saturdays).

[18]During the course of my fieldwork I was faced with possession in thirty-eight cases (five mediums were men). Thirty-three times the agent was identified as a deity; twenty-four times as a form of a *ṭhākurāṇī*, twice as Narasiṃha, and four times as ancestral spirit. I also watched several hundred possessed women during the final procession of Ṭhākurāṇī Yātrā, the biennial goddess festival of Berhampur. These numbers are not representative of possession in general since I specifically attended *religious* occasions that attracted *women.*

Then possession indicates that a woman favours one of them as her personal goddess or god, a preference that may overlap with the identity of the family deity. Deity possession at the house altar is usually a more or less private religious experience.[19] No special attention is paid to it, although neighbours will gradually get to know about it. For Basanti, who lived with her husband and children in a nuclear family, this encounter with God was a welcomed opportunity to share all kinds of day-to-day problems, whether concerning health or finance. However, she did not remember these incidents by herself. Rather her children told about her frightening appearance while serving Narasiṃha. Basanti was very happy (*khuśī*) when she learned about this, yet her husband remained indifferent to it.

In another family, a strange noise was heard from the *pūjā* room, where Sanju was busy with the daily worship of several deities. Since her childhood, she had been vulnerable to possession by Kāḷī and Narasiṃha. Initially her parents tried to save her from such physically exhausting experiences. When they learned from a senior relative that it was not a malevolent spirit (*bhūta*) but rather divine beings who were manifesting themselves in Sanju's body, she was given care of the house altar. After leaving school she spent several hours a day in prayers and worship on behalf of her extended family. Due to her slightly abnormal physique and poor health, she did not marry but continued to live in her parents' home. Yet her social status was high, since the prosperity of the family business (renting out mechanical equipment) was attributed to the regular divine presence in Sanju's body. Gradually, friends and neighbours came to ask for divine advice and—upon getting it—paid the young woman with food, clothes, and other gifts. One might speculate whether Sanju was forced into this role since, due to her physical deficiency, her parents could not find a suitable marriage partner for her. In fact, she planned to leave her family more than once (for different job offers and also to enter monastic life) but they refused to let her go out of fear that they would 'lose everything'.

> After one month he appeared in my mother-in-law's dream and asked her: 'Why do you just sit idle? We serve the public!' My mother-in-law could not understand anything. She didn't know how to answer people's questions. He replied: 'You just concentrate on me, call my name and I shall appear through your body.' (Nirmala, 47 years old, widow)

Sometimes, the capacity for divine possession is inherited within the family, for instance, if a child has died from smallpox and takes possession of his or her mother and of mothers in later generations. When Nirmala got married, she learned of her mother-in-law's regular possession by the spirit of a deceased son (Nirmala's husband's younger brother). 'I was scared to see this. I knew that the Lord had entered her body but still I was horrified . . . and avoided

[19]Studies of spirit and deity possession usually stress the performative aspect of this social phenomenon. From this angle, it is quite unusual for the possessed woman to be on her own. Nevertheless, others will notice and share their impressions.

the *pūjā* room. Then I got used to this. Since I was staying in this house, did I have any alternative?' The ancestral spirit was identified with Bāidhara, the son of Buṛhī Ṭhākurāṇī, the patron goddess of Berhampur.[20] This goddess is known, among other things, to induce, cure and embody smallpox (*basanta*), and anyone who fails to survive this disease is believed to be her son or daughter. At the age of thirty, Nirmala's husband died and a few years later her parents-in-law followed. By that time, Nirmala herself had started to develop divinatory skills. Once a week she answered people's questions and gradually gained a reputation as an oracle. In fact, the divination was the only way she could make a living and raise her four children. Although Nirmala enjoyed the financial benefits of her submission to Bāidhara, she also complained about the physical side effects. The divine encounter produced bodily pain, so Nirmala often avoided possession or limited its duration. At the same time she felt obliged to surrender to this god so as to guarantee divine satisfaction and hence blessing. She was looking forward to a daughter-in-law who could release her from this burden, yet she knew that she could not assume her cooperation. 'If she is very stylish, she probably won't like this. If we take measures in order to save my daughter-in-law from being possessed, then he won't come. Otherwise he will not leave her.'

Jyotsna (19 years old): 'Mother, Mother, who are you? . . . Mother, who has come?'
A woman blows on a conch, while others ululate.
Nila (17 years old, student): 'Who has come?
Hey you, who has come?'
Jyotsna: 'Tell us! If you keep quiet like this, then how will we know?'

Possession may occur during semi-public rituals shared by the women of one neighbourhood, for instance, on the occasion of the Jahni Oṣā, a votive rite undertaken by teenage girls to obtain a good husband.[21] For one month, unmarried girls meet every evening to worship the goddess Bṛndābatī. At some *pūjā* sites, though not at all regularly, one of the votaries becomes possessed. Then the girls have to find out who has appeared and why, i.e. what form the goddess has taken and whether her presence is the sign of her grace or anger. One evening, the identity of the deity and the subsequent divination were anything but clear. The votary who had at first impersonated Bṛndābatī as a part of the ritual (Fig. 16.1) started to shake her body in a very violent and unpredictable manner. The girls assumed that the goddess had appeared as Bāṭa Maṅgaḷā, a particularly frightening form of the goddess Maṅgaḷā often met at the roadside (*bāṭa*). Here Bāṭa Maṅgaḷā complained about the incorrect

[20]Bāidhara is worshipped under a sacred tree within the premises of the Buṛhī Ṭhākurāṇī temple. There devotees had donated a stone idol to him. At first sight he seems to be another form of Bhairaba (Sanskrit: Bhairava) who is also known as a guardian of the goddess. The head priest of the Buṛhī Ṭhākurāṇī temple distinguishes both deities though, drawing on the iconography of Bāidhara *vis-à-vis* Bhairaba in the nearby Śiba temple.

[21]For a detailed evaluation of this votive rite see Hauser 2008.

Figs. 16.1 and 16.2: A votary impersonates the goddess Bṛndābatī and becomes possessed by Bāṭa Maṅgaḷā

pūjā she had been offered (Fig. 16.2). Then the goddess started to stammer and to utter strange noises. She revealed herself as Jāṛī Mā, literally the 'Dumb Mother'. Finally, the possessor was recognized as Bṛndābatī herself, who, through her human host, addressed certain problems in the marriage negotiations of one participant. After half an hour the exhausted medium lay down and the girls completed the evening's regular programme of worship. The discussion as to the meaning of the prophecy continued over the following days. Since the divine utterances had been fragmented and ambiguous, nobody knew for sure whose 'brother had made a mistake', who exactly should be appeased, where

and in what way. Nonetheless, in this Jahni Oṣā group and others, the mere possibility of divine possession underlined the significance of the participants' religious practice. Girls felt they had a responsibility to perform votive rites whole-heartedly, since otherwise the goddess would enter their bodies and complain. Hence, their attitude towards possession was one of ambivalence, fear and appreciation at the same time.

> [The goddess] likes dancing, songs and everything. So if we don't dance in front of her, she will not appear at this place. (Babula, 29 years old, priest)

On some occasions divine possession is invited by aesthetic means such as rich decoration, figurative masks, elaborate costumes and artistic dancing.

Families who, because of a prospective marriage or for any other reason, wish to ensure the divine benevolence may take a procession out to the temple Būṛhī Ṭhākurāṇī. The priests of this temple, Oriya barbers by caste (Bhaṇḍārī), will organize these processions on suitable days in the month of *Caitra* (March/ April). They will invoke the divine generative power (*Śakti*) in one or more sacred pots that have to be carried by married women on behalf of the family. A few dancers, who remain hidden below huge *ṭhākurāṇī*-figures, will commence the pageant. A group of drummers follow. In their midst, a younger male member of the priest's family will dance, dressed up as the goddess Kāḷī. Moving a mask in front of his face, he interacts with the women who carry the sacred pots on their head. Then the remaining family of the sponsor, relatives and friends follow. While proceeding through the lanes of Berhampur, neighbours bow down to the pot bearer(s) and wash her/their feet with sacred water. Regardless of possession, these women are worshipped as an embodiment of the goddess. Moreover, the ritual specialist in the costume of Kāḷī will try to evoke the divine agency in the body of the pot bearer(s), and indeed some of them start to tremble, shriek or communicate in some other way. Neighbours may ask the possessed for their advice and prophecy, while others lay their babies on the road (Fig. 16.3). In response to this act of surrender, the living goddess is to step over them and thus show her grace. If a spectator becomes possessed, the priest will intervene and relocate the divine by 'cooling' the unprepared body with turmeric water.[22]

> [I told her:] 'If you are really powerful, then you have to come into my body.' . . . [Finally] the goddess entered my body, so won't I feel happy? (Rajeshvari, 58 years old, nurse)

There are several circumstances which influence whether and when a woman should invite or rather avoid goddess possession. During the three weeks of the biennial celebration of Ṭhākurāṇī Yātrā, a festival in honour of the patroness of Berhampur, night after night nine women from the Devāṅgī caste (Telugu silk weavers) carry sacred pots in a procession and are worshipped by the public as human manifestations of Būṛhī Ṭhākurāṇī.[23] In this context the goddess is banned from taking possession of the pot bearers. Just before the daily procession, a priest well versed in magic rituals (i.e. a tāntrika) will seal their bodies. Rather than by pragmatics (daily possession would be physically exhaustive), this rule is governed by the fact that Būṛhī Ṭhākurāṇī has 'adopted' the chief of the Devāṅgī as her father. Since a goddess may possess her children (i.e. devotees) but never her parents—here in a wider sense all Devāṅgī—she is not supposed to overwhelm the pot bearers. During the final night of the festival, however, any women of Berhampur seeking divine favour may go on a fast and join the nocturnal procession. In 2001, several thousands gathered for this event,

[22]For a thorough discussion of these processions see Hauser 2004b, forthcoming b.

[23]The various dimensions of this festival I have discussed elsewhere (Hauser 2005, 2006a, forthcoming a).

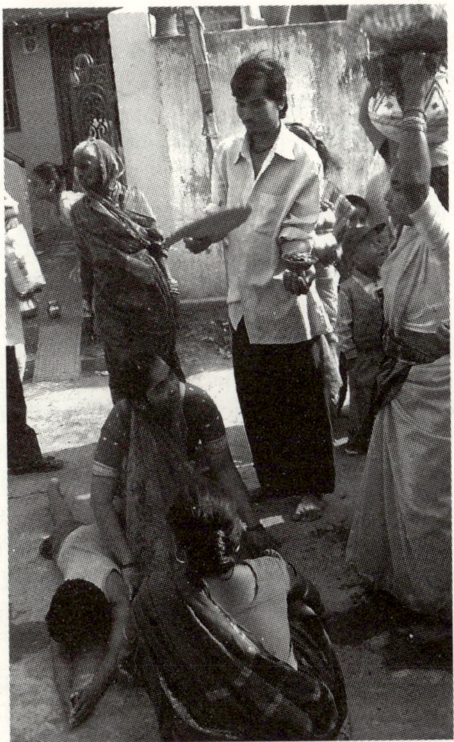

Fig. 16.3: The living goddess is to step over children and thus show her grace

each carrying a pot invested with the divine generative power (*śakti*). Since these women were not given similar protective measures, in the course of standing and walking in the crowd for hours, about 10 per cent of them became possessed. Whether overpowered by the divine or not, women appreciated this event as a significant religious experience, although due to the crowd the individual transformations were not paid any specific attention. After arriving at the Būṛhī Ṭhākurāṇī temple in the early hours of the morning, not only the sacred pot but also the remaining signs of possession were removed, again by sprinkling turmeric water to 'cool' the body.

The experience of possession is not restricted to particular castes or social strata. However, the majority of people in Berhampur and the surrounding area belong to the middle-ranking and lower spectrum of the caste society. They are basically artisans, small businessmen, agricultural labourers and farmers, or self-employed in the service industry. In regard to deity possession, caste and class identity does not matter that much.[24] These incidents move

[24]During fieldwork I spoke to possessed women from the following communities: Karaṇa (accountants), Oṛia (potters, etc.), Bhanḍārī (barbers, priests), Devāṅgī (weavers), Liārī (rice processors), Ḍaluā (betel merchants), Hāri (sweepers), Telaṅgā (bangle manufacturers, etc.), Gaura (milkmen), Haluā Brāhmaṇa (Brahman farmers) and Kārada (merchants). However, most families had given up their designated caste occupations.

Oriya- and Telugu-speaking devotees, women and also men. Yet possession is specifically associated with femininity. The preponderance of possessed women is explained by the goddess's preference for human beings who share her bodily substance through their sameness of sex and also the consumption of meat. (In southern Orissa only a very few people, Brahmans and non-Brahmans included, are pure vegetarians.) In general, deity possession is an *optional* proof of the divine that heightens religious experience and therefore is not limited to a specific ritual event. This may vary gradually if prophecy and therefore possession become a regular service on demand (as in Nirmala's case). The local discourse on divine possession involves only certain kinds of deities who are known for their hot temper and demanding character. Thus the man-lion-shaped Narasiṃha, a variety of *ṭhākurāṇī*s and deceased small-pox victims are likely to take possession.[25] Regardless of her or his mood, to experience the divine by means of the lived-in body is conceptualized in terms of pleasure (*khuśī*). It is not related to the overpowered individual, her living conditions or social situation. Being selected by a deity is understood to be a result of divine grace and thus may prove the piety of a woman. Yet divine possession is an ambivalent gift since it involves not only the voluntary surrender to an external agency but also demands unconditional physical self-denial.

On the basis of academic literature, it is difficult to judge whether the ethnographical examples given above are representative of female possession throughout Orissa. Moreover, this Indian state exhibits very considerable cultural diversity, with its dominant Oriya population in the plains, its well-established Telugu diaspora in the south and along the coast, and its various indigenous communities (Adivasi) in the upland interior. The rare and dispersed records on female possession all refer to institutionalized forms. Lynn Foulston mentions the example of a woman who is routinely possessed by the goddess within the premises of a Santoṣī Mā temple.[26] Every Friday, this ritual specialist assumes divine form, proven by eating fire. Being transformed, she is accredited with healing powers and thus draws large crowds of devotees, who seek help with medical problems and also in family affairs.[27] According to James M. Freeman, who analysed a fire walking ceremony that failed, deity possession seems to be a low-caste affair.[28] He describes a 70-year-old woman from the untouchable Bauri (Bāurī) caste who acts as a female 'shaman' (*kalasi*).[29] As a representation

[25]Conversely, the goddess Lakṣmī and male deities such as Nārāyaṇa, Rāma, Kṛṣṇa or Hanumān will not take a human form.

[26]Foulston 2002, 145-9.

[27]Although Foulston (2002, 104) does not provide any details on the background of the medium, she observes that the Scheduled Castes may attend this form of Friday worship but are forbidden to enter the sanctum of the goddess.

[28]J.M. Freeman 1981.

[29]The term derives from the word *kaḷasa*, the sacred pot carried by devotees. J.M. Freeman (1981, 311) translates the role of a *kalasi* (*kaḷasī*) as 'shaman' and as 'shamanistic curer'. As described above, to install the divine power in an earthen pot carried by devoted

of the goddess Banadurga, it was her task to guide the (male) firewalkers. 'She went into trance, trembling, stretching, and yawning, accompanied by loud drumming, blaring bagpipes and horns, played by Bauri-caste musicians, and a twirling dancing boy, dressed in a women's [*sic*] garb, performing the *patua* dance.'[30] Both instances of deity possession were observed in proximity to Bhubaneswar. In southern Orissa, to the best of my knowledge, this institutionalized form is considered the realm of the men, although in general women are believed to be more eligible for possession than male devotees.[31]

Deity possession among women of a Telugu fishing caste (Vāḍabalija), living along the shores of Orissa, is well documented. Elisabeth Schömbucher has provided an excellent analysis of the power and poetry of the divine words uttered by these female mediums.[32] The Vāḍabalija consider three classes of non-human beings as liable to possess women: (1) regional goddesses (in Oriya classified as *ṭhākurāṇī*) and addressed as 'mother' (Telugu: *ammavāru*); (2) Vaishnava male deities such as Narasiṃha; (3) immortal beings who have achieved the status of a demigod (Telugu: *vīruḍu*), such as victims of an untimely death.[33] The Oriya and Telugu women I met during fieldwork basically shared this classification. However, unlike in Berhampur, possession among the fisherwomen seems to be limited to a distinct therapeutic framework where a male priest (*dāsuḍu*) encourages a female medium (*bhakturālu*) to address the afflictions of various clients. The divine utterances of the possessed person constitute a dialogue that lasts for one or two hours. Its highly stylized and lyrical language inspired Schömbucher to analyse these possession séances as a verbal art, taking into account that the required skills might escape Western notions of aesthetics. In comparison, only *some* possessed women in Berhampur were speaking in tongues and employed familiar religious formulae, yet in a rather brief and much less articulated way.

The mass possession of women in public, as during Ṭhākurāṇī Yātrā, alludes to another type of nocturnal procession in the coastal zone of Andhra Pradesh. According to David Knipe these pageants are related to death and ancestor worship.[34] They are performed in honour of Vīrabhadra, a divine hero associated with the deification of ancestors who suffered a premature death (similar to

---

women is common ritual practice in Berhampur. Although I describe these women as pot bearers, they were not considered as *kaḷasī*, a term reserved for professional mediums (or 'shamans', in J.M. Freeman's parlance).

[30] J.M. Freeman 1981, 315.

[31] During the fire-walking festival (Jhāmu Yātrā) in the outskirts of Berhampur, a male priest cross-dresses in order to become an apt vessel for the goddess Ellāmmā, and only he walks on glowing coals. At a similar ceremony downtown, again a male ritual specialist embodies the goddess, yet the act of fire-walking itself has been abandoned (see Hauser 2007). At the yearly Daṇḍa Nāṭa performance, the goddess Kāḷī is known for possessing the male officiant (cf. Schnepel 2000).

[32] Schömbucher 1994a, 1994b, 1996, 1999, 2006.

[33] Schömbucher 1996, 243.

[34] Knipe 1989.

Būṛhī.Ṭhākurāṇī's smallpox victims). Ahead of those processions one finds musicians and dancers, who wear costumes to impersonate these departed heroes. A crowd of devotees follows. In the course of the night, some of these marchers get taken over by the spirits of deceased family members. According to Knipe it is 'most frequently younger mothers in their twenties and thirties, who sway or whirl, slowly at first, then quickly before they abandon the march and fall screaming to the ground.'[35]

Dialogues with immortal beings also characterize the religious practices of Adivasis in Orissa, such as the Sora, who live in the mountains bordering Andhra Pradesh. As Piers Vitebsky has demonstrated, it is again overwhelmingly, possessed women who utter the non-human voice of deceased relatives.[36] In this context the mediums are recognized as shamans (*kuran*) or rather as priestesses in their own right. However, the Sora's spirits (*ılda*) differ from the deified ancestors that are commonly worshipped by their Hindu neighbours.[37]

To make a thorough assessment of divine possession in Orissa, much more comparative research is certainly needed. With respect to the population in and around Berhampur, however, deity possession is not limited to specific religious events, social purposes or strata but rather serves as a general ritual act that might occur during various forms of worship. It is highly appreciated among women. As a religious idiom of its own, it proves the relevance of their pious dedication and specifically of those religious activities that scarcely find approval in brahmanical male discourse. Whether this commitment to deity possession reflects a regional development or rather hints at a hitherto silenced and gendered form of Hindu devotion is discussed in the next section.

FEMALE POSSESSION IN ACADEMIC DISCOURSE

The academic discourse on possession in South Asia is characterized by different theoretical and methodological approaches. Schömbucher distinguishes four interpretative models: (1) the psychological; (2) the sociological; (3) the cosmological and (4) the performative model of possession.[38] These different strands of argumentation reflect not only disciplinary preferences and a chronological development of research paradigms but also relate to different social contexts and phenomena that are discussed under the heading of possession.[39] Here I shall evaluate central positions taken in this literature regarding possession as a gendered practice.[40]

[35] Knipe 1989, 127-8.

[36] Vitebsky 1993.

[37] A collection of essays edited by Tina Otten and Uwe Skoda (forthcoming) will give several further examples of possession in tribal communities.

[38] Schömbucher 1993, 240.

[39] Similarly possession has been evaluated within studies on goddess worship, healing ceremonies and ritual dramas.

[40] For a review of the 'classical' academic positions followed in the 1950s, 1960s and 1970s see Schömbucher (1993).

Some of the pioneering studies on possession in South Asia conceive of these experiential states as a culture specific form and treatment of psychic disorder. The focus is on demonic possession, i.e. a form of body experience that is conceptualized in negative terms and demands exorcism. The afflicted person suffers from this state and shows mental and bodily signs of weakness that make normal life impossible and cause alarm in his or her relatives. Throughout the Indian subcontinent a variety of religious institutions specialize in the therapeutic cure of such illnesses and in this way testify to the prevalence of malevolent possession. Patients are not only taken to Hindu temples—as illustrated by Sudhir Kakar and, more recently, by Marine Carrin—but also to Buddhist shrines, graves of Muslim saints and to Christian pilgrimage centres.[41]

Although the patients suffering from demonic affliction are from both genders, academic scholars notice a preponderance of women. With reference to Varanasi, Jonathan Parry claims that about 70 per cent of victims are female, while over 80 per cent belong to the lower castes.[42] The main argument explaining demonic possession draws on Freudian psychoanalysis. The Indian female self is said to invite this exaggerated behaviour in order to deal with hidden desires, repressed emotions, guilt, fear and conflict—similar to the gendered phenomenon of hysteria in European medical discourse at the beginning of the twentieth century. To project 'the other' on to the demonic is regarded as a coping mechanism that is successfully dealt with in healing ceremonies, which aim to re-establish the self in relation to family and acquaintances. This approach is identified with psychoanalytically influenced scholars like Sudhir Kakar and Gananath Obeyesekere.[43] Although met with criticism—for instance concerning the Western bias—their influential studies keep on inspiring scholars.[44] Following this line, psychiatrist Antti Pakaslathi has pointed out that affliction by spirits is not limited to the underprivileged.[45] Exorcists of a north Indian temple instead attract clients with an 'average or better than average education', who 'belong to the higher castes' and who are of urban domicile. Regardless of social status, Sarah Caldwell suggests that female possession originates, among other factors, in the traumatic childhood experience of sexual abuse.[46]

Influenced by Ioan Lewis' deprivation theory, scholars identify demonic possession as a social phenomenon that allows subalterns to raise their voice

[41]See Kakar 1982, Carrin 1999, cf. Obeyesekere 1977, Pfleiderer 1988, 1994, Stirrat 1992.

[42]Parry 1994, 233.

[43]Kakar 1982, Obeyesekere 1977, 1981.

[44]For current psychological views from India compare Pakaslathi (1998) and Chandra Shekar (1989), for recent studies on demonic possession see Dwyer 2003 and Carrin 1999.

[45]Pakaslathi 1998, 164.

[46]Caldwell 1999, 228-33.

and pursue their interests against the hierarchy.[47] In a survey on popular Hinduism, Chris Fuller argues therefore that incidents of possession provide 'culturally tolerated opportunities to complain about female inferiority and subordination within Indian society'.[48] They serve women seeking to escape ill-treatment by their in-laws, to postpone an unwanted marriage or to claim authority in family decisions. Explorations by Claus, Gellner, Obeyesekere and Pfleiderer sustain this argument.[49] More recently, Isabelle Nabokov has questioned the effectiveness of this kind of 'subversion'.[50] With respect to a case study from Kerala, she claims that demonic possession does not provide women with a means to attain secondary gains but rather acts to keep them under control.

Looking at shamanic careers, scholars also recorded the transformation of previously suffering victims of demonic possession into ritual specialists, now in control of their ability to host a spirit. This institutionalization of possession may take the form of a regular oracular service at a shrine or of a public display of divine agency during religious festivals. Whereas the potential to gain control over non-human powers seems to be independent of gender and role expectations, female mediumship has raised academic attention fairly often. It will not come as a surprise that scholars concentrated on the socio-political impact of possession. Deprivation and severe troubles in life are often at hand to make sense of a professional approach to possession, since mediums themselves emphasize how the divine call has had a radically positive influence on hopeless economic, medical and social issues—a rhetoric that generally proves the power of a deity. The Rajasthani shaman described by Shail Mayaram, for instance, troubled by her alcoholic husband who, learning about her vocation, stopped drinking and assisted her in the management of a shrine.[51] Similarly Margaret Egnor traces the development of a low-caste construction labourer in Madras (Chennai) who, after suffering from poverty and considering suicide, was called by the goddess in a dream.[52] Becoming a divine servant did not only give her mental support. By means of possession she gradually emerged as a priestess of the goddess Māriamman, a ritual task that appeared to be a viable way of earning a living. Although some professional mediums may gain social reputation and practically intervene in family matters, caste and local politics, their memories and life-stories reflect first of all a religious discourse. Thus the scholarly comparison of a person's living conditions before and after the growth of mediumship skills risks underplaying the religious experience of a medium in her lived-in world. However, the *form* of possession seems to vary in accordance with social factors. According to David Gellner

[47]Lewis 1975.
[48]Fuller 1992, 233.
[49]See Claus (1975), Gellner (1994), Obeyesekere (1977) and Pfleiderer (1988, 1994).
[50]Nabokov 1997, 299.
[51]Mayaram 1999.
[52]Egnor 1984.

and Karin Kapadia the rising status of a medium mostly correlates to the class of divine power that takes possession of her (or him).[53] From that perspective, the identification of a non-human being—for instance a famous pan-Indian goddess—can be understood as a claim to authority.

The institutionalized dialogue with the divine is not limited to ritual specialists of low economic and caste status. Kathleen Erndl's studies on night vigils in honour of the mother goddess reveal that in northwest India, well-to-do and educated Brahman women may also experience possession and turn into 'living mothers'.[54] In any case, women's experience of possession and their gradual rise to expertise often initiates a complete change of life (whether intended or involuntary), i.e. giving up family ties and adopting an ascetic lifestyle. Still, it is anything but clear whether the scholarly preference for female mediums reflects the local gender distribution among this type of ritual specialists, or whether these women attract attention as exceptions to the rule. However, while studies on malevolent possession emphasize female *victims*, the women described here appear as strategic *agents* who manipulate their environment.

The problem with both the psychological and the sociological perspective on possession is, as Schömbucher has pointed out, that they regard these experiential states as a 'symbolic expression of other experiences'.[55] In her view, scholars should rather follow a 'performative approach to possession'.[56] They should consider the theatrical aspects of possession, the sequencing of the event, audience reactions and also the divine dialogues as cultural expression in its own right. This perspective was favoured in an exemplary way by Bruce Kapferer.[57] In his study on exorcism in Sri Lanka, he showed how aesthetics, creativity and humour contribute significantly to the experience and efficacy of the ritual act. Similarly, Richard Freeman emphasized that possession consists of learned and rehearsed gestures of possession rather than 'trance behaviour' of individuals.[58] On the basis of *teyyam*-performances, a ritual dance that culminates in the speaking in the voice of a god, he observed well-choreographed movements and highly structured recognizable utterances. Studies focusing on possession as a ritual and aesthetic performance—and thus as meaningful by itself—overwhelmingly identify male mediums to develop artful and ludic ways of expression. Schömbucher's work is exceptional since she considers the poetic potential and, in this respect, the authorship of possessed women.[59] Although academic literature gives more hints of a creative role of possessed women, scholars seemingly fail to recognize the possession episodes

[53]Gellner 1994, 38-9, Kapadia 1996, 433.
[54]Erndl 1993, 1996, 1997.
[55]Schömbucher 1993, 242.
[56]Schömbucher 1993, 257.
[57]Kapferer 1983.
[58]R. Freeman 1993, 124.
[59]Schömbucher 1996, 2006.

as a cultural site (co-)defined by female performers. Likewise Peter Claus describes women of a matrilineal community in Karnataka joining the performance of the Siri epic.[60] While mimetically re-enacting the suffering of the heroine, some of them are possessed. Yet according to Claus, these female participants 'are not true specialists because they do not see themselves essentially as priestesses to Siri'. To make it clear, I do not propose translating 'Western' concepts of personhood and art to South Asian contexts. Rather I wish to show how possessed women are represented in academic discourse and in what respect they are conceived of as subjects (compared with male mediums).

Socially widespread and mostly unobtrusive forms of deity possession, like those embedded in women's religious practices in southern Orissa, are rarely reflected by academic discourse. However, Mary Hancock's study of middle-class women in Chennai suggests that such an approach to possession is not limited by region.[61] She discusses how Smārta Brahman women develop mediumship skills in their devotion (*bhakti*) to a goddess, using these skills for private matters but also offering their help to others. According to Hancock, goddess oracles and their clients are found throughout all castes and social strata.[62] Similar to the Orissan examples given in the previous section, this form of religious practice is regarded as compatible with women's roles as mothers and wives.[63]

In academic discourse, divine possession is mostly recognized in its institutionalized form, i.e. related and limited to *specific* ceremonies (possession cults). Only rarely do scholars focus on possession as a type of ritual behaviour like, say, the singing of hymns. This is not only due to research methodology. Although formalized possession routines are to some extent predictable and

[60]Claus 1975, 56.

[61]Hancock 1995.

[62]Hancock 1995, 63, 70.

[63]Recently, Smith (2006) has applied the notion of possession to a continuum of experiential states of the body-mind complex. With reference to *bhakti* theology, he includes meditative and devotional practices that serve to evoke an emotional proximity to, if not complete absorption in the divine. His argument is in line with the findings of McDaniel (1989), who in a study on religious ecstasy among Bengali saints has shown how the emotional identification with a god is interlinked with the experience of being overpowered by a deity. 'In devotional ecstasy', McDaniel (1989, 3) explains, 'there is a permeability and openness uniting the person and the divinity, and a sharing of love between them.' Analysing theological texts, interviews and biographies of two female saints and three contemporary 'holy women' (*sādhikā*), she shows that these renunciants subscribe to a clear hierarchy of these altered states of the body (1989, 229). They privilege emotional experiences classified as *bhāva* (literally: mood, emotion, ecstasy) and downplay a rigid personality change conceived of as *bhor* (literally: engrossed, possession). Although both terms have their Oriya counterpart (*bhāba*, *bhoḷa*), people do not employ them to describe or classify experiential states like possession. However, in McDaniel's study women who have experienced the divine in this form are represented as subjects of their own with some freedom and self-determination.

thus suitable for systematic observation, the scholarly preference also reflects the social contestation of these experiential states within their own context. In the following, I show how local people ('informants') come to support ethnographer's scepticism as to the validity of possession as a *religious* experience and thus encourage the interpretation of possession as a representation of something else.

Both the psycho-medical and the sociological model of possession have, I argue, a counterpart in local folk theory. Ethnocentric assumptions deriving from (Western) psychoanalysis meet and apparently 'translate' Indian concepts on the female nature and vulnerability. Several scholars have rendered 'cosmological models of possession' (in Schömbucher's classification). They discussed South Asian characterizations of women as highly emotional beings, morally weak, attached to worldly desires, seducible and therefore likely to face possession.[64] These stereotypes are consistent with gendered concepts of the body, such as the menstrual impurity of women, their bodily permeability and specific 'openness'.[65] The sociological approach to possession as a subaltern strategy to acquire secondary gains corresponds in a similar way to 'emic' doubts on the reality of divine overpowering. In fact, deity possession is often subjected to critique and mockery.[66] Even the pious may challenge the authenticity of possession, the standard argument being that it is simply deprived individuals who try to win attention and wealth through this pretence. There is a certain amount of scepticism about the credibility of mediums and religious specialists, a stance taken and related to habitus (Bourdieu) and also to self-presentation.[67]

On the one hand, the perspective on possession is determined by caste and class, and thus reflects processes of status distinction. On the basis of fieldwork in Tamil Nadu, Kapadia distinguishes two clearly separated positions.[68] According to 'lower-caste ethos', possession is said to prove a person's piety and true love for God. Thus it constitutes one of the most important forms of *bhakti*. It contrasts with the brahmanical view that denies the religious significance of these bodily experiences and rather emphasizes liturgy authenticated by the Sanskrit scriptures.[69] Similarly Parry shows that from the

[64]See Kapferer 1983, 140; Gellner 1994, 39.

[65]Osella and Osella 1999, 186-91.

[66]See Hancock (1995, 70), Mayaram (1999, 122), Egnor (1984, 28), Kapadia (1996, 435).

[67]Gellner (1994, 39) recognizes another aspect that influences the social contestation of deity possession. According to his study in Nepal, the doubts as to the credibility of possession rise with the status of the possessing entity. The higher a deity, the more sceptical are people of claims to possession. Although this argument sounds convincing, it provokes tricky classificatory problems since the hierarchy of deities is itself a matter of context and perspective (on the 'multiple identities' of Durgā and Kāḷī, see McDaniel 2004, Chapter 4).

[68]Kapadia 1995, 124, Chapter 6.

[69]The orthodox standpoint, however, has been challenged by recently. According to

perspective of Brahman orthodoxy in Benares, spirit possession is considered as 'superstition' and, like impurity, reflects an inferior social status.[70] Nonetheless, Brahman priests may accept ritual specialists exorcizing demons, so long as they do not interfere with their own ritual competence and business, i.e. the negotiation with the divine. It seems that in many parts of the Indian subcontinent, 'high-caste' (or 'middle-class') discourse silences and openly devalues deity possession as an extrovert style of worship associated with the impure, uneducated, lower strata of society.[71] As a marker of class and caste distinctions, however, the relevance of possession is also subject to social change. Kapadia shows that divine possession may serve upwardly mobile middle-caste men (non-Brahman Tamils) to ritually back their new economic status.[72] As a result of this prestige, however, women are banished from these religious events.

On the other hand, the perspective on possession is related to the self-presentation of an interlocutor, whether medium or onlooker. Women who consider themselves to be a deity's vehicle are well aware that their own possession may be ridiculed. In Tamil Nadu, low-caste female possession is mocked at and made fun of.[73] According to Hancock, Smārta Brahman women under-emphasize their emotionally and aesthetically satisfying experiences during possession in order to avoid doubts being raised as to the genuineness of their transformation.[74] The fear of being stigmatized seems to particularly affect educated and high-caste people, who—refuting deprivation theory—actively participate in rituals that include and require possession in several parts of South Asia.[75] Regarding divine possession by men, William Sax points out that although high- and low-caste people are possessed, upper-caste people tend to deny it of themselves and attribute it to the subalterns.[76] However, the assessment of divine presence may also change in the course of time. Pious spectators who are swept away with emotion at the time of the possession episode, Kapadia notes, might later sneer at the alleged charlatans.[77]

Ethnographers who study possession are thus confronted with this *locally* contested practice. Their own scepticism as to the reality of this altered state of the body is likely to be manipulated by the respective standpoints of their interlocutors. With reference to anthropological studies on caste, Richard

---

Smith (2006), accounts of possession can be found in Vedic, Buddhist, Jain, Tantric and devotional literature, in the epics, in Sanskrit drama and also in medical texts.

[70] Parry 1994, 226-30.

[71] See McDaniel 1989, 240; Sax, cf. Smith 2006, 170.

[72] Kapadia 1996, 2000, 181-2.

[73] Kapadia 1995, 157 and 1996, 435; Egnor 1984, 28.

[74] Hancock 1995, 70.

[75] Scholars have documented brahmanical possession in Himachal Pradesh (Erndl 1993, Chapter 5, 1996, 1997), in Rajasthan (Pakaslathi 1998, 164), in Kerala (R. Freeman (1999, 165-70) and in Tamil Nadu (Kapadia 1995, 150-4).

[76] Sax, cf. Smith 2006, 170.

[77] Kapadia 1996, 430.

Burghart has argued that scholars tend to imitate the perspective of their mostly high-caste 'informants' (and research assistants, I would add) or, conversely, ignore and exclude their perspective altogether.[78] Although there is nothing like *one* brahmanical or upper-class view, the focus on the dynamics between researchers and their local counterparts in the production of ethnography suggests some self-criticism concerning the acknowledgement of possession as a form of religious experience. To give examples by two renowned scholars: As mentioned above, Gellner recognized how female mediums claim authority by identifying the possessing agent as a respected deity.[79] Yet when he concludes that this development was promoted by modern democracy, he seems to adopt the viewpoint of his (high-caste male?) Nepali interlocutors and ignores the perspective of mediums and their followers. Conversely, attending possession séances left an impressive mark on Erndl.[80] She decides 'to take seriously the notion of the Goddess as an agent herself rather than simply a symbol or projection . . . as an agent who interacts with both the person possessed and the devotees who worship her.' She obviously identifies with the devotees and, for her part, neglects the local scepticism about possession.[81] Both authors—in spite of their valuable contributions to the study of possession—seem to give preference to only one side of the coin. While wondering who actually is performing during possession episodes in Rajasthan, Ann Gold rightly recognizes '"The spirits themselves" might be a simple, valid response, but even speaking from within the culture, it is not the whole story.'[82]

CONCLUSION

Whereas the overview of scholarly approaches to possession gives some indication of the major social contexts through which possession in South Asia is constituted, the variety of situations that in southern Orissa may evoke divine possession seems to escape any of these patterns and rationales. It would be misleading to reduce this diversity on the basis of social factors. The overpowering by a divine agent can occur on several ritual occasions and serves as an optional proof of the divine that heightens the religious experience of mediums and onlookers alike. To communicate with the divine through one's own body is highly respected, particularly among women. It allows encountering the divine in an accessible form that resonates to one's own body

[78] Burghart 1990.

[79] Gellner 1994, 38, 41.

[80] Erndl 1996, 174-5.

[81] Only once Erndl (1996, 183) cursorily mentions that individuals might doubt the validity of deity possession.

[82] Gold 1988, 59. This social contestation of possession also alludes to a general anthropological problem: there is nothing like a singular emic voice. Moreover, performers, onlookers and also the ethnographer each produce their own arguments in relation to others.

and self-understanding. Orthodox high-caste women in principle share this religious discourse, yet only a few of them undergo this personal experience. The realm of devotion is rather defined by demographically dominant social groups. Although deity possession is hardly prevalent among the educated middle-class, it is not merely a sign of low status (unlike in Tamil Nadu, as suggested by Kapadia). At any rate, 'modern' interlocutors will carefully consider their self-presentation when rendering possession episodes. This does not outdate the relevance of deity possession as a religious idiom of its own.

Apart from deities that may 'jump upon' and 'dance' mortal beings, the Hindu cosmology in southern Orissa is populated by several uncanny supernatural entities that cause suffering and disease. On several occasions priests make use of a peacock-feather whisk to wipe out malevolent influences and to protect the human body. This 'brushing and blowing'(*jhaṛā-phunka*) is also performed by (male and female) mediums taken over by a goddess.[83] If possession occurs for the first time, people may call a ritual specialist well-versed in magical techniques (*tāntrika*) to find out whether this condition is caused by a haunting ghost (*bhūta*). Besides, possession is removed in the case of those persons who are not considered eligible to enter this experiential state. Unlike in parts of India with temples widely known for their exorcism rituals, in southern Orissa to drive away spirits, or rather to re-balance the human body is, in general, a two-to-ten minute affair that does not raise much attention. As shown above, there is no clear boundary between desired and harmful forms of possession. In both cases, the behaviour and expressiveness of the body is similar and, like during Ṭhākurāṇī Yātrā, even goddesses can be prohibited from entering pious women. However, certain types of psychophysical affliction are identified within a discourse on black magic (*guṇiā*) and thus regarded as a result of malevolent (super-)human manipulation.

As to the problem of whether this gendered form of divine possession can be considered an Orissan phenomenon, my analysis has raised several questions and can only suggest some answers that need further clarification. Certainly there are features that may account for the specific regional popularity of divine possession: the importance given to goddess worship (Shaktism) and the popularity of devotionalism (*bhakti*), which emphasizes individual experience of the divine. Yet the *intraregional* variety of possession practices should not be underestimated. At any rate, the previous sections indicated that the contrast between my observations in southern Orissa and the literature on possession also emerges due to the dynamics of anthropological knowledge production itself. Since the religious significance of deity possession is a locally contested issue, it is prone to being overlooked or devaluated by ethnographers. To them the local equivalent of academic psycho-medical and sociological arguments is tempting indeed. Therefore it is likely that women in other parts of Orissa,

[83]This ritual act is not limited to Orissa but commonly performed in popular and 'tantric' Hinduism (McDaniel 1989, 13; Gellner 1994, 31; White 2003, 259).

and even South Asia, may also appreciate the religious experience of divine possession, particularly in its non-institutionalized form.

To women in southern Orissa, divine possession is mostly synonymous with goddess possession. These incidents transmit fundamental cosmological knowledge about the similarities between and interdependence of women and female deities. Moreover, the occurrence of possession demonstrates the need to engage in the divine dialogue through prayers and elaborate forms of worship, so as to ensure that the goddess is pleased and will take care of her devotees and the territory they live in. Thus the practice of deity possession does not only express certain ideas about the self, the permeability of human bodies and communication with the divine. It also perpetuates Shaktism in its accessible and embodied form. This religious knowledge includes an inventory of images, observations, emotions and experiences that outline the character and power of female deities. It is re-enacted, spread and authenticated primarily by possessed women and their (male and female) exegetical supervisors. However, from an ideal 'high-caste male' perspective on Hinduism, this ritual practice can be seen to question hegemonic views on religion and society. Yet it would be highly misleading to regard the challenge of brahmanical (and academic) scholars as a self-conscious religio-political act intended by the respective women. The 'subversive' potential of possession is very limited.

In academic discourse, people who experience spirit possession are commonly regarded as weak personalities vulnerable to exterior forces. They appear to be under control, not only when in an altered state of consciousness, but also in their daily lives, a feature which often acts as a precondition for their possession. This is particularly so in the case of women, who are regarded as the creatures of demonic and divine powers. Their at times violent and desperate behaviour while under possession is interpreted as a reaction to their lack of recognition in and exclusion from many spheres of life. Although most scholars do not treat possession events solely as indigenous psychotherapy or a subversive form of social criticism but also focus on their aspect as cultural performance, they rarely associate women with aesthetic communication, ludic transgression, or ritual authorship.

REFERENCES

Assayag, J. and G. Tarabout (eds.) 1999. *La possession en Asie du Sud*: *parole*, *corps*, *territoire*, Collection Purusartha 21, Paris: ńcole des Hautes ńtudes en Sciences Sociales.

Behrend, H. and U. Luig (eds.) 1999. *Spirit Possession in Africa*, Madison: University of Wisconsin Press.

Boddy, J. 1994. 'Spirit Possession Revisited: Beyond Instrumentality', in *Annual Review of Anthropology* 23, 407-34.

Burghart, R. 1990. 'Ethnographers and Their Local Counterparts in India', in R. Fardon (ed.), *Localizing Strategies*: *Regional Traditions of Ethnographic Writing*, Washington, D.C.: Smithsonian Institution Press, 260-79.

Caldwell, S. 1999. *Oh Terrifying Mother: Sexuality, Violence and Worship of the Goddess Kali*, New York: Oxford University Press.

Carrin, M. (ed.) 1999. *Managing Distress: Possession and Therapeutic Cults in South Asia*, Delhi: Manohar.

Chandra Shekar, C.R. 1989. 'Possession Syndrome in India', in C.A. Ward (ed.), *Altered States of Conciousness and Mental Health: A Cross-Cultural Perspective*, Newbury Park: Sage, 79-95.

Claus, P.J. 1975. 'The Siri Myth and Ritual: A Mass Possession Cult in South India', in *Ethnology* 14, 47-58.

Dwyer, G. 2003. *The Divine and the Demonic: Supernatural Affliction and its Treatment in North India*, London: Routledge Curzon.

Egnor, M.T. 1984. 'The Changed Mother, or What the Smallpox Goddess Did When There Was No More Smallpox', in V. Daniel and J.F. Pugh (eds.), *South Asian Systems of Healing*, Leiden: E.J. Brill, 24-45.

Erndl, K.M. 1993. *Victory to the Mother: The Hindu Goddess of Northwest India in Myth, Ritual, and Symbol*, New York: Oxford University Press.

———1996. 'Seranvali: The Mother Who Possesses', in J.S. Hawley and D.M. Wulff (eds.), *Devi: Goddesses of India*, Berkeley: University of California Press, 173-94.

———1997. 'The Goddess and Women's Empowerment: A Hindu Case Study', in K. King (ed.), *Women and Goddess Traditions in Antiquity and Today*, Minneapolis: Fortress Press.

Foulston, L. 2002. *At the Feet of the Goddess: The Divine Feminine in Local Hindu Religion*, Brighton: Sussex Academic Press.

Freeman, J.M. 1981. 'A Firewalking Ceremony That Failed', in G.R. Gupta (ed.), *The Social and Cultural Context of Medicine in India*, Delhi: Vikas, 308-36.

Freeman, R. 1993. 'Performing Possession: Ritual and Conciousness in the Teyyam Complex of Northern Kerala', in H. Brückner, L. Lutze, and A. Malik (eds.), *Flags of Fame: Studies in South Asian Folk Culture*, Delhi: Manohar, 109-38.

———1999. 'Dynamics of the Person in the Worship and Sorcery of Malabar', in Assayag and Tarabout (eds.), 149-81.

Fuller, C.J. 1992. *The Camphor Flame: Popular Hinduism and Society in India*, Princeton: Princeton University Press.

Gellner, D. 1994. 'Priests, Healers, Mediums and Witches: The Context of Possession in the Kathmandu Valley, Nepal', in *Man* (n.s.) 29, 1, 27-48.

Gold, A.G. 1988. 'Spirit Possession Perceived and Performed in Rural Rajasthan', in *Contributions to Indian Sociology* (n.s.) 22, 1, 35-63.

Hancock, M.E. 1995. 'The Dilemmas of Domesticity: Possession and Devotional Experience Among Urban Smarta Women', in L. Harlan, and P.P. Courtright (eds.), *From the Margins of Hindu Marriage: Essays on Gender, Religion and Culture*, New York: Oxford University Press, 60-91.

Hauser, B. 2004a. 'Creating Performative Texts: The Introduction of Mangala Puja in Southern Orissa', in A. Malinar, J. Beltz and H. Frese (eds.), *Text and Context in the History, Literature and Religion of Orissa*, Delhi: Manohar, 203-38.

———2004b. 'Göttliches Gestalten: Zur Besessenheitserfahrung von Frauen in Orissa, Indien', in M. Schetsche (ed.), *Der maximal Fremde: Begegnungen mit dem Nicht-Menschlichen und die Grenzen des Verstehens*, Würzburg: Ergon, 139-60.

———2005. 'Travelling Through the Night: Living Mothers and Divine Daughters at an Orissan Goddess Festival', in *Paideuma: Mitteilungen zur Kulturkunde* 51, Special issue: 'When Darkness Comes...': Steps Toward an Anthropology of the Night (ed. B. Schnepel and E. Ben-Ari), Stuttgart: Kohlhammer, 221-33.

———2006a. 'Divine Play or Subversive Comedy? Reflections on Costuming and Gender at a Hindu Festival', in U. Rao and J. Hutnyk (eds.), *Celebrating Transgression: Method and Politics in Anthropological Studies of Culture*, Oxford and New York: Berghahn, 129-44.

———2006b. 'Periodisch unberührbar: Zur körperlichen Performanz menstrueller Unreinheit in Südorissa (Indien)', in U. Rao (ed.), *Kulturelle VerWandlungen: Die Gestaltung sozialer Welten in der Performanz*, Frankfurt am Main: Peter Lang, 73-105.

———2007. 'Tribal or Tantric? Reflections on the Classification of Goddesses in Southern Orissa', in G. Pfeffer (ed.), *Periphery and Centre: Studies in Orissan History, Religion and in Anthropology*, Delhi: Manohar, 131-52.

———2008. 'How to Fast for a Good Husband? Reflections on Ritual Imitation and Embodiment in Orissa, India', in K.-P. Köpping and A. Henn (eds.), *Rituals in an Unstable World: Contingency—Embodiment—Hybridity*, Frankfurt am Main: Lang, 227-45.

———Forthcoming a. 'Promising Rituals: Doing Gender in Southern Orissa (India)', Halle: Martin-Luther-Universität Halle-Wittenberg (Habilitation thesis).

———Forthcoming b. '(Re-) Calling the Goddess: The Emergence of Divine Presence', in T. Otten and U. Skoda (eds.), *Dialogues with Gods: Trance and Possession in Orissa/ Middle India*, Berlin: Weißensee.

Kakar, S. 1982. *Shamans, Mystics, and Doctors: A Psychological Enquiry into India and its Healing Traditions*, Bombay: Oxford University Press.

Kapadia, K. 1995. *Siva and her Sisters: Gender, Caste and Class in Rural South India*, Boulder: Westview Press.

———1996. 'Dancing the Goddess: Possession and Class in Tamil South India', in *Modern Asian Studies* 30, 2, 423-45.

———2000. 'Pierced by Love: Tamil Possession, Gender and Caste', in J. Leslie and M. McGee (eds.), *Invented Identities: The Interplay of Gender, Religion and Politics in India*, Delhi: Oxford University Press, 181-202.

Kapferer, B. 1983. *A Celebration of Demons: Exorcism and the Aesthetics of Healing in Sri Lanka*, Bloomington: Indiana University Press.

Keller, M. 2002. *The Hammer and the Flute: Women, Power and Spirit Possession*, Baltimore: Johns Hopkins Press.

Knipe, D.M. 1989. 'Night of the Growing Death: A Cult of Virabhadra in Coastal Andhra', in A. Hiltebeitel (ed.), *Criminal Gods and Demon Devotees: Essays on the Guardians of Popular Hinduism*, Albany: State University of New York, 123-56.

Kolenda, P. 1982. 'Pox and the Terror of Childlessness: Images and Ideas of the Smallpox Goddess in a North Indian Village', in J.J. Preston (ed.), *Mother Worship: Theme and Variations*, Chapel Hill: University of North Carolina Press, 227-50.

Lambek, M. 1989. 'From Disease to Discourse: Remarks on the Conceptualization of Trance and Spirit Possession', in C.A. Ward (ed.), *Altered States of Consciousness and Mental Health: A Cross-Cultural Perspective*, Newbury Park: Sage, 36-61.

Lewis, I. 1975. *Ecstatic Religion: A Study on Shamanism and Spirit Possession*, Harmondsworth: Penguin.

Mageo, J.M. and A. Howard (eds.) 1996. *Spirits in Culture, History, and Mind*, London: Routledge.

Mayaram, S. 1999. 'Spirit Possession: Reframing Discourses on the Self and Other', in Assayag and Tarabout (eds.), 101-32.

McDaniel, J. 1989. *The Madness of the Saints: Ecstatic Religion in Bengal*, Chicago: University of Chicago Press.

Michaels, A. 1998. *Der Hinduismus: Geschichte und Gegenwart*, München: Beck.

Nabokov, I. 1997. 'Expel the Lover, Recover the Wife: Symbolic Analysis of a South Indian Exorcism', in *Journal of the Royal Anthropological Institute* (n.s.) 3, 297-16.

Nuckolls, C.W. 1991. 'Deciding How to Decide: Possession-Mediumship in Jalari Divination', in *Medical Anthropology* 13, 57-82.

Obeyesekere, G. 1977. 'Psychocultural Exegesis of a Case of Spirit Possession in Sri Lanka', in V. Crapanzano and V. Garrison (eds.), *Case Studies in Spirit Possession*, New York: Wiley, 235-94.

———1981. *Medusa's Hair: an Essay on Personal Symbols and Religious Experience*, Chicago: Chicago University Press.

Osella, C. and F. Osella 1999. 'Seepage of Divinised Power Through Social, Spiritual and Bodily Boundaries: Some Aspects of Possession in Kerala', in Assayag and Tarabout (eds.), 183-201.

Otten, T. and U. Skoda (eds.) forthcoming. *Dialogues With Gods: Trance and Possession in Orissa*, Berlin: Weißensee.

Pakaslathi, A. 1998. 'Family-Centred Treatment of Mental Health Problems in the Balaji Temple in Rajasthan', in A. Parpola and S. Tenhunen (eds.), *Changing Patterns of Family and Kinship in South Asia*, Studia Orientalia, 84, 129-66.

Parry, J. 1994. *Death in Banaras*, Cambridge: Cambridge University Press.

Pfleiderer, B. 1988. 'The Semiotics of Healing in a North Indian Muslim Shrine', in *Social Science and Medicine* 5, 417-24.

———1994. *Die besessenen Frauen von Mira Datar Dargah: Heilen und Trance in Indien*, Frankfurt am Main: Campus.

Schnepel, B. 2000. 'Der Körper im 'Tanz der Strafe' in Orissa', in U. Rao and K.-P. Kopping (eds.), *Im Rausch des Rituals: Gestaltung und Transformation der Wirklichkeit in körperlicher Performanz*, Münster: Lit-Verlag, 156-71.

Schömbucher, E. 1993. 'Gods, Ghosts and Demons: Possession in South Asia', in H. Brückner, L. Lutze and A. Malik (eds.), *Flags of Fame: Studies in South Asian Folk Culture*, Delhi: Manohar, 239-67.

———1994a. 'The Consequences of not Keeping a Promise: Possession Mediumship among a South Indian Fishing Caste', in *Cahiers de Littérature Orale* 35, 41-63.

———1994b. 'When the Deity Speaks: Performative Aspects of Possession Mediumship in South India', in J. Kuckertz (ed.), *Jahrbuch für musikalische Volks- und Völkerkunde 15*, Eisenach: Karl Dietrich Wagner, 124-34.

———1996. 'Die Göttin und ihr Medium: Über Autorenschaft bei medialer Besessenheit', in R. van Queckelberghe and D. Eigner (eds.), *Jahrbuch für Transkulturelle Medizin und Psychotherapie: Trance, Besessenheit, Heilrituale und Psychotherapie*, Berlin: Verlag für Wissenschaft und Bildung, 241-55.

———1999. '"A Daughter for Seven Minutes": The Therapeutic and Divine Discourses of Possession Mediumship in South India', in Assayag and Tarabout (eds.), 33-60.

———2006. *Wo Götter durch Menschen sprechen: Besessenheit in Indien*, Berlin: Reimer.

Sered, S. 1994. *Priestess, Mother, Sacred Sister: Religions Dominated by Women*, Oxford: Oxford University Press.

Smith, F.M. 2006. *The Self Possessed: Deity and Spirit Possession in South Asian Literature and Civilization*, New York: Columbia University Press.

Stirrat, R.L. 1992. *Power and Religiosity in a Post-Colonial Setting: Sinhala Catholics in Contemporary Sri Lanka*, Cambridge: Cambridge University Press.

Vitebsky, P. 1993. *Dialogues with the Dead: The Discussion of Mortality Among the Sora of Eastern India*, Cambridge: Cambridge University Press.

White, D.G. 2003. *Kiss of the Yoginī: 'Tantric Sex' in its South Asian Contexts*, Chicago: University of Chicago Press.

CHAPTER 17

Social Representations 'In Between': Concepts of Society and Community in Orissa and Beyond

ULRICH DEMMER

INTRODUCTION

This chapter takes up one of the vital issues in the recent study of Orissan culture and society, namely, to seek a way out of centrist and dichotomous paradigms and examine subregional perceptions of the social and cultural fabric. In particular I ask how tribal communities perceive and construct society and the social environment. The present chapter will discuss this subject on the rather abstract level of social representation and the conceptualization of the social sphere—in other words, I ask, what kind of models do we find 'in between', and how do they relate to the dominant models of Indian social anthropology? Empirically I present a comparative perspective including the tribal cultures of Orissa and, on the other hand, a gatherer-hunter community of south India. These cultures will serve to show in detail how society and social relationships are modelled not only in quite specific but also in rather different ways.

MODELS OF SOCIAL LIFE

The question how people organize, represent, and model their social relations was and still is one of the central issues in South Asian as well as Orissan anthropology. This quest is dominated by, more or less, two 'master models'. One is, of course, that put forward most prominently by Louis Dumont.[1] As is well known, in his model of society, India is organized as a total system, with a consistent single pattern and prime values. Moreover, social relations are patterned by a clear-cut structure of oppositional ideas like purity-impurity and hierarchy-equality.

In recent times this image has come under new scrutiny, for example, by historians of the Subaltern Studies group[2] and by anthropologists like Nicholas

[1]Dumont 1970.
[2]Cf. Prakash 2000.

Dirks,[3] Veena Das[4] or Gloria Raheja.[5] Although one can certainly argue that the Dumontian thesis represents a rather structured concept of society, in particular the latter has advocated a social model that is no less accentuated. While Dumont foregrounded structure, system and a unity of values and ideas, Raheja's model underlines the openness, flexibility, and negotiated and contested character of relationships and values. Referring to praxis- and discourse-centred approaches, Raheja[6] views 'society not primarily in terms of structural fixities but in terms of the processes through which relationships are constructed, negotiated, and contested'.

However—and this concerns directly the issue of representation—these ideas and models run the risk becoming 'centristic' and dominating paradigms themselves. This, of course, is certainly not the intention of any of the authors just mentioned. Indeed, they are all aware of the dangers of essentializing ideas about society and social life. Moreover, they would certainly agree that, in order to prevent further essentializations, these ideas are explicitly to be seen as models themselves that need to be engaged with indigenous conceptions of social relations in every empirical case. In other words, though there is no question that all models (both scientific and indigenous ones) are constructed, whether society is also negotiated and contested needs to be shown as being based on empirical and local notions of culture and society. How, I ask, do these scientific 'master' models relate to indigenous ideas and representations of social life and society? To what extent, according to indigenous models, are social relations negotiated, flexible, and contested, or systematic, fixed, and rules-guided? This paper will address those questions and explore, based on field research among two Indian communities, how and what kinds of models these cultures construct.

It is in particular the late R. Burghart[7] and, when one shifts to Orissa, G. Pfeffer[8] who seriously began to take up those questions. Burghart[9] explicitly argued for a hermeneutic and what he called an 'intracultural' approach. He foregrounded the fact that social relationships are not only the object of scientists but also of the people 'on the ground', so to speak. Notwithstanding the fact that empirical models will always be subject to retranslation into the language of scientific discourse, from this point of view, rather than starting from a uniform and total concept of society, we expect a plurality of social representations 'on the ground'.

Thus, to cite just one instance, Burghart showed that eighteenth-century documentary sources from the kingdom of Nepal reveal 'that Dumont's theory,

[3]Dirks 2001.
[4]Das 1995.
[5]Raheja and Gold 1994.
[6]Ibid., 22.
[7]Burghart 1978, 1983.
[8]Pfeffer 1997.
[9]Burghart 1983.

for example, only pertains partially to Hindu society as it actually existed in its recent but pre-modern past. The evidence from royal, ascetic, and Brahmanical sources indicates', to Burghart, 'that the value of purity, far from being a sole fundamental value, both relativised and was relativised by other values'. Thus, 'the brahman, ascetic, and king each presented a hierarchical model of Hindu society and . . . each person claimed the supreme rank according to his own hierarchical model of social relation'.[10]

These findings modify Dumont's model of India in showing the extent to which local and regional perspectives vary and even may compete with one another. The same holds true for Orissa, where Pfeffer in particular argued for a comparative perspective which takes the diversity and unity of ideas and social practices as an object of study and not as a 'theoretical given'. Arguing that Dumont's single system approach, expressed, as it were, in terms of the *varna* system, tended 'to remove tribal categories from the agenda'[11] and that empirically tribal ideas may follow a 'different rationale when compared to the Hindu or "Western" order', he pleaded that we concern ourselves with 'the tribal idea of life'.[12]

These studies indicate a shift from a single system and centristic view to local perceptions and interpretations 'in between' the master models of Indian social anthropology, and they encourage the empirical study of the plurality and variety of models and social representations. This does not preclude, of course, that we look into the emergence of systematic patterns and configurations across cultures—it simply demands that one accounts for them in each specific case before one begins comparison on a higher cross-cultural level. This does not mean, however, that we must 'throw the baby out with the bathwater' and assume that neither Dumont's nor Raheja's models match the facts. As, for example, Vincentnathan makes clear,[13] the social concepts of the higher castes do closely correspond indeed to the ideas of Dumont.

Comparable evidence is provided by Hardenberg's study of the Orissan Nabakalebara ritual.[14] This performance, celebrated in the heart of Puri, while periodically instantiating the new birth of Jagannath, represents central ideas of the social order in quite Dumontian and classical Hindu terms. When the performers move into the forests while their families remain in Puri and 'at home', they are enacting prime oppositions in the social system, very much in Dumont's terms, namely, the contrast between 'people out of the world' and 'people in the world', between the ascetic and the householder, between the individual and society, between egalitarian relations and hierarchy and, if I understand correctly, also purity and impurity.[15]

[10]Burghart 1978, 519.
[11]Pfeffer 1997, 5.
[12]Ibid., 25-6.
[13]Vincentnathan 1993.
[14]Hardenberg 1999.
[15]Ibid., 417.

However, once we shift the view from the centre, its rituals and main deity to the regions 'in between', we encounter other models of social order and values. According to Vincentnathan's ideas, low-caste Dalit or Harijan groups often do not seem to follow the hierarchical and binary logic that is taken by many to be inherent in the Hindu system.[16] And when we turn to the broad spectrum of tribal communities, the expectation is great that here as well we will find specific models of the social order. In fact, as Pfeffer points out, 'a vast array of tribal and so-called scheduled caste people do not necessarily follow the *varna* model of social relationships'.[17] Thus, at the level of ideas, the difference between coastal and tribal Orissa is evident: 'the varna model is the frame of reference for all castes of the coastal area, but it cannot be discovered in the tribal hills at all. No estate of intellectual ritualists is opposed to the holders of secular power or segregated from the general peasant community'.[18]

> A more appropriate nomenclature would differentiate those who traditionally hesitate to communicate with the plains people and those who do not serve as accepted culture brokers within an ongoing symbiosis. The former are of a higher status and non-marriageable in relation to the latter.[19]

If we only concentrate on inter- and intra-tribal relations, it is the ideas of seniority, affinity, and reciprocity that govern tribal conceptions. Thus seniority is seen to order relations

> between subtribes and between clans and even at the village level members of a single clan subdivide into closely interrelated ritual groups of different standing. [...] status categories and groups are seen interrelated, mutually dependent seniors and juniors. [...][20]

And with respect to affinity, reciprocity, and symmetric exchange, we can see that

> the relationship between intermarrying lineages or between the living and the recently deceased is that of an overall symmetry. Temporarily the 'wife-givers' will have a status advantage that will be levelled [however] because of the rule of [...] reciprocity.[21]

THE KOYA

The Koya, who are also known as the Bison Horn Maria,[22] are settled in the southernmost part of Orissa in what is today Malkangiri district, and large

[16]Vincentnathan 1993.
[17]Pfeffer 1997.
[18]Ibid., 11.
[19]Ibid., 25.
[20]Ibid.
[21]Ibid.
[22]Cf. Grigson 1938.

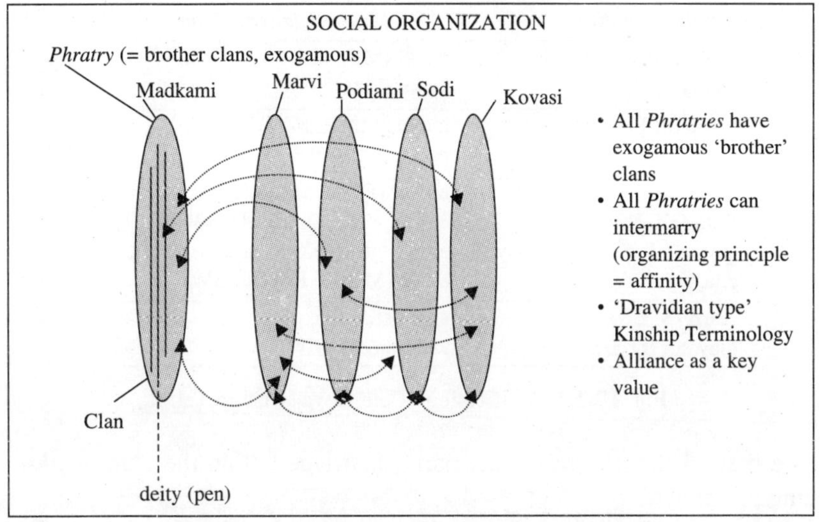

Fig. 17.1: The Social Organization of the Koya

sections also live in the eastern parts of Bastar in the neighbouring state of Chhattisgarh. The Koya I am referring to in this chapter live in the southernmost part of Malkangiri district, in settlements close to Mottu village.[23] As traditional slash-and-burn cultivators, they are farmers who practise cultivation (e.g. rice and millet), but they also herd cattle and buffalo or work in the fields of neighbouring farmers.

Linguistically the Koya language belongs to the Dravidian family of languages, which in Orissa embraces languages of tribal cultures like the Khond and Oraon and the many sections of the Gond.[24] The Koya communicate easily, however, in other local languages too, in particular Telugu. In fact, although without doubt a distinct language of its own, as Tyler shows, the Koya language itself is linguistically closer to Telugu then to any other language in the region.[25]

Koya society is organized in terms of what can be called a 'group model' of society. In contrast to, for example, the Jenu Kurumba of south India (see below), the Koya represent their social organization in the form of a clear-cut network of kinship-based groups. According to this model, their social organization consists of five exogamous *phratries*, namely Ko:vasi, Ma:di, So:di, Markami and Podiya:mi.[26] Each *phratry* in its turn is constituted by a number of patrilineal clans (*katta*), with each *phratry* and clan having their own totem. Both units, that is *phratries* and clans, are exogamous units, in the

[23]Cf. Demmer forthcoming.

[24]Cf. Tyler 1969, 1965.

[25]Tyler 1969.

[26]Grigson (1938, 306) mentions the *Kuhra:mi* (or *Kadiari*) *phratry* instead of *Podiya:mi*. My own inquiries, however, found no evidence of the former.

Parallel Relatives	*Cross Relatives (Affines)*
da:da:l (FF), emma (FM)	ta:ta:l (MF), ka:ko (MM)
tappe (F, FB), evva (FBW, M, MZ)	ma:ma:l (MB, FZH, WF, HF), po:ye (FZ, MBW, WM, HM)
enna (eB, FBeS), ekka (eZ, FBeD) tammund[/ṇḍ]u (yB, FByS), e:la:di (yZ, FByD)	ba:ta:l (FZeS, MBeS, eZH), en[/ṅ]ge (FzeD, MBeD, eBW) erund[/ṇḍ]u (FZyS, MByS, yZH), e:nda (MByD, FZyD, yBW)
marri (S, BS), maya:di (D, BD)	a:ne (ZS, DH), kodiya (ZD, SW)

Fig. 17.2: Classification of the Koya Kinship Terms

sense that all the *phratries* intermarry, marriage within the clan or *phratry* being prohibited.

While actual kinship on the personal level is certainly the dominant factor in the structuration of domestic and local units, locality is no longer thoroughly structured by clan affiliation. Even in the times of the early ethnographer Grigson,[27] this was no longer the case.

The linkages between the segments are determined by the kinship system, which is of the Dravidian type, differentiating all kin into two categories, namely those with whom one can have marriage ties and those with whom one cannot. The former category, of affinal relatives, is termed *akomama*. The latter category, those with whom marriage is forbidden, are the *dadabhai*.[28]

This classificatory system is employed on the clan level as well, so that ego has a number of *dadabhai* clans, with whom he or she cannot intermarry, and a number of *akomama* clans with whom marriage is conducted. This conforms to an overall Middle Indian pattern, where, as Pfeffer has pointed out, affinity is a key social principle organizing the society as a whole.[29] This is the case among the Koya too, where the category of *akomama* plays a central affinal role. Not only are the *phratries* seen as affinal categories but the clans too, since Koya can talk, for example, of *akomama* (affinal) clans. Moreover, as the analysis in the present chapter shows, actual kinship relationships, as well as both social and ritual life, are also based on 'affinity as a key value'. However, these kinship-based social structures are not fixed per se but have to be renewed and maintained. It is in rituals like the death ritual where the meaning and significance of this principal value is reinforced and kept alive.

The same holds true for relationships between humans beings, the deceased, and the deities, all of whom are seen as members of the society, which has an extended character. As among many other cultures in the world, Koya society

[27] Grigson 1938.
[28] Cf. Grigson 1938, 244-5.
[29] Pfeffer 1982.

is not confined to human beings but includes the dead and deities as well. Among the latter, it is in particular the clan deities (*pe*[*l*/*ē*]*n*) and the earth, worshipped as the village mother in every settlement, that are significant. All of these deities, that is, the clan deities as well as the village mother, influence the well-being of the community and are worshipped in the course of the many rituals (*padum*) that are associated with the fertility of the soil, prosperity and agriculture. Moreover, people also communicate and talk with them in times of difficulties. This 'divine discourse' is only practised in the séances, where Koya shamans embody the deities and act as their medium.

Like the deities, the dead too are regarded as important and active members of the society. In fact, they are really a part of everyday life. In every Koya house, the part of the storage room (*w*[/*v*]*ijalon*) where the 'pot of the departed' (*hanal kunda*) and the 'hearth of the departed' are set up is kept separate. Usually the dead are thought to live in the underworld, but during ceremonies and rituals they are thought to dwell in the pot, in front of which they are offered food, drink, and the smell of incense sticks. Moreover, in most of the *padum* that are associated with the prosperity of the land, the Koya also seek to maintain good relationships with the dead in order to secure fertility and well-being. The burning down of bushes on the land can also be done only with the help of the dead, because a burning log from their hearth must be used to kindle the bush fire. But even in everyday life, the dead are regarded as active beings with whom good relationships must be secured.

In sum, the Koya have a rather clear-cut idea of what their society looks like. According to the image represented in the death rituals, it is seen as a system of exchange and of marriage relations between groups, namely, the *phratries* and clans. Society, then, is seen here in terms of a group model of social order, which consists of five *phratries*, all connected through exchange and marriage relations. These relationships also include the other-than-human beings and, building on the kinship system and its normative implications, they are seen to constitute the basis for the exchange of services and gifts. Society is therefore conceptualized as a rule-guided system of exchange relations with relatively clearly outlined structures. Imagined as a network of exchange and alliance among rather clear-cut social categories, it is conceived to rest primarily on values like seniority, exchange, and affinity.

These findings correspond clearly to a whole spectrum of other tribal societies in Middle India, where affinity and exchange relations are the central parameters of the society.[30] In other cases, however, the idea of a group model of society is less pronounced and eventually shifts towards a notion of moral community which is based primarily on interpersonal kin relations rather than on groups and exchange.

The Orissan sections of the hunting-and-gathering Birhor, for example, seem to articulate such a social concept. According to study by Adhikary, the

[30]Cf. Pfeffer 1982.

Birhor draw a sharp contrast between internal relations and the broader Indian society.[31] The former, their own social configuration, is conceptualized in terms not of society, hierarchy, stratification, and status, but of personal relationships within a moral community:

> They divide their universe on the earth into disum and muluk. By disum they mean the region of hills and forests, their own territory, and by muluk, the peasant villages and the markets, the territory of 'other people'. The Birhor have developed adaptive strategies of participation and social interaction in these two sets of environment: a morally ordered gemeinschaft in disum and a rationalist-utilitarian gesellschaft orientation in muluk.[32]

Though we need not agree with the above thesis that a society is a rationalist-utilitarian environment, it is evident from Adhikary's descriptions that the Birhor do draw a contrast between it and the moral community. Making frequent reference to terms like 'groups' and what we call hierarchy, status, system and the like, the muluk indeed seems to refer to what we have called a group model of society. Unfortunately more details about the Birhor conception of community are not available. Therefore, it is necessary to travel to the furthest periphery beyond Orissa to obtain a fuller idea of how a moral community is conceptualized in contrast to 'society'. The Jēnu Kuṛumba in southern India present these ideas very explicitly.

THE JĒNU KUṚUMBA

The Jēnu Kuṛumba are numerically the largest gatherer-hunter people (around fifteen to twenty thousand people) in south India. Their home range stretches along the western side of the Ghat forests, which today form parts of Kerala, Tamil Nadu and Karnataka. These forests are the traditional foraging areas of the Jēnu Kuṛumba, but since the establishment of reserve and forest areas and the wildlife sanctuaries of Mudumalai and Bandipur (in the middle of this century), they have been deprived of their rights to forage in these forest regions. Today they are forced to live in settlements, comprising from one to twenty-five conjugal families each, on the periphery of the sanctuaries and reserve forest areas. In the latter they are, however, entitled to gather minor forest products (honey, tamarind, tree moss, soap nuts, etc.). Moving through the reserve forest areas in small, flexible camps, they gather these products throughout the year and usually sell them to non-tribal (private or public) agents. In addition they are employed as wage-labourers on tea and coffee plantations, farms or in wildlife sanctuaries.

As is typical of many gatherer-hunter cultures, the Jēnu Kuṛumba do not have either political or juridical institutions, such as chief, tribal council, village assembly, court, etc., nor do they have any corporate and stable groups like

[31] Adhikary 1984.

[32] Ibid., 22.

clans, moieties or the like. Social life is thus not based on a group model of society but unfolds exclusively on the level of the community and interpersonal relations.

The Jēnu Kuṛumba live in communities of approximately three hundred to four hundred people, scattered over a wide area. Sociality within the community is predominantly based on kinship relations, but in contrast to the micro-castes, the networks of the Jēnu Kuṛumba are not denoted by names nor situated in a hierarchical organization—therefore they do not exist as indigenous categories of the social order.[33] This, in turn, is related to the fact that an explicit representation of their society as a totality (be it as a verbalized model or in mythology) does not exist. Likewise the Jēnu Kuṛumba do not conceptualize a clan or moiety system for the network or for the *jāti* as a whole.

Since there are no lineages, unilineal or agnatic descent groups which act or define themselves as corporate units, the social order is not framed in a group model of society but rather in terms of interpersonal sociality. People in the network are situated in a chain of mutual obligations, a moral order of kinship which stresses filiative and affinal bonds. Affines or *ba:-mayika*, that is, all those who are bound together through repeated marriages (genealogical and terminological cross-cousins: ZH-WB, MB-ZS, FZ-BD, WF-DH, HM-SW, as seen in Fig. 17.2) should share among themselves and should support each other if one of them runs into difficulties (having no clothes, money, cigarettes, food, etc.).

As already noted above, as is typical of many gatherer-hunters, the Jēnu Kuṛumba have no headmen, no tribal council, or any other institution of political authority. Though all these features clearly differentiate them from the Koya, what they share with the latter is that concepts of social life and community are constructed most explicitly in death rituals. In fact, their death rituals[34] are organized around three 'key metaphors', which articulate a performed allegory of a moral community. In the first metaphor, the performance depicts their society as a moral community and a cooperative household. The second metaphor depicts it as an encompassing community that not only consists of the living, but also encompasses ancestors and the deceased as well. Finally, the third metaphor represents this encompassing community as a 'tradition of argumentation', where people are continuously required to engage in verbal debates on the values of community and the quality of actual social relations.

The Community as a Household

A death ritual takes the form of a successive number of symbolic actions or scenes. In the first sequence, called the 'cutting and bringing of leaves', all male participants walk in a kind of procession to a nearby river or waterhole.

[33]For these aspects and a general ethnography, see Demmer 2001a.

[34]See Demmer 2001b for a detailed description and analysis of the performance.

Guided by musicians who play a special tune, they go to collect branches with green leaves which are needed later on with which to build a small hut. The ancestor and the spirit of the dead person will be made to sit in this hut, being entertained with music, dance and food, and thus be made happy.

After reaching the river, the ritual priest (*yajman*) selects a special tree (*on*[/*ṅ*]*ge-mara*) with green leaves and performs a *puja* at its root. A little later, one of the younger participants climbs the tree and cuts down enough green branches with which to build a small hut. Thereafter all the other participants carry these branches ceremonially back to the ritual place. Holding the branches above their heads and accompanied by music, they walk in a line and shout joyfully. Once they have reached the ritual site, they circumambulate a prepared wooden frame anti-clockwise three times and place the leafy branches on the frame or simply drop them on to a heap. Then the musicians stop playing the first sequence.

After a period of rest, the second scene, called the 'bringing of water', is performed, in which everyone present walks back to the river, again in a kind of procession led by the musicians. The women carry water vessels while the ritual priest takes two small clay pots. After reaching the river bank, the *yajman* performs a *puja* (as before with an offering of bananas, coconut, incense and parched rice) in front of the water vessels and the small clay pots.

Then one of the small clay pots is ceremonially filled with water, and from now on the ancestor is said to reside in it. Later the whole group ceremonially returns to the ritual site. Two children carrying the small clay pots walk behind the musicians and are followed by three or four women carrying large water pots on their heads, which have already been filled with water from the river. When they approach the ritual site, the other male participants join them with foodstuffs (bags of rice, oil, vegetables, etc.), and firewood. Finally the group circumambulates the wooden frame and the heap of green branches three times, screaming loudly and joyfully in a rhythmic voice.

Immediately after the circumambulation, the small clay pots, the foodstuffs and the large water pots are set down and a fire is made with the burning firewood. Then the ritual priest builds a small hut (*udi-ma*[/*ā*]*ne*) with the green branches, and the two small clay pots are placed at its centre. If any green branches are left over, they are used to build a larger leaf hut alongside the small one. It is in the larger hut that the cooking, undertaken by some of the male participants, takes place. Finally, the *yajman* erects a wooden pole (*raṅga khambha*) in the vicinity of the *udi-mane*, adorns it with small green branches, and performs a *puja* in front of it. Then the musicians gradually start to play, and the people start to dance in circles around the *raṅga khambha*. This dancing lasts through the night, and the dancers will only take a break when the food is ready. First, the ancestor and the spirit of the dead will receive an offering of cooked food and incense. Then the living will also be served by those who have cooked the food. As with every other action in the ritual context, this communal eating is performed ceremonially, the people sitting and eating in a square.

Finally, the following day the unification of the dead and the deity is enacted ceremonially. The spirit and the deity, both still in their clay pots, are now brought in a procession, again led by the musicians, to a tree in the forest. At the foot of the tree the ritual priest places a small stone (approximately seven inches in height), performs a *puja* (as usual with incense, bananas, coconut, and parched rice), and then pours the water of both pots on to the stone. This is interpreted by the participants as their ultimate contribution to, as they say, 'making the spirit sit in the company of the deity'.

The death ritual thus articulates a key metaphor of this culture, namely, the community as a cooperative household. Through the process of the ritual, people realize an image of the community as a space of actually lived solidarity and cooperation. This concept is further developed in the wake of the discourses and dialogues within the performance. Thus, a good social life is imagined verbally as the 'pleasant and protected camp', as the 'cool spot', the 'shady place in the forest', or else is likened to the 'calm and peaceful camp under trees that offer shade'. Other verbal images depict it as a nest in which humans support one another 'like eggs in a nest that mutually support one another and prevent any from tipping over', and so forth. . . .

The Encompassing Community

The second image that is performed at the death ritual also relates to the Jēnu Kuṟumba conception of sociality. This metaphor depicts the community as an encompassing social fabric which includes not only the living but also the ancestors and the dead. According to the Jēnu Kuṟumba world-view, the ancestors and the dead live in the underworld. Nevertheless, the latter can interact and verbally communicate with the living. This, however, only happens in ritual contexts. In ritual performances the ancestors and the souls of the deceased can embody themselves in the shamans of the tribe, and thus embodied, they are able to interact with and to talk to their living relatives.

In the death ritual, this is performed in several scenes. In the first sequence it is the ancestors who distribute the green branches to the living. In fact, the living need the ancestors' cooperation to perform the first scene and bring the branches to the ritual site. The same holds true for the second phase. When the living have performed the *puja* at the river bank, they invite the spirits of the deceased to join the ritual. Moreover, when the spirits come and embody themselves in the shaman, participants also fetch water from the river and distribute it to the women. Without the support of the dead, the living cannot enact this second scene and are unable to bring the water to the ritual site. Thus the ancestors and the dead demonstrate their solidarity with the living and their membership of the moral community.

However, their relationship with the living is not a one-way street. The ancestors and the dead not only help and support the living, they also demand solidarity and assistance for their parting. Thus, as the performance proceeds, the ancestors may indicate with gestures that they want to drink a cup of water, or the dead may demand to smoke a *bidi*, a type of cigarette. Usually the living provide them with both. Apart from these 'worldly' desires, the supernatural beings, and in particular the dead, are shown to have very human feelings also. Thus they point out their sufferings and their need for help, bend down and hold the side that pains them, are given a stick to walk with if they indicate weakness, and complain, cry, or even embrace their close relatives. At other times, however, they also show their happiness and start to dance in a circle with their living relatives.

The most important act of solidarity, however, is the achievement of the death ritual itself. According to Jēnu Kuṛumba beliefs, a person continues to live after his death. Yet, the spirit of the dead needs to reach the underworld, where the ancestors and the other dead are already 'at home'. Otherwise the deceased will only exist henceforth as an angry and lonely spirit roaming around in the forests of the upper world. It is therefore the ultimate aim of the death ritual to help the dead reach the underworld and its inhabitants. From this it follows that the dead need the help and solidarity of their living relatives. This image is celebrated most elaborately in the final scene of the ritual.

After the nightly demonstration of good and happy relatedness between the living, the ancestors, and the dead, the living help the dead to move down into the underworld and join the ancestors. To achieve this, the participants bring both of the small water-filled jugs in which the ancestor and the dead are still dwelling to a tree in the forest. Once the procession reaches the tree, a small stone is decorated and a *puja* is performed. Finally, the *yajman* pours the water of both jugs on to the stone, and through this act the ancestor and the dead go down together into the underworld.

Another mode of visualizing the significance of the ancestors and the dead for the community is to underline and dramatize their presence. The act of embodiment is itself a dramatic performance. When the shamans are becoming possessed they tremble violently, stumble around, throw their arms up into the air or fall down to the ground. This latter, however, is always prevented by some of the relatives who stand close by and quickly catch them. Once the shamans are embodying the supernatural beings, their peculiar style of movement serves to focus attention on them. At these times the ritual site becomes a kind of arena, in the centre of which the shamans pace back and forth. Sometimes they stop walking, but even then they appear restless, their speech disjointed and breathless. Many of the living are accorded the role of spectators, keenly observing the shaman in the centre, but others are picked out by the shaman and brought forward to stand in a row facing him, in order that they may talk to the ancestors and the dead.

These performed images make it clear that the moral community not only rests on cooperation and solidarity, but that it is also basically an encompassing unit unable to exist without the support and moral guidance of supernatural beings. The 'good community' is only realized as an encompassing order which includes the ancestors and the dead as active, negotiating members of the social fabric.

This idea also emerges in verbal dialogues. People describe themselves as 'the children of the deities' or address the shamans as the 'favourite children' of the deities, 'sitting in their lap and being taken care of nicely'. In turn the deities are imagined as parents who hold human beings 'like children by their hand' and who keep the living 'like infants in their lap', 'lulling them to sleep like children', and so forth.

THE NEGOTIATED COMMUNITY

The third image depicts the community as being based on the discursive engagement of persons in dialogue. This is made visible in the very performance of the dialogues, which are not only public, but also highlighted, dramatized, and in fact 'staged' as an arena of debate. But this idea, which might be called 'dialogic sociality', is a crucial topic in verbal discourse as well. In fact, the reason why moral sociality must be dialogic in character is explained in discourse itself. First, speakers frequently state that they are in need of moral knowledge and orientation. Only if they are able to speak with non-human beings about 'what is good and bad' can they walk on the 'right and good footpath'. Without it, they lament, there is no justice, no allocation of responsibility, one cannot recognize the correct way of living with other people, etc.

One of the crucial features of social life that these dialogues point out, then, is that communal life is inherently uncertain and prone to dilemmas, its outcomes and overall development always open and at stake. The consequence of this is that, in order to live in a good way or, as the Jēnu Kuṛumba say, in a 'shady and protective camp', people are required to attend morally to one another. Moreover, in order to live such a moral life in a good way, people must respond to one another and constantly negotiate and justify their relationships and behaviour. What emerges in the death ritual is a concept according to which moral sociality is kept alive only through continuous engagement in public debate. What the Jēnu Kuṛumba discourse tells us, then, is that without debate, there can be no foundation (*nele*) for the moral community. The latter can thus be seen as a 'tradition of argumentation', where people continually argue with each other over who or what they are.[35]

CONCLUSION

This paper has explored empirically local conceptions of social order and society. In order to overcome centristic and dominating discourses, two rather marginalized tribal cultures were analysed, the ways in which they represent and articulate concepts of social life through ritual performance. The emerging models can fruitfully be related to the main paradigms that dominate Indian and Orissan anthropology.

[35]This concept is explained in more detail in Demmer 2006.

As it turned out, the Koya of southern Orissa present a concept of society that corresponds in certain aspects to the classical ideas put forward by Dumont and structuralist thought. In accordance with other Orissan cultures classified as 'tribal', they conceptualize their social fabric in terms of a kinship-based model and a system of exchange. In the performance of the death ritual, it is represented as having a relatively clear structure of interrelated segments and thus appears to be firmly organized in terms of a group model of society.

Other cultures, by contrast, like the Birhor of Orissa or the Jēnu Kuṛumba in south India, imagine their social world as a moral- and discourse-based community. In foregrounding negotiation and flexible relationships and in imagining their social environment as a moral community which must constantly be worked out through debate and argumentation, they come much closer than the Koya to Raheja's conceptualization of social life as an ongoing process of negotiation and contestation.

REFERENCES

Adhikary, A.K. 1984. *Society and Worldview of the Birhor: A Nomadic Hunting and Gathering Community of Orissa*, Calcutta: Anthropological Survey of India, Government of India.

Burghart, Richard 1978. 'Hierarchical Models of the Hindu Social System', in *Man* (n.s.) 13, 519-36.

———1983. 'For a Sociology of Indias? An Intracultural Approach to the Study of Hindu Society', in *Contributions to Indian Sociology* (n.s.) 17, 2, 275-99.

Das, V. 1995. *Critical Events: An Anthropological Perspective on Contemporary India*, Delhi: Oxford University Press.

Demmer, U. 2001a. 'The Social Structure of the Jēnu Kuṛumba', in G. Pfeffer and D.K. Behera (eds.), *Contemporary Society: Tribal Studies*, vol. 4, Delhi: Concept.

———2001b. 'Always an Argument: Persuasive Tools in Jēnu Kuṛumba Death Rituals', in *Anthropos* 96, 475-90.

———2006. 'The Rhetoric and Poetics of Ritual Performance: The Jenu Kurumba (A interactive multimedia cd-rom)', in U. Demmer, *Rhetorik, Poetik, Performanz: Das Ritual und seine Dynamik bei den Jenu Kurumba*. Berlin, New York: LIT.

———2007. 'Memory, Performance, and the Regeneration of Society among the Koya (Middle-India)', in A. Malinar and C. Mallebrein (eds.), *Time in India: Concepts and Practices*, Delhi: Manohar, 192-208.

Dirks, N. 2001. *Castes of Mind: Colonialism and the Making of Modern India*, Princeton: Princeton University Press.

Dumont, L. 1970. *Homo Hierarchicus: An Essay on the Caste System*, Chicago: The University of Chicago Press.

Grigson, W.V. 1938. *The Maria Gonds of Bastar*, London: Oxford University Press.

Hardenberg, R. 1999. *Die Wiedergeburt der Götter*, Berlin: Weissensee Verlag.

Pfeffer, G. 1982. *Status and Affinity in Middle India*, Wiesbaden: Steiner.

———1997. 'The Scheduled Tribes of Middle India as a Unit: Problems of Internal and External Comparison', in D.K. Behera and G. Pfeffer (eds.), *Contemporary Society: Tribal Studies*, vol. 1, Delhi: Concept, 3-27.

Prakash, G. 2000. 'Writing Post-Orientalist Histories of the Third World: Perspectives from Indian Historiography', in V. Chaturvedi (ed.), *Mapping Subaltern Studies and the Postcolonial*, London and New York: Verso.

Raheja, G.G. and A.G. Gold. 1994. *Listen to the Heron's Words: Reimagining Gender and Kinship in North India*, Berkeley, London: University of California Press.

Tyler, S.A. 1965. 'Koya Language Morphology and Patterns of Kinship Behaviour', in *American Anthropologist* 67, 1428-40.

———1969. *Koya: An Outline Grammar*, Berkeley and Los Angeles: University of California Press.

Vincentnathan, L. 1993. 'Untouchable Concepts of Person and Society', in *Contributions to Indian Sociology* (n.s.) 27, 1, 25-53.

CHAPTER 18

Dulduli: The Music 'Which Touches Your Heart' and the Re-enactment of Culture

LIDIA GUZY

INTRODUCTION

Dulduli is the name given to the regional tradition of instrumental orchestral music in western Orissa. In the traditional rural setting, it is known as *ganda baja* and is played exclusively by the (formerly) Untouchable communities of the Ganda (also called Pano).[1] The *ganda baja* is a ritual inter-village orchestra that carries with it indigenous concepts of rhythms, instruments and goddesses, and is associated with marriage alliances and religious ceremonies. Since the music combines gods and humans in a sensual manner, it is never absent during weddings or rituals for local gods and goddesses. In the urban setting, the inter-village orchestra transforms itself into *dulduli*, a form of folk art on stage, also known as Sambalpuri music. *Dulduli* players are generally urban middle-class musicians, who perform mainly on stage in a range of cultural contexts.

The present chapter, which represents work in progress,[2] describes a musical tradition in its diverse cultural settings and in a process of social change. In

[1]The phrase 'instrumental orchestra' signifies an ensemble of instruments with a choral character drawn from the different voices of the instruments, but in this context it does not signify any form of vocal ensemble. It is important to note that an instrumental orchestral tradition in South Asia is very different from the Indian traditional (classical) form of modal music. Modal music in classical Indian music is characterized by the individual solo performer and solo compositions (Daniélou 2004, 10-11); it lacks the choral character of instruments as voices which play together. The choral character of the South Asian orchestral tradition otherwise resembles classical European orchestras (chamber orchestra, opera orchestra, etc.). The differences from the classical European tradition lie in the fact that (a) the musicians are restricted to specific social groups or ethnic categories, (b) that the music is restricted to special occasions (Sachs 1923, 2-3), and (c) that it represents specific regional traditions of ensembles of regional instruments (see Sachs 1923, 3-11), for example, that known as the *Naykhibaja* of the Newar (Wegner 1988) or the *Damai baja* (Helffer 1969a/b), also known as the *Pancai baja*, of the Damai (Tingey 1994), both from Nepal.

[2]I am grateful to the German Research Council (Deutsche Forschungsgemeinschaft) for a generous research grant (from 2003 to 2005), which enabled me to conduct research in Sambalpuri music.

so far as music represents a society, it can only be understood in its specific cultural context.[3] This study thus attempts to differentiate between the rural and urban features of local music in western Orissa. When local performing arts evolve to become urban folklore on stage, the character of the cultural performances also changes. Urban folklore in western Orissa is directly connected with the music industry, the media, and the World Wide Web. Urban folklore is also related to the constitution and rise of regional ethnicity, in so far as this can be considered a political agent.

The first part of this chapter deals with the traditional settings of the instrumental orchestral music of western Orissa. The second part sketches a profile of the transformation of a performing folk art into urban folklore and thus draws attention to the political implications of music.

THE TRADITIONAL CONTEXTS OF DULDULI

Traditionally in western Orissa,[4] music and dance are embedded in the local belief system, where instruments and rhythms represent the speech of local goddesses. The voices of the different goddesses appear in different rhythms. In the rural context no socio-religious ceremony, such as marriage or *puja* to the gods and goddesses, can be celebrated without *baja*. The musicians are invited by means of the symbol of turmeric powder, which is sent to them by different local communities, such as the Binjal, Gouro, Dhol Khond, Mali, or Kulta, to perform in their villages. The music played by the Ganda musicians connects local communities, places, and religious concepts. In its linking and communicative function, it can be considered an inter-village orchestra, whose mediators are the Ganda musicians.[5]

The ensemble of the folk instruments is also called a *panchabadya*,[6] which itself refers directly to the five instruments assembled in the inter-village orchestra. The orchestra, consisting ideally of five instruments, might have between five and seven instrumentalists. The ensemble represents three categories of instruments: membranophones (*dhol*, *nissan*, *tasa*, also called *timkiri*), an aerophone (*mohuri*), and idiophones (*kastal/jhang* or *jumka*).

The ganda baja/panchabadya of western Orissa:

(1) *dhol*
(2) *nissan*
(3) *tasa* or *timkiri*
(4) *mohuri*
(5) *kastal/jhang* or *jumka*

[3]See Blacking 1973; Blacking and Kealiinohomoku 1979.

[4]The data drawn from Sambalpur and Bargar Districts, especially the rural Padampur and Boro Sombar region. I am thankful to Surendra Kumar Sahu from Padampur who assisted me in my research with that whole of his musical knowledge and devotion for the local music of this region.

[5]For comparison of the Pano in Koraput, see Pfeffer 1994, 14-20.

[6]See here the similarity with the Nepalese *pancha baja* of the Damai musicians (Tingey 1994).

DHOL

The *dhol*, which is the leading instrument, is a large membranophone. The large, long drum (90 cm to 1.5 metres in length) is made from the trunk of a tree and is stringed with cowhide (*gai chomora*) on two sides. The *dhol* also has strips of cowhide (*badi*) and rings for the strips (*kol kola*). The *tali* is the right-hand side skin and is made from calf's skin; the *dhaya*, the left-hand one is made from cowhide. *Tali* are slightly smaller (37 cm in diameter) than the *dhaya* (38 cm in diameter), and the left side is played with one rubber stick (*khanda/nara*) of around 40 cm in length. The *dhol* player is called the *dholya*, who typically directs all changes of rhythm played by the *ganda baja* group. All the rhythms are spontaneous, but they are still directed by the *dholya*. The musicians learn the rhythmic and melodic compositions by listening to various rhythms from early childhood on.

NISSAN

The *nissan*, another membranophone, has a tapered form like half a melon. It is often considered to be the most ancient instrument of the village orchestra. A *nissan* is made of wooden and iron sheets, and is played with two rubber sticks (*chimta*). The leather (*chipra*) that creates the sound is made of cowhide or goatskin, and is often decorated with colourful paintings.

The *nissan* is always played with maximum strength and thus has a deep, penetrating sound. In the Sambalpur area it is decorated with deer antlers, though these have begun to disappear, as deer hunting is now forbidden.

TASA

The *tasa*, a small membranophone, is a drum made from clay (*matul*) and stringed with cow's leather (*gai chomra*), called *mola*. Its shape is tapered to a base,[7] and it is played with two thin bamboo sticks. The sound the *tasa* makes is high and thin.

MOHURI

The *mohuri* is an oboe-like instrument. Its sound, the Ganda say, is a crucial element in changing the character of the music. Usually it is associated with the seductive voice of a capricious woman, but it can also be related to the desperate voice of a mother crying for her dead son.

KASTAL

The *kastal* or *jhang* are iron cymbals; the *jumka*, which may be used instead of the cymbals, is basically a rattle.

[7]The *tasa* has also leather strips.

All the instruments play together in both tune and rhythm. The most important criteria for a Ganda musician are to listen to what the other musicians are playing and to learn to play along with them. Playing *baja* also implies a sophisticated culture of listening. The musical specificity of the *ganda baja* seems to lie in its instrumental orchestral character. Through the beat of the right hand, *tali* side of the *dhol*, the *dhol* provides orientation for the *tasa*, which then beats a double rhythm. The beat of the left hand, *dhaya* side of the *dhol* provides orientation for the *nissan*, which then strikes a counter-rhythm to the beat of the *dhaya*. As the sound of the *mohuri* must often resemble the flirting of a women's voice, it is played in an extremely alluring way.

All the instruments in the inter-village orchestra are worshipped before being played. They themselves are used in the worship of gods and goddesses, but they also require worship.

Even if the orchestral character *ganda baja* can be compared with some structural features of the orchestral traditions of Nepal (Helffer 1969a/b, Tingey 1994, Wegner 1988), *ganda baja* seems to represent a regional specificity of western Orissa/Chhattisgarh.[8]

The Ganda Baja and the Worship of the Goddess

The *dhol*, *nissan*, and *tasa* are used in inducing trance. For instance, the *nissan* represents the voice of the goddess Nissani and thus becomes identical to her. This identification between drum and goddess can be observed in a Nissani temple near Padampur in Bargar District, where the goddess Nissani is considered to be, and where there are three *nissan* drums on the temple altar.

Ganda Baja and Boil: An Example of a Traditional Possession Cult

The relationship between *ganda baja* and the local worship of goddesses is illustrated by the local possession cult called *boil* in the Padampur/Borosombar region of western Orissa.

The Ritual Scene

Every Monday during Dasara (October) in the Boro Sombar region, when the Goddess Durga is to be worshipped, she appears in the body of her priest. At this time, *boil* comes upon the *pujari* (priest). Meanwhile the *ganda baja* accompanies the act of possession, which is embodied in the dance and speech of the priest.

[8]According to personal communication (August 2005) with Dr Nicolas Prévot, at the Department of Ethnomusicology in Paris, similar musical structures can be found in Chhattisgarh.

Definitions of Boil

Boil is a polysemic religious concept. It can be translated as either the 'divine dance' or the 'dance of gods and goddesses'. This concept refers to the religious specialist and his or her ritual involvement. The *pujari* who becomes *boil* is transformed into a sacred dancer of the Goddess Durga.

Boil can also be understood as the 'opening' of the local *pujari* to the entry of a divine power and can accordingly be identified with 'goddess spirit possession'.[9] *Boil* can also be translated simply as a divine power, a procreative and creative power, which comes upon the *pujari*. The phrases *boil asile* or *boil asi* (*boil* came) and *boil asibe* (*boil* will come) indicate the wild dance of the *pujari*, who, while dancing, represents and becomes *boil*. On the one hand, *boil* is a condition, a state of trance. On the other hand, it is the personified manifestation of the Goddess Durga. During *boil*, the *boil* himself may even completely lose control and fall down if he is not held or helped. Generally the *boil* of the Goddess Durga is a man, but a man with feminine attributes. *Boil* have long, open hair and wear a red sari during the *boil* ritual.

Boil charibe, jibe (*boil* will leave) signals the end of the ecstatic dance and the end of the presence of the divine power. After the divine power withdraws, the *boil* is left numb and then returns to his or her original state as the daily priest.

Ganda Baja Rhythms and the Ritual Transformation

The *ganda baja* is of central importance in the ritual transformation of the human priest into a *boil*, the divine manifestation of the Goddess Durga and of other goddesses and gods.

The concept of *bol* or *par*, the rhythm, plays a critical role in the ritual performance of *boil* possession. The trance itself is expressed in rhythms which become representative of the goddesses. The *ganda baja*, which is essentially polyrhythmic, leads the possession performance, particularly by playing the so-called *borua par*, the holy sixteen rhythms of *boil* possession.

Borua Par

The *borua par*, the rhythms of the divinely possessed, have a structure of sixteen rhythms, also called *sulo par*. *Sulo par* are the rhythms represented in the *boil*, the possessed priest (*pujari*) of a goddess. Different goddesses will appear via different rhythms (*par*) in the body of the possessed. *Sulo par*, the sixteen possession rhythms, represent sixteen different goddesses. The rhythms are named after the goddesses and are aurally recognized by the musicians.[10] Locally, the identifications of rhythms and goddesses can vary.

[9] Roche 2000, 288-95.

[10] Such as Durga Par; Maha Kali Par; Ma Magala Par; Ma Tarani Par; Oila Devi Par; Subakesi Par; Tulsa Devi Par; Bontei Devi Par; Chandraseni Par; Ganga Devi Par; Parvati Par; Lakshmi Par; Boiravi Par; Buri Ma Par; Patmeshwari Par; Samleshwari Par.

The *ganda baja* or inter-village orchestra accompanies the ritual of possession and the worship of the gods and goddesses. The music of the (formerly) Untouchable musicians in itself represents an 'Untouchable' entity of the sacred, channelling intangible local concepts of the divine as a wild, uncontrolled power, which is expressed by the rhythms and dance of the possessed priest. On the one hand, the *baja* transcends local communities in its function as a ritual inter-village orchestra. On the other hand, through its rhythmic expression of the transcendence, the *baja* enables the sensual experience of the local community and its communication with the holy sphere.

The Ganda Baja as an Expression of Local Identity

The *ganda baja* not only provides a form of religious expression, it also transmits to its listeners a strong emotional connection with local beliefs and identities.[11] To quote a Ganda musician: 'Listen to the *baja*. It touches your heart! It is the sound of the thunderstorm. It is the sound of your heart beat.' For all those whose life has been accompanied by *baja*, this music represents part of a local cultural totality, and as such the music reinforces a feeling of cultural interconnectedness. The inter-village orchestra can be considered a crucial component of cultural identity. As the *ganda baja* communicates with other cultural clusters—religious rituals and local communities—it signifies a feeling of local and religious identity. The ritual musical performance expresses an abstraction of the experience of the local community.

Having dealt with the topic of music and situated it in its traditional context, I shall now discuss recent transformations in an urban setting, where tradition is becoming more and more reinvented.

THE URBAN CONTEXT

In the urban context, the play of culture and local identity is expressed on stage. In urban western Orissa one can discern a high degree of creativity in the performing arts. Traditional music and dance are revitalized on stage and create a kind of urban folklore, the so-called Sambalpuri music. In Sambalpur it is striking that no less than two generations are searching for a 'lost cultural identity'. The second and third generations of urban migrants continually ask themselves what they have lost due to the industrialization and modernization of their world.

In this context, in recent years many cultural institutions and centres have appeared and grown in order to revitalize a 'forgotten' local culture. These cultural groups conduct research on traditional dance and music in order re-create these customs on stage in a proper traditional manner. The aim of this

[11] On the relationship between music and emotion, see Feld 1982.

wave of research in the most remote areas is to collect the 'wild' (yet not urbanized) rhythms and information about them before these traditions change or disappear. Many urban activists are going to the field and documenting these still vibrant traditions in remote villages, where they observe, learn, and finally teach their young urban students how to protect and understand their cultural identity through music and dance.

Cultural programmes, such as Loko Mohotsav, the annual Folklore Festival in Sambalpur, which started in 1998, deal with the changing world and with the persistent search for cultural identity. Modern media and technology are used to promote local cultural performances on stage and to transfer them to the World Wide Web. In various ways local musicians are invited to Sambalpur and encouraged to continue performing their local art traditions, for which they receive recognition and money.

The Loko Mohotsav in Sambalpur is an example of the ongoing process of creating and re-creating urban folklore on stage in a manner which connects it with a globalized world. In the Loko Mohotsav, local life is re-enacted and projected on to the global community. For urban cultural activists, west Orissan folklore is becoming one of the centres of musical and cultural expression. The sacredness of the traditional *baja* is being transformed into the sacredness of a performance which will be broadcast to the world.

Because of the vital work of these urban activists, art traditions are being preserved on stage, where, however, the re-enacted local traditions become fragmented by an earlier socio-cultural totality. On stage, the *dulduli* is no longer a ritual inter-village orchestra played by the (formerly) Untouchable Ganda. Instead it represents a regional folklore which is mostly being played by an urban middle class, who have migrated from the villages and have settled in the cities in the past two or three generations. Together with the cultural nostalgia being catered to by the music industry, the traditional *baja* has since become 'touchable'. With its tangibility, urban folklore is in danger of being transformed into an ever simpler and secular form of entertainment.

MUSIC AND ETHNICITY

Together with its cultural revival on stage, a growing regional ethnic awareness can be witnessed with regard to *dulduli* or Sambalpuri music. Ethnicity is the process of constructing group identity with regard to a constructed history, common origin, and culture.[12] The discourse on culture in western Orissa is strongly connected with its impact on music and language. Cultural and political activists are trying to combine language, music, and culture in order to construct a distinct regional and cultural identity. The regional uniqueness of Sambalpuri culture will be expressed by Sambalpuri music and language. Sambalpuri

[12]For definitions and discussion, see Guibernau and Rex (eds.) 1997; Waltzer, Kantowicz, Higham and Harrington 1982; Ben-Ami, Peled and Spektorowski (eds.) 2000.

music thus conveys political self-awareness and self-esteem. Potentially, this cultural distinctiveness may one day become the basis for the creation of Koshala,[13] an autonomous regional administration within India.

On stage, *dulduli* music demonstrates the cultural and political self-awareness of an urban middle class, since it reflects its relationship with local folk music and its power to create a regional ethnicity in urban western Orissa,[14] mirroring a recent example of cultural metamorphosis on stage. The former socio-ritualistic *ganda baja* is being transformed into secular Sambalpuri music, with implications for political, cultural, and regional distinctiveness.

[13] Koshala is the name of a mythological kingdom of this region.
[14] For comparisons, see Stokes (ed.) 1994.

REFERENCES

Ben-Ami, S., Y. Peled and A. Spektorowski (eds.) 2000. *Ethnic Challenges to the Modern Nation State*, Houndsmills and New York: Macmillan Press and St. Martin's Press.

Blacking, J. 1973. *How Musical is Man?* Seattle and London: University of Washington Press.

Blacking, M. and J.W. Kealiinohomoku (eds.). 1979. *The Performing Arts: Music and Dance*, Paris and New York: Mouton.

Daniélou, Alain 2004 (1975). *Einführung in die indische Musik*. Wilhelmshaven: Noetzel; 1st edn. Wilhelmshaven: Heinrichhofen.

Feld, S. 1982. *Sound and Sentiment: Birds, Weepings, Poetics and Song in Kaluli Expressions*, 2nd edn., Philadelphia: University of Philadelphia Press.

Guibernau, M. and J. Rex (eds.) 1997. *The Ethnicity Reader: Nationalism, Multiculturalism and Migration*, Cambridge: Blackwell.

Helffer, Mireille 1969a. 'Fanfares Villageoises au Nrpal', in *Objets et Monde* 9, 1, 51-8.

Pfeffer, Georg 1994. 'Music in Context: Ethnography and Meaning', in *Beiträge zur Musikethnologie* 30, 14-20.

Roche, David 2000. 'Music and Trance', in Alison Arnold (ed.) *Garland Encyclopedia of World Music*, vol. 5, *South Asia: The Indian Subcontinent*, New York: Garland Publishers, 288-95.

Sachs, Curt 1923. *Musikinstrumente Indiens und Indonesiens*, 2. Aufl. Berlin/Leipzig: Vereinigung Wissenschaftlicher Verleger Walter de Gruyter & Co. (Handbücher der Staatlichen Museen zu Berlin).

Stokes, M. (ed.) 1994. *Ethnicity, Identity and Music: The Musical Construction of Place*, Oxford and Providence: Berg.

Tingey, Carol 1994. *Auspicious Music in a Changing Society: The Damai Musicians of Nepal*, London: School of Oriental and African Studies.

Waltzer, M., E. Kantowicz, J. Higham and M. Harrington 1982. *The Politics of Ethnicity: A Series of Selections from the Harvard Encyclopedia of American Ethnic Groups*, Cambridge, Mass. and London: The Belknap Press of Harvard University Press.

Wegner, Gert-Matthias 1988. *The Naykhibaja of the Newar Butchers*, Wiesbaden: Franz Steiner Verlag.

CHAPTER 19

Discourses, History and Modernity: In Search of Orissan Civil Society

GEORG BERKEMER

The German people, united in its tribes. . . .[1]

This is the last of the Salzau Conferences of the Second Orissa Project. Allow me, therefore, in this essay, to bring up those matters which concern and trouble me most in Orissa, a place which has become our home away from home. I do not want to contribute scientifically to the already rich material on Orissa here, but rather shall use my time to formulate some thoughts on open issues from the point of view of a foreigner, a subaltern, and a historian.

From the beginning, this project was not able to do research in as wide a field as envisaged by its planners. It was crippled by the more or less complete absence of some key subjects such as sociology, and literary and political sciences. These, together with anthropology, philology and other subject areas, provide necessary partners and critical companions in the research of historians. This lack and some ill-timed cuts in the funding of our work on historiography have made it difficult to cover to our satisfaction such contemporary issues as are deeply rooted in one or more of Orissa's pasts. Orissa has at least three sets of such pasts: a partially ambiguous colonial past, a much cherished imperial past, and a multitude of local and subregional pasts—some contested, but mainly forgotten or disdained.

It is not only since the shift to post-modern paradigms that we have come to realize that any historical past is created by the present at least as much as the present is formed by the collectivity of such pasts. Consider the following example from places far away from Orissa, namely, Pakistan and Germany: in a two-part editorial in the *Daily Times* (Lahore) Georg Pfeffer[2] has described how horrified German visitors usually are when confronted with their Indian or Pakistani hosts' undiminished admiration of Adolf Hitler. While travelling, most of us Germans have had similar experiences, not only in South Asia, but also in Africa or South America. This naiveté is quite unsettling for a post-war German: Adolf the Horrible, the greatest of all mass murderers, the cause of

[1]Beginning of the Preamble of *The Reich Constitution* of 11 August 1919 (the Weimar Constitution) of the first German democracy.

[2]Pfeffer 2003.

unimaginable destruction and suffering, the personification of all the evil of the twentieth century—these epithets may suffice to illustrate the politically correct opinion about him in Germany—suddenly rises from his unknown grave as the nemesis of the British empire and ally to a host of freedom struggles most Germans either are in favour of, or have never heard of. After coming to grips with this embarrassment from his own past, the visitor from Germany usually understands that a different present indeed shapes a different past.

The past is often seen as a one-dimensional chain of events linked by cause and effect, leading straight to the New World Order after the end of the Cold War. The victory of global capitalism over its enemies is often presented as the natural precursor to global democracy and liberty. On the other hand, what our contemporaries have to endure in those countries that have been most affected by the recent global changes make many nostalgic for the good old times of stability and clear front lines. There are indeed problems with post-colonial and post-socialist democracy, new and untested, often imported from foreign parts as a ready-made commodity like crates of Coke and fleets of BMW cars. The American brand of democracy, a by-product of capitalism labelled 'Liberty' or 'Freedom', is indeed open to a fair amount of criticism. As Leonard Cohen, the Canadian poet, has put it: 'The poor stay poor and the rich get richer; that's how it goes, everybody knows.'

Globalization and capitalism, population pressure and unemployment, religious extremism and the consequences of the greenhouse effect . . . all this makes people feel insecure. The more you know about it, the less you like this little planet of ours. It is quite easy to call for the strong hand at the top or for the one and only ideology or creed that promises to keep the centrifugal tendencies at bay and the much cherished values of old intact.

In the Moscow daily *Prawda* of 8 May 2003 a commentator noted in the context of Iraq that for some countries the price of democracy is too high. And he asks: 'Isn't a dictatorship simply better for some peoples than democracy?'[3] We Europeans would deny this, but it is not easy to convince people facing seemingly insurmountable obstacles that there are other ways to solve their problems than resorting to *matsya-nyāya*, or following *avika-marga*, the way of the sheep. Not only in Russia, but everywhere from eastern Europe to Afghanistan, democracy is often seen as a liability, a burden to be shouldered for the sake of foreign capitalists or a newly rich minority.

Is all this relevant for Orissa? I think it is, even though, if one looks from the problems of the Near East to South Asia, India has recently been hailed as a haven of stability and is not counted among the likely candidates ready to sacrifice democracy for a strong national leader. India, it seems, has inherited the better part of the British colonial legacy by opting to become a constitutional and parliamentary democracy instead of adopting a presidential system. And Orissa—so snugly ensconced, despite its undeniable problems, in its memory

[3]Quoted in *Berliner Zeitung*, 9 May 2003, p. 4.

of a golden pre-colonial past and hopes for a better future—seems somewhat like a Switzerland in India. Rooted in its traditions and enjoying internal peace, it has indeed a few things in common with Switzerland—far-fetched as this comparison may seem at first glance: from the day of acknowledged nationhood, neither have ever lost their freedom, but have retained their traditions and struggled as an avant garde to find their own path into the future. Switzerland, however, has had a few centuries more to carry out this task, gaining freedom gradually between 1291 and 1648, while in Orissa many still remember the first and the second days of independence, in 1936 and 1947. There is more that the two states have in common than one may imagine: until the eighteenth century, the map of Switzerland consisted of territories of dominant, allied Sovereign Cantons (*Souveräne Kantone*) and their clients (*zugewandte Kantone*), interspersed with territories of shared authority and high mountains where state authority was merely a theoretical presence. This reminds one of Orissa's *garhjat* states. And not least is the fact that both have in their history as states so far avoided the dangerous, dark side of democracy, as we know it from both India and Europe.[4]

Does this dark side contain pitfalls which are all but unavoidable in the long run if a political system is to be founded on sentiments of national unity? Is democracy always based on the exclusion the 'other', i.e. of those groups whose language, culture, skin colour, religion, past, etc., do not fit the accepted norm? Europe was and still is full of such incidents, some centuries old, like the conflicts in Northern Ireland and in Kosovo, but many are less deep-rooted in the past than commonly assumed. I have quoted some examples in the call for papers for this conference to illustrate the fact that South Asia is not far behind in time in its creation of national sentiments based on allegedly 'ancient' traditions which were actually made up in the nineteenth or twentieth centuries. There is the strict refusal of Catalan nationalists to collaborate with the 'foreign' Spanish government in cultural matters, the outrage of Gaelic nationalists in the 1980s when cultural anthropologists showed that the alleged deep-rooted adversity against the 'Saxon' English was a fabrication, and there is the necessity to resort to cultural symbols produced in modern times in order to justify claims to ancient cultural independence (e.g. in the eighteenth-century Ossian in Scotland, the nineteenth-century Finnish Kalevala and the fabrication of an anachronistic Medieval 'French' or 'German' Empire, centred around the figure of Charlemagne or Karl der Grosse, etc.). Here, the past has been (re-) created as a support for the newest fashion in political thinking: nationalism.

I am not in favour of stating 'laws of history'—history in my opinion is an agglomeration of more or less unconnected contingent events and their long-term consequences, which are statistical and accumulative, and not determined

[4]Despite being culturally similar, Orissa has not yet let the Hindu-fascists add a chapter of communal mass murder to its history like Gujarat, nor has there been genocide in Switzerland like in Germany (see Anderson 1991; Mann 2006).

by any physical or metaphysical principle that we know of—but there seems to be a strong correlation between nation-building and strong sentiments against those who are seen as outsiders. There is a whole repertoire of actions which can make sure that everyone knows their place: to construct a handy conspiracy theory, to denounce the collaborators and the lukewarm, to sentimentalize one's own kind in language, culture, religion and the past—usually by evoking mother- or fatherlands and the biological equivalent of the nation (the *Volkskörper* or the Japanese *koku-tai*: the nation conceived as one collective body), to propagate the exemplary fate of the martyrs for the case at hand, and, in order to perpetuate the sentiment, to make sure that everybody knows that there are still some scores to be settled. There are territories still in the hands of the enemy (the *terrae irredentae*) and stray fellow countrymen to be gathered home into the fold ('Where Serbs Live There is Serbia'; Slobodan Milosevic). And again there is the bygone glory, the heroic days, the old empire to be resurrected. This list could go on and will inevitably end with horrors such as genocide, ethnic cleansing and the industry and bureaucracy of death, so masterfully put into homicidal practice in Germany during the Second World War. The twentieth century is full of such incidents, in Turkey, South Asia and later in Cambodia and the Balkans, to mention only a few.

While a good nationalist holds out the structural duality of 'us' *versus* 'them' and may as a politician win votes with such platitudes, praxis looks somewhat different. A colleague of mine who was a member of the municipal council of her home town found that, as soon as anyone from abroad starts to engage himself in communal activities such as sports or gardening clubs, welfare societies or political parties, the common interest can become stronger than the person's 'foreignness'. But there are degrees of this: the more somebody actively integrates himself, the easier is the process. The better he speaks the language, the longer he lives in the region (not in the country), the more he knows about local affairs, the more he 'becomes one of us'. The continuum has many dimensions. Take for instance Germany: depending on peoples' upbringing, there might be the problems of skin colour, country of origin, religion and of course education and wealth. Frenchmen, Dutchmen, Swiss, Austrians, Danes, Italians and a few others might be seen as less than half foreign, other EU citizens, especially when being Christian or not ostensibly non-Christian, and not dependent on the dole, will also have not much of a problem. Like them are Americans, Japanese, South Asians, South Americans and eastern Europeans. Integration is easier for individuals or single families than for larger groups, but virtually impossible for those who want to keep themselves aloof from the dominant culture.

While India is undergoing a new step in the formation of nationhood, in which a growing middle class discovers a common interest in modern, if not global, ideas and commodities, more traditional sectors of society demand the strengthening of region-based statehood. This discourse can also be observed in Orissa. As a Nation in a Nation, between 1936 and 1947 Orissa saw its share of conflicts between the proponents of statehood and the advocates of a nation-wide Independence movement. In 1936 Orissa, as the oldest of the language states of the Indian Union, represented a new dimension of statehood which set an example for others after Independence. This not only produced conflicts between the National Congress and several non-Congress governments, but also brought to light the backwardness of many of the Oriya-speaking princely states, where political awareness was rare and where the rulers had no interest in joining any quest for nationhood, be it within the Oriya movement or the INC. Now, two generations later, most of the old resentments have died down, but many of the problems Orissa has inherited from older times are still unsolved, and many new ones have arisen. The task in its quest for nationhood was and is not only to integrate Oriya-speakers of different social backgrounds, such as city, tribe, and countryside. There was also the task to turn Oriya from a peripheral 'dialect' in the Bengal Presidency or from a minority language without rights in Madras into a state language.

Much has been written about this cultural process of asserting the status of Oriya as a language of literary value as well as a tongue fit for school, administration and collective memory. Less, however, has been said about the inevitable result of this process of forming a national language: the very process of creating a centre within the Oriya-speaking tracts made 'deficient' those who do not speak the Oriya of the administrative elite of the centre. This, besides forming a national territory, is the one process which has been considered necessary for true nationhood all over Europe—with the exception of Switzerland—in the heydays of nationalism. It is the foremost distinctive mark a person carries, if not in their face, then on their tongue. From here arises the 'Dark Side of Democracy' whose excesses Orissa has so far avoided. However, no democratic state system remains free of it, and Orissa, as we shall see, has had its share of attempts to consolidate its centre at the expense of its peripheries.

Orissa is 'one' when the point of view is that of the centre, but 'diverse' when seen from its periphery. Then again, it seems to have many peripheries if we compare the cultural idioms in which these peripheries express themselves. As Flueckiger has shown, many of these peripheries have fuzzy boundaries which are not congruent at all with modern state boundaries. Over the centuries, traditional identities have been created and lost, amalgamated and split apart, and built layer upon layer of collective representations and memories. Any one of them can be taken up by interested parties, remodelled according to the latest fashion in self-representation, garnished with late modern or post-modern newsspeak, and delivered to the public as an urgent political or religious agenda.[5]

In Orissa, not much of this has made itself felt so far. Is there a danger that it may be ripped apart by centrifugal forces if certain 'peripheral' traditions

[5]See Flueckiger 1991, 1996; Flueckiger (ed.) 1991; Berkemer 2003.

unite with a modern political will to create a new political unit out of parts of Orissan territory? The Koshal movement is the best example here, the southern Desia another. It seems that the Koshal movement has started like the various Oriya movements a century earlier: as the brainchild of intellectuals who were dissatisfied with their personal career prospects and others' low regard for their local identity and cultural background in the political centres of their time. Getting away from these centres was one part of the agenda; finding a new focus in an old, but so far rather peripheral centre was another. From a Calcutta point of view, Puri was a 'centre out there', a nice place somewhere out in the sticks at the borders of the Bengal Presidency. But being the focus of a living tradition, one could build a new collective identity upon it.

Lacking such an old centre, however, the Koshal movement[6] may be in a less advantageous position. Here, as in the Oriya movement earlier, the combination of cultural tradition and historical construction with modern political ideas and means of dissemination are believed to do the trick. Whether it will is doubtful because, while the original Oriya movements took shape in the heyday of national sentiment, other issues are now to the fore. Globalization creates its own forms of modernity or post-modernity, and many of those to whom the intellectuals of a hundred years ago gave the only acceptable voice now have a whole set of strategies to choose from in order to make themselves heard. Political parties and ideologies, religious movements, NGOs, international human rights groups, terrorist cells, profit-seeking or non-profit business organizations—they can all provide a platform with which to link one's own small world with global ideas. The world which any contemporary in Orissa perceives as his 'own' is probably much bigger now than a hundred years ago, and emotional attachments that were once reserved for a very small part of the globe make themselves felt in a much wider context. Take, for instance, sports events, space flights, elections in a foreign country, the oil price or floods and earthquakes: things you know and have sentiments and opinions about become to a degree your own concern. This changing and widening point of view can also provide a means to 'modernise' outside mainstream society by helping to create the ability to think globally, or, in more scientific terms, to experience the relativity of one's own 'societal reference' and 'self-identity'.

Take, for instance, an example that Richard Eaton provides: there were Naga chiefs around 1880 who asked the British administration to send missionaries, even though they had no previous exposure to Christianity. The Nagas' explanation was that, in a world in which their fate was decided from as far away as London, they needed a god whose influence could be felt not only in their own area, but all over the British Empire. This is modernization by degrees. Maybe the Desia, when they are finally forced to take to political action against the exploitation and alienation of their land by national and

[6]Cf. S.K. Panda in this volume.

international industries, the logging mafia, the employees from the plains in the new industries and future oustees from land submerged by rising sea levels, will have a more 'modern' stance for their struggle to keep a foothold in their 'periphery'.

The Orissa Project has provided us with many data on social change showing how Orissa has opened up to the world. It seems to me that we are a long way from the 1980s, when even educated ladies would ask a visitor from abroad to bring them an American sari. The fictitious American sari is a good example of the universalization of one's own cultural frame of reference. Now, twenty-five years later, such ladies know from TV or personal experience that there are no saris in America. They have no problem to perform a process of relativization of their own frame of reference. I have seen tribals[7] in remotest Koraput discuss Osama bin Laden and the Taliban war in Afghanistan. News media provide information that allows everybody to compare their own situation with those of others, far and near.

I am not saying that things are better now than they were twenty or two hundred years ago, only that they are certainly different. For a long time in the past, the worlds of the common man and those of his rulers and spiritual leaders were parts of the same social system, or at least parts of very similar social systems. This prompted anthropologists like Robert Redfield to construct yet another of those dyadic oppositions which in the twentieth century seemed to explain the world of many societies: the Little *versus* the Great Tradition. Now the social reality in India is by far too complicated to be described in a sufficiently precise way by such a simple opposition. It became apparent in the first and even more so in the second Orissa Project that Orissa as a region was itself too complex for dyadic oppositions such as 'great' and 'little', 'tribal' and 'Hindu', 'modern' and 'traditional', 'centre' and 'periphery', etc.

Complex as social reality is and was, have we solved any of the terminological and nomological conundrums that faced British administrators when they tried to simplify the complexity they observed? As Bernard Cohn, Nicholas Dirks and others have demonstrated, the colonial powers have amassed whole archives of information which, taken at face value and transferred from the original context into a European one, is not much more than meaningless data and sometimes even accounts of grotesque intercultural misunderstandings.[8] I think that one of the few things we discovered is that only a few or perhaps even none of our terminologies and vocabularies have worked so far to make things easier to understand. We, the academics, are now more aware that we as 'experts' from all over the world are in the same situation as any other person: our understanding of what we study is very limited. But at least we are trained to express how we came to understand that we do not understand. We have

[7]The word 'tribal' is used throughout this essay as it is utilized as an administrative technical term provided by the Constitution of India. It is never meant as an analytical or 'scientific' term denoting a certain social or moral order.

[8]Cohn 1987, 1996; Cohn, Dirks 1988; Dirks 2001, 2006.

words to construct our at best partial solutions—that is, our academic training—as well techniques of deep immersion into that 'other' that we are studying. As long as we manage to surface again, our voice may be heard over yet another cultural divide: that between our world of academic area studies and a public 'at home' who might think that what we do is useless and a waste of money. How do we argue against such a utilitarian point of view when we are confronted with the question: what is the use of studying the other, when the other in the process of globalization is expected to become what we are already? Maybe the best answer is a question: what is globalization but a new form of cultural imperialism?

In our area of study, we may be confronted with global as well as more localized forms of cultural imperialism. I suppose that we all were dragged into rivalries between factions and contesting groups who want to make us a part of their arsenal of arguments against their opponents. Whether the RSS agitator who wants a foreigner to confirm his right to 'convert' tribals to Hinduism; the frustrated country school teacher who wants to get back to the city as soon as possible and needs somebody to commiserate with him; the fundamental Christian sectarian who wants 'uplift' by conversion but who does not see why the said foreigner does not support his absurd world-view; the disgruntled descendant of a zamindar who believes that everything was better way back when—they all have their strategies and arguments and maybe also a strong belief that theirs is the only solution to malnutrition, a lack of education, the wrong language, the lack of awareness of cultural heritage, etc. Going back to our levels of cultural imperialisms, we see that the common local people are in all these examples constructed as the 'other' which has to be linked with one's own level, the national in case of the RSS worker, the combination of global and sectarian in case of the missionary, the state-centralist in the care of the teacher and the subregional in that of the ex-zamindar.

All these people except the last have one feature in common: they all want to change somebody's future by creating a short cut between the small world of the local people and the wider world as they see it. In other words, they universalize their own existential particularism and its past. Thus they base their *raison d'être* on the same mental structure as any nationalism, European, South Asian, or otherwise. Their temporal frame is rarely a very long-term one—perhaps the time of a legislative period, the time until their retirement, the time period a money grant will last. But social change is a matter of generations rather than of years. There cannot be a highway to the future built by one group of people for others in lieu of tortuous and difficult paths of 'relativisation of self-identities'[9] and the realization of the relativity of one's own social and cultural categories.

Let us take a closer look at the last example in this file of disillusioned characters: the ex-zamindar or little king and his dispossessed descendant. He

[9] A phrase used by Arjun Appadurai.

is the only one whose complaints are not motivated by the peoples' stubborn refusal to embark on the one and only correct journey into the future. He rather tells tales of past ingratitude, and he and his brethren in spirit will recall the good old times when the king always had an ear open for the petitions of the subjects, and when judgements and sentences were passed and executed swiftly and justly according to a traditional law that was understandable to each and every one. It is easy to comprehend that such people may call for the strong hand in the way I described at the beginning of this essay. However, they do not long for a modern national leader like Saddam Hussain, but for the traditional ruler, who they believe to be the closest indigenous equivalent to the modern dictator. Such a figure in their traditional guise can definitely not be the solution to problems of change and modernity. The little king from the past might have been a nice figurehead in party politics during the formation of Orissa, but he was rarely a genuine politician due to his lack of any professional attitude.[10] Unfortunately we never had a political scientist in our Orissa Project who could have studied the political roles of the kings in the 1930s and compare them to contemporary minor royalty, the modern 'rajas' who get elected as MPs and MLAs. The kings of the twenty-first century might even become what their more conservative grandfathers were not: symbolic figures of a multi-faceted local modernity. What they share with their forefathers, however, is their potential role as integrators of diverse social systems on the local level.

Orissa, with its large tribal population and a Hindu majority split into many traditional and modern communities, its contrast between cities and rural areas, industrial belts, agricultural and forest economies, is presently building the monopolistic social infrastructure which, as a result of national and global trends of modernization for instance in Germany or France, gives whole countries that sort of suburban uniformity in architecture and mentality that provides all the necessary accoutrements of a boring life for boring people. One can only hope that Orissa is spared such a fate of becoming 'united' as yet another clone of uniformly modern society.

In what respect could the ongoing social and cultural changes be different in a globalizing Orissa as compared to most western countries? Some suggestions come to mind, based on three foci of change: (1) a local and regional within the state; (2) a national in India; (3) an international in the global world.

The state of Orissa still has on its soil what seems at first glance just a relic from a pre-modern past, something which most Western societies have eradicated in their course of modernization: a large population of 'others' who still have a considerable amount of autonomy. Orissa as a state has so far not done in a systematic way what other dominant social groups did throughout the world: to destroy either the physical existence or the cultural identity of

[10]Berkemer 2007.

the 'other'. The milder form, 're-education' into the dominant culture of those who were already socially marginalized has been a state programme for some time in countries such as Australia (Aborigines), Norway (Sami), Japan (Ainu) and Canada (First Nations).[11] The more brutal dislocation (Soviet Union, South Africa, USA, China) or outright state sponsored genocide as in Nazi Germany should not concern us here.

Entangled histories are a part of entangled identities. In our context of centres and peripheries or levels from local to global—and being aware that opposites and gradations are simplified models constructed for the sake of clarity—one can make up combinations of epithets which may seem nonsensical at first glance. Pairs of labels from a whole range of identity markers, such as 'Oriya', 'tribal', 'Hindu', 'Indian', 'Townsman', 'Villager', 'Muslim', 'Christian', etc., often conceived as sets of direct and mutually exclusive antonyms, which do not have spatial connotations *per se*, can be placed on a mental map of Orissa as provided by the centre. As history shows, however, what is now conceived as mutually exclusive, might not have been so in a certain period of time in the past.

Modernization in Orissa, however, inevitably has its impact on those who cannot or want not participate in the mainstream culture and society.[12] Following Akio Tanabe, who discusses the emergence of early modern Oriya patriotism from local patriotisms in this volume, we can ask what the difference may be between Oriya patriotism and Orissa patriotism.

Several questions follow therefrom: How does one express the entangled histories of the centres out there and other subaltern groups and localities in the languages and discourses of the superior powers? It is difficult enough to succeed in the attempt to give a voice to the subaltern for those who are trained to do so, the more difficult it is for the subaltern's voice to be heard at a centre where one more insignificant voice is just one more irritating factor.[13]

From the above-mentioned list of identity markers, some pairs appear to be more problematic on the level of the state of Orissa than on the level of the Indian nation: it is quite possible to be Indian and non-Hindu (e.g. a Muslim or atheist), or Indian and tribal (e.g. a Naga). In Nagaland, tribality is the state-level reference for ethnic identity.

Orissa is a more difficult case. Obviously, not everybody born in Orissa is automatically an Oriya. There are other requirements to be met beyond being

[11]This is not to say that there were not much more violent cases of 'solutions' in such countries as well as in those without such policies. I am just taking examples where state governments believed it was their task to 'civilize' or 'integrate' the marginalized. Death squadrons hired by cattle barons, mining, logging and oil companies, proxy and civil wars, etc., are a different matter.

[12]There are warning voices stating that even well-meaning changes of legislature can enforce the marginal status of the lowest (Kurup 2008).

[13]This is not to imply that the subaltern doesn't speak, or at least uses his means of communication to express his ideas and desires. It is just stating the fact that speaking alone does not constitute a dialogue, and even less a contribution to a dominant discourse.

born in the territory.[14] Does one need to speak Oriya? Not always, as one can be an Oriya—without knowing the language or being born there—by being the son (and maybe daughter?) of Oriya parents. But, it seems, this only works if you are a proper Hindu as well. One could assume that one criterion for true Oriya-ness is to be allowed to enter the temple of Jagannath in Puri.

So far, the construction excludes the tribals, the Muslims and Christians living in Orissa, and of course any 'foreigner'. When being a member of a minority community who are not allowed *darshan* there, maybe you have to love Orissa and Oriya culture to be an Oriya? And if so, what exactly is it, one is required to love? School books written in Oriya might provide an answer. And how much does it help to have visited an Oriya speaking school to pass that test for being a cultural Oriya? This may solve the issue for Muslims and Christians, and even for Indianized foreigners, since the identity construct contains the necessary loopholes. Therefrom follows, that Oriya patriotism or nationalism are constructs aiming for an imagined community in the sense of Benedict Anderson.[15]

But is it possible to be Oriya and tribal? In the case of Orissa, the state's foundation myth is so strongly based on constructions of linguistic and cultural unity, that this is hard to imagine. Those groups who were already inside the territory the Oriya movement struggled for, and whose members did not or could not help to make the patriotic dream come true, had to be labelled 'backward' in order to both deny them their own voice for the time being and make them eligible for uplift, i.e. give them the chance to join the already established mainstream voices. Such administrative thinking simply continues the old colonial categories.[16] In a Gandhian utopia, local tribality might go along with Oriya-ness or any other state level nationality in India, as long as the local level's cultural identity, its local values and ideas of autonomy are surrendered at the gate of the larger world of cultural and political patriotism.[17]

[14]This discussion can be found all over the world, and it is significant in the present context that it is the website Tamilnation.org where Ernest Renan's famous speech 'What is a Nation?' can be found on the net (Renan 1882, 1992). Renan argues for the *jus soli*, 'right of soil', according to which the territory of birth determines the citizenship, and against the *jus sanguinis*, 'right of blood', as in the German concept of 'objective nationality', whose basis is blood, race or language. See also literature and web discussions on meta-ethnicity.

[15]Anderson 1991.

[16]For a typical example how the dominant discourse uses such labels see Bulliya et al. 2001. Here much of the colonial attitude, e.g. John Stuart Mill's, towards India and its inability to govern itself (Mill 1977, 1990) is repeated on the micro level in the way the contemporary centrist administrator and functionary views the people at the peripheries. 'For the preceding reasons, it is in general a necessary condition of free institutions, that the boundaries of governments should coincide in the main with those of nationalities' (Mill 1977 [1859]: 548). According to Mill, not even in the European states of his time had this been achieved. There are numerous studies of failed interventions of the respective centres in present-day India (e.g. Kothari 1996; Kurup 2008, Meher 2001).

[17]Berkemer 2003; Fox 1989.

This Gandhian approach might be a patriotic vision, but it is neither modern nor democratic.

In today's reality, such a utopian tribality will only be possible in India/ Orissa, if the state administration and the majority of voters accept the local values as different, but important enough to be accepted as voices in the supra-local discourses.[18] Here again we come back to Switzerland, which recently (2008) was referred to as a role model for the future constitution of the republic of Nepal. Swiss national identity is indeed a mix of various linguistic, cultural, religious and historical backgrounds. It is an example of the survival of multi-ethnic societies in a modern and nationally defined, culture and society. Educational institutions[19] there provide their government and other interested parties with the information on such multicultural federal states.

It seems to me that subregional centres may be a key to both local autonomy and local modernity, both in the sense of the individual and the politico-religious and cultural units. Since local units below the regions and the state provide the first level of centrality above villages and small towns, they are also the first level on which different social groups have to interact with each other outside their own traditional and maybe self-created, social sphere. At this level, little kings come into the picture. But, as we know from various contributions in the previously published volumes of the Orissa Project as well as from contributions to this one,[20] religious cults, their officiants and the little kings in their role as 'first devotees' (*adi-sevaka*) and protectors of the goddess and her cult, can have different meanings for different people. What happens on the ground is being integrated in different systems of norms and values, tribal, Hindu, administrative, and others. These different interpretations of the same phenomenon indicate that we are confronted with a social reality in which social institutions have no totality any more. Here, for instance, the *boro/sano* (elder *vs.* younger) distinction, which permeates all of the traditional Middle Indian tribal world, is merely one hierarchy among others. Kinship continues to provide a frame of reference as on the local level, but wealth and political power, authority through traditional and modern education, and many other forms of social status make themselves felt as well.

There is still the chance in Orissa that the tribal social order will survive on the periphery of the historically grown traditional structure of the little kingdoms, with their networks of market towns and administrative centres.

[18]For an opposing voice to such multi/trans-cultural tolerance see Anonymous 2001.

[19]Foremost the Universities of Fribourg and Berne (Fleiner 2003, Kälin 1997, 2002, 2003, 2003a, 2004).

[20]Gutschow 2003, 2004, and in the present volume; Kulke 1980, 1984, 1984a, 1992, 1992a, 1993a, 1993b, 2004, 2006, and in the present volume; Mallebrein 1996, 1999, 2004, 2004a, 2004b, 2007, 2007a, and in the present volume; Nanda 1997, 1999, 2003, 2007, and in the present volume; Schnepel 1994, 1995, 1996, 2001, 2004; Skoda 2001, 2002, 2003, 2004, 2005, 2007, and in the present volume; Tanabe 1995, 1998, 1999, 2003, 2005, 2006, 2006a, and in the present volume.

That is, if the structural level I have introduced here in a somewhat essayistic way in the figure of the little king and his descendants, continues to exist and becomes recognized as a necessary counterpart and opponent to the central administration in Bhubaneswar. Maybe this development is already on its way. I do not know whether the new district boundaries follow old border lines by design or by administrative accident, perhaps because these lines are the only surveyed sections of some forested belts, or because they have been used as local boundaries ever since the abolition of the princely states and zamindaries.

These little kingdoms, which were the political clones of the empire and the units that kept its memory long after it was gone, were not its clones in terms of culture; rather, they were the focal points of local cultures and religious practices. From the point of view of the little kingdom, it is easy to see that there is a connecting line between forest cults and Puri Jagannath, a connection which, due to its polythetic nature, is easily overlooked from either one of two opposite ends. The memory attached to the little kingdoms is an ambiguous one: they were for a long time integrators of the local cultures and social systems within their sphere of influence, as well as a channel of influence from larger centres. They provided a mental map in terms of both geography and time for cults and wars, markets and collective memories. They gave people the chance to change social roles by channelling migrations and providing specialist occupations. To them were attached local epics, styles of textiles and painting, styles of speech and dialects. They provided the home for learned specialists of Astronomy, Dharmashastra and Ayurveda, for tantric knowledge and non-Brahman holy men, for *matha*s and temples. But in the twentieth century, their image became tarnished by the stand they took against popular campaigns. They were the focus of opposition to the national movement and all the Indian National Congress stood for, and they opposed all attempts at land reforms. This made the little kingdoms (more than the kings themselves) non-entities on the political map for a long time. While the kings continued to be integrating traditional figures on a somewhat reduced scale, they had little say in the way the central administration treated their former kingdoms.

There is one more aspect to the problem of the strong hand. While most people will probably agree that they themselves feel better under an elected leader, they might be tempted to deny that freedom to others. I remember, back in the 1980s, an article in *India Today* about the 'tribal problem' in Orissa and a politically very incorrect quotation from a state official who had—off the record, and hopefully as a joke—said that the best way to get rid of the tribal problem was to get rid of the tribals. We might conclude from this that one does not necessarily need a dictator to make sure that some people have no say about their own future. Neither the USA not the British empire have ever been totalitarian states, but in the first instance we have historical cases of large-scale genocide on the state's periphery in the nineteenth century, and in the latter we can at least say that some indigenous people, such as the Zulus, the Australian Aborigines, the Egyptians and Sudanese, the Burmese and of course many Indian groups, were denied their cultural and political autonomy, and in cases of 'white' colonies such as Australia, attempts at 're-education' and 'civilization' of indigenes in boarding schools and prisons were official state policy for some time. India is still using the old colonial administrative division between 'tribals' and the rest of the population. Insignificant as this may be from a modern anthropological point of view, it still constitutes a part of people's fragmented modern identities.

Would it be too utopian, too fantastic to hope that this middle ground, this stage between the local and the central, could bear the weight of one more dimension in addition to this already existing multi-dimensionality: the dimension of a functioning civil society? Can we imagine one person or group being tribal and a modern citizen both at home and outside? We can imagine it in the case of Hindus, Muslims, or Christians. We can do this under two conditions: (1) the existence of a civil society in which the principle of subsidiarity (or 'devolution' as the British say) is radically enforced: a flat bureaucratic hierarchy in which nothing that can be decided on a local level will be referred to a higher level; and (2) an awareness of one's own role as a world citizen and the relativity of one's own cultural and social position. This opens a door out of the trap of conflict over traditional identities in modern, essentialistic thinking.

On the other hand, I don't see how the roles of a traditional tribal and a traditional Hindu can be combined, because tribal social values and traditional Hindu social values are constructed as mutually exclusive in colonial times, and contradict each other on a fundamental level. That is why I don't believe that one can 'convert' tribals into traditional Hindus without destroying everything tribal society is based on. On the other hand, in a civil society one can be a religious Hindu and an 'ethnic' tribal, because there is—ideally—no collective pressure on the belief system.

These reflections have led us far away from harsh reality, but I think that an essay like this is the right place to turn the whole world upside down like an image and see whether it makes any more sense that way. And it does make more sense in this case because the modern 'tribal' actually exists. After a long history of bloodshed, displacement and racist oppression, in both Canada and the USA, Native American people, the First Nations of the continent, have successfully struggled for the right to determine for themselves how to integrate traditional ways of life into their existence as modern citizens. The situation in these countries is far from ideal, but it provides material for comparison with the Indian situation. Other countries, such as South Africa, Russia, Brazil, Great Britain and even Germany[21] and the EU, could be used for comparative studies and political models.

[21] I am referring here to the special privileges the German Constitution provides for the minorities of the Sorbs (people speaking a Slavonic language) in the federal states of Saxony and Brandenburg, and the Danish minority in the federal state of Schleswig-Holstein.

We cannot say that—as in post-modern epistemology—the result of our deliberations is only dependent on perspective. It is not a question of the personal point of view whether we emphasize the centrist or the local views of the world. In the realm of historical narratives this maybe so, but as soon as we think about the consequences, the dominant discourse comes into view and with it the politics of everyday life and its representation in political institutions.

REFERENCES

Agrawal, Arun and Elinor Ostrom 2001. 'Collective Action, Property Rights, and Decentralization in Resource Use in India and Nepal', in *Politics and Society* 29, 4, 485.

Anderson, Benedict 1991. *Imagined Communities: Reflections on the Origin and Spread of Nationalism*, London, New York: Verso Editions (1st edn. London 1983).

Anonymous 2001. 'Oriya Culture Needs a Facelift in Bordering Districts', in *The New Indian Express* (Chennai), Bhubaneswar edn., 15 April 2001, 5.

Banerjee-Dube, Ishita 2006. 'Blurred Boundaries: Religion and Politics in Orissa', in Brandtner and Panda (eds.) 2006, 263-78.

Banks, Marcus 1996. *Ethnicity: Anthropological Constructions*, London, New York: Routledge.

Barrier, N. Gerald 1985. 'Regional Political History: New Trends in the Study of British India', in Paul Wallace (ed.), *Region and Nation in India*, Delhi: Oxford University Press and Indian Book House, 111-52.

Barth, Fredrik 1969. 'Pathan Identity and Its Maintenance', in Fredrik Barth (ed.), *Ethnic Groups and Boundaries: The Social Organization of Culture Difference*, London: George Allen and Unwin, 117-34.

———1969a. 'Introduction', in Fredrik Barth (ed.), *Ethnic Groups and Boundaries: The Social Organization of Culture Difference*, London: George Allen and Unwin, 9-38.

Behera, Subhakanta 1995. 'Oriya and Oriyaness: Defining Identity of a Nationality', in *Orissa Historical Research Journal* 40, 1/4, 88-100.

Behura, Nabal Kishore 1999. 'Traditional Land Tenure and the Kandha of Orissa: A Case Study from Koraput', in *Banaja* 1999, 34-43.

Bennett, C.J. 1980. 'The Morphology of Language Boundaries: Indo-Aryan and Dravidian in Peninsular India', in D.E. Sopher (ed.), *An Exploration of India: Geographical Perspectives on Society and Culture*, Ithaca: Cornell University Press, 234-51.

Berkemer, Georg 2003. 'Borders, Lines and Cases: From Sīma to Sīmānta in South Orissa and Beyond: K.C. Panigrahi Memorial Lecture 2002, Ravenshaw College, Cuttack', in *Ravenshaw Historical Journal* 3.

———2007. 'The King's Two Kingdoms or How the Maharaja of Parlakimedi Finally Became the Ruler of Orissa', in G. Pfeffer (ed.) 2007, 341-59.

Berkemer, Georg and Margret Frenz (eds.) 2003. *Sharing Sovereignty: The Little Kingdom in South Asia*, Berlin: Klaus Schwarz.

Béteille, André 1998. 'The Idea of Indigenous People', in *Current Anthropology* 19, 2, 187-91.

Bhattacharya, Kumkum and R.K. Bhattacharya 2003. 'Tribes—State of Mind?', in *Journal of the Indian Anthropological Society* 38, 2/3, 159-65.

Brandtner, Martin and Shishir Kumar Panda (eds.) 2006. *Interrogating History: Essays for Hermann Kulke*, Delhi: Manohar.

Bulliya, G. et al. 2001. *Assessment of Health and Nutritional Profile Among the Elderly Population of Orissa Primitive Tribes* (Annual Report No. 2000-2001), Bhubaneswar: Regional Medical Research Centre.

Chacko, Pariyaram Mathew 2005. *Tribal Communities and Social Change*, Delhi: Sage.

Chakrabarti, Kunal 2000. 'Cult Region: The *Purāṇas* and the Making of the Cultural Territory of Bengal', in *Studies in History* (n.s.) 16, 1, 1-16.

Chandra, Kanchan 2001. 'Ethnic Bargains, Group Instability, and Social Choice Theory', in *Politics and Society* 29, 3, 337-67.

Chattopadhyaya, Brajadulal 1997. '"Autonomous Spaces" and the Authority of the State: The Contradiction and Its Resolution in Theory and Practice in Early India', in Bernhard Kölver (ed.), *Recht, Staat und Verwaltung im klassischen Indien*, München, Wien: Oldenbourg, 1-14.

———2004: 'State's Perception of the "Forest" and the "Forest" as State in Early India', in B.B. Chaudhuri and Arun Bandopadhyay (eds.), *Tribes, Forest and Social Formation in Indian History*, Delhi: Manohar, 23-38.

Chaudhury, Sukant Kumar 2004. *Tribal Identity: Continuity and Change Among Kondhs of Orissa*, Jaipur, Delhi: Rawat.

Colfer, Carol J. Pierce and Doris Capistrano (eds.) 2005. *The Politics of Decentralization: Forests, Power and People*, London: Earthscan Publications.

Cohn, Bernard S. 1987. *An Anthropologist among the Historians and Other Essays*, Delhi, Oxford, New York: Oxford University Press.

———1996. *Colonialism and Its Forms of Knowledge: The British in India*, Princeton: Princeton University Press.

Cohn, Bernard S. and Nicholas B. Dirks 1988. 'Beyond the Fringe: The Nation State, Colonialism and the Technologies of Power', in *Journal of Historical Sociology* 1, 1, 224-9.

Connor, W. 2004. 'A Few Cautionary Notes on the History and Future of Ethnonational Conflicts', in A. Wimmer (ed.), *Facing Ethnic Conflicts: Toward a New Realism*, Lanham: Rowman & Littlefield, 23-33.

Das, Vidhya 2003. 'Democratic Governance in Tribal Regions: A Distant Dream', in *Economic and Political Weekly*, 18 October 2003, 4429-32.

Devy, Ganesh N. 2006. *A Nomad Called Thief: Reflections on Adivasi Silence*, Delhi: Orient Longman.

Dirks, Nicholas B. 2001. *Castes of Mind: Colonialism and the Making of Modern India*, Princeton: Princeton University Press.

———2006. *The Scandal of Empire: India and the Creation of Imperial Britain*, Cambridge: Belknap Press of Harvard University Press.

Eaton, Richard M. 2000. 'Comparative History as World History', in R.M. Eaton, *Essays on Islam and Indian History*, Delhi, Oxford, New York: Oxford University Press, 45-75.

Embree, Ainslee T. 1977. 'Frontiers into Boundaries: The Evolution of the Modern State', in Richard G. Fox (ed.), *Realm and Region in Traditional India*, Delhi, Bombay, Bangalore: Vikas, 255-80.

———1989. 'Frontiers into Boundaries: The Evolution of the Modern State', in Ainslee T. Embree and M. Juergensmeyer (eds.), *Imagining India: Essays on Indian History*, Delhi: Oxford University Press, 67-84.

Fleiner, Thomas (ed.) 2003. *Multicultural Federalism: The Swiss Case*, Fribourg: Institute of Federalism.

Flueckiger, Joyce Burkhalter (ed.) 1991. *Boundaries of the Text: Epic Performances in South and Southeast Asia*, Ann Arbor: Center for South and Southeast Asian Studies.

———1991. 'Genre and Community in the Folklore System of Chhattisgarh', in Arjun Appadurai, Frank J. Korom and Margret A. Mills (eds.), *Gender, Genre, and Power in South Asian Expressive Traditions*, Philadelphia: University of Pennsylvania Press, 181-200.

———1996. *Gender and Genre in the Folklore of Middle India*, Ithaca: Cornell University Press.

Forsythe, Diana 1989. 'German Identity and Problems of History', in Elizabeth Tonkin, Maryon McDonald and Malcolm Chapman (eds.), *History and Ethnicity*, London, New York: Routledge, 137-56.

Fox, Richard G. 1989. *Gandhian Utopia: Experiments with Culture*, Boston: Beacon Press.

Goffman, Erving 1959. *The Presentation of Self in Everyday Life*, New York: Anchor Books.

Gregory, Robert J. 2003. 'Tribes and Tribal: Origin, Use, and Future of the Concept', in *Studies of Tribes and Tribals* 1, 1, 1-5.

Gutschow, Niels 2003. 'Ranpur: The Centre of a Little Kingdom', in G. Berkemer and M. Frenz (eds.) 2003, 137-64.

———2004. 'Ranpur Resolved: Spatial Analysis of a Town in Orissa Based on a Chronicle', in Malinar, Beltz and Frese (eds.) 2004, 67-92.

Judson, Pieter M. 1993. 'Inventing Germans: Class, Nationality and Colonial Fantasy at the Margins of the Hapsburg Monarchy', in *Social Analysis* 33, 1, 47-67.

Kälin, Walter 1997. 'Federalism and the Resolution of Minority Conflicts', in Günther Bächler (ed.), *Federalism Against Ethnicity*?, Chur, Zürich: Ruegger, 169-83.

———2002. *What Makes Decentralised Government Work? Lessons from Switzerland*, retrieved 3 February 2004 from www1.worldbank.org/wbiep/decentralization/library1/Kalin.pdf.

———2003. *Decentralised Governance in Fragmented Societies: Solution or Cause of New Evils?* Berne: University of Berne (http://www.federalism.ch/FTP-Mirror/summer_university_03/week_1/Kaelin_2.pdf; retrieved 21 June 2005, published as Kälin 2004).

———2003a. *Decentralization: Why and How*? Berne: Swiss Agency for Development and Cooperation (SDC), Federal Department of Foreign Affairs (http://www.ciesin.org/decentralization/English/General/SDC_why_how.pdf; retrieved 28 May 2007).

———2004. 'Decentralised Governance in Fragmented Societies: Solution or Cause of New Evils?', in A. Wimmer (ed.), *Facing Ethnic Conflicts: Toward a New Realism*, Lanham: Rowman & Littlefield, 300-14.

Kendall, Frances and Leon Louw 1987. *After Apartheid: The Solution for South Africa*, San Francisco: Inst. for Contemporary Studies.

Kimura, Masaaki and Akio Tanabe (eds.) 2006, *The State in India: Past and Present*, Delhi: Oxford University Press.

Kingsbury, Benedict 1998. '"Indigenous Peoples" in International Law: A Constructivist Approach to the Asian Controversy', in *American Journal of International Law* 92, 3, 414-57.

Kothari, Smitu 1996. 'Whose Nation? Displaced as Victims of Development', in *Economic and Political Weekly* 31, 24, 1476-85.

Kulke, Hermann 1980. 'Legitimation and Town-Planning in the Feudatory States of Central Orissa', in J. Pieper (ed.), *Ritual Space in India: Studies in Architectural Anthropology*, Art and Archaeology Research Papers (AARP) 17, London: AARP, 30-40.

———1984. 'Local Networks and Regional Integration in Orissa: Ritual Privileges of the Feudatory Rajas of Eastern India in the Jagannatha Cult of Puri', in Kenneth Ballhatchet and David Taylor (eds.), *Changing South Asia: Religion and Society*, Hong Kong: Asian Research Service, 141-8.

———1984a. 'Tribal Deities at Princely Courts: The Feudatory Rajas of Central Orissa and their Tutelary Deities (Iṣṭadevatās)', in Sitakant Mahapatra (ed.), *Folk Ways in Religion: Gods, Spirits and Men*, Cuttack: Institute of Oriental and Orissan Studies, 13-24.

———1992. 'Kṣatra and Kṣetra: The Cult of Jagannātha of Puri and the "Royal Letters" of the Rajas of Khurda', in Hans Bakker (ed.), *The Sacred Centre as the Focus of Political Interest*, Groningen: Egbert Forsten, 131-42.

———1992a. 'Tribal Deities at Princely Courts: The Feudatory Rajas of Central Orissa and their Tutelary Deities (Iṣṭadevatās)', in Sitakant Mahapatra (ed.), *The Realm of the Sacred*, Calcutta: Oxford University Press, 56-78.

———1993. *Kings and Cults: State Formation and Legitimation in India and Southeast Asia*, Delhi: Manohar.

———1993a. 'Kshatriyaization and Social Change: A Study in the Orissa Setting', in Kulke (1993), 82-92.

———1993b. 'Tribal Deities at Princely Courts: The Feudatory Rajas of Central Orissa and their Tutelary Deities (Iṣṭadevatās)', in Kulke (1993), 114-36.

———2004. 'The Making of a Local Chronicle: The Ranapur Rajavamsa Itihasa', in Malinar, Beltz and Frese (eds.) 2004, 43-66.

———2006. 'The Integrative Model of State Formation in Early Medieval India', in Kimura and Tanabe (eds.) 2006, 59-81.

Kumar, Krishna 1993. 'Educational Experience of Scheduled Castes and Tribes', in *Economic and Political Weekly* 18 (36/37), 1566-72.

Kumar, Sanjay and Stuart Corbridge 2002. 'Programmed to Fail? Development Projects and the Politics of Participation', in *Journal of Development Studies* 39, 2, 73-103.

Kundu, Manmath 2000. 'The Use of Minority Language by Majority Groups in a Multilingual Setting: A Case Study of the Non-Tribal Users of a Tribal Language in an Indian Village', in *Banaja* 2000, 42-6.

Kurup, Apoorv (2008): 'Tribal Law in India: How Decentralized Administration is Extinguishing Tribal Rights and Why Autonomous Tribal Governments are Better', *Indigenous Law Journal* 7, 1, 87-126.

Llobera, Josep 1989. 'Catalan National Identity: The Dialectics of Past and Present', in Elizabeth Tonkin, Maryon McDonald and Malcolm Chapman (eds.), *History and Ethnicity*, London, New York: Routledge, 247-61.

Mahapatra, Bishnu N. and Dwaipayan Bhattacharya 1996. 'Tribal-Dalit Conflicts: Electorial Politics in Phulbani', in *Economic and Political Weekly* 1996, 1, 13-20.

Mahapatra, Lakshman Kumar 1993. 'Customary Rights in Land and Forest and the State', in M. Miri (ed.), *Continuity and Change in Tribal Society*, Shimla: Indian Institute of Advanced Study.

———1998. 'Good Intentions or Politics Are Not Enough: Reducing Impoverishment Risks for the Tribal Oustees', in Hari Mohan Mathur and David Marsden (eds.), *Development Projects & Impoverishment Risks: Resettling Project-affected People in India*, Delhi: Oxford University Press, 216-36.

Mahapatra, Sitakant 1991. 'Development for Whom? Depriving the Dispossessed Tribals', in *Social Action—A Quarterly Review of Social Trends* 41, 3, 271-81.

Malinar, A., J. Beltz and H. Frese (eds.) 2004, *Text and Context in the History, Literature and Religion of Orissa*, Delhi: Manohar.

Mallebrein, Cornelia 1996. 'Dantesvari, the Family Goddess (kulasvamini) of the Rajas of Bastar, and the Dashara-Festival of Jagdalpur', in Axel Michaels, C. Volgesänger and A. Wilke (eds.), *Wild Goddesses in India and Nepal*, Berne: Peter Lang, 483-511.

———1999. 'Tribal and Local Deities: Assimilations and Transformations', in Vidya Dehejia (ed.), *Devi: The Great Goddess: Female Divinity in South Asian Art*, Washington: A. Sackler Gallery, 137-56.

———2004. 'Creating a *Kshetra*: Goddess Tarini of Ghatgaon and her Development from a Forest Goddess to Pan-Orissan Deity', in Mallebrein and Guzy (eds.) 2004, 155-65.

———2004a. 'Entering the Realm of Durga: Patkhanda, a Hinduized Tribal Deity', in Malinar, Beltz and Frese (eds.) 2004, 273-306.

———2004b. 'Ruler, Protector and Healer: The Clan Gods Sulia, Patkhanda and Sikerpat of the Kondh Tribe', in Mallebrein and Guzy (eds.) 2004, 143-53.

———2007. 'Maṇikesvari and Ḍokri: Changing Representations of Two Tribal Goddesses and the Dynastic Histories of Orissa', in Angelika Malinar (ed.), *Time in India: Concepts and Practices*, Delhi: Manohar, 203-34.

———2007a. 'When the Buffalo Becomes a Pumpkin: Animal Sacrifice Contested', in Pfeffer (ed.) 2007, 443-72.

Mallebrein, Cornelia and Lidia Julianna Guzy (eds.) 2004, *Facets of Orissan Studies*, Delhi: Kamla-Raj Enterprises.

Mallik, Basanta Kumar 2001. 'Making the Regional Identity: Oriya Mahabharata as a Marker of Time', in *The Fourth World* 14, 20-32.

Mann, Michael G. 2005. *Geschichte Indiens: Vom 18. bis zum 21. Jahrhundert*, Paderborn: Schöningh.

Mann, Michael 2006. *The Dark Side of Democracy: Explaining Ethnic Cleansing*, Cambridge: Cambridge University Press.

Mangaraj, Pranab 2003. *Rural Development and Political Participation Among Tribals*, Delhi: Anmol.

Meher, Rajkishor 2001. 'Degeneration of the Periphery under Hegemonic Development: The Case of Marginalization of the Aboriginal in a Tribal Region', in *Indian Social Science Review* 3, 2, 289-325.

———2003. 'Social and Ecological Effect of Industrialisation in a Tribal Region: The Case of the Rourkela Steel Plant', in *Contributions to Indian Sociology* 37, 3, 429-57.

———2004. *Stealing the Environment: Social and Ecological Effects of Industrialization in Rourkela*, Delhi: Manohar.

Mill, John Stuart 1977. 'Considerations on Representative Government', in *The Collected Works of John Stuart Mill*, vol. 19, *Essays on Politics and Society, Part 2* [*1859*], ed. John M. Robson, Martin Moir and Zawahir Moir, Toronto, Buffalo: University of Toronto Press, 371-577.

———1990. 'The East India Company's Charter', in *The Collected Works of John Stuart Mill*, vol. 30, *Writings on India* [*1868*], ed. John M. Robson, Martin Moir and Zawahir Moir, Toronto, Buffalo: University of Toronto Press, 31-74.

Mitra, Subrata Kumar 1998. 'Introduction', in Subrata Kumar Mitra and R. Alison Lewis (eds.), *Subnational Movements in South Asia*, Delhi: Segment Books, 1-13.

Mohanty, Bibhuti Bhusan 1997. 'State and Tribal Relationship in Orissa', in *Indian Anthropologist* 27, 1, 1-18.

Mojumdar, K. 1989. 'The Ganjam Agency, 1839-1900: Some Problems of Tribal Administration', in Pramodh Kumar Mishra (ed.), *Culture, Tribal History and Freedom Movement: Dr. N.K. Sahu Commemoration Volume*, Delhi: Agam Kala Prakashan, 149-63.

———1993. 'Bonded Labour in the Ganjam Agency: Dichotomy in British Tribal Policy', in *Studies in History and Culture* 1, 69-92.

Mubayi, Yaaminey 2006. 'Problematizing Heritage: Region, Religion and the Making of Cultural Identity', in Brandtner and Panda (eds) 2006, 279-90.

Nanda, Bikram Narayan 1989. *Towards a Social History of Highland Orissa*, Delhi: Nehru Memorial Museum & Library (Occasional Papers on Perspectives in Indian Development, 10).

Nanda, Chandi Prasad 1997. 'Mobilisation, Resistance and Popular Initiatives: Situating the Tribals of Koraput (1937-38)', in *Utkal Historical Research Journal* 9, 134-52.

———1998. 'Nationalist Politics and Popular Struggles in the Princely States: Rethinking Dhenkanal State (1937-39)', in *Studies in History and Culture* 6, 1/2, 35-60.

———1999. 'Mobilisation, Resistance and Popular Initiatives: Situating the Tribals of Jeypore Estate (1937-39)', in Subash Chandra Padhy and Shishir Kumar Panda (eds.), *Society, Culture and Polity in Eastern India*, Berhampur: Post Graduate Department of History, Berhampur University, 43-66.

———2003. 'Validating "Tradition": Revisiting Keonjhar and Bhuiyan Insurgency in Colonial Orissa', in Georg Berkemer and Margret Frenz (eds.) 2003, 205-20.

———2007. 'Marginal Texts, Marginal Men: The Social Mobility Movement of the Kudmi-Mahantas of Orissa', in Pfeffer (ed.) 2007, 393-16.

Nandy, Ashis 2006. 'Democratic Culture and Images of the State: India's Unending Ambivalence', in Kimura and Tanabe (eds.) 2006, 282-301.

Nayak, R. 2002. 'Towards Self-Governance: Tribal Development in Orissa', in *Social Action—A Quarterly Review of Social Trends* 52, 2, 186-99.

Orywal, Erwin 2002. 'Der Stammesstaat. Eine neue Form der politischen Organisation?', in *Zeitschrift für Ethnologie* 127, 57-76.

Pathy, Jagannath 1993. 'Was ist ein indigenes Volk?', in *Entwicklungspolitik* April 1993, 5-7.

Pathy, Suguna 2002. 'Destitution, Deprivation and Tribal "Development"', in *Economic and Political Weekly* 38, 27, 283-86.

Pati, Biswamoy 2006. 'Decolonised Orissa: Issues and Problems', in M. Brandtner and S.K. Panda (eds.) 2006, 303-30.

Patnaik, Himanshu Sekhar 2004. 'Sanskritisation: Myth or Reality for Orissa?', in *Utkal Historical Research Journal* 17, 37-44.

Pfeffer, Georg F. 1997. 'The Scheduled Tribes of Middle India as a Unit: Problems of Internal and External Comparison', in G.F. Pfeffer and D.K. Behera (eds.), *Contemporary Society: Tribal Studies: Prof. Satya Narayana Ratha Felicitation Volumes*, vol. 1, *Structure and Process*, Delhi: Concept, 3-27.

———1998. 'The Indian State and the Tribes of India', in *Journal of the Indian Anthropological Society* 33, 1, 77-86.

———1998a. 'The Own and the Other: Construction of Identity in Orissa', in *The Fourth World* 8, 15-25.

———2002. 'The Structure of Middle Indian Tribal Society Compared', in G.F. Pfeffer and D.K. Behera (eds.), *Contemporary Society: Tribal Studies*, vol. 5, *Concept of Tribal Society*, Delhi: Concept, 208-29.

———2003. 'War and Peace in South Asia: A Two-part Editorial', in *Daily Times* 31 January 2003 and 1 February 2003. Online address: http://www.dailytimes.com.pk/default.asp?page=story_31-1-2003_pg3_5 and http://www.dailytimes.com.pk/default.asp?page=story_1-2-2003_pg3_5 (last accessed 12 January 2009).

———2004. 'Tribal Society of Highland Orissa, Highland Burma, and Elsewhere', in Malinar, Beltz and Frese (eds.) 2004, 427-56.

———2007. 'Bailey's Khondh Structure on the Tribal Frontier', in Pfeffer (ed.) 2007, 249-71.

———(ed.) 2007. *Periphery and Centre: Studies in Orissan History, Religion and Anthropology*, Delhi: Manohar.

Pomeranz, Kenneth 1993. *The Making of a Hinterland: State, Society and Economy in Inland North China, 1853-1937*, Berkeley: University of California Press.

Ravinder Kumar 2002. 'India: A "Nation State" or "Civilization State"', in *South Asia* 2[illegible] 2, 13-32 (http://dx.doi.org/10.1080/00856400208723473, since: 01/08/2002, last accessed 18/10/2007).

Renan, Ernest 1882. *What is a Nation? Excerpts of a Lecture at Sorbonne, 11 March 1882.* Retrieved 10 February 2008, from http://www.tamilnation.org/selfdetermination/nation/renan.htm.

———1992. *Qu'est-ce qu'une nation? Et autres essais politiques*, Paris: Presses Pocket.

Rousseleau, Raphael 2003. 'Entre folklore et iosolat: le local: La question tribale en Inde, de Mauss à Dumont', in *Social Anthropology* 11, 2, 189-213.

Roy Burman and Bikram Keshari 2003. 'Indigenous and Tribal Peoples in World System Perspective', in *Studies of Tribes and Tribals* 1, 1, 7-27.

Sachchidananda 2004. *Man, Forest and the State in Middle India*, Delhi: Serials Publications.

Samal, Avinash 2006. *Governance and the Politics of Control and Management of Local Natural Resources: A Study in the Scheduled Areas of India.* Presented at 'Politics of the Commons: Articulating Development and Strengthening Local Practices', Chiang Mai, Thailand, 11-14 July 2003. Retrieved 28 October 2007 from: http://dlc.dlib.indiana.edu/archive/00001084/00/Avinash_Samal.pdf.

Sarkar, Mahua 2003. '"Community" and "Nation": Groping for Alternative Narratives', in *Economic and Political Weekly*, 27 December 2003, 5335-7.

Saunders, Cheryl 2003. 'Federalism, Decentralisation and Conflict Management in Multicultural Societies', in Raoul Blindenbacher and Arnold Koller (eds.), *Federalism in a Changing World—Learning from Each Other: Scientific Background, Proceedings and Plenary Speeches of The International Conference on Federalism 2002*, Montreal: McGill-Queen's University Press, 33-8.

Schnepel, Burkhard 1994. 'Goddesses, Kings and Tribals: Remarks on the Ritual Policy of a South Orissan Jungle Kingdom', in *Man in Society* 8, 19-36.

———1995. 'Durga and the King: Ethnohistorical Aspects of the Politico-Ritual Life in a South Orissan Jungle Kingdom', in *Journal of the Royal Anthropological Institute* 1, 145-66.

———1996. 'The Hindu King's Authority Reconsidered: Durga-Puja and Dasara in a South Orissan Jungle Kingdom', in G. Aijmer and A. Boholm (eds.), *Political Ritual*, Göteborg: Institute of Advanced Studies in Social Anthropology, 126-57.

———2001. 'Kings and Rebel Kings: Rituals of Incorporation and Dissent in South Orissa', in Hermann Kulke and Burkhard Schnepel (eds.), *Jagannath Revisited: Studying Society, Religion and the State in Orissa*, Delhi: Manohar, 271-96.

———2004. 'Goddesses, Kings and Tribals: Remarks on the Ritual Policy of a South Orissan Jungle Kingdom', in Nihar Ranjan Patnaik (ed.), *Religious History of Orissa*, Delhi: Indian, 291-309.

Segal, Daniel 1991. '"The European": Allegories of Racial Purity', in *Anthropology Today* 7, 5, 7-9.

Segal, Daniel and Richard Handler 1992. 'How European is Nationalism?', in *Social Analysis* 32 (December 1992), 1-15.

Sen, Padmaja (ed.) 2003. *Changing Tribal Life: A Socio-philosophical Perspective*, Delhi: Concept.

Shah, Mihir 2002. 'The Adivasi Question', in *The Hindu*, 2 April 2002, p. 10 and 3 April 2002, p. 10.

Sharma, Subhash 2004. 'Tribal Development in Jharkhand: A Multidimensional Critical Perspective', in *Studies of Tribes and Tribals* 2, 2, 77-80.

Skoda, Uwe 2001. 'Transfer of Children and Inter-group Relations in a Mixed Tribal and Caste Society', in *Adivasi—The Journal of the Tribal & Harijan Research-cum-Training Institute* 41, 51-60.

———2003. 'On a Tribal Frontier: Aghria-Gauntia as Village Kings', in G. Berkemer and M. Frenz (eds.) 2003, 181-203.

———2004. 'Ritual Friendship in a Converging Tribal and Caste Society', in C. Mallebrein and L.J. Guzy (eds.) 2004, 167-77.

———2005. *The Aghria: A Peasant Caste on A Tribal Frontier*, Delhi: Manohar.

———2007. 'Death Among the Aghria: Death and the Continuity of Life in a Peripheral Mixed Tribal and Caste Society', in Pfeffer (ed.) 2007, 223-48.

Soreng, Nabor 2007. 'Die Zerstörung der Adivasi-Kultur im industriellen Zeitalter', in Adivasi-Koordination in Deutschland e.V. (eds.): *Rourkela und die Folgen: 50 Jahre industrieller Aufbau und soziale Verantwortung in der deutsch-indischen Zusammenarbeit*, Heidelberg: Draupadi-Verlag, 69-87.

Srinivas, M.N. 1952. *Religion and Society among the Coorgs of South India*, Oxford: Clarendon Press.

Strong, Pauline Turner and Barrik van Winkle 1993. 'Tribe and Nation: American Indians and American Nationalism', in *Social Analysis* 33, 1, 9-26.

Sullivan, Patrick 2006. 'Introduction: Culture Without Cultures: The Culture Effect', *Australian Journal of Anthropology* 17, 3, 253-64.

Synnott, A. 1993. *The Body Social: Symbol, Self and Society*, London, New York: Routledge and Kegan.

Tanabe, Akio 1995. 'Remaking Tradition: The State Government and Martial Arts Competition in Orissa, India', in *Journal of Asian and African Studies* 48/49, 221-41.

———1998. 'Ethnohistory of Land and Identity in Khurda, Orissa: From Pre-colonial Past to Post-colonial Present', in *Journal of Asian and African Studies* 56, 75-112.

———1999. 'The Transformation of Sakti: Gender and Sexuality in the Festival of Goddess Ramachandi', in M. Tanaka and M. Tachikawa (eds.), *Living with Sakti*, Osaka: National Museum of Ethnology, 75-112.

———2003. 'The Sacrificer State and Sacrificial Community: Kingship in Early Modern Khurda, Orissa, Seen through a Local Ritual', in G. Berkemer and M. Frenz (eds.) 2003, 115-35.

———2005. 'The System of Entitlements in Eighteenth-century Khurda, Orissa: Reconsidering "Caste" and "Community" in Late Pre-colonial India', in *South Asia* 28, 3, 345-85.

———2006. 'Early Modernity and Colonial Transformation: Rethinking the Role of the King in Eighteenth and Nineteenth Century Orissa, India', in Kimura and Tanabe (eds.) 2006, 202-28.

———2006a. 'Recast(e)ing Identity: Transformation of Inter-caste Relationships in Post-colonial Rural Orissa', in *Modern Asian Studies* 40, 3, 761-96.

Thapar, Romila 2000. *Cultural Pasts: Essays in Early Indian History*, Delhi: Oxford University Press.

———2000a. 'In Defence of the Variant', in Thapar 2000, 1089-95.

———2000b. 'Regional History with Reference to the Konkan', in Thapar 2000, 109-22.

———2000c. 'Regional History: The Punjab', in Thapar 2000, 95-108.

———2000d. 'The Rāmāyaṇa Syndrome', in Thapar 2000, 1079-88.

———2004. 'Imagined Religious Communities? Ancient History and the Modern Search for a Hindu Identity', in David N. Lorenzen (ed.), *Religious Movements in South Asia, 600-1800*, Delhi: Oxford University Press, 333-59.

Tremblay, Reeta Chowdhari 1996. 'Nation, Identity, and the Intervening Role of the State: A Study of the Secessionist Movement in Kashmir', in *Pacific Affairs* 69, 4, 471-97.

Zola, Irving K. 1973. 'Pathways to the Doctor: From Person to Patient', in *Social Science and Medicine* 7, 677-89.

Contributors

SUSMITA ARP, freelance journalist, Hamburg, formerly Department of Indology, Hamburg University and Department of History, University of Kiel, Germany.

GEORG BERKEMER, Department of South Asian Studies, Humboldt University, Berlin, Germany.

BRAJADULAL CHATTOPADHYAYA, Kolkata, retired from Jawaharlal Nehru University, New Delhi.

GAGANENDRA NATH DASH, Bhubaneswar, retired from Berhampur University.

ULRICH DEMMER, Institute of Anthropology, University of Munich, Germany.

NIELS GUTSCHOW is specialized in architectural and urban history of Nepal and India, works and lives in Abtsteinach (Germany) and Bhaktapur (Nepal).

LIDIA GUZY, Institute of Religious Studies, Free University Berlin, Germany.

BEATRIX HAUSER, Visiting Professor, Cluster of Excellence 'Asia and Europe in a Global Context: Shifting Asymmetries in Cultural Flows', University of Heidelberg, Germany.

HERMANN KULKE, retired from University of Kiel, Germany.

CORNELIA MALLEBREIN, Department of Indology and Comparative Religion, University of Tübingen, Germany.

BASANTA KUMAR MALLIK, Department of History, Utkal University, Bhubaneswar.

CHANDI PRASAD NANDA, Department of History, Ravenshaw University, Cuttack.

SHISHIR KUMAR PANDA, Department of History, Berhampur University, Berhampur.

BISWAMOY PATI, Department of History, University of Delhi.

BHAIRABI PRASAD SAHU, Department of History, University of Delhi.

UWE SKODA, Assistant Professor, South Asian Studies, Aarhus University, Denmark.

AKIO TANABE, Graduate School of Asian and African Studies, Kyoto University, Japan.

GAYA CHARAN TRIPATHI, retired from Indira Gandhi National Centre for the Arts, New Delhi, National Fellow, Indian Institute of Advanced Studies, Shimla.

Index

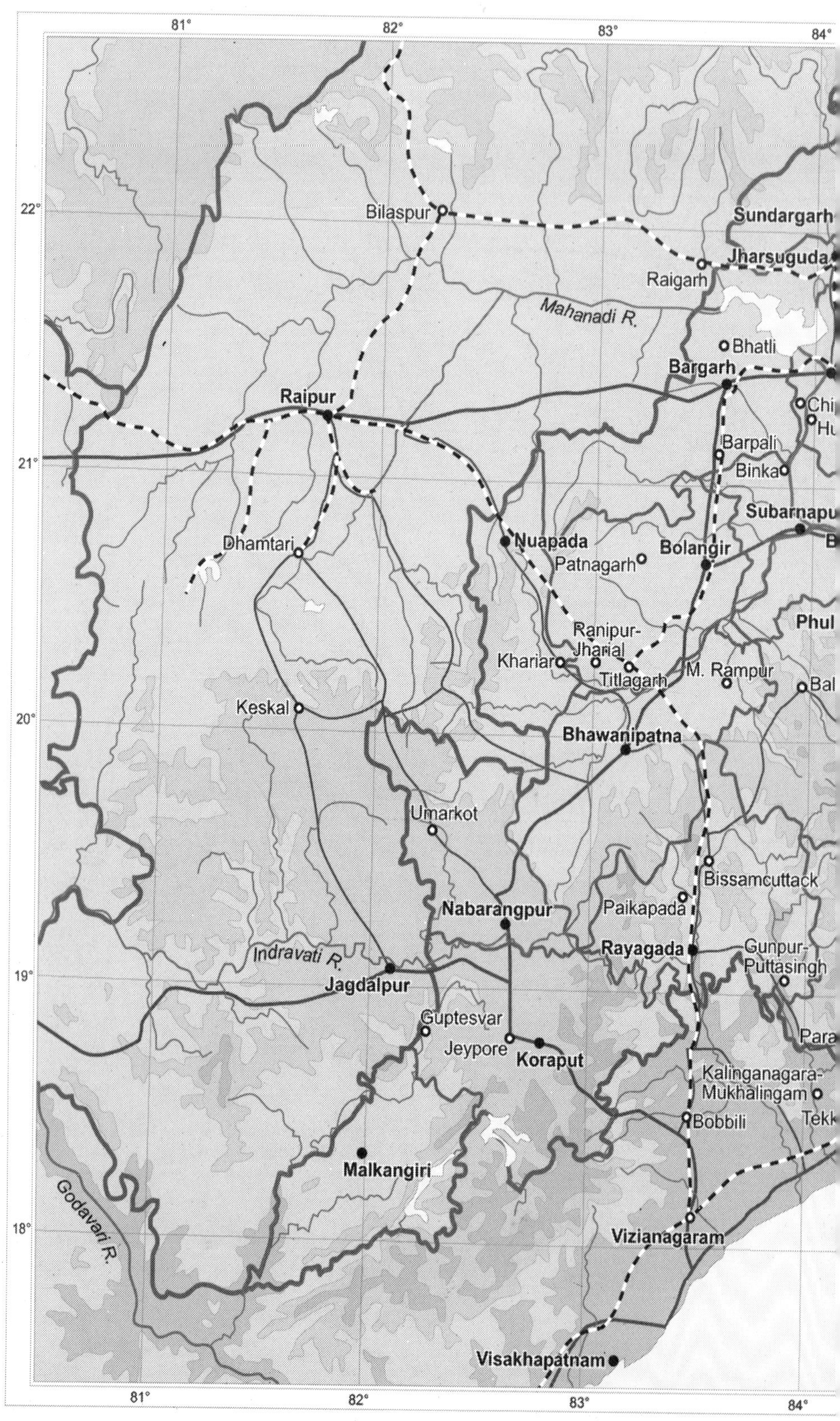
81°
82°
83°
84°
22°
21°
20°
19°
18°
Bilaspur
Sundargarh
Jharsuguda
Raigarh
Mahanadi R.
Bhatli
Bargarh
Raipur
Barpali
Binka
Subarnapu
Nuapada
Patnagarh
Bolangir
Dhamtari
Ranipur-
Jharial
Phul
Khariar
Titlagarh
M. Rampur
Keskal
Bhawanipatna
Umarkot
Bissamcuttack
Paikapada
Nabarangpur
Rayagada
Gunpur-
Puttasingh
Indravati R.
Jagdalpur
Guptesvar
Jeypore
Koraput
Kalinganagara-
Mukhalingam
Bobbili
Malkangiri
Godavari R.
Vizianagaram
Visakhapatnam